YALE LAW LIBRARY SERIES IN LEGAL HISTORY AND REFERENCE

OSCAR WILDE ON TRIAL

The Criminal Proceedings, from Arrest to Imprisonment

Joseph Bristow

Yale
UNIVERSITY
PRESS
New Haven & London

Published with support from the Lillian Goldman Law Library, Yale Law School.

Yale University Press books may be purchased in quantity for educational, business, or promotional use. For information, please email sales.press@yale.edu (U.S. office) or sales@yaleup.co.uk (U.K. office).

Set in Electra type by Newgen.
Printed in the United States of America.

Library of Congress Control Number: 2021950016
ISBN 978-0-300-22272-2 (hardcover: alk. paper)

A catalogue record for this book is available from the British Library.

This paper meets the requirements of ANSI/NISO Z39.48-1992 (Permanence of Paper).

10 9 8 7 6 5 4 3 2 1

To Daniel P. Williford

Personality is a very mysterious thing. A man cannot always be estimated by what he does. He may keep the law, and yet be worthless. He may break the law, and yet be fine. He may be bad, without ever doing anything bad. He may commit a sin against society, and yet realize through that sin his true perfection.
—Oscar Wilde

I am a born antinomian. I am one of those who are made for exceptions, not for laws.
—Oscar Wilde

CONTENTS

Part II *Regina v. Oscar Wilde and Alfred Taylor*: A Reconstruction of the Proceedings

Part III After the Trials

ILLUSTRATIONS

PREFACE

There is no question that the three trials the forty-year-old Irish writer Oscar Wilde endured at London's Central Criminal Court (Old Bailey) in spring 1895 remain legendary. They resulted in the brutal incarceration of a brilliant author who had reached the peak of his dramatic powers when the jury concluded that he was guilty of acts of gross indecency with other men. Such were the homosexual acts prohibited by the eleventh section of the Criminal Law Amendment Act 1885. This terrible outcome was the unanticipated result of a hazardous libel action that Wilde had taken out against John Sholto Douglas, 9th Marquess of Queensberry. On 18 February 1895, Queensberry had left an insulting visiting card at the Albemarle Club, London, where Wilde was a member. The marquess handed the card to Sidney Wright, the hall porter. Wright, who saw what was written on the card, placed the document inside an envelope and put Wilde's name on the outside. In a notorious misspelling, together with some shaky grammar, Queensberry had hurriedly accused Wilde of "posing [as a] Somdomite." The irate aristocrat, who had been harassing Wilde for months, wished to bring the fêted playwright's intimacy with his third son, Lord Alfred Douglas, to a decisive end.

Once he collected Queensberry's visiting card ten days later, an indignant Wilde—whose lawyer had previously complained about the marquess's provocative behavior—proceeded to sue. Soon after Wilde had instigated the libel case, either Queensberry or his solicitor, Charles Russell, hired two former police detectives who possessed detailed knowledge of London's sexual subcultures. Through these seasoned investigators, the defense team obtained astonishing amounts of evidence that showed Wilde's sexual tastes were not just those of a man who (if we correct the wording of the insult) was "posing as a sodomite." Russell concluded that Wilde broke the law because he had committed acts of gross indecency with at least a dozen young males, several of whom were prostitutes and extortionists. Without delay, the energetic attorney compiled a comprehensive list of witness statements that formed the basis of the plea of justification. As the phrase suggests, the plea aimed at justifying the marquess's allegation, which was a criminal offense. On 30 March, Russell entered the plea on Queensberry's behalf. Meanwhile, the solicitor arranged for the young men who had given witness statements to be subpoenaed, just in case the occasion arose when their testimony might support Queensberry's plea. (As it turned out, during the libel case none of these witnesses was called.)

Wilde's libel suit against Queensberry, which began at the Old Bailey on Wednesday, 3 April 1895, and finished two days later, did not result in a conviction. Since the marquess's defense presented such detailed accounts of Wilde's involvement with London's queer social circles, Wilde's senior counsel, Sir Edward Clarke, eventually advised his client to withdraw the charge. This was a precarious outcome that ruined Wilde financially. Straightaway, Queensberry organized a campaign to ensure that the government would prosecute the Irish author. He urged Russell to hand over the shorthand reports of the proceedings that had been specially commissioned, together with the substantial set of witness statements, to the Hon. Hamilton ("Ham") Cuffe, the director of public prosecutions—the government officer who serves under the attorney general and the solicitor general. The wealth of documentation quickly persuaded three other members of the government to issue a warrant for Wilde's arrest: Herbert Henry ("H. H.") Asquith, the home secretary (the senior minister in charge of law enforcement, prisons, and probation in England and Wales), took this action in consultation with Sir Robert Reid, the attorney general (the supervisor of the prosecution of criminal offenses), and Sir Frank Lockwood, the solicitor general (the deputy of the attorney general). The unanticipated arrest, which occurred within hours of the withdrawn libel suit, set in motion a lengthy pretrial hearing followed by two criminal trials that took place in quick succession. Beginning on 26 April 1895, the first trial, in which Wilde was tried alongside the thirty-three-year-old Alfred Taylor, who had provided him with assorted sexual contacts, failed on a technicality. Several weeks later, the retrial, in which Wilde and Taylor were tried separately, led to Wilde's incarceration for two years in solitary confinement with hard labor: the seldom-given maximum sentence under the 1885 law. On his release, Wilde traveled to the Continent, where he spent the remainder of his life in France and Italy. Up to and including his untimely death on 30 November 1900, when he had recently turned forty-six years of age, Wilde never revisited the country that had punished him so harshly.

As *Oscar Wilde on Trial* sets out to demonstrate in much greater detail than before, the legal injury inflicted on Wilde is astounding. His chastening experience during the pretrial hearing and subsequent two criminal trials not only resulted in a conviction that shook him to the core; these hearings also proceeded at times in ways that proved confounding both to his close friends and to a handful of legal observers. By drawing on a broad range of recently digitized newspaper sources, as well as ones that are still not accessible through digital media, the present study tracks the events that led up to Wilde's arrest on the evening of Friday, 5 April 1895, resulted in his sentencing on the afternoon of Saturday, 25 May 1895, and concluded with his release from jail on Tuesday, 19 May 1897.

Oscar Wilde on Trial addresses our current knowledge of the Crown prosecution of Wilde, his personal life and professional career prior to the trials, the proceedings that stretched across just over seven weeks, and the post-trials punishment that he endured at three different English prisons. The introductory discussion explains the courtroom events that resulted in Wilde's incarceration. Thereafter, the initial remarks outline the legal background to his conviction for committing acts of gross indecency. This was a newfangled and ill-defined phrase that for the first time became part of the legislative idiom in 1885. Gross indecency, which embraced any form of sexual contact between men, counted as a misdemeanor, whereas the much older criminal offense of sodomy, which dated from the Buggery Act 1533 (25 Hen. 8 c. 6), counted as a felony.

The rest of *Oscar Wilde on Trial* is divided into three parts. Part I focuses on Wilde's personal and professional career, from the time he studied classics at Trinity College Dublin and later at Magdalen College, Oxford, until the moment he decided to launch into his libel suit against Queensberry. Chapter 1 pays close attention to Wilde's evolving sexual interest in other men during a period when he established himself as a talented literary author with an attractive wife and two young sons. Subsequently, chapter 2 looks closely at the period that began with Wilde's intense intimacy with Douglas. Moreover, the discussion draws attention to the two men's mutual interest in an evolving homophile literary subculture. The chapter proceeds to an account of the circumstances that resulted in Queensberry's insulting visiting card accusing Wilde of posing as a sodomite. The analysis concludes with the reasons that brought about the withdrawal of Wilde's libel suit on 5 April 1895, his discreet departure from the Old Bailey that morning, and his subsequent arrest at the Cadogan Hotel, Sloane Street, later that day.

"*Regina v. Oscar Wilde and Alfred Taylor*: A Reconstruction of the Proceedings" makes up part II of *Oscar Wilde on Trial*. Readers will see at once that the reconstruction of the proceedings in part II generally adopts a style that differs from the approach taken by the preceding chapters. There is good reason for this shift. Chapters 3, 4, and 5 try to maintain fidelity to the late Victorian discourse of a range of printed sources that provide reports on the prosecution all the way from the pretrial hearing to the conviction. Part II elucidates the manner in which the press followed the staggering revelations that emerged in the course of the Crown's protracted case. The present volume tries to reproduce as judiciously as possible the information that late Victorian readers at the time could discover about these startling trials. In part II, the commentary also addresses the noticeable moments of discomfort that sundry newspaper editors expressed when they were faced with sexually explicit testimony about London's queer underworld. Without question, the heavily edited reports that appeared in 1895 often take a rather discontinuous turn that can sometimes make it difficult to discern where a lawyer's examination or cross-examination begins and where exactly it ends. Wherever possible, signposts have been placed within the reconstructed proceedings in order to clarify where each attorney starts, finishes, and on occasion resumes his line of questioning. The annotation to the courtroom exchanges is extensive, since the documentation sheds light on details that may be unfamiliar to readers. Many of the notes explain relevant legal cases, as well as such particulars as the network of streets, the major landmarks, and the main institutions of Victorian London.

Part III, which departs from the reconstruction of the proceedings, considers the impact of the trials on the remaining five-and-a-half years of Wilde's comparatively short life. Chapter 6, "Imprisonment," begins by analyzing the diverse ways in which commentators immediately responded to Wilde's sentence. Many of their remarks were hostile. There were, however, a small number of dissenting voices. Skeptical reporters as well as correspondents with the press raised exigent questions about the proceedings, especially the presentation of evidence by individuals who admitted their involvement in the criminal world. These critics on occasion posed queries about the fairness of the legislation under which Wilde had been convicted. Once Wilde entered jail, journalists began to address the repercussions that harsh prison life had on Wilde's mental and physical health. Especially callous was the refusal of the prison authorities to grant Wilde access to books other than John Bunyan's *Pilgrim's Progress* (1678) and the Bible. Relief came in the form of a limited number of books that a Member of Parliament ensured were made available to him. It took more than a year, however, before Wilde obtained, through a change of governor at H.M. Prison Reading, the writing materials for which he had also peititioned. Once he had access to pen and paper, he in due course set to work on the long prison letter, addressed to Alfred Douglas, that eventually became known as *De Profundis*. This document, which counts among the most significant memoirs about the experience of incarceration under the separate system (i.e., solitary confinement), offers an invaluable retrospective on the events that culminated in the trials.

The coda, "Release," considers Wilde's various attempts at restoring his personal and professional affairs in the months after he had completed his sentence. He lived in exile, moving between France and Italy, where he eventually found it impossible to sustain his creativity. Toward the end of 1900, Wilde died in debt, as well as in great physical distress from an infection of a ruptured eardrum that created an opportunity for the meningoencephalitis that killed him.

In many respects, *Oscar Wilde on Trial* serves as a complement to Merlin Holland's *Irish Peacock and Scarlet Marquess: The Real Trial of Oscar Wilde* (2003). Holland's expert volume reproduces the longhand transcription of the exhaustive shorthand reports that Queensberry commissioned during Wilde's libel case. Yet, unlike the document that Holland has edited, there are no comparable shorthand records of the Crown prosecution. As a consequence, my task has been to reconstruct the full complexity of the proceedings from diverse (often highly detailed) printed sources. Through the critical adaptation of these materials, *Oscar Wilde on Trial* aims to give a much completer account of the trials than those that exist in the four extant editions. Here, a few comments on these preceding works are in order, since each one plays a role in the reconstruction of the Crown prosecution that is presented below.

The first of these four volumes, *The Trial of Oscar Wilde: From the Shorthand Reports* (1906), appeared six years after Wilde died in Paris. Charles Carrington—a publisher who traded mostly in clandestine erotica in the French capital—issued this very uneven but nonetheless revealing account. It remains uncertain if Carrington himself had any editorial hand in the selective reconstruction of the proceedings that appears in the publication. The book that Carrington issued, which offers glimpses of major incidents in the courtroom exchanges, claims (as the subtitle suggests) to reproduce sections from a set of shorthand reports, although the provenance of those records is mentioned nowhere in its pages. Importantly, the 1906 volume draws attention to one feature of the trials that some later studies downplay. *The Trial of Oscar Wilde* makes it clear that at least two of the witnesses testified that Wilde had committed sodomy with them. Even though the numerous press reports of the Crown prosecution refrained from printing the word "sodomy," the newspapers of the day every now and then suggested that witnesses used this highly sensitive term. To be sure, the 1906 transcript suffers from serious muddles about names, places, and events that it splices together through ham-fisted editing. There is, however, every reason to believe that *The Trial of Oscar Wilde* is based on a shorthand record of some kind, since even the erratic representation of selected examinations and cross-examinations at the Old Bailey reproduces proper names and street names in a phonetic style.

In 1912, Christopher Sclater Millard—whose impressive publications earned him a reputation as the greatest Wilde scholar of his generation—issued anonymously *Oscar Wilde: Three Times Tried*. Amounting to 484 pages, this imposing volume contains little in the way of annotation, even though Millard's intermittent commentary is often invaluable. Particularly in relation to the first criminal trial that Wilde endured, Millard's study includes exchanges and details that are absent from other archives. His attentive and meticulous reconstruction is the work of a practised bibliographer—although it should be noted that his knowledge of Wilde's career drew on the discoveries of another gifted independent researcher, Walter E. Ledger, who avoided public attention. I have reproduced Millard's findings in those instances where other accounts are not as thorough as his own. Throughout, Millard keeps a close eye on historical information that reveals the political stakes involved in the Crown's determination to secure a conviction. Millard's purpose, as he states in a concise "Preface," is "to give a fair picture of the trial," as well as to "clear . . . the man's figure from the filthy web of lies which has entangled it" ([London: Ferrestone Press, 1912], vii–viii). In principle, Millard's approach is fair-minded. Still, he suppresses any mention of sodomy. Moreover, there is another area where he understandably proceeds with a due measure of caution. In 1912, Millard labored under an obligation not to say anything that might offend the surviving close associates of Wilde's, especially Alfred Douglas, whose personal history with the Irish author, especially in the 1910s, touched on acute sensitivities. (By this time, Douglas, who had married Olive Custance in 1902 and converted to Catholicism in 1911, proved extremely defensive about his homosexual past. His politics had grown correspondingly reactionary.)

After World War II, H. Montgomery Hyde—in what became the most widely circulated book of its kind—compressed the contents of Millard's *Oscar Wilde: Three Times Tried* for a new generation of readers. Hyde's liberal borrowings from Millard came to public attention in a 1967 judgment on a long-delayed copyright case, which involved a dispute about the individual or company that owned the transcript of the proceedings. At the time, Justice Plowman opined: "Hyde's account of the proceedings of the trials was substantially copied from the account in 'Three Times Tried,'" though Hyde "did a good deal of editing"

(*Warwick Film Productions Ltd. v. Eisinger and Others* [1967], 1 c. 1969: 524–25). Hyde admits as much when he states that while Millard's account stands as "the fullest record of the trials which had hitherto appeared," it fails to provide "the necessary introductory background" that would permit "the evidence to be correctly appreciated" (*The Trials of Oscar Wilde*, Notable British Trials [London: William Hodge, 1948], 14). Hyde asserts that even though "the traditional sense of fair play can scarcely be said to have been very pronounced during these trials," it is still the case—when viewed in strict accordance with the 1885 law—that "there can be little if any doubt that Wilde was justly convicted" (13). As I show here, in 1895 this was not an opinion shared by every section of the press. To a few contemporary observers, it looked as though Wilde had been treated inequitably, since there were many unanswered questions about names, places, and persons whose identities were shrouded throughout the proceedings. To his credit, Hyde, who served as an Ulster Unionist Member of Parliament campaigning for homosexual law reform in the 1950s, took a fairly liberal approach to Wilde's behavior. His support for such reform, together with other progressive causes, eventually cost him his political career. Nonetheless, in the 1962 revision of his study for Penguin Books, Hyde continues to speak of Wilde's sexuality in largely negative terms: "The precise mode in which Wilde's peculiar inverted instincts found satisfaction is of interest from the medico-legal viewpoints" (*Oscar Wilde*, Famous Trials 7 [Harmondsworth: Penguin, 1962], 60). Hyde's guarded language, even for its time, strikes a rather wary, if not embarrassed, note. His phrasing was also, for 1962, somewhat out of date. At the point that Hyde's volume came out, social attitudes toward homosexuality had already begun to shift decisively away from this old-fashioned method of pathologizing eroticism between men. In our present century, political standpoints on same-sex attraction have transformed so much that there is no longer any need to apologize for Wilde's honorable desire to enjoy intimacy with other males, particularly in the face of unwarranted legal prohibition.

The reconstruction of the proceedings in *Oscar Wilde on Trial* has largely involved following Millard's lead by synthesizing the admittedly piecemeal but still numerous reports that appear in a broad range of British newspapers. Especially important among the most vigilant newspapers is the *Star*, the radical halfpenny evening paper that rose to fame shortly after it was first published in 1888, when it featured Ernest Parke's reports on the police's failure to catch the suspect eventually known as "Jack the Ripper" in the East End of London. Under Parke's resourceful editorship, the *Star*—which became closely associated with the investigative New Journalism of the time—brought a sharp critical eye to the merciless prosecution. Equally observant about the injustice that Wilde suffered was *Reynolds's Newspaper*: a Sunday broadsheet that stemmed from the Chartist movement much earlier in the century. This remarkable weekly approached the trials with far greater latitude than most of its contemporaries, since it made space for such items as readers' correspondence that pointed to Wilde's progressive political sentiments and his wrongful treatment by the law.

Miscellaneous newspapers including the scandal-mongering *News of the World* had no difficulty in publishing hostile editorials on Wilde's ordeal in court. Even so, the dailies and weeklies carrying the most comprehensive coverage tended to be more descriptive than judgmental in their journalistic methods. This is true of newspapers such as *The Times*, the *Echo*, and the *Sun*, as well as regional ones that reported on the trials with a measure of independence from the centralized press agencies. (The *Western Mail* from Cardiff is one such example, and the *Manchester Courier* is another.) Then again, there were editors who found the courtroom revelations so repulsive that they pledged themselves to minimizing the public's exposure to such unseemliness. The conservative *St. James's Gazette*, to cite one instance, immediately recoiled from the libel proceedings and had little to say about the Crown prosecution that subsequently unfolded. Even though the newspaper acknowledged its obligation to report "the result of the trial," it took the moral high ground when it came to relating the evidence: "We are no fanatical purists," it proclaimed, "no believers in that 'cloistered virtue,' as Milton calls it, which shrinks from contact with the ugly facts of Nature and Life. But some things there are best not spoken" ([anon.], "In Camera," *St. James's Gazette*, 4 April 1895: 3).

Other periodicals adopted different stances when presenting the most scintillating particulars of Wilde's ordeal. The *Illustrated Police Budget* and the *Illustrated Police News* appealed to readerships that were eager to learn as much as they could about the specifics of this astounding case. Both of these papers capitalized on the public's interest in shocking crimes, especially homicides, self-murders, abductions, robberies, and tragedies at sea. (The *Budget* also carried regular features on prizefighters.) Moreover, they included striking woodblock prints, which—through the use of this antiquated technique—injected a spontaneous hand-drawn drama into such exhilarating episodes. These papers touted their privileged contact with members of the prison service and the London Metropolitan Police. Their fly-on-the-wall style of reporting exists nowhere else.

By comparing the assorted parts of the courtroom exchanges that a diverse group of newspapers chose to record in April and May 1895, it has been possible to create a much fuller picture of the Crown prosecution in *Oscar Wilde on Trial* than we find in the earlier studies of 1906, 1912, 1948, and 1962. (The present volume is also more comprehensive than *The Trials of Oscar Wilde, 1895* [2001], edited by Tim Coates, which presents comparatively short extracts from reports on the Crown prosecution of Wilde.) Since the press was mainly the outlet that mediated the extraordinary proceedings against Wilde, I have tried, wherever possible, to preserve the journalists' tone and wording. It has not, however, except in one or two cases, been possible to incorporate the coverage that appeared in foreign newspapers, especially the extensive reporting in France and in the United States, both of which have been the subject of important studies. The Irish press, especially the *Freeman's Journal* and *United Ireland*, which had maintained a strong interest in Wilde's evolving career in London, reported thoughtfully on the trials. In particular, *United Ireland*, edited by William O'Brien, a leading proponent of Home Rule, was quick to see the political dimensions of the confrontation that took place between Queensberry's defense counsel Edward Carson (a diehard Unionist) and his contemporary from college Oscar Wilde (a committed nationalist) during the libel trial. Meanwhile, in Paris two English-language newspapers—the *Galignani Messenger* and the *Paris Herald* (the European edition of the *New York Herald*)—at times served as proof that journalists based outside Britain made observations that were more liberal in their outlook than those of their British counterparts. Here and there, I draw on these sources to focus attention on matters that are invisible in the British reports.

Besides identifying each and every source, I have taken the liberty of modernizing occasional details in certain newspaper articles, simply to increase their accessibility. (An example would be the representation of street names. "Regent-st." in the original has become "Regent Street" in the text below.) This is equally the case with materials quoted from sources prior to 1800, where the use of staves and the capitalization of nouns and verbs have been modernized. I have inserted punctuation where it would otherwise prove somewhat difficult to parse a longer sentence. Such emendations are registered in the notes. Since the press regarded trials of this type as rather theatrical affairs, journalists often pepper their reports with stage directions that remind us of moments in the proceedings when a particularly startling admission created, to take a representative example, a "*sensation in court*." Directions of this type, which also alert us to the tone that a lawyer or a witness adopted when the exchanges grew intense, have been maintained.

Readers may rightly question whether late-nineteenth-century newspapers can reliably provide accurate insights into the astonishing courtroom events that made Wilde's name into such a source of both national and international scandal. Under no circumstances can we view such journalism, regardless of how observational and neutral it often appears, as a transparent account of the truth. Each paper had its political predilections, editorial preferences, and reporting practices. Moreover, journalists sometimes made divergent assumptions about the events that unfolded in the courtroom, especially with respect to Wilde's demeanor and state of mind. In any case, all of the press accounts that have been assembled here involved editors and subeditors abbreviating and condensing shorthand records of the proceedings. Had such records been published in their entirety, they would have far exceeded the amount of text that could be contained within the limited column inches available. Nonetheless, there is a further noticeable aspect of the abundant reports of the trials. Many of them strove, in the face of considerable pressures to exercise discretion, to reveal the more unmentionable aspects of the homosexual acts that various leading witnesses had described.

The comparative openness of the journalism of the time arguably came at a moment before the transition to a more moralistic tone that increasingly dominated the press in the later 1890s. In 1933, the novelist and memoirist Compton Mackenzie saw 1895 as a pivotal year when affordable newspapers were still more forthright in their reporting than they became in a later, more censorious period. Mackenzie, whose early writings reflect on the legacy of aesthetes such as Wilde, recalls at length how, at the time of Wilde's suit against Queensberry, he was almost run down as a child by an Atlas omnibus while hurriedly crossing Piccadilly Circus to grab a copy of a well-known afternoon daily:

> I was nearly run over because I had turned my head away from the direction of Regent Street in order to read a *Pall Mall Gazette* placard waved by an excited newsboy who was shouting in a shrill voice, "Libel action by famous author against well-known peer! Verdict!" Even to a boy of twelve that sounded exciting. As a result of that verdict Oscar Wilde was arrested in the Cadogan Square Hotel, and the deplorable case took its course. In those days newspapers were not printed for family reading; they were father's possession, and father was presumed to be able to read in his newspaper without blushing what read in a book would have made him explode with outraged pudor [i.e., proper sense of shame or modesty]. We nice moderns who are inclined to deprecate the devotion and care with which *The News of the World* collects every Sunday morning for the tired working-man the sexual offences of the previous week, have forgotten the freedom that the Press allowed in the days before Mr. Alfred Harmsworth revolutionized journalism by producing a paper that could be read not merely by father but by the rest of the family. The *Daily Mail* was still a year away from birth when the Oscar Wilde case was being fully reported in the papers without any attempt even to soften

> details that printed in a book would have sent the author and publisher to gaol. (Compton Mackenzie, *Literature in My Time* [London: Rich & Cowan, 1933], 79–80)

For this reason, children such as Mackenzie "knew every detail of the case" (80). In his view, even though the "shock to respectability was too great" for there to be "any open sympathy with Wilde," his generation for the most part sensed "that there was something wrong with a civilization which attributed so much importance to an eleventh commandment, *Thou Shalt Not Be Found Out*" (80). By this account, even parents could not entirely protect their charges from homosexual scandal. As Mackenzie suggests, the national mood of the press shifted considerably when Alfred Harmsworth's halfpenny *Daily Mail* began publication in 1896. To Holbrook Jackson, in his informative study of 1890s art and culture, the *Daily Mail* not only appealed to "the political prejudices and aspirations of the average man"; its loud conservative moralizing voice also "openly fanned the Jingo flame" in the spirit of a populist imperialism (*The Eighteen-Nineties: A Review of Art and Ideas at the Close of the Nineteenth Century* [London: Grant Richards, 1913], 63).

In light of these remarks, *Oscar Wilde on Trial* draws conclusions about the press coverage in 1895 that diverge from the inferences that Ed Cohen makes in his ambitious study *Talk on the Wilde Side: Toward a Genealogy of a Discourse on Male Sexualities* (1993). Cohen asserts that the printed sources that he has analyzed suggest that Wilde's trials involved evasions and circumlocutions about the sexual activities that had taken place with a dozen or so young men. As a result, Cohen advances the following claim about the apparent difficulties that the courts and the newspapers had in voicing the distasteful eroticism in which Wilde had indulged: "So while the courtroom proceedings circled around the unarticulated implication that Wilde had sought the sexual services of the men named in the plea of justification, the newspapers were challenged to report this testimony without actually revealing any of its very titillating substance" ([New York: Routledge, 1993], 144). Both parts of this statement require a measure of correction.

To be sure, journalists faced serious challenges regarding what they could and could not put into print. Yet the proceedings, as later evidence would reinforce, were not always so tame. As I have mentioned above, our comprehension of Wilde's unsuccessful libel suit radically transformed when Merlin Holland issued his edition of the longhand transcription of the shorthand reports that Queensberry had commissioned for his own purposes. Carson had no hesitation in talking about sex between men when he asked Wilde to explain the reasoning behind a passage of dialogue from *The Picture of Dorian Gray*: "Do you think that, taken in its natural meaning, would suggest that what they were talking about was a charge of sodomy?" (*Irish Peacock*, 102). The barrister repeatedly pressed Wilde to admit to the sexual activities that Queensberry had itemized in the plea of justification. Of Walter Grainger—who was seventeen when Wilde hired him as an under-butler at a vacation home that he rented during the summer of 1893—Carson wished to know: "did you ask him to come into your bedroom?" "Never," Wilde retorted, "in my life" (209). Unwilling to let the matter drop, Carson persisted: "Or into your bed[?]" (209). Such statements demonstrate that it was not quite the case that Wilde's intimacies remained "unarticulated" at the Old Bailey. On more than one occasion, Carson wanted to know if Wilde had placed his "person between the legs" of his young male acquaintances (118). Once the male sex workers appeared as witnesses for the subsequent Crown prosecution, the testimony became even more graphic, in ways that suggest that they were primed to speak openly of having committed "sodomy," even though Wilde was not charged with committing this felony. "Sodomy" was an almost unreportable word in the press. The same is true of the term "sodomite." Nevertheless, editors now and again made these offending words evident through carefully situated em-dashes and asterisks.

At this juncture, a few commments are in order about sexual terminology, since the vocabulary that I use touches on sensitivities about the critical categories that appear most apposite for approaching and interpreting Wilde's personal life. I wish to remove any misapprehensions about my frequent references to Wilde's homosexuality, since this particular term—whether in the late Victorian period or afterward—carries certain complications, not least the idea that it defines a specific type of identity. The term was not anachronistic when Wilde was sent to jail. By 1893, the homophile campaigner John Addington Symonds, who had absorbed the idea of homosexuality from the Austro-German sexologist Richard von Krafft-Ebing's *Psychopathia Sexualis* (1886), had started to employ it in his confidential correspondence with like-minded individuals, including the English socialist Edward Carpenter. We can see its appearance, too, in French sources, such as the magazine *Mercure de France*, which in 1896 spoke openly about "l'amour hétérosexuel" and "l'amour homosexuel" ([anon.], "Journaux et revues," *Mercure de France*, 20 [1896]: 393). Yet the label "homosexual," as historians have observed, soon became associated for some time with prejudiced clinical attitudes. For many medical specialists, a person's erotic attraction to his or her own sex manifested a congenital pathology that defined the very core of one's abject subjectivity. Hence there has long been good reason, in many different contexts, to advert to other labels that do not carry the taint of illness or disease. One such word is "gay," which during the late 1960s transformed from a term initially linked with Victorian female prostitution to an identity that politicized sexual subjects could own with pride. Another is "queer." The epithet "queer," which bore considerable stigma during the Victorian *fin de siècle,* underwent radical transformation in the 1990s, when activists reclaimed and re-signified it, in order to provide more expansive opportunities to articulate non-normative sexual practices and presentations of gender.

These descriptors or labels, in their original usage, were not—on the evidence we have—terms that Wilde ever embraced. (After the trials, his preferred term was "Uranian": a *fin-de-siècle* word that associates same-sex love with heavenly bodies.) For the purposes of the current language that we employ to analyze the history of sexuality, however, terms such as "homosexual," "gay," and "queer" prove more neutral than the one that gained greatest purchase among medical specialists from the 1890s through the 1950s. The idiom in question is "sexual inversion," which advances the belief that women who love women and men who love men constitute inverts: figures whose sexual soul is supposedly at odds with their anatomically designated sex. This concept was established in the English-speaking world through the eminent sexologist Havelock Ellis's remarkable series of case studies, *Sexual Inversion* (1897), which subsequently became the first volume in his imposing *Studies in the Psychology of* Sex (1897–1928). To be sure, there were modern writers such as Radclyffe Hall, who identified strongly as a sexual invert. Moreover, historians have in recent decades analyzed the development of the concept in relation not to homosexuality, but to the development of transgender forms of sexual being and gender identity. Even so, "sexual inversion" for decades addressed what specialists largely agreed was a congenital pathology. "Inversion," the term that Hyde prefers to employ, is therefore not pertinent, historically or theoretically, to an account of Wilde's sexuality.

For the past quarter of a century, many different institutions of power in the western world have succeeded (not infrequently in the face of hostile resistance) in disentangling homosexual behaviors from medical charactizations that view such desires as a form of psychiatric disease. Briefly, the term "homosexual" is no longer freighted these days with the insinuations of ill-health, debility, or even degeneracy frequently associated with once-influential paradigms such as sexual inversion. Be that as it may, the word nonetheless endures to some extent as a restrictive category, one that does not always provide the fullest picture of Wilde's intimate passions. In what follows, the term "homosexual" is reserved for discussions of his erotic encounters with other men. In no respect do I regard Wilde—when we look at the broad sweep of his career—as an exclusively homosexual or fundamentally gay man, although it is unmistakable that his desires inclined over time toward younger males. (There is anecdotal evidence that the poet Ernest Dowson persuaded Wilde to visit a female prostitute in June 1897, a few weeks after his release from jail. Robert Harborough Sherard recalls that "Dowson took [Wilde]—in the hope of wooing him back to natural ways, to the brothel at Lègué Dieppe[,] an experience which Wilde described as a supper of cold mutton" [Sherard, "To A. J. A. Symons," 13 May 1937, Clark Library, MS Wilde, S551L S988, Box 62, Folder 25].)

Wilde's career evinces noticeable transitions in his patterns of intimacy, which ultimately courted considerable danger through sexual contact with younger males whose criminal activities were known to the police. He proved, however, undaunted by the perils involved in this type of sexual contact. As we can see from Wilde's correspondence with his future literary executor Robert Ross, in his final years he refused to apologize for his erotic attraction to his own sex. Despite his compromised health and precarious finances, he continued to pursue the company of male youths, in ways that reveal that he felt no shame because some "people [were] being horrid" about him, including those hotel guests whose complaints about his presence were sufficiently loud that the management asked him to leave the premises (*The Complete Letters of Oscar Wilde*, ed. Merlin Holland and Rupert Hart-Davis [London Fourth Estate, 2000], 1019).

Hotel managers, however, were not always troubled simply by the idea that Wilde's unwelcome notoriety might offend other guests. The audacious life that he led often came, in a different sense, at a high price: the risk that he would be unable to pay his bills. In any case, Wilde—long before the trials—ran up many debts at the luxurious venues where he had reserved rooms. His failure to settle his debts sometimes resulted in writs, ones that not only led to the sale of his household goods but also contributed to his bankruptcy. For this reason, my discussion refers at various moments to Wilde's income and expenses. Undeniably, it proves challenging to provide direct monetary equivalents between the value of pounds sterling in the 1880s and 1890s, on the one hand, and the corresponding value in the same currency and in U.S. dollars in our own time, on the other hand. It is, however, reasonable to note that in the late nineteenth century it was possible for an individual to live comfortably on an income of £300 per annum. Very roughly, this amount has a real-price value of £31,500 and $44,000 in the present day. From the perspective of labor earnings, though, that annual amount comes to a much higher sum in relation to current parameters of income: £123,000 or $172,000. When we discover, then, that Wilde lavished £85 on a dinner that he enjoyed with Alfred Douglas at Paillard's, Paris, it is clear that the bill ran into what would be, by today's calculations, thousands of British pounds or U.S. dollars. To be sure, this was an exception even in Wilde's customary extravagances. It nevertheless gives a fair indication of the large sums with which he was willing to part when either his generosity or profligacy got the better of him.

If, in the process of researching this study, one point has become clear, it is this: Oscar Wilde, whose defiant homosexuality persisted as such an affront to society, was by no means tried fairly. The proceedings of the pretrial hearing and two criminal trials demonstrate that the Crown pursued a conviction on debatable legal grounds, especially where the contentious corroboration of evidence was concerned. The lurid courtroom discussion of Wilde's sexual practices also derived from the abundant witness statements that Queensberry's attorney collected, through dubious means, in support of his client's plea of justification. It appears that the witness statements from the young men were extracted after the solicitor had exerted considerable moral pressure. This was, for example, plausibly the case with Herbert Tankard, the fifteen-year-old page boy who had served Wilde at the Savoy Hotel in March 1893. In his plea, the marquess claimed that Wilde had taken "indecent liberties" with the teenager (Holland, *Irish Peacock*, 289). The same may have been true of the seventeen-year-old Walter Grainger, whom Wilde employed while he was writing *An Ideal Husband* at a large rented home in Goring-on-Thames later that year. Grainger disclosed that Wilde came into his bedroom: "he worked me up with his hand and made me spend [i.e., ejaculate] in his mouth." He stated, too, that Wilde had browbeaten him by stating that he would go to jail should anyone discover their sexual intimacy. As Neil McKenna has rightly observed, "If Grainger was telling the truth, Oscar's threats reflect little credit upon him, and today would be condemned as a classic stratagem of sexual abuse" (*The Secret Life of Oscar Wilde* [London: Century, 2003] 240).

Still, as McKenna also acknowledges, Russell wrested statements of this kind from witnesses who were almost certainly told that it was in their best interests to cooperate. It is likely that when the veteran private detectives tracked down these vulnerable individuals, none of whom had much education, they reminded them that they might be prosecuted and imprisoned for their close association with Wilde. It also seems possible that Russell or Queensberry used the services of another lawyer, Bernard Abrahams, whose clients included blackmailers, to assist in coercing witnesses to make statements. At the same time, it is evident that the marquess made sure funds were available to suborn witnesses in return for the desired testimony. As we see below (179), different observers have concluded that sums were paid to Charles Parker, Alfred Wood, and Edward Shelley, all of whom confessed to having experienced sexual intimacy with Wilde. Moreover, certain reporters remarked that the leading male witnesses with the most questionable backgrounds, such as Charles Parker, appeared finely turned out with fresh sets of clothes, just so that they could masquerade as models of respectability.

That Russell managed to obtain these distressing statements from witnesses most probably under duress and with inducements from the marquess gives one pause. The situation speaks as much to the legal threats that these young men suffered from Russell as it does about the sexual advances that Wilde made on them. Moreover, the fact that these statements—which were sold at Christie's, London, in 2001—are still not available to the public means that it will take some time before we can obtain a fuller sense of the techniques that Russell implemented. Access to these documents might clarify, for example, why Jane Margaret Cotter, a Savoy Hotel chambermaid, declared that she had found "a common boy, rough looking, about 14 years of age" in Wilde's bed two years earlier. The same is true of the statement that the freelance masseur Antonio Migge made about noticing a teenage boy in Wilde's bed, though under cross-examination he could not remember the color of the unidentified young man's hair. At present, it remains difficult to assess Russell's methods. Currently, we are limited to snippets from the witness statements recorded in newspaper reports from the time of the Christie's sale, such as the one in the *Guardian* (https://www.theguardian.com/uk/2001/may/06/books.booksnews). The other main glimpses of these witness statements appear in *The Life of Oscar Wilde* by McKenna: the only researcher, I believe, who has had the opportunity to review these materials.

These small slices of documentation raise suspicions about Russell's tactics. When one reads such sensational statements as Cotter's and Migge's, it is hard not to imagine that money may well have changed hands. Why, we might ask, would Wilde permit a chambermaid and a masseur to espy such flagrant indiscretions? And why did these otherwise insignificant individuals agree to divulge such indelicate observations about events that had taken place more than two years previously? Similarly, the proceedings reveal that Cotter mentioned that she had reported the excrement stains on the bed linens and in the bathroom to the housekeeper. Yet any concerns that the befouled sheets may have aroused were taken no further. At present, it proves difficult for us to fathom the trustworthiness of this kind of testimony from the hotel staff. Even Justice Wills—

who meted out the harshest available sentence to Wilde because of his outrage at the sexual disclosures made in court—called their evidence into question.

Besides the witness statements, there are no other comparable documents that shed light on the men who cooperated with Russell and his team. No memoirs appear to have survived. Some of the young men who either exploited or benefited from Wilde's company, including Alphonse Conway, William Parker, and Alfred Wood, disppeared from the record. Small bits and pieces of information, however, illuminate the lives that a few of these individuals went on to lead. Tankard, the youngest person to give a statement to Queensberry's solicitor, eventually became the landlord of a public house in Whitechapel. He died, with an estate of over £7,000, in 1946. Meanwhile, Edward Shelley, a publisher's clerk who had literary ambitions, pursued an uneven military career; he married a wealthy widow in 1937 and died in 1951, aged seventy-seven, at Hertford (see Thomas Mallon, "A Boy of No Importance," *Biography* 1, no. 3 [1978]: 65–81). Walter Grainger, by comparison, married in 1902 and went on to have three children; he worked as a dispatch porter in Whiteley's department store. He died in 1935. Frederick ("Fred") Atkins, who traded in extortion and prostitution, continued to perform as a comedian. Reports in the *Stage* indicate that Atkins had roles in Alfred Mason's *Dainties* in 1920 and in *Scenes and Screams* at the Royal Theatre in December 1927. Little is known about the Parker brothers. Hyde observes that in 1907 the Irish diplomat and writer Sir Shane Leslie encountered the former blackmailer and sex worker Charles Parker, down and out, on the Dundalk–Dublin road (H. Montgomery Hyde Collection, Harry Ransom Center, quoted in Holland, *Irish Peacock*, 318).

There were at least two individuals who refused to comply with Russell's demands. Sydney Mavor, who came from a respectable family, had a passion for cross-dressing and an interest in the music-hall stage. He went on to teach English at Hurstpierpoint College, a private boys' school in Sussex, from 1917 to 1925 (see Peter King, *Hurstpierpoint College, 1849–1995: The School by the Downs* [Bognor Regis: Phillimore, 1997], 157). Mavor died, after he was struck by a car at age eighty-five, at Upton Lovell, Warminster, Wiltshire, in 1952. By comparison, the other individual who refused to testify againt Wilde, Alfred Taylor, ended up suffering the same sentence as his friend. After his release, Taylor, the onetime heir to a cocoa manufacturing fortune, disappeared almost entirely from view. He made his way to the United States. Alfred Douglas claimed that when he was staying in a Chicago hotel during the 1920s, he called for a floor waiter and Taylor answered (see Richard Ellmann, *Oscar Wilde* [New York: Knopf, 1988], 478). Nothing else is known about Taylor's later life.

In the end, what is most remarkable about the mishandled trials is that Wilde—even when he was enduring the hardships of solitary confinement—expressed no regrets about the time that he spent with the young men who testified against him. In the long, recriminatory letter that Wilde wrote from prison to Douglas, he impenitently recalled his intimacy with the youths whom he had entertained at restaurants, hotels, and his family home, and on whom he had lavished expensive gifts, including silver cigarette cases: "I don't," he insisted in the work that became known as *De Profundis*, "feel at all ashamed of having known them" (*The Complete Letters of Oscar Wilde*, 759). To the end of his days, Wilde understood that in expending much energy and money on the various males he called the "brightest of gilded snakes," he had not—regardless of whatever the law may think—done anything conceivably wrong.

ACKNOWLEDGMENTS

My interest in Wilde's harrowing experience at the Old Bailey arose in 2011 when Ella Dzelzainis (Newcastle University) kindly invited me to give a plenary presentation at the "Taking Liberties" conference, hosted at her university, on 15–16 June 2012. My preparation for that symposium, together with the research for a subsequent essay that appeared in *Feminist Theory* in 2016, inspired me to develop the present study. I first presented sections of my discussion about Wilde's involvement in two magazines, the *Spirit Lamp* and the *Chameleon*, in a plenary talk, "Oscar Wilde and Queer Modernity: Oxford, 1892–1895," at the annual conference of the Victorian Interdisciplinary Studies Association of the Western United States (VISAWUS), Portland, Oregon, in November 2013. My thanks go to Diana Maltz (Southern Oregon University) and Kristin Mahoney (Michigan State University) for the generous invitation to speak at this event. I am grateful to the audience at the School of Law, University of Toronto, whose faculty and students offered responses to the presentation I made on this topic in March 2014. Simon Stern and Patrick Keilty were gracious hosts during my visit there. Selected materials relating to the Fitzroy Street raid in August 1894, the extortionists and sex workers who served as witnesses in the Wilde trials, and the assault on writer and composer Cotsford Dick were delivered as a plenary presentation at the Australasian Victorian Studies Association (AVSA) conference, "Victorian Margins," 7–9 July 2016. Jock MacLeod (Griffith University) and Meg Tasker (Federation University) offered generous hospitality at Ballarat, Victoria, during the AVSA symposium. I appreciate the hospitality that Deaglán Ó Donghaile and Gerry Smyth, who organized the "Marginal Irish Modernisms" conference at Liverpool John Moores University, 8–9 September 2016, gave to me when I presented my research on the Dublin Castle affair.

I am grateful, too, to Ana Parejo Vadillo (Birkbeck, University of London); Rebecca N. Mitchell (University of Birmingham); Daniel Brown, Mary Hammond, and Justine Pizzo (University of Southampton); Peter Stoneley (University of Reading); and Matthew Ingleby (Institute of English Studies, University of London) for inviting me to make presentations on aspects of my research for *Oscar Wilde on Trial*. My thanks must go as well to James Lingwood (Artangel) for making arrangements for me to present my research in the lecture series accompanying the installation "Inside: Artists and Writers at Reading Prison" (4 September–4 December 2016). Laurel Brake (Birkbeck, University of London) graciously provided an instructive response to my presentation on "Oscar Wilde and the Liberal Party," which I made at the IES on 28 October 2016. Part of the "Coda" was delivered in a paper, "Oscar Wilde and the Homoeroticism of Italy and Sicily: Naples, Capri, Taormina, Palermo," given at the NAVSA/AVSA Supernumerary Conference held at La Pietra, Florence, 17–20 May 2017. I am also grateful to have had the opportunity to present parts of this research at the conference "Victorian Stakes and Stakeholders," held by VISAWUS at Seattle on 6–9 November 2019.

Substantial portions of my research for *Oscar Wilde on Trial* have developed from sources held at the William Andrews Clark Memorial Library, University of California, Los Angeles, which houses the largest archive of materials relating to Wilde's life and work anywhere in the world. Scott Jacobs arranged for scans to be made from the invaluable scrapbook of press cuttings from the *Star* and *Daily Telegraph*, as well as several other newspapers. Philip Palmer, the former head of research services, also made various important items available to me during the temporary closure of the Clark from April 2015 to January 2018. Rebecca Fenning Marschall directed me to relevant items in the Clark's collections. I appreciate as well the assistance of Aric Nair. At UCLA, I remain grateful to Barbara Fuchs, who between 2011 and 2016 directed the Center for 17th- & 18th-Century Studies, for providing funds to support research assistance. During the early stages of research, Grace A. Ballor assisted my inquiries by transcribing an album of newspaper cuttings from the *Star*. Paul Cella scrupulously checked many details in my initial reconstruction of the proceedings; moreover, he located invaluable information about the individuals who featured in the trials, and identified sundry important sources in the American and feminist press. At the Young Research Library (UCLA), Jenny Lee and Monalisa Sanchez processed many requests for interlibrary loans, Christopher Brennan went to great lengths to obtain electronic copies of British newspapers, and Matthew Johnson ensured that I had access to e-books. Molly Haigh assisted with the reproduction of many of the figures. Lynda Tolly and Hillary Gordon at the Grace M. Hunt Memorial English Reading Room at UCLA gave me access to numerous important sources. At UCLA's Hugh and Hazel Darling Law Library, Stephanie Anayah and Lynn McClelland provided invaluable assistance. Marissa Kings-Garwig at the University of California, Southern Regional Library Facility assisted with reproducing two of the figures.

My knowledge of Wilde's presence in the early 1890s student press at Oxford derives from the research that Andra Lim undertook for her prizewinning research paper in "The Wilde Archive" capstone seminar English 184 (winter 2013). While preparing this book, I was particularly indebted to the students who enrolled in the Honors Collegium seminar "London and the Culture of Male Homosexuality, 1870–1900," which I taught during spring 2015. The members of this class—Jessica Arizmendi de la Torre, Robin Chang, Alyssa Dorn, Maxwell Fleer, Rosemary Flores, Matthew Holland, Shannon Kanegawa, Elias Lawliet, Nicolette Jin Olson, Alexa Savalas James, Tori Jean Schmitt, Layla Stirewalt, Sadaf Tabatabai, and Yuyu Zhu—shared their insights with great thoughtfulness. I also wish to thank Ashley E. Truong, who audited the class, for her helpful comments. In winter 2016, I benefited from the observations that the graduate students in English 252 ("Victorian Sexual Scandals") made during our discussions of prominent controversies that took place in London between 1870 and 1895. I am grateful to the following seminar members: Oriah Amit, Jacqueline Barrios, Kristen Cardon, Jessica Cook, Vivian Delchamps, Rebecca Ehrhardt, Kersti Francis, Misho Ishikawa, Robert Mendoza, Samantha Morse, Jené Pledger, Emma Spies, and Darby Walters. During spring 2018, I discussed the contents of this book with the students enrolled in Honors 151, "Victorian Sexual Scandals": Ryan Anderson, Rebecca Barrett, Brooke Collins, Pauline Demerjian, Christine Guanzing, Richard Hatch, Darby Hughes, Simone Montgomery, Mercedes Navarro, Annie Nicholson, Rachel Paul, Bernice Perdomo, Josselin Rivas, Victoria ("Tori") Roderick, Alexandra ("Lexi") Van Ligten, and Jordan Wimbish. Louise Brown offered much-appreciated guidance on my translations from the French. In the UCLA English department, the officers handling finance—Laura Clennon, Frank Figueroa, Feng Huang, Nicole A. Liang, and Brianna Miller—assisted me with both the administration of my research funds and my travel arrangements to London. Research at The National Archives, Kew, and the Eccles Bequest, British Library, was kindly sponsored through a generous UCLA Council on Research grant from the Academic Senate for the year 2015–16.

Colette Colligan (Simon Fraser University) generously shared her research on the Parisian English-language newspapers the *Galignani Messenger* and the *Paris Herald*, which published certain details of the trials that did not appear in

British sources. I appreciate her thoughtful responses to a near-final draft of my account of the proceedings. Phyllis Weliver (St. Louis University) illuminated a musical reference. Rebecca N. Mitchell, with whom I co-authored a previous study of Wilde's career, made thorough responses to my earliest attempt at reconstructing a transcript of the trials. I wish to thank her for the photographs of a copy of the *Oxford Magazine* that she kindly consulted at Trinity College Dublin Library, and for a transcription of materials relating to Charles Russell's records of Wilde's professional contracts, which are held at the Bodleian Library, University of Oxford. Diana Maltz alerted me to assorted important points about Wilde's career that I mention in this volume. I remain indebted to Marysa Demoor (Ghent University) for presenting me with a copy of the invaluable *Dictionary of Nineteenth-Century Journalism* (2009), which she co-edited with Laurel Brake. Mark W. Turner (King's College London) located and copied an issue of the *Church Reformer* held in the university library. Kimberley Smith, at the City of Westminster Archives Centre, shared information about the Paddington Free Library. Lindsay Smith (University of Sussex) alerted me to the significance of Louis Umfreville Wilkinson's memories of his correspondence with Wilde about the trials. Alexandra Milsom (Hostos Community College, City University of New York) assisted me with bibliographical information about the John Murray tour guides. Neil McKenna graciously answered a query about the witness statements that Queensberry's attorney collected before the marquess's libel trial. Yvonne Ivory (University of South Carolina), with whom I have co-edited a textual edition of Wilde's works, directed me toward significant German sources.

John Stokes (King's College London) furnished a letter of introduction so that I could consult British Library, Western Manuscripts, Loan MS 122. Tim Hitchcock (University of Sussex) and Sharon Howard (University of Sheffield) provided guidance on sources that illuminate the procedures for jury selection at the Old Bailey in the nineteenth century. Julia Peers and Lucy Sussex directed me toward databases containing a range of Australian and New Zealand reports on the Wilde trials. Otto Rauchbauer (University of Vienna) alerted me to materials on Shane Leslie's interest in Wilde. Clare Barlow (Tate Britain) shared with me references to materials held in The National Archives. Graham Earnshaw (Earnshaw Books) and Mark Samuels Lasner (University of Delaware) exchanged their thoughts on the career of Edmund Trelawny Backhouse. Ellen Crowell (St. Louis University) shed light on the role that the bibliophiles connected with Ye Sette of Odd Volumes had on Wilde's social life. Gregory Mackie and Katherine Kalsbeek kindly arranged for scans from *Poetry of the Crabbet Club* (1892) to be made from the copy held at the Department of Rare Books and Special Collections, University of British Columbia Library. Michael Seeney illuminated the careers of Maurice Salis Schwabe and More Adey. Barry Walsh of the Friends of the Metropolitan Police Historical Collection directed me to Peter Kennison's historical study of policing in central North and South-west London. Oriah Amit (UCLA) consulted the "Bad Debts, 1884–1906" folder of James Lock and Co., which is housed at the London Metropolitan Archives. I am grateful to Philip Burnett and to the Master and Fellows of University College, Oxford, for granting permission to refer to an article on Charles Alan Fyffe held in the college library. Xavier Giudicelli (Université de Reims Champagne-Ardennes) generously arranged for me to receive an electronic copy of his 2013 article on the *Spirit Lamp*; he also advised me on my transcriptions from the French. Alastair J. L. Blanshard (University of Queensland) shared with me a recent essay that addresses the relations between Karl Heinrich Ulrichs's definition of the *Urning* and Plato's *Symposium*. Alex Murray generously sent me a copy of Jeffrey Dudgeon's study of H. Montgomery Hyde. Mack Gregg shared information about Alexander Francis's comments on the Crown prosecution of Wilde. Both John Kirwan and Eoin Swithin Walsh offered their thoughts on the suggestion that the court papers relating to Wilde's trials might have perished in the firebombing that destroyed the home of Hamilton ("Ham") Cuffe, 5th Earl of Desarts, Desart Court, Co. Kilkenny, in 1923. Tim Coates graciously shared his considerable knowledge of the "blue books" that include reports on the trials, which are now housed at the premises of TSO Williams/Lea Tag, Normanton, Humberside, U.K. Lisa Surridge (University of Victoria, British Columbia) brought the collection of Cecil O. D. Branson, Q.C., to my attention; Branson's library contained several titles that I had not previously consulted. I remain particularly grateful to the staff of the Department of Collection Care at The National Archives for ensuring that I had access to materials that they were preparing for an exhibition. Ceri Richards at the Department of Special Collections, University of Reading Library, arranged for me to examine materials held in the Robert Harborough Sherard Collection. The Department of Rare Books and Special Collections at Princeton University Library furnished me with a copy of *The Great West-End Scandal: Oscar Wilde Exposed*, which M. Elton published in April 1895. Martin Beisly (Martin Beisly Fine Art, London) kindly sent me a copy of his 2019 catalogue, *William Powell Frith, R.A. (1819–1909): The Private View at the Royal Academy, 1881*. Elizabeth Adams, Librarian at University College, Oxford, identified items for me to consult in the Robert Ross Memorial Archive. Charlotte Berry, Magdalen College, Oxford, enabled me to consult a scrapbook of newspaper cuttings in the H. Montgomery Hyde collection. Mary-

Louise Rowland (Hurstpierpoint College) arranged for me to obtain a copy of Peter King's study of the school.

Special thanks go to Nicholas Frankel (Virginia Commonwealth University), Neil Hultgren (Calfornia State University, Long Beach), and Sean O'Toole (Baruch College, City University of New York), who read my first complete reconstruction of the criminal proceedings from start to finish; their generous feedback was invaluable. Simon Stern has liberally shared numerous references with me, many of which relate to the legal history of the period. Gregory Mackie offered a helpful response to my concluding remarks in the coda. Merlin Holland advised me on various matters relating to the different records of the trials that were published in 1906, 1912, 1948, and 1962. The anonymous readers who generously shared their insights in two sets of reports have assisted in ensuring that specific details, especially ones regarding points of law, are accurately represented in the discussion.

As my notes should make clear, I have learned greatly from the research of knowledgeable scholars who have advanced our understanding of the challenges that Wilde faced in April and May 1895. Linda Stratmann's *Marquess of Queensberry: Wilde's Nemesis* (2013), which presents fresh information about the role that John Sholto Douglas played in Wilde's downfall, proved especially illuminating. Several other biographers—Maureen Borland, Franny Moyle, Julie Speedie, and Caspar Wintermans—have produced irreplaceable scholarship that has strengthened my knowledge of Wilde's connections with Robert Ross, Constance Wilde, Ada Leverson, and Alfred Douglas, respectively.

The staff members at Yale University Press deserve my fullest acknowledgment for their expert guidance. The executive editor, William Frucht, responded thoughtfully to each phase of this project as it developed from concise proposal to completed manuscript. Ann-Marie Imbornoni, who maintained a close eye on the smallest details, shepherded the final manuscript through production. Charlie Clark at Newgen answered my numerous inquiries. Robert Whitelock undertook the demanding copy-editing. Do Mi Stauber completed the comprehensive index.

Small amounts of material reproduced in the present volume have appeared in previous essays of mine: "Oscar Wilde: The Man, the Life, the Legend," in *The Palgrave Guide to Oscar Wilde*, ed. Frederick S. Roden (Basingstoke: Palgrave, 2004), 6–35; "'All men kill the thing they love': The Realistic and Romantic Contexts of *The Ballad of Reading Gaol*," in *Approaches to Teaching Oscar Wilde*, ed. Philip E. Smith (New York: Modern Language Association, 2008), 230–47; "Introduction," in *Wilde Discoveries: Traditions, Histories, Archives*, ed. Joseph Bristow (Toronto: University of Toronto Press, 2013), 3–39;

"Oscar Wilde's Unfinished Society Plays: *Mr. and Mrs. Daventry, A Wife's Tragedy*, and *Love Is Law*," in *Oscar Wilde's Society Plays*, ed. Michael Y. Bennett (New York: Palgrave Macmillan, 2015), 51–74; "The Blackmailer and the Sodomite: Oscar Wilde on Trial," *Feminist Theory*, 17, no. 1 (2016): 41–62; "Oscar Wilde, Ronald Gower, and the Shakespeare Memorial," *Etudes anglaises* 6, no. 1 (2016): 7–22; "Homosexual Blackmail in the 1890s: The Fitzroy Street Raid, the Oscar Wilde Trials, and the Case of Cotsford Dick," *Australasian Journal of Victorian Studies* 22, no. 1 (2017), https://openjournals.library.sydney.edu.au/index.php/AJVS; and "Introduction: Oscar Wilde and the Cultures of Childhood," in *Oscar Wilde and the Cultures of Childhood*, ed. Joseph Bristow (London: Palgrave Macmillan, 2017), 1–39. Selected materials in my discussion of Wilde's broken friendship with Rennell Rodd appear in the volume titled *Epigrams, Lectures, and "L'Envoi,"* in the Oxford English Texts edition of *The Complete Works of Oscar Wilde*, which I have co-edited with Yvonne Ivory and Rebecca N. Mitchell. My thanks go to Palgrave Macmillan, the Modern Language Association, University of Toronto Press, Sage Journals, Klincksieck (Cairn International), AVSA, and Oxford University Press for permission to reprint those materials here.

Merlin Holland, the executor of Oscar Wilde's estate, kindly granted permission for the reproduction of passages from correspondence that remain in copyright, and for extracts quoted from *Irish Peacock and Scarlet Marquess*. Jullianne Ballou arranged for copies of Edward Shelley's and Arthur Clifton's respective items of correspondence to be made from the collections held at the Harry Ransom Center. Quotations from these sources are reproduced here courtesy of the Harry Ransom Center, the University of Texas at Austin. Lord Alfred Douglas's unpublished materials are reproduced courtesy of the Executors of the Literary Estate of Lord Alfred Douglas © John D. Stratford and John Rubinstein. Caroline Gould, executor of the estate of Robert Baldwin Ross, generously granted permission to quote from an unpublished letter to Louis Umfreville Wilkinson.

The figures have been taken from the following collections. Figs. 1 and 2: The National Archives, Kew. Fig. 3: akg-images. Figs. 6, 7, 8, 9, 21, and 25: William Andrews Clark Memorial Library, University of California, Los Angeles. Figs. 13 and 15: Joseph Bristow's private collection. Fig. 4: British Museum. Figs. 5, 10, 12, 14, 20, 23, and 24: Charles E. Young Research Library, University of California, Los Angeles. Fig. 16: Look and Learn History Picture Archive. Figs. 11, 18, and 19: Alamy. Fig. 17: British Library. Fig. 22: British Newspaper Archive.

I give special thanks to Daniel P. Williford, to whom the volume is dedicated, for providing impeccable research assistance in preparing this complicated manuscript for submission to the press. He shared his bibliographical expertise and focused his attentive copy-editor's eye on my final drafts—all of which gained immeasurably from his insights. Moreover, Dr. Williford identified several sources that were integral to my discussion. Andrea Acosta, who served in the same capacity during the 2019–20 academic session, assisted with many of the finishing touches to the project, as did Elyse Brusher in her role as graduate student researcher in fall 2020. My deepest gratitude goes to Helen Deutsch, the director of UCLA's Center for 17th- & 18th-Century Studies from January 2017 to December 2020, for sponsoring this generous and much-appreciated research assistance.

Throughout the writing of *Oscar Wilde on Trial*, my partner, Blaine Ashton Noblett, shared his legal acumen with me. Our two long-haired dachshunds, Leo and Sabrina, were loyal companions during the time that I spent on the present volume.

J. E. B.
Los Angeles

INTRODUCTION

It is no use of my addressing you. People who can do these things must be dead to every sense of shame, and one cannot hope to produce any effect upon them. It is the worst case I ever tried.

—*Sir Alfred Wills, Central Criminal Court (Old Bailey), 25 May 1895*

I have no doubt we shall win, but the road is long, and red with monstrous martyrdoms. Nothing but the repeal of the Criminal Law Amendment Act would do any good. That is the essential. It is not so much public opinion as public officials that need educating.

—*Oscar Wilde, "To George Ives," postmark 21 March 1898*

As Oscar Wilde once remarked, one can't go about abusing Heliogabalus, censuring Cesar Borgia, or scolding Nero. These figures have passed into the sphere of Art. So has our spectacular genius, Oscar Wilde. But the essential difference is that he was a man incapable of being either cruel or hard. The most soft-hearted, carelessly-generous and genial of men, his great fault was weakness, and, with all his brilliance, a fatal want of judgment. Yet he is like them because he has become a legend. He was always a legend. He always will be.

–*Ada Leverson, "Reminiscences: The Importance of Being Oscar," 1930*

Late in the afternoon on Saturday, 25 May 1895, at London's Central Criminal Court (also known as the Old Bailey), the clerk of arraigns addressed the jury.[1] He asked if its twelve members had reached a verdict about Oscar Wilde. The defendant, a gifted forty-year-old Irish writer from a noted Protestant nationalist family, had recently risen to the heights of the literary profession through a series of outstanding works. In the past few years, Wilde had garnered attention for a controversial novel (*The Picture of Dorian Gray* [1890, revised 1891]); a book of sophisticated critical essays (*Intentions* [1891, revised 1894]); four successful society comedies (beginning with *Lady Windermere's Fan* [1892]); a one-act French-language Biblical drama, *Salomé* (1892); and three impressive volumes of short stories. Once the clerk had posed his question, the foreman replied: "We have."[2] The clerk then began the first in a series of blunt inquiries: "Do you find the prisoner at the bar guilty of an act of gross indecency with Charles Parker at the Savoy Hotel on the night of his first introduction to him?" (397). The answer was clear: "Guilty" (397). "Do you find him," the clerk asked in turn, "guilty of a similar offence a week later?" "Guilty" (397). "Do you find him," the clerk reiterated, "guilty of the offence at St. James's Place?" (397). The foreman answered this and three further questions in the affirmative.

The offense in question was a misdemeanor specified in the eleventh section of the Criminal Law Amendment Act 1885: "*Outrages on decency*. Any male person who, in public or private commits, or is a part to the commission of or procures (*a*) or attempts (*b*) to procure the commission by any male person of, any act of gross indecency (*c*) with another male person, shall be guilty of a misdemeanor, and being convicted thereof shall be liable at the discretion of the court to be imprisoned for any term not exceeding two years, with or without hard labour" (48 & 49 Vict. c. 69 s. 11). This clause appears in what was a comprehensive piece of legislation, which in most other respects sought both to increase the age of consent in relation to acts involving heterosexual intimacy from thirteen to sixteen and to regulate female prostitution. More to the point, the main provisions of the 1885 act had been rushed into Parliament in troubled reaction to a recent scandal about the sex-trafficking of young girls in London. The scandal in question had made headlines over several days in the investigative journalist W. T. Stead's exposé that he called, echoing Revelation 17:5, "The Maiden Tribute of Modern Babylon."[3] The hasty parliamentary debate to pass the 1885 bill, which a skeptical commentator in the 1920s vividly recalled as a "panic measure," resulted in one of the major acts that consolidated the English criminal law during the nineteenth century.[4] Evidently, Justice Alfred Wills must have known the provisions of the 1885 act well, since in the first year of its implementation he meted out no fewer than twenty sentences under it, in connection with thirty-three cases brought before Leeds Assizes.[5]

The eleventh of the twenty sections, which forbade acts of "gross indecency" between males (even in private), had been introduced into the hurried bill as something of an afterthought by the Radical MP Henry ("Labby") Labouchere. The section, for the first time, conjured the expression gross indecency for legislative purposes. Once we turn to the background to Labouchere's adaptation of the term, we can see why the amendment had such success in terrorizing and incarcerating thousands of queer men until the clause was partly decriminalized through the Sexual Offences Act 1967 (Eliz. 2 c. 60). The 1967 law eliminated private consensual sexual acts between male civilians twenty-one years of age and older as a misdemeanor.

Prior to Labouchere's clause the phrase gross indecency was not uncommon in discussions of impropriety. It had been employed for decades to allude to a broad range of offensive activities that commentators thought it advisable to condemn, including illicit sexual behaviors. In 1767, for example, Floyer Sydenham, in his English edition of Plato's dialogues, employs it exactly in this context. He remarks that in the *Symposium* the final speech that we hear from Alcibiades—a male object of Socrates's affection—is one that scholars have not rendered into English "for fear of the offence it may reasonably give to the virtuous from the gross indecency of some part of it."[6] The fear, clearly enough, involves references to sexual love between older and younger men in Ancient Greece. By comparison, in Adam Smith's *Wealth of Nations* (1776) the phrase occurs when he discusses what he calls the "liberal or loose system" of morality that arises during periods of prosperity. For Smith, there are times when individuals are less likely to disapprove of vices associated with pleasure, provided that these are "not accompanied with gross indecency."[7]

Not long after the turn of the nineteenth century, mentions of gross indecency arose with greater regularity in the press to describe, at least informally, such diverse phenomena as disorderly conduct involving damage to property or sexual harassment, the opening of a murderer's shallow grave, and a man's intercourse with his wife and her sister in the same bed.[8] Closer to the time of Labouchere's Amendment, the term continued to have sundry applications. Gross indecency could refer to such differing matters as the objectionable libretto to Richard Wagner's *Parsifal* (1882), the occasional vulgarity of the French poet Pierre-Jean de Béranger, and the public cross-dressing of a bearded male plumber from Eltham who was charged with unlawful possession of female apparel.[9] Still, there was one point on which these distinct usages converged. In the numerous accounts that adopt the phrase, gross indecency consistently captures disregard for social respectability.

Every now and again, journalists commented on court cases that employed the term as a means of gesturing toward unutterable sexual behaviors. The Queen's Bench, for instance, heard a protracted libel case that the sixty-eight-year-old Revd. William Chamberlaine of Keevil, Wiltshire, brought against the Revd. E. L. Barnwell, a clergyman in nearby Melksham, who had accused him of committing "acts of gross indecency . . . toward various young women and young men, his parishioners."[10] The proceedings involved multiple allegations that the vicar had indulged in unnatural offenses. One of Chamberlaine's sons testified that Barnwell had informed him that the accusations against the vicar of Keevil amounted in general "to a case of sodomy."[11] Several other trials from this period show how the phrase "gross indecency" recurred when the charges involved sexual activity between men. In commentaries on a well-publicized 1878 case against the fifty-six-year-old Henry Ford (an erstwhile respected clerk of the peace in Devon) for indecent assault on males, the phrase "acts of gross indecency" emerged at the Old Bailey.[12] Justice Hawkins adverted to it when summing up his doubts concerning the evidence given by one of the young soldiers who had testified about the unwelcome advances that Ford had made to him in the vicinity of Exeter Barracks. By comparison, in 1880 forty-seven individuals were arrested at a "fancy dress party" where some of the male guests wore female attire. At the Manchester Police Court, the officers who had raided this event claimed that they witnessed "gross indecency between the men and the supposed women."[13] The partygoers "were charged with soliciting and inciting each other to commit a nameless offence, and conspiring to assemble at a particular place, there to incite and solicit each other."[14]

Labouchere appropriated the widely used preexisting phrase and bound it to what had for years been its power to evoke an unspecified set of exclusively male homosexual acts. In any case, the vagueness of Labouchere's appeal to gross indecency, which subsequently left much to the courtroom's imagination, embraced any conceivable male homosexual misdeed. Further still, the number of witnesses required to prove that the crime had occurred was reduced to one—so long as their testimony could be corroborated about the time, place, and context in which the indeterminate homosexual act had taken place. Besides the difficulties involved in specifying what gross indecency signified, an additional aspect of the term warrants attention. It appears that Labouchere blended the adjective that defined the concept of gross negligence (found in commercial contracts) with the definitions of indecency to be found, for example, in the Towns Improvement (Ireland) Act 1854, which legislated against "[e]very Person who wilfully and indecently exposes his Person, or who commits any Act contrary to public Decency" (17 & 18 Vict. c. 103 s. 72). As we bear these matters in mind, it is vital to note that in 1885 the phrase "gross indecency" entered the law in a far from deliberative manner. Labouchere's clause proceeded so hastily, and with such minimal discussion in a poorly attended House of Commons, that historians have speculated about the degree to which he believed his amendment (and perhaps the embarrassments involved in engaging too lengthily with its substance) would undermine a contentious piece of legislation that a number of politicians feared might threaten personal liberties.[15] No one, however, spoke against it.

As the records of the Old Bailey show, gross indecency operated as a generalized subcategory of sodomy: itself a word—one that was not always gender-specific (or, for that matter, species-specific)—that had by the turn of the nineteenth century proved hard to preserve in records of courtroom examinations. The main obstacle facing journalists who reported on allusions to sodomy during Wilde's cross-examination originated in earlier nineteenth-century shifts in propriety and decorum that made it difficult to consign the word to print. If we pause for a moment on the legal prohibitions on intimacy between men, we can see why the late Victorian move toward basing convictions on gross indecency occurred with increasing frequency in the courts. Ever since gross indecency came to define such a misdemeanor in 1885, there has been no clear understanding of what it should particularize, whether it is supposed to refer to anal penetration or another kind of sexual congress including fellatio, kissing, or masturbation. Even so, in 1897 the sexologist Havelock Ellis felt confident enough to assert that "'gross indecency' between males usually means some form of mutual masturbation."[16] From Ellis's viewpoint, it was hard to imagine that this type of sexual activity could amount to a criminal offense: "However shameful, disgusting, personally immoral, and indirectly anti-social it may be for two adult persons of the same sex, men or women, to consent together to perform an act of sexual intimacy in private, there is no sound or adequate ground for constituting such act a penal offence in law."[17] Given that certain jurors might also have had similar thoughts about the potentially harmless meaning of gross indecency, the carefully groomed leading witnesses were likely told not to make any explicit reference to the ill-defined phrase. Instead, whenever they described an offending homosexual act, the witnesses adverted to the much older and arguably more disconcerting term sodomy. The development of this felony in English law reveals why it became such a charged word in Wilde's case, where the counts were focused, at least technically, on the unspecified misdemeanor of gross indecency.

Initially, sodomy was criminalized through Henry VIII's Buggery Act 1533 (25 Hen. 8 c. 6). At that point, sodomy, which was fairly interchangeable with buggery as an exploit involving non-heterosexual forms of penetration, covered both humans and animals. Wayne R. Dynes reminds us that by the time Edward Coke issued *The Institutes of the Laws of England* (1644), buggery had become an unspeakable act: Coke characterized it as "a detestable and abominable sin, amongst Christians not to be named."[18] Very probably, Coke had in mind the reference by Thomas Coventry, Lord High Steward, to the "offences, which a Christian scarce ought to name" during the arraignment of Mervyn Tuchet, 2nd Earl of Castlehaven, on 25 April 1631, for raping his wife and committing acts of sodomy with two male servants.[19] Moreover, Coke states that buggery includes oral and anal sex between men, intercourse between males and animals, and copulation between women and beasts. By comparison, by 1717 an updated edition of Thomas Blount's well-known *Law-Dictionary and Glossary* extended the Latin phrase *carnalis copula contra Naturam* to unnatural acts of "a Man with a Woman."[20] William Blackstone, in his foundational *Commentaries on English Law* (1765–69), was so taken aback by what he called this "infamous *crime against nature*, committed either with man or beast" that he could not even bring himself to employ the word sodomy.[21] To Blackstone, whose terminology elaborates upon Coke's earlier phrasing, this was "a crime not fit to be named; '*peccatum illud horribile, inter christianos non nominandum.*'"[22] Hereafter, given the influence that Blackstone's *Commentaries* exerted on later accounts of English law, the climate in which social observers might write about sodomy grew more inhibited than before.

At the same time, the manner in which English law both defined sodomy and made convictions upon it went through miscellaneous transformations. By 1781, in order to verify a conviction for sodomy a court required at least two witnesses to testify that an act of oral or anal penetration had resulted in ejaculation. The Offences against the Person Act 1828 marked a decisive change in this regard. The requirement of verifying the emission of seed was removed from the law. "The new provision on proof," Paul Johnson observes of the 1828 act, "originated in an amendment by a committee of the whole house of commons to the bill, at the behest of Home Secretary Peel."[23] On this basis, it was deemed easier to secure a conviction for buggery and related crimes. The Offences against the Person Act 1861 reiterated that a conviction of an "unnatural offence" against the person, including sodomy, did not have to verify, according to section 63, "the actual emission of seed in order to constitute a carnal knowledge" but could be based on evidence of penetration alone (24 & 25 Vict. c. 100). The crime therefore depended on the public witnessing of a specific physical act.

There were also significant changes in the punishments for sodomy or buggery in the respective laws of 1828 and 1861. Section 18 of the 1828 legislation stated "that every person convicted of the abominable crime of buggery, committed either with mankind or with any animal, or aiding or abetting such crime, shall suffer death as a felon" (9 Geo. 4 c. 31). Importantly, the 1861 act abolished the death penalty for sodomy, even though many years had already passed since such a penalty was imposed. (The last men to be hanged for committing sodomy were James Pratt and John Smith, who were executed in November 1835 after receiving a death sentence under the fifteenth section of the 1828 law.[24]) Section 62 of the 1861 act used the established legal phrase "indecent assault upon any male person" to proscribe, in a generalized fashion, sexual intercourse between men. The wording, especially when applied in collocation with the phrase "unnatural offence," had sufficient semantic elasticity to redouble the disgust customarily associated with male homoerotic practices.

By the looks of it, it may appear as if these legal shifts brought about a relaxation in punishment. Between 1828 and 1885, in spite of everything, the law had witnessed a movement away from sodomy as a capital crime, on the one hand, to gross indecency as a misdemeanor carrying a maximum sentence of twenty-four months, on the other hand. This is not, however, a progressive pattern. Charles Upchurch, in his study *Before Wilde* (2009), points out that these reforms were scarcely as decisive as they might at first seem, since it remained difficult under the legislation prior to 1885 to attest that sodomy had taken place. Instead, the majority of cases that came before the courts involved sentences for attempted sodomy (a crime that emerged through the Threatening Letters Act 1825 [6 Geo. 4 c. 19]), which usually carried a two-year jail term. "Between 1811 and 1860," Upchurch writes, "there were 864 trials for attempted sodomy held in the London criminal courts, compared with only 116 cases of sodomy. One reason for this disparity was that the proof needed for an attempted-sodomy charge was easily acquired or invented."[25] Upchurch provides an example from 1842 that shows how easy it was to convince the police that a reprehensible sexual act has taken place: "Henry Webb . . . spent two nights in a Bow Street holding cell after Thomas Addy pulled him toward an officer in Covent Garden and said, 'I give this gentleman in charge for an indecent assault.'"[26] No further proof was needed.

There was further unevenness in the modifications that were made to the laws affecting sexual acts between men. Over time, the eleventh clause of the 1885 legislation notched up thousands of convictions. Wilde was correct when he confided to the penal reformer and advocate of homosexual rights George Ives that "the road is long, and red with monstrous martyrdoms." By the 1890s, dozens of men had been convicted under the 1885 prohibition.[27] Still, Labouchere's Amendment did not displace the 1861 ban on sodomy. The felony, it is hard to believe, stayed on the statute books for the next 142 years. It took until the Sexual Offences Act 2003 before homosexual offences were removed from statutory law. Many convictions for sodomy at the Old Bailey took place during the decades following the Criminal Law Amendment Act had passed.[28] Even in the post-World War II era, it was not uncommon for men convicted of "unnatural offences" to be sent to prison for periods of three to thirteen years.[29] Moreover, even when sodomy was not the explicit charge, there were indictments (particularly in provincial courts) against "unnatural offences," although occasionally these related to bestiality.[30] All the same, in the closing years of the nineteenth century convictions for sodomy were far less common in the Central Criminal Court than those where defendants were tried on the charge of gross indecency. Wilde's sentence for violating Labouchere's Amendment was one of the most extreme. Never, it seems, until Wilde stood before Justice Wills, had the Old Bailey heard a jury reach a verdict on six counts involving acts of gross indecency—even though some of the witnesses, on the evidence we have, defined their erotic intimacy with Wilde exclusively in relation to sodomy.[31]

As the clerk of arraigns continued with his questions to the foreman, the only relief from the list of counts on which the defendant had been charged came at the conclusion of the verdict. The courtroom knew that Wilde could not be convicted on the seventh and final count concerning an individual in his early twenties named Edward Shelley, who had no links with the criminal class to which the other young main witnesses belonged. Shelley admitted that he had slept with Wilde at the Albemarle Hotel, near Piccadilly, in central London, during February 1892. (Shelley did not, it appears, mention sodomy.) Throughout the proceedings, it became manifest that Shelley—who had previously been employed as an office junior at one of Wilde's publishers—suffered from a history of mental instability. Such disclosures threw his distressing testimony into doubt. This was a matter to which Justice Wills had drawn attention two days before he sentenced Wilde. At that point, Wills also stated that there were no grounds upon which Shelley's evidence could be corroborated. There was, it appeared, no one to confirm that Wilde's dinner invitation to Shelley entailed an act of gross indecency. The *Daily Telegraph* recorded Wills's misgivings about taking Shelley's testimony into serious consideration: "[Wills] could see nothing—apart from what Shelley had himself said—in the admitted facts that which was inconsistent with a perfectly honourable relationship, and the letters [from Wilde] put in by Shelley were immensely against the notion that there was anything dishonourable between them. He entertained a perfectly clear view, therefore, that it was his duty to withdraw the case of Shelley from the jury."[32]

On this basis, the foreman agreed that Wilde was "[n]ot guilty on that count" (397). In principle, the judge's unwillingness to take the evidence of Shelley, who was the only leading witness one might characterize as socially respectable, had the potential to strengthen Wilde's position. Yet the jury concluded that they had, in the end, every reason to trust the individual word of two men—Charles Parker and Alfred Wood—who admitted in court that they had committed sodomy with Wilde, were connected with the world of male prostitution, and had perpetrated the crime of blackmail.[33] Moroever, the jurors agreed to convict Wilde even though another leading witness, a habitual criminal named Frederick ("Fred") Atkins, perjured himself in the first trial when he denied his involvement in a ploy to blackmail an unsuspecting man seeking sexual contact with him. Wilde's defense exposed Atkins as a liar.

There was, it is important to note, nothing unusual in the English courts permitting witnesses with dubious reputations to corroborate one another's evidence. As John H. Langbein observes, there had been a corroboration rule operating within the judicial system since at least the 1730s that allowed individuals convicted of wrongdoing to give testimony against those who had also perpetrated crimes. Under this principle, "[a]n apprehended criminal was excused from prosecution in exchange for testifying against former confederates."[34] In such a situation, questionable witnesses of this type were protected from prosecution because they provided evidence that, more often than not, would be hard to extract by other means. By permitting corroboration of this kind even from potentially treacherous sources, the courts therefore provided a safeguard against witnesses perjuring themselves. Importantly, this working principle had become a mandatory rule by the nineteenth century.[35]

In Wilde's trials, however, the jurors were not faced, in the strictest sense, with felony witnesses. None of these blackmailers and sex workers—despite the fact that they were obviously enmeshed in London's criminal world—had been sentenced for these activities. Even if Fred Atkins, Charles Parker, and Alfred Wood had taken risks that sometimes involved brushes with the law, they had been repeatedly successful in blackmailing their clients, often to great profit, with impunity. In such circumstances, Queensberry's solicitor, Charles Russell, ensured that these villains were coached to provide mutally reinforcing testimony that strengthened the prosecution's case. Assuredly, these witnesses' evidence appeared tainted to skeptical onlookers. Wilde's senior counsel, Sir Edward Clarke, insisted that the very fact that such men had admitted "their participation in such practices" as sodomy "ought to disentitle their evidence to the slightest credence" (279). Their testimony, however, still proved admissible. As far as the jurors could tell when they took considerable time discussing Wilde's case on Saturday, 25 May 1895, if the evidence against the defendant had been corroborated, as Justice Wills claimed it had, Wilde should be found guilty.

Once the foreman of the jury had declared that Wilde was guilty on all but the final charge, the knowledgeable defense moved briskly to forestall an impatient Justice Wills from rushing headlong into passing sentence. "I have to suggest to your lordship," said Sir Edward Clarke, who had done everything within his power to defend Wilde, "that you will not pass sentence until the next sessions. There is a demurrer [i.e., objection] on record, which has to be argued, and I submit that it would be well to postpone passing sentence in order that that argument may be considered" (397).[36] Immediately, the respected attorney J. P. Grain made an identical petition on behalf of his client: the thirty-three-year-old Alfred Taylor, who had been tried alongside Wilde for committing the same crime with a number of the same men. The judge, however, would not countenance any deferral of what he regarded as the "worst case" that he had "ever tried." In the sternest of tones, Justice Wills rounded on Taylor and Wilde: "That you, Taylor, kept a kind of male brothel it is impossible to doubt; and that you, Wilde, have been at the centre of extensive corruption of young men of the most hideous kind, it is equally impossible to doubt. I cannot, under such circumstances, do anything except pass the severest sentence which the law allows, and in my judgement, it is totally inadequate to such a case as this. The sentence on each of you is that you be imprisoned and kept to hard labour for two years" (399).

This was the terrible outcome of not one but three trials, during the course of which Wilde plummeted from the height of his literary fame into an abyss of social disgrace. Once the evidence had mounted against him, he rapidly transmuted from an illustrious playwright, with two outstanding comedies (*The Importance of Being Earnest* and *An Ideal Husband*) running concurrently on the London stage, to a pariah whose secret intimacies, including liaisons with male prostitutes and seasoned blackmailers, stunned the world. At the time, there was no case like it. The conviction understandably did untold amounts of damage to Wilde's reputation. Moreover, it had injurious consequences for his wife, Constance, who ensured that their two children escaped the humiliating verdict by taking refuge on the Continent. Once she and her sons were settled abroad, all three were known by the family name Holland. This was a complex stratagem—one that confused both of Wilde's boys—to dissociate themselves, irreversibly, from the husband and father who had dishonored them.[37]

For reasons that bear careful consideration, the official shorthand records of the trials that sent Wilde to jail have always been missing. At no point have their whereabouts been discovered, although there has been—as I mention below—speculation about their fate. Their omission from the public record comes starkly into view when one consults the Old Bailey Online (*OBPO*) website, which reproduces the proceedings of London's Central Criminal Court from 1674 to 1913. The two entries that exist—the one for the first trial, the other for the second—contain the scantest amount of information. In each case, we see the dates of the trials, with the first one taking place on "*Friday and Saturday, April 26th and 27th, and Monday, Tuesday, and Wednesday, April 29th, 30th, and May 1st*, 1895," and the second one occurring on "*Monday, May 20th, and Five Following Days*."[38] The entries also provide basic facts about the attorneys. In both of these trials, Sir Edward Clarke, who maintained great standing in the legal profession, served as Wilde's senior counsel, with Charles ("Willy") Mathews and Travers Humphreys as his juniors. (Grain acted as Taylor's senior counsel.) In the first trial, Charles Frederick ("C. F.") Gill, supported by Horace Avory, led the prosecution. Meanwhile, in the second trial Sir Frank Lockwood, the solicitor general, acted as the Crown prosecutor, with Gill and Avory supporting him. Many of these attorneys had achieved the status of celebrities, given the prominence of the headline-making cases upon which they built their much-publicized careers. Their characteristic gestures, idiosyncrasies of dress, and styles of comportment take vivid shape in the memorable caricatures that cartoonists such as John Paget Mellor and Leslie Ward furnished for *Vanity Fair* (see figures 11, 12, 13, 14, 15, 20, 23, and 24 [114, 117, 122, 144, 201, 306, and 307 below]).

Since there were technical problems with the inconvenient way in which the twenty-five counts had been combined in the indictment, the first trial foundered. The Crown originally chose to try Wilde and Taylor together on counts that brought together some charges relating to conspiracy (a felony) and others to gross indecency (a misdemeanor). This joinder (as it was called), if not unprecedented, created incoherence, especially regarding the risk that the defendants might give evidence that could be used against them. On the one hand, section 20 of the 1885 law aimed to expand the right of the accused by permitting them to testify under oath. On the other hand, the law of conspiracy prevented the accused from giving evidence, since such testimony might serve against their interests. At the start of the first trial, Wilde's defense took pains to draw the judge's attention to this potential conflict. Clarke's well-reasoned arguments, however, were unsuccessful.

In any case, since Taylor's and Wilde's ostensibly shared crimes did not relate to each and every charge, the judge eventually agreed to remove the counts of conspiracy. This situation created additional complications for the jury. Once the conspiracy charges had been withdrawn, Justice Arthur Charles posed four questions (with subdivisions) that he wished the jurors to address, each of which focused on whether sexual acts had taken place between various parties. Although the press reported the general questions, we have no knowledge about the specific subdivisions in the judge's inquiry (see 291). At any rate, matters were compounded for the jury when Clarke outwitted the blackmailer Frederick Atkins so that this disreputable witness ended up perjuring himself. Even though Clarke and his team had gathered intelligence about Atkins's criminal activities, the twenty-year-old comic performer brazenly denied that his landlady had contacted the police to investigate a disturbance that involved an attempt at blackmailing a gentleman. Once the police officers who had been called to Atkins's lodgings appeared at the Old Bailey, it was evident that Atkins had lied under oath. In these messy circumstances, it is hardly surprising that the jurors could not reach agreement on the four questions. Accordingly, Justice Charles ordered a retrial. The retrial, which reiterated much of what had already been heard, involved trying Taylor and Wilde solely under the 1885 law, with the one man receiving his sentence discretely after the other. The records of the Old Bailey summarize the fact that the two men were tried together in the first trial and then separately in the retrial. No additional details appear. The exchanges that transpired in the courtroom, which occasionally follow these summaries in the official record, remain absent.

One question naturally arises from this series of events. Why did the official shorthand reports of such a heavily publicized case vanish from the record? The obvious answer relates to the sensitive contents of not only these two trials but also an earlier one that precipitated the Crown prosecution. On 1 March 1895, Wilde had initiated a headstrong libel suit against John Sholto Douglas, the 9th Marquess of Queensberry: an ill-mannered Scottish aristocrat who was at the time best known for his association with the rules of modern boxing. Queensberry was the indignant father of Wilde's young male lover, Lord Alfred Douglas, who was twenty-four years old when these legal events came to a head. Queensberry detested the intimate relationship that Wilde had developed with Lord Alfred. On 18 February 1895, Queensberry alleged, on a badly scrawled visiting card left at one of Wilde's social clubs, that the celebrated Irish author was "Posing as a Somdomite" (figs. 1 and 2).[39] The insult was the culmination of the marquess's harassing behavior, which had worsened over the course of twelve months. Regardless of the misspelling and the apparently omitted words, which were sure signs of Queensberry's impetuousness, the accusation was clear. The marquess had charged Wilde with behaving like (though not, it seems, actually being) a sexual criminal. This was a point that the marqess reiterated to his daughter-in-law Minnie: "What I say, and have already told them [i.e., Douglas and Wilde] is that it is as bad to pose as such a thing, and to give everyone reason to talk as they are doing, as being actually criminal."[40] Even if the card was a

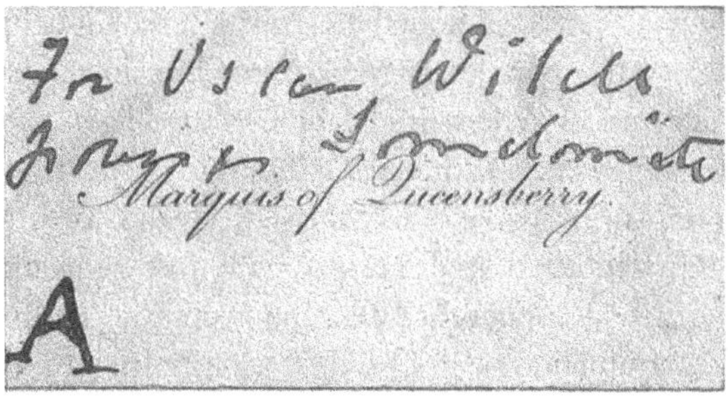

Fig. 1. Visiting card left by John Sholto Douglas, 9th Marquess of Queensberry, for Oscar Wilde at the Albemarle Club, London, 18 February 1895.

Fig. 2. Envelope for the visiting card left by John Sholto Douglas, 9th Marquess of Queensberry, addressed by Sidney Wright for Oscar Wilde at the Albemarle Club, London, 18 February 1895.

hurried affair, Queensberry had nonetheless given some thought to the accusation of posing as a sexual offender. As Marc-André Raffalovich put it in his contemporaneous account of Wilde's trials, the libel had been shrewdly worded: "Notez l'habileté. Il ne l'accuse pas d'actes impossibles à prouver, mais de poser comme s'il s'en rendait coupable" (Note the skill. He did not accuse him of acts that are impossible to prove, but of acting as if he were guilty of them).[41] More than anything else, the loudmouthed allegation was unequivocal in expressing Queensberry's determination to end Wilde's intimate friendship with the third of the marquess's four sons.

The uncouth card followed an earlier episode when the marquess had been foiled in his attempt to cause a commotion at the premiere of Wilde's comedy *The Importance of Being Earnest*. The play had opened to very good reviews at London's fashionable St. James's Theatre on 14 February 1895. Although Wilde's experienced solicitor C. O. Humphreys told him that the "threats and insulting conduct" that the marquess had displayed at the St. James's were not outrageous enough to warrant legal action, the attorney reassured his client that "such a persistent persecutor" as Queensberry would eventually give the aggrieved party "another opportunity sooner or later of seeking the protection of the Law."[42] The visiting card, which Wilde collected ten days after the marquess had deposited it, was sufficiently insulting to set the legal wheels in motion. "I don't see anything now," Wilde told his loyal friend (and former lover) Robert Ross, "but a criminal prosecution."[43] Like the trials that resulted in Wilde's prison sentence, the libel case—which lasted two-and-a-half days in early April 1895—took place at the Old Bailey. Similarly, the records of the Old Bailey in session present nothing of the libel proceedings. As with the official shorthand reports of the Crown prosecution of Wilde and Taylor, the transcription of the exchanges in court has gone missing. (This fact is of great interest, since the court transcript of the libel proceedings was read aloud, exhaustively from the start to finish, in the two trials that resulted in the conviction of Wilde and Taylor.) In the brief notice we find about the libel trial, there is a terse explanation for the absence of the proceedings. "*The details of the case*," we learn, "*are unfit for publication*."[44] We learn as well that Queensberry, who benefited from the skills of a gifted Queen's Counsel, Edward Carson, was found not guilty. The jury added that the publication of Queensberry's criminal libel through the visiting card, which he had explained in a lengthy plea, was not only justified but also justified for the "Public Benefit," according to the Libel Act 1843 (6 & 7 Vict. c. 96 s. 6).

There is a further piece of information in the court record that points to the circumstances that ensured the failure of Wilde's case. "*At the close of the prosecution,*" we read, "*and whilst* MR. CARSON *was opening for the defence,* SIR EDWARD CLARKE *interposed and stated that he had consulted with his client, and was prepared to accept a verdict of* NOT GUILTY."[45] To the observers who followed this trial attentively, the hazardousness of Wilde's prosecution had become patently evident not long after the proceedings began. Queensberry's defense did everything within its power to demonstrate that Wilde was undoubtedly a "Sodomite." The marquess's attorney, Charles Russell, and his senior counsel, Edward Carson, advanced this punishing argument by drawing attention to his liaisons with a dozen young men, as well as focusing the jury's mind on the questionable desires (especially the homoerotic undercurrents) that appeared in selected literary writings by Wilde. What readers of the widespread newspaper reports of the libel case were not able to see was that Carson alluded, at crucial moments in his dogged cross-examination, to the word "sodomy" and its derivative "sodomitical," since he wished to show that the marquess was not mistaken in libeling Wilde. Although it would be inaccurate to claim that such language never made its way into the columns of newspapers at the time, these terms were often deemed far too sensitive to introduce into most publications. It was perhaps on this basis that the proceedings of the libel trial were removed from the record. There are other possible reasons for their disappearance. Charles Tattersall has entertained the prospect that the director of public prosecutions, Hamilton ("Ham") Cuffe, 5th Earl of Desart, took all of the records of both the libel trial and the ensuing criminal prosecution with him after he retired from his post in 1908. Had Cuffe appropriated the records in this manner, they would, Tattersall suggests, have been destroyed on 22 February 1923 when the Irish Republican Army firebombed the earl's imposing Georgian mansion, Desart Court, in County Kilkenny, Ireland.[46] No one, however, knows about their destiny.

The libel trial, together with the laborious Crown prosecution that ensued, brought to light many aspects of Wilde's private life that had stayed unknown even to some of his oldest and closest friends, as well as (for many years) his wife. (Wilde's children were not aware of the precise nature of their father's crimes until they were adults.) The proceedings, moreover, spurred renewed attention to those aspects of his literary works that had boldly explored male homoerotic themes during the past six to seven years. These developments in Wilde's career ran in tandem with profound changes in his personal universe, chiefly—as I show in chapter 1—those that took place a few years into his marriage. Even if there is a possibility that Wilde may have enjoyed intimacies with other men during the time that he spent studying classics (first at Dublin, and then at Oxford), it is certain that in the later 1880s he combined his domestic routine and his professional obligations with same-sex liaisons, ones that gathered in number—as well as measures of danger—until the advent of the trials.

The most significant of these relationships was the passionate one that he forged with the Marquess of Queenbsberry's third son, Lord Alfred Douglas: a boyish-looking, athletic, and poetically gifted Oxford undergraduate who had for a while been sexually active with men of his own age. Wilde, as eyewitnesses at the university could tell, appeared indiscreet in the affair that he conducted with this privileged and petulant individual known to his intimates as "Bosie" (derived from "Boysie," his mother's nickname for him). At Oxford, Douglas gained a polemical reputation for transforming a humdrum student magazine, the *Spirit Lamp*, into a largely homoerotic literary periodical. Bosie, with whom Wilde soon endured an unstable and spendthrift relationship, aroused his older lover's strongest poetic passions and, after a year or so of fervid friendship, provoked the greatest frustrations. In their affair, which was a sexually open one, Wilde modeled himself as an intellectual and artistic mentor to Bosie. (Douglas, after all, was an admiring undergraduate when he first met Wilde.) At the same time, Bosie, since he was impulsive, arrogant, and reckless, brought Wilde into close contact with a homoerotic underworld of untrustworthy prostitutes and perilous pleasures. Their relationship, in which Douglas took many of the sexual leads, integrated—to lesser and greater degrees—two different types of intimacy. On the one hand, Wilde and Douglas cultivated elements of the Socratic ethos, whereby the older male exercised ethical care for his younger lover. On the other hand, they intensified their interests in pursuing intimate relationships with young men, some of whom—as we have seen—were sex workers and extortionists.

Wilde's intense personal relationship with Douglas, which also had a significant literary dimension, enabled him to expand his homosexual contacts, especially through Alfred Taylor, whom he had met—by way of one of Bosie's sexual partners—in September 1892. The sociable Taylor, about whom we know comparatively little, supplemented his family allowance with fees from procuring male sex workers for well-off clients. He soon provided Wilde with a steady stream of young men. One or two were respectable individuals such as Sydney Mavor, who had an enthusiasm for cross-dressing. Even though Wilde bestowed gifts upon Mavor, it is uncertain whether he handed over cash. (Mavor, whose family had a private income, appears to have made loans to Taylor.) Others, however, came from a different class and required payment for sexual services, although of sums that are sometimes hard to determine. Among the most precarious intimacies of this kind that Wilde enjoyed was with Alfred Wood. A hardened criminal in his early twenties, Wood accidentally found four of Wilde's impassioned letters to Douglas in a set of clothes that the young lord had given him so that he was (we must presume) properly dressed for dinner. Not surprisingly, Wood had little hesitation in using one of these in an attempt to blackmail Wilde.

Extortion of this type, as the press from time to time revealed, was a staple of queer subculture in Britain, particularly across London. Wilde's trials demonstrated that male sex workers who traded in blackmail reaped lucrative rewards from entrapping men who responded to their overtures. One of the reasons that criminals found their trade so profitable had much to do with the law that forbade any form of erotic contact between men. Not only was the 1885 legislation under which Wilde was tried so far-reaching that it had the power to convict consensual erotic acts that had taken place even in private; it was also a law that intensified the conditions (in the words of the homophile writer John Addington Symonds) for "obvious incitement to false accusation."[47] Furthermore, this world of blackmail, in which victims were reluctant to report the crime to the police, proliferated in an era when males who enjoyed erotic contact with their own sex were also well aware of several fear-inducing scandals. On occasion, however, victims of homosexual blackmail resorted to the law to fend off these bullies.

Section 47 of the Larceny Act 1861 made it a felony to "accuse or threaten to accuse, either the person to whom such accusation shall be made or any other person, of any of infamous or other crimes lastly hereinbefore mentioned, with the view or intent . . . to extort or gain from the person so accused" (24 & 25 Vict. c. 69 s. 47). As he executed his duties at the Old Bailey, Justice Wills was scarcely unaware of the pervasiveness of this type of extortion and the severe punishments that could result from this crime. Four months before he passed judgment on Wilde's case, Wills had imposed a tough sentence on twenty-year-old Harry Turner for three attempts at blackmailing his former employer, Walter Hugh Silver: a member of a well-known firm of London merchants that traded principally in outfitting the military. In his summing-up on 28 January 1895, Wills expressed considerable ambivalence about the case, since Turner claimed that Silver had been responsible for committing "abominable offences," ones that provided the rationale for the blackmailing efforts.[48] Without question, Wills viewed Turner's allegations, which implicitly referred to the unspeakable crime of sodomy, as an outrage. All the same, the judge appeared even more disconcerted by the fact that a man of Silver's professional standing should even have had the temerity to bring charges. In Wills's view, such an action was in extremely poor taste because it associated the plaintiff publicly with a vile sexual crime:

> Mr. Justice Wills said the offence was one of the worst known to the law, and in that court, on at least one occasion, he had felt that the case justified the infliction of the maximum punishment, which was penal servitude for life. Many a man, added his Lordship, would prefer being murdered to having such atrocious allegations made against him, and there had been many a man, too, who, having once yielded to extortion, found that suicide afforded the only possible escape from persecution. The difficulty which a Judge experienced in dealing with such a crime was that there was no way by which the possible truth of the charge could be ascertained, as that would, of course, affect the sentence. In this case, there was a suspicion—he would say a strong suspicion—but it was the most cruel circumstance of all that the person who was the subject of the threats could not completely clear himself, and so he became the victim of a lasting stigma. Were it not for his youthfulness the prisoner would have to undergo a very long term of imprisonment. As it was, a severe sentence was required, and he would have to endure seven years' penal servitude.[49]

These remarks reveal Justice Wills's deep-seated prejudice, since he implied that it might perhaps be more understandable if Silver had taken his life than brazen it out with his young adversary in court. The audience in the Old Bailey, it appears, was startled by the severity of Turner's sentence, perhaps because the penalty was motivated by the implication that there had at some time been sexual intimacy between the older man and his former employee.

It is worth bearing Silver's case against Turner in mind when we consider the alarming circumstances that led to Wilde's conviction. Four months later, a group of extortionists had their questionable testimony upheld in the name of sentencing Wilde to a two-year prison term. In Wilde's case, Justice Wills's preparedness to countenance the depositions of these scoundrels—witnesses who also readily admitted to similar misdeeds without any legal consequences—forces attention on how indefensible the verdict was on that Saturday afternoon in May 1895. By that point, Wills had no misgivings whatsoever about the lasting stigma that would ruin a man of Wilde's professional renown. That the stigma was immediate and ineradicable motivated a crime that took place in the week leading up to Wilde's conviction, when three blackmailers appeared before the Great Marlborough Street Magistrates' Court for attempting to extract funds from a Putney hairdresser, Westley Francis, after they had apprehended him in a street near a public urinal on Oxford Circus in the West End of London. (Presumably, the three men assumed that Francis appeared as an easy target in a restroom of this kind, since such venues served as homosexual cruising grounds.) Once the case reached the Old Bailey the following month, Francis testified that his adversaries claimed to have been police detectives who declared that he was under arrest because this was "an Oscar Wilde business."[50] Each of these felons, who were convicted of demanding money through menaces, received a five-year sentence. These episodes recurred with regularity and persisted for decades. Many men, however, were not successful in surmounting the threats that went along with this kind of crime. The menacing nature of extortion is treated intrepidly in Basil Dearden's film *Victim* (1961), starring Dirk Bogarde, which was released at a time—especially in light of the Wolfenden Report (1957)—when public attitudes in Britain gave increasing support toward homosexual law reform.[51]

Homosexual blackmail was not invented with the passing of Labouchere's Amendment. Without doubt, men who enjoyed sexual intimacy with other men had for decades been prey to extortion.[52] On this basis, recent historians, such as H. G. Cocks, have gone so far as to assert that Labouchere's "efforts did not change the law in a dramatic fashion."[53] But the legal shift from "indecent assault on any male person" in 1861 to the charge of gross indecency twenty-four years later broadened vulnerable men's susceptibility to prosecution. The expanded reach of the law, by introducing such vague language characterizing sexual conduct between men in private, made the allegation of a crime far more plausible. By comparison, the accusation of sodomy, while incurring harsher sentencing under the provisions of the 1861 act, as we can tell from Upchurch's findings, was more difficult to support. The point that needs to be borne in mind is that at the time of Wilde's trials the trade in blackmailing men who had sex with other males was rife in London.

In a thought-provoking pamphlet titled *Gentle Criticisms on British Justice*, which dates from around July 1895, J. H. Wilson provides a blistering analysis of the Crown prosecution of Wilde. Wilson boldly asserts that Labouchere has become the "patron-saint" of the "20 to 30 blackmailers" who operate around the neighborhood of Piccadilly.[54] "They gratefully recognize," Wilson states, "that they owe their entire existence to that gentleman. They drink to the health of 'good old Lab.'"[55] Regardless of Wilson's hyperbole, the 1885 law buttressed the existing culture of silence and secrecy that encircled male homosexual behaviors. The point is clear when we see the English homophile socialist Edward

Carpenter commenting in 1908 that the "Act of 1885," which had "undertaken a censorship over private morals," "opened wider than ever before the door to a real, most serious social evil and crime—that of blackmailing."[56]

Labouchere's clause, which increased attention to male homosexual offenses, created the conditions not only for blackmail but also for assorted humiliating scandals that either destroyed or threatened to ruin the reputations of men, including ones who had established themselves in their professions or came from privileged backgrounds. The 1885 legislation, which followed closely on the heels of the widely publicized Dublin Castle affair, formed the backdrop to three other cases that received notice in the press during the years leading up to Wilde's conviction.[57] These controversies, which sometimes led to sensational headlines, included one in 1889 that exposed the activities of titled gentlemen frequenting a male brothel based in central London (known as the Cleveland Street scandal); another in 1893 that involved a libel suit that a Liberal parliamentary candidate took out against his Tory opponent (*Gatty v. Farquharson*); and a third one, also in 1893, that sent the Conservative politician Edward de Cobain to jail for twelve months. As we can see from the trials that attended these incidents, which are discussed in chapter 1 (60–67), nobody—not even members of the country's social elite—was necessarily immune from police investigation and the workings of the law. These three cases in turn formed part of a much greater awareness of non-conforming sexual practices and styles of gender presentation among men across the length and breadth of the nation.

The 1880s and 1890s were decades when members of the public gained increasing insights into the urban queer subcultures that supported intimacy between men, whether in brothels, at fancy-dress parties, or at cruising grounds such as the roller-skating rink in Knightsbridge. To be sure, Wilde was not known for attending the cross-dressing gatherings that overlapped with the music-hall networks taking place in different localities of the metropolis. But he mingled with many men, including Taylor, who did. The point to bear in mind is that Wilde's participation in these groups was nevertheless somewhat marginal. Richard Ellmann, in his influential 1987 biography, misled readers by implying that Wilde himself practiced cross-dressing, on the basis of a photograph with a caption that read: "Wilde in costume as Salome."[58] The image, which Ellmann probably found in the H. Roger Viollet photo-library in Paris, in fact features a Hungarian diva, Alice Guszalewicz (née Farkas), in a 1907 performance of Richard Strauss's *Salome* (1905): a compelling opera based on a German translation of Wilde's 1892 one-act biblical tragedy.[59] In the photograph, the female opera singer, it must be admitted, bears a passing resemblance to Wilde's rather heavyset physique. Even so, the idea that Wilde enjoyed wearing female attire quickly inspired a series of academic elaborations of Ellmann's baseless suggestion, in ways that made it appear that there was plausibility in the idea that the Irish writer's contacts with a network of young, men-loving men signified that he must have engaged in transgender practices.[60] Justice Wills, as his final comments show, labored under a parallel misapprehension. He concluded that Wilde had been "at the centre of extensive corruption of young men." The judge maintained the distorted belief that Wilde played a central role in this sociable community.

By spring 1895, Wilde had nonetheless gathered a range of sexual contacts in London's subcultural queer world—one whose fearless insubordination fascinated him. Since his libel suit followed in the wake of contentious cases involving gross indecency, his appeal to the law may well look as if it was seriously misjudged on both his own and his attorneys' behalf, given the fact that Queensberry's defense team promptly managed to dig up a wealth of inculpating evidence. But, then, Wilde is unlikely to have gone ahead with the suit unless he believed, no matter how fallaciously, that he could exonerate himself. Here, a brief outline of the trial and its terrible consequences casts into relief why Wilde's decision to pursue the charge of libel turned out to be so hazardous. As chapter 2 reveals in greater detail, the materials that Queensberry's solicitor amassed in order to support his lengthy plea of justification were so overwhelming that it became apparent that Wilde's prosecution could only founder. This was a demoralizing outcome that made Wilde responsible for such hefty legal costs that they compounded the prospect of bankruptcy.

With regard to the libel trial, it took until the early twenty-first century before modern readers had a comprehensive grasp of the probing research that informed Queensberry's plea, together with the lengths to which Edward Carson went in his cross-examination to demonstrate that the marquess had libeled Wilde for the public benefit. In 2003, Merlin Holland published his impressive edition of a long-lost courtroom transcript of the libel trial. Holland's volume clarified for the first time the numerous occasions when Carson made such damning references to sodomy when interrogating Wilde on many aspects of the author's personal life and literary career.[61] Carson's persistent inquiries about sodomy, owing to the shifts in decorum that we have already acknowledged, were not reported verbatim in the press. Without having witnessed the proceedings, no reader of newspapers in 1895 could grasp the frequency with which Carson kept referring to sodomy. Not only was Wilde quizzed about his rendezvous with a dozen or so young men; Carson also pressured him on the imputed immorality of his writings, especially works such as *The Picture of Dorian Gray*, which had triggered moral outrage in parts of the British press when it first appeared in June 1890. Noticeably, Carson did not adhere entirely to the script laid out in Queensberry's plea. Never once did he advert to the term "gross indecency" when inquiring into Wilde's liaisons with these young males, since the libel technically involved the question of whether Wilde was posing as a sodomite. Having questioned Wilde about the unspecified "sins" that his protagonist Dorian Gray commits in the course of the narrative, Carson followed up with this comment: "you left it open to be inferred, I take it, that the sins of Dorian Gray, some of them, may have been sodomy?"[62]

As we see in chapter 2, Carson's line of questioning sought to uncover any trace of evidence that might substantiate Queensberry's accusation. Still, the marquess's plea also had another purpose: it justified the allegation by referring to the crime of gross indecency, and not the more severely punishable crime of sodomy. The text exploited the ambiguities inscribed in the 1885 law at the same time as it intimated that Wilde, as the libel declared, was presenting himself as a sodomite. Through a tactical circumlocution, the plea declared that Wilde had successfully solicited and incited young men to commit "sodomy and other acts of gross indecency and immorality," but added that the only crime that had been committed involved those "other said acts of gross indecency and immorality."[63] Matthew Sturgis has observed that "[t]he wording nimbly relieved the defence from the difficult business of proving that 'sodomy' had actually occurred."[64] Only toward the end of the plea did the marquess state that Wilde had "committed the offences aforementioned and the said sodomitical practices" with seven young men.[65] Even then, during the libel trial Carson's use of the epithet "sodomitical" arguably evoked something more than a type of sexual congress that required public witnessing, as would have been the case with the provisions of the Offences against the Person Act 1861. (The resonant adjective emerged whenever Carson wished to characterize Wilde's purportedly immoral cultural tastes, especially the author's predilections for a "sodomitical novel" or a "book putting forth sodomitical views."[66])

The Crown prosecution revealed that Queensberry's plea had in retrospect been cannily designed so that it could serve, if needed, as the basis of a future indictment against Wilde. (This was exactly its purpose when the grand jury found true bills [i.e., indictments] against both Wilde and Taylor on Tuesday, 23 April 1895.[67]) By the 1890s, as we have seen above, it was much more common to secure charges against homosexual activity on the grounds of gross indecency according to the 1885 law than to authenticate sodomy on the basis of the 1861 legislation. The plea makes it clear that, even though gross indecency was a misdemeanor and not a felony like sodomy, these legal shifts showed that the opportunities to assail sexual intimacy between males had broadened. To this day, Wilde counts as one of the foremost figures among an estimated 50,000 or so men who suffered greatly through the implementation of the Labouchere Amendment.[68]

Even so, making fuller sense of what happened to Wilde at the Old Bailey, from the moment of his arrest to the time of his conviction, entails more than unearthing from these sources the extraordinary turns of courtroom events that generated such immense interest in the press. It is hard to comprehend Wilde's motivation for initiating a perilous libel suit against Queensberry, unless we grasp the professional ambitions and sexual desires that he pursued, from the time he excelled as a student of classics to the moment he collected the marquess's offensive visiting card. This central aspect of his career is the subject of chapters 1 and 2, which appear below in part I of *Oscar Wilde on Trial*.

Part I

OSCAR WILDE ON TRIAL

Social Background, Cultural Context, Legal Process

1

OSCAR WILDE'S REMARKABLE CAREER: PROFESSIONAL AMBITIONS, SEXUAL ADVENTURES

> [H]e could appreciate the fun of the show, for he related how once, when he and his wife were walking along Kings Road, Chelsea, an urchin stared at them and shouted derisively "'Amlet and Ophelia out for a walk, I s'pose!" To which he returned "My little fellow, you are quite right. We are."
>
> —*Hesketh Pearson, The Life of Oscar Wilde* (1946)

This chapter examines Oscar Wilde's developing interest, during the late 1880s and early 1890s, in pursuing sexual liaisons with a diverse group of males in their teens and twenties. My discussion begins with his initially happy marriage, which began in May 1884, to the talented Irishwoman Constance Mary Wilde (née Lloyd), whom he had met—through a friendship between their Dublin families—three years before. By looking closely at Wilde's growing desire to enjoy intimacy with his own sex, which became evident three years into his wedded life, the present discussion explores the circumstances that resulted in the severe harassment that he suffered at the hands of John Sholto Douglas, 9th Marquess of Queensberry. The account that unfolds here leads up to the months preceding the libel suit that Wilde, in unguarded fashion, took out against the belligerent marquess. What becomes observable is that Wilde's earliest homosexual affairs developed within, not in spite of, his marriage, which was for some time based on mutual ties of affection and respect. The young married couple embodied the height of modern aesthetic taste. They would bedazzle bystanders with their elegant, finely colored outfits. Undoubtedly, the anecdote that we find in the epigraph, in which a working-class imp taunted them with a reference to Shakespeare's *Hamlet*, stretches credulity. Be that as it may, it would be mistaken to extract from this tall tale that the finely accoutered pair were simply playing roles in what steadily transmogrified, in the longer term, into a domestic calamity. Even when periodicals such as *Punch* more than intimated that Wilde and Douglas were conducting an affair (this unwelcome publicity came to attention in late 1894), the husband and wife still appeared together at public gatherings, with journalists often noting their stylish attire.

Although Wilde seized on opportunities to invite young men to sleep with him at Tite Street when his family was absent, he sought out some of his most precarious homosexual attachments in the rooms that he had reserved at different hotels. Nevertheless, he did not at first see a conflict between integrating his affection for lovers such as Bosie and maintaining his position as both a father and a spouse. As we see below, Wilde sought to create a balance, as best he could, among three different parts of his busy career. There was, to begin with, his domestic life, which involved the social world he occupied with Constance; the raising of their two young sons, Cyril and Vyvyan; and the maintenance of their fashionable residence in Chelsea. Soon after he married, Wilde made increasing efforts to concentrate on his profile as an accomplished man of letters who could excel in a broad repertoire of genres. On top of these considerable demands, he became connected with the queer subcultural circles that thrived, in the face of serious legal threats, throughout the metropolis. This aspect of his private universe led to intimacies with several male sex workers and hardened extortionists who were, as he remarked in prison, "wonderful in their infamous war against life."[1] These competing bursts of activity, at a time when he came into the public eye as one of the preeminent dramatists of the 1890s, took place during an era when homosexual scandal unsettled the upper reaches of English society as never before. This was the period when, as a family man, Wilde espoused himself—as unapologetically as possible—to an art and life that championed men's passion for their own sex.

"YOU MUST GET MARRIED *AT ONCE!*" OSCAR WILDE, DOMESTIC LIFE, AND LITERARY SUCCESS

By the middle of 1881, when Wilde met his future wife, he had a well-publicized reputation—if not a fair measure of notoriety—as a well-heeled man-about-town. He was also known for his academic brilliance. He had graduated with a rare double first in Literæ Humaniores (the interdisciplinary degree in Classics and modern social thought known as Greats) from Magdalen College, Oxford. At the time that Wilde's intimacy with Constance Lloyd flourished, he may not have had much personal income but he had achieved celebrity as a flamboyant aesthete (the lily was a characteristic boutonnière), as well as a raconteur famed for his matchless skills in conversation. He had also published effusive poems, a few of them in praise of noted actresses, including Lillie Langtry ("Lily of love, pure and inviolate!"), Ellen Terry ("O Portia! take my heart"), and Sarah Bernhardt (who, in the lead role of Racine's *Phèdre* [1677], presents "the loveless lips which men kiss in Hell").[2]

So great was the attention that Wilde had attracted because of his striking public image that he featured as a central figure in *The Private View at the Royal Academy, 1881* (1883), a stylistically conservative painting by the well-established William Powell Frith (fig. 3). Here, as Frith's painting shows, Wilde's reputation largely rested on his visibility as the figurehead of the popularized and much-satirized Aesthetic Movement. In this crowded spectacle that brings together dignitaries of the age (Frith himself included), Wilde's illuminated face is close to the foreground. Behind him, the assembled company includes such men as the novelist Anthony Trollope, the artist George Du Maurier, the poet Robert Browning, and the liberal premier W. E. Gladstone, amid many others whose faces are not as strongly recognizable as Wilde's. Placed firmly before the viewer, Wilde is surrounded by sundry ladies in "aesthetic" attire (the type of brightly colored gown that offered greater freedom of movement than the tightly corseted couture of the day), together with one of their young children. Two of his other female acolytes, along with a little girl who appears to be copying her mother's notetaking, are in the left of the panel, where the eyes of one of

Fig. 3. William Powell Frith, *The Private View at the Royal Academy, 1881* (1883). Oil on canvas, 102.9 × 195.6 cm.

these female art-lovers look upward at the paintings hanging from the gallery's soaring walls. This particular young woman, who is draped in a luxurious green fabric, noticeably sports on her breast a sunflower: another of the extravagant blooms that Wilde had occasionally worn on his lapels at social events.

Meanwhile, there is an assortment of gentlemen in sober dress, including the established journalist G. A. Sala, some of whom glower at Wilde. Noticeably, the tall and elegant aesthete ignores them. His own gaze turns in a different direction, toward the artworks arranged on the gallery's walls. Unquestionably, Sala's disapproval suggests that certain members of this elite have doubts about this fashionable upstart. It is, though, equally discernible that Wilde, whose lofty figure attracts attention in the scene, is not the object of overall scorn or satire, even if Frith himself appeared to have little respect for the "well-known apostle of the beautiful."[3] In his memoirs, which appeared later in the 1880s, Frith remarked, without mentioning Wilde's name, that the painting sought to "hit the folly of listening to self-elected critics in matters of taste, whether in dress or art."[4] Regardless of Frith's dismissive comments, what grabs our attention in *The Private View* is the young aesthete's vibrant figure as he dispenses his critical wisdom, just as he had done at other openings of exhibitions in London. By 2 February 1885, after it had been acquired by the Dorset solicitor and brewing company executive Alfred Pope, *A Private View* was sufficiently well known for the printmaker Henry Graves to produce a photogravure of the painting. The photogravure, which Graves aimed at a large popular market, includes a numbered guide identifying thirty-two (about two-thirds) of the celebrities assembled at this prestigious gathering (fig. 4).[5]

At the time that Frith's painting came before the public, Wilde was evidently an eligible young man. He stood out in a crowd of dignitaries and he captured the attention of women. Among the other affairs that Wilde treasured was with Florence Balcombe—the daughter of an English lieutenant—whom he met in August 1875. Even though he had never been officially engaged to Balcombe, he parted with precious gifts, including a gold cross that he had bestowed upon her, most probably at Christmas 1876. In September 1878, he politely asked her to return the trinket because it enshrined the "memory of two sweet years" ("the sweetest of all the years of my youth") that they had spent together.[6] Three months later, Balcombe married Wilde's contemporary from Dublin, Bram Stoker, whose literary fame also came into its own during the *fin de siècle*, with his famous novel *Dracula* coming out in 1897. Wilde had, in 1880, it seems, proposed to Charlotte Montefiore, the sister of one of his Oxford peers, who refused him. Equally intense was his flirtation with the seventeen-year-old Violet Hunt, later known as a successful author and suffragist who had affairs with

Fig. 4. Numbered guide to Henry Graves, photogravure of William Powell Frith, *The Private View at the Royal Academy, 1881* (1883), 1 February 1885. Paper, 30.48 × 20.54 cm.

modernist writers including Ford Madox Ford, W. Somerset Maugham, and H. G. Wells. In a 1926 memoir, Hunt records that she "as nearly as possible escaped the honour of being Mrs. Wilde."[7]

There were, however, commentators who found much to mock in what they saw as Wilde's posturing. Particularly risible, especially to the skeptics who observed his mannered persona, were his attempts to be taken in earnest as a gifted poet. His poetic aspirations increased in pace at Oxford, where he received the prestigious Newdigate Prize for his poem on a set topic, *Ravenna*. The least kind reviewers of his first book, *Poems* (1881), believed that his poetry too loudly echoed that of his Pre-Raphaelite idols: "Swinburne and Water[!]," the satirical magazine *Punch* memorably exclaimed.[8] Similarly, his efforts in making his name as a dramatist to some degree misfired: *Vera; or, The Nihilists* (1880), which focuses on radical attacks on the Russian tsar, never managed to reach the London stage, although in 1883 it played for a week—in a production starring the respected American actress Marie Prescott—in New York City. Still, these literary ventures hardly placed him in the public eye in the same way that his eye-catching image as a dashing aesthete drew attention in the press. This Aesthetic Movement, which had been germinating in the 1860s before Wilde capitalized on it, had for the past few years been the butt of many jokes in George Du Maurier's memorable caricatures, which aroused plenty of humor in *Punch*. And in light of his *Poems*, Linley Sambourne—another of *Punch*'s acclaimed humorists—mocked him as the "Æsthete of Æsthetes" (fig. 5).

These sendups did much to inspire two comic operas, F. C. Burnand's *Colonel* (1881) and Gilbert and Sullivan's *Patience* (1881), in which aspects of Wilde's persona as a self-appointed champion of art for art's sake (often known as aestheticism) were clear to see. Rightly sensing that the young aesthete presented good commercial opportunities, the theatre entrepreneur Richard D'Oyly Carte invited Wilde to deliver lectures on aspects of the Aesthetic Movement, in the name of both complementing and promoting the North American tour of *Patience*. Wilde, who at the time had no lecturing experience, agreed to Carte's contract. He took elocution lessons from the actor Hermann Vezin, designed an appropriate costume, which he donned as a marketing tool, and (for much of the time) presented himself in this garb as just the type of ostentatious aesthete that these comic operas had envisioned. During a profitable, year-long lecture tour that took him from coast to coast, he spoke—not always as audibly as he might have done—on such matters as "The English Renaissance of Art" (largely a tribute to the Pre-Raphaelites) and "Art and the Handicraftsman" (on the Arts and Crafts Movement). The famous photographs that the studio of Napoleon Sarony took in New York City of Wilde in his aesthetic apparel, just as he was about to start his tour, were immediately copyrighted as the only images of the young lecturer that could be sold at the countless venues where he made his presentations. These portraits—which present him in languid poses, memorably dressed in such quaint items of clothing as velvet breeches, silken hose, and opera pumps—ensured that he immediately turned into a familiar icon (fig. 6). Since his presence and performance made him look like the doyen of British aestheticism, his financial prospects were excellent. One of the main reasons that Wilde agreed to turn himself into such a spectacle—which set the American press abuzz and gave rise to further caricatures and parodies—was that it promised to put him on a firm financial footing. In London, he had accrued considerable debts, given his lack of steady income and his high expenditures. After his father (the eminent ear surgeon Sir William Wilde) died in 1876, the lack of family money was a source of hardship for his mother (a revered poet) and older brother (a budding journalist), both of whom, in a few years' time, deserted Dublin for London.

In January 1883, when he returned from New York City to London, Wilde's every move was put under scrutiny by the press, especially as he came back into the public sphere in a very different guise. Edmund Yates's magazine, the

PUNCH'S FANCY PORTRAITS.—No. 37.

"O. W."

"O, I feel just as happy as a bright Sunflower!"
Lays of Christy Minstrelsy.

Æsthete of Æsthetes!
What's in a name?
The poet is WILDE,
But his poetry's tame.

Fig. 5. Linley Sambourne, "Punch's Fancy Portraits.—No. 37," *Punch*, 25 June 1881: 298. Sambourne's allusion to the Christy Minstrels refers to "The Big Sunflower" (1868), by Bobby Newcomb, which became the signature song of the blackface performer Billy Emerson, who dressed as a dandy in brightly colored clothing. The link between Wilde's aestheticism and blackface minstrelsy was exploited in various caricatures and trade cards that circulated in the United States during Wilde's year-long lecture tour of North America in 1882.

Fig. 6. Studio of Napoleon Sarony, New York City, full-length portrait of Oscar Wilde in knee breeches, 1882. Photograph, 17 × 11 cm.

World: A Journal for Men and Women, which had published some of his early poems, was so taken with Wilde's change in appearance that it created—after he had returned from a three-month residence on the Continent—a verse celebrating the fact that "he has left behind him in Paris all his esoteric properties, including his luxuriant locks, and now arrays himself in nothing more eccentric than the costume and coiffure of the boulevards": "Our Oscar is with us again, / He is changed who was once so fair! / Has the iron gone out of his soul? O, no; / It has only gone over his hair."[9] Now donning much more sober attire, he soon greeted British and Irish audiences with lectures on "The House Beautiful," as well as his "Impressions of America." Constance Lloyd, who renewed her romance with Wilde in the summer of 1883, heard him deliver both of these talks at the Gaiety Theatre, Dublin, in November. Toward the end of the month, she blissfully told her brother Otho Lloyd to prepare himself "for an astounding piece of news": "I am," she exclaimed from Ireland, "engaged to Oscar Wilde and perfectly and insanely happy."[10]

Otho Lloyd's response was circumspect, not least because Wilde could not command the resources to support a household. Moreover, Otho Lloyd, who had been a contemporary of Wilde's at Oxford, knew well the contentious reputation that the young aesthete had established there through his affected passions for chic blue china and aesthetic costume. Although she had been brought up in a well-off family (her father was a well-known English barrister who died in 1874), as a young woman Constance Lloyd relied on a modest annual allowance of £250 from her paternal grandfather. (This modest sum was almost enough to ensure a middle-class individual could live comfortably.) Constance's mother, who had already wrangled with the father-in-law about financial support for her two children, remarried in 1878 and remained at times distant from Constance and Otho. The benevolent, though cautious, grandparent who had ensured that Constance had enough means to live on each year, agreed to a marriage settlement through a trust, which meant there were sufficient funds for the young lovers to wed. (The settlement, as Wilde confirmed many years later during his bankruptcy hearing in November 1895, yielded about £800 a year.[11]) Even then, the monies were to be advanced on the condition that Wilde defrayed outstanding debts of £300. It seems that at an early point in 1883 Wilde had borrowed the large sum of £1,200 from a moneylender called Edwin Levy.[12] As the proceedings of the trials made apparent, this was a pattern that dogged Wilde to the end of his days, and during the weeks immediately before he appeared at the Old Bailey this habit put him in peril with his creditors.

How, then, did Wilde respond to the impending marriage to Constance Lloyd? In January 1884, he struck a poetical (though, one might also say, slightly hollow) tone when he wrote to his dear friend Langtry, whom he had met not many years before through the Marlborough House circle around the Prince of Wales: "I am going to be married to a beautiful young girl named Constance Lloyd, a grave, slight, violet-eyed little Artemis, with great coils of heavy brown hair which make her flower-like head droop like a flower, and wonderful ivory hands which draw music from the piano so sweet that the birds stop singing to listen to her."[13] To be sure, much of this smacks of fanciful banter. But the letter still gives the impression that Constance Lloyd, in many ways, had for him the appeal of a somewhat innocent aesthetic object. At the same time, Wilde turned a skeptical eye on the sentimentality that was supposed to infuse traditional romance. "We are of course," he quipped to the American sculptor Waldo Story, "desperately in love."[14] He followed up the hyperbole with an equally droll comment on the messages that he and his beloved exchanged while he was "civilising the provinces" through his "remarkable lectures": "we telegraph to each other twice a day, and the telegraph clerks have become quite romantic in consequence."[15] Here, too, he presents Constance as picture perfect: "quite young, very grave, and mystical, with wonderful eyes, and dark brown coils of hair."[16] She was, too, serious-minded. Constance had already developed an earnest interest in alternative forms of spirituality, which would lead to meetings of the Theosophical Society and membership of the Hermetic Order of the Golden Dawn, both of which were significant in the occulture of the period.

During her engagement, Constance's letters show that she was besotted. Wilde's frequent absences from London while he lectured in the provinces brought pain to her heart. "I cannot," she wrote, "bear to be an hour away from you: Do believe that I love you passionately with all the strength of my heart and mind: anything that you asked me to do, I would in order to convince you and make you happy."[17] Her phrasing, if fired by intense romantic passion, intimates her desperation to win him over. The sizeable marriage settlement, which later became such a source of contention during Wilde's prison sentence, gave him a firm measure of financial security. It would, however, be incorrect to claim that it made him a wealthy man. Unquestionably, he was attractive. In his late twenties, Wilde cut a fine figure, as we can tell from the impressive portrait that the American painter Harper Pennington presented to him as a wedding gift in 1884 (fig. 7). Here, Wilde adopts a self-assured stance, with one hand on his left hip and the other planted firmly on a silver-topped walking stick, in a composed manner resembling the posture of King Charles I in Anthony van

Fig. 7. R. G. Harper Pennington, *Portrait of Oscar Wilde* (1884). Oil on canvas, 176.78 × 91.5 cm.

Dyck's famous painting *Le Roi à la chasse* (c. 1635). Toward the end of May 1884, Constance and Oscar married in St. James's Church, Sussex Gardens, in West London, after which they crossed the Channel for their honeymoon in Paris, where her wardrobe complemented—if at times outshone—his stylish outfits. When his first son, Cyril, was born in June 1885, Wilde was elated. He told Norman Forbes-Robertson—the English actor with whom he had traveled in 1879 to greet the French tragedienne Bernhardt after her Channel crossing—that the "baby is wonderful"; "[i]t also has a superb voice," he wryly observes, noting that the infant's booming cries are "essentially Wagnerian."[18] "You must get married *at once*!," Wilde declares, in a tone that, if teasing, perhaps belies a more serious undercurrent.[19]

The larger question, given the course that Wilde's busy career would take, was the degree to which Constance Wilde knew about her husband's evolving erotic interests. In her thoughtful biography, Franny Moyle comments: "What Constance understood of homosexuality at this stage is impossible to know."[20] What remains indisputable, however, is that Constance was much more than a fey Artemis with a drooping "flower-like head." As Moyle points out, Constance established herself as a talented children's writer, a political campaigner, and an editor of her husband's wittiest sayings: she was "a high-profile figure, whose beauty was widely acknowledged, whose activities were often reported in the press and whose appearance and outfits were also monitored for the sake of an intrigued public."[21] At a private view at the New Gallery in 1888, for instance, a reviewer took note of her elegant appearance: "Mrs. Oscar Wilde, in yellowish green, looked charming."[22] Moreover, from an early point in her marriage Constance earned respect as a leading proponent of the dress reform movement, which aimed to relieve women of the restrictive fashions that enjoyed such vogue during the 1870s and 1880s. In 1886, just to give one of many examples, a journalist remarked on the prominent role she played at a meeting of the Rational Dress Society at Westminster Town Hall, where she presented a motion: "That some reform is much needed in women's dress, in order to make it more convenient and at the same time more graceful."[23] From 1888 to 1889, she likely edited all six issues of the *Rational Dress Society's Gazette*.

Together as a married couple, Oscar and Constance shared a modestly sized but finely appointed home at 16 (now 34) Tite Street, Chelsea, which the avant-garde designer E. W. Godwin decorated for them. They moved there at the start of 1885. (The imposing Pennington portrait took pride of place in the drawing room.) In this modern residence, Wilde ambitiously sought to sustain what ultimately turned out to be an unworkable model of modern marriage. Fascinatingly, Adrian Hope, one of her distant in-laws, who later became ward to her two sons, recorded that at a dinner party in April 1885 Constance ventured that in wedlock "it should be free to either party to go off at the expiration of the first year."[24] Wilde, according to Hope, contributed to the discussion by showing "distinct leanings to a system of Contract for 7 years only, to be renewed or not as either party saw fit."[25]

This conversation took place when Constance was expecting Cyril in 1885. Within a year, the second child, Vyvyan, was born. The two boys were educated on the top floor of the Tite Street home, which was dedicated to both the daytime and nighttime nursery. It is perhaps easy to forget, given the incalculable scandal of Wilde's conviction, that he devoted plenty of attention to his sons. Just over two months before he left jail, he told his friend More Adey that he hoped he might have the opportunity to see them, especially Cyril: "I always was a good father to both my children."[26] But there was no chance that he could enjoy their company ever again. Cyril and Vyvyan certainly missed him. In a moving memoir published during the centenary of Wilde's birth in 1954, Vyvyan Holland recalls his loving parent with great fondness: "Most small boys adore their fathers, and we adored ours; and as all good fathers are, he was a hero to us both. He was so tall and distinguished and, to our uncritical eyes, so handsome. There was nothing about him of the monster that some people who never knew him and never even saw him have tried to make him out to be. He was a real companion to us, and we always looked forward to his frequent visits to our nursery."[27]

As Holland's touching memories also reveal, the Tite Street home was a busy hub of social activity. His mother's receptions attracted illustrious members of the artistic, political, and social elite: "Henry Irving, Sir William Richmond, R.A., Sarah Bernhardt, John Sargent, John Ruskin, Lillie Langtry, Mark Twain, Herbert Beerbohm Tree, Robert Browning, Algernon Swinburne, John Bright, Lady de Grey, Ellen Terry and Arthur Balfour." Furthermore, Holland recalls, "[a]ll of the Pre-Raphaelite Brotherhood were in attendance."[28] These were lasting social contacts. At the premiere of Wilde's second society comedy, *A Woman of No Importance* (1893), a journalist noted that Constance Wilde shared the stage box with the leading Conservative politician Arthur Balfour and the eminent Pre-Raphaelite painter Edward Burne-Jones.[29] Without a doubt, she and her husband were exceptionally well connected.

Particularly significant were their ties to dignitaries in the Liberal Party. In 1888, journalists took note of the Wildes' presence at various gatherings of party members. They were counted, for instance, among the noted persons in an audience of 300 people who attended the South Kensington Women's Liberal Association to meet Catherine Gladstone; the topic was the much-debated Local

Government Bill. Later in 1888, Wilde appeared at an "at-home" organized by the Eighty Club, the political organization that took its name from the year of its founding; the club was established in 1880 "with the object of promoting Liberal Education, and of stimulating Liberal organization," and its membership consisted of gentlemen who were "willing to give assistance by speaking at Public Meetings and by delivering Lectures on political subjects."[30]

The Eighty Club proved especially important to Wilde because it delivered lectures in favor of Gladstone's controversial policy of Home Rule for Ireland. Wilde's membership of this club, which was largely the preserve of political figures, began in 1887; it enabled him—as Thomas Wright has noted—to "promote his dream of Irish parliamentary independence through English party politics."[31] Wilde wrote passionately on Home Rule. In an 1889 review of J. A. Froude's *Two Chiefs of Dunboy* (a historical novel about eighteenth-century Ireland), Wilde observed, at a time when the coercion acts were creating severe conflicts in a nation fighting for its independence from Great Britain, that English prejudice against a restless Irish population had become acute. "There are," he wryly remarked, "some who will welcome with delight the idea of solving the Irish question by doing away with the Irish people."[32] Home Rule clearly mattered to Constance Wilde as well. In 1888, she stood among a small group of society women who played an active role in the Old Irish Market Place exhibit at Olympia, West London.

These social and political endeavors occurred during the period when Wilde was coming into his own as a professional writer. Even though he began publishing reviews as a twenty-three-year-old Oxford student (his larger-than-life presence at the opening of London's fashionable Grosvenor Gallery, which he wrote about in detail, is a case in point), it took until the mid-1880s before he made his mark as a respected journalist. During this phase of his professional life, which gradually superseded his earlier career as a lecturer, he established himself as a regular contributor to the *Pall Mall Gazette*: a gentlemen's evening newspaper that had a progressive Evangelical, W. T. Stead, at the helm. The immensely wide reading that he had undertaken at Oxford prepared him well to produce authoritative (and at times sharp-witted) reviews of such diverse literary works as John Addington Symonds's *Renaissance in Italy* (1875–1886) (Symonds, he says, "has something of Shakespeare's sovereign contempt for the masses"), the English poet William Morris's translation of the *Odyssey* (he praised its "freedom from affection and commonplace"), and his idol Walter Pater's *Imaginary Portraits* (1887) (these stories, he remarks, show that the Oxford don Pater ranks as "our greatest artist in prose").[33] Wilde's final contribution to the newspaper was a review of four undergraduate poets at Oxford, where the "summer term," he amusingly recalls, "teaches the exquisite art of idleness."[34] By the time this notice came out on 24 May 1890, he had contributed no fewer than 135 pieces to this and other periodicals, including the *Dramatic Review* and the *Speaker*.

During the late 1880s, Wilde became a magazine editor in his own right. He transformed, with considerable flair, an ailing journal called the *Lady's World* into the intellectually ambitious *Woman's World*. Under his two-year leadership, he ensured that this substantial monthly magazine appealed to educated women readers with broad cultural and political interests. The opening numbers contained contributions from an emergent generation of gifted writers, including Amy Levy, A. Mary F. Robinson, and Olive Schreiner, as well as essays from well-established figures such as Anne Thackeray Ritchie and his mother, Lady Jane Francesca Wilde. Constance Wilde also made two contributions, one of which promoted rational dress for girls in kindergarten ("a divided skirt either buttoned on to the stays or made with a Princess bodice").[35] Besides discussing topics such as the women's colleges at Oxford, the *Woman's World* carried a monthly fashion column.

The advances that Wilde achieved in journalism soon paved the way for his even more successful career as a literary author. Several years after he had settled into his marriage, his brilliant short fictions—including "Lord Arthur Savile's Crime" (1887, revised 1891) and "The Canterville Ghost" (1887, revised 1891)—debuted in the *Court and Society Review*. Not long afterward, his first collection of fairy stories, *"The Happy Prince" and Other Tales* (1888), which contains such classics as "The Selfish Giant," appeared in a beautifully presented edition from the publisher David Nutt. Shortly thereafter, in January 1889, his great essays "Pen, Pencil and Poison" and "The Decay of Lying" attracted attention in the influential *Fortnightly Review* and the *Nineteenth Century*, respectively. This was, by any account, an astonishingly productive time for him, and it spurred a series of evermore imposing writings that blazed a trail right up to the moment he entered the Old Bailey. In 1891 alone, Wilde published four substantial volumes, including a revised and expanded version of *The Picture of Dorian Gray*; his second collection of fairytales, *A House of Pomegranates*; *"Lord Arthur Savile's Crime" and Other Stories*; and *Intentions*.

As Wilde's literary career flourished, it led to a series of theatrical successes. Even if reviewers could quickly tell that Wilde had taken some of the elements of his first society play, *Lady Windermere's Fan*, from recognizable sources (Richard Brinsley Sheridan's *School for Scandal* [1777] was one and *Françillon* [1887] by Dumas *fils* was another), his wit proved irresistible. This was exactly the impression that the sparkling drama made on A. B. Walkley, one of the most knowledgeable theatre critics of day, who had his breath taken away by the chutzpah with which Wilde injected fresh life into familiar character types and well-worn plots, whose origins the dramatist had scarcely bothered to conceal:

> Mr. Oscar Wilde . . . is a gentleman who devotes brilliant talents, a splendid audacity, an agreeable charlatanry and a hundred-Barnum-power of advertisement, to making a change in old customs and preventing life from being monotonous. He does this in innumerable ways by his writings, his talk, his person, his clothes, and everything that is his. He has aimed at doing it in his play, *Lady Windermere's Fan*, and has been, to my mind, entirely successful. It is by no means a good play: its plot is always thin, often stale; indeed, it is full of faults—oh! dear, yes! glaring faults—faults that would leap to the eyes of the man in the street or the old applewoman around the corner. Yet, again it *is* a good play, for it carries you along from start to finish without boring you for a single moment.[36]

In 1892, *Lady Windermere's Fan* enjoyed an impressive run of 197 performances, and it possibly earned him as much as £3,000. The following year his next comedy, *A Woman of No Importance*, which opened at the Haymarket Theatre Royal, ran for 113 performances between April and August. The leading critic William Archer, who was well known for his defense of Henrik Ibsen's controversial plays, went so far as to remark of this and Wilde's preceding drama: "Mr. Wilde has no rival among his fellow-workers on the stage."[37] Admittedly, Archer did not regard either work as a masterpiece. Yet he maintained that the two comedies were of "an altogether higher order" than those of Wilde's contemporaries.[38] Such plays contained the hallmark wit on which Wilde's reputation often rests to this day, as we can see in the dandyish figure of Lord Illingworth, a libertine who makes much of the philosophy of the superficial. "A well-tied tie," he memorably informs his illegitimate son Gerald, "is the first step in life."[39] Such unforgettable lines gave the impression that the finely accoutered Wilde could have spoken these thought-provoking words himself.

With his literary star in the ascendant, Wilde's personal life went through various transformations that increased the distance between himself and Constance, especially after the birth of their second child. As a number of their friends realized, when the boys were small the parents had begun to row. In her memoirs, the Australian opera singer Nellie Melba recalls a poignant story that Wilde divulged to her: "He had been talking to me about his little sons. 'I was telling them stories last night,' he said, 'of little boys who were naughty and who made their mothers cry, and what dreadful things would happen to them unless they became better, and do you know what one of them answered? He asked me what punishment could be reserved for naughty papas, who did not come home till the early morning, and made mother cry far more?'"[40] The marriage, by all accounts, was failing.

Alfred Douglas recalled that in 1892, when he had become sexually involved with Wilde, his lover "was not very kind to his wife."[41] Douglas, however, took pains to note that Wilde "certainly had been (as he often told me) very much in love with her, and the marriage was purely a love match."[42] Moyle entertains the idea that Wilde's diminishing interest in his spouse was connected with "post-natal complications after Vyvyan's birth [that] left Constance unable to have full sex."[43] This view emerges most graphically in the dismal account that Frank Harris supplies in his sensational 1916 biography. The following passage claims to be an accurate report of an intimate conversation with Wilde that took place at some point in 1898. Wilde, in this troubling confession, admitted that he could no longer love Constance when she started to bear children:

> When I married, my wife was a beautiful girl, white and slim as a lily, with dancing eyes and gay rippling laughter like music. In a year or so the flower-like grace had all vanished; she became heavy, shapeless, deformed; she dragged herself about the house in uncouth misery with drawn blotched face and hideous body, sick at heart because of our love. It was dreadful. I tried to be kind to her; forced myself to touch and kiss her; but she was sick always, and—oh! I cannot recall it, it is all loathsome . . . I used to wash my mouth and open the window to cleanse my lips in the pure air. Oh, nature is disgusting; it takes beauty and defiles it: it defaces the ivory-white body we have adored, with the vile cicatrices of maternity; it befouls the altar of the soul.[44]

Most likely, Harris's recollections exaggerate various regretful sentiments that Wilde had probably confided to him one or two months after Constance died, at the age of forty, from botched surgery. But no matter how much Harris amplifies Wilde's disgust, this passage points to a matter that scholars have recently considered in careful detail: namely, that Constance had from 1889 been experiencing difficulties with mobility.

Then again, after the birth of their two sons Oscar and Constance were not entirely disaffected with each other. As we can tell from the manuscript of Wilde's fairytale "The Selfish Giant," they cooperated with each other, since the document is written in Constance's hand—a fact that points to either her co-authorship of the tale or her role as a secretary in preparing the stories for the press. Further, the fact that Wilde three years afterward dedicated to her his second, beautifully decorated book of fairy stories, *A House of Pomegranates*, is an additional indication of how much she mattered to him. Moreover, they continued to take vacations together as a family in the country, though these also involved homosexual liaisons that occurred behind Constance's back. In the summer of 1893, for example, when Wilde rented a large property called The Cottage at Goring-on-Thames, she confided to her older cousin, Lady Georgina Mount-Temple, that she was puzzled about why he was so distant from her: "I cannot make out whether it is my fault or Oscar's that he is so cold to me and so nice to others . . . His butler knows his other plans and I know nothing."[45]

By this juncture, Wilde appears to have been conducting an intimate affair with his teenage servant Walter Grainger, who had previously worked in a similar capacity for Bosie in Oxford. What is more, Douglas—who had recently left the university without a degree—had now become a fixture in Wilde's life. Serious stresses (both emotional and literary) developed at this point in Wilde's volatile relationship with him. Still, during this difficult phase of his marriage Wilde sought to strike a balance between his family commitments, his professional obligations, and his intimacies with other men. Even if Constance may not have yet completely faced the fact that her husband's withdrawn behavior had much to do with his preoccupation with the young men in his employ, it was evident to Cyril and Vyvyan's governess, Gertrude Simmonds, that some kind of surreptitious activity was afoot between Wilde and his male servants. Simmonds, too, gave a statement to Queensberry's solicitor, in which her comments referred to her witnessing Wilde's familiarity with George Hughes, the boy who looked after the boats: "Mr. Wilde had hold of his arm and was patting his shoulder familiarly."[46]

Although such information indicates that Wilde did not always conduct himself with due discretion, he knew that his wife and children, especially their privacy, had to be protected from intrusions by the press. In 1889, he was irritated to discover that Herbert Vivian, in a mischievous column in the daily *Sun*, had—among other things—recklessly reported on private conversations he had enjoyed with Wilde in various places, including a meeting of the Eighty Club. Most offensive was the journalist's readiness to record, without Wilde's permission, some anecdotes about Cyril and Vyvyan: "I plaster the walls of their rooms," Wilde is said to have told the journalist, "with texts about early rising and sluggards, and so forth, and I tell them that, when they grow up, they must take their father as a warning, and occasionally have breakfast earlier than two in the afternoon."[47] The revelations that followed about Wilde's oldest boy crossed a line: "Cyril . . . not yet a lustrum old, bewildered his family one morning by announcing that he did not mean to say his prayers any more. It was pointed out to him that he must pray to God to make him good, but he demurred that he did not want to be made good at all, and was not going to pray for what he did not want."[48] After an altercation with his father, Cyril, we learn, offered a compromise, stating that "he wouldn't mind praying to God to make baby good."[49] Wilde was prompt to express his displeasure on reading this. "[Y]ou," Wilde sternly informed him in July 1890, "have given pain to a lady, to whom you have had the honour of being introduced, my wife, by writing about our children in the public press."[50]

No matter how much the married couple strove to defend their dignity, it was clear to those who observed them that there were reasons that they appeared to be separating. The problems in their relationship emerge in *A Willing Exile*: an otherwise inconsequential novel that one of Wilde's bitterest critics, the queer writer Marc-André Raffalovich, published in 1890. In this exercise in poking fun at Wilde's social milieu, Oscar and Constance appear in the guises of Cyprian and Daisy Brome. Telltale details reveal that Wilde is the target of Raffalovich's strenuous satire. At one point, the narrator remarks on Cyprian's obsession with his image: "He was struggling with a complicated buttonhole, composed of half-a-dozen orchids, white lilac and daphne, and getting it to keep in a position by pinning it in two places to his coat."[51] A little later, we discover that the Bromes' family residence is infested with countless male companions, all of whom appear to have little interest—like Cyprian himself—in anything but their looks. The clueless Daisy, it appears, finds it hard to know what to make of them: "Cyprian was, or seemed to be, intimate with countless young men; they were all curiously alike. Their voices, the cut of their clothes, the curl of their hair, the brims of their hats, the parties they went to."[52] In the end, she develops an affair with the altogether manlier Clarence Holford, and her personal life promises to thrive once the effete Cyprian's health finally declines.

Raffalovich's plot was prescient. Wilde caused grave social embarrassment when he treated Constance contemptuously in front of his lover Alfred Douglas and the young French author Pierre Louÿs at the Albemarle Hotel, at the time when *A Woman of No Importance* premiered in April 1893. When she arrived with the mail that had been sent to their family residence in Tite Street, Constance asked Wilde if he intended coming home. In response, he callously replied that he no longer knew the address. She left in tears. Louÿs, to whom Wilde had dedicated the French edition of *Salomé*, found the episode so offensive that he brought their friendship to an end.

Perhaps unsurprisingly, once these distressing experiences began to circulate Constance sought out alternative sources of affection. In 1894, when she was preparing *Oscariana* (a collection of Wilde's epigrams), she appears to have developed romantic affections for a younger man, Arthur Humphreys, the general manager of Hatchards, who issued the volume that year. "I do love you dear Arthur," she wrote tenderly in August 1894, after he had visited her during a family vacation at Worthing. "[H]ow dear and delightful you have been to me to-day. I have been happy, and I do love you dear Arthur . . . You have been a great dear all the time quite perfect to me, and dear to the children, and nice to Oscar too, and so I love you."[53] Granted, the love of which Constance writes has much to do with the deep affection that Humphreys had shown to herself and her family. But it also suggests that she desired Humphreys—who was equally unhappy in his marriage—because her husband's fondest attachments were no longer with her. By this point, Constance had probably come to acknowledge that her spouse's passions were for members of his own sex, especially Douglas, whose company had for some time constituted a serious emotional and financial drain on Wilde's life.

Even during this prosperous period, Wilde spent far more than he earned. At the very point when he should have been able to exult in his wealth, Wilde was fleeing hotels where he had failed to pay his bills, just as he was receiving writs from creditors who demanded that he settle invoices for silver cigarette cases and other jewelry that he had bestowed upon his male lovers. His expenses were enormous. By Wilde's own reckoning, between the fall of 1892 and his imprisonment he spent "£5,000 in actual money" when he was in Douglas's company.[54] As J. Robert Maguire has observed, in the months leading up to the trials the Irish dramatist had been reaping a substantial annual income of £2,000; yet even with these handsome resources, Wilde faced huge debts, having "been served writs amounting to £400."[55] He had many costs to cover for hotel accommodation in London, Paris, and elsewhere. The numerous bills, as Donald Mead has pointed out, included one for £8 19s. 6d. from the Metropole Hotel, Brighton, where he had been staying with Douglas during 4-8 October 1894.[56] Dinner on the first night amounted to £1 10s. 6d. Even the unpaid amounts on the grocery bills for Wilde's family home grew steadily from 1892 onward. The day before the libel trial began, the account book held at Channon's stores—which supplied Wilde with his favorite champagne, hock, and seltzer—shows that he owed the company £37 15s. 5d., though it also records that on 22 March 1895 a payment of £15 was credited to the account.[57]

Such expenditures took an increasing toll on Wilde's life. On 1 March 1895, just one month before the libel trial began, Wilde was so desperate for funds that he pawned pieces of jewelry, which raised £10 2s. 6d.: a sum he promptly used to support a short vacation with Douglas in Monte Carlo. Further, even if it had become more perceptible that Wilde maintained an unconventional marriage, the rumors about his private habits put Constance under intolerable stress. And, as we will see below, once Wilde experienced alarming harassment from the Marquess of Queensberry because of his increasingly public intimacy with Lord Alfred, he found himself the object of an unbearable accusation that he decided—ill-advisedly—to fight in court.

The next section takes a long view on the intellectual, creative, and personal circumstances that first engaged Wilde's interest in male homosexuality in the 1870s and finally introduced him to Edward Shelley, the first of the young men whose intimacy with Wilde came to attention during the libel case. These developments in Wilde's personal life occurred at a time when scandals about men who enjoyed sexual contact with other men were the subject of widely publicized legal actions.

"I ADORED YOU MADLY, EXTRAVAGANTLY, ABSURDLY": OSCAR WILDE'S EVOLVING HOMOSEXUAL CAREER

In what circumstances, then, did Wilde devise an uncompromising way of life that provided him with opportunities to enjoy intimacy with a broad range of young men in their teens and twenties? Part of the answer may lie in an intriguing anecdote that his devoted friend Ada Leverson—who had given him refuge in her home while he was on bail prior to the second criminal trial—recalled, with a refreshing lack of embarrassment, in 1930. The story concerns an epiphany that supposedly came to Wilde outside a well-known department store located in the hubbub of Piccadilly Circus:

> When he first married, he was quite madly in love, and showed himself an unusually devoted husband. He never left his wife for an hour, and she adored him in return. A few months after their marriage, she went shopping, and Oscar accompanied her. He waited for her outside Swan and Edgar's while she made some long and tedious purchase.
>
> As he stood there full of careless good spirits on a cold sunny May morning, a curious, very young, but hard-eyed creature appeared, looked at him, gave a sort of laugh, and passed on. He felt, he said, "as if an icy hand clutched his heart." He had a sudden presentiment. He saw a vision of folly, misery and ruin. And remained in a depressed state for the rest of the evening.[58]

Even though Leverson's story looks apocryphal, it draws attention to the geographical location that was pivotal in many of the male sexual contacts that he made. In his history of rent boys who worked in this area, Jeremy Reed imagines the opportunities that this notorious part of central London held for Wilde. Besides the erotic prospects that the promenade at the Alhambra Theatre, in neighboring Leicester Square, offered to men in search of sex, the places where Wilde enjoyed intimacy included hotels such as the Albemarle and Savoy; restaurants such as Kettner's and the Solferino in Soho; and, very possibly, the St. James's bar.[59] All of these venues were within striking distance of Piccadilly Circus. Reed reminds us, for example, that the fashionable Café Royal, which was no more than 100 yards away, played a crucial role in Wilde's erotic networking. There, he met the minor music-hall comedian Frederick Atkins (also known as Fred Denny) in October or November 1892, as well as Alfred Wood in January 1893. The "Dilly"—as it was known to the sex workers who operated on this territory—played a crucial role in what Reed terms the "sexual psychogeography" of Wilde's London.[60] The street features prominently in an early chapter of Wilde's *Picture of Dorian Gray*, where the protagonist confides to his mentor, Lord Henry Wotton, about a stroll he took through an area where shoppers commingled with prostitutes: "I used to look at every one who passed me, and wonder with a mad curiosity, what sort of lives they led. Some of them fascinated me. Others filled me with terror. There was an exquisite poison in the air."[61]

Wilde's evolving interest in homosexual culture derives from key moments in his college education, which began in October 1871 at Trinity College Dublin. His inquiries into Greek love assuredly influenced how he fashioned himself as a benevolent older man who bestowed favors upon younger males. Particularly important to Wilde was his tutor, John Pentland Mahaffy: the prolific scholar of classical studies, who became a fellow in 1864 and took the chair in ancient history seven years later. Even though Wilde eventually expressed frustration with the Unionist lens through which Mahaffy filtered his views on classical antiquity, at Trinity Wilde performed an instrumental role in the development of his tutor's first major publication, *Social Life in Greece from Homer to Menander*. The prestigious house of Macmillan & Co. brought out Mahaffy's study in 1874, the same year that Wilde was awarded the college's Berkeley Medal for Greek. In the preface to this volume—which appeared just after Wilde had proceeded to a second degree in Classics at Oxford—Mahaffy gave his thanks to his recent pupil, who counted among the individuals who "made improvements and corrections all through the book."[62]

Mahaffy's discussion is remarkable for the boldness with which he approaches the intimacy between the ἐραστής (the male lover) and the ἐρώμενος (the male beloved): the cross-generational structure of desire that created intimacy between an older and younger citizen. He first introduces this passionate bond between males at the moment he turns to a discussion of "Greek culture in its highest development in Athens," and he immediately focuses on Plato's dialogue *Char-*

mides, whose title is taken from the name of the exquisite youth who arouses Socrates's interest.[63] As Mahaffy points out, the dialogue opens when Socrates returns from a military campaign and then makes inquiries about the "new beauties" that have "appeared in the Gymnasia."[64] Socrates does this, Mahaffy adds, "just as we should ask what new belles had appeared at the balls of the season in Dublin."[65] "The appearance of Charmides," he adds, "is described just as we should be describing the reigning belle at a flower show—surrounded by a crowd of gentlemen in attendance, and causing quite a sensation when she comes in."[66]

To be sure, in his study Mahaffy later ventures a comment that intimates that he should perhaps apologize for alluding to a matter that might appear indelicate to modern sensibilities. "To us," he says, "these things are so repugnant and disgusting, that all mention of them is usually omitted when treating of Greek culture."[67] Still, no sooner has he admitted these misgivings than he reminds us (with an explicit cross-reference) about the passage where he has already observed that modern heterosexual customs are perhaps not so very different from classical homosexual ones. These audacious words stayed the same in the many later editions of *Social Life in Greece*. But there was, as Lawrence Danson has discerned, an area of the book that Mahaffy took pains to revise. When Mahaffy's study first came out, he admitted that in modern society "there is generally a feeling of wonder and of disgust that so highly-wrought natures should have tolerated such strange and unnatural attachments."[68] Although he readily acknowledged his contemporaries' revulsion toward Greek love, he still advanced this fearless point: "As to the *unnatural*, the Greeks would answer probably, that all civilisation was unnatural, that its very existence presupposed the creation of new instincts, the suppression of old, and that many of the best features in all gentle life were best because they were unnatural."[69]

It is noticeable that this comment, together with other parts of his text that endorse this insight, disappeared from all later editions, as did Mahaffy's tribute to Wilde in the preface, which instead alerted the reader that the "discussions of Greek morals" had been amended so that the volume could now serve as "school and family reading."[70] Danson proposes that "it's hard not to spot Wilde's 'contribution'" in the offending sentence.[71] On this view, in the summer of 1874, when Wilde was transitioning from Trinity College Dublin to Magdalen College, Oxford, Mahaffy's prizewinning student had acquired a sophisticated understanding of Greek love. He acknowledged that ancient and modern societies have deemed aspects of sexuality to be either "natural" or "unnatural," depending on conventions that differ from one culture to another.

Wilde entered Oxford to read Literæ Humaniories when curricular reforms had brought about significant changes in the approach that tutors made to the works of Plato in particular. In her study of Oxford Hellenism, Linda Dowling reminds us of the determination with which Benjamin Jowett—who held the Regius Chair in Greek from 1855 to the time of his death in 1893—was "an agent of revolutionary change at Oxford"; Jowett embraced, for the first time, the openly homoerotic dialogues such as *Phaedrus*, *Symposium*, and *Charmides* on the curriculum.[72] Although Jowett was hardly a proponent of Greek love, he introduced these reforms as part of a broader move toward the greater intellectual latitude in many areas of Oxford life. These advances understandably had special resonance for homosexually inclined men.

Especially significant for Wilde was the university tutor Walter Pater's responsiveness to male same-sex attraction. A retiring man, Pater—who held a fellowship at Brasenose College, and had no responsibilities for Wilde's education—established his name (and also provoked an outcry) with a collection of superlative critical essays, *Studies in the History of the Renaissance* (1873). Pater's brilliant volume explores the art and thought of Pico della Mirandola, Michelangelo Buonarroti, and Leonardo de Vinci, among several others, in order to draw attention to the "outbreak of the human spirit" (especially "the worship of the body") that defined the cultural rebirth that Jules Michelet, much earlier in the century, associated with the late medieval and early modern period.[73] Pater's volume, which demonstrates his supreme skills as a prose stylist, enjoyed a measure of notoriety for its brief but pointed "Conclusion," which reads like a manifesto advancing the view that we must uphold "the love of art for art's sake" because it arouses intense moments of "poetic passion" as well as the "desire for beauty."[74]

Yet there were other aspects of Pater's volume that were arguably more intrepid in their discussion of ardent human passion. Notably, one of his chapters focuses on the eighteenth-century German archaeologist and art historian Johann Joaquim Winckelmann, who expressed an "affinity with Hellenism" that "was not merely intellectual."[75] Winckelmann's intellect, Pater asserts, had "subtler threads of temperament . . . inwoven in it," a truth borne out "by his romantic, fervid friendships with young men."[76] Such phrasing, which was perhaps too scholarly to meet with any moral objections from Pater's readership, counts among the boldest statements about male homosexual desire to be found in English literature from the 1860s and 1870s.

One might argue that the strong homoerotic current and emphasis on physical pleasure that flows through Wilde's *Picture of Dorian Gray* owes much to the leads that Pater had taken. "Be always searching," Lord Henry advises his friend, "for new sensations. Be afraid of nothing."[77] Although Wilde's novel does not transcribe these words from Pater's writings, they resound with the spirit of Pater's "Conclusion": "What we have to do is to be for ever curiously testing new opinions and courting new impressions, never acquiescing in a facile orthodoxy." Admittedly, Wilde was known to have made quips about Pater's reserved manner. Vincent O'Sullivan, the American poet who befriended Wilde at Oxford in the early 1890s, recalls Wilde's wry response to a lecture that Pater had given in London: "At the end, said Pater, 'I was rather afraid that people had not heard me.' 'We overheard you,' answered the ready Oscar, perhaps a little disdainfully."[78] From the time of their initial meeting in late October 1877, some months after Wilde had sent him a copy of his review of the Grosvenor Gallery, their personal exchanges, however, stayed for the most part respectful. As the record of the libel trial reveals, Pater advised Wilde to reconsider "a certain passage" in *The Picture of Dorian Gray*—one that touched on male homoeroticism—that "was liable to misconstruction."[79] Pater, Wilde told the court, was "the only critic of this century" whom he "set high."[80]

Besides trying to make his mark as an art critic, Wilde devoted part of his time at Oxford to establishing his profile as a poet. In his earliest poems, one can readily detect traces of homoerotic desire. This is true of his much-revised sonnet "The Grave of Keats," which originally appeared as the tailpiece to an article in the Catholic *Irish Monthly*. In the final version, which appeared in *Poems*, his speaker lauds the brilliant English poet, who died at the young age of twenty-five, as a venerated "Martyr"—one who was "fair as Sebastian, and as early slain."[81] Moreover, he remarks that Keats had the "sweetest lips since those of Mitylene."[82] These lines bring together homoerotic classical references. Sebastian, the third-century Christian martyr who was murdered by his presumed former lover, the Emperor Diocletian, had—especially through the art of the Renaissance painter Guido Reni—become for various late Victorians an icon of homosexual desire. This element is evident in the crucial commentary that originally prefaced the sonnet. In his discussion of Keats's burial site, Wilde expounds upon what he experienced when contemplating it in the Protestant Cemetery, Rome: "a vision of Guido's St. Sebastian came before my eyes as I saw him at Genoa, a lovely brown boy, with crisp, clustering hair and red lips, bound by his evil enemies to a tree."[83] This luscious description goes on to remind us of the extraordinary manner in which Guido's art presents the young man—one whose body is "pierced by arrows"—"raising his eyes with divine, impassioned gaze towards the Eternal Beauty of the opening heavens."[84] Matched with the lyric intensity of the lesbian poet Sappho, who dwelt at Mitylene, Wilde's discussion suffuses his image of Keats with an erotic luxuriance that is unquestionably queer.

The same can be said of his description of the "Grecian lad" who is the focus of the longer poem, "Charmides," whose Platonic title reminds us of the dialogue that features Socrates's surging desires. Here, too, we witness the boy's "crisp brown curls," as he begins a voyage that leads to a series of perverse encounters, including an episode where he makes passionate love to the "grand cool flanks," "the crescent thighs," and "the bossy hills of snow" of a statue representing Pallas Athene.[85] "Charmides," which first appeared in *Poems*, was so audacious in its depiction of sexual passion that it eventually came between Wilde and a friend who opened his eyes to the queer life of London. The person in question was the society portraitist Frank Miles, whom Wilde had met at Oxford. Miles, who was two-and-a-half years older than Wilde, came from a wealthy family in Nottinghamshire, where his father served as a senior member of the clergy. Although Miles, who probably encountered Wilde sometime in 1874 or early 1875, was not an Oxford undergraduate, he was nonetheless well-ensconced in the social networks of the university. Just as we do not know the precise circumstances of their initial encounter, no one has ever established with certainty that Wilde and Miles were lovers. In an unreliable biography, Rupert Croft-Cooke records, without providing any source, that in 1892 Alfred Douglas learned "that Frank Miles had been his predecessor in Oscar's affections."[86] Meanwhile, in *The Secret Life of Oscar Wilde* Neil McKenna asserts that the two fast friends, who visited each other's family homes, were "unlikely to have been monogamous" and that theirs must have been an erotic affair: "They had sex with each other," he insists, "and with other people."[87] By comparison, Molly Whittington-Egan contends that for both men the bond between them was "their first serious special friendship."[88] From her perspective, Wilde might have maintained a much healthier attitude toward homosexuality had Miles not enabled the "disastrous encounter" with a somewhat older man, Lord Ronald Sutherland Gower.[89] Gower, the youngest son of the Duke of Sutherland, was an aspiring sculptor whose greatest achievement was the imposing Shakespeare Monument, which the town councilors of Stratford-upon-Avon unveiled in the grounds of the Memorial Theatre in 1888. (Wilde made a speech in Gower's honor.[90]) "Gower," Whittington-Egan says, "was an extreme corrupting influence on Oscar and Frank."[91] The reason, she avers, is undeniable: "Gower was a grossly reckless frequenter of 'rough trade'"; "his example," she adds, "led Oscar on to that use of boys in low life which has seemed inappropriate and so puzzled and repelled."[92]

These are strong words, and they are in all likelihood misplaced. The friendship with Gower was not exactly disastrous. For a start, it put Wilde in contact (as did his intimacy with Miles) with the artistic world of London. In his review of the opening of the Grosvenor Gallery, Wilde draws attention to a painting by the eminent artist John Millais: "a head of a young man with delicate aquiline nose, thoughtful, oval face, and artistic abstracted air, which will be easily recognized as a portrait of Lord Ronald Gower."[93] Wilde would have known, too, that Gower was fearless in defending his reputation against sexual slurs. In 1879, Gower went to the Queen's Bench to fend off a serious attack that had appeared in a gossip-mongering magazine, the *Man of the World*. The fashionable periodical had published an article headed "A Loathsome Scandal." Although it dared not mention the aristocrat's name, the journalist insinuated—through well-chosen information—that Gower was the object of contempt: "It is within the recognizance of the men of the world that allegations of a most serious character have recently been made against two *aristos*, allegations of so serious a character that if proved true the delinquents are not only cast outside the pale of society, but are excluded from the sympathy of humanity . . . . One delinquent is of high descent and has young domestic ties. The other, equally well born, has claims beyond those which are merely hereditary, and has been regarded as a man, not only of refined tastes and studious habits, but as an artist of somewhat more than ordinary ability."[94]

In the face of this insult, Gower submitted an affidavit in which he declared his identity, place of residence, and family descent: "I am thirty-three years old," the document went on to state, "and unmarried. I am an artist, and for the greater part of my life have devoted much of my time to artistic studies, and my habits would naturally be described as studious. . . . [U]nder no circumstances," he declared firmly, "have I been guilty of any such acts of practices as were referred to, or of any unnatural, unmanly, or disgusting acts or practices whatever."[95] Even though Gower's counsel, Sir Henry James, was eager to press for libel, the Lord Chief Justice ruled that the case should be dismissed once there was denial under oath.

Gower and Wilde maintained a friendship through the 1880s. Its significance perhaps accounts for the fact that Gower's mannerisms and physical features appear in Wilde's portrait of Lord Henry Wotton in *The Picture of Dorian Gray*. In 1893, the artist Roger Fry observed that when he set eyes on Gower, he "recognized [him] at once as the original of Lord Henry in *Dorian Gray*."[96] Even if Lord Henry unwittingly spurs Dorian Gray's criminal activities, it is doubtful that Gower wielded the same influence on Wilde. As things stand, there is no evidence that Gower provided contacts for Wilde in what was known as rough trade around Piccadilly Circus. By comparison, there is documentation that reveals the reasons that the close friendship with Miles came to an end in 1881. Not long after leaving Oxford, Wilde moved into rooms with Miles at 13 Salisbury Street, and he later resided in the home that Miles commissioned E. W. Godwin to design, Keats House, in what had become an artists' colony in Tite Street. Together, the friends enjoyed the company of the Marlborough House set connected with the Prince of Wales. Among the many society women who sat for Miles was the prince's onetime mistress, Lillie Langtry. She was, as we know from Gower's memoirs, a visitor to Salisbury Street. Despite these strong social ties, a rift developed between Miles and Wilde. Canon Miles wrote sternly from Bingham Rectory to Wilde, stating that the time had come for his son to break off relations with his roommate. The avowed reason had nothing to do with any knowledge the canon may have had of Miles's sexuality. It appears that Wilde's "Charmides" had caused offense: "there are passages which give pain and distress to minds even of my wife's age and class."[97] The two men thus parted ways.

Wilde sought to establish one further intimate friendship with a male peer. In the late 1870s, he enjoyed the company of Rennell Rodd: a recent graduate in Greats from Balliol College, Oxford, where he, like Wilde, had won the Newdigate Prize, on this occasion for a poem on Sir Walter Raleigh. Later known as a career diplomat, Rodd—who was four years younger than Wilde—spent much of his social life after leaving Oxford in the circles that Wilde enjoyed. Even though Rodd had been introduced to Wilde at the university ("[t]here was an immediate fascination in the unconventional freedom of his brilliant conversation"), it was in London that their relationship fared well.[98] Rodd visited Wilde at 13 Salisbury Street, and Wilde in turn furnished Rodd with an introduction to the American artist James Whistler, who in March 1881 had returned from Venice to reestablish his practice at 13 (later 33) Tite Street.

Rodd, who subsequently assisted Whistler with printmaking, had already struck up a literary connection with Wilde. They became close friends. The year before Rodd graduated from the university, Wilde accompanied him on a vacation in La Roche, Belgium. The following year, Rodd and Wilde traveled once more together, this time to the Loire. Differences, however, began to arise between them. In later life, Rodd recalled that on reading Wilde's *Poems* he asked his friend "to eliminate one or two passages which violated" Rodd's "sense of taste."[99] During Wilde's lecture tour of North America, they eventually fell out. "He had," Rodd recollects, "spontaneously offered to take my little book of poems with him and have it published in America."[100] It was this project that ended their friendship.

Wilde found an American publisher for Rodd's *Rose Leaf and Apple Leaf* (1882), which reprinted most of the poems in *Songs in the South*, which had appeared in London in 1881, while adding nine new ones. The volume came out from J. M. Stoddart, an editor based in Philadelphia, in an extravagant edition that Wilde described as "a *chef d'oeuvre* of typography."[101] But Wilde went to further lengths with this fine-looking volume. *Rose Leaf and Apple Leaf* carried a long prefatory essay by him titled "*L'Envoi*," in which Wilde celebrates the "enthusiasm for beauty which is the secret of Hellenism" before recalling how he and Rodd had spent time together in France—"'matching our reeds in sportive rivalry,' as comrades used in the Old Sicilian days."[102] Such words caused Rodd unease. In particular, Rodd came to regret the effusive dedication that Wilde had inserted into the volume: "TO OSCAR WILDE—'HEART'S BROTHER'—THESE FEW SONGS AND MANY SONGS TO COME."[103] To the English poet Algernon Charles Swinburne, Wilde's phrasing resounded with the passion that the Macedonian nobleman Hephaestion declared for the "all-conquering Alexander."[104] Swinburne was not alone in finding this expression of devotion too forthright. Once Rodd received a copy, he wrote directly to Stoddart, where he began by thanking the publisher for the "great care and delicacy" of the printing and binding before conveying his misgivings about both his dedication and the substance of Wilde's "*L'Envoi*": "I am not overpleased with the way in which I find myself identified with much that I have no sympathy with . . . there is one thing in it that has annoyed be excessively, and had I had a proof I should not have allowed it to stand. The dedication is too effusive. I have written to Mr. Wilde on this score, but if he does not write to you, I must ask you as a personal favour to see to it. I want to have it removed from all copies that go out for the future."[105]

By this point, in a pattern that injured a noticeable number of Wilde's closest male friendships, Rodd decided to make a break with Wilde, very likely because a mocking notice in the *Saturday Review* thought it ridiculous that Rodd was supposed to be the exemplar of Wilde's "New Renaissance" in art. The elaborate binding and Japanese-style decorations, together with Wilde's prefatory essay, suggested to the *Saturday* that Rodd's poems were "not quite unworthy of the mystic cover," especially since the "flowery components" of his poetry dwelt "in a haze of green and rose."[106] Rodd, who was eager to establish his name as a poet, clearly could not take this kind of attack. "A letter which I wrote to him," Rodd reminisces, "in which I also warned him of the harm which he felt he was doing to himself by his extravagant performances in America, gave profound offence."[107] In April 1883, Wilde mentioned to a new acquaintance, Robert Harborough Sherard—who always claimed not to have any knowledge of Wilde's homosexuality before the trials—that although Rodd was "the true poet," the gifted author of *Rose Leaf and Apple Leaf* was also "the false friend."[108]

Wilde's gravitation toward physical encounters with other men appears to have emerged in the early stages of his marriage. The strongest evidence that he attempted to connect intimately with a younger male emerges in his correspondence with Henry Currie Marillier: a twenty-year-old scholar of classics at Peterhouse, Cambridge, whom Wilde had known five years before. After receiving an invitation to watch Marillier and his fellow students perform in a production of Aeschylus's *Eumenides,* Wilde responded: "I have a very vivid remembrance of the bright enthusiastic boy who used to bring me my coffee in Salisbury Street."[109] At this earlier time, Marillier—a "blue-coat boy" who wore that distinctive attire at Christ's Hospital, Horsham—had been lodging at Miles's home, where Wilde was teaching him Greek.[110] Later in 1885, after he had delivered a lecture at Newcastle upon Tyne, Wilde divulged to the undergraduate Marillier how much he treasured the hours that they had spent together: "I have never learned anything except from people younger than myself, and you are infinitely young."[111] "You have the power," Wilde declared in a similarly enthusiastic missive sent the following week, "of making others love you."[112] He asked, too, for the young man to send a photograph of himself. The next month Wilde's choice of language gave a sure indication that he was passionate about the undergraduate. "You too," he effused to the artistically minded Marillier, "have the love of things impossible—ἔρως τῶν ἀδυνάτον—*l'amour de l'impossible* (how do men name it?)."[113] (The French version of this phrase comes from the homophile John Addington Symonds's poetry and prose.[114]) No sooner had Wilde alluded to such impossible desires than he started speaking rapturously, in terms that echo a famous line in Pater's "Conclusion," of "[o]ur most fiery moments of ecstasy."[115] The erotic connotations should have been clear to Marillier, who—although he allowed the friendship to continue for a short while—maintained a respectful distance from Wilde.

Far more significant, though in some ways harder to construe, is the intimate relationship that Wilde began with the seventeen-year-old Robert Baldwin Ross. "There has," Jonathan Fryer observes, "been endless speculation about how Robert Ross and Oscar Wilde first met."[116] Frank Harris, who thrived on telling tall tales, fueled the legend of Wilde's risk-taking career by stating that the two men met in a public lavatory.[117] The truth was far less sensational. Ross's widowed mother, Eliza (the daughter of the Canadian political leader Robert Baldwin) enjoyed such a strong social relationship with the Wildes that she let her youngest son lodge with them for three months while she traveled abroad. In 1886, Ross stayed as a paying guest at the small Tite Street home while taking a two-year course at W. B. Scoone's, a crammer in Covent Garden, which prepared him for his entrance examination to King's College, Cambridge. Exactly where Wilde and Ross enjoyed their intimacy remains uncertain. "It should not be assumed," Fryer states, "that Oscar and Robbie conducted a passionate, clandestine affair on the premises."[118]

Wilde's intimacy with Ross marked not only a turning point in his homosexual outlook; their relationship also spurred him into increasingly confident representations of desire between men. In his correspondence, Wilde suggests that he had consulted Ross at length about his ingenious story "The Portrait of Mr. W. H.," which unfolds an intriguing tale around a long-discredited theory that claims that the cryptic "W. H."—whose initials refer to the "ONLIE BEGETTER" in the dedication of Shakespeare's *Sonnets*—was Willie Hughes, a handsome boy-player in the Bard's troupe. This hypothesis, which Edmond Malone (in response to his contemporary Thomas Tyrwhitt) first aired in 1780, depends in large part on the belief that the line in Sonnet 20, "A man in hew all hews in his controlling," contains puns on the young actor's last name.[119] Meanwhile, this piece of short fiction, which appeared in *Blackwood's Edinburgh Magazine* in July 1889, was at this juncture Wilde's boldest attempt to give legitimacy to the idea that a male object could fuel the greatest literary passion in other men. Cleverly, the narrative explores not just the postulation that Shakespeare harbored a desire for "Mr. W. H."; it adopts, too, an ironic perspective on the three young characters in the story (the unnamed narrator, his friend George Erskine, and Erskine's erstwhile pal Cyril Graham), all of whom express, if at different points in their lives, the belief that Shakespeare's dedicatee was indeed—as we also find in a term from Sonnet 20—"the master-mistress of Shakespeare's passion."[120] Each of these men in turn is captivated so completely by the theory that it appears they would do anything they could to authenticate it—even to the point, in Graham's case, of forging an Elizabethan portrait of "Mr. W. H." The unnamed narrator finds it impossible not to be seduced by the belief, as Graham was, that "W. H." was "some wonderful boy-actor of great beauty, to whom [Shakespeare] intrusted the presentation of noble heroines."[121] Assuredly, at no point does Wilde intimate that the Bard consummated his passion for the young actor.

Wilde's deepening friendship with Ross was central to the development of the "Portrait," as we can see from a letter written just after the tale appeared in *Blackwood's*. "[T]he story," Wilde told Ross, "is half yours, and but for you would not have been written."[122] "Now that Willie Hughes has been revealed to the world," he adds cryptically, "we must have another secret."[123] Exactly what their new "secret" could have been is hard to tell. But what we know for sure is that Wilde held fresh ambitions for producing a longer and bolder story that explored the relations between an older and a younger man. By the end of

1889, Wilde informed the American editor Stoddart—who had expressed interest in the possibility that the Irish author might contribute a work of fiction to the transatlantic *Lippincott's Monthly Magazine*—that he had "invented a new story"; "I am," Wilde noted, "ready to set to work at once on it. It will be ready by the end of March."[124]

The work that emerged was *The Picture of Dorian Gray*, which the popular American monthly brought out in June 1890. To a classically trained reader, the homoerotic currents that run throughout the narrative are evident from the start. In the opening chapter, the painter Basil Hallward confides to his friend Lord Henry Wotton about the extraordinary experience that he has undergone when working on his portrait of the consummately beautiful Dorian Gray. "He is all my art to me now," Hallward declares, after Lord Henry has told his friend that the picture is the artist's "best work."[125] Yet to Hallward the force of Dorian Gray's inspiration is so enthralling that it threatens to consume him. As Hallward admits, he has "put too much of" himself into the portrait to feel confident in exhibiting it in public.[126] The reason that Hallward harbors such fears emerges in the revealing allusions he makes. Dorian Gray's overwhelming beauty, he tells Lord Henry, has suggested to him "an entirely new manner of art," one that—as we can quickly discern—is queer in nature: "What the invention of oil-painting was to the Venetians, the face of Antinoüs was to late Greek sculpture, and the face of Dorian will some day be to me. It is not merely that I paint from him, draw from him, model from him. Of course I have done all that. He has stood as Paris in dainty armor, and as Adonis with huntsman's cloak and polished boar-spear. Crowned with heavy lotus-blossoms, he has sat on the prow of Adrian's barge, looking into the green, turbid Nile."[127]

As one can see, Dorian Gray has been the subject of Hallward's artworks on classical topics, including the figure of Paris, who betrayed the nymph Oenone in favor of Helen, and Adonis, who was the beloved of Venus. Yet these two myths of other-sex passion are intermixed with that of Antinoüs, the object of the Emperor Hadrian's desire. This theme quickly resurfaces in the next chapter. No sooner has Lord Henry met the attractive Dorian Gray—who has returned to Hallward's studio so that the painter can add some finishing touches to the portrait—than he starts mentoring the younger man on the imperative to pursue one's life without any moral inhibitions: "The aim of life is self-development. To realize one's nature perfectly,—that is what each of us is here for."[128] And just to make the origins of this philosophy unambiguous, Lord Henry insists that everyone should savor such perfection, since "the world would gain such a fresh impulse of joy that we would forget the maladies of mediævalism, and return to the Hellenic ideal."[129] That this innovative mode of art signals a return to a world that celebrates pagan aesthetics, which are infused with homoerotic desire, is evident in this short piece of dialogue. Moreover, Lord Henry informs his new companion that it is vital to enjoy life at the peak of one's youthful beauty: "You have only a few years left in which really to live. When your youth goes, your beauty will go with it, and then you will suddenly discover that there are no triumphs left for you."[130] "Live!" he insists, "Live the wonderful life that is in you."[131]

Unquestionably, Lord Henry has no idea of the malign influence that such wisdom will exercise on his newfound friend, who panics at the thought of losing his good looks. In a fantastical maneuver, Wilde's novel shows how Dorian Gray exchanges his flawless outward appearance for that of the perfect image on the portrait that Hallward gives him, and which the young man at one point tells the artist that he has destroyed. The truth, however, is that Dorian Gray preserves the picture, which will haunt him to the end of his days. Once he has stored it in the schoolroom of his home, his demeanor retains the timeless appearance of the exquisite young man whose beauty Hallward has captured, and his beauty persists while he makes his way through London committing increasingly heinous crimes. At the same time, the painting gradually adopts a gruesome visage that reflects the appalling crimes that the elegant young man has perpetrated. The unsightly nature of the picture prevents him from showing it to anyone, especially Hallward, who at one point changes his mind and tells Dorian Gray that he wishes to exhibit it. "Have you noticed in the picture," Hallward asks, with heavy dramatic irony, "something that you did not like[?]"[132] Here Hallward takes the opportunity to make a confession about the obsessive desire that he had experienced while he was working on the portrait: "It is quite true that I have worshipped you with far more romance of feeling than a man usually gives to a friend. Somehow, I had never loved a woman. I suppose I never had time. Perhaps, as Harry says, a really '*grande passion*' is the privilege of those who have nothing to do, and that is the use of the idle classes in a country. Well, from the moment I met you, your personality had the most extraordinary influence over me. I quite admit that I adored you madly, extravagantly, absurdly."[133] Hallward's longings could not be more explicit. This was, as Edward Carson revealed during the libel trial, an especially sensitive passage that Wilde chose to revise carefully when he reprinted the novel—in an expanded version—in 1891.

Later in the story, once rumors have unnerved high society about Dorian Gray's misdemeanors, Hallward returns to his friend's residence. Wilde's protagonist leads the painter up to the schoolroom to witness the horrific spectacle that we have already glimpsed in the intervening chapters. What Hallward sees there terrifies him. "Years ago," Dorian Gray says, "when I was a boy . . . you met me, devoted yourself to me, flattered me, and taught me to be vain of my good looks."[134] Matters worsened, he recalls, when Lord Henry "explained to me the wonder of youth."[135] As he stares at the artwork, Hallward is aghast: "God! what a thing I must have worshipped! This has the eyes of a devil."[136] Grotesque, hideous, evil—the portrait has come to represent the horrors of Dorian Gray's criminal actions. At this point, Dorian Gray sinks a knife into Hallward's neck. Thereafter, once he has blackmailed the scientist Alan Campbell to remove Hallward's body without trace, Campbell—who implicitly fears the public exposure of his queer desires—takes his own life. Ultimately, Wilde's maddened eponymous character recoils from the distorted picture that stands before him: "Why was the red stain larger than it had been?" he wonders. "It seemed to have crept like a horrible disease over the wrinkled fingers."[137] Impulsively, he picks up the blade with which he has murdered Hallward and plunges it into the painting. At this juncture, a further transformation takes place. The moment Dorian Gray's servants hear the commotion, they enter the schoolroom. There they discover "hanging upon the wall a splendid portrait of their master as they had last seen him."[138] On the floor, by stark contrast, they find "a dead man, in evening dress, with a knife in his heart."[139] "He was," the narrator adds, "withered, wrinkled, and loathsome of visage. It was not until they had examined the rings that they recognized who it was."[140]

Once Wilde's *Picture of Dorian Gray* appeared on London's bookstands, Ross enthused about its success: "80 copies," he told Wilde, "were sold in one day at a Strand booksellers, the usual amount being 3 a week in that part."[141] Yet, as Ross also observed about his fellow members at the Savile Club, "Dorian Gray . . . is said to be very dangerous."[142] He was right, as a quick succession of hostile reviews demonstrated. The *St. James's Gazette*, which often took the moral high ground when faced with sexual matters, claimed that the execrable stench that Wilde's story made in *Lippincott's* was too strong to warrant sustained critical attention: "Not being curious in ordure, and not wishing to offend the nostrils of decent persons, we do not propose to analyse *The Picture of Dorian Gray*."[143] Meanwhile, the *Daily Chronicle*, which was noted for its more liberal perspective, characterized Wilde's fiction as "a tale spawned from the leprous literature of French *Décadents*."[144] It was left to the Tory *Scots Observer* to be more direct about what appeared so offensive in the work. "The story," it said, "deals with matters only fitted for the Criminal Investigation Department [CID] or a hearing *in camera*."[145] Just to make these innuendoes unmistakable, this critic—though willing to admit that Wilde has "brains, and art, and style"—states that if he continues to "write for none but outlawed noblemen and telegraph boys, the sooner he takes to tailoring (or some other decent trade) the better for his own reputation and the public morals."[146]

Through these terse comments, the *Scots Observer* was referring to the Cleveland Street affair, which had created a hullaballoo in the press from late 1889 through spring 1890. Since this was the most widely publicized homosexual scandal prior to Wilde's trials, it is worth dwelling for a moment on its most prominent aspects, which draw attention to the ways in which the upper classes sought to close ranks in the face of investigative journalism. The case, which eventually attracted notice when Wilde was composing *The Picture of Dorian Gray*, became known to the police quite by accident in the summer of 1889. Constable Luke Hanks, who was attached to the General Post Office in the City of London, learned that a telegraph messenger-boy named Charles Thomas Swinscow had large amounts of extra cash about his person. Hanks discovered that Swinscow reaped these rewards after a post office clerk, Henry Newlove, had introduced the youngster to Charles Hammond: a pimp who kept a male brothel at 19 Cleveland Street in the fashionable West End. Further inquiries revealed that two of Swinscow's young coworkers, George Wright and Charles Thickbroom, had also earned additional money from performing sexual services. Once the police put the premises under observation, Chief Inspector Frederick Abberline of the CID applied for a warrant to arrest Hammond and Newlove; the charge was that the two procurers "did unlawfully, wickedly and corruptly conspire, considerate and agree to incite [the three messenger-boys] to commit the abominable crime of buggery against the peace of Her Majesty the Queen."[147] At the same time, the surveillance of the building revealed that one of the visitors was Lord Arthur Somerset: a major in the Royal Horse Guards. The third son of the 8th Duke of Beaumont, Somerset had for two years been extra equerry to the Prince of Wales, an office that gave him control of the prince's stables at Marlborough House. Very soon, Abberline realized that his investigation was uncovering activities that risked unsettling the highest echelons of society.

In an interview with the Irish prostitute Jack Saul, the inspector learned that another titled gentleman, Lord Euston, had been a regular visitor at Cleveland Street. "He is not," Saul commented, "an actual sodomite. He likes to play with you and then 'spend' [i.e., ejaculate] on your belly."[148] Even though the attorney general Sir Richard Webster decided that proceedings should be taken against Somerset (along with a procurer, George Veck, who masqueraded as a priest), the Home Office became disconcerted at the prospect of a high society scandal breaking in the press. Matters worsened for the authorities when they arrested Veck, since they found letters that a teenager named Algernon Allies had written petitioning for funds and mentioning a "Mr. Brown." In this thickening plot, Hanks traveled to Sudbury, Suffolk, where Allies—a former houseboy at the Marlborough Club who lost his job when caught stealing money—had returned to his family. The interview led to the disclosure that "Mr. Brown" was indeed Somerset, who had been sending him money orders through the mail. Somerset, who first met Allies at the Prince of Wales's home, Marlborough House, sought to assist the youngster by introducing him to Newlove, with whom the teenager lived for a few months. These details revealed that any legal steps that the director of public prosecutions might take against the high-ranking Somerset would lead to severe public embarrassment.

Even though on 11 September 1889 Newlove and Veck (though not Hammond, who had escaped to the Continent) were committed for trial at Great Marlborough Street Magistrates' Court, the police court—in a conspicuous delay—took two more months before it issued a warrant for Somerset's arrest. In the interim, the press showed little interest in the procurers and the telegraph messenger-boys, while Somerset's well-connected friends made complaints to James Munro, the Metropolitan Police Commissioner, that Inspector Abberline was putting pressure on the *Pall Mall Gazette* to publish a report on the case. At any rate, there was not much prospect of arresting Lord Arthur. On 1 September 1889, a police officer who visited Hyde Park barracks in search of the royal equerry learned that Somerset was on four months' leave of absence in Europe, though it was true that Lord Arthur returned over two weeks later to England on a visit that included meetings with both the Prince of Wales and his commanding officer. Tensions mounted when Somerset's attorney, Arthur Newton, told Hamilton Cuffe (who was, at the time, the assistant director of public prosecutions) that there would be even more serious consequences if the case against his client did not come to a halt. Moreover, Newton stated that Prince Albert Victor (better known as Prince Eddy), the heir to the throne, would become involved. Not surprisingly, Newton started advising assorted high-ranking men to abscond from the country. The rumors, especially the unfounded ones about Prince Eddy, sent jitters through circles close to the court. At this juncture, there were other maneuverings going on, including Hammond's escape on the S.S. *Pennland* to New York City, from where he undertook a long journey to Seattle. Meanwhile, Veck received nine months with hard labor, while Newlove was sentenced to four months and the same. Both were tried under the eleventh section of the 1885 Criminal Amendment Act. Still, the lord chancellor, the Prince of Wales, and the prince's leading courtier Sir Dighton Probyn (after a discussion with the prime minister, Lord Salisbury) expressed various misgivings about the prosecution of Somerset. Only in mid-October, when the pressure on Lord Arthur had become truly threatening, did the aristocrat flee Britain once and for all.

On 16 November 1889, when the police obtained a warrant for Lord Arthur's arrest, Ernest Parke—a well-known journalist on the radical *North London Press*—went into print declaring that not only Somerset but also Euston were linked with the male brothel on Cleveland Street. Euston forthwith hired Sir George Lewis to apply for a judgment under the Newspaper Libel Act 1888. In the meantime, Parke's solicitor secured H. H. Asquith and Frank Lockwood for the defense. Toward the end of November 1889, the case against Parke was heard at Bow Street Magistrates' Court, where Euston declared that he had visited 19 Cleveland Street after Hammond presented him with a card that advertised "*poses plastiques*": a euphemistic term for female nudes. At this point, Parke's criminal trial was set to take place at the Old Bailey the following month. These revelations inflamed the press. *Reynolds's Newspaper* observed that "[t]he existence amongst us of a Sodomite institution is a matter of far more serious nature that his lordship [i.e., Lord Euston], judging by the way in which he gave evidence, would seem to think."[149] "The most severe measures the law will admit of," the reporter went on to remark, "should be resorted to in order to stamp out practices of an unnatural and revolting shape too hideous even to be mentioned."[150]

In the meantime, the director of public prosecutions (Augustus Stephenson) set about obtaining summonses against Newton, Newton's assistant Frederick Taylorson (who had been trying to remove Allies abroad), and an interpreter (Adolphe De Gallo) at the police court where Newlove and Veck's case had been heard. The charge was that all three of these individuals, by attempting to contact the messenger-boys and shepherd them out of the country, had tried to pervert the course of justice. As we can see, this rapid turn of events led to no fewer than three concurrent actions or potential actions relating to the scandal. By 15 January 1890, when Parke's trial for criminal libel came before the Old Bailey, Jack Saul gave such graphic responses during the examination-in-chief that the press could not bring itself to reproduce them. Saul divulged how he first met Euston, whose name he did not know for some time. "I picked him up just as I might have picked up any other gentleman," Saul said to Sir Charles Russell during the cross-examination.[151] "When," Sir Charles inquired, "did you first learn Lord Euston's name?."[152] "About a fortnight or three weeks after the first occasion on which Lord Euston visited 19 Cleveland Street," Saul replied.[153] When Russell inquired who it was that revealed Euston's identity,

Saul stated that he learned it from "Lively Poll": a drag moniker, one imagines, for a friend called Carrington.[154] Seldom had the London courts been exposed to such revelations.

Certain sections of the press rallied to support Parke, with H. W. Massingham—who at the time edited the radical *Star*—setting up a defense fund for the embattled journalist. Parke, in particular, had an ally in Henry ("Labby") Labouchere, the Radical MP who had engineered the clause that outlawed "gross indecency" in 1885. In his journal *Truth,* Labouchere stated that he was determined that the clause should not be used "against obscure people" so that "people in a high position [were] allowed to violate it with impunity."[155] Meanwhile, when it came to the case against Newton, Taylor, and De Gallo, Labouchere had already spoken in anger against the prime minister and the home secretary for their procrastination in prosecuting Somerset. He said the delays amounted to "a noisy attempt to close the stable door after the steeds have been allowed to issue from the stable."[156] Labouchere also stated that he was appalled that "a wretch like Saul" was "to be allowed to swear away the honour and good name of a person with impunity, without any action on the part of the Public Prosecutor"; the situation, Labouchere observed, was "an insult to law and justice."[157] Moreover, Saul's impenitent testimony, in which he expressed his frustration that Hammond had allowed "boys of good position in the Post office in the house [i.e., 19 Cleveland Street]" while he "had to walk the streets" to earn his keep, provoked Labouchere's indignation.[158]

By the end of February 1890, Labouchere's allegations that the government under Lord Salisbury had engaged in a cover-up—one that had permitted Somerset to flee the country—resulted in the the MP's suspension from the House of Commons. The *Pall Mall Gazette* had such sympathy for Labouchere's remonstrations that it contended that "the fullest inquiry should be made" into the ways in which Lord Salisbury's government had handled this immensely controversial scandal.[159] In the interim, regarding the two trials in process, Parke's resulted in his imprisonment for twelve months without hard labor. *Reynolds's* voiced astonishment at the idea that Euston won his case on the basis of his "*ipse dixit*": "The evidence of the witnesses who testified having seen him several times," it noted, "was ridiculed by Sir C[harles] Russell as being that of persons in a very low grade of life."[160] "Surely," the editor sarcastically remarked, "he did not expect that the Archbishop of Canterbury would appear in the box and testify to having the Earl coming to or going from that den of infamy."[161] After many delays, in May 1890 Newton's case was eventually heard at the Queen's Bench, a lower criminal court than the Old Bailey, where he pleaded guilty and duly received a sentence of six weeks for committing a "first-class misdemeanor."[162] All of this information reveals that in the month before *The Picture of Dorian Gray* appeared, the Cleveland Street scandal remained fresh in the minds of Wilde's readership.

Although the prominent newsvendor W. H. Smith withdrew copies of *Lippincott's Monthly Magazine* from its shelves once unpleasant notices appeared in the press, Wilde proved undeterred in presenting his novel once again before the public. His first foray into reasserting his faith in his story was the publication, in February 1891, of the "Preface to 'Dorian Gray,'" which Harris, who capitalized on controversy, issued in the *Fortnightly Review*. The "Preface" constituted a deliberate provocation, since it reads like a manifesto summarizing precisely those points that Wilde had already made in the rebuttals that he submitted to the letters columns of the *Daily Chronicle*, *St. James's Gazette*, and *Scots Observer*, all of which had condemned the scarcely veiled homosexual subtext of his novel. As Wilde pointed out to W. E. Henley, who edited the hostile *Scots Observer*, readers tend to bring to artworks whatever they choose to see. "It is the spectator," he said, "and not life, that art really mirrors."[163] Wilde repeated exactly the same phrasing in the "Preface," while also defending his artistic practice by pointing out, in another well-known line: "Those who find ugly meanings in beautiful things are corrupt without being charming."[164] Moreover, the "Preface" gives voice to various other controversial ideas that reiterate Wilde's commitment to art for art's sake. "There is no such thing," he declares, "as a moral or an immoral book. Books are well written, or badly written. That is all."[165] The document, which flatly opposes the view that art should have moral utility, concludes with this blunt statement: "All art is quite useless."[166] Defying his critics, Wilde revised the "Preface" for an augmented version of *The Picture of Dorian Gray* (it contained six additional chapters) that the British distributor of *Lippincott's*, Ward, Lock & Co., brought out a few months later in a single volume. The edition features a fine binding and frontispiece by Wilde's close friend, the young queer artist Charles Ricketts.

Soon after, Wilde took the opportunity to defend *The Picture of Dorian Gray* in person when he accepted an invitation from the fifty-year-old anti-imperial activist, poet, and horse-breeder Wilfrid Scawen Blunt to attend the exclusive Crabbet Club. Although the club did not have an official membership, it hosted parties for rising politicians and young intellectuals whose company Blunt enjoyed at his fine country home in Sussex. On 4 July 1891, Wilde joined the jamboree, which included such leisurely activities as strolling through the grounds and entering poems in set-topic competitions. He spent the evening in a verbal jousting-match with the Conservative statesman George Curzon. Blunt records that Curzon played "with astonishing audacity and skill upon

[Wilde's] reputation for sodomy and his treatment of the subject of Dorian Gray. Poor Oscar sat helplessly smiling, a fat mass, in his chair."[167] Blunt adds that in response Wilde "gradually warmed to an amusing and excellent speech . . . . The discussion went on a long time between them, and I doubt if anything better of its kind was ever heard, even from Disraeli in his best days."[168] Blunt's tribute reminds us of Wilde's redoubtable rhetorical skills. But it is also evident from Blunt's journals that this exchange with Curzon caused Wilde unease, and—even though it appears he made contributions to the two privately printed collections titled *Poetry of the Crabbet Club*—Wilde never returned to this elite society.[169] The Crabbet Club included such prominent men as the Conservative MP George Wyndham, the Liberal politician Lewis Vernon ("Loulou") Harcourt, and the antiquarian Charles Tindal Gatty, each of whom had good reason to take a strong interest in the trials that occurred four years later, since all of them were close to the centers of political power. As we will see later, it was at the House of Commons, on 5 April 1895, that Wyndham apprised his cousin Douglas of the warrant issued for Wilde's arrest. Similarly, the bisexual Harcourt—whose father was chancellor of the exchequer under both Gladstone and Rosebery—kept a close eye on the Crown prosecution against Wilde, since he advised the attorney general, Sir Robert Reid, to focus on the activities of James Dennis Burton: "an infamous blackmailer who is supposed to have been the original employer of the boys who are the witnesses for the prosecution in the OW case."[170] Most significant of all, however, was Gatty's connection with this close-knit circle linked with the Crabbet Club. In summer 1893, Gatty launched into an action against a political opponent who had intimated—during a tough election campaign—that he had many years before been expelled from the distinguished private school Charterhouse because of a homosexual misdemeanor.

The high-profile libel case of *Gatty v. Farquharson*, which came to the Queen's Bench Division of the High Court of Justice in June 1893, seldom features in discussions of the homosexual controversies that arose in the years immediately preceding Wilde's trials. This is rather surprising, given that the proceedings involved the two attorneys who later represented the opposing parties in the retrial at the Old Bailey that sent to Wilde to prison. On this occasion, Lockwood (the leading Liberal, who was knighted the following year) acted on Gatty's behalf, while the former solicitor general Sir Edward Clarke defended Henry Farquharson, the standing Conservative Member of Parliament for West Dorset. Fifteen months previously, Farquharson had made an ad hominem attack on Gatty, the opposing Liberal candidate, during the electoral campaign for the constituency. The case was straightforward. Lockwood opened by stating that the plaintiff's suit was not in any respect linked with political matters; instead, the grievance related to the fact that Farquharson had said at a campaign meeting in March 1892 that "there were schoolfellows of [Gatty's] living in Dorset who were at Charterhouse with him, and remembered him."[171] This was an unpleasant piece of hearsay for a political rival to put into circulation.

Once Gatty had learned about what happened, he consulted with his close friend Wyndham for advice on the best way to rebut Farquharson's allegation. His request for a retraction of his opponent's shameful remarks resulted in an exchange of correspondence, in which Farquharson claimed that the rumors did not originate with him. Gatty, who was clearly inflamed by the situation, threatened to publish the letters between himself and Farquharson, which he duly did in a pamphlet. The document also included a letter from Dr. William Haig-Brown, the long-serving headmaster of Charterhouse, who said "there was no truth in the statement that [Gatty] had been expelled" from the school.[172] In response, Farquharson exacerbated the conflict by informing Gatty: "If you are really so anxious to set [the rumors] at rest, why do you not refer to those of your schoolfellows now resident in Dorsetshire, who could so easily confirm or contradict the rumours of which you complain? Instead of adopting this very simple course, it seems you are attempting to shelter yourself behind a correspondence with me."[173] Matters escalated when Farquharson claimed that he had received a telegram from one of Gatty's former classmates, which the Conservative candidate said he would publish with Gatty's permission, so long as Gatty signed an agreement to take no legal action against him. Gatty declined to cooperate. Eleven days before the election, Gatty issued a writ for libel, which he quickly followed with a placard headed "Caution to Electors." On 15 June 1892, when Farquharson won the election, he indulged his supporters with passing comments on the contents of a telegram that supposedly confirmed that the Liberal candidate "had been expelled from West Dorset."[174] Lockwood pointed out that the telegram, which had eventually been found, actually stated that "if not expelled" from Charterhouse, Gatty had been "called upon to leave" the school.[175] After three days, the jury returned a verdict finding that Gatty should receive the huge sum of £5,000 in damages, although this amount was halved when Clarke unsuccessfully petitioned the Court of Appeals for a fresh trial.

Had Lockwood not handled the prosecution so well, *Gatty v. Farquharson*—which also drew attention to the plaintiff's "scandals in connection with printers' boys" at a local newspaper in Yeovil—could have caused even further embarrassment to the former Liberal candidate.[176] But, as the proceedings reveal, Gatty had the strength of the establishment behind him, which left his private character intact. It is not unreasonable to suggest that in pursuing his own libel suit, Wilde believed that his personal dignity would be protected at the Old Bailey. If he labored under any such impression, he was profoundly mistaken. Even though Wilde mingled with the leading members of the Liberal Party, he had begun to take—as his dealings with the Crabbet Club revealed—too many risks among the political elite in defending what Blunt called "sodomy." Further, his determination to make more and more sexual contacts with younger males ensured that it was increasingly difficult for him to defend his "private character." Wilde's homosexual affections were gaining greater visibility in London society. Gatty, from what we can tell, committed no indiscretions of the kind that were evident to Wilde's closest observers.

From the late 1880s to the early 1890s, when Wilde's career went from strength to strength, his intimacies included one with Frederick Althaus, the son of a German professor who taught at University College London. It appears that Wilde met Althaus at the Crown public house on Cranbourn Street, near Charing Cross Road, sometime in 1888. The bohemian clientele that gathered there struck Max Beerbohm, in a witty letter he sent to Reggie Turner, as "a literary tavern full of young nameless poets and cocottes and old men who have been ministers of the Church of England and are no longer."[177] The extant correspondence from Althaus shows that the older man's attentions flattered him: "I appreciate your kindness to me," Althaus remarks, "which I feel positively ashamed of in no way being capable of reciprocating but I can only assure you that I hardly know a greater pleasure than being in your society."[178] The following year Althaus asked Wilde whether he might be interested in traveling to Eastbourne, a seaside resort where one could take pleasure "lying on the cliffs in flannels."[179] The relationship, however, petered out. (By September 1892, Althaus says to his "dear Oscar" that he has "seen or heard nothing" of him "for ages."[180])

The relationship with Althaus bears comparison with a much briefer but nonetheless resonant encounter that Wilde enjoyed, perhaps for a single day, in summer 1888 with the aspiring English author Richard Le Gallienne, who would later introduce a 1907 American edition of Wilde's complete works. Le Gallienne, a man of immense ambition, distinctive hairstyle, and chiseled looks, soon became a staple part of 1890s literary culture, to which he contributed prolific amounts of poetry, criticism, and fiction. In June 1888, Wilde inscribed a copy of *Poems* to Le Gallienne, whom he boldly addressed as "poet and lover."[181] In turn, Le Gallienne responded with an affectionate poem: "With Oscar Wilde, a summer day / Passed like a yearning kiss way."[182] While the homoerotic nature of this exchange is undeniable, it sounds as if this (as

Matthew Sturgis surmises) was likely a matter of "poetical posturing by both parties."[183] As Wilde's correspondence shows, he saw himself as a mentor to an up-and-coming disciple who in part modeled his striking dandyish persona on the older, increasingly established writer. Still, Wilde's unrestrained amatory language belongs to a larger pattern of forthright sentiments that he bestowed on younger men who charmed him.

By this time, Wilde had begun to learn more about the queer subculture of London, and not without complications. In early 1889, he had a flirtation with the young American writer Clyde Fitch, who wrote over-the-top letters to the older man ("Your love is the fragrance of a rose," he effuses).[184] It was probably in the summer of 1889, when Wilde's interest in Althaus and Fitch had lapsed, that he first enjoyed the acquaintance of John Gray: a handsome, largely self-taught man in his early twenties, who began his career as a metalwork apprentice at the age of thirteen before taking evening classes. Gray's prodigious self-education enabled him to advance to a position in the civil service and later to the post of reference librarian in the Foreign Office. At the same time, this remarkable autodidact, who became conversant with French and Latin, was making his mark as a literary talent. His career as a writer, which involved developing connections with the habitués of the Rhymers' Club (a circle of male poets who met in London) and translating the works of several noted modern French authors (Arthur Rimbaud, Stéphane Mallarmé, and Paul Verlaine), in part thrived under Wilde's auspices. So eager was Wilde to sponsor the young man that he reached an agreement with the publisher John Lane to defray the costs of Gray's exquisitely printed and bound first collection of poetry (much of it adapted from French sources) named, after the delicate Renaissance drawing technique, *Silverpoints* (1893). The unique volume, which featured rather small type, very wide margins, and the unusual dimensions of a Persian saddle-bag book, featured on its lizard-green boards a striking design by the young gay artist Charles Ricketts. As several reviewers observed when it appeared, *Silverpoints* was the quintessential manifestation of modern literary Decadence.

Still, for all his devotion to Wilde, Gray eventually held conflicted feelings about the favors that the older man had vouchsafed to him. In many respects, Wilde treated the good-looking Gray as a protégé: a perception that a London newspaper articulated in a review of Gray's lecture "The Modern Actor," which he had delivered at the Playgoers' Club on 7 February 1892. Shortly afterward, Wilde disclaimed any such idea that Gray was his minion: he informed the *Daily Telegraph* that he sought Gray's acquaintance because the young man "had already a perfected mode of expression both in prose and verse," which owed nothing to any influence that he might have had.[185] Wilde's clarification was urgent, since Gray had grown uneasy at the suggestion—one touted in the *Star* the day before he gave his lecture—that he was "said to be the original Dorian of the same name."[186] Once Gray threatened to sue for libel, the paper promptly apologized for the "erroneous impression" that it had given.[187] The damage, however, was done. The situation deteriorated further when Gray, who suffered a mental breakdown in the later part of 1892, finally rebelled against Wilde.

No doubt the less-than-discreet in-jokes within Wilde's cenacle had begun to touch Gray's nerve. Beerbohm, whose gift for satire could overstep the mark, had already courted danger in the *Anglo-American Times*, where he published a tongue-in-cheek article intimating that Wilde's passion for Hellenism made him into nothing less than a modern-day Greek philosopher: "If he had lived in the days of Socrates he would surely have been impeached on a charge not only of 'making the worse cause appear the better'—for paradox as a method is never acceptable to the many—but also of 'corrupting the youth,' he would have been condemned, and would have drunk the hemlock under protest, and one of the corrupt—perhaps Mr. John Gray—would have written another *Phaedo* in his memory."[188] The very notion that Gray (a potential Phaedo to Wilde's Socrates) counted among the youths upon whom Wilde had sexually preyed went too far.

By this juncture, however, Gray had taken pains to distance himself entirely from Wilde. On 4 January 1893, Gray signed a fresh contract with the publisher, which absolved Wilde of any financial responsibility for *Silverpoints*. Around the same time, Raffalovich—who had written bitterly against Wilde in *A Willing Exile*—began a non-sexual but deeply loving relationship with Gray, which lasted through the end of their lives. Within a matter of years, Gray elected to join the priesthood, having converted to the Church of Rome in February 1890. From 1898 to 1901, the independently wealthy Raffalovich, himself a Catholic convert, supported Gray's training at the Scots College, Rome, and he later assisted in the funding of his companion's church, St. Peter's, Morningside, Edinburgh, where Canon Gray preached until his death in 1934.

One of the literary works that Gray had translated was *Le Baiser* (1887), a one-act play by the French author Théodore de Banville, which the English poet rendered into alexandrine couplets. On 4 March 1892, Gray's version of the drama, which was well received, appeared as *The Kiss* at the Royalty Theatre, in a program arranged through J. T. ("Jack") Grein's Independent Theatre Society. Wilde, who attended the performance, almost certainly brought with him Edward Shelley, the clerk who worked at the offices of Elkin Mathews and John Lane, the company with which Wilde had established a publishing relationship. Wilde had already, on 20 February 1892, taken the teenager to the premiere of *Lady Windermere's Fan*, where Shelley was in the company of Wilde's circle of homosexual men, including More Adey, Reggie Turner, and Maurice Salis Schwabe. Wilde possibly made overtures to Shelley in late 1891 when he was negotiating with Mathews the reissue of the remaining stock of *Poems*, which had appeared a decade previously. The plan was to remove the original title page, half title, and binding, and then replace those parts of the volume with materials designed by Charles Ricketts, whom Wilde had befriended—together with Ricketts's personal and professional partner, Charles Haslewood Shannon—shortly before "The Portrait of Mr. W. H." was in print.

What differentiated Shelley from all of the other young men with whom Wilde had been intimate was that this publisher's assistant, who slept with him on more than one occasion at the Albemarle Hotel in February 1892, stood—at least at the beginning of the Crown prosecution—as the most respectable and plausible witness. As the libel proceedings revealed, Wilde dedicated considerable time to treating Shelley not only to theatre performances but also to an exhibition at Earl's Court, dinners at the Café Royal and Kettner's, and supper at his Tite Street residence (where Shelley met Constance). In addition, Wilde gave Shelley sums of money, including one to cover the train fare to Cromer, where Wilde vacationed with his family in August and September 1892. (Shelley did not take up the invitation.) Moreover, Wilde made presentation copies of his works to Shelley, since he was a young man—as Wilde explained to Edward Carson—who "seemed most interested" in the author's literary writings.[189] Eventually, at Mathews and Lane's premises on Vigo Street the chaffing that Shelley received from his coworkers about the interest Wilde had taken in him became unbearable. This was the main reason that Shelley quit his job in 1893. At the same time, his resentful behavior toward Wilde also broke up their intimacy.

Once Shelley disappeared from Wilde's life, the erotic contacts he made with young men rendered him increasingly vulnerable to different types of exploitation. Even though Wilde tried, in later years, to cast blame on Bosie for some of the hazards that beset him during this new phase in his erotic attachments, he also admitted that he alone was responsible for his sexual pursuits: "Desire, at the end," he wrote from prison in early 1897, "was a malady, or a madness, or both. I grew careless of the lives of others. I took pleasure where it pleased me and passed on."[190] Before moving to the tensions that led to the perilous courtroom conflict with Queensberry in April 1895, I now turn to the homosexual rendezvous that Wilde made between February 1892 and summer 1893, in part owing to his relationship with Douglas. These were the connections that formed the core of the Crown prosecution's allegations, which claimed that Wilde had repeatedly perpetrated the crime of gross indecency.

"FEASTING WITH PANTHERS": ALFRED DOUGLAS, ALFRED TAYLOR, AND THE WORLD OF HOMOSEXUAL BLACKMAIL AND MALE PROSTITUTION

The difficulties that beleaguered Wilde's intimacy with Shelley, no matter how wretched they turned out to be, pale considerably beside the very different ones that developed at this time with Douglas. This intimate relationship, which was more impassioned and exasperating than any other that Wilde had experienced, provides the context in which he enjoyed introductions to a broad network of young men, some of whom were interested in drag parties, while others traded in blackmail and prostitution. (There was a group that dedicated itself to both.) In *Without Apology*, Douglas recalls his initial meeting with Wilde, which took place during his second year at Magdalen College, Oxford, where he was studying—with little motivation—Greats: "During the 'Vac' [in June 1891] Lionel Johnson, who had been at Winchester with me and with whom I formed a great friendship at Oxford when he was at New College (two years senior to me), took me to Wilde's house in Tite Street. It was Lionel, a great scholar, who took a 'double first' at Oxford, and who was also a poet of a very high order, who originally lent me *The Picture of Dorian Gray* to read just before I met Wilde. I read it at Magdalen and was passionately absorbed in it."[191]

Wilde and Douglas were not involved with each other again until spring 1892. Bosie reached out to Wilde to gain assistance with a blackmailing incident at Oxford. It appears that he had a written a foolish letter to a young man. Although the precise details have never been unearthed, it is known that Wilde came to Douglas's rescue by parting with £100, which Sir George Lewis handled on his behalf. From this point onward, their intimacy deepened, although the physical dimension was not, from Douglas's point of view, appealing. In 1984, H. Montgomery Hyde published a revelatory letter that the fifty-four-year-old Douglas had sent to Harris. In this letter, which dates from 1925, Douglas disclosed that first as a pupil at Winchester College and then as an Oxford undergraduate he "had been neither better or worse" than his contemporaries.[192] Hardly an ingénu, Douglas was "perfectly familiar" with what is "euphemistically called 'the schoolboy nonsense' that goes on among boys at school and college."[193] Even though, he observes, Wilde started "laying siege" to him during their initial encounter, it took a further six months—after Wilde had stayed at Douglas's rooms in Oxford—before he "gave in" to the older man. "It is hateful to me," he says, "to write of such things, but I must be explicit. Sodomy never took place between us, nor was it thought or dreamt of. Wilde treated me as an older boy treats a younger one at school, and he added what was new to me and was not (as far as I know) known or practised among contemporaries: he 'sucked' me." Moreover, he told Harris: "I never liked this part of the business . . . After a time he tumbled to the fact that I didn't like it all and very soon 'cut it out' altogether."[194]

Assuredly, this counts among the most candid records of Wilde's homosexual practices. Still, it is worth bearing in mind that Douglas made these admissions when he had been married for over twenty years, and had been a Catholic convert, with a reactionary outlook, for over a decade. In this light, one is led to wonder whether Douglas's frank remarks are disingenuous regarding either the absence of anal penetration or the abrupt cessation of their lovemaking. At the same time, there is little reason to doubt that his sexual intimacy began, as he recalls, when—after an evening of supping and drinking—he visited Wilde at 2 o'clock in the morning at Tite Street: "After about two hours['] discussion he induced me to stay the night in a spare bedroom and in the end he succeeded in doing what he wanted to ever since the first moment he saw me."[195] This event presumably occurred in April 1892. Even if it was the case that Douglas refused further physical intimacy with Wilde, the fact that two men were often seen in each other's company made it appear, to some eyes, that they were a couple.

Around this time, Wilde's bond with Bosie focused on his one-act French-language tragedy *Salomé*, which draws on recognizable French sources, including Gustave Flaubert's tale "Hérodias" (1877). Wilde had great hopes for this play, which for him broke entirely new ground both formally and linguistically. The complex drama, which situates the young female protagonist in a relay of looks and desires that spin out of control, concentrates on her yearning for the body of the imprisoned John the Baptist (called Iokaanan in the drama). Over and over, Salomé tells the imprisoned John the Baptist, who dwells in a submerged cistern: "Je baiserai ta bouche, Iokanaan" (I will kiss your mouth, Iokanaan).[196] Once her stepfather, Herod Antipas, has put the saint to death, she makes the constant demand, "Donnez-moi la tête d'Iokanaan" (Give me the head of Iokanaan), which culminates in her whirling dance with St. John's severed head.[197] Her triumphant performance, however, does not survive the orgiastic climax that it represents. Instead, the dance inspires the sexually frenzied Herod, who is maddened by his lust for Salomé, to command his guards to murder her.

Quite unexpectedly, the examiner of plays Edward Pigott-Smyth censored *Salomé*. In principle, the main reason for banning the drama related to the fact that since the time of Henry VIII biblical figures under English law were forbidden from representation on the stage. But when we see that Pigott-Smyth found the work to be "half-Biblical, half-pornographic," it becomes evident that much about Salomé's rapacious desires caused him alarm.[198] Wilde deplored the ban. Particularly galling was the much-publicized news that he had arranged for Sarah Bernhardt to take the leading role in a production scheduled to occur at London's Palace Theatre, which—in these embarrassing circumstances—had to be aborted. At the time, Bernhardt was the leading tragedienne of the Paris and London stage. Infuriated, Wilde stated in an interview that if the ban continued, he would become an exile: "I shall leave England and settle in France, where I will take out letters of naturalization." "I will not," he added, "consent to call myself a citizen of a country that shows such narrow mindedness in its artistic judgments."[199] Just to clarify his stance, he also observed: "I am not English, I'm Irish, which is quite another thing."[200] Exhausted, he departed, at Bosie's invitation, for the luxurious German spa town Bad Homburg vor der Höhe. There, Wilde had the company of Douglas's mother, and her father Alfred Montgomery (who took a disliking to him).

Not long after Wilde had returned to England, he began work on *A Woman of No Importance* in a farmhouse that he had rented at Felbrigg, near Cromer, where Constance (and, on occasion, the children) came to stay. In August, Douglas announced he would join them. After Constance departed with their sons, the handsome young aristocrat stayed another ten days, further strengthening his closeness with Wilde. Later on, Douglas had no hesitation in joining Wilde's family when they were spending time in the country.

Now that Wilde was frequently in Douglas's company, his homosexual attentions roved widely. He became immersed in the homoerotic world that Russell's detectives uncovered when seeking incriminating evidence that would justify Queensberry's accusation. Even though it is difficult to confirm the circumstances in which Wilde first encountered Schwabe (he was a known quantity among Wilde's close friends such as Turner), Bosie was apparently the initial point of contact. Schwabe, a scion of a wealthy industrial Lancashire family, had been involved in a romantic affair with Douglas. We know that Schwabe, who was obviously well connected with the queer subcultures of London, introduced Wilde to the procurer Alfred Taylor, who had lodgings at 13 Little College Street, Westminster. It was there that the sociable Taylor held sex parties, drag shows, and even—in an episode that a witness vividly recalled in court—a mock wedding ceremony with Charles Spurrier Mason, whom Wilde knew socially, if not intimately. These lively events, which were euphemistically referred to as tea parties in court, took place behind muslin-covered windows in rooms suffused with incense. Given the questionable reputations of the various individuals with whom he mingled, Taylor's rooms (as a landlady revealed at the Old Bailey) came under police surveillance. The bankrupt Taylor, who had squandered an immense fortune of £45,000 that he had inherited from his father's cocoa business in 1883, earned fees from pimping.

The first sexual contact that Taylor successfully made for Wilde was with the twenty-six-year-old Sydney Arthur ("Jenny") Mavor: the son of a well-known equestrian veterinary surgeon. Mavor, who had an interest in cross-dressing and music-hall performance, joined Wilde, Bosie, and Schwabe for dinner at Kettner's restaurant in Soho. Very soon, in a gesture that became a pattern when Wilde rewarded those partners who had received his money for sex, he sent the youth a silver cigarette case. The gift, inscribed "S. A. Mavor, Esq.," had been purchased from William Thornhill, New Bond Street, on 3 October 1892. Later that month, Wilde invited Mavor to join him at the Albemarle Hotel, where they presumably enjoyed physical intimacy. Mavor, though, as Douglas later observed, refused to admit in court that he had slept with Wilde; as Douglas recalled, before the pretrial hearing began, Douglas told this well-educated young man: "When counsel asks you the questions, deny the whole thing, and say you made the statement because you were frightened by the police."[201] Among the young men who entered the witness box, Mavor stood alone in flatly denying that any indecencies had taken place with Wilde.

If Mavor emerged as trustworthy, the next sexual partner that Taylor supplied most definitely did not. The young man in question claimed to be Frederick ("Fred") Atkins, though he went by other names, most commonly Fred Denny: this was the identity that he gave in a court appearance in 1894 and the one he used when performing music-hall numbers on stage. Atkins, who later committed perjury during Wilde's trials, met Wilde in November 1892.[202] At the time, this impish eighteen-year-old was a seasoned criminal who had been living for more than two years with an older man, James Dennis Burton. As we have seen above, the politically well-connected Loulou Harcourt informed the attorney general about Burton's felonious activities. Burton, he said, had played a central role in wresting funds from men seeking sex with the young male prostitutes who, unbeknownst to these patrons, were operating in league with this veteran blackmailer.[203] Atkins, who amused the court when he declared that he earned his living as a bookmaker's clerk and a billiard-marker, made most of his income as an extortionist who attracted unsuspecting punters back to the lodgings that he shared with Burton. (On occasion, it seems, Atkins plied his trade as a cross-dressed prostitute as well.) Once he had welcomed a client into his rooms, an outraged "uncle" Burton would promptly appear, making all sorts of threats against the gentleman for having taken sexual advantage of his supposed "nephew." They terrorized the client, sometimes stripping the man naked, if he failed to part with the large sums that they demanded.

This was a routine familiar to other homosexual blackmailers in London. The practice became public knowledge in an article about the well-known extortionist William Allen that appeared in *Reynolds's Newspaper* in 1898. As Allen revealed, the victims of extortion were drawn from all walks of life: "amongst others who have been through my hands have been several lords, honourables, M.P.'s, naval and military officers, clerics, barristers, solicitors, J.P.'s, bankers, wine merchants, civil engineers, authors, Americans, and foreigners of almost every nationality, not excepting black men."[204] Whenever they could, a blackmailing duo would rob a victim of any materials—including letters, envelopes, and pocket books—that disclosed names and addresses. This was how Atkins and Burton conducted their business. Their main tool of intimidation was that they would have no hesitation in alleging that the gullible patron had attempted to commit indecencies on the supposedly innocent Atkins. The teenage Atkins combined these blackmailing exploits, which were exposed in court, with engagements doing turns as a comedian on the provincial stage. (In all likelihood, he sometimes appeared as a female impersonator when performing comedy acts in the music-halls.) Moreover, as he admitted, he assisted in taking bets on the horse-racing circuit, which was one of Burton's other dubious sources of remuneration.

It remains impossible to determine how much of this reprehensible history Wilde had learned when he hosted a dinner for Atkins, Schwabe, and Taylor at the Italian restaurant in the Hôtel de Florence. Yet there is no question that Wilde immediately took a shine to the shameless youngster. Events moved swiftly, as Atkins revealed in his rascally manner to the court during the pretrial hearing: "Wilde asked if I would like to go to Paris with him as his private secretary. I said 'Yes,' and we went two days later by the Club Train from Victoria" (182). What transpired after Wilde and Atkins arrived at a private hotel on the Boulevard des Capucines made for sensational disclosures during the Crown prosecution. In a show of calculated naïveté, Atkins began by recalling with excitement the scrumptious meal that he had enjoyed at the Café Julien ("The best I ever had in my life"), the visit to a fashionable hairdresser where he had his coiffure curled ("Wilde spoke in French to the barber"), and the fact that Wilde pressed a coin into his hand ("Wilde gave me a louis and permission to go outside") (182).

Even though Atkins never tried to practice blackmail on Wilde (he admitted to returning a letter that he had received from him), one of Atkins's associates,

Alfred Wood, had no hesitation in doing so. Once again, Wood, who was particularly treacherous, belonged to Taylor's milieu, and it seems that Wilde came across him at a gathering in 13 Little College Street. (Taylor deposed that Atkins introduced him to Wood in February 1892.) As with Wilde's involvement with Shelley and Atkins, it was left to the libel trial, together with each phase of the Crown prosecution, to reveal Wood's involvement in the extortion that he and two of his confrères attempted on Wilde. In January 1893, Douglas, who had no doubt been sleeping with Wood after Taylor had introduced them to each other, passed him on to Wilde. As a consequence, Wilde issued an invitation, and Wood accordingly joined him at the Café Royal. This rendezvous led to lunch at either Kettner's or the Florence. Thereafter, the two men proceeded to Wilde's home on Tite Street, where—as Wood later calmly testified—they enjoyed what seems to have been mutual masturbation. There were further encounters, including a visit to Wilde's rooms at the Savoy Hotel in March 1893, which—if Wood is to be believed—involved the ill-defined term sodomy. Around this period, Wood tried to extort funds from Wilde, on the basis of some sensitive documents he had stumbled across. While he was staying at Douglas's rooms on High Street, Oxford, Wood accidentally discovered a sheaf of love letters that Wilde had written to Bosie. He found the documents in a set of clothes that Douglas had given him so that they could (so it seems) adjourn, properly dressed, for dinner.

One of these adoring epistles, which likely dated from January 1893, had reached Bosie while Wilde was staying with his family at Lady Mount-Temple's home in Babbacombe, Devon. Wilde composed this passionate document, which became a showpiece in many parts of the proceedings, after he had received a copy of Douglas's sonnet "In Sarum Close." The poem, which is set in the cathedral city of Salisbury, Wiltshire, where Douglas's mother resided, features an overwhelmed voice that recalls that "Love"—no matter how exhausting passion can prove—continues to play on the "passionate strings" of his heart.[205] In the sestet, Douglas's speaker appeals to his beloved: "help me, or I die, / To bear Love's burden; for that load to share / Is sweet and pleasant."[206] Together, the poet says, the two of them must stand side by side as "neighbour jewels in Love's coronet."[207] Such phrasing, clearly, amounts to Douglas's effusion of his longing for Wilde. This is the finely crafted reply that Wilde made to Douglas's overwrought lines:

> My Own Boy,
>
> Your sonnet is quite lovely, and it is a marvel that those red rose-leaf lips of yours should have been made no less for the music of song than for madness

of kisses. Your slim gilt soul walks between passion and poetry. I know Hyacinthus, whom Apollo loved so madly, was you in Greek days.

Why are you alone in London, and when do you go to Salisbury? Do go there to cool your hands in the grey twilight of Gothic things, and come here whenever you like. It is a lovely place—it only lacks you; but go to Salisbury first.

Always, with undying love, Yours

Oscar[208]

Douglas took up Wilde's invitation to join him in Devon in mid-February 1893. Bosie's visit to Babbacombe, where the private tutor Campbell Dodgson accompanied him, resulted in the first bitter row with Wilde. Their argument set a pattern for much of the time that they subsequently spent together. The reason for the acrimony remains obscure, though Croft-Cooke surmises that the source of the conflict arose from Douglas "mischievously pulling [Wilde's] leg at times."[209] (On this view, Wilde took himself a little too seriously when Bosie ragged him.) Whatever the cause, it left a wound so deep that the pain becomes evident in the long dashes punctuating a letter that Wilde found difficult to write. Here, in full, is the appeal that Wilde made to Douglas in March 1893 from the Savoy Hotel:

Dearest of all Boys—Your letter was delightful—red and yellow wine to me—but I am sad and out of sorts—Bosie—you must not make scenes with me—they kill me—they wreck the loveliness of life—I cannot see *you*, so Greek and gracious, distorted by passion; I cannot listen to *your* curved lips saying hideous things to me—don't do it—you break my heart—I'd sooner be rented [i.e, blackmailed] all day, than have you bitter, unjust, and horrid—horrid—I must see you soon—you are the divine thing I want—the thing of grace and genius—but I don't know how to do it—Shall I come to Salisbury—?—There are many difficulties—my bill here is £49 for a week! I have also got a new sitting-room over the Thames—but you, why are you not here, my dear, my wonderful boy—? I fear I must leave; no money, no credit, and a heart of lead—Ever your own

Oscar[210]

Not long after Douglas received the letter, it fell into Wood's perfidious hands.

Even though Wilde, when placed under Clarke's examination during the libel trial, declared that Wood never made "a direct demand" for money in return for the letters, he had to negotiate the situation carefully when he met the young extortionist at an appointed time in Taylor's rooms.[211] This meeting tested Wilde's skills in handling such a delicate situation, and, in the circumstances, he managed to keep the potentially high costs down to size, especially as he had already resorted to his attorney Sir George Lewis, who had promptly contacted Wood, only to receive no reply. At various points of the libel proceedings, the court learned that after the meeting at 13 Little College Street Wilde handed Wood sums of £15 and £5. Yet rather than admit that he paid Wood these amounts either for sexual favors or under the threat of exposure, Wilde contended that he had made these gifts for an entirely different matter. The purpose of the £15, Wilde maintained, when responding to Carson's inquiries, was to secure the young man a safe passage to America, where he wished to restart his life with a clean slate. After a farewell lunch at the Florence, Wood petitioned Wilde for even more money, since the blackmailer maintained that £15 "would land him almost penniless in New York."[212] As a consequence, Wilde parted with another £5. These monies, which amounted to a considerable sum, eventually enabled Wood to cross the Atlantic on 1 April 1893, where he stayed for just one month (though in full employment, it seems). Wood, however, soon came back to his old hunting-ground. After he returned to London in May 1893, Wilde appears to have stayed clear of him, which is not surprising, given that the threats of blackmail escalated soon after Wood had embarked on his voyage to America.

Wood, who was well integrated into London's homosexual circles, had by this time received substantial amounts of cash from working in league with the young but seasoned extortionists William Allen and Robert Cliburn. At one point, Wilde's love letters to Douglas came to Allen's attention. Once he had read the documents, Allen returned all of them to Wood, apart from the letter (quoted above) that Wilde had written in response to "In Sarum Close"; Allen told Wood that this letter was "quite hot enough," and he arranged for his business partner, Cliburn, to confront Wilde about it at the stage door of the Haymarket Theatre, where *A Woman of No Importance* had been running for several nights.[213] According to the testimony that he gave during the libel proceedings, Wilde told Cliburn that he could not be bothered to engage with him. (Allen or Cliburn had already mailed a copy of the passionate missive to Herbert Beerbohm Tree, the actor-manager who was directing the production.) Undeterred, Allen then called at Wilde's family home in Tite Street. "I suppose," Wilde recalled saying to Allen on the doorstep, "you have come about my beautiful letter to Lord Alfred Douglas."[214] He told Allen that it was foolish for a blackmailer to mail a copy to Beerbohm Tree, who—as a loyal friend—had duly handed it over to Wilde. Allen, it seems, retorted by stating that he had been offered £60 for the original letter. Derisively, Wilde refused to be intimidated: "If you take my advice you will go to that man and sell my letter to him for sixty pounds . . . I myself have never received so large a sum for any prose work of that very small length."[215] In the end, when Allen could tell that Wilde was unafraid, he declared that he "hadn't a single penny."[216] Wilde parted with a half-sovereign (worth 10s.) and bade Allen to be on his way. These events took an even more unexpected turn when Cliburn appeared on the doorstep five minutes later and handed the letter back to a bemused Wilde. Given this turnabout, Wilde wanted to understand the reason for Allen's unexpected act of generosity: "Well, he says that you were kind to him and there is no use trying to rent you."[217] Wilde's refusal to be "rented"—a verb that was linked not just to extortion but also prostitution—reveals Wilde's audacious attempt at beating the blackmailers at their own game.

As we can tell, Taylor's circle held increasing liabilities for Wilde. This was especially the situation when Taylor put Wilde in contact with the Parker brothers, Charles and William, in February 1893. On this occasion, Taylor's procuration involved scouting the busy St. James's bar in Piccadilly. This was a haunt of male and female sex workers. Taylor discovered one of his friends, a publisher's clerk named Edward Harrington, in the company of the teenage Parkers, who claimed in court that they had previously held positions as a groom and a valet, respectively. After buying them a drink, Taylor arranged to meet with them at his rooms, most probably with the goal of enjoying sex with both of them, since it appears that they lodged for a short time at 13 Little College Street. One way or another, Taylor ushered the Parkers to a dinner that Wilde hosted in an upstairs room at Kettner's.

During the first criminal trial, William Parker recalled the antics that took place over a splendid meal, where Wilde also treated his guests to cigarettes and champagne. Wilde, he said, paid all of his attention to Charles, who playfully accepted a preserved cherry from Wilde's mouth. Wilde took the cherry back into his own mouth, and this trick was repeated three or four times. At the end of the repast, Wilde allegedly announced: "This is the boy for me" (167). Four years later, when he languished in jail, Wilde reflected on the lavish manner in which he had regaled these young villains: "People thought it dreadful of me to have entertained at dinner the evil things of life, and to have found pleasure in their company. But they, from the point of view which I, as an artist in life, approached them, were delightfully suggestive and stimulating. It was like feasting with panthers. The danger was half the excitement."[218]

There were other male objects of erotic interest. As Russell discovered, the young men to whom Wilde made overtures for sexual favors included Ernest Scarfe, Walter Grainger, and Herbert Tankard. Scarfe, who had turned twenty-five when he came back from fifteen months in the goldfields of Australia in early 1893, was another man whom Taylor procured for Wilde, this time in April that year. Like Charles Parker and various other young men mentioned in Queensberry's plea, Scarfe visited Wilde at Geneux's private hotel.[219] Meanwhile, the fifteen-year-old Herbert Tankard was serving as a page boy when he met Wilde in March 1893 at the Savoy. For reasons that are uncertain, Grainger—who was employed by Wilde as his under-butler during the summer of 1893—did not give evidence, even though the confession he made to Russell appears to have been the only one to suggest that Wilde coerced this partner into sexual activity by making threats that the young man would suffer jail time should he ever disclose what had been going on between them. McKenna has questioned why Grainger's admissions did not attract closer attention during the libel trial and the Crown prosecution: "Did [Queensberry's solicitors] 'prompt' Grainger to record these threats of dire consequences? If it was a prompt, why was Grainger the only one of the witnesses persuaded to speak of threats?"[220] Grainger had been told to be present at the Old Bailey, since he was seen in the vicinity of the courts. The same is true of Scarfe. Exactly why they did not take the stand remains a matter of speculation.[221] Very possibly, Grainger's testimony would too readily implicate Douglas's homosexual adventures, which were—as I elaborate throughout the following sections—dangerous ground upon which to tread. In the meantime, it was noticeable that Douglas's older brother, Percy Sholto Douglas, arranged for a watching brief to be held during the libel proceedings, since he had befriended Scarfe while they were making the journey back to London after spending time in Australia. In the circumstances, Queensberry's solicitors had to make sure they did not generate any needless controversy that risked shifting the focus away from Wilde's culpability onto Alfred and Percy Douglas.

Little is known about Wilde's other young male intimates. Tankard, at the time of the trials, had escaped across the Channel to Calais, where he had found a post in a hotel. Neither do we have much evidence of Wilde's involvement with the actor Harry Barford, who visited him a few times at St. James's Place. This is equally true of his relations with another young actor, Sydney Barraclough, whom he wanted Beerbohm Tree to cast in the role of the young man Gerald in *A Woman of No Importance*: "It is absurd," Wilde told Barraclough, on hearing the director's refusal, "that I can't have the boy that I want in the part."[222] There is also material that reveals that during the months when Grainger was employed by Wilde, Douglas brought back to The Cottage the sixteen-year-old Claude Dansey, who in later life earned fame as a spymaster working for MI5.[223] While the details are murky, it appears that Douglas sought to rescue Dansey from a sexual imbroglio involving Robert Ross at the boy's school in Bruges. As it turned out, once he was retrieved from Ross's clutches Dansey enjoyed sex with both Wilde and Douglas at The Cottage, and then Douglas paid for the schoolboy to enjoy an extra night with a female sex worker. This information suggests that Wilde may well have enjoyed intimacy with several other young men, given the number of those of whom we have some knowledge.

Slightly less opaque, however, are the aspects of the intimacy that Wilde developed with the sixteen-year-old Alphonse Conway, whom he met with Douglas at Worthing, a seaside town in Sussex, in August 1894. The summer vacation in this holiday resort, where Constance had secured the lease on a residence named The Haven, reveals how Wilde strove to balance his professional writing (he drafted *The Importance of Being Earnest* there), playtime with his sons (boat trips with Cyril, as well as building sandcastles on the beach), awarding prizes at one of the Worthing festivals (the competition was for the best-decorated boats at a Venetian fête), and allotting his time both to his family (Constance spent five weeks there before the boys returned to school) and to Douglas (who visited The Haven three times and stayed, on the final occasion, in the town until early October). Antony Edmonds points out that the relationship that evolved with Conway "was very different from any other in Wilde's life," and there is no question that it was different—insofar as the affair neither resulted in the distress that Shelley had suffered nor involved Taylor providing the means of contact.[224] This was not, as Edmonds observes, a relationship similar to the ones where Wilde rejoiced in "feasting with panthers." Instead, at Worthing Wilde expressed "an unmistakeable undercurrent of affection" for the working-class teenager, as we can ascertain from his courtroom testimony.[225]

Wilde first encountered Conway among a group of teenagers who assisted in the dragging of a boat, one that Wilde had rented, down the beach to the water. This new companion went with Wilde on fishing trips, and the friendship extended to a tea party at the Marine Hotel, as well as one with Wilde's children at The Haven. Not one to lose a sexual opportunity, Wilde invited Conway to take a leisurely walk with him one evening toward nearby Lancing. In the witness statement that Russell extracted, Conway recalled that Wilde "took hold" of him, undid his fly, and masturbated him until he "spent."[226] This activity was repeated during the next day or two. Once Constance had departed from The Haven, Wilde invited Conway to dine there, and on three occasions they retired to bed together. Toward the end of September, Wilde asked Conway to join him on a special excursion to Brighton, where they stayed at the Albion Hotel. There, too, according to the witness statements, sexual intimacy took place. "He acted as before," though on this occasion he "used his mouth."[227]

It seems unlikely that, if Conway performed sexual favors, he did so for fees. But Wilde parted, it appears, with £15 during their relationship, and he gave Conway presents, including the requisite inscribed cigarette case, a signed photograph of himself, a fancy walking stick, and two books with seafaring themes. (*Treasure Island* was one of these titles, which perhaps indicates that Wilde appreciated Conway's interest in joining the merchant navy.) Edmonds contends that Conway "can hardly have been appalled by what happened" during his initial and subsequent sexual liaisons with Wilde.[228] Still, one can never tell for sure. The admittedly limited evidence that we have about this affair suggests that Wilde's spontaneous generosity cast something of a spell over Conway, whose subsequent history is unknown. Besides his witness statement, after the trials Conway—like quite a few of the other young men who entered Wilde's life—vanished from the record.[229]

If, however, we will never really understand whether Conway reciprocated Wilde's affections, what happened around this time with Douglas—a companion whom he found increasingly difficult to handle and even harder to escape—is altogether more palpable. The exhausting presence of Bosie in Wilde's career, for which Wilde bore a strong measure of responsibility, also had a powerful literary dimension that was arguably as significant as the one that led him toward a promiscuous homosexual life with the "panthers" who dined with him in Soho and slept with him at the Savoy. Moreover, these two aspects of his intense affair with Lord Alfred stirred up an emotional whirlwind that exposed what Ada Leverson called Wilde's "fatal want of judgment."[230] The glaring irony about this momentous attachment is that while it created the conditions that triggered Wilde's libel action, it was the most enduring relationship whose intimacy no one dared to explore in court.

The next chapter considers the increasing tensions that developed in Wilde's passion for Bosie, which not only drained him of resources and led to emotional fatigue but also included important literary collaborations, ones that reveal their commitment to developing a modern homoerotic literary culture. Even if, in the end, Queensberry expressed his anger at his son Alfred for publicly parading his affair with Wilde at venues such as the Café Royal, he was additionally aware that the two men's names stood closely together in the literary world. The marquess's animosity toward Wilde deepened as the intimate friendship with Douglas attracted attention in the press. As we will see in chapter 2, Wilde became entangled in a plot that Queensberry had designed so that the Irish author would receive the severest punishment.

2

OSCAR WILDE AND ALFRED DOUGLAS: THE SCANDALOUS AFFAIR THAT INFLAMED THE MARQUESS

LORD WINDERMERE: What is the difference between scandal and gossip?

CECIL GRAHAM: Oh! gossip is charming! History is merely gossip. But scandal is gossip made tedious by morality.

—*Oscar Wilde, Lady Windermere's Fan (1892)*

Commentators have seldom been forgiving toward Alfred Douglas's headstrong contribution to the collapse of his lover Oscar Wilde's career in spring 1895. The consensus is that Bosie wreaked havoc by insisting that Wilde take decisive action against the reviled John Sholto Douglas, 9th Marquess of Queensberry: the young lord's belligerent father, whose hounding of the male couple had increased during the two years preceding Wilde's libel suit. More to the point, the petulant Douglas has often appeared as a grasping and feckless narcissist who bled Wilde dry of funds, in ways that resulted in massive debts and a stream of writs from creditors. Some of Wilde's closest friends, especially his literary executor, Robert Ross, concluded that the exploitative, moody, and capricious Douglas should have been separated from the vulnerable older man many months before the ill-advised libel case.

Frank Harris was the first to make public this hostile approach to Bosie's behavior when he observed in his 1916 biography (whose publication Douglas suppressed in Britain): "As soon as Oscar Wilde began to entertain [Douglas] . . . his expenses became formidable, and soon outran his large earnings."[1] "It was weakness in Oscar and not strength," Harris went on to remark, "that allowed him to be driven to the conflict by Lord Alfred Douglas."[2] Moreover, Harris gives the impression that once Wilde's ill-judged case against Queensberry foundered, Douglas's unwillingness to urge Wilde—as many friends had done—"to leave the country at once to avoid scandal" was largely responsible for Wilde's arrest.[3]

To Harris, the most disgraceful aspect of Douglas's fickle behavior became painfully manifest when Wilde's two-year prison sentence began on 25 May 1895. In his view, Bosie had so little compassion for Wilde that he ultimately neglected a man who had, through thick and thin, been a self-sacrificing partner. During the two years that Wilde languished in solitary confinement, Douglas noticeably stayed incommunicado with the prisoner. The undependable Bosie's silence might suggest that he was spurning the man who had taken every step to protect him from an outraged and browbeating father. To Harris, Douglas's treacherous conduct was consistently destructive: "Alfred Douglas had driven [Wilde] to the prosecution, and then deserted him and left him in prison without using his influence to mitigate his friend's suffering or his pen to console and encourage him. The abandonment was heartless and complete."[4]

As Harris knew well, from the start of the libel trial against Queensberry through the subsequent Crown prosecution of Wilde, Douglas experienced no brushes with the law. Never once was Bosie invited to take the stand. And when it appeared that Douglas might be in danger of prosecution, he followed Wilde's advice to abscond and seek refuge in France. Even the jurors could discern that it appeared peculiar that the charges brought against Wilde might equally pertain to the untouched Douglas. As the foreman remarked to Justice Wills: "[I]t seems to us that if we are to consider these letters [from Wilde to Douglas] as evidence of guilt, and if we adduce any guilt from these letters, it applies as much to Lord Alfred Douglas as to the defendant" (393).[5] In response, the judge abruptly discounted the very idea of venturing such a suggestion: "Lord Alfred Douglas, as you all know, went to Paris at the request of the defendant, and there he has stayed, and I know absolutely nothing more about him. I am as ignorant in this respect as you are. It may be that there is no evidence against Lord Alfred Douglas—but even about that I know nothing" (393). Such comments intimate that it was not only Wilde who wished to protect Douglas from harm; Justice Wills's remarks also insinuate that perhaps Queensberry had engaged in behind-the-scenes negotiations with the establishment to make sure that Wilde was pilloried instead of Bosie. Assuredly, we cannot confirm whether such inveigling took place. Still, the judge's refusal to admit any evidence against Douglas makes it appear as though there was a cover-up.

On the basis of such information, Douglas should have shouldered much of the burden that he had foisted upon his enraptured lover. This is a somewhat distorted perspective. Modern critics have proved largely unwilling to acknowledge that Wilde was not only besotted with Bosie's physical attractiveness. Neither was it a relationship rooted in ongoing sexual contact between them. Nor, for that matter, was it an affair in which Wilde was bamboozled by the young man's extravagant whims. Central to Wilde's fascination with Douglas was the young lord's unquestionable talent as a poet, which resulted in publications where their names appeared close together. As Wilde's statements in court show, he respected Douglas as a consummate artist. This point came to the Old Bailey's attention when attorneys read aloud a letter that Wilde sent to Bosie in early 1895, where he responded to the young poet's verse "In Sarum Close": "Your sonnet is quite lovely. It is a marvel that those red rose-leaf lips of yours should be made no less for the music of song than for the madness of kissing" (77).[6] In the second trial against Wilde, the lead prosecutor, Sir Frank Lockwood, asked: "Do you think that was a decent way for a man of your age to address a man of his?" (367). "It was," Wilde countered, "a beautiful way for an artist to address a young man of culture and charm. Decency does not enter into it" (367). This excerpt from Wilde's correspondence demonstrates that he conceived of his intimacy with Douglas as not so much erotic as aesthetic. The finely composed letter suggests that Wilde looked upon Bosie as both an artist and an artwork.

In significant respects, the excitement that Wilde felt toward Douglas was as much connected with their literary interests as it was with the homosexual opportunities that Bosie's wealth of contacts opened up for him. Their attachment, it is worth remembering, originated in the great impression that Wilde's only novel, *The Picture of Dorian Gray*, left on Douglas's mind. Upon receiving a copy from Lionel Johnson, a close friend from Winchester College, Douglas read it no fewer than nine times. Once Douglas finally met Wilde at Tite Street, the attractive Scottish aristocrat was smitten, though not—as Bosie took pains to point out many years after Wilde's death—in the sense of "physical admiration."[7] "[T]he dazzling brilliance and spell-weaving enchantment of his conversation completely outweighed in my eyes the disadvantages of his appearance."[8] At the same time, we need to bear in mind that Bosie's memories, like Wilde's, were selective in their rendering of the past. "There was nothing I would not have done for him," Douglas adds.[9] "It is a mere commonplace to say," he declares, "that I would gladly have died for him, or gone to prison in his stead."[10] Both remarks remain open to question.

Still, the dynamics of their intimacy appear pretty unambiguous. Largely because of the intense feelings that sprang from Douglas's awe in the presence of the older man, together with Wilde's corresponding infatuation, their evolving intimacy suffered many perilous upheavals. It is therefore misleading to attribute to the temperamental Douglas the onus of blame for the events that triggered Wilde's decision to sue the volatile Queensberry for criminal libel. Their union, which endured periods of great devotion followed by ones tarnished with saddening betrayals, was more intricate and textured than it might at first appear. Theirs was a busy, adventurous, and luxurious life marked by a great measure of codependency. Together, Douglas and Wilde made rather poor decisions at the same time as they insisted that they could defy the social customs and punitive laws that sought to discipline their desires. As Nicholas Frankel has observed, the moment has come to even out the historical bias against Bosie: "Douglas has too often been represented as a callous and heartless Judas or Iago figure who spurred Wilde on to not one but two disastrous and fateful actions, before abandoning Wilde each time to face the consequences alone."[11]

Wilde himself bears a degree of responsibility for the ways in which this deeply negative view of Douglas developed over the years. The belated appearance of the long letter that Wilde wrote in prison, which was afterward widely known as *De Profundis*, did much to shore up Harris's belief that Bosie was the driving force behind the misjudged libel suit and the subsequent arrest. In the early months of 1897, as readers could finally see when the complete text became public in 1962, Wilde generated a highly detailed account of the affair, which is often at its most startling when one discovers the degree to which he memorized the times, places, and transactions involved in each phase of their intimacy. With the apparent gift of hindsight, Wilde makes many memorable claims about the ways that he allowed Douglas's foul and exploitative behavior to dominate him: "The basis of character is will-power," he intones, "and my will-power became absolutely subject to yours. It sounds a grotesque thing to say, but it is none the less true."[12] Such words, when we put them in perspective, give one pause. Was it really the case that Wilde permitted his subjection to Douglas's spendthrift habits and petulant outbursts? Did not Wilde have some accountability for the vast quantities of money he squandered on meals, fine wines, and jewelry in Douglas's company? Was not Wilde party to the seemingly reckless decisions that they made in the months that culminated in the libel trial? Both men participated in the steps that resulted in Wilde's legal action. Their bond, even if Wilde tried to end it when their rows flared out of control, was a mutual, unbreakable one. Practically nothing could shatter it, even during a busy professional period when Wilde's two society comedies—*An Ideal Husband* and *The Importance of Being Earnest*—gave him the financial resources to make a clean break with the man whose presence in his life he continued to desire. Instead, their attachment endured in the face of testing situations. The sections that follow reveal that Wilde was not discreet in presenting

Douglas to the world as an intimate friend who meant much more to him than a youthful companion. The conflict with Queensberry, as we see here, would never have arisen unless there was growing acknowledgment that Bosie and Wilde were lovers.

"WRITE TO ME SOON, YOU HONEY-HAIRED BOY!" WILDE, DOUGLAS, AND THE "LOVE THAT DARE NOT SPEAK ITS NAME"

De Profundis is no ordinary letter. Instead, as Ian Small has contended, this highly crafted document aimed "to form (in some way) a literary work, or the basis of a literary work" intended for publication.[13] Six weeks before his release from jail, Wilde asked Robert Ross "to have it type-written . . . on good paper such as is used for plays, and a wide rubricated margin" that "should be left for corrections."[14] Still, as commentators such as Rupert Croft-Cooke have observed, Wilde's epistolary tone in this seemingly well-considered memoir is often "theatrical and exaggerated," and there is—as we can also see when balancing Wilde's recollections against other records—an inclination throughout the letter to misrepresent what were unmistakably painful memories.[15] "I allowed you to dominate me," Wilde repeatedly informs Douglas, "and your father to frighten me."[16] Without doubt, Wilde targets these reproaches as much at himself as he does at Bosie. Yet Wilde spouts so much bile elsewhere in this document that it is hard not to conclude that he lays the larger part of the blame for his sentence firmly on his impulsive companion. "I should have got rid of you," Wilde writes.[17]

Be that as it may, amid these reproaches there are observations that reveal how and why the bond between the two men proved almost indissoluble. One of the surest signs of Wilde's unshakable devotion to Bosie, no matter how many quarrels it had to withstand, is that the young Scottish lord meant far more to him—even if they were no longer sexually involved—than any of the males on whom he bestowed the customary cigarette cases and other trinkets. By spring 1893, it had become Wilde's habit to indulge each and every one of Douglas's expensive tastes. As he looks back on the debts that escalated during this time, Wilde recollects, in succulent prose evoking the luxurious living that he relished on these occasions, the "Savoy dinners—the clear turtle-soup, the luscious ortolans wrapped in their crinkled Sicilian vine-leaves, the heavy amber-coloured, indeed almost amber-scented champagne—Dagonet 1880, I think."[18] Particularly improvident was a "special little present" that Wilde commissioned at the Bond Street jeweler Henry Lewis, in order to celebrate the opening of *A Woman of No Importance*: "dainty sleeve-links—four heart-shaped moonstones of silver mist, girdled by alternate ruby and diamond for their setting."[19] Wilde inconsolably recalls that Bosie "sold them for a song a few months afterwards."[20] The pawning of the cufflinks, Wilde recollects, is all the more poignant because he had never been able to settle the bill for this fancy item, which was the most expensive gift that he had ever conferred on anyone.

Later in the year, Wilde celebrated their affair in a set of photographs that were taken in Campbell Gray's studio on Edgware Road: a company well known at the time for making portraits of celebrities, politicians, and (in later years) royalty (figs. 8 and 9).[21] As we can see from these images, the two men are nicely attired, with Bosie sporting a boater and white flannels, while a somewhat portly Wilde dons a finely tailored suit featuring his characteristic boutonnière. In both pictures, Wilde assumes a dominant position. In fig. 8 he asserts himself by standing upright, with his left foot planted firmly on the bench, while in fig. 9 his left arm circles behind Douglas. In many ways, the two photographs project the idea that Wilde wished to model this affair on Greek male love. This was, in principle, the paradigm that both men believed shaped their relationship. As Douglas wrote after the trials, in a letter that he withdrew from publication in the Parisian *Mercure de France*: "I am proud to be what I am, proud to have been so much loved by a great man, and proud to have suffered so much for him."[22] "There is," he goes on, "a certain philosopher called Plato, whose words are vaguely remembered even in this civilized age. He has spoken of the love I have for Oscar Wilde and he has for me as 'the beginning of wisdom.'"[23] But as we know from the carefree manner in which they passed along sexual partners such as Wood, theirs was not an intimacy based exactly on the erotic discipline that Socrates attempts to instill in the young male citizen whose education is the focus of Plato's dialogues such as *Phaedrus*.

Their relationship was also based, in its earliest phase, on the respect that Bosie expressed for Wilde's literary abilities, in relation not just to *The Picture of Dorian Gray* but also to the one-act tragedy *Salomé*.[24] In the final issue of the *Spirit Lamp*, Douglas bestowed great praise upon the drama; it was a "a perfect work of art, a joy for ever."[25] Later in 1893, after Douglas had departed without a degree from Oxford, Wilde bequeathed him a task that eventually led to further rancor between them. He urged Bosie to translate *Salomé*, which—in the face of the ban on its staging in England—had appeared in February that year, in a jointly published edition, from the Librairie de l'Art Indépendant in Paris and from Elkin Mathews and John Lane in London. By

Fig. 8. Photograph of Oscar Wilde and Alfred Douglas (1893).
Studio of Campbell Gray, 88 Edgware Road, London. 13.5 × 9.5 cm.

this time, Wilde had taken out a lease on The Cottage, Goring-on-Thames, apparently at Douglas's request. It was there that Bosie worked on rendering Wilde's not entirely steady French into a stirring idiom that resembles the august prose of the King James Bible. In the meantime, Wilde, who found writing plays challenging, made slow progress drafting the society comedy that became *An Ideal Husband*.

This was an expensive and stressful summertime. The rental on this large residence, together with the costs of Wilde's own servants as well as Bosie's, came to a colossal £1,340.[26] To be clear, Wilde had a good stream of income from *A Woman of No Importance*, which had opened in mid-April. Moreover, he and Bosie spent plenty of time together in this home close to the river. Harris, in one of his more plausible anecdotes, recalls hearing Wilde good-humoredly divulge

Fig. 9. Photograph of Oscar Wilde and Alfred Douglas (1893). Studio of Campbell Gray, 88 Edgware Road, London. 14 × 9.5 cm.

what happened one sultry afternoon when Bosie stripped naked in order to cool down:

> Bosie proposed that I should turn the hose pipe on him. He went in and threw his things off and so did I. A few minutes later I was seated in a chair with a bath towel round me and Bosie was lying on the grass about ten yards away, when the vicar came to pay us a call. The servant told him that we were in the garden, and he came and found us there. Frank, you have no idea of the sort of face he pulled. What could I say?
>
> "I am the vicar of the parish," he bowed pompously.
>
> "I'm delighted to see you," getting up and draping myself carefully, "you have come just in time to enjoy a perfectly Greek scene."[27]

Still, Bosie's company involved as many frustrations as it did pleasures. Apart from these amusements, Wilde was stuck in a predicament where not only were the expenses immense; his now almost habitual rows with Bosie also led to the impetuous young man's dismissal from the residence, although this was only—as it turned out—on a temporary basis.

As Wilde looked back from prison on Douglas's infuriating behavior, which led to the young lord's expulsion from The Cottage, he bitterly regretted the reconciliation that soon followed. In June 1893, he remembers, there was a particularly unpleasant episode:

> Some of your Oxford friends came to stay from a Saturday to a Monday. The morning of the day they went you made a scene so dreadful, so distressing that I told you that we must part. I remember quite well, as we stood on the level croquet-ground with the pretty lawn all round us, pointing out to you that we were spoiling each other's lives, that you were absolutely ruining mine and that I was evidently was not making you really happy, and that an irrevocable parting, a complete separation was the one wise thing to do. You went sullenly after luncheon, leaving one of your most offensive letters behind with the butler to be handed to me after your departure. Before three days had elapsed you were telegraphing from London to beg to be forgiven and allowed to return. I had taken the place to please you. I had engaged your own servants at your request. I was always terribly sorry for the hideous temper to which you were really a prey. I was fond of you. So I let you come back and forgave you.[28]

It is noticeable that these aggrieved words from *De Profundis* preface an even deeper source of resentment on Wilde's part. "Three months later still, in September, new scenes occurred, the occasion of them being my pointing out the schoolboy faults of your attempted translation of *Salomé*. You must by this time be a fair enough French scholar to know that the translation was as worthy of you, as an ordinary Oxonian, as it was of the work it sought to render."[29] No surviving letters from summer 1893 shed further light on Wilde's belief that Douglas's translation undermined the great pride that he took in his French-language drama. What appears indisputable, however, is that Wilde had serious concerns about the contractual aspects of Douglas's adaptation, which had already gone into production with Mathews and Lane. Troubled, Wilde sought advice from Charles Kains-Jackson, a literary-minded attorney who had, since 1888, edited the *Artist and Journal of Home Culture*: a periodical that took increasing risks through publishing homophile writings, including a selection of Douglas's early passionate lyrics. We still do not know how Wilde became acquainted with Kains-Jackson, but Wilde turned to him for legal advice in the early 1890s. On 6 November 1893, he telegrammed: "Wish to consult you professionally on *Salomé* business."[30]

In all likelihood, Wilde wanted to know the most appropriate way of presenting Douglas's contribution in the English edition. A dispute seems to have broken out between him and Douglas over the wording that should appear on the title page. The problem was that Douglas's name had originally enjoyed pride of place there. In the end, Wilde's dedication—"TO MY FRIEND | LORD ALFRED BRUCE DOUGLAS | THE TRANSLATOR OF MY PLAY"—was the only credit given to the translator's handiwork. As a consequence, Douglas felt rebuffed. Merlin Holland and Rupert Hart-Davis, in their annotation to Wilde's telegram, quote an embittered letter from Douglas to Lane, in which Douglas says that he "realised that the difference between the dedication to *Salomé* to me by the author and the appearance of my name on the title-page is the difference between a tribute of admiration from an artist and a receipt from a tradesman."[31] Bosie, who had produced a stylish text, clearly grasped that Wilde—no matter how much passion the Irish dramatist might express for his young male companion—most probably valued his art above everything else.

Besides the persistent difficulties in Wilde's intimacy with Douglas, there were other sources of pressure that made the English edition of *Salomé* contentious. Boldly, Mathews and Lane had commissioned the controversial young artist Aubrey Beardsley to furnish full-page illustrations to complement Douglas's translation. These also met with Wilde's displeasure. Beardsley, who had little time for either Wilde or Douglas ("Both of them are really dreadful people"), intimated to Ross that the wrangle over the edition had become tedious: "I suppose you heard about the *Salomé* row. I can tell you I had a warm time of it between Lane and Oscar and Co. For one week the number of telegraph and messenger boys who came to the door was simply scandalous. I really don't know how matters stand now. Anyhow Bozie's [*sic*] name is not to turn up on the Title. The book will be out soon after Christmas. I have withdrawn three of the illustrations and supplied their places with three new ones."[32] One can tell from Beardsley's quips, which evoke the memory of the telegraph boys in the Cleveland Street scandal, that he has well aware of Wilde's predilection for young men. In any case, the independent-minded Beardsley found Wilde hard to take seriously. As this letter shows, some of Beardsley's artworks had been deemed unsuitable for the edition. Even though Wilde declared to the well-known actress Stella Campbell that Beardsley's drawings were "quite wonderful," the ones that carictaure Wilde show little sympathy for the dramatist.[33] Beardsley's fun-poking images of Wilde appear in the bloated face of the moon, in the obese and lustful figure of Herod Antipas, and in the bottom-right-hand corner of a drawing titled *Enter Herodias*, where Wilde's face protrudes beneath an American Indian owl-mask, while his hidden right hand clutches what appears to be either the Rod of Asclepius or Hermes's caduceus. According to Roger Fry, Ross told him that Wilde "*loathed* the drawings to Salome but dared not say so."[34] Charles Ricketts suggested that Wilde was more forgiving. He recalled that Wilde had confided to him: "Aubrey's designs are like the naughty scribbles a precocious schoolboy makes on the margins of his copybooks."[35]

The rows that intensified over *Salomé* noticeably came to a head when Wilde had resolved to disentangle himself, once and for all, from Douglas. On 9 November 1893, he wrote a letter of great concern to Douglas's mother, Lady Sibyl Montgomery, Marchioness of Queensberry, in which he claimed that her third son—who remained "sleepless, nervous, and rather hysterical"—might "come to grief of some kind," unless he went "abroad for four or five months, to the Cromers in Egypt if that could be managed."[36] (Evelyn Baring, 1st Earl of Cromer, was agent and consul general in Egypt.) Whatever truth one might find in Wilde's anxieties for Douglas's wellbeing, it is also evident that he needed a reprieve from an affair that had proved emotionally and financially draining. As for Douglas, it appears that he agreed to leave England in an attempt to allay his personal and professional anxieties. His letters show that he was deeply troubled by the plight of other men whose lives were destroyed when allegations about their homosexual practices led to criminal prosecutions under the 1885 act. "I have just seen in the papers," Douglas wrote to the penal reformer George Ives, who later founded the secret homophile Order of Chaeronea, "the horrible account of the poor wretched man who was charged with 'indecently assaulting' a boy or two boys. It seems to me one of the horrible and inhuman laws, and reading it has made me feel quite ill."[37] This episode, he says, reminds him of "[t]he terrible death two years ago of [Charles Alan] Fyffe (the Oxford history man)."[38] In July 1891, Fyffe—a life fellow of University College, Oxford, who was married with three small children—had been charged at Guildford Assizes "with committing acts of gross indecency with another male person in a railway carriage on the London, Horsham, and South Coast railway."[39] Even though the grand jury threw the case out of court, Fyffe had already made an attempt on his own life in May 1891. The injuries that he suffered were followed by his death the following February. In another letter on a similar matter, this time to Kains-Jackson, Douglas petitions this friend that he is deeply concerned about "a poor man Barnard who is waiting his trial for an assault on a boy."[40] The man in question, Douglas adds, is a roommate of the actor and author Roy Horniman. "Do for my sake," he pleads with Kains-Jackson, "try and do something, and see Horniman about the poor chap."[41] This correspondence shows that Douglas was well aware of the serious legal danger that any man courted should his homosexuality become exposed. "I am very unhappy about other things as well as this," he adds, before giving his contact information in Cairo.[42]

The plan to place Douglas at a considerable remove from the emotional turmoil of London proceeded well, at least for a while. The idea was that, with Cromer's support, this directionless descendant of a noble family would acquire professional stature by serving as an honorary attaché at the British embassy in Constantinople. (Cromer made the request but, in the end, the ambassador refused.) In the meantime, Wilde was left to try to clean up the financial mess that he had created. His debts had begun to sting him as never before. In early December, he told Douglas that he was at the mercy of "vulture creditors."[43] At the same time, however, Wilde was making decisive advances with his writing. He had published both *Lady Windermere's Fan* and the French edition of *Salomé*. He was also, from October 1893 onward, renting rooms at Geneux's hotel in St. James's Place, where he not only made progress with *An Ideal Husband* but also entertained a string of young male visitors.

This more manageable world of literary work and sexual pleasure, though, did not last long. Douglas grew bored whiling away his time in the Middle East. Cromer confessed that he found Douglas "a useless boy full of all sorts of . . . willful nonsense."[44] Douglas wanted to return to England before taking up in June, as he had at one point planned, an unpaid position under Lord Currie at the embassy in Constantinople. From Paris, he made various entreaties to see Wilde. His forays included a telegram to Constance urging her to persuade Wilde to write to him. There was, too, as Wilde remembered, "a telegram of some ten or eleven pages in length" sent to Tite Street.[45] Wilde, faced with this barrage, finally capitulated, and he agreed to meet Bosie, without making his plans explicit to Constance. Once again, Wilde footed the bills for what turned into an eight-day sojourn. Hyde observes that this escapade cost him £150.[46]

In every respect, as Wilde recalled in jail, Douglas's demeanor expressed "unfeigned joy," as well as "contrition, so simple and sincere."[47]

In *De Profundis*, Wilde's resentful memory of the way in which he allowed himself to "consent to renew" his friendship with Douglas precedes one of the most ominous sentences in his dramatic retelling of their life together.[48] "Two days after we had returned to London," Wilde recollects, "your father saw you having luncheon with me at the Café Royal, joined my table, drank of my wine, and that afternoon, through a letter addressed to you, began his first attack on me."[49] This disquieting turn of events became public knowledge during his libel suit against Queensberry. Wilde's eminent counsel, Sir Edward Clarke, had several items of vindictive correspondence between Queensberry, his son Alfred, and his former father-in-law put in as evidence. As Douglas noted in his *Autobiography*, ever since Lady Sibyl divorced his father in 1887, he had not seen the marquess "more than a dozen times."[50] Relations were equally precarious with his eldest son Francis, Viscount Drumlanrig, with whom Queensberry was not on speaking terms, and also with his second son Percy (who, at the time, was seeking his fortune in Australia), whose recent marriage the marquess had only lately acknowledged. Like Bosie, his older brothers Francis and Percy sided with their mother after the break-up. Clarke, who thought the acrimonious letters would cast Queensberry in a negative light, began by reading aloud the cudgeling missives that the indignant father had sent to Bosie. The first piece of correspondence, which is the one Wilde mentions in *De Profundis*, berates Douglas for indulging publicly in a "most loathsome and disgusting relationship."[51] "I now hear," Queensberry declares, "that [Wilde's] wife is petitioning to divorce him for sodomy and other crimes."[52] In reaction to this explosive correspondence, Douglas fired off a mocking telegram that declared insolently: "WHAT A FUNNY LITTLE MAN YOU ARE."[53] Once the furor reached Lady Sibyl's ears, she ensured that Bosie was sent off to Florence. Wilde followed a few weeks afterward, and he stayed there with Douglas until the end of the month.

Douglas's departure for Italy, however, did not see tempers cool. The marquess remained agitated with his family. Especially ill-natured was Queensberry's epistle to Alfred Montgomery, the father of his ex-wife, and a close friend of the Prince of Wales. The marquess, who was prone to paranoia, assumed that Montgomery was plotting against him. In July 1894, Queensberry told Montgomery that he deplored the support that Lady Sibyl gave to Alfred in the thick of this "stinking scandal": "your daughter's conduct is outrageous."[54] Particularly unpleasant was Queensberry's ire at the fact that Montgomery's beloved grandson Francis had been granted, on 22 June 1893, a peerage as the 1st Baron Kelhead. A month later, Francis was appointed as a lord-in-waiting to Her Majesty by Lord Rosebery, who at the time was foreign secretary in prime minister W. E. Gladstone's last administration. The peerage came at the behest of Gladstone and the Queen. The marquess was aggrieved because in 1880 he had been excluded as an elected representative Scottish peer in the House of Lords, since he refused to sign an oath of allegiance to the sovereign. (The marquess, an avowed atheist and secularist, detested "such religious tomfoolery."[55]) "I am fully convinced," Queensberry told Montgomery, "that Rosebery—Gladstone—Royal insult that came to me through my other son, that she [i.e., Lady Sibyl] worked that."[56] This was, by any account, a painful letter to air at the Old Bailey in April 1895, since Francis, as we see below (99), had died in a shooting incident six months before.

Wilde's libel case against the marquess disclosed how badly the harassment had escalated during the summer of 1894. In late June that year, Queensberry appeared unannounced with a stockbroker named Edward James Pape at Wilde's family home in Tite Street, Chelsea. As Wilde explained during the fraught libel proceedings, his servant informed him that Queensberry and Pape were waiting for him in the library. Queensberry, Wilde recalled, rudely told him to "[s]it down" as soon as he entered. Wilde, according to his recollection of this unpleasant episode, had refused to be intimidated: "I said, 'I don't allow you to talk like that to me or anyone to talk like that to me in my house or anywhere else.' I said, 'I suppose you have come to apologise for the statement you made about my wife and myself in the letter you write to your son.' I said, 'I could have you up any day I chose for criminal libel for writing such a letter.' He said, 'the letter was privileged as it was written to my son.' I said to him, 'How dare you say such things as you do about your son and me?'"[57] This account provides a tempered version of what really happened. In *De Profundis*, Wilde reminds Douglas: "your father, with his bully, or his friend, between us, had stood uttering every foul word his foul mind could think of, and screaming the loathsome threats he afterwards with such cunning carried out."[58] Faced with these accusations, Wilde stated that all of these allegations were lies. In the end, Queensberry sought to terrorize him: "If I catch you with my son together in any public restaurant, I will thrash you."[59] Such threats were too much for Wilde to bear. "I said to him," he recounted in court, "'I don't know what the Queensberry rules are, but the Oscar Wilde rule is to shoot on sight.'"[60] This incisive comment, which prompted laughter in court, revealed how egregious the marquess's bullying had become.

The prospect of gunfire turned into a reality when Douglas informed Queensberry that he was carrying a "loaded revolver," which he said he would readily use if his outraged father did not desist.[61] "If O. W. was to prosecute you in the Central Criminal Court for libel," Bosie warned his father, "you would get seven years' penal servitude for your outrageous libels."[62] In prison, Wilde recalled that Douglas's taunting of the marquess had spun out of control, not least because the loaded gun exploded at a public venue, causing grave embarrassment: "All you could think of (besides of course writing him insulting letters and telegrams) was to buy a ridiculous pistol that goes off at the Berkeley, under circumstances that create a worse scandal than ever came to *your* ears."[63] (It remains uncertain whether the gunfire at the restaurant was accidental or deliberate.) At the time, however, Wilde was so incensed that he turned to Sir George Lewis to see if the eminent attorney would support an action against Queensberry. Much to Wilde's chagrin, Sir George, who had served his interests in the past, responded on 7 July 1894 by stating that the marquess was his client. As Linda Stratmann observes, Bosie's cousin George Wyndham, the Conservative Member of Parliament whom Wilde knew through the Crabbet Club, had shortly before advised Wilde against suing the marquess, since it would cause a scandal in the family.[64] Wyndham made this appeal at the behest of his cousin Lady Sibyl, who wanted the affair to be kept out of the public eye.

By this point, Wilde appeared dauntless. He had begun, on Ross's recommendation, to rely on an experienced solicitor, C. O. Humphreys, who dealt in criminal cases, to handle his legal affairs. Over several months, Wilde petitioned Humphreys to see if there were grounds upon which to establish a libel case against Douglas's father. Repeatedly, Humphreys stated that he could not support taking the matter to court. It was only when Wilde discovered that Queensberry had walked not many steps from his hotel to deposit the insulting visiting card at the Albemarle Club that Humphreys put the legal machinery in motion.[65] Humphreys, it seems, had little sense of the perils involved in supporting Wilde's case.

Queensberry's hatred of Wilde was enmeshed in his diehard anger toward Rosebery, which involved intimidating behavior that was arguably worse than the brutish manner in which he had treated Wilde. Not long after Francis had given his maiden speech in the House of Lords in June 1894, Queensberry tracked Rosebery to Bad Homburg, with the express purpose of a confrontation. At the elite resort, which drew wealthy members of high society, Sir George Lewis advised Rosebery to retire to his hotel room in order "to avoid any collision with a lunatic."[66] Meanwhile, the Prince of Wales, who was no doubt aware that the marquess had been parading through the streets making threats against his enemy, was relieved to learn that Queensberry had decided against causing any further disturbance. The chief of police in the spa town had already warned the pugilistic aristocrat against carrying out his alarming threats.

Rosebery's close attachment to Francis Douglas, as I have mentioned above, came to a tragic conclusion. Francis's death on 18 October 1894, from a gunshot wound through his mouth that shattered his lower skull, has long been a subject of speculation. Stratmann, who provides the most detailed assessment of the evidence to date, reminds us that Francis's death came exactly a month after he had confided to Rosebery that he would soon announce his engagement to Alexandra ("Alix") Ellis, the third daughter of Major-General Arthur Ellis, equerry to the Prince of Wales. Alix's uncle Edward Stanley (the Conservative Member of Parliament for Bridgwater, Somerset) invited the engaged couple and their families to meet friends at his residence, Quantock Lodge. During a shooting party, Francis separated from his companions in order (so they assumed) to look for a wounded bird in an adjacent field. Late in the afternoon, when Francis appeared to be missing, the men who went in search of him found his corpse. "He lay motionless on his back," Stratmann notes, "his body parallel with the hedge, his head turned slightly to the right and concealed in the brambles. The gun lay across his stomach, the muzzle towards the hedge, and his arms were stretched out, his hands some distance from his sides."[67] Understandably, no one connected with Viscount Drumlanrig wanted the least suspicion to be cast upon the cause of death. At Quantock Lodge, the coroner concluded that the fatal injury was the result of Francis's attempt to return to his party through a gap in the hedge. This is the view that Douglas presents in the sonnet that he wrote in memory of his brother: "Shall I cheat you," the speaker says, "who never did a wrong / To any man?"[68] As Stratmann observes, however, the verdict of accidental death failed to take into account that the position of the deceased's body, together with the fact that the bullet was fired upward into his mouth, pointed to self-murder.

Why did this happen? Stratmann reckons that a plausible diagnosis comes from Francis's nephew, also named Francis Douglas (the 11th Marquess of Queensberry), who claimed that the death was the result of a "highly nervous temperament."[69] This viewpoint runs unequivocally against the theory that Francis took his life because Queensberry—who had done his utmost to harass Rosebery at Bad Homburg—was taking steps to blackmail Rosebery, who had recently been elected prime minister. From this perspective, the hotheaded aristocrat sought to destroy the politician's career lest a scandal break about Rosebery's sexual involvement with the marquess's heir apparent.

The suggestion that Queensberry was hellbent on exposing Rosebery's homosexuality came to attention many years later when scholars discovered Edmund Trelawny Backhouse's fanciful memoirs. A minor member of the nobility, Backhouse was a contemporary of Douglas's, first at Winchester and then at Oxford, before departing for China, where he established himself as a western expert on the Qing Dynasty and a favorite of the empress dowager. In "The Dead Past," which he composed a few years before his death in 1944, Backhouse characterizes Rosebery as "an unsated lover of his own sex."[70] Ever eager to convert fiction into fact, Backhouse conjures a memory of meeting Rosebery during a soirée at the politician's "magnificent Berkeley Square mansion" in November 1892.[71] Early in their friendship, Backhouse claims, Rosebery divulged his sensational personal history to him:

> His marriage with a Rothschild [Hannah de Rothschild] had brought to him over a million sterling; he had been a devoted husband and Lady Rosebery's death in 1890 had been, to quote Louis XIV's "bon mot" on the decease of the Spanish Consort, *le seul chagrin qu'elle m'eût jamais causé* [the only grief she had ever caused me].
>
> He told me that after his bereavement in 1890 he was staying in his Neapolitan villa and when visiting the blue Grotto at Capri became attracted, *à l'instar de Tibère* [just like Tiberius], to an Italian *ephebus* who was disporting himself in utter nakedness at that historical post sacred to love and lust. He then for the first time revelled in the beauty of the masculine posterior which was to become his dominant passion, perhaps not even yielding place to his bookloving propensities which were literally his second nature.[72]

As he unleashes this fantasy about Rosebery's personal life, Backhouse fabricates a further tall tale, one that supposedly accounts for Francis's suicide. He claims that the bisexual Loulou Harcourt, who was ensconced in Liberal party politics and well acquainted with London's queer subcultures, decided to inform Queensberry that "relations between prime-minister and secretary were scarcely platonic."[73] As a result, Queensberry set "private detectives to work," and soon he "obtained very damaging evidence of a carnal bout after a supper party at Bourne End on the River Thames."[74] "Queensberry," Backhouse elaborates, "wrote to the prime-minister threatening exposure in a letter to the republican owner of Truth, Mr. Henry Labouchere, Lord Rosebery's inveterate enemy, unless he resigned office and severed relations with Drumlanrig."[75]

In his unsparing study of Backhouse's recollections, Hugh Trevor-Roper draws the conclusion that these intriguing works are "pure fantasy throughout—and yet fantasy which was spun with extraordinary ingenuity around and between true facts accurately remembered or cunningly bent to sustain it."[76] To Neil McKenna, however, Backhouse's arresting claims sound as if they have more than a ring of truth about them. "If," McKenna hypothesizes, "Trelawny Backhouse's account of the affair is correct, Drumlanrig must have been desperately manoeuvring to try and save Rosebery's career and find a way out of a seeming impossible situation. His proposal of marriage to Alix Ellis may have been his best hope of averting scandal."[77]

The problem with entertaining this view is that we still have no evidence that Rosebery had homosexual leanings, let alone a passion for Francis. To be sure, there was parliamentary gossip about Rosebery. Tim Healy, the Irish nationalist Member of Parliament, records in his memoirs that he approached the solicitor general, Sir Frank Lockwood, asking him not to pursue a second Crown prosecution against Wilde. Lockwood responded by saying that there would be no need to try Wilde a second time were it not for the fact of the "the abominable rumours against [Rosebery]."[78] Meanwhile, when Rosebery's health collapsed soon after his attempt to resign as prime minister on 19 February 1895, there was plenty of gossip about the real cause of his debility. Frederick William Lambton, 4th Earl of Durham, for example, divulged the following to Reginald ("Regy") Baliol Brett, 2nd Viscount Esher, who knew much about the queer circles in the upper echelons of society: "the Newmarket scum [i.e., the racing set] say that R[osebery] never had the influenza, and that his insomnia was caused by his terror of being in the Wilde scandal. Very charitable."[79] Such tittle-tattle aside, there remains nothing in Rosebery's documents to confirm these suspicions. Leo McKinstry, in his definitive biography, contends "that in none of [Rosebery's] papers . . . is there the smallest indication that he felt any guilt about or involvement in the tragedy."[80] As McKinstry also observes, the only suggestion that might indicate that a dread of homosexual exposure drove Francis to take his own life comes from a comment of Loulou Harcourt's on the announcement of the engagement to Alix Ellis: "It makes the institution of matrimony ridiculous!"[81] Then again, Harcourt's sniping, as McKinstry suggests, might have been motivated by different reasons—either "the brevity of the courtship, Queensberry's eccentricity, Drumlanrig's perceived frivolity, or the couple's financial prospects, since Queensberry was notoriously mean, and General Ellis had no private income."[82]

Two days before Francis died, Wilde turned forty. The birthday occurred when Wilde was suffering further stress from his affair with Bosie. During a visit to Brighton, where they stayed at the Grand Hotel, Douglas fell ill with influenza, and Wilde—who recalled providing the patient "with every luxury of fruit, flowers, presents, books, and the like that money can procure"—nursed him attentively.[83] No sooner had Douglas recovered than Wilde reserved private rooms in which to finish writing *An Ideal Husband*. But once he tried to settle into his work, he also succumbed to the virus, suffering from what he portrayed at the time as "a sort of malarial fever."[84] Bored, Douglas neglected his lover. "The next two days," Wilde remembered in jail, "you leave me entirely alone without care, without attendance, without anything."[85] The only time Bosie appeared in the room was purely "for money."[86] The moment Wilde tried to put pressure on Douglas to show some care, Bosie's response was resentful: "You accused me of selfishness in expecting you to be with me when I was ill; of standing between you and your amusements."[87] Soon after, when his fever broke and he was able to look after himself, Wilde learned that Bosie had run up expenses at the Grand Hotel. These were charged to Wilde's account.

This depressing existence contrasted with the opulent lives of the two leading characters in *The Green Carnation*: an anonymously published satirical *roman à clef* that draws on aspects of *The Picture of Dorian Gray* in order, as the *Globe* put it, to "burlesque . . . with singular success, the 'Wildean' cult."[88] Brought out at the end of September 1894, this flippant novel—which was one of the earliest works by the popular writer Robert Hichens—takes its title from the artificially colored bloom that Wilde and his young male coterie sported as boutonnières at a number of dramatic premieres, including an Independent Theatre Society production in February 1892.[89] The green carnation caught the attention of reporters, though none disclosed that it connoted a man's passion for his own sex. The hints that the protagonists share similar queer desires, however, are scarcely hidden.

Early in the novel, Lord Reggie Hastings, whose demeanor caricatures aspects of Douglas's public image, also bears more than a passing resemblance to Dorian Gray, especially with reference to his finely furnished residence. "This evening," the narrator notes, "Reggie stood before the mirror till the Sèvres clock on the chimneypiece gently chimed seven. Then he drew out of their tissue paper a pair of lavender gloves, and pressed the electric bell."[90] Once he starts riding around in a hansom through the fashionable West End, Reggie passes "an elderly gentleman with a red face and small side whiskers."[91] Earlier that day, we learn, Reggie "has received a long and vehement diatribe from his parent, showering abuse upon him . . . . He had replied by wire—'What a funny little man you are.'"[92] Such phrasing shows that Hichens, who had spent time with Douglas in Egypt, had privileged access to Bosie's queer milieu.

If Reggie embodies an attractive blend of Bosie and Dorian Gray, his counterpart Esmé Amarinth presents a more familiar aspect of Wilde, who comes before us as "a big man" spouting witty aphorisms. "I was born epigrammatic," Amarinth declares, "and my dying remark will be a paradox. How splendid to die with a paradox upon one's lips!"[93] Like Lord Henry Wotton, Amarinth plays the role of a beguiling mentor to his young companion. "No, Reggie," he says, in tones that hardly match Lord Henry's well-honed rhetoric, "do not marry unless you have the strength to be a bad husband."[94] Despite the derivative nature of Hichens's prose, at least one thoughtful reviewer—who grasped that the work was "apparently intended as a satire on Mr. Wilde"—ventured the idea that it might, perversely, have been conjured by Wilde himself.[95] Wilde was quick to disabuse the *Pall Mall Gazette* of the idea that he was "the author of *The Green Carnation*": "I invented that magnificent flower," he announced, "[b]ut," he went on, "with the middle-class and mediocre book that usurps its strangely beautiful name I have, I need hardly say, nothing whatsoever to do."[96] Such comments, however, barely distracted attention from Hichens's *succès de scandale*. In the weeks that followed, after the *Daily Chronicle* had announced that Hichens was the author, a reporter remarked that *The Green Carnation* "threatens to rival [E. F. Benson's] 'Dodo' in popularity."[97]

Hichens's diverting satire, though hardly as poised as Wilde's stylish aphorisms, lampooned its subjects in a tone that was for the most part benign. The same, however, could not be said of a disparaging full-page feature in *Punch*, which was much more pointed in suggesting that Douglas and Wilde were not only lovers but also seducers of young men. Titled "The Decadent Guys (a Colour-Study in Green Carnations)," the article turns to the occasion of Guy Fawkes Night (traditionally celebrated in England on 5 November, with displays of fireworks) in order to represent the "collapsed forms" of Wilde and Douglas as miserably cloth-stuffed "guys" (fig. 10). These "guys," since they are like the ones thrown onto bonfires commemorating the foiling of the 1605 Gunpowder Plot, are ready, in their dilapidated condition, to be cast into the flames. Here, in the cartoon placed at the center of this send-up, Wilde appears in the guise of Fustian Flitters, wearing a beaten-up top hat, while Douglas materializes as Lord Raggie Tattersall, donning a raggedy boater. Both of them, in the style of the literary decadents whose sleazy eroticism had been a subject of debate in the press, are sagging over the ropes that bind them, the moment before they are about to be set alight. Instead of green carnations, the two "guys" have uncomplimentary cauliflowers stuck in their lapels.

Even though the image indicates that society has begun to yawn at Wilde and Douglas's notoriety, the narrative is little short of spiteful: "See Raggie," says Mr. Flitters, "here come our youthful disciples! Do they not look deliciously innocent and enthusiastic? I wish though, we could contrive to imbue them with something of our lovely limpness."[98] Once the youths arrive, Lord Raggie muses: "Beautiful rose-coloured children! . . . how sad to think they will all grow up and degenerate into pork-butchers, and generals, and bishops, and absurdly futile persons of that sort."[99] A little further on, we hear Fustian take pride in his spineless, if not degenerate, manhood: "Perhaps to be vertebrate is

Fig. 10. "J. B. P." [John Bernard Partridge], cartoon for "The Decadent Guys (a Colour-Study in Green Carnations)," *Punch*, 10 November 1894: 224.

to be normal, and the normal is necessarily such a hideous monstrosity. I love what are called warped and distorted figures. The only real Adonis nowadays is a Guy."[100] The hostile wording, it does not take much to grasp, implies that this effeminate pair share the same homoerotic desires. "The Decadent Guys" certainly left an impression on Wilde's arch-enemies. Once the libel trial collapsed, the conservative *National Review*, which the imperialist W. E. Henley edited, expressed "a deep debt of gratitude toward the Marquess of Queensberry for destroying the High Priest of the Decadents."[101] As the phrasing hints, by the mid-1890s the term decadent had in one or two quarters become a byword not only for a Bohemian littérateur but for a homosexual one as well.

"The Decadent Guys" understandably caused Constance grief. Still, she tried to put a brave face on the open secret that her profligate husband was conducting affairs with younger men. Once the children had returned home from school, she concentrated on preparing for the Christmas celebrations. She also sought to rebuild the public image of her family life. Franny Moyle observes that "[a]n extensive interview with her in the 24 November edition of *To-Day*, a popular magazine edited by Jerome K. Jerome, must have served as some welcome positive publicity for the Wilde marriage."[102] The interviewer, having taken note of each and every artwork arranged in the finely appointed Tite Street sitting room, concludes the article by sharing with the readership "a glimpse into Mrs. Oscar Wilde's tastes and surroundings" through her autograph book, which she opens at the "dedicatory verses" that her spouse has inscribed on the opening page: "I can write no stately proem, / As a prelude to my lay; / From a poet to a poem, / That is all I say."[103] Besides Wilde's dedication, the journalist scrutinizes other entries by such eminences as Arthur Balfour, Henry Irving, and John Ruskin.

A few weeks later, however, *To-Day* protested the publication of what it viewed as a disreputable new magazine called the *Chameleon*, which was "issued from Oxford, and published by a West-end firm."[104] Even though it must have been Jerome who decided to refrain from mentioning the names of the contributors to this journal, he firmly condemned the contents: "The publication appears to be nothing more nor less than the advocacy for indulgence in the cravings of unnatural disease."[105] Among the authors included in the first and only issue of the *Chameleon*, which had a print run of just 100 copies, were Douglas and Wilde. Wilde's thought-provoking list of epigrams, "Phrases and Philosophies for the Use of the Young," took pride of place. A handful of these sharp-witted aphorisms strike a scarcely covert homoeotic tone: "*There is something tragic about the enormous number of young men there are in England at the present moment who start life with perfect profiles, and end by adopting some useful profession.*"[106] These sayings, which finish with an amusing reversal of moral contempt toward vanity ("*To love oneself is the beginning of a life-long romance*"), are harder hitting than another catalogue of irreverent epigrams that Wilde had recently published, this time in Frank Harris's *Saturday Review*.[107] In "A Few Maxims for the Instruction of the Over-Educated," Wilde's phrases sound similar to the droll lines that sparkle in his society comedies. "Dandyism," he proclaims, "is the assertion of the absolute modernity of beauty."[108]

More rebellious in the *Chameleon*, though, were the two sexually unapologetic poems that Douglas had placed there. In the sonnet titled "In Praise of Shame," the poetic voice recalls a mystical nighttime experience with a phantom called "Shame," who inspires him to declare: "Of all sweet passions Shame is loveliest."[109] By comparison, Douglas's second (and much longer) poem, "Two Loves," makes an altogether more trenchant point about the delectable nature of "Shame." In this dramatic monologue, the speaker recounts a visionary experience, in which he met a naked youth, with pale, white skin and deep red lips, who approached him in a state of rapture: "he . . . / . . . caught my hand and kissed my mouth" before feeding the speaker grapes.[110] "Come," this youth said to him, "I will show thee shadows of the world."[111] Immediately, two figures appeared. The first, who shielded himself from the light, "sang of pretty maids / And joyous love of comely girl and boy."[112] By contrast, there was a despondent "comrade that walked aside"; "his head," we learn, "Was wreathed with moon-flowers pale as lips of death.[113] The strangeness of this "wan and white" presence encouraged the speaker to inquire: "What is thy name?."[114] The moment the wraith-like spirit declared that the answer was "Love," his bedazzled companion flatly contradicted him: "He lieth, for his name is Shame."[115] "I am true Love," the same figure continued, "I fill / The hearts of boy and girl with mutual flame."[116] The poem ends with the memory of the "wan and white" figure resigned to humiliation: "Have thy will," he said. "I am the love that dare not speak its name."[117] Once Queensberry read his son's poems in this new magazine, he immediately denounced the "filthy gibberish" of this resonant final line—"'The love that dare not breathe its name,' meaning Sodomy."[118]

In Wilde's trials, both his "Phrases and Philosophies" and Douglas's poetry formed part of an extended debate about the questionable nature of Wilde's literary works, including *The Picture of Dorian Gray* and "The Portrait of Mr. W. H." At the Old Bailey, Wilde was asked to explain such resonant phrases as "I am the love that dare not speak its name." The same was true of a short story titled "The Priest and the Acolyte," which appeared anonymously in the *Chameleon* (its signature was a cryptic "X"). (The story was not by Wilde but by an ambitious Oxford undergraduate, John Francis Bloxam, who edited the magazine.) In this tale, where a priest falls passionately in love with a young male altar server, the older man murders the child by dispensing poison in a wine-filled chalice. Once the boy has perished from this perverse celebration of communion, the priest takes his own life. In the end, they lie entwined before God: "On the steps of the altar was stretched the long, ascetic frame of the young priest, robed in the sacred vestments; close beside him, with his curly head pillowed on the gorgeous embroideries that covered his breast, lay the beautiful boy in scarlet and lace."[119]

Jerome's protests about the *Chameleon*, if sending out a warning shot, hardly impeded Wilde's next theatrical conquest. By the end of December 1894, Wilde was in attendance at the fashionable Haymarket Theatre for the rehearsals of *An Ideal Husband*—for which he had received an advance of £500. Once the New Year festivities had concluded, the play, which was his third society comedy on the West End stage, enjoyed a spectacular premiere. He provided tickets for Douglas, Ross, and Ross's brother Aleck, as well as for the publisher William

Heinemann. As for the drama itself, reviewers were quick to observe that this new society comedy struck a chord that differed from the repartee that had dominated *Lady Windermere's Fan* and *A Woman of No Importance*. To be sure, the *Athenæum* found Wilde's enduring penchant for epigrammatic dialogue a bit tiresome (such maxims were "the trappings of a vigorously ridden hobby-horse of affectation"); nevertheless, it remained "difficult to be angry with the author or displeased with his play."[120] The performances, especially with the gifted actors Charles Hawtrey, Julia Neilson, and Lewis Waller in the leading roles, ensured that it was an exultant production.

To some commentators, the serious topics that emerge in *An Ideal Husband* marked a refreshing advance in Wilde's art. As a drama that focuses on the twin themes of honesty in modern marriage and the crime of blackmail, it presents an otherwise happily married couple, Sir Robert Chiltern and Lady Chiltern, whose domestic bliss and social standing suddenly fall under serious threat of political corruption. The crisis blows up when Mrs. Cheveley, who has long been a rival of Lady Chiltern's since their schooldays together, inserts herself into a party that the couple are hosting. Mrs. Cheveley, who conforms to the character type known as the adventuress, seizes upon the opportunity to speak in private with Sir Robert, a barrister who has risen to the office of under-secretary for foreign affairs. Once Mrs. Cheveley, who is recently arrived from Vienna, meets Sir Robert, she threatens to expose the fact that years ago he amassed a huge fortune of £85,000 by selling a Cabinet secret to the late Baron Arnheim ("a Stock Exchange speculator"); the baron, we learn, was at one time her paramour.[121] According to Mrs. Cheveley, in order to keep this fraud a secret Sir Robert must agree to support an ill-advised canal scheme in Argentina ("I have invested very largely in it," she insists).[122] "Scandals," she remarks mockingly, "used to lend charm, or at least interest to a man—now they crush him."[123]

The *Stage*, which appreciated Wilde's "very powerful and interesting story," claimed that even if the play was "heavily weighted with forced wit and paradoxical nonsense," it nonetheless amounted to his "best work," one destined for "a long and successful run."[124] William Archer, the great defender of the English stage from censorship, especially liked the dandyish Lord Goring's remark: "vulgarity is simply the conduct of other people."[125] Such phrasing proved that "there is in this a world of observation and instruction."[126] Constance agreed. Noting its "most tremendous success," she informed her mentor Lady Mount-Temple that *An Ideal Husband* was "the most beautiful play he has written."[127] The optimistic ending, which involves the triumphant suppression of scandal in the name of preserving the Chilterns' marriage, must have had special resonance for the woman publicly known as Mrs. Oscar Wilde.

Given the attention that *An Ideal Husband* attracted, Wilde—just as his wife had done the previous month—made himself available to interviewers. Not long after his comedy opened, Wilde allowed the journalist Gilbert Burgess to conduct a spirited conversation with him. Reproduced in the *Sketch*, their exchanges present Wilde as a major literary figure, one who has no qualms about capitalizing on his preeminence. Yet rather than become explicitly boastful about his talents, Wilde places the responsibility for his genius firmly upon the public's shoulders. "The public," he states firmly, "makes a success when it realises that a play is a work of art. On the three first nights I have had in London the public has been most successful, and had the dimensions of the stage admitted of it, I would have called them before the curtain."[128] "Most managers," he adds, "leave them behind."[129]

Wilde's tone, however, became more bullish in an interview that appeared in the *St. James's Gazette*. On this occasion, he made several carping remarks about the inferiority of theatre critics. "They should be pensioned off," Wilde declaims, "and only allowed to write on politics or theology or bimetallism, or some subject easier than art."[130] With this wholesale condemnation in place, Wilde defends himself squarely against a charge that critics had every now and then leveled at his playwriting: "Have you heard it said that all the characters in your play talk as you do?"[131] In reply, Wilde says: "In the case of a dramatist also an artist it is impossible not to feel that the work of art, to be a work of art, must be dominated by the artist. Every play of Shakespeare is dominated by Shakespeare. Ibsen and Dumas dominate their works. My works are dominated by myself."[132] Such uncompromising sentiments made it manifest that, even if Wilde maintained an honest belief in the integrity of his art, he was not averse to comparing himself with the Bard. Humility, it goes without saying, was not—insofar as his literary works were concerned—a virtue in which he indulged.

Later in February 1895, Wilde wrote to Ross, thanking his friend for his assistance in writing up this self-regarding interview. The letter came from the well-appointed Hôtel d'Europe, Algiers, where he had been staying with Bosie for over a week. "There is a great deal of beauty here," Wilde told Ross. "The Kabyle boys are quite lovely."[133] "Bosie and I," he added, "have taken to haschish."[134] By this point, Wilde's interest in pursuing intimacy with younger men had transformed into an intoxicating form of sex tourism. The most thorough account we have of Wilde and Douglas's time in Algeria appears in the French author André Gide's controversial memoir, *Si le grain ne meurt* (1924). Gide, whose recollections reveal his apprehensiveness toward his own homosexual feelings, discloses how, in February 1895, he discovered Wilde's and Douglas's names in the guest book at the hotel where he was staying. Even though Gide was at first reluctant to be in Wilde's company (he made haste for the local station only to think twice about his action), he soon caught up with the Irish author, whom he had met first in Paris in November 1891 and then again in Florence in May 1894.

Not long after he started conversing with Wilde in Algiers, Gide for the first time came across Bosie, who appeared to fill Wilde with rapture ("d'autant moins qu'il semblait mettre une certaine affectation à ne louer de Bosy que la beauté" (especially as he seemed rather affectedly to make a show of praising nothing but Bosie's beauty).[135] Within days, Wilde and Douglas had endured one of their formidable rows, a conflict that became apparent when Gide encountered them in a local hostelry. "Douglas entra dans la salle," Gide recalls, "enveloppé dans un manteau de fourrure dont le col relevé ne laissait passer que son nez et son regard" (Douglas came into the bar, wrapped in a fur coat, with the collar turned up so that one could only see his nose and his eyes). "Il passa contre moi, comme sans me reconnaître, se campa en face de Wilde, et, d'une voix sifflante, méprisante, haineuse, lança d'une haleine quelques phrases dont je ne compris pas un mot; puis brusquement tourna les talons et sortit" (He brushed past me as if he didn't recognize me, placed himself in front of Wilde, and in a hissing, hateful voice, threw out a few sentences, of which I did not understand a word, then abruptly turned around and exited).[136] Wilde told Gide that Bosie never did anything but make scenes like that, almost as if to suggest that Wilde took pride in such displays of rancor. It was during this period that Wilde confided to Gide that something dreadful awaited him on the horizon: "J'ai été aussi loin que possible dans mon sens, me répétait-il. Je ne peux pas aller plus loin. A présent il fait qu'il arrive *quelque chose*" (He told me, "In my opinion, I've gone as far as I can. I can go no further. *Something* has to happen now").[137]

As Wilde knew, trouble was brewing. On 3 February 1895, he left Algeria, while Bosie stayed there, in love with a young man whom he ended up punishing for sexual betrayal. Once Wilde arrived in London, the rehearsals for his fourth society comedy, *The Importance of Being Earnest* (amusingly subtitled *A Trivial Comedy for Serious People*), had already begun, ahead of their expected schedule. There was a strong reason that George Alexander at the St. James's Theatre hastened *Earnest* into production. The American author Henry James's drama *Guy Domville* (1895) had opened to an embarrassing premiere on 5 January that year. James, after he walked on the stage to take the customary bow at the end of the opening night, had to withstand jeering from the audience, with someone in the topmost balcony shouting "rotten."[138] By this time, Wilde had taken rooms at the Hotel Avondale, off Piccadilly, where he was entertaining a teenager named Tom Kennion.[139] Complimentary tickets were sent to friends, including Constance's recent object of passion, Arthur Humphreys. "I hope," Wilde wrote to Kennion, "you will enjoy my 'trivial' play. It is written by a butterfly for butterflies."[140] His expectations were correct. The production was about to follow on the heels of *An Ideal Husband* as a further theatrical triumph. All the same, there was one hazard Wilde had to avoid. Once he learned from Lady Sibyl that Queensberry had obtained a seat for the opening night, he urged the theatre manager to write to Carter's Hotel, where the marquess was staying, with a message stating that "the seat given to [Queensberry] was already sold," together with the promise of a refund.[141] "This will," Wilde recognized, "prevent trouble."[142] Had the marquess known where Wilde was residing, he would no doubt have created a commotion there as well. Wilde was canny enough to see that, even if Queensberry's ticket had been revoked, his antagonist would probably attempt to cause an uproar through some other means. Fearing violence, he wisely informed the police.

On the opening night, which took place when snow was falling on St. Valentine's Day, Queensberry and a henchman (very possibly a prizefighter) sought to gain entrance to the St. James's Theatre. But with twenty police officers on guard, it became impossible for the marquess to barge his way into the building. In the end, Queensberry had to abandon in the snow what Robert Harborough Sherard called the "phallic bouquet" of vegetables that the marquess had hoped to throw over the footlights at Wilde.[143] The attempted intimidation was sufficient for Wilde to ensure that C. O. Humphreys should take action against the indignant aristocrat. The solicitor, however, stated that the theatre management would not cooperate: "Had Lord Queensberry been permitted to carry out his threats you would have had ample ground for instituting a prosecution against him."[144]

Regardless of Queensberry's hostile behavior outside the St. James's, the first night, as A. E. W. Mason notes, was "an indubitable wow."[145] Reviewers were deeply impressed by this dynamic comedy that brings together two bachelors who appear to know each other so well that the one who calls himself "Ernest" intends to propose to this ostensibly best friend's first cousin, Gwendolen Fairfax. The only problem for "Ernest" is that Algernon ("Algy") Moncrieff, soon after he has welcomed this pal into his flat, discovers that the prospective fiancé also goes by a different name. The truth is that "Ernest" is a ploy that John ("Jack") Worthing uses in order to escape his domestic responsibilities to his young ward, Cecily Cardew. Jack soon makes a slip when he leaves behind a silver cigarette case in Algy's apartment. Once his servant Lane has retrieved the item for his friend, Algy reads a puzzling inscription on it: "From little Cecily, with her fondest love to her dear Uncle Jack."[146] In one of the funniest moments in the play, Jack declares that Cecily is his aunt. At once, Algy observes that he cannot comprehend "why an aunt . . . should call her own nephew her uncle."[147] Flummoxed, Jack has no alternative but to confess the truth: "my name is Ernest in town and Jack in the country."[148] At this country home, as we see later, Jack has beguiled his ward, Cecily Cardew, into believing that he has to go to town because of the antics played by his brother Ernest. Algy, however, is the last person who should decry Jack's dishonesty. He, too, resorts to alibis that enable him to take refuge from the domestic world, which his formidable Aunt Augusta (Lady Bracknell) rules with an iron rod. "I have invented," he tells Jack, "an invaluable permanent invalid called Bunbury, in order that I may be able to go down into the country whenever I choose."[149]

As the plot beautifully unfolds, we relish the confusions that lead both Gwendolen and Cecily to believe that they are in love with the same individual named "Ernest." Equally funny are Algy and Jack's respective efforts to resume their true identities, which involve the ultimate (and magnificently far-fetched) revelation that the infant Jack—whom his late guardian Thomas Cardew had recovered from a handbag accidentally abandoned in a cloakroom at London's Victoria Station—was, prior to his existence as a foundling, christened Ernest. Even more amusing is the fact that Jack in the end just happens to be Algy's brother: the false identity, Ernest, that Jack once assumed while in town. With the tables so neatly turned, the comedy casts into relief—through a seemingly trivial pun—the most serious consequence of its marvelously overwrought plot: "I've now realized for the first time in my life," Jack informs his newfound family members in the final line of the play, "the vital Importance of Being Earnest."[150]

Even A. B. Walkley, who had recently complained that *An Ideal Husband* reused threadbare theatrical devices not even worthy of the French dramatist Victorien Sardou, delighted in this fast-paced scenario. In an astute piece of criticism, Walkley grasped how the ingenious plot, which thrives on ludicrous coincidences and double identities, so capably generates exceptional comic effects:

> Take the capital situation of the farce. John Worthing, who is John in the country and (for the old reason) "Ernest" in town, determines to kill off his imaginary brother Ernest, and arrives at the country-house clad in complete mourning. The mere sight of him in this garb sets us off laughing. For we guess at once what he is going to do; and we have just seen his bosom friend arrive at the house in the assumed character of the very Ernest who is now

> to be given out as dead. Why do we laugh? Because, knowing what we do, we recognise John's conduct as absurd; but, on the other hand, we recognise it, given only his knowledge, as natural. So with all the actions of the play.[151]

Many other commentators were similarly awed. "In brilliant dialogue," the *Sketch* exclaimed, "Mr. Wilde is without a rival; and how versatile an artist he is! Not only a poet, an essayist, a novelist, 'an amateur of beautiful things and a *dilettante* of things delightful,' but one of the most brilliant playwrights of modern times."[152] Such kudos elevated Wilde to the pinnacle of his career.

Queensberry remained restless. Stratmann suggests that the marquess was stung into his next violent action after a tense confrontation with his son Percy at Carter's Hotel. During this meeting, Queensberry remonstrated with Percy about the homosexual scandal that enveloped Bosie and Wilde, only to discover that Percy flatly defended his brother and promised to shoot his quarrelsome father if the attacks did not cease. Once he had ordered Percy out of his rooms, the marquess performed the deed that precipitated Wilde's libel case. "[I]t was," he recalled, "that very day that driven almost to desperation I left that card on Oscar Wilde and brought matters to a head."[153] Queensberry took a short walk next door to the Albemarle Club. He handed the offending item to the hall porter, Sidney Wright: "For Oscar Wilde posing Somdomite."[154] "It is open to question," Stratmann notes, "whether Queensberry's message, written in a state of some agitation, was what he intended to write."[155] "There was," she adds, "no legal counsel on hand."[156] Whatever lack of deliberation was involved, the card triggered not only the lethal libel suit but also the longer chain of events that led—three and a half months later—to Wilde's incarceration.

THE MARQUESS'S LIBEL

Queensberry's visiting card languished at the Albemarle Club for no fewer than ten days, and it would have probably gone unnoticed for two or three weeks had Wilde not found himself trapped in London. As we know from *De Profundis*, Wilde had planned on departing for Paris. But on 28 February, when Sidney Wright handed him the card, the hotel manager would still not release his luggage:

> On that fatal Friday [1 March 1895, the day that Wilde initiated his libel suit], instead of being in [his solicitor's] Humphreys's office weakly consenting to my ruin, I would have been happy and free in Paris, away from you and your father, unconscious of his loathsome card, and indifferent to your letters, if I had been able to leave the Avondale Hotel. But the hotel people absolutely

> refused to let me go. You had been staying with me for ten days: indeed you had ultimately, to my great and, you will admit, rightful indignation, brought a companion of yours to stay with me also: my bill for ten days was £140. The proprietor said he could not allow my luggage to be removed from the hotel till I paid my account in full. That is what kept me in London. Had it not been for the hotel bill I would have gone to Paris on Thursday morning.[157]

Instead of traveling to the Continent, the cash-strapped Wilde expressed his despair about Queensberry's card to Ross: "My whole life seems ruined by this man. The tower of ivory is assailed by the foul thing."[158] Promptly, Ross came that evening to Wilde's hotel, and he wisely discouraged his friend from taking action. The following day, Bosie offered contradictory advice, since he was eager to see his father charged with the crime. Together, the three men entered Humphreys's office on 1 March. Humphreys wished to know if there was any truth in the allegation. Once Humphreys heard Wilde categorically deny the accusation, the attorney assured him that if Wilde was innocent, the case would succeed. They agreed on terms. Humphreys needed an advance of £150. Humphreys promptly obtained a warrant for Queensberry's arrest. Such confidence in Wilde's innocence also convinced the distinguished lawyer Sir Edward Clarke (fig. 11) to serve as senior counsel for the prosecution. Clarke, together with his junior counsel, required £500 for his services. Two years later, Clarke recalled that Wilde had given him "his word of honour as a gentleman that there was no foundation whatsoever for the charges wh[ich] were afterwards so completely proved."[159]

"The question why," Hesketh Pearson observed in 1946, "[Wilde] ever embarked on such a course, and why he maintained it after recognising the danger, has troubled many people, and no satisfying answer has yet been given."[160] In Pearson's view, the root cause was Wilde's "nature"; there was, he reckons, a "histrionic capacity being part of that emotional life which never reached maturity."[161] Ellmann amplifies this belief by venturing that Wilde had an "inclination to betray himself."[162] From this perspective, Wilde's apparent tendency to place himself in such a vulnerable position belonged to his larger fascination with experiencing life through heightened, self-dramatizing roles. "The role of victim," Ellmann writes, "was only one among several, including the dandy and the apostle of joy, through which he could see himself passing."[163] Even if we question these speculations, there were, as Ellmann acknowledges, palpable forces conspiring against Wilde. Especially pressing was Douglas's zeal in taking vengeance against his infuriated father ("there was no resisting Douglas's fierceness").[164] Certainly, Bosie had insisted that Lady Sibyl and Percy cover the legal

Fig. 11. "Spy" [Leslie Ward], cartoon of Sir Edward Clarke, *Vanity Fair*, 11 June 1903.

costs. (Neither mother nor son, it transpired, would defray these sums.) From a financial viewpoint alone, the lawsuit looked inadvisable. Although Wilde had received as much as £800 in advances from Alexander, his debts had become enormous. Creditors were clamoring for the various amounts that he owed them.

Still, it appears that Wilde may have believed that his headstrong action against the marquess would forestall the exposure of his intimacies with a host of younger men. Sir Edward Hamilton, joint permanent secretary to the Treasury, who was close to Rosebery, drew this conclusion. He remarked in his journal at the end of Wilde's libel trial: "He [i.e., Wilde] is said to have been aware that the Police has been watching him for some time, and that he took proceedings in the hope that he would win in the action which he brought against so crack-brained a man as Queensberry, and that he would thus stave off Police proceedings."[165] Wilde might have thought that he needed to deter interference from police officers, since their discoveries would only implicate Bosie, whom both he and the marquess wished to protect from culpability. There is, to a greater and lesser degree, a grain of truth in all of these suggestions, since a measure of each is likely to have impelled Wilde to sue Queensberry. What remains unambiguous is that Wilde proceeded in a defiant spirit, refusing to be broken by the sexual rules and financial restrictions that placed firm limits on the ambitious life he wanted to lead.

Queensberry was arrested at Carter's Hotel on the morning of Saturday, 2 March 1895. Detective Inspector Thomas Greet escorted him to Great Marlborough Street Magistrates' Court, where Humphreys declared that his client had been suffering the "most cruel persecution" at Queensberry's hands for the past ten months.[166] The proceedings were brief. Although Sir George Lewis, who represented the marquess on this occasion, warned that "when the circumstances of this case are more fully known, you will find that Lord Queensberry acted as he did under feeling of great indignation," the contending parties concurred that John Sholto Douglas should be allowed to stay a free man on the basis of his own recognizances of £1,000.[167] Humphreys also wanted to secure a surety (a term that meant bail), which a ship-owner named William Tyser offered to the tune of £500. "Lord Queensberry," Lewis said on behalf of his client, "is not going to run away."[168] As matters turned out, however, it was Sir George who deserted Queensberry. No sooner had Lewis represented the marquess in court than this eminent lawyer—who had assisted both Wilde and Douglas on some difficult occasions in the past—returned the brief to Queensberry. "In the whole of Lewis's career," John Juxon writes, "there is no incident remotely resembling this one."[169] The reasoning behind Lewis's decision has led to conjecture. In all probability, he had no desire to act against a man whose personal life he knew more about than he would have wished. This situation meant that the marquess had no counsel once the magistrate adjourned the hearing until the following week.

The abandoned Queensberry spent his time walking adrift on The Strand, where he sought any solicitor whose offices stayed open. On the Saturday afternoon, he had (from his point of view) the good fortune to stumble across a young partnership, Russell and Day, at 37 Norfolk Street. At the time, the thirty-one-year-old Charles Russell was still at the beginning of a promising career, which in later decades would match the success enjoyed by the legendary Sir George Lewis. (These days Charles Russell Speechlys LLP, one of the largest legal companies in Britain, is a direct descendant of the partnership Russell had with Day.) The second son of the recently appointed Lord Chief Justice (Baron Russell of Killowen), Russell showed himself to be exceptionally adept in handling Queensberry's defense. Russell, who took the business at once, moved expeditiously. He consulted with his father for advice on the most capable barrister who would vindicate the marquess's accusation. Lord Killowen, who had been the leader of the English Bar when he previously served as attorney general, made a bold recommendation.

The gifted lawyer whom Sir Charles proposed to his son was Edward Carson (fig. 12), the Liberal Unionist Member of Parliament for Dublin University. In the past few years, Carson had moved from Ireland, where he was appointed as a Queen's Counsel in 1889, to London, where he was called to the English Bar in 1892. Carson arrived in London with a formidable reputation behind him. As the Crown prosecutor in Ireland, a post he assumed in 1887, he earned the memorable nickname "Coercion Carson" because of his determination to suppress nationalist insurgency. He was ruthless in implementing the harsh Coercion Acts that removed trial by jury in order to punish and imprison nationalist agitators. Once installed in the British Parliament, he delivered a maiden speech that demonstrated his exceptional skills when challenging the political proponents of the nationalist Plan of Campaign in Ireland, which from 1886 to 1891 sought to contest the eviction of tenant farmers who were withholding rents from unscrupulous landlords. Carson's performance won a resounding endorsement from the prominent Liberal Unionist Joseph Chamberlain, who congratulated him on his "splendid speech": "It was," Chamberlain added, "the best debating speech I have heard for some time."[170]

Carson's relocation to London, where in Westminster he roundly opposed Gladstone's second Irish Home Rule Bill (1893), was unprecedented in the legal profession. No other Irish Q.C. wished to command the same authority in the different legal practices of the English courts. As his biographer, Edward

Fig. 12. "Lib." [Liborio Prosperi], cartoon of Edward Carson, *Vanity Fair*, 9 November 1893.

Marjoribanks, observes, it was within weeks of his calling to the English Bar that Carson applied to the Liberal lord chancellor to serve as an English Q.C. "The Chancellor," Marjoribanks notes, "replied that there was no precedent for giving of a silk gown to a barrister of a few weeks' call."[171] This situation, which in part stemmed from Carson's refusal to be intimidated by English judges, lasted until June 1894, when he finally had the honor of taking silk. In the interim, he made his mark as a shrewd cross-examiner, especially in a case at Guildford Assizes, where he represented the *Evening News*, which Havelock Wilson—a trade union leader and Liberal Member of Parliament for Middlesbrough—had charged with libel. In an exposé of corruption, the newspaper accused Wilson of exploiting the dues that members of the National Amalgamated Sailors' and Firemen's Union had paid into the coffers. Even though the jury agreed that Wilson had been libeled, they awarded him a humiliating farthing's damages. The press reported widely on Carson's knack at grinding down the plaintiff, which turned out to be so injurious to Wilson that he was led out of the court shaking with tears.

A direct contemporary of Wilde's at Trinity College Dublin, Carson did not, during his undergraduate days studying law, display the same academic brilliance as his literary peer. Neither was he a close acquaintance of Wilde's. Assuredly, the two men belonged to the college's Historical Society. Moreover, both students came from well-known Dublin families. But they lost the limited amount of contact that they once had when the prizewinning Wilde departed for Oxford, without a degree from Trinity, in 1874. Marjoribanks records that the next occasion when Carson encountered Wilde took place in February 1893. As he made his way to the House of Commons, "a fine carriage, drawn by two horses, narrowly missed him and splashed him with mud."[172] In a spirit of apology, Wilde jumped out of the vehicle and offered to shake the man's hand. At this point, Wilde inquired: "Hullo, Ned Carson, how are you?" "Oscar," Marjoribanks observes, "was friendliness itself." "Come and dine with me one day," Wilde said, "in Tite Street."[173] Carson, it appears, did not take up Wilde's offer.

This shared history, however, formed only one of the various reasons that Carson initially felt disinclined to accept the brief. There were other difficulties, too. Besides not wanting to oppose a former classmate in court, Carson needed to know more about the evidence, which in early March 1895 remained in short supply. For Russell as well, the scant information about Wilde's personal life posed a severe challenge. Since this was a charge of criminal libel, Queensberry's plea would have to justify that he made this insulting allegation in the public interest. As Hyde remarks, all that the young solicitor had in his arsenal were copies of the "two letters to Alfred Douglas and Wilde's published writings."[174]

Convinced that further evidence could be unearthed, Russell—who chose not to offer the brief to any lawyer but Carson—worked with two skillful private detectives, Frederick Kerley and John Littlechild. The task facing these former police inspectors was to identify the young men with whom Wilde had conducted intimate affairs. The sleuths were well chosen, since both men had far-reaching acquaintance with London's criminal world. In the memoirs he published in 1894, Littlechild had already capitalized on discussing sensational episodes from the early stages of his enthralling career. "I must admit," he told an audience fascinated by crime, "that the expert forger, the ingenious swindler, and the inventive genius of roguery are each and all very interesting studies."[175] By comparison, Kerley—who had retired from the CID fifteen years before—

apprehended the infamous cross-dressers Ernest Boulton and Frederick Park (known to their circle as Fanny and Stella) when they were leaving the Strand Theatre on 28 April 1870. The charge against Boulton and Park, both of whom wore outré female attire, was that they had been conspiring to commit sodomy. Kerley's longstanding knowledge of London's queer subcultures ensured that he was able to follow important leads that unraveled the homosexual network to which Wilde, if only marginally, belonged.

Even though Carson learned about the startling early results of this snooping, he was still indisposed to represent Queensberry. Marjoribanks claims that the Irish Member of Parliament was definitely convinced that Wilde was "a public danger and pest, and a disgrace to his native land."[176] At this point, Carson already understood far more about his former classmate's personal life than Wilde ever imagined. Still, Carson went forward on the marquess's behalf. At the adjourned hearing on 9 March 1895, Carson, together with his junior counsel (and Irish compatriot) Charles Frederick Gill (fig. 13), represented Queensberry, while Humphreys spoke on behalf of Wilde. "Great interest," *Lloyd's Weekly* observed, "was manifested in the proceedings, and there were numerous applications from persons of position asking to be accommodated with seats."[177] No sooner had Wilde entered the court than the magistrate, Mr. Robert Miles Newton, asked Bosie to leave. In response to Humphreys's inquiries about his name, profession, education, and acquaintance with Douglas's family, Wilde maintained an imperturbable demeanor. "All this," *Reynolds's* noted, "Oscar deposed with ponderous gravity, standing in a characteristic attitude, with his left hand on his hip, and his right, holding his gloves, resting on the head of his cane. He was quietly dressed in a dark Chesterfield overcoat, with collar and cuffs of black velvet."[178]

As matters moved to the offending card, however, it became clear that the magistrate harbored doubts about the degree to which Queensberry's allegation warranted the exposure that would emerge from a trial. He retired from the court with Humphreys and Carson in order to see if the attorneys could reach a settlement. They refused. Carson was eager to raise the profile of the case by pursuing a cross-examination of the kind that should have been preserved for the criminal prosecution. "How long," Carson asked Wilde, "have you known Lord Alfred Douglas?"[179] Before Wilde could respond, Newton and Humphreys made the point that such an inquiry was inappropriate at this stage. Humphreys referred Carson to the case of *Regina v. Carden* (1879), which ruled that any cross-examination involving the hearing of evidence was not permitted. Carson, who would not be stopped in his tracks, claimed the case in question stated that an attorney "should not cross-examine with reference to the plea of

Fig. 13. "Spy" [Leslie Ward], cartoon of Charles Frederick Gill, *Vanity Fair*, 9 May 1891.

justification."[180] Still, he pointed out that *Regina v. Carden* "goes no further"; "[i]t does not," he added, "take away the ordinary right to cross-examine upon the question of guilty or not guilty." Carson proceeded to argue that, if the case was sent to trial, he would want to "ask certain questions to show how it was that Lord Queensberry came to write this card." Queensberry's purpose, Carson insisted, was "to do everything in his power to put a stop to the connection of his son with Mr. Oscar Wilde."[181] These exchanges were reproduced in miscellaneous newspapers. None of them, though, made explicit reference to the "certain foul epithets," as the *Pall Mall Gazette* called them, inscribed on the "uncovered card" that Wilde had collected from his club.[182]

Events moved apace. On 26 March 1895, a grand jury, which met at the Old Bailey to see if Wilde had a case to be answered, returned a "true bill" (i.e., an indictment) against Queensberry. Two days later, a hearing at the same court—where Carson and Gill appeared for the defense, and Sir Edward Clarke and Charles ("Willie") Mathews represented Wilde—scheduled the trial date. The *Globe* reported that "[u]nder ordinary circumstances the case would have been stood over to the next sessions, subject to the sanction of the court, in order to put in the plea of justification within a week of the next Sessions."[183] Queensberry, however, had expressed a wish to expedite the trial without delay. Mathews agreed, as did Justice Richard Henn Collins (fig. 14). The judge "thought it was very desirable that a case of this kind should be disposed of as quickly as possible."[184] Such urgency communicated the belief that the unseemliness of the alleged libel should not be allowed to fester even more. In all probability, the prospect of moving the case ahead speedily may have struck Wilde's counsel as one it would be wise not to argue against. A hastened trial would restrict the amount of time that Queensberry's defense could devote to digging up additional evidence in order to bolster the view that the accusation was in the public interest. On Saturday, 30 March, as promised, an amended plea of justification was ready. The plea not only identified ten of Wilde's sexual partners; it also made reference to "a certain immoral obscene work . . . entitled *The Picture of Dorian Gray*" and an "immoral and obscene work . . . entitled *The Chameleon*."[185] Both publications, this document claimed, represented "the relations[,] intimacies and passions of certain persons of sodomitical and unnatural habits[,] tastes and practices."[186]

By the time of the libel trial, most of the youths named in the plea had been subpoenaed. They had also, it appears, been carefully prepared should the moment arrive when they were called to give evidence. Exactly how they had been placed in this position bears close consideration, since both their commitment to testify at the libel trial and the nature of the evidence some of them gave during the Crown prosecution indicate that they were under considerable pressure to cooperate with Russell. Not long after Wilde was sent to jail, Douglas reflected on the ways in which Queensberry's solicitor and his two private detectives had treated these witnesses. In the letter that he prepared for the *Mercure de France*, Douglas claims that his father "went to clever and unscrupulous solicitors and spent two or three thousand pounds" to make sure the job was done thoroughly.[187] "The principal witnesses," Douglas explains, "were either

Fig. 14. "Quiz" [John Paget Mellor], cartoon of Justice Richard Henn Collins, *Vanity Fair*, 14 January 1893.

blackmailers or male prostitutes. They were approached by detectives who told them: 'If you will give evidence against that man you will receive a certain sum, and you will be screened from being prosecuted yourself; if you refuse to co-operate, you will in all probability be arrested.'"[188]

J. H. Wilson, in a forthright pamphlet that Wilde's supporters persuaded him not to make public, drew similar conclusions from the investigations that he undertook, shortly after Wilde's imprisonment, into Russell's questionable methods. Wilson claims that Russell threatened a witness—a man who was known to have perpetrated blackmail—with arrest by a police detective sitting in an adjacent room. In this situation, unless a witness produced the necessary evidence, he would himself be subject to prosecution. "This extortion of evidence by terror," Wilson sharply observes, "has a suspicious family resemblance to blackmailing itself. . . . By all means disbelieve a blackmailer's word, even when he has no interest to lie, but do not accept it, when he has been coerced."[189] Not all of the named individuals, however, were available to testify. Two years before, Maurice Schwabe had left for New Zealand before moving to Australia. Herbert Tankard held a position across the Channel in Calais. Still, Russell and his team had sufficiently intimidated Wilde's sexual partners to make sure they were ready to take the stand. They also paid them fees.[190]

There was, however, one crucial contact of Wilde's whose significance only emerged once the libel trial was in progress. The identity of this individual arose from Kerley's discussion with the actor and playwright Charles Brookfield, who had played the minor role of Lord Goring's valet in *An Ideal Husband*. Brookfield, who had with Jimmy Glover previously staged an unsparing burlesque of Wilde's *Lady Windermere's Fan* in 1892, directed Kerley toward an unidentified female prostitute who understood the places that Wilde frequented. She put Kerley in touch with Sophia Gray, the landlady at 3 Chapel Street, who had in her possession a trove of materials that he realized would substantiate Queensberry's allegation. Gray revealed that Alfred Taylor had taken rooms at the property during the second half of 1893. The spendthrift Taylor, however, failed to pay his rent. Accordingly, Gray withheld some of his belongings, including a leather hatbox, which was stuffed with documents. Once he had inspected this item, Kerley discovered that it contained checks, letters, and telegrams, including communications from Wilde. This was by far the greatest find that Russell's team had unearthed, since the materials inside—which referred to Atkins, Sydney Mavor, and others—indicated that Taylor served as a procurer of young men. As the courts would learn, Taylor played a principal role in a queer social circle whose company Wilde enjoyed. Kerley's discovery, however, did not occur in time for inclusion in Queensberry's plea.

What, we might wonder, went through Wilde's mind between the adjourned hearing that took place on 9 March 1895 and the plea that Russell submitted three weeks later? He continued to behave dishonestly to his lawyers. Just as he and Douglas had put the solicitor C. O. Humphreys's mind at rest that the libel had no basis, so too did they give the same reassurances to Sir Edward Clarke and Charles Mathews. In 1953, Travers Humphreys—when recalling how he was "given a brief as an extra junior to take a note of the evidence in this *cause célèbre*"—clarified that both Clarke and Mathews fully grasped the perils ahead should the defense present materials that might exonerate the marquess: "Reluctant as counsel were to embark upon what is always a dangerous step—prosecution for libel where the proposed defendant has already stated in effect his intention to plead justification, as Queensberry had—neither felt that the client's instructions could be ignored."[191] "[T]here was," Travers Humphreys insists, "nothing in the way of general knowledge of Wilde's homosexual proclivities."[192] Caspar Wintermans surmises that Wilde may have suggested there "was an exact parallel with his own case against 'Q'" and that of *Gatty v. Farquharson*.[193] Clarke, however, as we have seen in chapter 1 (66–68), had been unsuccessful in his defense against Gatty.

Wilde refused to hide from the public. On Monday, 1 April 1895, he, Douglas, and Constance attended a performance of *The Importance of Being Earnest*. This was, Sturgis observes, "an act of defiance."[194] By all accounts, Constance was visibly agitated. The theatre manager, Alexander, took the opportunity to urge Wilde to depart for the Continent. A handful of Wilde's other close friends expressed their apprehensiveness about the probable outcome of the suit. Harris was one. Even though he tends to embroider his memories with the benefit of hindsight, Harris claims that he had sufficient knowledge to understand that the two pilfered love letters to Bosie that had come to Queensberry's attention constituted enough evidence for Wilde to lose his case. "Take it from me, Oscar," Harris recalls saying, "you have not a ghost of a chance."[195] Harris states that, shortly before the trial opened, he invited Wilde to join him and George Bernard Shaw for lunch at the Café Royal to discuss the likelihood that the defense would annihilate Wilde's prosecution. Over their meal, Harris offered this advice:

> You should go abroad, and, as ace of trumps, you should take your wife with you. Now for the excuse; I would sit down and write such a letter as you alone can write to The Times. You should set forth how you have been insulted by the Marquis [*sic*] of Queensberry, and how you found out very soon that this was a mistake. No jury would give a verdict against a father, however mis-

> taken he might be. The only thing for you to do is therefore to go abroad, and leave the whole ring, with its gloves and ropes, its sponges and pails, to Lord Queensberry. You are a maker of beautiful things, and not a fighter. Whereas the Marquis of Queensberry takes joy only in fighting. You refuse to fight with a father under these circumstances.[196]

In 1910, Shaw had already mentioned that Harris offered this wise counsel, though Shaw stated that the discussion took place "on the eve of the Queensberry trial."[197] By this juncture, Wilde had reached a point of no return. Douglas burst in upon their conversation. Once he had heard what had passed, he protested Harris's opinion: "Such advice shows you are no friend of Oscar's."[198]

REGINA v. *JOHN SHOLTO DOUGLAS*: THE LIBEL TRIAL

There was an air of heightened anticipation when the libel proceedings began on the morning of Wednesday, 3 April 1895, at the Old Bailey. Wilde, if we are to believe his earliest biographer, Robert Harborough Sherard, arrived in grand style. "Oscar Wilde, the prosecutor," Sherard wrote in 1906, went "down to the court in a brougham with two horses and liveried servants."[199] Sherard, who later endured a rift with Wilde over the writer's extramarital affairs in 1897, believed such an arrogant display revealed that the plaintiff's "psychopathia was at this moment perilously tending towards megalomania and what that portends."[200] The *Pall Mall Gazette* suggested, contrary to Sherard's impression, that the moment Wilde took his seat at the solicitors' table, he maintained a dignified demeanor: "There was none of that tendency to flippancy on Mr. Wilde's part which some thought they detected at the police court. He was intensely grave."[201]

The court was packed. According to one journalist, it was "almost crowded to suffocation."[202] "People begged, bullied, and bribed for admission," the *Star* observed, "and the junior bar passed in on its wig and choked all the passage ways."[203] The attorneys who assembled in the courtroom were Sir Edward Clarke, Q.C., Mr. Charles Mathews, and Mr. Travers Humphreys (instructed by Mr. C. O. Humphreys) for Wilde; and Mr. Edward Carson, Q.C., Mr. C. F. Gill, and Mr. Arthur Edmund Gill (instructed by Mr. Charles Russell), who were present for the Marquess of Queensberry. Mr. Edward Besley, Q.C., and Mr. J. L. Monckton held watching briefs on behalf of Percy Sholto Douglas. Percy Douglas had legal representation because he knew one of the young men, Ernest Scarfe, who was mentioned in Queensberry's plea of justification. Scarfe, who was not called to give evidence, was referred to on several occasions in the subsequent proceedings (see, for example, 310 and 374 below). Meanwhile, the press could not bring itself to spell out the specifics of Queensberry's accusation. All that the *Pall Mall Gazette* would dare to mention was that the visiting card charged Wilde with "'posing as' A CRIMINAL OF A PARTICULARLY ODIOUS DESCRIPTION."[204] There was a further striking aspect to the assembled parties in the courtroom: many of them were Irish. This was not, it must be said, a point that struck English journalists as significant. It was left to the nationalist *United Ireland* to observe: "Irishmen were pretty much *en evidence* in this remarkable case. Mr. Wilde and Mr. Carson are Dublin men. Mr. Gill . . . is also an Irishman. So is Mr. Justice Henn Collins."[205] This shared background, however, hardly meant that the defense team and the judge had much else in common with Wilde, whose political orientation, especially on the question of Home Rule, contrasted with their unionist affiliations.

Clarke opened for the prosecution by outlining his distinguished client's career, his publications, his friendship with Alfred Douglas, and the blackmailing episode involving the letters that Alfred Wood had stolen. These observations culminated in the perfectly reasonable argument that it was "surely the most strange inference" to think that *The Picture of Dorian Gray* should reveal "Mr. Oscar Wilde as being a person showing himself to be addicted" to the "vices and weaknesses of which Dorian Gray is guilty," simply because Wilde was the author of the novel.[206] It was left to Mathews to examine the only witness for the prosecution, Sidney Wright, who explained that he had handed Queensberry's card to Wilde on 28 February. Clarke then proceeded to his examination of Wilde, who commented on Queensberry's harassment of him, as well as Wood's attempt at extortion. In the course of their exchanges, Wilde stated unequivocally that he was not the author of "The Priest and the Acolyte," a work he regarded as "bad, indecent literature."[207]

Yet Wilde's principled claims on art became difficult to substantiate. Carson began by pursuing a clever strategy to suggest that the plaintiff could not be trusted to tell the truth: "You stated at the commencement of your examination that you were thirty-nine years of age. I think you are over forty, isn't that so?" The query understandably put Wilde on his guard: "I have no intention of posing for a younger man at all." Carson capitalized on the ambiguity of Wilde's reply, since their exchange immediately led to another query of this kind: "do you happen to know what age Lord Alfred Douglas was or is?" Since Wilde failed to be precise in his response ("I think he will be twenty-five his next birthday"), Carson intimated that Wilde paid little heed to his responsibilities as an older man for a younger one.[208] Moreover, Wilde's apparent fuzziness in his otherwise innocuous comments on his own and Douglas's respective ages suggested that his subsequent answers might suffer from the same inexactitude.

Once Carson clarified a few matters regarding the venues where Wilde had enjoyed Douglas's companionship, he turned his sights on the *Chameleon*, particularly the "improper suggestions" that he detected in Douglas's poem, "Two Loves," and the homoerotic story "The Priest and the Acolyte," whose authorship remained unclear. Carson, however, reserved his most trenchant inquiries for Wilde's "Phrases and Philosophies for the Use of the Young." Even though Clarke would object that "[w]e are not dealing here with matters of literary criticism or literary taste," Carson proved dauntless in probing Wilde's oeuvre for instances of revealing criminal evidence, not artistic worth.[209] As a seasoned hand in deflecting moralistic criticism of his art, Wilde stood his ground fairly well. In the process of bombarding Wilde with questions about the slightest trace of "sodomitical" sentiment in these "Phrases," Carson would recite one of the amusing aphorisms aloud and then ask Wilde to defend it against the charge of immorality. "Listen sir," Carson commanded, as if he were about to teach Wilde a lesson of some kind. "Wickedness," Carson said, quoting one of Wilde's wittiest "Phrases," "is a myth invented by good people to account for the curious attractiveness of others." As often happened during this part of the proceedings, such sayings met with amusement in the courtroom. "Most stimulating to thought, I should say," Wilde declared. "If one tells a truth," Carson stated, this time reading aloud another of Wilde's epigrams, "one is sooner or later to be found out." "Yes," Wilde declared with breezy confidence, "that is a very pleasing paradox, but I don't set any high store on that as an axiom."[210] As members of the audience were chuckling at these retorts, Wilde's shining literary wit, whenever it could, outsmarted the defense.

Yet as he proceeded with the unremitting cross-examination, Carson's probing analysis of Wilde's deftly written works succeeded in wrong-footing the author. On more than one occasion, Wilde protested Carson's presumption that his works of fiction were direct expressions of personal sentiments. Marco Wan reminds us that Wilde "explicitly told Carson that [Carson's] attempt to read literature as legal evidence was a futile task because it was based on the realist assumption that life provided the only definitive meaning to a work of art."[211] "[Y]ou must remember," Wilde reiterated later in the exchanges, "that novels and life are different things."[212] But the moment Carson sought to align Wilde's homoerotic writings with the various sexual liaisons that he had allegedly enjoyed with young men, the reputedly "sodomitical" author made several small but fateful slips. Once Carson turned his attention to noteworthy passages in the 1890 text of *The Picture of Dorian Gray*, which had drawn so much wrath from critics who objected to its homosexual insinuations, Wilde found himself caught off-guard. Especially susceptible to Carson's inquiries was the passage where the adoring painter Basil Hallward says to the perpetually beautiful (though always treacherous) Dorian Gray: "I quite admit that I adored you madly."[213] "Have you," Carson inquired, "ever loved a young man, some twenty-one years younger than yourself, madly?" The question hit home. "No," Wilde answered, in an agitated state, "not madly, not madly."[214] This pivotal moment arguably took the trial out of Wilde's hands.

Once Carson adverted to one of the passionate letters that Wilde had written to Douglas, the telltale wording in *The Picture of Dorian Gray* seemed to strike a highly personal note. Carson selected various phrases from this intimate missive. "I know," Wilde professed to Douglas, "Hyacinthus, whom Apollo loved so madly, was you in Greek days."[215] The allusion to the Greek myth counted among Wilde's favorite classical references when honoring male homosexual love. After he had drawn the court's attention to similar sentiments in the correspondence, Carson asked Wilde: "Do you think that is a proper kind of letter to write?"[216] "It is a poem," Wilde declared defiantly, "and I have written other beautiful letters to Lord Alfred Douglas."[217] The statement, in principle, was true, since the French poet Pierre Louÿs had elaborated this line into a sonnet that appeared in Douglas's literary journal, the *Spirit Lamp*.[218] Yet, as Carson knew well, the letter had a contentious history. The moment Carson began asking about the financial premium one might put on this item of correspondence, which Wilde proudly described as a "beautiful letter" that constituted a "poem," the proceedings took a turn for the worse. Once Carson inquired if Wilde still had the reply that Douglas made to this "beautiful letter," Wilde appeared panicked that a copy of Douglas's correspondence might be in circulation. "Let me see—let me read the letter—let me see the letter," he exclaimed.[219] It transpired that Carson, who had been taunting Wilde, did not in fact possess it. But the wily lawyer caused tremendous unease by implying that he might have it on hand. "How much would you give now," Carson queried, "if you could get a copy?"[220] It was a foreboding inquiry.

Here the exchange returned to the delicate topic of the stolen letters that Clarke had already broached. Carson wanted to gain the fullest insights into Wilde's precise knowledge of homosexual blackmail. The relationship that had developed between the middle-aged author and the young blackmailer involved more than a reconciliation over the letters that Wood thieved from the suit of clothes Douglas had given him. Under Carson's exacting cross-examination, Wilde admitted that he had handed Wood various sums of money, from £2 to

£16, which might well have amounted to more than £40 in total. These expenditures, the court learned, had preceded the interviews that took place over the love letters. Such payments, Wilde tried to explain, were not for buying back pilfered correspondence. Yet when he was pressed to account for the reasons why he had parted with these not inconsiderable amounts, the court must have suspected that sexual services were involved. Wilde nonetheless insisted that he was following Douglas's instructions "to be kind to the young man." "He was," Wilde said of Wood, "in want of a situation and he wanted helping."[221] There was, Wilde revealed, a prehistory to his interview with Wood. Wilde had, as he gradually disclosed, become acquainted with him in early 1893, some weeks before the encounters with the blackmailers William Allen and Robert Cliburn. As Carson suggested, the unemployed Wood—who claimed to be a former clerk—had ties to the sociable Taylor, whom Wilde had known for a few months. Carson had evidence that Wood had at one time stayed for a while at Taylor's rooms in Little College Street, and Carson wanted to determine whether Taylor had procured Wood for Wilde. According to Wilde, the backstory differed. He maintained that his first encounter with Wood came in response to Douglas's request that he find a position for the young man. Douglas, Wilde recalled, encouraged Wood to go to the fashionable Café Royal on Regent Street: "Alfred Wood came in," he said, "and knowing me by sight, as many people do, came over to my table, and produced the telegram."[222] It transpired that once Wilde had met Wood at the café, he offered the young man supper at the Italian restaurant in the Hôtel de Florence on Rupert Street, Soho.

Carson wanted to know if anyone else, such as Taylor, had attended the dinner. At this juncture, he handed a paper to Wilde on which a name was written, which was clearly too sensitive to be uttered aloud: "Was that gentleman present on any occasion when you dined with him?"[223] As the Crown prosecution disclosed, the person in question was Maurice Salis Schwabe. Since Schwabe, as the lawyers knew, was the nephew-in-law of the solicitor general, Sir Frank Lockwood, the very mention of his name may well have pointed to the idea that Wilde's intimacies were too close to the center of power for comfort. Once Wilde stated that the unidentified gentleman was not present at the dinner in Rupert Street, the exchanges moved to highly contentious inquiries about Wood. "Did you," Carson probed, "ask him to your house in Tite Street?" "Never," Wilde replied.[224]

By this point, since this information did not appear in Queensberry's plea of justification, Wilde must have realized that a confession had very recently been extracted from Wood. Carson asked Wilde no fewer than three times whether he had ever entertained Wood at Tite Street. Once he had belabored Wilde with further inquiries about the different lodgings that Wood had used in early 1893, Carson set his sights on the substantial sums that Wilde had given to this young criminal. He commented that the theft of the correspondence had aroused such consternation that Wilde had consulted Sir George Lewis, with the goal of writing a solicitor's letter to Wood. As Carson pressed harder on this issue, the court discovered that in mid-April 1893 Cliburn had burst in upon Wilde at a dress rehearsal of *A Woman of No Importance*. "Did you think he was blackmailer?" Carson asked. "Connected," Wilde responded, "yes."[225] This was the nearest admission that Wilde was willing to make about the fact he had been negotiating with an extortionist. Yet in trying to deny that blackmail was Cliburn's principal aim, Wilde had begun to sound disingenuous. The more he attempted to explain a situation in which he had given various sums to men whom he swore had not tried to pressure him to part with money, the more difficult it became for anyone to believe that these funds came from a wellspring of generosity. There was something so amiss in the evidence that Carson shifted the focus to Wilde's numerous relationships with other young males. The list of these contacts was remarkably long, and he set before the court his knowledge of the dates, times, and places of these alleged encounters with a very high level of detail.

From this moment onward, Carson subjected Wilde to a fierce grilling about the occasions when these rendezvous had taken place. The encounters fell between the later months of 1892 and the middle of 1894. Meanwhile, the court learned that the assignations came to pass in sundry hotels, lodgings, and restaurants. The first in this inventory of Wilde's sexual partners was Edward Shelley, who at the time was employed by John Lane, one of Wilde's publishers. "Did you," Carson asked, "in February 1892 become fond of their office boy?"[226] It proved, at first, difficult to extract a straightforward answer. "I say I object to your description of Mr. Edward Shelley," Wilde observed, as if to suggest that the term "office boy" was demeaning. Carson brushed aside this response in order to confirm Shelley's age. He wished to know as well if Wilde thought Shelley a "good-looking boy": "No, I wouldn't call him so—an intellectual face," Wilde said.[227] The questioning then targeted Wilde's intimate knowledge of the clerk: "Did you put your hand on his person?"[228] Wilde denied that any such activity had taken place, though he admitted that he had spent extensive amounts of time in Shelley's company.

Once Carson had dispensed with Wilde's intimacy with Shelley, he turned to the affair with Alphonse Conway. Besides presenting in court three of the gifts that Wilde made to the young man (a signed photograph, an inscribed cigarette case, and a copy of W. Clark Russell's seafaring novel *The Wreck of the Grosve-*

nor [1877]), Carson went so far as to display two other items before the jury. The day's proceedings, in the words of the *Morning*, "culminated in a scene of excitement when Mr. Carson produced the clothes and walking-stick which Mr. Wilde admitted having given" to Conway.[229] Carson then confronted Wilde with a blunt inquiry about the visit to the Albion Hotel, Brighton: "Did [Conway] come into your bed that night?" The punishing cross-examination ended with a jolt when Carson posed a further threatening question: "Did you ever take another boy to the Albion?"[230]

Press reports varied in their opinions of Wilde's performance. The *Pall Mall Gazette*, for instance, withheld its judgment on the content of the exchanges by focusing instead on their quality. "The lawyer," it observed, "is a master of legal dialectic," while "Mr. Wilde is an excellent witness, in the sense that he appreciates all questions without any difficulty."[231] By comparison, the *Evening News* devoted much of a column to a list featuring Wilde's epigrammatic "gems," some of which had been aired in court; such wit served to balance the paper's descriptive account of the "strange and queer persons" whose names and activities had arisen during the proceedings.[232] Then again, Wilde failed to impress the liberal-minded *Daily Chronicle*. Kudos went instead to Queensberry's senior counsel, whose formidable skills in putting Wilde on the defensive drew the paper's resounding admiration: "under the cold white light of Mr. Carson's ruthless cross-examination [Wilde] became very restless, grew almost soprano in his denials and incessant in his gestures, and at last appealed for protection to the judge, claiming to be allowed certain suggestions with an absolute, positive denial once and for all, instead of being 'dragged through the ignominy' of denying every 'suggestion.'"[233] Since there is no other record of Wilde's appeal for "protection," one casts a measure of doubt on this otherwise thorough report. Still, the journalist leaves the impression that at moments during the ordeal Wilde was rattled.

On the morning of Thursday, 4 April 1895, Carson resumed his remorseless interrogation by trying to excavate as much information as he could about Wilde's visits to Alfred Taylor's rooms at 13 Little College Street. Many of Carson's questions must have taken Wilde aback, since they drew on the letters and telegrams that Kerley had recently retrieved from the hatbox that Sophia Gray, Taylor's landlady, had seized from Taylor many months earlier. Although Carson wanted to extract Wilde's thoughts on the unusual interior of Taylor's rooms (especially the fine furnishings, the "double set of curtains drawn across the windows" day and night, and the "strongly perfumed" atmosphere), he was mainly interested in the various homosexual contacts that Taylor had procured for the author: "How many young men," Carson asked, "did he introduce to you?"[234] It took a while before Wilde stuttered a possible figure: "I should think six—seven—eight."[235] "I like the society of young men," Wilde protested unrepentantly. "I delight in it."[236]

Once Carson moved through an inventory of the men whom Taylor had supplied for Wilde, he explored the plaintiff's personal history with Charles Parker. He asked Wilde to recall an incident that supposedly took place after an evening party held in a private room at a Soho restaurant in March 1893. "After dinner," Carson inquired, "did you say, turning to Charlie and in the presence of Taylor and in the presence of William his brother, 'This is the boy for me'?" "Most certainly not," Wilde remonstrated.[237] "Did you ever," Carson asked probingly, at a later point of the proceedings, "bring any boys into your bedroom at the Savoy?" "No, sir," Wilde replied, in one of many flat denials of such shocking allegations.[238] These and other similar queries followed a grilling that persisted in disconcerting Wilde. When put under pressure to remember a teenage servant named Walter Grainger, whom he had met through Douglas in 1893, Wilde was faced with the following provocation from Carson: "Did you ever kiss him?" "Oh, no, never in my life," Wilde declared in flustered tones, only to follow up with a remark that disclosed his sexual predilection for young males: "he was a peculiarly plain boy."[239] This already unfavorable situation worsened when Wilde confessed that he had indulged in no such intimacy because Grainger was "so very unfortunately—very ugly."[240]

Carson unflinchingly probed the broad extent of Wilde's private contacts of this kind. There was, for example, Wilde's friendship with the twenty-year-old Atkins, whom Wilde described as a "pleasant, good-natured fellow who was going on the music hall stage."[241] Wilde, the jurors learned, had taken Atkins on an all-expenses-paid trip to Paris. On this occasion, Wilde commented that he had shared Atkins's company with the mysterious individual whose identity was kept secret ("the gentlemen whose name you handed up to me").[242] Besides learning about a meeting at the Café Royal, the courtroom heard that Atkins, the unmentionable Schwabe, and himself occupied rooms in a private hotel located at 29 Boulevard des Capucines. Wilde confirmed that he had dined at the Café Julien, and when asked whether he had paid for Atkins's hair to be fashionably curled, he denied it, since that would have been a "silly thing" for Atkins to do. Ever ready to demonstrate that he knew the places in Paris familiar to Wilde, Carson went to so far as to ask if the coiffure, which Atkins presumably had mentioned in his witness statement, was styled "[a]t Pascal's the hairdressers under the Grand Hotel."[243] Clearly, the investigations into Wilde's personal life had burrowed deep into the French capital.

Doggedly, Carson concentrated on further names that elaborated the breadth of Wilde's encounters with young men. One of them, as we have seen, was Conway. Another was Ernest Scarfe, a young man of twenty-five whom Wilde had met in December 1893, not long after Scarfe had returned from the gold diggings in Australia.[244] Wilde's point of contact with Scarfe, as with Charles Parker and William Parker, was Alfred Taylor, who had brought the young man to see Wilde at Geneux's private hotel in St. James's Place. "Did you ever kiss him?" Carson asked, "[o]r attempt to have indecencies with him?" As usual, Wilde denied the allegations. He conceded, however, to having given Scarfe a cigarette case. "It is," Wilde stated boldly, "my custom to present cigarette cases." (The defiant remark prompted laughter.) The court was likely taken aback when Carson produced the item for all to see. "This was it?" he queried.[245] "I have," Wilde responded, in an attempt to regain his composure, "given so many cigarette cases I can hardly verify them."[246]

The same was true of a similar item that Wilde had bestowed on Mavor. In October 1892, having known the man for just one month, Wilde spent—as Carson had learned from the vendor's ledger—"four pounds eleven shillings and sixpence" on a cigarette case, inscribed to "S. A. Mavor." "What did you give him the cigarette case for?" Carson inquired, in tones that probably insinuated that the item might have been presented in return for sex. This idea became more evident when Carson elicited the following information about Wilde's relations with Mavor: "He stayed with me at an hotel in Albemarle Street."[247] "Did any indecencies take place between you?" Carson predictably inquired.[248] The fact that Wilde admitted that Mavor had brought his luggage, when it was the case that it would only have taken this guest twenty minutes to drive to his Notting Hill home, cast doubt on Wilde's calm-and-collected claim that the stay-over was simply a sign of his desire for companionship. "Yes," Wilde said, "it amused him to be my guest, it is a very nice, charming hotel."[249]

Carson concluded his cross-examination by dwelling for some time on the month-long stay that Wilde enjoyed at the Savoy in March 1893. He focused on the statement that Antonio Migge, a freelance masseur at the hotel, had made to Russell about an unidentified boy who was allegedly spotted in Wilde's bed. Carson then quizzed Wilde about the periods he had spent in a Paris hotel, this time not in Atkins's company: "did you bring boys into your bed?" "Never," said Wilde.[250] The term "boy," even though it was occasionally used to refer to men in their early twenties, resonated with the sense that Wilde might have been engaging in sex with males who, if they were in other-sex relationships, would be considered underage. Carson seized on the opportunity to find out the way that Wilde might define a "boy." Wilde declared, should anyone have thoughts to the contrary, that it meant a young man in a specific age range. "I have many friends in Paris," he proclaimed, "from eighteen to twenty."[251]

Once Carson had concluded his cross-examination on the Thursday morning, Clarke tried to rebalance the regrettable turns that had taken place in the proceedings. He began by reading aloud the browbeating correspondence that Queensberry had sent to both his son Alfred and his former father-in-law, Alfred Montgomery. These dismaying private letters, Clarke assumed, would give the desired impression that Wilde was right not to capitulate to Queensberry's demand that the friendship with Douglas should come to an immediate end: "I thought it right," Wilde said, "to entirely disregard it."[252] The same idea, it seemed, could be made when Clarke alluded to Wilde's public defense of *The Picture of Dorian Gray* in July 1890. To those hostile critics who had imputed that the novel was a sexually corrupt work, Wilde made pointed repudiations. Clarke, too, drew attention to the fact that the line from the 1890 text of the novel, in which Basil Hallward admits to Dorian Gray that he adores him "madly, extravagantly, absurdly," was carefully revised in the 1891 version. In response to Carson's previous suggestion that "some people upon reading the book . . . might reasonably think that it did deal with sodomy," Wilde had already stated that he had emended a passage that was "liable to misconstruction."[253] He said he had done so on the advice of the recently deceased Walter Pater: the eminent Oxford critic whose writings left a deep impression on Wilde's thinking about art. Once he had read aloud the corrected excerpt, Clarke declared that the matter was settled: "I think substantially, my lord, that closes the passage."[254]

There were other concerns, especially Wilde's links with Charles Parker and Alfred Taylor, that Clarke addressed in a similarly exculpatory spirit. He mentioned, as Carson had done before, that both of these men had been arrested (along with eighteen other male partygoers) in the Fitzroy Street raid, which had occurred on 12 August 1894. Wilde, who appears not to have had any foreknowledge of the party, said that he had learned about the arrests through a press report in the *Daily Chronicle*, as well as from intelligence that he had gathered from Taylor himself: "He told me that it was a benefit concert that he had been given a ticket for, that when he arrived at the house there was dancing going on and he was asked to play the piano, that two music hall singers were expected to arrive in costume."[255] At the height of the festivities, the police came in and apprehended the guests. Clarke wished to suggest that the fines a magistrate had imposed upon the attendees were for "having music and dancing only."[256] Yet, as Carson had already intimated, the police raid involved detaining a group of queer men, some of whom were known criminals and blackmailers.[257] The cross-dressed Arthur Marling, who appeared in the police court wearing a stunning black-and-gold gown, was a point of reference. "Isn't Marley," Carson had previously asked, getting the performer's name slightly wrong, "a notorious sodomite?"[258] Wilde claimed, quite honestly, that he had no knowledge of the man, just as he had no acquaintance with anyone else who attended the party, besides Parker and Taylor. To Clarke, who stressed that the charges against the arrested men were summarily dropped, it was crucial that Wilde agree there was no "imputation of blame" on Taylor for what had happened at the party. "None," Wilde said. "I thought it a most monstrous thing."[259] As we can tell, Carson was making every effort to associate Wilde with the arrested revelers.

Clarke then turned to samples of the correspondence that Wilde had received from Shelley. "I have had a very horrible interview with my father," Shelley had written on 27 March 1893, "[t]he stupid brutal insults of Vigo Street [the publishing business that he had recently left] are preferable to this."[260] Even though the court learned that Shelley subsequently secured a modest position in the City of London, the clerkship did not pay him enough to survive. Each subsequent letter that Clarke read out in turn articulated the young man's neediness: "Will you try," Shelley petitioned Wilde on 14 June 1894, "to get me something to do[?]"[261] In one missive after another, Shelley's tone grew increasingly desperate. As he heard these sad declarations spoken in court, Wilde admitted that he had given Shelley £5. The final item of correspondence, which dated from 28 August 1894, contained the following bleak line: "I am afraid sometimes that I am not very sane."[262] Wilde assured Clarke that his relations with Shelley, who seemed unhinged, were never sexual.

As Clarke referred to the young men whose company Wilde had enjoyed, he made a point of confirming the innocuous nature of these friendships. Conway, the court discovered, had attended "a children's tea" while Constance Wilde was present.[263] And when it came to Alfred Wood, Fred Atkins, Charles Parker, and William Parker, Clarke wanted Wilde to acknowledge that he had no "reason whatever for suspecting them as immoral or disreputable persons."[264] "None whatsoever," Wilde stated flatly.[265] As Clarke moved toward wrapping up his examination, he drew attention to the fact that Wilde had for many months been working with C. O. Humphreys to see if a solicitor's letter might bring Queensberry's hostilities to a close. He pointed out that on 11 July 1894 Humphreys had said that his client was ready to give the marquess "the opportunity of retracting [his] assertions and insinuations in writing, with an apology for having made them. If this be done at once, it may prevent litigation."[266] The jury therefore discovered that the present libel action marked the outcome of a deepening antagonism that Wilde had done his best to neutralize. Humphreys's letter, as a further document showed, turned out to be futile. On 18 July 1894, after a meeting with Humphreys, Queensberry stated that the time had arrived for himself to hand over incriminating evidence about Wilde "to the police authorities."[267]

At this moment, when Clarke asked Wilde to confirm whether he had taken any notice of the marquess's threat, a juror interrupted the proceedings with a request for information. The jury wished to know whether the editor of the *Chameleon* counted as a "personal friend" of Wilde's—presumably because of Wilde's presence in a journal that included "The Priest and the Acolyte," which had been the focus of Carson's earlier cross-examination.[268] In response to this inquiry, Wilde stated that had never seen or heard anything about the story before it was in print, though he stated that he had met the young editor, who was also the author of the short fiction, at the rooms of a friend.[269] On that note, the evidence for the prosecution came to an end, with no one else called to the stand. The only proviso that Clarke wished the judge to grant was the opportunity "to call evidence in rebuttal" of any further claims that the defense might make.[270] Justice Collins assented to this request, though he commented, in words that implied there were matters afoot that could further undermine the plaintiff's case: "It may possibly be that some evidence might be sprung upon you."[271]

The possibility of "some evidence" springing forth upon Wilde was very strong. When Carson opened his case for the defense, he made it manifestly clear that he was ready to call a long line of witnesses who would testify that Taylor was a procurer of lads "for sodomitic purposes."[272] "You will hear," he said, "the kind of life that this man Taylor lived, the extraordinary den he kept in Little College Street with its curtains always drawn."[273] This lurid description assuredly evoked an image that Taylor had been running a male whorehouse in a seamy area close to the Houses of Parliament. No sooner had Carson raised the specter that Atkins, the Parker brothers, and Wood might enter the witness-box than he proceeded to lambast Wilde's writings, the impassioned letters to Douglas, and the dubious connection with the *Chameleon*. All of these documents, Carson claimed, proved that the Irish author "was either in sympathy with, or addicted to, immoral and sodomitic habits."[274] He then returned once more to *The Picture of Dorian Gray*, on this occasion reading aloud the long passage where Dorian Gray's mentor, the aesthete Lord Henry Wotton, charms the fine-looking young man with deftly cadenced phrases that advocate forgetting "the maladies of mediævalism, and return[ing] to the Hellenic ideal."[275]

The Hellenic ideal, from Carson's perspective, was implicitly a byword for sodomy. As he took up much of the Thursday afternoon with subjecting Wilde's novel to a ham-fisted critique of the Ancient Greek love of male beauty, Carson wanted to demonstrate that *The Picture of Dorian Gray* was the "story of a man corrupted by another man and who by such corruption is brought to commit, or the book suggests he has committed, the sodomitic vice of which we will hear a good deal more."[276] For the rest of the available time, Carson threw into doubt Wilde's disarming account of the various meetings that had taken place with the trio of blackmailers: Wood, Allen, and Cliburn. The truth, he contended, would be heard from Wood himself. "Wood," he commented ominously, "will describe to you—I am not going to anticipate it now—how time after time Mr. Oscar Wilde, almost from the commencement of the acquaintance, adopted filthy and immoral practices with him."[277]

At 10.30 a.m. on Friday, 3 April, when Carson resumed his vigorous case for the defense, it became obvious that the trial threatened to enter an excruciating phase. Wilde now faced the prospect of the sundry young men who had been identified and questioned by Kerley, Littlechild, and Russell entering the court and divulging, one after another, each and every sexual act they had performed with him. It appears that the letter Wilde had arranged to be hand-delivered to Constance at Tite Street was written at this point. He urged her not to permit anyone to enter his bedroom or sitting-room. "See no one," he told her, "but your friends."[278] Wilde feared the worst. Particularly troubling on that Friday morning was the likelihood that Charles Parker would testify. Characterized by Carson as "a respectable, credible witness," this scoundrel had been serving as a gunner in the Royal Artillery for the past six months.[279] Carson solemnly presented Parker as a soldier who "now bears . . . an excellent character."[280] Parker should, Carson intoned, be recognized as a spotless member of Her Majesty's armed forces: "He comes here and he will come here with great reluctance. Tracked out and asked the truth which was brought home to him by the knowledge we had, he has to tell truth, and I regret that he has to come here, and I regret that I shall have to examine him in connection with my learned friends to prove all this before a prurient public, who will be in no wise benefited by hearing the details of his evidence."[281]

At this point, Carson transferred the court's attention to Conway, upon whom Wilde had lavished various gifts: "he procures him a set of clothes and he dresses him up like a gentleman"—all in the name, it seems, of making Conway look as if he were a "proper person" with whom Wilde could associate in public.[282] At the moment the court might have assumed that Conway was also waiting in the wings to take the stand, Clarke approached his colleague, tugged him by the sleeve, and asked if they might confer for a moment. There was not, as Clarke knew, any point in pursuing the case further. He advised Wilde to depart from the courtroom, which Wilde did (discreetly) through a side door.

In an essay reflecting on the events that transpired the moment the libel trial collapsed, Alfred Douglas suggested that an acquaintance had been waiting in the street outside the Old Bailey to alert Wilde to the activities that Queensberry's defense team had been undertaking in order to secure witnesses for a Crown prosecution. As Douglas observed, Russell had been working closely with Bernard Abrahams, whose underhand business involved brokering deals between male blackmailers and their queer victims:

> The principal witnesses [in the criminal trials that followed the failed libel suit] were without exception either blackmailers or male prostitutes. They were approached by detectives who told them: "If you will give evidence against that man you will receive a certain sum, and you will be screened from being prosecuted yourself; if you refuse to co-operate, you will in all probability be arrested." This procedure has been described to me by persons who have been approached in that way. One of them came of his own accord to forewarn Mr. Wilde against what was going on. This is what he told me in the presence of two witnesses: "After the proceedings at the Police Court I was standing in the street when Mr. Bernard Abrahams came up to me and asked me if I was willing to go to ——'s office to denounce Mr. Wilde under oath.
>
> "I don't see why I should," I replied. "I have never had any dealings with Mr. Wilde in my life."
>
> "'Oh, that doesn't matter,' said Abrahams. 'If you will do as you are told, you will have no cause for complaint.'"
>
> Mr. Bernard Abrahams, a well-known lawyer and notorious blackmailer, was employed by Lord Queensberry's solicitors to carry out much of the dirty work.[283]

If this warning was indeed given, it appears that it took effect. At this point, Wilde had to determine his next steps, which involved responding to pleas from friends urging him to abscond by crossing the English Channel.

Once Wilde had exited from the Old Bailey, Clarke did his utmost to mitigate the considerable damage that the failed suit had wrought upon his client. In an unavoidable move that financially ruined Wilde, Clarke resolved that the case should be dropped, since it was now unmistakable that the proceedings were about to move on to "long evidence," in mortifying ways that would lead to "an investigation of matters of the most appalling character." "I now," he continued, "interpose to say that on behalf of Mr. Oscar Wilde I would ask to withdraw from the prosecution." Clarke's request entailed a significant qualification: the verdict of "Not Guilty" should refer only to "that part of the particulars which is connected with publication of *Dorian Gray* and the publication of the *The Chameleon*."[284] Justice Collins would not countenance such a proposal: "There can be no terms; there can be no limitation; the verdict must be 'guilty' or 'not guilty.'"[285] Once the judge agreed with Carson that the defense was prepared to accept the verdict, the clerk of the court turned to the foreman of the jury to respond to their conclusion about Queensberry's allegation. "You say that the defendant is 'not guilty' and that is the verdict of you all?"[286] In the process of assenting, however, the foreman added a phrase that was arguably an even more problematic one for Wilde. Just before the proceedings came to an end, Justice Collins mentioned, as Carson had also requested, that Queensberry could only be cleared of the crime if the libel had been published for the benefit of the public. "Yes," said the foreman, "and also that it was published for the public benefit."[287]

In principle, the only matter left to arrange was the discharge of Queensberry and the confirmation of Wilde's responsibility for the costs. The *St. James's Gazette* noted that the marquess "was very warmly greeted by an enormous crowd when he left the court."[288] Matters, however, hardly stopped there. Queensberry, Russell, and sections of the press had their own ideas about exploiting Wilde's libel suit even further for the public benefit. At 11.15 a.m., once Queensberry left the court a free man, events began moving rapidly against Wilde.

WILDE'S ARREST

Soon after Wilde's libel trial concluded in abrupt failure, Justice Collins wrote to congratulate Carson on doing such a fine job of the defense: "I never heard a more powerful speech or a more searching [cross-]exam[ination]."[289] The consensus was that Carson's performance had been a tour de force. Still, *United Ireland*, given its political antipathy to Carson, found much to deplore in what it believed was his scheme for ingratiating himself with the English judiciary:

> Mr. Carson, Q.C., has been very much lionised over his remorseless cross-examination of Mr. Oscar Wilde. He has been successful, undoubtedly, in turning that notorious person from the position of a plaintiff in a court of justice to that of a prisoner in the dock, and *dénouements* of that kind are most entertaining to the John Bull fraternity. We have little interest in Mr. Carson's success, and we cannot admire very much the methods by which he has grown into prominence as a lawyer. He was one of the most offensive and

> intolerant of the gang of unscrupulous law-hacks who did the odious work of Mr. [Arthur] Balfour in the days of his coercion, and he is one of the bitterest enemies to legislation in favour of Ireland of any that sit on the benches of the House of Commons.[290]

The paper noted that Carson had reputedly declared "he never had a much easier case."[291] It went on to note wryly the apparent compliment that Carson paid to Clarke's own dignified prosecution: "the opening part of the case," Carson said, "was, under the circumstances, and in face of the tremendous difficulties under which he laboured, a real masterpiece."[292] There is more than a hint of sarcasm in this account of Carson's presumed condescension.

As for Clarke, he recalled that he had "hoped and expected that [Wilde] would take the opportunity of escaping the country"; "I believe," Clarke added, "he would have found no difficulty in doing so."[293] Harris claims that Mathews spoke privately to Wilde earlier on the Friday morning. "If you wish it," Mathews is supposed to have said, "Clarke and I will keep the case going and give you time to get to Calais."[294] Clarke and Mathews, had they harbored these sentiments, were hardly alone in entertaining this prospect. Immediately, the press received public statements from both Queensberry and Russell. The marquess shared with reporters the warning that he had sent to Wilde: "If the country allows you to leave, all the better for the country; but if you take my son with you, I will follow you, wherever you go, and shoot you!"[295] Later, the *Sun* carried a report that Queensberry (who evidently thought twice about the wording of this missive) wished to correct the idea that he had fired off this letter directly after the trial: "The message was sent some days ago, and not after the trial ended. Lord Queensberry did not say he would shoot Mr. Wilde. What he said was that if he persuaded his misguided son to go with him, he would feel quite justified in following him, Wilde, and shooting him, did he feel inclined to do so. And were he worth the trouble."[296] As Stratmann points out, the marquess's principal aim was to separate Lord Alfred from Wilde; he also wished to have no part in any prosecution, since he was already in debt because of the considerable legal costs that his defense had incurred.[297]

Both the press and the police believed that Wilde would head to a port. With journalists tracking his every move, Wilde traveled to the Holborn Viaduct Hotel, which, according to the *Illustrated Police Budget*, he reached at "about half-past eleven."[298] As observers would have gathered, the location of the hotel was advantageous. Only a few minutes' drive from the Old Bailey, it occupied the frontage of Holborn Viaduct Railway Station (opened in 1874); the station was a terminus for the London, Chatham, and Dover Railway. From here, Wilde could have readily made his way to the major Channel seaport of Dover, should he have tried to defy the police by attempting the crossing to France.

Reynolds's Newspaper, which carried extensive coverage of Wilde's appearances in court, provided a thorough account of his journey to the hotel:

> Before the carriage had stopped at the door of the hotel, he thrust his arm and a gold-headed cane out of the window, and signalling to a man who stood there, apparently waiting, hoarsely cried, "The verdict, not guilty!" Afterwards, Lord Alfred Douglas was also seen to go into the hotel.
>
> There is some ground for supposing that the "prosecutor" had appointed the Viaduct Hotel as a rendezvous with his particular friends. Within half an hour of his arrival there, several gentlemen arrived hurriedly, and were conducted at once to the rooms which have been reserved for Mr. Wilde since Thursday. The brougham [a four-wheeled carriage], with two smart little brown horses, was driven slowly up and down the viaduct, pausing once while the coachman received instruction from Lord Alfred Douglas, who came out bare-headed with the hall porter. These movements were closely watched in a number of interests, and it is reported that Scotland Yard [i.e., the headquarters of the London Metropolitan Police] was keeping a provisional eye on the hotel.[299]

The *Echo* added information about the crowds that had congregated so that they could witness Wilde's movements: "Outside the hotel and at the approach to Holborn Viaduct Station a dense crowd had assembled. The rumour was that Wilde intended to make a dash for the Continent by the 5.30 train. This was at eleven o'clock in the forenoon."[300]

Wilde had lunch at the hotel, which was close to his solicitors' offices, from 12.30 p.m. to 1.30 p.m., with Ross, Bosie, and Percy Douglas.[301] The three supporters, like Clarke, also advised Wilde to flee the country, though Wilde resisted the idea. Nearly all of Wilde's friends and family members were astonished that he stayed put. Max Beerbohm was baffled. "Poor Oscar!," he wrote to Ada Leverson from New York City: "Why did he not go away while he could?"[302] As Merlin Holland has pointed out, *Bradshaw's Railway Guide* reveals that there were cross-Channel departures until 9.45 p.m. that evening.[303] Possibly, Wilde realized that the authorities would impede him from traveling to France. The *Daily Telegraph,* for example, reported that once the warrant had been issued "the police sent out a description of Mr. Wilde . . . and all the termini in London were watched by detectives." "The description," it added, "was also sent by telegraph to the chiefs of police in British ports, with urgent requests that he might be arrested at sight."[304]

It is not known whether Wilde received these warnings. By the time he had sat down for luncheon with his friends at the Holborn Viaduct Hotel, he could tell that he was in a serious quandary. He knew for certain that he could not face the press. *Reynolds's Newspaper* reported that Percy Douglas spoke on behalf of his brother and Wilde to a reporter from the *Sun*:

> Lord Douglas of Hawick said Mr. Wilde felt quite unable at the moment to bear seeing anyone. The young lord, however, added that on Mr. Wilde's behalf he was willing to answer any questions he could. He was, he said, himself, together with his brother, Lord Alfred, under subpoena for the prosecution. He himself would have been quite willing to go into the box, and his brother was most anxious to be allowed to do so, and was exceedingly grieved that Mr. Wilde had prevented him. It was to prevent that—and because he felt that "no man could bear to have every little act of indiscretion of his life, and every word and thought produced against him they perverted in the basest way and placed in the worst possible light," that Mr. Wilde had resolved to retire from the prosecution.
>
> "You may say from me myself," went on Lord Douglas of Hawick, "that I, and every member of our family, excepting my father, disbelieve absolutely and entirely the allegations of the defence. It is, in my opinion, simply a part of the persecution which my father has carried on against us ever since I can remember. I think Mr. Wilde and his counsel to blame for not showing, as they could have done, that was the fact."[305]

Percy Douglas added that Wilde "had no thoughts of immediately leaving London, and would stay to face whatever might be the result of the proceedings."[306]

In light of Percy Douglas's comments, Wilde issued a statement to the *Evening News* about his unwillingness to allow Alfred Douglas to take the stand during the trial:

> It would have been impossible for me to have proved my case without putting Lord Alfred Douglas in the witness-box against his father.
>
> Lord Alfred Douglas was extremely anxious to go into the box, but I would not let him do so.
>
> Rather than put him in so painful a position I determined to retire from the case, and to bear on my own shoulders whatever ignominy and shame might result from my prosecuting Lord Queensberry.[307]

It is perhaps a sign that Wilde was so unsure of his next move that he made a visit to the offices of his onetime solicitor Sir George Lewis, who had washed his hands of Queensberry. "I am powerless to do anything," Lewis is reported to have told Wilde. "If you had the sense to bring Lord Queensberry's card to me in the first place," Lewis observed, "I would have torn it up and thrown it in the fire, and told you not to make a fool of yourself."[308] Wilde returned from Lewis's offices in Ely Place to the nearby Holborn Viaduct Hotel, and then traveled in a brougham behind Douglas, his brother Percy, and Ross to the London and Westminster Bank in St. James's Square. Douglas jumped out of his cab and cashed a check made out to "Self" for £200.[309] The *Echo* reported that during this part of the afternoon a cab containing two detectives followed Wilde's carriage "down Holborn Viaduct, up Hatton Garden, again back to Holborn Circus, and then to Ely Place."[310] Wilde, meanwhile, drove on to the Cadogan Hotel, 75 Sloane Street, which he reached shortly after 3.00 p.m. The reason for heading to this hotel was that Douglas had been staying there, according to Harris, "for the past four or five weeks."[311] At the Cadogan Hotel, Wilde had the support of Alfred Douglas, Robert Ross, and another loyal friend Reggie Turner. Wilde asked Ross to visit Constance and inform her of what happened. "Ross did this," Harris reports, "and had a very painful scene: Mrs. Wilde wept and said, 'I hope Oscar is going away abroad.'"[312]

In the meantime, Russell had been moving briskly, at Queensberry's urging, to encourage the director of public prosecutions to arrest Wilde. Once the libel trial collapsed, Russell presented the Hon. Hamilton Cuffe with the following letter, which also quickly appeared in the press:

> 37 Norfolk Street, Strand
>
> To Hon. Hamilton Cuffe, Esq.,
> Director of Public Prosecutions
> The Treasury, Whitehall
>
> Dear Sir,—
>
> In order that there may be no miscarriage of justice, I think it my duty at once to send you a copy of our witnesses' statements, together with a shorthand copy of the trials.
>
> Yours faithfully,
> Charles Russell[313]

Cuffe immediately took action. He spoke with the home secretary (H. H. Asquith), the attorney general (Sir Robert Reid), and the solicitor general (Sir Frank Lockwood). Asquith determined that Wilde should be arrested. By 3.30 p.m., Inspector Brockwell of Scotland Yard, accompanied by Mr. Angus Lewis from the Treasury, which provided legal services to central government departments, made their way from Whitehall to Bow Street Magistrates' Court, where they appeared before Sir John Bridge (fig. 15) in order to apply for a warrant to

Fig. 15. "Spy" [Leslie Ward], cartoon of Sir John Bridge, *Vanity Fair*, 25 April 1891.

apprehend Wilde. The magistrate was so troubled by the allegations that he adjourned his court and traveled with Brockwell and Lewis to the Treasury, where he could consult the documents that Russell had prepared on Queensberry's behalf. On returning to court just before 5.00 p.m., Sir John Bridge signed the warrant, which he handed to Brockwell.[314] The inspector proceeded to Scotland Yard, where, within ten minutes of his arrival, a message was relayed to all district stations of the Metropolitan force: "Oscar Wilde is wanted by the police." Brockwell handed the warrant to Detective Inspector Charles Richards and Detective Sergeant Allen, who took a cab to the Cadogan Hotel.

Douglas had been deeply troubled by the prospect of Wilde's arrest. Sometime during the afternoon, he departed from the Cadogan Hotel in order to visit the House of Commons, where he wished to discover the moves that the government had made: "I went . . . to see my cousin, George Wyndham, and asked him to find out what the authorities intended to do. Wyndham saw me in the lobby and, after making enquiries in the House, came out and told me that Sir Robert Reid had told him there was to be a prosecution. I went back to the Cadogan Hotel and found there, not Oscar Wilde, but a letter in which he told me he had been arrested and would have to pass the night at Bow Street, and asking me to see various people on the question of bail, and also to come to Bow Street to try and see him."[315] In Douglas's absence, journalists lined Sloane

Street awaiting the arrest. By 5.00 p.m., Thomas Marlowe, a sympathetic reporter from the *Star*, asked if he could communicate urgent news to Wilde at the hotel. Since Wilde declined to meet the journalist, Marlowe informed Ross that a tape message had reached his newspaper stating that a warrant had been issued.

Shortly after 6.00 p.m., the police officers Richards and Allen entered the hotel in order to escort Wilde to the police headquarters. The *Morning Leader* claimed that the hotel staff informed Richards that Wilde "was not there"; "[t]his," the paper added, "was to ward off what was thought to be a necessary intrusion." The officer in turn stated that "it would be dangerous to trifle with him."[316] He thus made his way to Wilde's rooms. The *Echo*, which claimed to rely on an eyewitness account, described Wilde's reaction when "they found their man": "In the room were two young men. Wilde was seated by the fireplace in a saddle-bag chair, calmly smoking a cigarette. He raised his inquiring eyes to the intruders. Inspector Richards said, "Mr. Wilde, I believe?" Wilde languidly responded, "Yes! Yes!" According to our enterprising contemporary, from which we still quote, the floor of the room was strewn with some eight or nine copies of evening papers which had evidently been hastily scanned and then thrown aside."[317]

The *Illustrated Police Budget*, which also noted that Wilde was found "calmly smoking a cigarette and drinking a brandy and soda," conjured a similar image of his arrest; it printed an illustration in which miscellaneous newspapers—including, conspicuously, a copy of the *Star*—are scattered across the carpet of Room 53 (fig. 16).[318] As we know from Richards's testimony during the pretrial hearing, he and Allen informed Wilde of the charges: "We told the prisoner: 'Mr. Wilde, we are police officers. A warrant has been issued for your apprehension for committing some indecent offence with a male person.' He said: 'Yes. Where shall I be taken?' I told him: 'You will have to go with me now to Scotland Yard, and then on to Bow Street.' The prisoner asked: 'Can I have bail?' And I replied: 'I don't think you can.'"[319]

Before departing from the Cadogan, Wilde left the following letter for Douglas, who was still at Westminster:

> My dear Bosie, I will be at Bow Street Police Station tonight—no bail possible I am told. Will you ask Percy, and George Alexander and [Lewis] Waller, at the Haymarket, to give bail.
>
> Would you also wire Humphreys to appear at Bow Street for me. Wire to 41 Norfolk square, W.
>
> Also, come to see me. Ever yours Oscar[320]

Fig. 16. "The Arrest of Oscar Wilde: The Pet of London Society, One of Our Most Successful Playwriters and Poets, Arrested on a Horrible Charge," *Illustrated Police Budget*, 13 April 1895: 8.

Around this time, Ross also received Wilde's instructions to visit the family home in Tite Street in order to salvage the manuscripts of several works, including an unfinished play, *A Florentine Tragedy*, which Wilde had recently been developing. Once Ross and a friend (possibly Adey) entered Wilde's study, they were not able to locate the materials Wilde requested, but witnessed instead "all of the published MSS . . . lying about in various fragmentary states."[321] To Ross, one thing was clear: "someone familiar with the author's writing had been there before us."[322] Russell's henchmen had likely broken into the property in hopes of locating any documents in Wilde's handwriting that might provide further evidence of his criminal activities. At this point, Ross bundled items of Wilde's clothing into an overnight bag.

After the arrest had taken place, the Central News Agency issued a bulletin: "The warrant for the arrest of Oscar Wilde was executed by Inspector Richards, of Scotland Yard, who, with Sergeant Allen, proceeded to the Cadogan Hotel, Sloane Street, shortly after six o'clock, and arrested the prisoner. He appeared somewhat surprised when the charge was read over to him, but he made no reply, and was immediately taken to New Scotland Yard and handed over to Inspector Brockwell, who held the warrant."[323] "Wilde," the *Illustrated Police Budget* went on to note, "then passed over to a couch, picked up his overcoat, and was assisted in putting it on by one of the young men present. Carefully he lifted and adjusted his hat. He grasped his suede gloves in one hand and seized his stick with the other." The same newspaper added that just before his departure in police custody, Wilde "threw away the end of a cigarette" and took "a fresh one from his silver case, lit by a match given him by one of his young friends." At this point, Wilde informed the officers: "I am now, gentlemen, ready to accompany you."[324]

In the *Paris Herald*, which claimed to have insider knowledge of Wilde's arrest, there was a report on what happened when the officers Brockwell and Allen escorted Wilde from the Cadogan Hotel. Especially important was the French newspaper's observation that Wilde left the premises carrying a copy of the controversial literary quarterly the *Yellow Book*. This allegation had serious implications for a magazine whose risqué contents had already made it synonymous, at least for disapproving commentators, with a questionable style of literary decadence: "Picking up and taking with him a number of the *Yellow Book*, which lay on the table, he then put on his coat and hat, and accompanied the detectives in a cab to Scotland Yard. It then became evident that he had been drinking heavily. After he left the cab, he nearly fell and reeled somewhat as he crossed the pavement."[325] As it turned out, the *Paris Herald*, together with various other papers, was mistaken about the yellow-covered publication that

Wilde had under his arm. (To this day, we do not know which yellow-backed volume Wilde had with him at the Cadogan Hotel.) The headlines, however, had a severe impact on the *Yellow Book*, its publisher John Lane, and Lane's relations with Wilde.[326]

The *Illustrated Police Budget*, which kept a vigilant eye on the smallest details, commented that Detective Allen hailed a four-wheel cab ("['No. 13,031'] from the rank in Cadogan Square"), and once the journey began the cabman "cried out to some of his brethren, 'I've got him inside.'"[327] The report recorded that the cab made its way to Scotland Yard via Hobart Place, Buckingham Palace Road, and St. James's Park.[328] By comparison, the *Western Mail* printed a number of widely circulated accounts from press agencies on the events that followed Wilde's arrival at the police headquarters: "The accused was the first to alight from the vehicle and walked direct into the station, followed by the detectives. He was attired in a long black frock coat, dark trousers, and silk hat. His demeanour was that of a gentleman self-confident of his own innocence of the charge alleged against him."[329] The *Illustrated Police Budget*, however, observed that Wilde seemed ruffled: "In alighting he missed the carriage step and nearly fell to the stone pavement. Quickly recovering his position and still retaining between his teeth the cigarette which he was smoking, he dived his hand into his pocket and pulled out some money for the purpose of paying the cabman. Detective Allen interposed. 'I'll pay.' 'No! No!' said Wilde. 'Allow me if you please,' but on being informed that it was a way they had of paying for the conveyance of prisoners Wilde returned the coins to his pocket."[330]

The minute Wilde entered Scotland Yard "with his hands in his pockets," he heard the charges against him.[331] Thereafter, the police officers escorted Wilde to Bow Street Magistrates' Court just after 8.00 p.m. This eyewitness account appeared in the *Illustrated Police News*:

> [Wilde] was at once placed in the dock and charged by Inspector [Edwin] Digby of committing acts of gross indecency with certain male persons, to wit, one Chas. Parsons [*sic*] and others on a certain date, and divers other dates and places.[332] While the charge was being read, the prisoner leaned over the dock, still keeping his hands in his pockets, and appearing unconcerned. The prisoner did not make any reply to the charge, and he was removed for the night to an ordinary cell. Soon after Wilde had been removed to the cell, a man drove up in a hansom cab, bearing a portmanteau containing some of the prisoner's clothes, &c. He carried the bag into the station, but the police would not permit him to leave it, and he had to carry it away again. Lord Alfred Douglas also paid a visit to Bow Street in the course of the evening.

> When the four-wheeler containing Wilde and the police inspectors drove up in front of Bow Street station, several newspaper reporters were waiting there, but there was no excitement of any kind, and the prisoner was not recognized by anybody save the reporters. It is understood that evidence of a formal character only will be tendered today (Saturday).[333]

The same newspaper provided further insights into Douglas's visit to Bow Street and Wilde's experience in his cell there:

> Lord Alfred Douglas visited Bow Street, and asked to bail out Wilde; this was, of course, refused. Wilde was requested to give up any articles he had upon him. He, without a word, turned out his pockets. A few loose coins, a pencil case, and twenty five-pound notes were all he had upon him. The notes were kept by the police, with the remaining articles, except the pencil, being returned to him. Then he was conducted to the cell, one of those on the ground floor of the building. It is furnished in the usual manner, with a chair, a table, and a wooden bench fixed against the wall. "How am I to sleep?" asked Oscar. In reply, a constable brought in a few rugs he had collected in the living rooms of the men adjacent to the station, and throwing them on the bench, indicated that that would be the bed for the night. The prisoner was allowed to secure special food, and he sent to the Tavistock Hotel for a dinner of soup, fish, chicken and a small bottle of champagne. For this the prisoner displayed only the slightest partiality. He slept very lightly, and now and then paced his cell. As soon as morning broke, he stepped up to the door of his cell, and catching sight of the constable who had been watching him during the night, had a brief conversation with him. At eight o'clock a messenger arrived from the Tavistock Hotel again with breakfast.[334]

The *Echo* added: "This consisted of bread and butter. The coffee he drank. But the solid food he returned untouched."[335] Meanwhile, the *Illustrated Police Budget* recorded that once he had awoken at 6.00 a.m., Wilde "asked if could smoke": "When told it was against the rules, he seemed much surprised."[336] As he witnessed Wilde's plight in prison, Douglas feared what lay in front of his lover. From the Cadogan Hotel, he wrote urgently to George Ives: "I cannot see Oscar to give him anything, not even some poison to kill himself with. I should be glad to learn that he is dead. I think he had died before this terrible thing happened."[337]

Amid the reports of Wilde's imprisonment were commentaries on the fate of his two comedies, *An Ideal Husband* and *The Importance of Being Earnest*, which had been enjoying successful runs for many weeks at the Theatre Royal Haymarket and the St. James's Theatre, respectively. By this point, Wilde's name had begun to disappear from theatre posters, as the *Western Mail* observed in a meticulous response to the libel trial:

> In order to obtain a practical opinion as to how far the verdict is likely to affect the plaintiff's position as a dramatist, a "St. James's Gazette" representative waited upon Mr. H. H. Morell, of the Haymarket Theatre. Mr. Morell (writes the pressman) assumed an air of imperturbability, and pointed to a large poster. "That is the only answer I can give."
>
> I looked at the poster, which bore the words, "On Saturday, the 13th of April, 'An Ideal Husband,' will transfer to the Criterion theatre."
>
> "I fancy," I said, "I observe a change—an omission. You seem to have departed somewhat from the customary form!"
>
> "Quite true. The author's name has disappeared from the bills, nor does it figure any longer in the advertisements in the daily papers."
>
> "The fact is not without significance."
>
> Mr. Morell smiled. "The press and the public must, of course, form their own conclusions as to its importance. Let me repeat, I am always charmed to see you, but this afternoon—I am out."
>
> The hint was too strong not to be taken, and from the Haymarket I crossed to the St. James's Theatre, where, after a brief delay, Mr. George Alexander expressed himself ready to see me.
>
> "I can guess your object in coming in," he at once remarked, "but I have really little or nothing to say. I need hardly, however, impress upon you the fact that our play, 'The Importance of Being Earnest,' is the most innocent one in the world, and does not contain a line that could hurt the tenderest susceptibilities. I am free to admit that when first this scandal was bruited about, the business here was in some measure affected, but since then it has returned to normal condition. Whether the revival of the unhappy business will cause any change the future must be left to show."
>
> "You know, perhaps," I said, "that your neighbours, Messrs. Waller and Morell, have withdrawn Wilde's name from their bills and advertisements?"
>
> "The same step," answered Mr. Alexander, "has been taken by myself in regard to the latter, and will also take effect in the case of the former as soon as the printers can complete the alterations."
>
> On the question of the "St. James's Gazette"'s action in closing its columns to the publication of evidence given in court, Mr. Alexander was exceedingly emphatic. "It was quite the right thing to do," he said. "It is a crying shame that such nauseous and disgusting details should be left open to the perusal of men, women, and children, of all sorts and conditions, and I heartily applaud the course taken by the "St. James's Gazette."[338]

The productions of Wilde's two comedies were affected differently by the verdict of the libel case and his subsequent arrest. *An Ideal Husband* transferred to Charles Wyndham's Criterion Theatre, Piccadilly, where it ran until Saturday, 27 April 1895. On its last night, *An Ideal Husband* was advertised as "Oscar Wilde's successful play."[339] Wyndham, noticeably, demanded that Wilde's name stay on the bill. By comparison, *The Importance of Being Earnest* ran for eighty-six performances through Wednesday, 8 May 1895. Wilde's name did not appear on the bills for the remainder of its run. Alexander made a considerable loss of £289 8s. 4d. on the first season of *The Importance of Being Earnest*; "it was not until the year 1909–1910," Mason observes, "that the comedy made its triumphant success."[340] Yet, as Michael Seeney has pointed out, Wilde's society comedies (including *Lady Windermere's Fan* [1892] and *A Woman of No Importance* [1893]) continued to open at different London theatres and at many different regional venues both during and after the criminal proceedings, all the way through March 1908. The Waller and Morell Company, for example, opened *An Ideal Husband* at the Grand Theatre, London, on 1 July 1895, as well as at Morton's Model Theatre, London, on 23 September 1895, while the Charles Hawtrey Company opened the same play at the Lyric Theatre, London, on 16 December 1895.[341]

At any rate, one or two commentators expressed consternation at the removal of Wilde's name from the posters at both the Haymarket and the St. James. The *Sketch* reported that the popular dramatist Sydney Grundy, known for such dramas as *The New Woman* (1894), had written to the *Daily Telegraph* protesting the action: "I wonder," Grundy remarked, "on what principle of law, or justice, or common sense, of good manners, or Christian charity, an author's name is blotted from his work."[342] A related point, the *Sketch* also noted, had recently appeared in the *Westminster Gazette*, which contended that, while it was understandable that an "illogical sentiment should be strong" in obliterating Wilde's name, it was true that "no one has discovered any taint of corruption in these plays."[343] "We cannot see," the *Westminster Gazette* opined, "that the sternest morality requires us to deny that the plays are good."[344] By the time the paper made this judgment, however, the public had already been exposed to the first and second day of the pretrial hearing, the proceedings of which exposed the startling evidence that would be elaborated—in repetitive amounts of detail—in the two criminal trials that followed.

Part II of *Oscar Wilde on Trial* begins by unpacking the grueling experience that Wilde endured during his arraignment on Saturday, 6 April 1895 and through his committal for trial, which ended thirteen days later.

Part II

REGINA *v.* OSCAR WILDE AND ALFRED TAYLOR

A Reconstruction of the Proceedings

3

THE PRETRIAL HEARING: ARRAIGNMENT AND COMMITTAL OF OSCAR WILDE AND ALFRED TAYLOR AT BOW STREET MAGISTRATES' COURT

> Oscar Wilde lost his case and was put in gaol. I was forced to leave the country, and Lord Queensberry became the idol of the English people. He was cheered in the streets; the newspapers extolled in him leading articles, and dinners were given in his honour. Lord Queensberry "had justified himself," that is to say, had proven "to the court's satisfaction" that what he had written on the card left at Mr. Wilde's club was true.
>
> How did he pull it off?
>
> He went to clever and unscrupulous lawyers and he spent two or three thousand pounds. It is the easiest thing in the world. Provide me with two thousand pounds and, with the help of the same solicitors, I will undertake to collect enough evidence to bring an action against all and sundry, high or low, starting with the Prime Minister downwards.
>
> The principal witnesses were without exception blackmailers or male prostitutes.
>
> —*Lord Alfred Douglas, "Oscar Wilde," September 1895.*

We have seen in chapter 2 that, within a matter of hours, on Friday, 5 April 1895, Oscar Wilde's predicament suffered an astonishing reversal. In the morning, he was still in the third day of an arduous prosecution against the Marquess of Queensberry, who had branded him as a sodomite. By 11.15 a.m., the evidence against Wilde was so great that his suit collapsed, which led to his discreet exit from the courtroom before the jury determined that the libel was justified. Later in the afternoon, the police arrived at the Cadogan Hotel, Sloane Street, with a warrant for Wilde's arrest. Thereafter, he endured an unanticipated night in prison faced with the fact that the Crown was about to commit him for trial. The populist *News of the World*, which scornfully observed Wilde's startling reversal of fortune, took pleasure in the humiliating fact that his name had immediately been "removed from all programmes and all advertisements" for the London productions of his two well-received comedies, *An Ideal Husband* and *The Importance of Being Earnest*.[1] As the paper reveled in the scandal, it conjured a theatrical metaphor to show that Wilde's successful plays were no longer the most compelling drama of his career. "Here then with the end of the libel suit the first act of the terrible drama ends. Already the curtain has risen on the second act, with the situation of the principals. The third is yet to come."[2] The *Morning* similarly capitalized on the idea that Wilde's downfall had now taken center stage: "Oscar Wilde as a dramatist had discovered the art of drawing the public. People laughed at, as well as with, him, but they crowded to his plays. And now the farce has turned to tragedy."[3] Constance Wilde also lamented her husband's plight in much the same terms. In a letter sent two weeks after his arrest, from Lady Mount-Temple's home in Babbacombe, Devon, she informed her palmist, Mrs. Robinson: "What a tragedy for him who is so gifted."[4] The prosecution that followed became a test of endurance. Since Wilde was refused bail not only at Bow Street Magistrates' Court but also during the the first Crown prosecution against him, he ended up spending no fewer than thirty-two nights in jail: the first in a cell at the police court, and the remainder at H.M. Prison Holloway.[5]

Even though the pretrial hearing took up only three days (6, 11, and 19 April 1895), the proceedings, as the dates show, were spaced out across two weeks. The start of the proceedings marked the second of fourteen days of fatiguing courtroom appearances, which eventually led to his incarceration after the best part of seven weeks had elapsed. In the present chapter, we see that Wilde's appearance at the Bow Street Magistrates' Court, which exposed the range of his outlawed homosexual activities, especially during the 1892–93 period, presented graphic testimony of a kind that seldom came to public attention. Given that Wilde enjoyed celebrity status as a leading dramatist, this was no ordinary hearing. The lengthy revelations, which included Alfred Wood's calm and collected statement that Wilde committed sodomy with him at the family home on Tite Street, were so astounding that some commentators began to wonder whether such a barefaced witness might incriminate himself through the open admission that he, and not just the defendant, had broken the 1885 law. Just as striking were the disclosures of two of the other witnesses—Charles Parker and Frederick ("Fred") Atkins—whose admissions, like those of Alfred Wood, revealed their intimate involvement in the criminal world of homosexual blackmail. These confessions, which gripped the nation, ensured that the magistrates' court was packed with reporters, along with members of the public who relished the spectator sport that arose from such scandals.

In these taxing circumstances, in which Wilde was now betrayed by a series of young men on whom he had bestowed many favors, he understandably had much on his mind. Besides the prospect of long-term imprisonment, in addition to the immense burden of debt that he had to bear, the welfare of his wife and children weighed heavily upon him. His letters to Constance from this period, which have gone missing, would no doubt shed light on his deep concern for her and their sons' welfare. Constance's level of distress was intense: "What is to become of my husband who has so betrayed and deceived me and ruined the lives of my darling boys?"[6] Once she could no longer return to Tite Street, friends and relatives rallied round to give her financial support. Apart from spending time with Lady Mount-Temple, she moved from the home of her aunt, Mary Napier, to rooms on Hyde Park Terrace, and, a few weeks later, to her friend Eva Roller's residence in south London. Protecting her sons from the scandal was imperative. She withdrew her eldest child, Cyril, from the modern coeducational school Bedales, and she promptly sent him to relatives in Ireland, while she kept her younger son, Vyvyan, by her side. Constance, who was beleaguered by her husband's creditors, had already started discussions with the eminent lawyer Sir George Lewis about the steps that she should take to ensure that Wilde made no claim on the substantial life interest (namely, the proceedings from a trust) that she brought to their marriage.

Amid these upheavals, the magistrate Sir John Bridge flatly refused Wilde bail. There was a strong reason, apart from the desire to prevent Wilde from attempting to flee the country, for not bailing the defendant. To be sure, Wilde had access to sufficient funds, as well as the backing of individuals who were willing to enter into recognizances with sureties. (Sureties were guarantees from associates that lessened the possibility that the accused would abscond.) Still, the important point to note is that the charges involved not only Wilde's committing homosexual offences; he was also deemed to be in conspiracy with Taylor. As the *Standard* put it, Wilde "was charged with indecent conduct with various persons," while Taylor was charged "with conspiracy with Wilde to procure the committal of these offences."[7] Since it was frequently left to the justice's discretion to determine whether bail should be granted, the charge of conspiracy (a felony) on top of gross indecency (a misdemeanor) likely swayed the decision to refuse bail. As James Fitzjames Stephen observed in 1883, it was the Indictable Offences Act 1848—one of the decisive moves to consolidate English criminal law—that granted a justice the discretion "either to bail or refuse to bail any person accused either of felony or of any common misdemeanour except libel, conspiracies other than those named [i.e., receiving property stolen or obtained by false pretenses], unlawful assembly, night poaching and seditious offences."[8] Section 23 of the act clarified that a justice had the discretion to admit bail to individuals who were charged with "any felony" (whether the intention to commit or the actual committing of, for example, an assault) or specific behaviors such as the "willful or indecent exposure of the person" (11 & 12 Vict., c. 42). Long before the prosecution of Wilde began, there had been a growing legal discussion about the degree to which the arbitrariness of a magistrate's discretion could undermine fairness in granting bail. This debate led to the reforms of the Bail Act 1898 and culminated in those of the Criminal Justice Act 1967.[9]

The withholding of bail, which followed the shock of Wilde's imprisonment in H.M. Prison Holloway, took a serious toll on his ability to withstand, both mentally and physically, the pretrial hearing. Such stubborn opposition from the magistrate gave the impression that Wilde was guilty before he was committed for trial. More than a month passed before Sir Charles Edward ("Baron") Pollock agreed that the prisoner should be bailed, so long as there was a recognizance from Wilde himself of £2,500 with two sureties amounting to £1,250 each. In the meantime, the press made much of the purportedly favorable conditions that Wilde enjoyed in cell "B. 24." The *Daily Telegraph* noted that he occupied "one of the better-class cells," and added that for the "payment of a nominal amount—about 1*s* a day" the prison regulations permitted "meals to be sent" to him by his friends from a nearby hotel.[10] Journalists also relished making fun of the gossip that surfaced about Wilde's hearty dinners in "B. 24": "'You are starving me,'" he was reputed as saying to a warder, "after consuming a large plate of chicken."[11] "Tell them," he supposedly said, "to send larger comestibles."[12] This, however, was a tall tale that conflicted with accurate reports about Wilde's refusal to eat the substantial dinners that were delivered to him. As various journalists noted, there was the grave issue of the impact that prison life was already having on his mental and physical health. The Exchange Telegraph Company transmitted the news that on Wednesday, 10 April 1895, "Wilde was seen by the prison doctor several times."[13] The *Star* had by this point reported that at 11.00 p.m. during his first night in Holloway, Wilde "complained of insomnia"; a doctor subsequently administered a "sleeping draught, but to no purpose."[14] The prison authorities, according to the *Sun*, harbored fears for his wellbeing: "Yesterday," it had already remarked on Monday, 8 April 1895, "he was in a gloomy, depressed state, and as a precautionary measure, unknown to him, he is being specially watched, lest, in an access of despair, he should attempt to take his life."[15] "He greatly misses," this report went on to note, "his indispensable cigarette."[16]

Wilde was allowed visitors, at the rate of one per day. In 1929, Douglas—who was later to be criticized for his supposed negligence of Wilde during this harsh period—stated: "I used to see Oscar every day at Holloway in the ghastly way 'visits' are arranged in prisons. The visitor goes into a box rather like the box in a pawnshop . . . and opposite, facing each visitor, is the prisoner whom he is visiting."[17] The truth is that Douglas saw Wilde with a little less frequency than he claims. The *Star* observed that on 6 April 1895 Douglas "sought to see him, but prison regulations did not permit more than his legal adviser being admitted."[18] At the same time, Douglas's visits, which Wilde cherished, proved harrowing. "Poor Oscar," Douglas recalls, "was rather deaf. He could hardly hear what I said in the babel. He looked at me with tears running down his cheeks and I looked at him."[19] The noisiness of the visiting room also made it difficult for prisoners to discuss their affairs with counsel. In any case, Wilde's lawyers had scarcely enough time during these visits to prepare him properly for the onslaught of the prosecution. He was not in the best condition to face cross-examination. In court, Wilde often looked miserable and exhausted. His appearance became increasingly disheveled.

There was, however, some significant relief from the legal strain that Wilde was under. The press reported, after the first day of the hearing, that Sir Edward Clarke, who was not present at Bow Street on 6 April 1895, had written to Wilde's solicitors, Messrs. Humphreys, Son, and Kershaw, offering to defend their client without a fee:

April 6th, 1895

Dear Sir,

Having regard to the events of yesterday I think it right to say that if Mr. Oscar Wilde would like me to defend him at his trial my services shall be at his disposal, and in respect of services so offered I, of course, shall not accept any fees. Will you kindly communicate with Mr. Oscar Wilde and ascertain his wishes?

Faithfully yours,
Edward Clarke[20]

It was this type of gesture that earned Clark the cognomen "Bayard of the bar."[21] Clarke's junior counsel, Travers Humphreys and Charles Mathews, followed his example. Both had also served under Clarke during the miscarried libel suit. These two lawyers represented Wilde, in Clarke's absence, when the hearing began.

In the meantime, from the Crown's vantage-point the committal of Wilde and Taylor for trial could not have gone more smoothly. Queensberry's attorney, Charles Russell, had already primed a stream of witnesses, including several male prostitutes, landladies of boarding houses, and assorted hotel staff, to give evidence against Wilde should they have been called during the libel suit. As the hearing rapidly approached, Russell worked closely with the prosecution to ensure that five young men in particular—Frederick Atkins, Charles Parker, William Parker, Edward Shelley, and Alfred Wood (fig. 17)—would not hold back when alluding to the erotic acts that they had either performed with Wilde or witnessed him performing with other males. The Parker brothers and Wood were also prepared to divulge their knowledge of Taylor's sociable circle of queer men.

Alfred Taylor, whose arrest had occurred the morning after Wilde's, was escorted into the dock ten minutes after the proceedings had commenced. The

Fig. 17. ["E. J. S."], illustration of Oscar Wilde, Alfred Taylor, Charles Parker, Edward Shelley, and Frederick Atkins, *News of the World*, 14 April 1895: 7.

Fig. 18. "The Wilde–Queensberry Case and How It Ended,"
Illustrated Police News, 13 April 1895: 1.

Illustrated Police News featured this as a central episode in Wilde's downward path since the failure of the libel trial (fig. 18). Like Wilde, Taylor had taken no action to flee the country. Neither did he comply with the pressure that Russell had placed upon him to betray Wilde. According to Douglas, Taylor had refused to be drawn by Queensberry's attorney into giving evidence against the Irish writer: "Taylor . . . had [like the other subpoenaed witnesses] been approached by the opposite side. If he had consented to testify against Wilde, he would not have been prosecuted. But he behaved like a true gentleman, and was rewarded with two years' hard labour."[22] At the time, Taylor had no legal representation, although by the second day of the hearing Douglas had sent "£50 to defend Taylor" to Arthur Newton, a lawyer who had—among other controversial cases—defended Lord Arthur Somerset during the Cleveland Street scandal of 1889–90.[23] Once Taylor was under remand, he and Wilde were accused of perpetrating the same crimes. The two men learned that they were to be tried together.

The Treasury, which had its own group of government attorneys on which to draw, chose to hire a lawyer outside its ranks. To one or two commentators, this was an unexpected decision. In 1929, the legal historian Edward Maltby reflected on the Treasury's appointment of Charles Frederick ("C. F.") Gill, the Irish barrister who had served as Queensberry's junior counsel during Wilde's libel suit, to lead the prosecution: "There was some surprise that the Government did not send down one of its Law Officers to prosecute."[24] The likeliest reason that the authorities turned to Gill is that Carson had made it known that he would refuse the brief. Edward Marjoribanks states that Carson "would have nothing to do with the case," since a "prosecution"—involving what was a "filthy business"—constituted "a different matter" from his leading role in the defense of Wilde's libel action against the marquess.[25] The appointment of Gill made sense, insofar as he was well acquainted with the inculpating evidence that had arisen during the libel proceedings. Still, as Maltby also states, "it was generally agreed that the case was too big for Gill."[26]

As we can tell from the reconstruction of the courtroom exchanges below, Gill was not able to match the rhetorical deftness of Carson, whose skills he attempted to emulate. Especially clumsy were his efforts to stifle witnesses when they were about to refer to Alfred Douglas by name. Moreover, Gill repeatedly asked leading questions that would scarcely be countenanced in a modern court of law. At one point, his examination of Charles Parker posed the following inquiry about Taylor's lodgings: "Did you see the woman's dress at either of those places?" (170). Once again, in this fashion he asked Edward Shelley: "While you were in the room, did he kiss you?" (185). Such questions on behalf of the prosecution elaborated bits and pieces of information that were not relevant to the witness testimony, and they apparently—on the materials we have to go on—passed without objection. At the same time, Gill did not hesitate to pounce on Arthur Newton, who defended Taylor, when it came to asking Charles Parker whether the witness knew that Frederick Atkins worked as a comedian: "I do not know for what purpose this mode of cross-examination is being indulged in" (185). Gill's objection was that a query of this kind might imply Atkins was not suited to give evidence. Based on the available reports on the pretrial hearing, it very much looks as if Gill was not impeded in pursuing his examination through what were at times debatable methods.

FIRST DAY: SATURDAY, 6 APRIL 1895

On the morning of Saturday, 6 April 1895, at Bow Street Magistrates' Court, Wilde was charged on a warrant before Sir John Bridge with committing offenses under section 11 of the Criminal Law Amendment Act 1885.[27] At 10.30 a.m., the court informed the reporters who had been besieging the pavement outside that the hearing would be held in the small upper court, also known as the Extradition Court. The *Echo* observed: "Constables had been placed on duty for the purpose of coping with the throng."[28] The newspaper also noted that one of Wilde's closest friends tried to deliver a bag filled with supplies to him before the courtroom opened its doors:

> The first of Oscar Wilde's friends to arrive was Mr. More Adey, of Hornton Street, Kensington. He drove up in a cab with a large portmanteau, containing a complete change of linen and a suit of clothes. These he attempted to take into the building by the police entrance on the right, but was there referred to the station. The inspector in charge, however, refused to allow the articles to be handed to the prisoner. "It is against the rule," was his dictum. "Mr. Wilde is completely dressed, and he must go before the magistrate in that condition. "Can I see him?" was the next question, and again a reply was returned in the negative. "Certainly not; it is against the orders. You must make your application to the magistrate; neither can we accept any responsibility for the clothes if they are left in our charge.[29]

The *Illustrated Police News* reported that Mr. Charles ("Willie") Mathews "appeared at a quarter past ten, and immediately applied to the gaoler to show him the way to the prisoner."[30] It appears that Wilde had been escorted from the station house adjacent to the court through the backyard from "the gaoler's room, separate from the other prisoners."[31] Thereafter, the jailer and Wilde, according to the *Illustrated Police Budget*, "ascended by a private staircase to the cells behind the Extradition Court."[32]

Once the court opened its doors at 10.30 a.m., there was a rush to find a seat in a very crowded chamber. The *Echo* calculated that "there could have been little short of 200 persons who were vainly struggling for admission."[33] *Reynolds's Newspaper* reported that the court "was so crowded that the ushers had to take chairs in to accommodate the comers."[34] The journalist also remarked that the court "was filled with men only," apart from an unidentified woman "quietly dressed in black, with close-fitting jacket and small bonnet, slightly relieved with a few violets," who was "shown in from the prisoners' entrance, and given a seat immediately behind the prisoners' dock."[35] Among the crowd was Sir Augustus Harris, manager of the Drury Lane Theatre, who entered in a fur coat and silk hat.

For its part, the *Illustrated Police Budget* took special note of Wilde's entrance: "About twenty minutes to eleven o'clock the door by which the prisoners enter the Court was opened, and Oscar, hat in hand, and the suede gloves between his fingers, entered the Court. He was conducted by Mr. Bush [the jailer] to the dock at each end of which stood a policeman."[36] Once inside the dock, Wilde placed his silk hat on a chair before leaning forward to engage in a short, animated conversation with Mr. Travers Humphreys. "The Court, small and oppressive," this reporter noted presciently, "represented a scene that will one day become history. In the dock, looking haggard, tired, and troubled, stood Oscar Wilde, the man who had materially assisted to make the dramatic history of the nineteenth century, and who practically was better known for his 'peculiar' literary ability than any man of the present day."[37] One source reported that Wilde "nodded familiarly" to Sir Augustus, "but that magnate of the theatrical world deliberately turned his back upon the playwriting celebrity."[38] The *Galignani Messenger* observed that Mr. Edward Besley, Q.C., with Mr. J. L. Monckton, maintained watching briefs on behalf of Percy Sholto Douglas.[39] Both attorneys, as we have seen in chapter 2 (125), had kept this responsibility during Wilde's libel suit.

Sir John Bridge took his seat at 11.00 a.m. A number of commentators noted that Wilde, who wore "a black frock-coat and dark trousers," displayed "no great concern at any time during the proceedings."[40] *Reynolds's Newspaper*, however, claimed that Wilde "stared round uneasily, and fidgeted incessantly, stroking his face with his brown suede glove."[41] The *Globe* remarked: "The charge sheet was signed by Inspector T. Brockwell, and on it was further stated that the prisoner was taken into custody by Inspectors Brockwell and Richards at new Scotland Yard, and that the property found on him included twenty £5 notes. The charge was taken by Sub-Divisional Inspector Digby, of the E Division, at Bow Street Police Station."[42]

Without further ado, Mr. C. F. Gill, instructed by Mr. Angus Lewis of the Treasury, spoke for the prosecution. At the start of the proceedings, Mr. Travers Humphreys, under the instruction of his father C. O. Humphreys, defended Wilde. To the *Illustrated Police Budget*, there was a notable figure in court whose distress was patently evident: "One important personage—Lord Alfred Douglas—sat at the solicitors' table, looking the very semblance of the image of misery. He spoke to no one and no one spoke to him."[43] Gill explained that he was there to prosecute the prisoner on a series of charges of inciting to commit or of committing certain gross indecencies under the eleventh section of the Criminal Law Amendment Act. In his opinion, there was no good purpose served by going into these matters in an opening speech. Gill stated that he would merely indicate the general character of the evidence that he proposed to produce before Sir John and the nature of the charges, while the question of what the prisoner would ultimately be committed upon depended on the evidence produced.

The first charge, Gill explained, involved acts of indecency that took place on 13 or 14 March 1893 at the Savoy Hotel, where Wilde had taken rooms from

2 to 29 March that year.[44] Gill clarified who Wilde's associates were at the time. He commented that in March 1893 Alfred Taylor occupied the upper part of a house at 13 Little College Street, Westminster, which Wilde visited habitually.[45] As Gill proceeded, the court learned that toward the end of February or beginning of March that year, William Parker (an unemployed valet) was with his younger brother, Charles Parker (a former groom), when Taylor approached them in the St. James's restaurant. At this venue, Taylor offered the brothers a drink, took down their addresses, gave them his own address, and informed them that Wilde could provide them with money. After two or three further meetings with the brothers, Taylor received a telegram from Wilde, asking him to bring the Parkers to a private room at Kettner's restaurant, Soho, where all four of them dined together.[46] Once they had enjoyed what Gill described as a sumptuous repast, Charles Parker drove with Wilde to the Savoy Hotel. Gill stated that Wilde plied Charles Parker with drink, and then parted with £2. According to Gill, Wilde met Charles Parker several times afterward, visiting the young man's lodgings at 7 Camera Square, Chelsea, and giving him money, as well as a gold ring and a silver cigarette case.[47] In addition, Gill remarked that Charles Parker now led a respectable life, and thus it was painful that the youth's story had to be recounted in court. Moreover, according to *Reynolds's Newspaper* Gill stated that Wilde "had the audacity to commit these offences at the Savoy Hotel, at a hotel in Piccadilly, and even at his own house in Tite Street, when his family were away"; "Charles Parker," the paper added, "a slight, fair, young fellow of medium height, well dressed, who stated that he had been a valet, was the first witness."[48] By comparison, the *Manchester Courier* noted: "He is a fair young man with a slight moustache, 19 years old and rather tall and slim. He was dressed in a dark blue suit, black tie, long and light brown racing overcoat, and tan-coloured gloves."[49] These details revealed that the defense had gone to some expense to ensure that this star witness looked well turned-out.

MR. C. F. GILL: Are you nineteen years of age?[50]

CHARLES PARKER: Yes, sir.

GILL: You were formerly in service as a valet?

CHARLES PARKER: Yes.

GILL: Did you leave that employment at the end of February 1893?

CHARLES PARKER: Yes.

GILL: Have you a brother named William Parker?

CHARLES PARKER: Yes. He was out of employment at the same time. He had been a groom, and his last occupation was that of a butler.

GILL: Do you remember being in company with Taylor and going into the St. James's restaurant?

CHARLES PARKER: Yes.

After ten minutes, Gill's examination was interrupted. The *Daily Chronicle* noted: "the police made a communication to him, and he then informed the magistrate that the man Alfred Taylor, whose name had so frequently cropped up during the proceedings at the Old Bailey, had just been arrested, and as he was charged with conspiring with Mr. Wilde in inciting a number of lads to the commission of offences, he had better be brought up and placed in the dock."[51] Sir John Bridge assented to this suggestion. At this point, the *Western Mail* noted, Wilde's counsel posed the following question to the magistrate:

TRAVERS HUMPHREYS: May I ask you, Sir John, how long you propose to sit today?

SIR JOHN BRIDGE: I propose to sit within reason so long as we have witnesses to go on with.[52]

Following a pause lasting a few minutes, Taylor was brought into the court and placed in the dock next to Wilde. "Taylor," the *Daily Chronicle* observed, "is a dark, clean-shaven, good-looking man of medium height and build, with clear-cut features, fresh complexion, and blue eyes."[53] The press also noted that Taylor was fashionably dressed: "he wore a long fawn overcoat, and carried a bowler hat in his hand."[54] Wilde received his fellow prisoner with a bow, and Taylor smiled and bowed in return. After rising to let Taylor pass to the other end of the dock, Wilde sat down again, while Taylor stood leaning forward and smiled sneeringly at the witness. Inspector Brockwell had been given the warrant for Taylor's arrest, which took place at Taylor's lodgings at 25 Denbigh Street, Pimlico, at 10.30 that morning.[55] The *Illustrated Police News* remarked: "A search of Taylor's rooms was made, and a large number of telegrams found. It is said that many of the letters afford information to the police as to other persons, but the police are naturally reticent, and state the documents seized have not yet been examined."[56]

Charles Parker's brief evidence was read one more time, and Gill's questions continued about the reasons why Taylor wished to introduce the young man to Wilde.

GILL: For what purpose?[57]

CHARLES PARKER: When I met Taylor, he told me that Oscar Wilde was a "good man."

GILL: What did you understand by that expression?

CHARLES PARKER: Good for money, I suppose.

SIR JOHN BRIDGE: But why did he say he wanted to introduce Wilde?

CHARLES PARKER: Because he likes boys. (*Sensation in court.*) I was introduced to Mr. Wilde two days later.

GILL: After a time did you go to Little College Street, near the Houses of Parliament?

CHARLES PARKER: At the restaurant, Taylor gave my brother the address. I went there with my brother. I cannot remember who admitted us to the house. Inside, I saw Taylor's rooms. There were three rooms—a bedroom, a drawing room, and a kind of kitchen. The drawing room was well furnished. The bedroom had a low bed in it—no more than a foot or a foot and a half from the ground.[58]

GILL: Do you remember whether the rooms at the time you went there were lit up?[59]

CHARLES PARKER: No.

GILL: Was anyone there but Taylor?

CHARLES PARKER: No.

GILL: At what time did you go to Taylor's rooms?[60]

CHARLES PARKER: It was about 11 o'clock in the morning when we went there.

GILL: What did he say to you?

CHARLES PARKER: That he had arranged for me to be introduced to Mr. Wilde, either at Kettner's restaurant or the Solferino.[61]

GILL: When were you to be introduced?

CHARLES PARKER: In the evening, at dinner, at half-past seven. Nothing more was said, and all three of us left the house together. That evening, my brother and I went to the restaurant, whichever it was. We went upstairs to a private room. Previously, we had met Taylor at the St. James's bar.[62]

GILL: Was there a table laid for dinner?

CHARLES PARKER: Yes, for four. The table was lighted with candles, with red shades.[63]

GILL: Did the prisoner Wilde shortly after come in?

CHARLES PARKER: Yes.

GILL: Had you ever seen him before?

CHARLES PARKER: Never. Taylor introduced us, and we had dinner together.

GILL: Was it a good dinner?

CHARLES PARKER: Yes, a very good dinner. We had champagne.

GILL: Did you smoke?

CHARLES PARKER: Yes, cigarettes.

GILL: Did you see who paid for the dinner?

CHARLES PARKER: I saw Wilde write out a cheque.

GILL: At the end of the dinner, did Wilde ask you anything?

CHARLES PARKER: He said: "This is the boy for me. Will you come to the Savoy Hotel with me?"

GILL: Did you go?

CHARLES PARKER: Yes, we drove in a hansom. It was about ten o'clock. We went to the second or third floor of the hotel.

GILL: When you got to the rooms, where did you go?

CHARLES PARKER: Into the sitting room. No one else was there. Drink was brought into the room.

GILL: What did he order?

CHARLES PARKER: Whisky and soda were brought for two.[64]

GILL: After the waiter who brought them had gone away, what did Wilde say to you?

CHARLES PARKER: "Come into my bedroom." There was a door leading to a bedroom, from the sitting room.

GILL: Did you undress?

CHARLES PARKER: Yes.

GILL: Both of you?

CHARLES PARKER: Yes.

SIR JOHN BRIDGE: Did you take them all off?

CHARLES PARKER: Yes.

GILL: Both went naked into bed?

CHARLES PARKER: Yes.

GILL: I don't propose to take this further, Sir John, in any detail. (*To Charles Parker.*) Acts of indecency took place between you in the bed?

CHARLES PARKER: Yes. I was there about two hours. He gave me £2 and told me to come again in about a week. I went. It was about eleven o'clock at night. I was shown to the same room—his sitting room. We went into the bedroom afterward, and the same kind of thing took place as had taken place before. I remained about an hour and a half. Then I dressed and went away. He gave me £3 that time.

SIR JOHN BRIDGE: Did he say why £3 instead of £2?

CHARLES PARKER: Oh, he told me to buy some clothes. I saw Wilde again from time to time. I forget how I got to the St. James's Street address. I went there in the afternoon between four and five o'clock. I had tea with Wilde. Afterward we went into his bedroom, but not into bed. Acts of indecency took place. Sometimes I went to St. James's Street every day.

GILL: Did you have lunch there?

CHARLES PARKER: Yes, I went to the Crystal Palace with Wilde after meeting him at St. James's Place, and had lunch with him.[65] I have dined at Solferino's and Kettner's with him alone.

GILL: Do you recall going with him to music halls?

CHARLES PARKER: Yes, he was in a box at the Pavilion.[66]

GILL: Afterwards, where did you go?

CHARLES PARKER: I went with him to St. James's Place. He let himself in with his keys, and I went with him. Similar acts took place, and we came out and left the place together. We drove part of the way to Park Walk, Chelsea.[67] I got out, and he drove on. I had a room at 50 Park Walk.

GILL: Did Wilde ever come there?

CHARLES PARKER: Yes, once.

GILL: Did he walk or come by cab?

CHARLES PARKER: By cab.

GILL: Did he come into your room?

CHARLES PARKER: Yes.

GILL: Did he keep the cab waiting?

CHARLES PARKER: Yes.

GILL: Your room was a bedroom?

CHARLES PARKER: Yes. Nothing took place on that occasion.

GILL: What time was it?

CHARLES PARKER: It was at night.

SIR JOHN BRIDGE: Why did he come?

CHARLES PARKER: Just to see me.

GILL: After that there was some unpleasantness with the landlady, and you left?

CHARLES PARKER: Yes.

GILL: How far is it from Tite Street to Camera Square?

CHARLES PARKER: I think about half an hour's walk.[68] I think he visited me at Camera Square, but I am not certain. I visited him once at the Albemarle Hotel.[69] I was taken there by—[70]

GILL: Never mind. I don't want to introduce any other name into the case.[71] Did you see Wilde there?

CHARLES PARKER: Yes.

GILL: When did you last see Wilde before these matters took place?

CHARLES PARKER: About eight or nine months ago. He was driving past in a hansom near Trafalgar Square.[72] He stopped, shook hands, and spoke. He asked me how I was. He said I was as pretty as ever. (*Parker laughed.*)

GILL: Did you ever go to any of Taylor's tea parties?[73]

CHARLES PARKER: Yes, in Chapel Street.[74]

GILL: Were you with Taylor when you were arrested last year in connection with the Fitzroy Square affair?[75]

CHARLES PARKER: Yes.

GILL: And after that incident did you give up all companionship of this kind?

CHARLES PARKER: Yes.

GILL: Have you seen Wood at Taylor's?

CHARLES PARKER: No.[76]

GILL: Have you seen Atkins?[77]

CHARLES PARKER: Yes.

GILL: Did you see the woman's dress at either of those places?

CHARLES PARKER: No. I did not see Scarfe at St. James's Place.[78]

GILL: When you went to St. James's Place, were you always alone?

CHARLES PARKER: Nearly always.

GILL: Did you pawn the silver cigarette case and ring?

CHARLES PARKER: Yes. After I ceased companionship with these people, I went into the country, where Mr. Charles Russell came to me for the other case.

At this point, Mr. Travers Humphreys arrived. The lawyer had appeared for Wilde at the Central Criminal Court during the libel case against Queensberry. Humphreys conversed with the prisoner Wilde as he passed behind the dock. Afterward, he announced that he was in attendance in order to defend Wilde, but he stated that the charge had so taken his client by surprise that he was not prepared at this point to cross-examine Charles Parker. Humphreys added that he was not sure if cross-examining Parker would be necessary here, but he added that if he needed to cross-examine the witness, he would give the prosecution notice.

Charles Parker was then bound over for £80 to appear at the Sessions.[79]

Taylor, who had no legal representation, reserved his right to cross-examine Charles Parker.

The court then adjourned for half an hour.

At two o'clock, the court resumed, and William Parker, the older brother of Charles Parker, was called.

GILL: You are the brother of Charles Parker?[80]

WILLIAM PARKER: Yes.

GILL: And formerly in employment as a groom?

WILLIAM PARKER: Yes.

GILL: In March 1893, were you and your brother without employment?

WILLIAM PARKER: Yes.

The witness proceeded to explain his first meeting with Taylor.

WILLIAM PARKER: I remember being spoken to at the St. James's restaurant by the prisoner Taylor. He was a complete stranger to me.

GILL: How did he introduce himself to you?

WILLIAM PARKER: He was standing beside us for some time, and then he entered into a conversation with us and asked us to have a drink.

GILL: Did he mention anyone's name?
WILLIAM PARKER: He mentioned Oscar Wilde's name.

Gill tried to entice the witness to say why Oscar Wilde's name was mentioned, and for what purpose. But William Parker said he could not remember any particular words that had been used, though he said that he understood the sense of what was said, and the intention of the introduction. Pressed as to what the intention was, William Parker declared: "The same as women." (His phrasing implied that he was expected to provide the services that a female prostitute offered to a male client.) The *Morning Leader* noted the evident stress that William Parker was under: "The witness was obviously much affected by the position in which he was placed, and had to sit in the witness box owing to faintness."[81] Eventually, William Parker was able to corroborate his brother's evidence.

WILLIAM PARKER: Taylor got my name and address on this paper, which was in my handwriting, and he should like to introduce us, as Oscar Wilde was a good man for money.[82]
SIR JOHN BRIDGE: Money for those who were the same as women?
WILLIAM PARKER: Yes.
SIR JOHN BRIDGE: What women?
WILLIAM PARKER: Women that walk the streets.
SIR JOHN BRIDGE: The money was for the same as those women?
WILLIAM PARKER: Yes.

Gill asked William Parker to speak about the incident involving the call at Taylor's rooms, the appointment for dinner the same night, and the introduction to Wilde, who made the request to Charles Parker in the presence of William Parker, and the departure of Charles Parker and Wilde together.

GILL: When you went to Little College Street, did you see Taylor there?[83]
WILLIAM PARKER: Yes.
GILL: Was an appointment then made to meet Oscar Wilde?
WILLIAM PARKER: Yes. Afterwards my brother and I went to a restaurant, and we dined with Taylor and Wilde in a private room. It was a good dinner, and we had champagne. After dinner the prisoner invited my brother to go to the Savoy with him, and they went away together.
GILL: Was that the only occasion when you saw Wilde?
WILLIAM PARKER: Yes.
GILL: What did you do afterwards?
WILLIAM PARKER: I went down Piccadilly with Taylor.

MR. TRAVERS HUMPHREYS: (*To Sir John Bridge*) I do not think it is necessary for me to cross-examine the witness on behalf of Mr. Wilde. (*To William Parker*) Cannot you give us the date in March when the dinner took place?[84]

WILLIAM PARKER: No, I can't.[85]

SIR JOHN BRIDGE: When the prisoner Wilde and your brother went out, did they leave you behind?

WILLIAM PARKER: Yes, sir.

GILL: Taylor might like to ask a question.

ALFRED TAYLOR: No, I don't wish to say anything at present.

The next witness was Mrs. Ellen Grant, caretaker of the house at 13 Little College Street, where Taylor had been a tenant for eighteen months.[86]

ELLEN GRANT:. I am the wife of William Alfred Grant. The prisoner Alfred Taylor occupied rooms in that house from January 1892 to August 1893. The rooms consist of a bedroom, bathroom, sitting room, and kitchen, for which he paid £3 a month. The rooms were furnished very nicely. The linen in the bedroom was very good. The windows were very dark, especially in the sitting room. Art muslin was strained over the glass, and there were dark curtains and muslin curtains. There was no daylight. It was lit by candles. There was no bedstead; it was a spring mattress on the ground. He furnished the place himself. He kept no servants.

GILL: Did he cook for himself?

GRANT: Yes.

GILL: Was he visited by many gentlemen?

GRANT: Yes, a great many gentlemen.

GILL: Were they young?

GRANT: Yes, quite young.

GILL: He had no wife?

GRANT: I was always given to understand he was a bachelor. No woman lived with him there.

GILL: How old were the young gentlemen who called?

GRANT: From sixteen upwards. If Taylor was dressed, he opened the door himself; if not, I did.

GILL: Have you seen ladies' clothes there?

GRANT: Well, wigs and things for fancy dress.[87] But no ordinary dress. Taylor was fond of scent and burning scent. There were large numbers of scent bottles.

The *Sun* noted how Grant's comments prompted an outburst of laughter from Taylor when she also recalled that "she had seen his night-shirt fastened with a gold brooch."[88]

GRANT: The gentlemen who came used to come to tea. I do not recognize the other prisoner as having been at the rooms.

SIR JOHN BRIDGE: Stand up, Wilde.

Wilde stood up; but Ellen Grant still said she failed to identify him. Immediately, Wilde sank back into his seat in the corner of the dock and spread out his arms, partially hiding his face, as he had done through almost all of the proceedings.

GRANT: I have heard Alfred Taylor speak of his friend Oscar.[89]

Gill then put the names of several young men mentioned during Wilde's libel suit to Ellen Grant, and she said that two or three of them were at Taylor's rooms for a few days at a time; these young men slept with Taylor and shared his rooms.

GRANT: There were tea parties—always men—and I heard Taylor addressing one as "Oscar" and others as "Charlie dear," etc. On one occasion, I allowed a gentleman, who said he was a friend of Taylor's, to see the rooms; but I afterwards learned that he was a police sergeant. (*Laughter in court.*) I knew the house was being watched, and the police sergeant visited shortly before Taylor left. Taylor left suddenly, telling me on the Saturday and leaving on the Sunday. He left no papers or telegrams behind. He never told me what his occupation was.

SIR JOHN BRIDGE: There was no brass plate upon the door?[90]

GRANT: Oh no. He said he was a gentleman.

Alfred Wood, a fair young man dressed in black, was the next witness. Gill began his examination by asking him several questions about himself and his acquaintance with Taylor.

ALFRED WOOD: I am a clerk. I know the prisoner Taylor, and was staying with him in Little College Street in January 1893. I had been out of employment about a week. I did not know that Taylor had any legitimate employment whatever.

GILL: Do you know the other prisoner?

WOOD: Yes, I know Oscar Wilde.

GILL: When did you make his acquaintance?

WOOD: At the Café Royal, and I think it must have been sometime in January 1893.[91] It was about three months before I went to America. I was alone when I met him. It was about nine o'clock in the evening when I met him. We went to the Florence in Rupert Street, and there we had supper together in a private room.[92] We had champagne. After supper, we went to, I think, Tite Street. He said his family were at Torquay.[93] We went into the house. There seemed to be nobody about, and he let himself in by a latchkey. We went to his bedroom, and there we had something to drink. I stayed for three or four hours.

GILL: Did acts of indecency take place there?

WOOD: Yes.

Here Travers Humphreys rightly objected to what he claimed was a leading question. Sir John Bridge said it would not assist the prisoner Wilde to have details, but since the objection had been raised, the witness would have to state the facts.

WOOD: He committed sodomy upon me.[94] My only excuse is that I was worse for drink at the time.

GILL: Did you make further visits to Tite Street and did further acts of indecency take place?

WOOD: Yes, similar acts took place after supper, and drink was plentiful.

SIR JOHN BRIDGE: Where did the supper come from?

WOOD: Mr. Wilde and I went down to the pantry and found it. I did not see any servant in the house.

SIR JOHN BRIDGE: Had you seen Mr. Wilde before?

WOOD: I had seen him at Taylor's rooms in Little College Street. I was lodging at Langham Street, having a bed and sitting room combined.[95] Wilde called on me there one afternoon and stayed about twenty minutes. I do not recall any indecencies taking place there. I later took rooms at 4 Great Russell Street. Wilde gave me money on several occasions, £3 and £4 at a time, and also gave me a watch and a chain. Our acquaintance ceased when I went to America, in March 1893.

GILL: How did your leaving come about?

WOOD: I told Taylor that I would like to get away from these people.

SIR JOHN BRIDGE: Who do you mean by these people?

WOOD: Wilde and others.

GILL: Let us leave others out at present. You had become acquainted with others who had attended these tea parties at Taylor's, and some of them are out of the country at present?

WOOD: Yes.

GILL: You wanted to go abroad, and told Taylor so?

WOOD: Yes. I heard Taylor telling him that I wanted to go to America, and Wilde asked me if I had any letters, and I said yes. Taylor sent me a telegram to meet Wilde, and I went to his rooms. Wilde then gave me two £10 notes and two £5 notes.

GILL: Did you give him any letters then?

WOOD: He asked me for them; he seemed very anxious to get them.

SIR JOHN BRIDGE: Did you give him any letters of his that day?

GILL: Not his, Sir John—other people's.[96]

WOOD: The next day I lunched with Wilde at the Florence. That was the last time I saw him. He sent me £5 by messenger after the lunch. I have been to the Savoy to see Mr. Wilde. I know Mavor.[97]

The next witness to be called was the twenty-eight-year-old Sydney Arthur Mavor: "a tall youth," the *Illustrated Police Budget* commented, "and well dressed."[98] Mavor said that he had made Taylor's acquaintance in 1892, and that he had visited Taylor in Little College Street. The young man added that in September 1892 he dined with Wilde, Douglas, and Taylor at Kettner's. About a week later, Wilde sent Mavor a silver cigarette case. Later still, Mavor received a message asking him to meet Wilde.

GILL: At an hotel?

SYDNEY MAVOR: I don't remember.

GILL: Come. We have the hotel books, you know.

MAVOR: I don't know the date. It might have been October. It was at the Albemarle Hotel. Mr. Wilde was waiting when I arrived, and I found that he had taken rooms, and a bedroom for me as well. My bedroom led from Mr. Wilde's bedroom.

GILL: And what took place there?

MAVOR: Nothing.

GILL: Did you not make a statement to Mr. Charles Russell?[99]

MAVOR: No. Mr. Russell asked me a lot of questions, but I did not think he had taken down my answers.

SIR JOHN BRIDGE: Why did you stay all night at the Albemarle Hotel?

MAVOR: Because it was so late. I went there to stay all night. Mr. Wilde paid the hotel bill.

Mavor admitted that he had stayed three times at Taylor's rooms, and that he had slept in the same bed as Taylor. Moreover, Mavor stated that he called Wilde "Oscar," and that Wilde called Mavor "Sydney."

The next witness to be called was Antonio Migge, who declared he was a "professor of massage," a freelance masseur who serviced guests at the Savoy Hotel.[100] In his testimony, Migge stated that he had been to Wilde's rooms to provide massages from 16 to 20 March 1893. One morning, when he entered after knocking, he witnessed a young man of between sixteen and eighteen years of age in the bed. At the time, Wilde informed Migge that there was no need for the masseur to stay any longer, since Wilde's health was good that morning. Migge never attended Wilde again. The last witness to be called was Jane Margaret Cotter. Cotter, a chambermaid at the Savoy Hotel, claimed that she had discovered a young man occupying the same bed.[101]

Once Cotter stepped down from the stand, Gill said that was as far as he proposed to go that day.[102] After a consultation, the prisoners were remanded until 11 o'clock on Thursday, 11 April. Travers Humphreys requested bail, saying that sureties could be offered to any amount; he remarked that all day Friday Wilde had known that a warrant might be issued for his arrest and that he had not made any attempt to get away. Gill opposed the question of bail. Sir John Bridge said he could not grant bail, and he added that Wilde should consult with his solicitor at Holloway.

> SIR JOHN BRIDGE: There will be no bail under any conditions, but I may be able to consider the matter next Thursday. There will be every opportunity to converse with him in prison. It is not a case for bail.[103]

Wilde sighed heavily as he heard the decision. After a short consultation with his counsel, Wilde followed his fellow prisoner out of the dock through the prisoners' door, where he was led to one of the cells below. Sir John Bridge gave Wilde permission to speak to several friends.[104] It was expected that Wilde would be afforded the privilege of a cab to Holloway, but since no one appeared to supply the money for it, he and Taylor were driven away in an ordinary police van to the prison. Wilde spent five nights in Holloway before his next court appearance. The *Illustrated Police Budget* noted the conditions of his cell:

> [T]he accused has been provided with a comfortably furnished cell. It has a well-upholstered bedstead, table, two chairs and washstand, and is in close proximity to the cell in which that unfortunate gentleman, Major Parkinson, committed suicide some months ago. In the case of Oscar Wilde, the small oval looking-glass has been removed. Arrangements have been made by the friends of Oscar that he is to be supplied with his meals from a local caterer, and that entertainer of persons in durance vile has been told to provide his customer with the best things he can possibly obtain. By the rules of the prison, the accused will be able to empty half a bottle of wine *per diem*, but smoking is strictly forbidden. The prisoner will be allowed to see his solicitor daily, and a friend on visiting days.[105]

Wilde's diet was also the subject of sustained scrutiny. After he had been in his cell for half an hour, the *Sun* noted, he was asked whether he needed food to be brought into the jail:

> He replied in the affirmative, adding that his friends would, the following day, make all the necessary arrangements. Giving the money to a warder told off for the purpose, Oscar, at his own request, was supplied with a fried sole, a boiled chicken, and a half-pint of claret. The fish was pierced with a fork, turned over and left undisturbed. The chicken was roughly dissected, one or two mouthfuls taken, and then sent away. Oscar drank the wine with avidity, and asked for more, but was informed that the regulations only permitted half a pint per diem.
>
> Yesterday morning, following a rather sleepless night, Oscar breakfasted off ham and fried eggs and coffee. A pint of liquid was sent in, and about half the quantity consumed. The solids were about half demolished. Cold grilled fowl, tomatoes, and salad, and bread, constituted the Sunday dinner, together with a half-pint bottle of claret. Whether the cooking or the surroundings destroyed the prisoner's appetite is impossible to say; but the meal, like that of the preceding evening, left his room with almost the same weight as it entered. He eagerly drank the bottle of wine. For tea, poached eggs on toast, water cress, and a pint of tea was supplied.[106]

Meanwhile, the *Illustrated Police Budget* went on to describe Wilde's daily routine at Holloway on those days when he was not in court. The report draws attention to the hour when he arose ("six o'clock"), the time he spent thereafter cleaning his room ("[f]or this service the prisoner receives 1s. a week"), and his breakfast time ("half-past seven o'clock," when "tea, ham, and eggs, or a chop, toast, and bread and butter arrives from a well-known restaurant in Holloway").[107] Wilde, the *Budget* observes, "pays for the food, and, within reason, can eat and drink what he pleases." By 9.00 a.m., Wilde exercised in the yard. Thereafter, he returned to his cell in order to read the newspapers, for which he also paid. On the days when he was not in the dock, he stayed there until noon, when his lunch arrived from the same local restaurant: "It consists of a cut off the joint, vegetables, cheese, and biscuits and water, or one glass of wine." After this repast, Wilde went once more to the exercise ground for an hour. Once back in his cell, he returned to reading the press. From time to time, his close friends and his solicitor visited him. By 6.00 p.m., his dinner was delivered: "It consists usually of soup, fish, joint, or game, cheese, and half a pint of any wine he chooses to select." After dinner, he sat once again in his chair: "the agony he endures at not being allowed even a whiff at his favourite cigarette," the journalist opined, "must be agony indeed." Once 8.00 p.m. came around, the warder brought a lamp into the cell. One hour later, the warder returned, giving Wilde five minutes to undress and get into bed. "He complies," the reporter notes, "but with a sigh." After Wilde turned in for the night, the warder removed the lamp, bolted and locked the door. The journalist divulges that Wilde slept poorly: "he is out of bed most of the night, and in unstockinged feet paces the room in apparently not too good a mood." "Yes, poor Oscar," the commentator adds, "I do pity you."[108]

SECOND DAY: THURSDAY, 11 APRIL 1895

Oscar Wilde of 16 Tite Street, Chelsea, and Alfred Taylor of 25 Denbigh Street, Pimlico, were again brought up at Bow Street Magistrates' Court on Thursday. Sir John Bridge took his seat on the bench at 11 o'clock. The prisoners were immediately placed in the dock. As with the first day of the hearing, Mr. C. F. Gill, instructed by Mr. Angus Lewis, prosecuted on behalf of the Treasury; Sir Edward Clarke, Q.C., MP, and Mr. Travers Humphreys, instructed by Mr. C. O. Humphreys, defended Wilde; Mr. Arthur Newton appeared for Taylor.[109] The Hon. H. C. Cuffe, the public prosecutor, occupied a seat on the bench.[110] The *Star* reported: "Sir Edward Clarke arrived rather late by way of the public staircase, wearing a summery grey frockcoat and a general air of Easter vacation."[111] The newspaper also observed that before Wilde appeared, he could be heard asking: "Is Sir Edward Clarke here?" "Yes," replied the sergeant jailer. Wilde still wore "the dark grey overcoat with the velvet collar and cuffs" in which he had previously appeared in court, while Taylor—"[c]lean-shaven and pink-shirted"—"had more than ever the appearance of a valet."[112]

On the charge sheet, Wilde was described as a gentleman and Taylor as of no occupation. The small Extradition Court in which the charges were heard was again densely crowded. The *Illustrated Police News* commented: "Wilde looked careworn and much older than he appeared last before the Court. Taylor, on the other hand, looked all the better for his imprisonment. His cuffs and collar were spotlessly white; his face clean-shaven, and his hair carefully brushed. Wilde's hair was not so carefully brushed as usual."[113] *Reynolds's Newspaper* noted that Wilde, who appeared much paler than on the previous occasion, bowed respectfully to the magistrate as he entered the dock. According to the same report, Taylor seemed unconcerned, and smiled at the apparent interest that his appearance excited. Among the people in the court were the theatre impresario Augustus Harris and the editor and popular author Jerome K. Jerome.

At 11.05 a.m., when Sir John Bridge took his seat, Clarke rose at once.

CLARKE: In this case, I appear with my friend, Mr. Humphreys, in defense of Mr. Wilde. I have had the opportunity to read the depositions taken at the first hearing last Saturday.[114] I was much obliged to you for allowing the cross-examination of the witnesses to stand over. On consideration of the matter, I have decided not to ask for the witnesses to be recalled for cross-examination because I feel it would not affect the result so far as this court is concerned, and I think it desirable on all grounds that we should have as few adjournments as possible. I shall probably adopt the same course with regard to witnesses to be called, and not cross-examine them. I have told my learned friend Mr. Gill this, with a view to shorten the inquiry.

SIR JOHN BRIDGE: It is absolutely incumbent upon all of us to get the matter over as quickly and speedily as possible.[115]

ARTHUR NEWTON: I would be obliged to ask for the witnesses to be recalled in order that I might cross-examine them on behalf of Taylor.

Charles Parker was the first witness who was recalled. "He was," the *Star* observed, "respectably dressed, apparently in new clothes."[116] The smart attire immediately raised suspicions about the ways in which these witnesses had been groomed for the roles that they were expected to play. More Adey, who later took much of the responsibility for Wilde's legal affairs during the two-year prison sentence, confided to a correspondent that "Charles Parker appeared in the court in suit of clothes given him by Lord Queensberry."[117] Still, it took until 1963 before C. H. Norman made public the belief that the authorities had compensated witnesses for the prosecution by handing Parker and Wood "£5 a week from the day of Wilde's arrest," when the usual payment was 5s.[118] Shelley reportedly received a total of £22 1s.; this was approximately half the annual salary that he had earned at Mathews and Lane's publishing partnership in Vigo Street.[119] In private correspondence, Norman contended that these handsome witness fees came out of Queensberry's pocket.[120]

Charles Parker gave his name and said he was born in 1874.[121] He added that he had been in his current employment for nearly eight months. Newton proceeded to ask Charles Parker various questions. He wanted to know whether a man named Harrington had introduced Parker to Taylor.[122] Newton also questioned Parker about his knowledge of Frederick Atkins.[123]

NEWTON: Were you not arrested in Fitzroy Square last August?

CHARLES PARKER: Yes.

NEWTON: Were you a friend of many of the men who were arrested there?

CHARLES PARKER: No, I only knew one. That man was Taylor.

NEWTON: Did a man named Harrington introduce you to Taylor?

CHARLES PARKER: I was not introduced to Taylor by a man named Harrington. Taylor first accosted me at a restaurant.

Parker added that he had made a statement about this case to Mr. Russell the solicitor, and he believed it was true.[124] Newton continued the cross-examination.

NEWTON: Were you afraid when you made that statement that you would be brought into the libel case?

CHARLES PARKER: Not at all.

NEWTON: You knew that you had committed illegal acts over and over again, and might be prosecuted?

CHARLES PARKER: I was not aware of it.

NEWTON: As a fact, you had committed indecencies with men?

CHARLES PARKER: Not before I met Mr. Wilde.

NEWTON: Did you not know you might be prosecuted for it?

CHARLES PARKER: Yes.

NEWTON: With regard to the dinner, at which four of you were present, did you not know that it was Taylor's birthday?

CHARLES PARKER: I didn't know that it was Taylor's birthday when I was first taken to dine with Wilde.

NEWTON: Am I right in saying that nothing was said by Mr. Wilde to you about going to the Savoy in Taylor's presence?

CHARLES PARKER: He asked me in Taylor's presence, but I do not know whether Taylor heard it.

Charles Parker added that on his second visit to the Savoy, Taylor had nothing to do with it.

NEWTON: Did you know Atkins?

CHARLES PARKER: Yes.

NEWTON: Is he not a notorious blackmailer?

CHARLES PARKER: I don't know.

NEWTON: How long have you known him?

CHARLES PARKER: About three years.

NEWTON: What is his occupation?

CHARLES PARKER: A comedian.

GILL: I do not know for what purpose this mode of cross-examination is being indulged in. If it is for the purpose of preventing the man coming here as a witness, it will not succeed. If it is pursued, I shall go into other cases against Taylor.[125]

NEWTON: I am entitled to test this evidence and to show that this man Parker is an associate of the most notorious and depraved characters in London.

SIR JOHN BRIDGE: Go on.

NEWTON: You say you do not know what Atkins is?

CHARLES PARKER: No.

NEWTON: Why did you leave the service in which you engaged as a valet?

CHARLES PARKER: The gentleman could not afford to keep me.[126]

NEWTON: Did he not say you had stolen some of his clothes, and discharged you as a thief?

CHARLES PARKER: No. It was after I left that he said I had stolen the clothes.

NEWTON: Did you steal a sovereign that came for Taylor?[127]

CHARLES PARKER: No.

NEWTON: Just before that, did you not get £30, in conjunction with two other persons, by threatening to accuse a gentleman of a crime?[128]

CHARLES PARKER: I didn't. The others gave it to me.

NEWTON: They extorted it from a gentleman?[129]

CHARLES PARKER: I think that is right.

NEWTON: They extorted more than £30?

CHARLES PARKER: I think so.

NEWTON: That was your share?

CHARLES PARKER: Yes.

NEWTON: Substantially, it was hush money, was it not?[130]

CHARLES PARKER: They didn't tell me it was to keep my mouth shut.

NEWTON: And was it you who had committed indecency with the gentleman who paid the money?

CHARLES PARKER: Yes.

NEWTON: Then it was hush money to prevent your saying anything about it?

CHARLES PARKER: They did not tell me it was to keep my mouth shut.

SIR JOHN BRIDGE: Isn't that substantially what it was?

CHARLES PARKER: I don't know what they gave it to me for. They only told me who it came from.

On this exchange, *Reynolds's Newspaper* commented: "The quiet, assured tone in which Charles Parker made this remark stunned the court. Wilde, leaning back in the corner of the dock, with a dull lifeless expression in his eyes, took no notice. Taylor pretended to be delighted."[131]

NEWTON: Did you not ask Taylor to introduce you to Wilde?

CHARLES PARKER: No. He asked me if I would like to be introduced to Wilde, and I said I would.

NEWTON: How long had you been out of employment when you met Taylor?

CHARLES PARKER: Two or three weeks.

NEWTON: Had you been in constant employment before that?

CHARLES PARKER: Always.

Gill proceeded to redirect the examination of Charles Parker.

GILL: Until you met Taylor, did you know such men as have been referred to existed?

CHARLES PARKER: I knew there were such men.

GILL: But had you been brought into contact with them?

CHARLES PARKER: No.

GILL: From the time you made Taylor's acquaintance up to the time of the arrest in Fitzroy Square did you see Taylor frequently?

CHARLES PARKER: Yes.

GILL: After Taylor left Little College Street, did he let you live in Chapel Street?

CHARLES PARKER: Yes.

Newton said that he desired to ask certain questions of William Parker and the landlady of 13 Little College Street, but he did not propose to ask anything of Alfred Wood or Sydney Mavor. Gill remarked that the witnesses mentioned were not present, since no notice had been given, but he would secure their attendance.

Frederick Atkins was the next witness to be called. The *Star* described him as "a pale-eyed, pimply-faced lad of 20, in a green cord waistcoat with pale blue spots, a blue oxford shirt, and a jacket of rough brown tweed."[132] Gill began his examination.

ATKINS: I knew Taylor and his rooms at Little College Street. Taylor introduced me to Wilde in November 1892, when all three of us and another gentleman dined together at the Florence Hotel in Soho.[133] Wilde asked if I would like to go to Paris with him as his private secretary. I said "Yes," and we went two days later by the Club Train from Victoria.[134] Once we arrived in Paris, we went to 29 Boulevard des Capucines, a private hotel, where Wilde had a bed-sitting room and I had a bedroom.[135] There was a door connecting both rooms. Wilde told me to beware women, as they ruined men.[136] (*Laughter in court.*) The next day we lunched at the Café Julien, and in the afternoon, we went to the Grand Hotel to get our hair done.[137] Wilde spoke in French to the barber, who began to curl my hair. (*Laughter.*[138])

GILL: What kind of dinner was it?

ATKINS: The best I ever had in my life.

Everybody in court laughed. Taylor increased his grin. Even Wilde smiled.

ATKINS: After dinner, Wilde gave me a Louis and permission to go outside.[139]

GILL: To go to the Moulin Rouge?[140]

ATKINS: No. He told me not to go there. But I went. (*Laughter in court.*[141]) I got back at half past two in the morning, and I found Schwabe with Wilde. At half past nine, Wilde came and sat on the edge of my bed, and he talked to me about women. He told me not to have anything to do with them.

It was conceivably at this point that Atkins alluded to the fact that he participated in a sexual act with Wilde. As the *Illustrated Police News* observed: "[Atkins] went on to describe what took place there, but the details are totally unfit for publication."[142] Presumably, Atkins used the word "sodomy," which Wood also appears to have used in his testimony about his visit to Wilde's home on Tite Street.[143] Gill continued his examination by focusing on the gifts that Wilde habitually made to the young men with whom the defendant had enjoyed intimacy.

GILL: Did he buy you a present while you were in Paris?[144]

ATKINS: Wilde gave me a silver cigarette case.

GILL: Did he give you any money?

ATKINS: Yes, £3, as soon as we got back to Victoria, where we parted. I afterwards went to Tite Street, after a letter I got from Wilde. I took the letter with me. When he saw me, he asked for the letter, and I gave it to him.[145]

GILL: Did he say anything about the visit to Paris?

ATKINS: He told me not to say anything about it. Wilde afterwards visited me while I was having tea with a friend—a young man. I introduced him to Wilde.

GILL: How did you make the acquaintance of Taylor.

ATKINS: I was introduced to him.

GILL: What did Taylor call you?

ATKINS: He and Wilde called me "Fred." One night when we were at a hotel, Wilde kissed the waiter.[146] He asked me if I wanted to go to Paris.

GILL: What happened then?[147]

ATKINS: He put his arm round my neck.

GILL: What else?

ATKINS: He put his arm round Douglas.

GILL (*quickly*): Never mind that. Keep to what he did to you.

Newton proceeded to cross-examine Atkins.

NEWTON: Do not mention any name. But were you not introduced to Taylor by the gentleman who was in Paris?[148]

ATKINS: Yes.

NEWTON: And did not that gentleman also introduce you to Mr. Wilde?

ATKINS: No.

NEWTON: Did not some other gentleman introduce you to Mr. Wilde?[149]

ATKINS: Yes.

NEWTON: At the time you were introduced to Taylor, were you leading the same kind of life as you are now?

ATKINS: Yes.

NEWTON: What is that?

ATKINS: I am a comedian and a bookmaker's clerk. (*Laughter in court.*)

NEWTON: For years past, have you been living with a man named Burton?

ATKINS: Yes.

NEWTON: Committing immoral acts with various persons, and then getting money from them?

ATKINS: Never. I have never got money in that way.

NEWTON: Do you seriously say that you have not, on more than one occasion, extorted money from men by threatening to accuse them of crimes?

ATKINS: I never have.

NEWTON: Has Burton?

ATKINS: Not to my knowledge.

SIR JOHN BRIDGE: Did you ever do any secretarial work for Wilde in Paris?

ATKINS: Yes. I wrote something about *A Woman of No Importance*.

Once Gill took the opportunity to reexamine Atkins, the court learned more about the sleeping arrangements in the Paris hotel. The magistrate asked for clarification.

SIR JOHN BRIDGE: Was the person in bed with him a man or a woman?[150]

ATKINS: A man.

GILL: He was the man who introduced you to Taylor?

ATKINS: Yes.

The next witness to be called was Edward Shelley, the young man whom Wilde met at his publishers Elkin Mathews and John Lane at The Bodley Head, and whom Carson in the libel trial dubbed an "office boy."[151] The *Star* referred to Shelley as a "tall, heavy-framed, with a square jaw and a distinctly 'intellectual face,' as Wilde said of him at the Old Bailey . . . . In spite of the stifling closeness of the court, he wore a heavy double-breasted reefer overcoat, tightly buttoned."[152] Gill began his examination.

GILL: When you worked for Mr. Mathews, what were your wages?

EDWARD SHELLEY: They were 15s. a week at first, and were raised afterwards to £45 a year.

GILL: When did you first meet Mr. Wilde?

SHELLEY: I met him when he called to discuss the reissue of his volume of poems. Afterwards, in February 1892, he sent me a note asking me to join him at the Albemarle Hotel. We had dinner together in a public room. We had plenty of wine at dinner, enough to excite me. After dinner we went to his sitting room, where we drank wine, talked, and smoked until half-past one or two in the morning. Mr. Wilde asked me to stay the night.

At this point, Shelley became exceedingly distressed and proceeded with great difficulty.

SHELLEY: I did not know the man. Since it was far from my home, I thought that Mr. Wilde, who had been kind to me, called me clever, and flattered me, was going to put me up for the night.

GILL: While you were in the room, did he kiss you?[153]

SHELLEY: Yes, just as I was going into the bedroom.

GILL: Was he a man for whom you had a great admiration for his talent?

SHELLEY: Yes, and he always professed to be fond of me and flattered me.

GILL: Did you stay there the night?

SHELLEY: Yes.

GILL: Sleeping in the same bed?

SHELLEY: Yes. The next night we went to the Independent Theatre, where we had a box, and we dined together in his sitting room at the Albemarle Hotel.[154] We also went to the Prince of Wales's Club, to Kettner's, and the Café Royal.[155] Wilde wrote letters to me at my place of work. But I destroyed everything he gave me except books. I received books from Mr. Wilde, including a large edition of *Dorian Gray*.[156] I tore out the title pages because of the inscriptions that he wrote on them. I kept the books. Wilde also arranged for me to go to Paris. But I was not able to get off work. Sometime in 1893 I wrote a letter to Wilde regarding the conduct he showed towards me, and I said I wished not to see him again. It was after writing that letter that I destroyed the letter Wilde had sent me.

NEWTON: Taylor is a stranger to you?[157]

SHELLEY: Yes, quite a stranger.

Throughout Gill's examination of Shelley, Wilde maintained an inscrutable countenance. His suede gloves hung from his fingers as he fixed his gaze blankly at the wall behind the magistrate. Shelley left the witness box holding a highly polished silk hat and rattan cane.[158]

Three further witnesses were called before lunch. Mrs. Lucy Rumsby was the landlady of 50 Park Walk, Chelsea, where Charles Parker had occupied a small back room for several weeks. She gave him notice because of a complaint from another lodger. Mrs. Rumsby had seen Parker call on a friend in Chapel Street. A young man had called once or twice to visit Parker, but since her eyesight was so bad, she could not recognize him. Thereafter, Mrs. Margery Bancroft, whom the *Sun* described as "a fancifully attired young woman," stated that she had lodged in the house for eight years, and added that Taylor—who at the time lived at 3 Chapel Street—frequently called for Parker.[159] She recalled that on one occasion late at night, a cab drew up at the door, and she saw Parker and Wilde alight. Park Walk was ten minutes on foot from Tite Street. But Wilde, she added, came in a cab.[160] Both prisoners were ordered to stand up, and Mrs. Bancroft insisted that she recognized both of them. In response, Wilde remained impassive, while Taylor grinned. Mrs. Bancroft added that she had her suspicions, and it was on the basis of her complaint that Parker was sent away.[161]

Mrs. Sophia Gray, the landlady of 3 Chapel Street, gave similar evidence.[162] She rented two rooms to Taylor from August to the end of 1893, and she had seen both Parker and Wilde there. Parker had stayed all night and slept in the same bed. Taylor had an accident, and Wilde came to see him. She also mentioned that Taylor's sister-in-law came to visit him.[163] When Taylor left, she held onto some of his effects in order to pay off the debts he owed her. One of these items was the hatbox containing letters, which she tried unsuccessfully to sell.[164] The witness handed over the hatbox to Mr. Fred Kerley, who represented Mr. Charles Russell, Lord Queensberry's solicitor. Sophia Gray testified that Taylor never seemed to have any occupation, and he had not many callers. There were, she added, perhaps two or three young men who had called at different times. She knew nothing about the Little College Street establishment.

NEWTON: You are not in the habit of asking questions about your lodgers' business?

SOPHIA GRAY: Oh, no. I knew he was a man of respectable family. He always acted as a gentleman in my place.

GILL: You never saw any ladies there?

GRAY: Oh, no, sir. (*Laughter in court.*)

The court adjourned for luncheon.

At two o'clock, Mary Applegate was called.[165] She was a servant employed at the house where the witness Atkins had been living.[166] There had, she stated, been a picture of Wilde in Atkins's room. She recognized Wilde as a man who had visited Atkins there on two occasions. Thomas Price, a waiter at Geneux's private hotel, 10 and 11 St. James's Place, said that Wilde reserved two rooms there in October 1893, and kept them until April 1894. Price remarked that Wilde had many visitors there, principally young men. Price's response to Gill's examination threatened to cause embarrassment.

THOMAS PRICE: Among the young men were—

GILL: Ha! Never mind names just now. Was Charles Parker among these?

PRICE: Yes.
GILL: Taylor?
PRICE: Yes, once.
GILL: Atkins?
PRICE: Yes, several times—two or three.
GILL: A lad named Scarfe?
PRICE: Yes, several times.
GILL: A lad named Barford?[167]
PRICE: Yes.

Reynolds's Newspaper remarked: "What the names were [that] Mr. Gill did not wish mentioned after suggesting this list was a point which raised considerable curiosity."[168]

M. Aloys Louis Vogel, proprietor of the Albemarle Hotel, informed Gill about Wilde's visits to the establishment.[169]

ALOYS LOUIS VOGEL: It was Mr. Wilde's habit to finish his plays at the hotel, and to produce them from there. Wilde had many young men calling upon him, and at first it was thought that they came from the theatres. But something raised our suspicions, and I made up my mind that Mr. Wilde should no longer be a guest at our hotel. Wilde had a small bill outstanding. I instructed my solicitor to take advantage of that to sue Mr. Wilde for it. But Mr. Wilde did not take the hint, and he had to be sued for a second little account. Mr. Wilde always had a private sitting room with a bedroom opening off it. To my annoyance, Mr. Wilde was admitted to my hotel from 1 to 17 January this year, while I was away. I again pressed Mr. Wilde for money, and, failing to obtain it, I issued a writ.[170]

The next witness, Mrs. Annie Perkins—formerly a housekeeper at the Savoy Hotel, now retired to Southsea—gave evidence about Wilde's stay there.[171] She said that a servant told her something about the condition of the sheets on Wilde's bed.[172] The magistrate wished to know more.

SIR JOHN BRIDGE: What did you see on the sheets?
ANNIE PERKINS: I refused to look at them.

The witness who followed Annie Perkins was Charles Elkin Mathews, former business partner of John Lane at The Bodley Head. Mathews deposed that both he and Lane had their attention called to Shelley's friendship with Wilde, whose books they were at the time publishing. He was aware of one letter that Wilde addressed to Shelley. Mathews stated that the publishers took no action, although Shelley left his position.[173]

At this moment, Detective Inspector Charles Richards was called; on the evening of 5 April, he went with Detective Sergeant Allen to the Cadogan Hotel, Sloane Street, where he arrested Wilde. Richards gave a detailed response to Gill's inquiry.

CHARLES RICHARDS: We told the prisoner: "Mr. Wilde, we are police officers. A warrant has been issued for your apprehension for committing some indecent offence with a male person." He said: "Yes. Where shall I be taken?" I told him: "You will have to go with me now to Scotland Yard, and then on to Bow Street." The prisoner asked: "Can I have bail?" And I replied: "I don't think you can." At Scotland Yard, I handed the prisoner over to Inspector Brockwell, who had the warrant. Later in the evening, I went to 25 Denbigh Place, Pimlico: the address that Taylor gave when he was charged. I searched Taylor's rooms, and among other things I found a gold brooch, which Taylor used to fasten his nightshirt, and eight pairs of trousers.[174]

GILL: Was there anything peculiar about the trousers?

RICHARDS: Yes. Seven pairs had the sewing of the pockets cut on one side, so that anyone could pass their hands straight through. (*Sensation in court.*)

Inspector Brockwell was the next witness. He provided an even more detailed account of the arrest.

THOMAS BROCKWELL: When Wilde was handed over into my custody, I read over the warrant to him. Wilde put out his hands and said: "Let me read it." I said: "No. I can't do that. If there is anything you do not understand I will read it to you again." Wilde then asked what dates were mentioned. I told him: "March 29, 1893, and divers other days." Wilde made no further reply. He was searched, and on him we found letters and memoranda and three writs. Among the papers were an envelope addressed to "Sydney Mavor, Esq.," and a penciled note:

Dear Syd,—
I could not wait any longer. Come on at once to see Oscar, 16 Tite Street, Chelsea, I am there.—

Yours,
Alf Taylor.

There was another note from Taylor to Wilde, referring to Inspector [John G.] Littlechild, the retired police officer who prepared the evidence for the Marquess of Queensberry's case. The letter ran:—

Dear Oscar:—
When I left home yesterday I left a note, as I told you, for Sydney Mavor if he called. Littlechild, the detective, called shortly after I left, and, as I was

out, asked to write a note. So he was shown into my room, where the letter for Sydney was. When I returned last night I found the enclosed letter, and the letter I had written to Sydney had been opened. In its place was one from Littlechild saying that he wished to see me next morning.

Yours,
Alfred Taylor.

I also found upon Wilde the following letter from Littlechild to Taylor:

APRIL 2.

Dear Sir,—
I wanted to see you, but to-morrow morning will do. I will be on the look-out for you at the Old Bailey at ten.

—Yours truly,
J. G. Littlechild.

There was also a letter signed Harry Bartlett,[175] and two writs were by jewelers for jewelry and cigarette cases. I also found upon Wilde twenty £5 notes and a cheque-book on the London and Westminster Bank. I was present at Bow Street on the morning of the 6th when Taylor was brought in. When Taylor was arrested, he seemed surprised, but not at the arrest. "Is that the only charge?" he asked. "I don't know," I replied.

Detective Sergeant William Harris of the "A" Division was the next witness.

WILLIAM HARRIS: Taylor had been known to me for some time.[176] In May '93, I kept observation for seventeen or eighteen days on the house in Little College Street. During that time, I gained entry to his rooms. The windows were draped, and the rooms and staircase were heavily draped. On the morning of the 6th, I saw Taylor leave the house in Denbigh Place. Last Saturday, when I tapped Taylor on the shoulder and took him into custody "for committing indecency with male persons," he said, smilingly: "Very well; I expected you last night. What are you going to do?" "I shall take you to Bow Street," I replied. On arrival there, the warrant was explained, and Taylor was brought before the magistrates." I found upon Taylor a copy of the subpoena to attend the Central Criminal Court during the hearing of the *Wilde v. Queensberry* case.

Newton cross-examined the police officer.

NEWTON: Do you know that he attended every day?
HARRIS: I do not.

Alfred Wood was the next witness to be recalled.[177] Gill examined him. Wood stated that the letter found in Taylor's hatbox was one that Wood had written from America to Taylor. In that particular item of correspondence, Wood had mentioned the name of Burton. But he said that he did not remember whether Taylor knew Burton.

GILL: In the letter, you write: "Tell Oscar he can send me a draft for an Easter egg."[178] (*Laughter in court.*) Did Taylor ever answer that letter?
WOOD: No, sir.
GILL: Have you ever received money from Taylor?
WOOD: No. I borrowed five shillings from him once, and paid it back.
GILL: Has he given you money by cheque?
WOOD: No.

A cheque bearing Wood's name was then produced in court, but Wood said that it never came to him.

The final witness of the day was Mr. George Frederick Claridge, clerk to Messrs. Walter Thornhill and Co., silversmiths, who testified that on 3 October 1892 Wilde purchased a silver cigarette case, and asked him to engrave it "S. A. Mavor, Esq."[179]

Gill said he did not propose to go further that day. He would ask for a further remand until Friday. With respect to the course that Clarke had adopted, Gill did not think it would be necessary for him to occupy the court very long.

Travers Humphreys and Arthur Newton made strong applications for bail.

TRAVERS HUMPHREYS: I beg to apply for bail on the grounds I gave last week.
SIR JOHN BRIDGE: I shall allow no bail.

Newton applied for bail on Taylor's behalf; he stated that his client belonged to a very respectable family.

SIR JOHN BRIDGE: In a case of this kind, a man's respectable connections are not in any way a reason to let him out on bail—quite the contrary.[180]

Sir John remanded the prisoners until twelve o'clock the next day.

The press provided supplementary reports about events surrounding the outcome of the second day of the hearing. The *Western Mail* noted:

A Central News telegram from New York says:—Mr. John Lane, publisher, of London, writes to the Central News agent as follows[181]:—"The details of Oscar Wilde's case have not been extensively reported here, but private cabled advices inform me that it has been stated in court that I introduced Shelley to Oscar. Allow me to say that I did not know Wilde except by sight until he became an active partner with Elkin Mathews in February 1892. At that time Shelley had been clerk to Mathews for a whole year, and acting in that capac-

> ity, Shelley had already made the acquaintance of Wilde. My relations with Wilde have been entirely of a business nature. I have never introduced anyone to him. On the contrary, I have frequently declined to do so. My attitude towards him is quite well known. After seeing the papers here on my arrival last Sunday, I immediately cabled to my manager to withdraw all of Wilde's books, and not merely his name from the title pages."[182]

Lane was shaken by these reports. Later in the month, he wrote from New York City to the Irish author George Egerton (Mary Chavelita Dunne Bright)—who, at the time, commanded a high reputation—that he had been "terribly worried re Oscar-Beardsley-Yellow Book": "Imagine my surprise," he added, "when I was cabled ten days ago that Oscar had stated in court that I introduced him to Shelley."[183]

Elsewhere, Wilde's literary contemporaries enjoyed gossiping about his sexual humiliation. W. E. Henley, whose *Scots Observer* had expressed such antipathy to the publication of *The Picture of Dorian Gray* in 1890, confided to his colleague Charles Whibley that the pretrial hearing had not only exposed Wilde's reprehensible actions but also shown his foolishness in not remaining on the Continent:

> Yes: the Bugger at Bay was on the whole a pleasing sight. The air is alive with rumours, of course, but I believe no new arrests will be made, & that morality will be satisfied if Oscar gets two years; as of course he will. Why he didn't stay at Monte Carlo, once he got there, God alone knows. Seeing that he was cognizant of all these arseholes out of place, & that, despite his cognizance, he returned to face the music, & play the Roman fool to Carson's destiny, I can only conjecture that, what between personal & professional vanity, he was stark mad. Be this as it may, he is mad no more. Holloway & Bow St. have taken his hair out of curl in more senses than one. And I am pretty sure that he's having a damn bad time.[184]

From Henley's unsparing viewpoint, it was only right that the once-pretentious Wilde should suffer his comeuppance.

THIRD DAY: FRIDAY, 19 APRIL 1895

As early as 10 o'clock a large crowd had assembled outside Bow Street for the purpose of hearing the prosecution of Oscar Wilde and Alfred Taylor, who were charged under section 11 of the Criminal Law Amendment Act.[185] The number of spectators continued to increase until shortly before 11.00 a.m., when it was announced that Sir John Bridge would not commence the hearing of the remand until noon. The *Sun* described the scene outside the police court: "Long before ten o'clock, the pavement adjacent to the police court and beneath the piazza of Covent Garden Theatre began to be lined with people. By eleven o'clock there was a large crowd on each side of the way. Strange to say, many of these curious spectators waiting for the arrival of the prisoners were women. The great majority, however, were young men, and several of them—a very large number altogether—were well dressed, even fashionably dressed, men."[186] As the front page of the *Illustrated Police News* reveals, Wilde (also known by his cell number, "B. 24") had been "HOOTED BY THE MOB" (fig. 19). The vivid drawing displays a surging horde that includes a group of behatted ladies and gentlemen raising their hands and voices in disapproval. Meanwhile, in the top-right-hand panel, Taylor casts a troubled glance at a rather corpulent Wilde staring into the middle distance of the courtroom, while in the panel below a physician takes the ailing inmate's pulse in H.M. Prison Holloway.

The case was once again held in the Extradition Court. By 11.30 a.m., even though almost all of the available space was occupied, the public were still admitted until the court was packed. Mr. C. F. Gill, instructed by Mr. Angus Lewis of the Treasury, prosecuted. Sir Edward Clarke and Mr. Travers Humphreys defended Wilde. Mr. Arthur Newton appeared for Taylor. Mr. J. P. Grain, Q.C., represented Mavor, should he be called. Mavor was a tall young man, clean-shaven, and with a slight cast in his eye. He appeared in court dressed in the height of fashion, with an immaculate black frock coat, a brilliant silk hat, and a deep 4-inch collar. It was ten minutes past noon by the time Gill arrived, and at 12.20 p.m. Sir John Bridge and Sir Edward Clarke were still missing. Sir John did not take his seat until 12.30 p.m. This was about the time when Wilde and Taylor, who had been conveyed to Bow Street in the police van, entered the court. The *Illustrated Police Budget* captured "a bird's-eye view of the court as the two prisoners st[ood] forward in the dock":

> Seated on the Bench, in a very high-backed chair, is the impassive and learned Sir John Bridge. In front of him on the desk are bundles of papers and innumerable books. Sir John does not lean forward on the desk, but lays back in his chair, crosses his hands, and listens intently to the evidence put before him. On a lower disc, placed immediately below the magistrate, sits the clerk of the court, whose duty it is to inscribe in a big book, which he has on a desk in front of him, all the statements made by the various witnesses. On the floor, but edging on the lower extremities of the clerk's desk, is a big table. On the extreme right sits Mr. Gill, the Treasury counsel, and near to him is Mr. Angus Lewis, a Treasury solicitor who is responsible for the preparation of the

Fig. 19. "Oscar Wilde at Bow Street," *Illustrated Police News*, 20 April 1895: 1. The cover juxtaposes Wilde's plight to that of the Liberal MP Jabez Spencer Balfour, whom the British police had arrested in Argentina for amassing a huge fortune through business fraud. At the time, the police were escorting Balfour back to London. After a long spell of detention in H.M. Prison Holloway, Balfour eventually stood trial at the Queen's Bench Division of the High Court of Justice in November 1895, where he was sentenced to fourteen years of penal servitude.

> cases. On Mr. Gill's left sits Sir Travers Humphreys, who, in the absence of Sir Edward Clarke, is defending Oscar Wilde. Next to him is Mr. J. P. Grain, who holds a watching brief on behalf of the witness Mavor, the lad who was ambitious in going on the music-hall stage. Mr. Arthur Newton, the solicitor who is defending Taylor, and Mr. Smythe [*sic*], holding a watching brief on behalf of someone "unknown" to the public, complete the list of eminent men interested in the case who sit on the counsel bench. The table before them is strewn with papers and documents, the major portion of which seem to belong to Mr. Gill. Immediately behind the advocate's bench is the dock, and in this Wilde and his companion, Taylor, stand, looking not as is their wont, the free and easy men about town. One has the appearance of abject despondency, and stares into space as if trying to read his destiny there; the other smiles occasionally, and is apparently in high spirits. To people who study human nature but very slightly, it is at once apparent that both Taylor's spirits and smiles are forced, and that he is but acting a part. In short, the two prisoners do not by a long way look happy.[187]

The *Sun* took note of additional details about the witnesses: "The two Parkers stood in the doorway laughing, one with his hat cocked on one side of his head, the other, the younger one, with his hat perched back balancing on his neck."[188] Especially noticeable in his appearance was Mavor: "the young fellow who so cheerfully gave two distinct and opposite versions of his stay with Wilde at the Albemarle Hotel."[189] Mavor "stood prominently in the front glaring around with the same self-assurance as though he were singing one of his songs. Dressed! He was a perfect dude. A great high stand-up collar, an inch higher than ordinary people wear; a glossy silk hat and an excellent frock coat. He was one of 'these poor boys' that Mr. Carson so often and vehemently referred to in the Old Bailey Trial."[190] The reporter's wry tone suggests that these young men had been carefully spruced so that they at least looked respectable when their staggering evidence variously scandalized and titillated the courtroom.

Charles Parker was called again and reexamined by Gill. This witness remembered staying at Little College Street. He did not, however, recall Taylor making an improper proposition to him. After he was pressed on the matter, Charles Parker stated that he did remember Taylor making such a proposal, and he said that he had seen Charles Spurrier Mason at Taylor's rooms in Little College Street.[191] He stayed at Chapel Street with Taylor for about a fortnight, during which time Taylor made a similar proposition to him. In response, Taylor laughed contemptuously at some of Charles Parker's statements, but his color heightened, and for the first time he betrayed uneasiness. At this juncture, Charles Parker recounted a more remarkable episode, in which Taylor and Mason went through a ceremony of mock marriage. Taylor, he said, wore female garments. Mason played the bridegroom, and the ceremony was followed by a wedding breakfast.

Newton cross-examined Charles Parker. He inquired if the time to which the witness was referring was the beginning of 1893. William Parker, the older brother of Charles, was the next witness to be recalled. Gill asked William Parker if it was about two years ago that he stayed with Taylor. William Parker confirmed that he had stayed with Taylor, who had attempted indecencies with him. "Am I to speak plainly?" he asked Newton.[192] *Reynolds's Newspaper* remarked that the "evidence was quite unreportable, and that the manner of delivering it was revolting."[193] William Parker's testimony, the *Star* observed, visibly troubled Taylor. According to this newspaper: "Taylor sneered, and affected to smile at [William Parker's] statements, but he presently placed his face on his gloved hands, on the front of the dock, and made a careful study of the floor."[194] Mr. Newton asked the same question, and William Parker replied that it was two years ago that he stayed with Taylor.

Frederick ("Fred") Kerley, whom the press noted as a former police inspector, was the next witness.[195] Kerley responded to Gill by stating that he acted for Messrs. Day, Russell, and Co. in respect of certain inquiries, and he visited 3 Chapel Street and took a written statement from Mrs. Sophia Gray, who afterwards handed him a leather hatbox containing cheques, telegrams, tradesmen's bills, etc., some of which were produced in court. The papers included cheques payable to Sydney Mavor, one for 30s. and another for £2 2s. There were two telegrams. One read: "Cannot manage the dinner tomorrow; am so sorry.—OSCAR." And another read: "Obliged to see [Herbert Beerbohm] Tree at five o'clock. So don't come to the Savoy. Let me know at once about Fred.—OSCAR."[196] There was also a New Year's card from Sydney Mavor to Taylor.

The next witnesses focused on the prisoner's finances. Charles Robinson, a bookkeeper at the Savoy Hotel in the Strand, where Wilde stayed from 2 to 29 March 1893, produced a duplicate of the bill that was handed to Wilde for that period. He stated that Wilde had originally occupied Rooms 361 and 362 before moving to Rooms 343 and 346.[197] Subsequently, Theodore Leith, a clerk at the Marylebone branch of the London and Westminster Bank, displayed a certified copy of Taylor's account from 1 January 1892 to 29 December 1893, at which date the account was closed. Leith was the first witness to divulge Taylor's full name: "Alfred Waterhouse Somerset Taylor." Reginald Walter Brooks, another clerk from the same branch, furnished a copy of Wilde's account from 1 January 1892 to 9 April 1895.

John William Lehmann, a shorthand writer, who, in conjunction with Ebenezer Howard, took shorthand notes of the trial at the Old Bailey of *Regina (Wilde) v. Queensberry*, handed over a transcript of the notes that he had taken.[198] Howard then testified to taking a portion of the notes on *Regina (Wilde) v. Queensberry*, which was also given over and put in as evidence. These testimonies closed the case for the prosecution. Gill handed the transcripts to Sir John Bridge, observing that he had marked the passages upon which he sought to have the prisoners committed for trial. At this point, Sir John read them to himself. The time had come for Gill to ask Sir John to commit the prisoners for trial.

Travers Humphreys wished to know what the charges were regarding Wilde's committal for trial. John Alexander, the magistrate's clerk, read out the list, which alleged that Wilde had committed acts of gross indecency, and had conspired for that purpose with Taylor. Taylor was charged with conspiring with Wilde to procure persons for the commission of indecent offenses, and with attempting to commit indecent offenses.

SIR JOHN BRIDGE: Now you have heard the offences of which you stand charged and the evidence given against you, do you wish to say anything in answer to the charge? You are not obliged to say anything, and whatever you do say will be taken down in writing and may be used in evidence against you at your trial.[199] Do you wish to say anything, Wilde?

WILDE: No, not at present, your worship.

On Wilde's reply, the *Illustrated Police Budget* commented: "There was not a trace of emotion, and the cultured voice was under perfect control."[200]

SIR JOHN BRIDGE: Do you, Taylor?

NEWTON (*standing up*): Before my client answers the question, will you allow me, Sir, to take your ruling upon the question as to whether there is any evidence to meet the graver charge.[201] I hope before you commit Taylor, you will come to the conclusion that the only evidence given against him came from two discredited persons.

SIR JOHN BRIDGE: Their evidence has been corroborated.

NEWTON: I respectfully submit, Sir John, that there is no corroboration as to particular offences.

SIR JOHN BRIDGE: Not as to particular dates, but generally.

NEWTON: Considering the nature of the alleged crimes, and that they are alleged to have been committed about three years ago, I do submit that this is not a case to go to the Central Criminal Court, so far as Taylor is concerned.

SIR JOHN BRIDGE (*sternly*): That does not alter the case at all. A crime is always a crime.

TRAVERS HUMPHREYS: I must now ask, Sir, that Wilde be admitted to bail. You can understand that there are witnesses to be obtained for the defence, and it is very difficult for Mr. Wilde to communicate with persons and prepare his defence unless he is to have the facilities of a man at liberty. I think that the case is really one for bail.

SIR JOHN BRIDGE: It is a matter within my discretion, and I cannot grant bail.

NEWTON: With regard to Taylor, in addition to what I said last week, I should like to say that he was living at the same address during the trial of the Queensberry case at the Central Criminal Court, and he attended the case every day, and made no attempt to avoid arrest.

SIR JOHN BRIDGE: In deciding what to do with a case of this kind, I have to use my discretion according (in the words of a great judge) to the evidence given and the gravity of the accusation. With regard to the gravity of the case, I think there is no worse crime than that with which the prisoners are charged. As to the evidence, all I shall say is that I do not think it is slight, and I shall therefore refuse bail.[202]

At this juncture, the prisoners were then formally committed to take their trial at the next Sessions of the Central Criminal Court. *Reynolds's Newspaper* observed: "The prisoners showed no disappointment at this decision, which could not have surprised them. They were immediately removed to the cells, and later in the afternoon were taken back in the prison van to Holloway."[203]

The day after the pretrial hearing came to an end, the *Morning* published a report contesting what other newspapers had stated about the prospect that Scotland Yard would make any further arrests. "It appears," the journalist reported, "that up to three days ago there was the possibility of a gentleman whose name was mentioned during the late Old Bailey proceedings being placed beside Oscar Wilde in the dock at Bow Street yesterday; but all action was suddenly dropped—for what reason it is impossible to say. No new arrests seem now to be in contemplation."[204] "It is stated," this commentator proceeded to remark about an unnamed individual who would not appear in court, "that one gentleman, who would give important evidence against Wilde and Taylor has left England for the 'benefit of his health.' He has, it is added, left no address behind."[205] The unknown witness counted among several men who realized it was in his best interests to leave the country. In 1929, Alfred Douglas recalled: "The day before the trial came on I left the country, because I was asked to do so by Sir Edward Clarke, who said that my presence in London was prejudicial to his client."[206] It was also true that Douglas remained in potential legal peril if he continued to be as attentive as he had been to the imprisoned Wilde during the hearing. Douglas, however, later resented the advice. In middle age, he claimed that if Clarke "had called him as a witness"—as Douglas had implored—Clarke "would in all probability have saved Oscar."[207] By the time Douglas left for France, Wilde had spent a further six days in Holloway since Sir John Bridge had committed him for trial.

The next chapter focuses on the proceedings of the first criminal trial, which began on Friday, 26 April and ended on Wednesday, 1 May 1895.

4

THE FIRST CRIMINAL TRIAL: *REGINA* v. *WILDE AND TAYLOR*, CENTRAL CRIMINAL COURT (OLD BAILEY)

> The trial of Oscar Wilde and Alfred Taylor was begun at the Old Bailey this morning. As at the extraordinary case that was heard at the last sessions only three weeks ago, when Wilde was prosecutor and the Marquess of Queensberry was in the dock charged with criminal libel, the public interest in the proceedings was intense. The Old Court was thronged. The gallery, as before, was from an early hour packed with a most unusually well-dressed crowd. Yet there could hardly have been one among the dense mass wedging themselves within the walls who did not feel that before them was to be carried out to its bitter end the tragedy of a brilliant genius and the tragedy of a wasted life. Of all the trials, and there have been many sad ones, heard within these historic walls, there has never been one more saddening than this. So terrible is it, that it is impossible to realise at the full the whole of its awful import.
>
> —*[Anon.], "Wilde and Taylor at the Old Bailey," Sun*

Once Oscar Wilde and Alfred Taylor had been committed for trial at Bow Street Magistrates' Court on Friday, 19 April 1895, the legal machinery could not have moved more briskly. The proceedings began just one week after the hearing had finished. The present chapter opens with the hectic sequence of events that took place during the intervening seven days. On the following Tuesday, 24 April, the grand jury found true bills on all twenty-five counts of the indictment.[1] Wilde's solicitors, Humphreys, Son, and Kershaw, informed the Press Association that he would plead not guilty.[2] Their intention, they said, was to fight the case to the end, and they expressed confidence in winning.

Still, the moment they appeared in court Wilde's attorneys pursued an entirely different strategy when representing their client. They made an application to postpone the trial at the Old Bailey on Wednesday, 25 April. On this day, Wilde and Taylor were brought in the same van from H.M. Prison Holloway to the courthouse, and their names appeared on the list of prisoners for trial before the recorder.[3] For an unexplained reason, they were not brought up to plead before the judge, although Taylor consulted briefly with his counsel, John Peter ("J. P.") Grain at the back of the dock in the New Court.[4] On behalf of Wilde's defense, Mr. Charles ("Willie") Mathews handed the judge, Justice Arthur Charles (fig. 20), an affidavit, drafted by the solicitor Robert H. Humphreys, stating that they needed another month of preparation in order to secure a fair trial.

Mathews pointed out that the libel trial against the Marquess of Queensberry had only terminated on 5 April. On the same day, Mathews added, Wilde was arrested. Thereafter, the prisoner had been brought before Sir John Bridge on Saturday, 6 April, Thursday, 11 April, and Friday, 19 April. On this last day, Wilde had been committed for trial. Mathews noted that Wilde's lawyers had not obtained full copies of the police depositions until the afternoon of Saturday, 20 April. He also remarked that the grand jury had not returned the true bills against Wilde and Taylor until the previous day. In these straitened circumstances, Mathews observed, Wilde was not ready to proceed with his defense. He argued that the present application for the postponement was based on the further ground that, in the current state of public feeling, a fair trial could prove hard to obtain. In the affidavit, Humphreys contended that the lapse of a month would give sufficient time for the hostility to subside and therefore increase the chances of an impartial hearing.

Grain, however, stated that he was instructed to defend the second prisoner, Taylor, and could not concur with Mathews's application, since Taylor desired to have the case tried at the earliest possible moment. Thereafter, Mr. Charles Frederick ("C. F.") Gill, on behalf of the Crown, commented that he had to oppose the application to postpone the trial as strongly as he could. He noted his surprise that such an application should be made after the hearing at Bow Street, where Wilde's leading counsel, Sir Edward Clarke, declared that his client wished to have the case brought to trial in good time. To that end, Gill pointed out, the magistrate had been appointed promptly, in order to ensure that the prisoners be committed to the present sessions. Regarding Wilde's lack of preparedness, Gill remarked that the plea of justification in the case against the Marquess of Queensberry had been delivered as long ago as 30 March. The plea, he noted, was carefully drawn as an indictment, which accurately informed Wilde of the nature of the charges made against him.[5]

Fig. 20. "Spy" [Leslie Ward], cartoon of Justice Arthur Charles, *Vanity Fair*, 4 February 1888.

The presiding judge asked if the prisoners were charged with any offenses not mentioned in the Marquess of Queensberry's plea of justification. Gill replied that, on the contrary, the plea of justification included much that was now charged against the prisoners. "There are many reasons," Gill stated, "why I oppose the application. In a case of this kind, it is important that witnesses should give their evidence as soon as they possibly can. I oppose it on the ground that there might be a miscarriage of justice if the case were not soon brought to trial."[6]

Mathews said that Humphreys had told him that the proceedings at Bow Street had been taken expediently because it was in the public interest, and that Wilde expressed no anxiety at facing trial during these Sessions. According to the *Daily Chronicle*, Mathews observed that Queensberry's plea of justification "dealt with uncertain dates and uncertain acts."[7] For his part, Mathews said that he did not know whether this application would be opposed. He pointed out, however, that Wilde was in custody. He urged that it was an invariable rule that where a prisoner under such conditions made it apparent that he was not prepared for trial, a postponement would be granted. (As the judge implicitly understood, the difficult conditions in which attorneys were permitted to communicate with their clients in prison created obstacles in discussions about the defense's strategies.)

In response, Justice Charles said that he had listened carefully to the application, and that he had read Humphreys's affidavit. He declared that he did not feel that he could accede to the application after reviewing these materials. Moreover, the judge stated that he could not believe that the prisoners would be prejudiced by trial at these sessions as compared with any other, and it was now clear that the carefully worded plea of justification, which had been delivered as long ago as 30 March, employed language that defined the charges that were now made against the prisoners. (As we have seen above, the only crime that Queensberry's plea claimed Wilde to have committed involved those "other said acts of gross indecency and immorality."[8]) Further, he remarked that the prisoner Taylor did not concur with Wilde in the desire for a postponement. The trial would begin on the morning of Friday, 26 April 1895. There were additional reasons to begin the trial expediently. As the *Illustrated Police Budget* acknowledged: "All the witnesses in the case who are to appear against Wilde and Taylor are being closely protected and watched by detectives, so as to assure their attendance at the Old Bailey next week."[9] The authorities feared that the young men who had enjoyed intimacy with Wilde, or at least been involved in the homosexual circles he moved in, might abscond.

Once the Crown prosecution opened at the Old Bailey, the pressure on Wilde had already intensified considerably. He had been languishing in custody for three weeks. To make matters worse, in order to satisfy different creditors, his household effects, on the instructions of the sheriff, were sold at auction on Wednesday, 24 April 1895. The family's belongings, including books, artworks, and items of furniture, went for modest prices in the crowded parlor of the family residence that he leased at 16 Tite Street, Chelsea. This chaotic sale attracted widespread attention. The *Daily Chronicle* focused, as did many other papers, on the most striking of the numerous lots: "The most interesting article sold was an antique mahogany writing table, fitted with flaps, a rising slope, and a draw-out desk, stated to have been at one time the property of [Thomas] Carlyle": the famous Scottish man of letters who had died in 1881.[10] It fetched 14 guineas. The total sale of 114 lots, Donald Mead concludes, came to £295.[11] At the point when Wilde's precious worldly goods were dispersed (several of the artworks remain missing to this day), he also learned that he was not going to see his children. On the day the trial began, Constance had arranged for a French governess to chaperone their two sons to the village of Glion, near Montreux, in Switzerland. There is no record that Constance had visited her husband in prison since his arrest. In the meantime, Alfred Douglas, under legal advice, had recently left the country.[12] Further, Wilde's close supporters More Adey, Robert Ross, and Reggie Turner had already been residing in France for the past few weeks. They counted among a number of fearful queer men who, unsettled by Wilde's imprisonment, sought refuge on the Continent.

Before addressing the detailed record of the proceedings that began on Friday, 26 April 1895, it is important to register the legal quandaries that arose in a trial that occupied five full days (26, 27, 29, and 30 April, and 1 May 1895). From the start, Wilde and Taylor realized that their line-up of experienced lawyers was gaining little traction in its efforts to convince Justice Charles about the imprudent structure of the lengthy indictment. The twenty-five counts on which both men were charged constituted what the lawyers called a joinder: a combination of accusations involving conspiracy, on the one hand, and gross indecency, on the other hand. There were technical complications, which Clarke explicated before the court, in combining these charges in the same indictment, since there were different protocols regarding the ways that defendants could or could not give evidence in relation to the two distinct crimes. To begin with, defendants always had the right not to give evidence. In cases involving charges of conspiracy, the accused could not be called upon to give evidence, even if they desired to do so—although the Criminal Evidence Act 1898 relieved that restriction.[13] Meanwhile, those indicted with gross indecency were classified as competent but not compellable witnesses. The situation therefore was a somewhat contradictory one. No matter how hard Clarke tried to substantiate his point by citing significant test cases, Justice Charles refused to countenance the view that the dissimilar provisions in the law of conspiracy and in the Criminal Law Amendment Act 1885, respectively, might undermine the trial. The appeal against the joinder thus proved ineffective.

It was also on the third day that a series of remarkable exposés transpired through Clarke's searching cross-examination. Clarke laid bare the fact that Charles Parker, who claimed that Wilde committed sodomy upon him in different locations, had as recently as August 1894 been involved in a blackmailing exploit with two experienced extortionists, Alfred Wood and William Allen. In this episode, an unnamed man, whose identity Clarke treated with discretion, had engaged in a sexual act with Charles Parker. Most probably when the sexual partners were physically intimate, Wood and Allen burst in upon them. The blackmailers then intimidated the gentleman with threats, subjected him to a roughing-up, and forced him to pay a substantial sum of £300 or £400. Most likely, the solicitor Bernard Abrahams, who counted extortionists among his clients, brokered a deal with the nameless victim.[14] For his part in this offense, the teenage Parker received £30: this was a fact that he freely divulged during the trial. This was not the only piece of blameworthy intelligence that Clarke had discovered about this petty criminal. Clarke questioned the young man about the theft of clothes from a former employer. Moreover, Clarke asked him about a residence on D'Oyley Street, an anonymous composer, and a gentleman named Thurr. These exchanges scratched the surface of Charles Parker's deeper involvement in wresting property and funds from older—presumably homosexual—men.

The same was true of Wood, who testified, just as he had done during the pretrial hearing, to the sexual acts that he had performed with Wilde. This witness readily confessed his involvement with Charles Parker and William Allen in the blackmailing incident that had taken place nine months before. More important, however, Wood admitted that he had discovered passionate letters from Wilde to Douglas. As the public had learned during Wilde's libel proceedings against Queensberry, once Wood had appropriated these epistles from Douglas's belongings, he quickly handed the items over to Allen. In turn, Allen used one of the letters in an attempt at extorting money from Wilde. The press was aghast at the calm and collected manner in which the well-spoken Wood alluded to his sexual offenses and his corrupt behavior. Noticeably, Clarke acknowledged that he needed to exercise caution when pressing Wood for information about his social contacts. This was the situation regarding the name of Wood's former employer, where the young man held the position of junior clerk. Instead of causing undue embarrassment by publicizing the name, Clarke asked Wood to write it down discreetly on a piece of paper.

The dubious background to the snappily dressed twenty-year-old Frederick ("Fred") Atkins turned out to be even more serious. There were liabilities, both for the prosecution and the defense, with this amusing and high-spirited witness. In the pretrial hearing, Atkins had already declared that during his November 1892 adventure in Paris with Wilde he espied the Irish author in bed with Maurice Salis Schwabe: the nephew-in-law of the solicitor general, Sir Frank Lockwood. (Schwabe, as we have seen, fled the country to escape scandal in 1893.) Further, Atkins's denials that he had ever enjoyed sexual relations with Wilde, who took him to a hairdresser to have his hair fashionably curled, sounded improbable. In any case, Atkins's puckish humor, which had prompted ripples of laughter at Bow Street, threatened to appear too charismatic. Clarke knew that he must hamper Atkins's skillful theatrics. To obstruct Atkins in his path, Wilde's defense had gathered intelligence about this witness's complicity with a well-established blackmailer, James Dennis Burton, who had probably turned sixty at the time of the trial. Clarke had received plenty of troubling information about Atkins and Burton's joint exploits: their extortion of a "foreign gentleman" in the seaside resort of Scarborough, an escapade that took them to Nice, and their blackmailing of a man named Driver. Besides, Wilde's defense had also uncovered a case in which Atkins had lured an unidentified "Birmingham gentleman" to his rooms on Tachbrook Street (237). On this occasion, Atkins had most apparently been posing cross-dressed as a prostitute. Once the unsuspecting client had paid for Atkins's sexual services, Burton appeared, and the victim suffered the routine terrorization. The gentleman, however, resisted the assault. When the landlady heard the commotion, she entered the rooms. Before her eyes were Atkins and the customer in a state of undress. Immediately, she contacted the police. As a result, Atkins and Burton were escorted to Rochester Row station. Records were kept, though charges were dropped. One must assume that the "Birmingham gentleman" could not endure what would have been a humiliating prosecution.

The moment Clarke drew this incident to Atkins's attention, the witness denied that he and his blackmailing partner had been apprehended. Within a matter of hours, however, C. O. Humphreys had gathered sufficient evidence from the police records on the episode that a document was passed up to Justice Charles. On reading it, the judge hauled Atkins back onto the witness stand. At this point, Clarke took the opportunity to rehearse once more his questions about this crime. Just at the point where Atkins renewed his protestations, Clarke pointed to the courtroom presence of the two police constables who had arrested both him and Burton and charged them with "demanding money from a gentleman with menaces" (246). Since it was unmistakable that Atkins had perjured himself, Justice Charles summarily dismissed the impudent witness from court.

There were additional difficulties with another leading witness. Justice Charles could already see that it was going to prove challenging to corroborate Edward Shelley's testimony. It had become evident that Shelley, who once again admitted to committing sexual acts with Wilde, had suffered such mental distress that it cast doubt on his reliability. More troubling, though, were the questionable depositions that the subsequent stream of witnesses gave in relation to Wilde's sexual activities with other men. The proceedings featured what were brief appearances from hotel staff and landladies who had already taken the stand during the pretrial hearing. Their role in the prosecution, however, became evermore significant, especially in the retrial that began on 20 May 1895. In particular, the lurid statements that the employees at the Savoy made, principally with reference to the stains they descried on the bed linens some two years before, occurred at a crucial moment. Their evidence caught the courtroom's attention at the same time that the judge resolved that the jury should not countenance the striking admissions that Atkins and Shelley had offered about Wilde's homosexual indiscretions.

The most strenuous part of the trial involved the attorneys taking turns to read aloud a longhand transcription of the official shorthand report of the proceedings in Wilde's libel case against Queensberry. Technically, this tedious exercise, which occupied hours upon hours in court, made sense insofar as it reminded the jurors of the laborious evidence that had been given in relation to the marquess's plea of justification. Even so, as Clarke pointed out, there was much in the record of Edward Carson's cross-examination of Wilde that appeared irrelevant to the twin charges of conspiracy and gross indecency: "The whole of it being read will meet with no objection on my part, but I would suggest for your consideration that it is clear that there is a great deal in that evidence which has nothing whatever to do with the case, especially with regard to literary discussion and with reference to persons whose names have never been mentioned in this case" (253–54). The reading, which included all of Carson's inquiries into the "sodomitical" aspects of Wilde's works that the jurors presumably had not read, drew to a close on the third day. By this point, the case for the prosecution came to an end. At this juncture, when the court had been fatigued by the relentless details of Wilde's failed libel suit, Clarke handed to the judge a formal demurrer about the joinder, which resulted in the withdrawal of the conspiracy charges.

By the fourth day, Clarke was vindicated. Gill, who lacked foresight in upholding the joinder, eventually admitted: "I have come to the determination not to ask for a verdict on counts of the indictment charging conspiracy. Of course, I do that having in my mind that no evidence has been given here at all which was not directly material to the other charges" (258). As the proceedings show, it was impossible to substantiate the seven counts stating that Wilde and Taylor had conspired to commit acts of gross indecency. To begin with, there was the respectable Shelley, who had never had contact with the parties held at Taylor's rooms in 13 Little College Street and who had no record of extorting funds from gentlemen. The foreman of the jury stated that his members acknowledged that Taylor and Shelley had never been acquainted.

The time therefore arrived for Clarke to make the case for the defense, and he asked Wilde to declare under oath that the evidence that had been heard against him was false. "There is no truth whatsoever in any of these allegations," Wilde remarked flatly, "no truth whatsoever" (263). Once Gill completed his examination of Wilde, he stated that he had wanted the court to endure the whole "literary discussion" from the libel proceedings. Perhaps the most memorable moment of this trial occurred when Gill asked Wilde to interpret the concluding line of Douglas's homoerotic poem "Two Loves," which had appeared in the short-lived literary magazine the *Chameleon* in December 1894. Gill posed a question that Carson had not: "What construction can be put on the line: 'I am the love that dare not speak its name'?" (266). In "Two Loves," such unutterable desire is that of a man for another male. At this grueling point of the trial, Wilde rallied his strength to deliver a finely modulated speech. "'The love that dare not speak its name' in this century," he said, "is such great affection of an elder for a younger man as there was between David and Jonathan, such as Plato made the very basis of his philosophy, and such as you find in the sonnets of Michelangelo and Shakespeare" (266). As Wilde enlarged upon the imposing artists and philosophers who had celebrated this currently "misunderstood" but "noblest form of affection," his eloquence not surprisingly left a deep impression on the courtroom. The satirist and caricaturist Max Beerbohm, who attended the proceedings, remarked: "Oscar has been quite superb. His speech about the Love that dares not tell his name was simply wonderful, and carried the whole court right away, quite a tremendous burst of applause."[15] The clapping appears to have been louder than the audible hissing from the mischief-makers in the gallery.

From this point onward, Wilde held his own until Gill shifted attention to the evidence that the staff at the Savoy had given. Flustered, Wilde declared that it was "childish" (269) to interrogate him on testimony from a housekeeper, a chambermaid, and a masseur about whom he had no memory at all. Gill proceeded to quiz Wilde about the host of young men with whom he was alleged to have enjoyed intimate contact. The names included individuals who were not present in court, such as Herbert Tankard, who was now working in Calais, and Alphonse Conway, whom Wilde had befriended at Worthing. Gill unleashed a barrage of questions about this long list of young men, to which Wilde produced a series of unequivocal denials about his erotic involvement with them. In the face of these accusations, Clarke did his best to remind the court of these leading witnesses' untrustworthiness: "I reminded you that these men—the Woods, the Parkers, the Atkinses, the whole tribe of them—flourish in so frightful a trade, because a man who has been tempted into any sort of guilt would rather give his whole fortune, rather exile himself from his country, than allow the thing to be suggested against him" (278). Clarke took the position that the defendant had acted nobly when opposed by witnesses who had given nothing but tainted testimony. In the end, the jury found itself unable to agree upon four questions (listed below [290]) that Justice Charles had posed to them. After some wrangling, Clarke managed to persuade the judge to ask the foreman if the jury found the defendants not guilty on the withdrawn charges of conspiracy. The jurors' lack of agreement on the counts of gross indecency resulted in a retrial. From every angle, the available reports on the proceedings reveal that this was an ineptly handled prosecution.

FIRST DAY: FRIDAY, 26 APRIL 1895

As the press observed, public interest in the trial of Wilde and Taylor was prodigious.[16] Since many individuals had been waiting for a while before the doors of the Old Court opened at 10.00 a.m., there was a rush for seats. The courtroom was teeming, as we can see from a poster advertising the *Illustrated Police Budget* (fig. 21). "The jury," the *Sun* commented, "was put into the box at 10.20, and their names were called over by Mr. Henry Avory Read, the Clerk of Arraigns. It was an intelligent, good-looking jury, as London juries for important cases nearly always are."[17] Mr. Charles Frederick ("C. F.") Gill, Mr. Horace Avory, and Mr. Arthur Edmund ("A.") Gill were in charge of the prosecution, on behalf of the public prosecutor. Wilde was defended by Sir Edward Clarke, Q.C., Mr. Charles ("Willie") Mathews, and Mr. Travers Humphreys; Mr. John Peter ("J. P.") Grain and Mr. Paul Taylor appeared for the prisoner Taylor; and

Fig. 21. "Scene at the Old Bailey: The Most Sensational Trial of the Century." Detail from poster advertising the *Illustrated Police Budget*, 4 May 1895.

Mr. Leonard Kershaw held a watching brief for the witness Sydney Mavor. All of the counsel was early in attendance.[18] Mathews passed down through the dock to the cells, doubtless to see the prisoner Wilde. At 10.30 a.m., Justice Arthur Charles entered the court in his scarlet robes, bowed to the jury and the Bar, and then took his seat to the right of the Rt. Hon. Sir Joseph Renals, lord mayor of the City of London. In the court were present the Hon. Sir Arthur Charles, a justice of Her Majesty's High Court of Justice, and assorted other officials, including aldermen of the City of London, sheriffs, and under-sheriffs. In the calendar, Wilde's age was given as forty, and he was described as an author; Taylor's age was stated as thirty-three.[19]

The prisoners were brought into the dock. The *Illustrated Police News* observed a noticeable change in Wilde's physical appearance: "He had lost a great deal of flesh. His face looked almost bloodless, and his eyes heavy and weary. He entered the dock with faltering steps."[20] Wilde nonetheless tried to present himself elegantly. He wore the dark overcoat and suede gloves that had been his attire throughout his appearances in court. Moreover, he carried his scrupulously brushed silk hat. For the first time, Taylor donned an overcoat of light brown cloth with a collar of slightly darker velvet, and he wore suede gloves like Wilde. As usual, Taylor was neatly presented, but his fresh-colored face wore a much more serious expression than when he was first brought up at Bow Street. Wilde carried in his hand a small blue volume, possibly a volume of his poems, which he placed on the ledge of the dock before him.[21] He straightened himself up and sighed as he looked over at the bench.

Mr. Henry Avory Read, the clerk of arraigns, summarized the twenty-five counts in the indictment against the prisoners. The *Justice of the Peace* itemized the counts as follows:

> Eight of these counts charged Wilde with committing acts of gross indecency with certain (named) male persons, two counts charged Taylor alone with similar offences, four counts charged Taylor with procuring the commission by Wilde of acts of gross indecency with said male persons, two counts charged Taylor with attempting to procure the commission of acts of gross indecency by certain mentioned male persons with him (Taylor), and two counts charged Wilde and Taylor with attempting to procure the commission of acts of gross indecency by another male person with Wilde. All the above-mentioned charges are under section 11 of the Criminal Law Amendment Act, 1885. The remaining seven counts of the indictment charged Wilde and Taylor with conspiracy to procure the commission of Wilde of the above offences.[22]

Read, the clerk of arraigns, called upon Wilde to plead first.

Sir Edward Clarke at once rose to take a preliminary objection to his client being called upon to plead at all.[23] The *Justice of the Peace* recorded in detail Clarke's demurral of the indictment. Clarke stated that the twenty-five counts could not be lawfully joined together:[24]

> CLARKE: On the counts which allege the commission of offences under the Criminal Law Amendment Act 1885, the defendants are competent witnesses (section 20);[25] on those counts which charge conspiracy they are not competent witnesses. If the defendants are called, and give evidence on the set of counts under the Criminal Law Amendment Act there is no limit imposed by the act as to the cross-examination to which they may be subjected, and that cross-examination may be used against them.

Clarke cited *R. v. Payne and others, L. R. 1 C. C. R.* 349.[26]

> CLARKE: In *R. v. Owen*, 20 *Q. B. D.* 829, the objection was not taken before plea, but after the verdict of the jury had been given, the defendant having given evidence without any objection having been taken by himself or his counsel.[27] I submit that the defendants are entitled to be charged either for an offense on which they can, or for an offense for which they cannot give evidence, as the cross-examination of the defendants might tend to affect the minds of the jury with reference to the conspiracy counts, if they are tried on the indictment as it now stands.[28]

Grain, for the defendant Taylor, did not add anything.

> GILL: The only charges beyond those under the Criminal Law Amendment Act are those charges of conspiracy to commit the very acts they are charged with actually committing. *Regina v. Owen* shows conclusively that the indictment is properly framed.[29] *Regina v. Wealand*, 20 *Q. B. D.* 827 also supports this contention.[30]

In response, Clarke stated that in the case of *R. v. Owen* the defendant was allowed to give evidence, and he was convicted of a common assault, as it was only on the indictment of indecent assault that he could give evidence. The objection was taken after the verdict, and the finding of the jury was sustained. The present case, Clarke submitted, was different because the objection was taken before the prisoners were called upon to plead.

Gill, in reply, said the prisoners were charged with acts of gross indecency, on which they could give evidence.[31] The only other charge against them was one of agreement as to committing or attempting to commit these misdemeanors.

To give evidence on the first would undoubtedly leave them open to cross-examination on both, but there was no hardship, Gill said, in the prisoners being indicted on counts so nearly similar. Clarke said he was not discussing hardships, but a point of law. In response, the justice ruled over the objections to the joinder because there were precedents that demonstrated that there was no conflict when it came to defendants' giving evidence when charged at once with a misdemeanor (gross indecency) and a felony (conspiracy).

JUSTICE CHARLES: The defendants are here charged on two sets of counts: (1) on counts under section 11 of the Criminal Law Amendment Act 1885; (2) with conspiracy to commit those offences.[32] Under the first set of charges, the defendants are competent witnesses, but not under the second. The contention on behalf of the defendants practically amounts to this: that these counts cannot lawfully be joined, because on some of them the defendants can give evidence, and there is no limit to the cross-examination, and, therefore, they would be supplying evidence upon the conspiracy counts on which they are neither competent nor compellable witnesses. Prior to the act of 1885, such counts as these might clearly have been lawfully joined. Has it made any difference to the law of criminal pleadings that now, on some of the counts, the defendants have been made competent witnesses, and not on others? *R. v. Payne* obviously differs from this case; there it was decided that when two prisoners were indicted and tried together, one was not a competent witness for the other. I do not lose sight of the observations made in that case by *Blackburn*, J., as to cross-examination. *R. v. Wealand* has not much relevance to the present case; there the indictment was under section 4 of the Criminal Law Amendment Act, 1885, but only supported the charge of indecent assault, a charge on which, if it had stood alone, the unsworn statement of the child could not have been received as evidence. The defendant was convicted of indecent assault under the powers given by section 9 of the act, and the Court of Crown Cases Reserved was of opinion that the conviction was right, because on the indictment as presented the unsworn evidence was admissible.[33] No doubt it is an anomaly, but still the anomaly exists. In *R. v. Owen*, there were two counts, one for common assault, and one for indecent assault. On the first count, the defendant was not a competent witness; on the second count he was a competent witness. The defendant gave evidence and was convicted of a common assault. The court heard that this conviction was proper. It does not seem to have occurred to the judges that there was a misjoinder of counts in any way. The fact that the Legislature had made the defendants competent witnesses on some charges, has not altered

> the general law as to the joining of counts, and has not altered the law as to criminal pleading. Though I feel the inconvenience, and concur with the remarks of Lord *Coleridge*, C.J., in *R. v. Wealand*, I am not authorised to say that by law these counts cannot be joined.[34]

According to the *Illustrated Police Budget*, "[a]ll through the speech . . . [Wilde] did not move a muscle, and after a time gave one the impression of a man who was becoming rapidly bored. In some like position, Oscar sat hour after hour. He never spoke, laughed, or scowled, but stared incessantly into vacancy, and so on for two long days."[35]

Read, the clerk of arraigns, addressing the prisoner Wilde, then said: "Oscar Fingal O'Flahertie Wills Wilde, do you plead guilty or not guilty to the indictment which you have heard read?"[36] Wilde replied: "Not guilty." Taylor was next called upon, and he rather huskily replied in the same words. Both prisoners were then provided with chairs in the dock. Clarke at once rose again and submitted that the court should now exercise the discretion that it had, and that it should call upon the prosecution to elect on which set of counts they would proceed, whether on the conspiracy or on the other counts. He referred to *Regina. v. Boulton*, 12 *Cox C. C.*; to *Regina v. Burch and Another*, 4 *F. & F.* 407; and to *Regina v. Murphy*, 8 *C. & P.* 297.[37] Gill responded by saying that the question of election was entirely for the discretion of the judge.

> JUSTICE CHARLES: In my previous judgment, I expressed my view of the inconvenience that undoubtedly exists, but I do not think that I am authorized here in putting the prosecution to their election. The case is distinguishable from the cases referred to, and I see no reason to call on the prosecution to elect.

The trial then proceeded on the whole indictment.

Gill opened the case for the prosecution. With regard to the nature of the case, he was sure that the jury had read and heard much. He asked them to dismiss from their minds anything they knew about the case, and to listen to the evidence brought before them with impartiality. Gill narrated the history of Wilde's legal actions from 1 March, when the defendant took out a warrant for the arrest of the Marquess of Queensberry on a charge of libel, to the collapse of the case against the marquess through "certain disclosures" made in the hearing of the case, and the subsequent story of the arrest and the committal. Gill described the nature of the offenses with which the men were separately and jointly charged. Briefly, they were against Wilde for acts of indecency and against Taylor for procuring facility for Wilde to commit indecency, and also with himself committing indecency. The *Star* observed: "[Gill] appeared to classify [Wilde and Taylor] as principal and procurer respectively, and [he] made it a merit on the part of the prosecution that the way in which the indictment was drawn would permit them to answer the charge of conspiracy as well as the charge under the Criminal Law Amendment Act."[38] The judge immediately interposed.

> JUSTICE CHARLES: No, Mr. Gill. I do not agree to that at all. If they give evidence they may be cross-examined on the whole case, but they will only be entitled to give evidence in chief on the counts of the indictment under the Criminal Law Amendment Act.[39]

Gill then proceeded to remind the jury of the facts of the two previous trials with which the public was acquainted, and to analyze the charges against the prisoners.[40] Wilde, he said, was well known as a dramatic author and generally as a literary man of unusual attainments.[41] Wilde had resided, Gill continued, until his arrest at a house in Tite Street, Chelsea, where his wife lived with the children of the marriage. Taylor had numerous addresses, but for the time covered by these charges he had dwelt in Little College Street, and afterward at Chapel Street. Gill described Taylor's rooms at Little College Street, with their heavily draped windows; their candles burning on through the day; and the languorous atmosphere, heavy with perfumes.[42] Although Wilde had a house on Tite Street, he had at different times occupied rooms in St. James's Place, the Savoy Hotel, and the Albemarle Hotel.[43] Gill stated that it would be shown that Wilde and Taylor were in league for specific purposes.

Thereafter, Gill explained the specific allegations to the prisoners. As he analyzed the indictment, he stated that the first nine counts referred to misconduct with Charles Parker and William Parker, the next three to Frederick Atkins, the next five to Alfred Wood, two more to indictments at the Savoy Hotel, two to the young man named Mavor, three to charges of conspiracy, and the last to Wilde's conduct regarding Shelley.[44] He gave particulars of the dinner at the Soho restaurant and afterward the visit that Wilde and Charles Parker made to the Savoy Hotel. Gill followed the relations between Wilde and Parker on later dates, and he commented also on Taylor's association with the Parker brothers. Wilde, he asserted, had not hesitated, soon after his first introduction to Taylor, to explain the purpose of their acquaintance.[45] Taylor was familiar with several young men who were in the habit of giving their bodies, or selling them, for the purpose of sodomy. It appeared that there were various youths engaged in what Gill called this abominable traffic, and that one or all of them were known to Taylor, who went about and sought out for them men of means who were willing to pay heavily for the indulgence of their favorite vice. Gill endeavored to show that Taylor himself was given to sodomy and that he had himself indulged in these filthy practices with the same youths as he agreed to procure for Wilde. Thereafter, Gill touched upon Wilde's visits to Taylor's rooms, and he laid bare the circumstances attending these visits. On nearly every occasion when Wilde called on Taylor, a young man was present with whom Taylor committed the act of sodomy. Gill mentioned the names of the sundry young men connected with these facts.

At this juncture, Gill proceeded to explain that when Taylor vacated his rooms at 3 Chapel Street in order to take up lodgings at 25 Denbigh Street, Pimlico, he left behind miscellaneous compromising papers that would be produced in evidence against the prisoners. He added that in due course there was abundant corroboration of the statements on the young men who were involved. Gill pointed to the peculiarities in the case of Frederick Atkins. The young witness, he said, had accompanied Wilde to Paris, and there was no doubt whatsoever that Wilde had in the most systematic way endeavored to influence Atkins's mind toward vicious courses, and that Wilde had also endeavored to mold Atkins to his own depraved will. Subsequently, Gill went on to describe the relations that existed between Wilde and another young man, Alfred Wood. Gill then made special allusion to the remarkable manner in which Wilde lavished money upon Wood prior to the young man's departure for America.

Here, Gill referred to another of Wilde's young male friends, Sydney Mavor, about whom the jury would form their own conclusions after they heard the evidence. Among other things to which Gill wanted the jury to direct careful attention was a letter in pencil that Taylor had written to Mavor.[46] The communication ran as follows:

> Dear Syd,—
>
> I could not wait any longer. Come on at once to see Oscar, 16 Tite Street, Chelsea, I am there.—
>
> Yours,
> Alf Taylor.

Gill observed that the use of Wilde's first name in such a familiar way suggested the intimate nature of the acquaintance between Mavor and Wilde, who was, he added pointedly, old enough to be Mavor's father.[47]

After he had commented on this communication, Gill conceded that there was a difference about Wilde's acquaintanceship with Shelley, whom Wilde met in the shop of his publishers, Messrs. Mathews and Lane, where Shelley was employed.[48] This was, he stated, an acquaintance with a literary side, but it went through the same stages. Gill concluded with assurance that the evidence he was going to present would justify the jury in finding the prisoners guilty on all counts of the indictment. He then called his first witness.

Reynolds's Newspaper observed: "There was no sound in the court, except the moving of the people in their seats, when Gill sat down—no expression one way or another, as so frequently marked the Queensberry trial. But when, as immediately followed, the first witness was called, and Charles Parker stepped forward, the vulgar curiosity to get a good view of the fellow caused several of the well-dressed men in court to produce opera-glasses! They did not appear proud of the act; they did it as furtively as they could, and then hid the glasses in their hats or beneath their coats."[49] Meanwhile, the reporter from the *Illustrated Police Budget* commented on Charles Parker's fine appearance: he was dressed in "a serge suit, with a high white collar and neat black bow," while his "hair was carefully parted down the centre and greased into shape on a low receding forehead . . . . In his left hand, he carried a hard felt hat."[50] "His manner in the witness box," this reporter noted, "was subdued and respectful, and all his answers were given in mono-syllables, uttered in a tone, so low, indeed, that the judge had often to ask him to speak a little louder."[51]

Under Gill's examination, Charles Parker deposed that prior to his acquaintance with Taylor he was employed as a valet. His brother, William Parker, was a groom. He then proceeded once more to give in detail the process by which Taylor introduced himself at the St. James's restaurant. Charles Parker stated that Taylor started a conversation with him and his friends, and Taylor insisted on "standing" the cost of their drinks.[52] As they were talking, Parker recalled, Taylor drew attention to the female prostitutes who frequented Piccadilly Circus: "I don't understand sensible men wasting their money on painted trash like that. Many do, though. But there are a few who know better. Now," Taylor added, "you could get money in a certain way easily enough if you cared to." Charles Parker said that he understood Taylor's meaning, and that he made a coarse reply.

GILL: I am obliged to ask you what it was you actually said.

CHARLES PARKER: I do not like to say.

GILL: You were less squeamish at the time, I daresay. I ask you for the words.

CHARLES PARKER: I said that if any old gentleman with money took a fancy to me, I was agreeable. I was terribly hard up.

GILL: What did Taylor say?

CHARLES PARKER: He laughed and said that men far cleverer, richer, and better than I preferred things of that kind.

GILL: Did Taylor mention the prisoner Wilde?

CHARLES PARKER: Not at that time. He arranged to meet me again, and I consented.

GILL: Where did you first meet Wilde?

CHARLES PARKER: At the Solferino restaurant.[53]

GILL: Tell me what transpired.

CHARLES PARKER: Taylor said he could introduce me to a man who was good for plenty of money. Wilde came in later, and I was formally introduced. Dinner was served in a private room.

GILL: Was the dinner a good dinner?

CHARLES PARKER: Yes. The table was lighted by shaded candles. We had champagne with our dinner, and brandy and coffee afterwards. Wilde paid for the dinner.

GILL: What was the nature of the conversation?[54]

CHARLES PARKER: General, at first. Nothing was then said as to the purposes for which we had come together.

GILL: And then?

CHARLES PARKER: Subsequently, Wilde said to me: "This is the boy for me. Will you go to the Savoy Hotel with me?" I consented, and Wilde drove me in a cab to the hotel. He took me first into a sitting room on the second floor, where he ordered some more drink—whisky and soda. Wilde asked me to go into his bedroom with him.[55]

GILL: Let us know what occurred.

CHARLES PARKER: He committed the act of sodomy upon me.

GILL: With your consent?

The witness did not reply.

CHARLES PARKER: Before I left, Wilde gave me £2, telling me to call at the Savoy in a week. I went there about a week afterwards about 11 o'clock at night. We had supper, with champagne. Wilde on that occasion committed the same acts as on the first occasion. I stayed about two hours. When I left, Wilde gave me £3. I remember subsequently going with my brother to 13 Little College Street. We slept there with Taylor. Taylor told me on that occasion that he had gone through a form of marriage with Mason.

GILL: Did he say who acted as the woman?

CHARLES PARKER: Yes, he said he did—that he was in a woman's dress, and that they had a wedding breakfast.

Charles Parker then gave evidence about Taylor's proposals to him about engaging in acts of indecency, which he resisted.[56]

CHARLES PARKER: I had a bedroom at 50 Park Walk, Chelsea. Wilde visited me there about 11.30 p.m. or twelve. The same thing occurred as at the Savoy.[57] I was asked by Wilde to imagine that I was a woman and that he was my lover. I had to keep up this illusion. I used to sit on his knees and he used to play with my privates as a man might amuse himself with a girl. Wilde insisted on keeping up this make-believe. He drove away in a cab, after staying about a quarter of an hour. After that incident, my landlady gave me notice to leave, and I left.

GILL: Apart from money, did Wilde give you any presents?

CHARLES PARKER: Yes. He gave me a silver cigarette case and a gold ring. Wilde said to me: "I don't suppose boys are different to girls in acquiring presents from them who are fond of them."[58]

GILL: You pawned the cigarette case and the ring?

CHARLES PARKER: Yes.

GILL: Where else have you been with Mr. Wilde?[59]

CHARLES PARKER: To Kettner's restaurant.

GILL: What happened there?

CHARLES PARKER: We dined there. We always had a lot of wine. Wilde would talk of poetry and art during dinner, and of the old Roman days.

GILL: On one occasion, you proceeded from Kettner's to Wilde's house?

CHARLES PARKER: Yes. We went to Tite Street. Wilde let himself in with a latchkey. I remained the night, sleeping with the prisoner [i.e., Wilde], and he himself let me out in the early morning before anyone was about.

GILL: And where else?[60]

CHARLES PARKER: I visited Wilde at St. James's Place. Taylor gave me the address. Wilde had a bedroom and sitting room opening into each other. I have been there in the morning and to tea in the afternoon.

At this juncture, Charles Parker described a sexual act that took place with Wilde at Geneux's private hotel.[61]

CHARLES PARKER: I remember dining with Wilde at Kettner's and then going to the London Pavilion. We went back to St. James's Place where the same thing occurred as before.

GILL: Where else have you visited this man?

CHARLES PARKER: At the Albemarle Hotel. The same thing happened then.

GILL: When did your last interview take place?

CHARLES PARKER: I last saw Wilde about nine months ago when walking in Trafalgar Square. Wilde was riding in a cab. He stopped and spoke to me. He alighted from the hansom.

GILL: What did he say?

CHARLES PARKER: He said: "You are looking as pretty as ever." He did not ask me to go anywhere with him then.

At this point of the proceedings, the *Star* observed: "Wilde leaned over the front of the dock to whisper a few sentences into the ear of Mr. Charles Mathews, who nodded and left the court"; this newspaper also noted that throughout this cross-examination "Wilde . . . gazed at [Charles Parker] fixedly, showing no embarrassment or feeling."[62] Furthermore, the *Star* commented: "Almost as if by accident Mr. Gill elicited a piece of evidence against Wilde more revolting than anything which had yet been told in the case."[63]

GILL: During the period of your acquaintance with Wilde, did you frequently see Taylor?[64]

CHARLES PARKER: Yes.

GILL: Who else did you meet at Little College Street?

CHARLES PARKER: Atkins, Wood, and Scarfe, amongst others.

GILL: Did you continue your acquaintance with Taylor until the raid at Fitzroy Square? You were arrested?

CHARLES PARKER: Yes.

The *Star* commented on this point of the proceedings: "When Mr. Gill went on to refer to the arrest of the witness and Taylor in the Fitzroy Square raid in August 1894, Mr. Grain rose for the first time and quietly protested against the introduction of matter extraneous to the indictment. 'Surely I have enough to answer!' he said. Mr. Gill said he only desired to show that after that incident the witness ceased his acquaintance with Taylor, and went into the country, where he enlisted in the Army."[65]

Gill continued with the examination.

GILL: When did you cease your association with Taylor?

CHARLES PARKER: In August 1894. I went away into the country, and took up another occupation.

JUSTICE CHARLES: What was the occupation?

CHARLES PARKER: I enlisted, and while I was with my regiment, I was seen by the solicitor of Lord Queensberry, who took down my statement.

GILL: Until you became acquainted with Taylor, had you ever been mixed up in the commission of indecent acts?

CHARLES PARKER: No. Never.

Charles Parker's response closed the examination-in-chief of this witness, and the court adjourned for luncheon.[66] The *Star* remarked that Wilde looked positively ill.[67] Taylor, however, was apparently more cheerful, and he made an effort to scrutinize carefully various people who were up in the public gallery, as if looking for someone. There was an interval of half an hour.

After lunch, when the court resumed, Clarke proceeded with his cross-examination of the witness.

CLARKE: On what day did you enlist?

CHARLES PARKER: On September 3.[68]

CLARKE: When were you seen in the country in reference to this case?[69]

CHARLES PARKER: Towards the end of March.

CLARKE: Who saw you?

CHARLES PARKER: Mr. Russell.

CLARKE: Was there no examination before that?

CHARLES PARKER: No. That was the first I had heard of these matters. I enlisted in my own name. I do not know how Mr. Russell found me out.

GILL: Did you state at Bow Street that you received £30 not to say anything about a certain case?

CHARLES PARKER: I stated at the police court that I received £30, part of monies extorted from a gentleman with whom I had committed acts of indecency. I received the £30 a few days before I was arrested in August 1894.

CLARKE: I don't ask the name of the gentleman from whom the money was extorted, but I do ask the names of the two men who got the money, and gave you £30.

CHARLES PARKER: Wood and Allen.[70]

GILL: Where are Wood and Allen living now?[71]

CHARLES PARKER: I could not tell you where Allen is now. He used to live in Crawford Street.[72] Wood is a witness in this case, I know.[73]

Around this point, Gill concluded the examination, and Clarke began the cross-examination of Charles Parker by refocusing attention on the address where the blackmailing episode occurred.

CLARKE: Where were you living then?[74]

CHARLES PARKER: In Crawford Street.[75]

CLARKE: When had the incident occurred in consequence of which you received the £30? How long before?

CHARLES PARKER (*after long hesitation*): I cannot think. About two weeks before.

CLARKE: You had indecent behavior with the gentleman in question?

CHARLES PARKER: Yes, but only on one occasion, at Camera Square.

CLARKE: Where you were living?

CHARLES PARKER: Yes.

CLARKE: Did the gentleman come into your room?

CHARLES PARKER: Yes.

CLARKE: By your invitation?

CHARLES PARKER: He asked me if he could come.

CLARKE: And you took him home with you?

CHARLES PARKER: Yes.

CLARKE: You say positively that Mr. Wilde committed sodomy on you at the Savoy?[76]

CHARLES PARKER: Yes.

CLARKE: But you have been in the habit of accusing other gentlemen of the same offence?

CHARLES PARKER: Never, until it has been done.

CLARKE: I submit that you blackmail gentlemen.

CHARLES PARKER: No, Sir. I have accepted money, but it has been offered to me to pay for the offence. I have been solicited. I have never suggested this offence to gentlemen.

CLARKE: How much did Wood and Allen tell you they got?

CHARLES PARKER: About £300 or £400.

CLARKE: Was that the first sum of money for such a thing that you had received?

CHARLES PARKER: Yes.

CLARKE: What did you do with the £30?

CHARLES PARKER: Spent it.

CLARKE: And then went into the army?

CHARLES PARKER: I spent it in a couple of days.

Clarke went on to ask Charles Parker about a former employer. At Clarke's request, Charles Parker wrote down the name and address of his late employer, from whom he was alleged to have stolen clothing.[77]

CHARLES PARKER: I was in that gentleman's service as valet for nine or ten months. I did not leave the place without a character.[78]

CLARKE: Did you not say that your employer had stated that you had stolen some clothes?

CHARLES PARKER: Yes.

CLARKE: How did you know that he had said so?

CHARLES PARKER: He wrote and told me so, and asked me to send their things back, which I did. They were not clothes; they were shirts and collars.

CLARKE: Well, I call them clothes. Do you have a written character?

CHARLES PARKER: Yes. That is so.

CLARKE: Did you ever live at D'Oyley Street, Chelsea?[79]

CHARLES PARKER: No. Never.

CLARKE: Did you know a person named Thurr?[80]

CHARLES PARKER: No.

CLARKE: When Taylor asked you if you ever went with men and got money for it, did you understand what he meant?

CHARLES PARKER: Yes.

CLARKE: You had heard of such things before?

CHARLES PARKER: Yes.

CLARKE: Then it was with the intention of entering upon such practices that you called upon Taylor?

CHARLES PARKER: No.

CLARKE: Then why did you call upon him?

CHARLES PARKER: Because he asked me to.

CLARKE: You meant to go with men and get money?

CHARLES PARKER: Yes.

CLARKE: You understood the practices you were going to enter upon?

CHARLES PARKER: Yes. I told Wilde that I wanted to get some employment on the stage. I knew that Wilde was a dramatist, and had much to do with theatres; and I suggested that he might help me.

CLARKE: When you allowed yourself to be introduced to Mr. Wilde, you knew perfectly well the purpose for which the introduction was made?

CHARLES PARKER: Yes.

CLARKE: At the dinner, Mr. Wilde was the principal conversationalist, I suppose?

CHARLES PARKER: Yes.

CLARKE: And you found him a brilliant and amusing talker?

CHARLES PARKER: Yes.

Clarke inquired about the visits to the Savoy Hotel, and Wilde's visits to Park Walk, with the apparent object of showing that all of the prisoner's movements were open and undisguised.[81]

CHARLES PARKER: On the first visit to the Savoy, Wilde locked the bedroom door. I did not see any servants as I left the hotel. I went away in a hansom. As to the second visit, Wilde told me the night and the time to come again. I found Wilde occupying the same rooms. I gave my name, and the hall porter showed me up by the lift. Wilde on this occasion, too, locked the bedroom door. The waiter who served the supper, of course, saw me there.[82]

CLARKE: There was no concealment about your visit, was there? You gave your name, were shown up, and in going away you did not attempt to avoid any of the servants?

CHARLES PARKER: That's so.

CLARKE: Had other people besides Wilde been to see you at Park Walk?

CHARLES PARKER: Yes. Taylor used to call upon me, in the morning.

CLARKE: Did Wood come?[83]

CHARLES PARKER: No. I knew Allen only a little while before I enlisted. About the same time, I became acquainted with Cliburn.[84]

CLARKE: If you did not know either of them before that, from whom did you hear about the letters which Wood had?[85]

CHARLES PARKER: I can't remember. I heard that Wood had gone to America, and that he had in his possession some letters written by Mr. Wilde. I thought he had taken them away with him.

CLARKE: Did you hear how Wood got possession of them?

CHARLES PARKER: Yes.

CLARKE: From whom did you hear that?

CHARLES PARKER: I don't remember.

CLARKE: Did you hear that Wood had got £20 or £30 from Mr. Wilde for some letters?

CHARLES PARKER: I did not hear that he got the money. I heard from someone, I cannot remember from whom, that Wood got the letter out of some clothes which were given to him by Lord Alfred Douglas. I never saw the letters.

CLARKE: Were Wilde's rooms on the ground floor at St. James's Place very public rooms?

CHARLES PARKER: Yes. There were men-servants about. The sitting room was a sort of library. There were a good many books about.

CLARKE: Do you suggest that in rooms such as you have described and so situated this kind of conduct went on again and again?

CHARLES PARKER: Yes.

CLARKE: There was not the smallest concealment about your visit with Mr. Wilde to the music hall?

CHARLES PARKER: No.

CLARKE: You shared a box with him at the Pavilion?

CHARLES PARKER: Yes.

Once he had elicited this information, Clarke appeared satisfied and sat down.[86] Mr. J. P. Grain, on behalf of Taylor, proceeded to cross-examine the witness.

GRAIN: Do you know a person named Harrington?[87]

CHARLES PARKER: I know a person named Harrington. I made his acquaintance at the skating-rink at Knightsbridge some time before I met Taylor.[88]

GRAIN: Now were you not introduced to Taylor by Harrington?

CHARLES PARKER: No. I think Harrington was at the St. James's bar, but he did not make the introduction.

GRAIN: Did Wood frequently visit you at Camera Square?

CHARLES PARKER: Yes.

GRAIN: Are you quite sure that the sum of £30 mentioned by Sir Edward Clarke is the only sum you have received under similar circumstances?

CHARLES PARKER: Yes.

GRAIN: Had Wood ever suggested persons to you from whom he might obtain money, and that you might participate in it?

CHARLES PARKER: No.

GRAIN: Quite sure of that?

CHARLES PARKER: Yes. Quite. I was hard up at the time, but not in debt. I had a few shillings in my pocket.

GRAIN: Did you say at Bow Street that when you stayed with Taylor at 3 Chapel Street every night for a fortnight—"He did nothing to me and I did nothing to him?"

CHARLES PARKER (*after much hesitation*): I suppose I must have said so.

GRAIN: About six months after you made the acquaintance of Taylor, did you go to Paris?

CHARLES PARKER: Yes.

GRAIN: Did you go with a composer?[89]

CHARLES PARKER: Yes.

GRAIN: An operatic composer?

CHARLES PARKER: Yes.

GRAIN: How long were you with that person in Paris?

CHARLES PARKER: About a month. I went with him as a valet. He paid me two guineas a week.[90] I lived at a different place to the gentleman, but went every morning to his residence to valet him.

GRAIN: Do you know a person of the name of Burton?

CHARLES PARKER: Yes. I knew that Atkins and Burton were living together at the same place.

GRAIN: Did you go to Monte Carlo with Burton?

CHARLES PARKER: Yes, in 1894. We only stayed a few days.

GRAIN: Did Wood go with you?[91]

CHARLES PARKER: No.

Gill then reexamined the witness.

GILL: Did you know Lord Alfred Douglas?

CHARLES PARKER: Yes. Taylor introduced me to him. I know that the letters referred to belonged to Lord Alfred Douglas.[92] Until I met Taylor, I did not know Atkins, Wood, Allen, Cliburn, or Burton.

GILL: When did you first make the acquaintance of Wood?
CHARLES PARKER: About six months before he went to America.
GILL: When Mr. Russell found you in the country, he asked you if your statement was true?[93]
CHARLES PARKER: Yes.
GILL: Did you desire to be a witness in the case?
CHARLES PARKER: No.

Charles Parker stated that he had been twice to the Savoy Hotel with Wilde, and once before he had enlisted.

JUSTICE CHARLES: I understood you had only been to the hotel twice.

Both Clarke and Grain remarked that they understood the same.

JUSTICE CHARLES: When was it you paid this third visit?
CHARLES PARKER: In the summer of 1893.
JUSTICE CHARLES: But that is a long time before you enlisted.

Charles Parker made no reply.

After giving evidence for almost three hours in the witness box, Charles Parker was dismissed.[94] Gill called William Parker to testify. William Parker, under Gill's examination, corroborated his brother's evidence about the first meeting with Taylor in the St. James's bar, together with the subsequent dinner with Wilde at the Solferino.[95] On one occasion, William Parker said, he had slept at Little College Street with his brother and Taylor in the same bed, and he described an attempt that Taylor made to commit what the press referred to as a felonious act. (There is some probability that William Parker uttered the unmentionable word "sodomy.") The witness then stated that he went twice to Little College Street. Shortly afterward, he said, he took employment in the country. These answers concluded Gill's examination.

At this juncture, Clarke began his cross-examination of the witness.

CLARKE: What employment did you go into?
WILLIAM PARKER: I went into a groom's situation.

William Parker went on to state that he was present at dinner with Taylor and Wilde.[96] Wilde, he said, paid all of his attention to Charles Parker, who accepted a preserved cherry from Wilde's own mouth. Wilde took the cherry back into his own mouth, and this trick was repeated three or four times. William Parker recalled that, after his brother went off to Wilde's rooms at the Savoy, he stayed behind with Taylor, who said: "Your brother is lucky. Oscar does not care what he pays if he fancies a chap."

CLARKE: Where did you go after the dinner with Wilde?[97]

WILLIAM PARKER: After going away from the dinner, I went home after having a drink or two.

CLARKE: Hadn't you had enough at the dinner?

WILLIAM PARKER: I know when I have had enough.

CLARKE: Did you know that when you went to the dinner at Kettner's or the Solferino with your brother that you were to be treated as women, and that you were to have money for it?[98]

WILLIAM PARKER: That was what I understood.

At 3.45 p.m., the next witness appeared. This was Ellen Grant, the caretaker who resided at 13 Little College Street. Under Gill's examination, she stated that she was not the landlady, but said that she and her husband leased a portion of the house in which Taylor had rooms. For a few weeks, she said, she had assisted Taylor in his household duties. He had no female servant and did his cooking with a gas stove. Taylor's rooms, she observed, were curtained and draped, and no daylight was admitted. He had no gas lighting, but lit his rooms by oil lamps and candles with colored shades over the light. The bed was a sprung mattress, which lay on the floor of the bedroom. Grant maintained that she had seen women's shoes and stockings, as well as "Mr. Taylor's wig"—a fair-haired woman's wig with curls. His nightshirt was fastened with a gold brooch. She knew that among his visitors there were no women, but various young men aged from sixteen to thirty. She had seen Alfred Wood there. Grant claimed that Wood had stayed with Taylor for three weeks. Sydney Mavor frequently stayed in the house. So did Charles Mason and one Ernest Macklin.[99] Grant said that Taylor and his gentlemen friends used to call one another "Charlie dear," "My dear boy," etc. There were frequently parties.[100] She had heard them talk to a person whom they called Oscar. A sergeant of police visited the house in May last year, and she showed the sergeant the rooms in the house. Taylor had several women's brooches.

CLARKE: Was Mr. Wilde ever in the house?[101]

ELLEN GRANT: I never saw Mr. Wilde in the house.[102]

GRAIN: You understood that the wig and other things were used by Taylor for fancy dress?

GRANT: Yes, fancy dress.[103]

The court learned that Taylor left his rooms at Little College Street in August 1893.

The next witness was Lucy Rumsby, who stated that Charles Parker lodged with her at 50 Park Walk. Wilde, she recalled, was there only on one occasion, when he stopped for one or two minutes. She said that she gave Charles Parker notice after something she heard.[104]

Margery Bancroft, a tenant of the house, stepped forward. She stated that late one night she saw Wilde leave the premises. She knew Wilde because he had previously been pointed out to her. The next witness, Sophia Gray, testified that Taylor lodged with her at 3 Chapel Street. Wilde was there on only one occasion, when he stopped for a few minutes. Fred Kerley, the retired detective inspector, said that among the documents that Taylor had left behind was a piece of paper on which Charles Parker, when he was at the St. James's restaurant, had written Taylor's address.

The next witness to be called was Alfred Wood. "He is," the *Illustrated Police Budget* noted, "slightly taller than both of the Parkers, and though . . . the best educated, has the worst record."[105] Horace Avory examined Wood for the prosecution. Once he was sworn, Wood explained his background.

ALFRED WOOD: I was formerly a clerk. In January 1893, I was not in any occupation. I first knew Taylor about that time.

HORACE AVORY: When did you go to Little College Street to live?

WOOD: In January 1893. I stayed about three weeks.

AVORY: Where did you sleep there?

WOOD: In the same room with Taylor. There was only one bed.

AVORY: When did you first know Wilde?

WOOD: I was introduced to him by a gentleman at the Café Royal.

AVORY: Who was the gentleman?

WOOD: Must I give the name?

AVORY: Yes.

WOOD: Lord Alfred Douglas.

AVORY: Had you known Lord Alfred before?

WOOD: I had seen him at Taylor's rooms.

AVORY: What took place when you were introduced to Wilde?

WOOD: I was introduced by telegram.

JUSTICE CHARLES: You would have led anyone to believe that you were personally introduced.

WOOD: In consequence of the telegram, I went to the Café Royal at 9.00 p.m. Wilde was sitting down. He spoke to me first. "Are you Alfred Wood?" he asked. I said, "Yes." Then he offered me something to drink, and I had something; and then he invited me to go round to the Florence in Rupert Street to dinner. I went with him, and we dined in a private room.

AVORY: What kind of meal was it?

WOOD: Very nice—one of the best to be got.

AVORY: What wine did you have?

WOOD: Champagne. After dinner, I went with Wilde to 16 Tite Street. There was nobody about the house, to my knowledge. Wilde let himself in by a latchkey. We went up to the bedroom, where we had hock and seltzer.[106]

Wood then stated that he committed a sexual act with Wilde.[107]

AVORY: Did he give you any money that night?

WOOD: Yes, at the Florence. About £3 I think it was. He said he thought I must need some money to buy things with. The money was given before any suggestion was made about going to Tite Street. I stayed at his house about an hour. He asked me to meet him again at the corner of Tite Street. Two or three days afterwards, at about 11.00 p.m., I went to the corner. Wilde came up in a cab, and we both went to the house. I did not see anyone about the house. I had some chicken in the pantry, and afterwards went to the bedroom, where we had something to drink. I don't remember committing any act of indecency that night. I stayed only a very short time. I don't remember that I ever went again to Tite Street.

AVORY: Did you ever meet Wilde again?

WOOD: He once came to my room in Langham Street.[108]

AVORY: Did you know he was coming?

WOOD: Yes.

AVORY: How did you know?

WOOD: He came by appointment. He took me out to buy me a present. He bought me half a dozen shirts, some collars, and handkerchiefs, and a silver watch and chain. Before he took me out, we had some tea.

AVORY: Has he given you money on any other occasion?

WOOD: Yes. He has given me £2 or £3 when he has met me.

AVORY: Up to what time did your acquaintanceship with Wilde go on?

WOOD: Up to the end of March.

AVORY: How did it cease?

WOOD: I told Taylor that I would like to get away from a certain class of people, and I think he mentioned it to Wilde, who gave me £30. I saw Wilde at Taylor's rooms.

AVORY: What took place between you?

WOOD: Wilde asked me if I wanted to go away to America. I said, "Yes," and then he said he would give me the money. "You have," he said, "some letters I should like to get back," and he gave me £30.

AVORY: In what form?

WOOD: Two £10 notes and two £5 notes.

AVORY: Was it a fact that you had any letters of his in your possession?

WOOD: Yes. I don't remember how many, nor do I remember giving them back to Wilde. I might have put them on the table.

AVORY: Did the letters belong to you?

WOOD: No. They were letters I found in some clothes Lord Alfred Douglas had given me. They were letters from Wilde to Lord Alfred. I saw Wilde at the Florence the next day. He had invited me to lunch with him there.

AVORY: What sort of lunch was it?

WOOD: Very nice lunch. We had champagne. At lunch, Wilde said, "£30 is very little to go to America with, and I will send you £5," which he did by messenger. I went to America two or three days afterwards.

Wood identified a letter that Kerley had found to be one that Wood had written from America to Taylor: "Tell Oscar that if he likes he can send me a draft for an Easter egg—Burton and Douglas were at Liverpool for the races."[109]

AVORY: Do you know a lad named Sydney Mavor?

WOOD: Yes. I met him at Taylor's rooms. He was known there as "Sydney."

At 5.00 p.m. the court was adjourned until the following morning at 10.30 a.m.[110]

SECOND DAY: SATURDAY, 27 APRIL 1895

Reynolds's Newspaper opened its commentary on the second day of the proceedings with a vivid depiction of the court:

> The crowd in the galleries was as great yesterday as on the preceding day, and briefless young barristers were there galore, looking very fine in wig and gown. They occupied all of the spare seats, and some even sat on the stairs of the Court or stood at the sides of the seats with arms akimbo, as if they were persons of some importance. Why the court should be filled with these legal luminaries or otherwise, whilst reporters are compelled to stand in crowded, out of the way corners where work can be done only under difficulties, is best known to the court officials.[111]

All members of counsel engaged in the case were early in attendance. Mr. Charles Mathews again passed through the dock to consult with Wilde in the cells below.[112] There was no demonstration when the van arrived at the Central Criminal Court this morning. Punctually, at 10.30 a.m. Mr. Justice Charles took his seat upon the bench and resumed the trial. At the same moment, Wilde and Taylor, who wore the same clothing as on the day before, were placed in the dock where they took opposite seats. Wilde leaned his arm upon the corner of the dock and rested his head heavily upon his hand. Taylor resumed his singular smile, but Wilde seemed utterly broken down. At no stage of the proceedings was there any perceptible communication between the two. Wilde seemed oblivious of Taylor's presence, but Taylor occasionally looked across at his companion.

Alfred Wood went once again into the box, and he was cross-examined by Sir Edward Clarke. Wood stated that he went to America in 1893, and returned the following year.[113] In 1893, Wood said, he informed Wilde that he wished to get away from the class of persons he had associated with. On this basis, he received £30 from Wilde. According to *The Trial of Oscar Wilde*, during the cross-examination Wood stated: "Wilde saw his influence to induce me to consent. He made me nearly drunk. He used to put his hand inside my trousers beneath the table at dinner and compel me to do the same to him. Afterwards, I used to lie on a sofa with him. It was a long time, however, before I would allow him to actually do the act of sodomy. He gave me money to go to America."[114] The *Morning* noted that, at the point where Wood admitted receiving large sums from Allen's "blackmailing operations," he delivered his responses in a tone of "utmost nonchalance."[115]

CLARKE: Did you return to respectable employment when you came from America?

WOOD: I was taken ill on my return, and I have not been in any describable employment since.

CLARKE: Charles Parker told us that you and a man named Allen got £300 or £400 out of a gentleman, and gave him £30.

WOOD: I did not give it to him.

CLARKE: Well, tell us, did you get £300 from a gentleman?

WOOD: Not me. Allen did.

CLARKE: You were a party to it?

WOOD: I was there, yes.

CLARKE: Do you mean by that that you came into the room whilst the gentleman was there with Parker?

WOOD: I did not. Allen went in first.

CLARKE: At all events, Allen and you got £300 or £400 from the gentleman?

WOOD: Yes.

CLARKE: And you gave Parker £30?

WOOD: I did not. Allen might have done. I don't know the exact amount he got.

CLARKE: How much did you get?

WOOD: £175.

CLARKE: What for?

WOOD: Well, it was given me by Allen.

CLARKE: Then Mr. Wilde's giving you £30 to get away from this class of person had not a very satisfactory result?
WOOD: I was in employment all the time I was in America.

(The witness appeared to be chewing something while this evidence was taken.[116])

CLARKE: How did you live when you came back?
WOOD: On some money left me by my father. I was not of age when I went to America.
CLARKE: Was that money spent before you had the £175?[117]
WOOD: No.
CLARKE: When were you last in respectable employment in England?
WOOD: A short time before I met Mr. Wilde.
CLARKE: Give me the date.
WOOD: It is so long ago I do not remember it.
CLARKE: Write on a slip of paper the name of where you were last employed, and the date.
WOOD: I do not want it disclosed.
CLARKE: It will not be disclosed.

Wood wrote down the name. The slip was handed to the judge and passed on to counsel.

CLARKE: But you have not given the date.
WOOD: I cannot recollect it.
CLARKE: What were you there?
WOOD: A junior clerk.
CLARKE: Now, did you leave there in 1891?
WOOD: I cannot say. I think it must have been at the end of 1892.
CLARKE: Since then, have you ever had a salary from anybody in England?
WOOD: No.
CLARKE: What did you live on, then?
WOOD: Money left me by my father.
CLARKE: How long had you known Allen?
WOOD: Just before I went to America.
CLARKE: At what date was it that you came into possession of the letters of which you spoke?
WOOD: Between January and March 1893.
CLARKE: How long had you had them?
WOOD: Only a few days.
CLARKE: What?
WOOD: They were lying about my rooms for a long time.

CLARKE: Did you hand them to anybody else?

WOOD: No.

CLARKE: Did you receive a letter from Sir George Lewis?[118]

WOOD: Yes.

CLARKE: Before that, had you any of those letters copied?[119]

WOOD: No. Not to my knowledge was one copied.

CLARKE: When you gave the letters back, or left them on the table, or whatever it was you did, did you know that there was one which you did not hand back?

WOOD: Yes.

CLARKE: Where was that one?

WOOD: Allen had it.

CLARKE: Did you give it to him?

WOOD: No. He took it out of my pocket.

CLARKE: Did it remain in Allen's possession?

WOOD: I don't know. I did not want to have it back.

CLARKE: Did you say at the police court that you were the worse for drink when you went on the first occasion with Mr. Wilde to Tite Street?

WOOD: Yes.

CLARKE: Were you the worse for drink?

WOOD: Yes.

CLARKE: How long before you were examined at the police court did you make a statement to someone—a solicitor, for instance?

WOOD: It was just after the arrest of Lord Queensberry.

CLARKE: Who came to see you about taking your statement?

WOOD: Mr. Littlechild, the detective.

CLARKE: How did he find you out?

WOOD: I don't know.

CLARKE: Have you ever, since you came back from America, visited Charles Parker?

WOOD: Yes, at Camera Square.

CLARKE: Have you stayed there?

WOOD: No.

Gill began the examination of Wood.[120]

GILL: At the beginning of 1893, your father was still alive?

WOOD: No.

GILL: When you were at home, with whom did you live?

WOOD: My mother.

GILL: Had you been guilty of any acts of indecency before you knew Wilde?

WOOD: No, not with any man until I went to Little College Street.

GILL: How did you get the letters?

WOOD: I found them in the pockets of some clothes which were given to me at Oxford.[121]

GILL: Did Allen take more than one of the letters?

WOOD: Yes.

GILL: And did he give them all back but one?

WOOD: Yes.

GILL: Did you know that he was keeping back one?

WOOD: Yes.

GILL: Were the people from whom you wanted to get away, when you went to America, people whose names have been mentioned here?

WOOD: Some of them were, and there were others.

GILL: What did you mean by the class of people you had been mixed up with?

WOOD: I meant not only Wilde and Taylor, but several others whose names have not been mentioned.

Grain proceeded to cross-examine Wood.

GRAIN: When you first met Mr. Wilde, it was because of a telegram?

WOOD: Yes.

GRAIN: The telegram was not from Taylor?

WOOD: No.

JUSTICE CHARLES: He said yesterday whom it was from.

The coolness with which Wood conducted himself continued to surprise the press. As the *Morning* put it: "After giving his evidence Wood remained in court, seemingly in no way abashed by the undisguised disgust with which he had been regarded by the judge and everybody else."[122]

The next witness was Thomas Price, a waiter from Geneux's private hotel at 10 and 11 St. James's Place. Price stated that Wilde had rooms at the hotel from October 1893 to April 1894. He observed that the rooms were located on the ground floor and consisted of a communicating bedroom and sitting room. Price recognized Taylor, whom he had seen on one occasion at St. James's Place. Moreover, Charles Parker, who came to Wilde's rooms five or six times, asked for Mr. Wilde and was shown to the rooms. Charles Parker, Price stated, lunched there once. Price added that he knew Atkins by sight. Atkins, Price remarked, had stayed there twice. In addition, Scarfe had called about five or six times, and Barford about the same number. Wilde, the waiter noted, had a latchkey, but he never slept there more than a dozen times. He said that Wilde generally arrived about eleven o'clock in the morning, did some literary work, and returned in the afternoon.

Frederick Atkins, who was the next to step forward, put in a spirited performance that regaled the court with the adventures he had enjoyed with Wilde.[123] As the press revealed, this roguish young man had recently been at the center of a well-publicized scandal. The *Morning* paid attention to Atkins's ostentatious dress and the questionable reputation that came before him: "'Fred Atkins' was called. There answered to the requisition a somewhat burly, clean-faced young fellow, wearing a long blue Newmarket coat, which, when opened, disclosed the corduroy waistcoat much affected by 'horsey' people nowadays. His appearance was a revelation to certain onlookers in court. He described himself as a bookmaker's clerk; but he was quickly recognized as 'Fred Denny,' a low comedian of the minor music halls, and the prosecutor in which a collateral member of a noble family and his wife were convicted of robbing him of a number of valuables, including a cigarette case. 'Fred Atkins' answered questions in a raucous voice."[124]

Horace Avory began his examination.

AVORY: How old are you?

ATKINS: I am twenty years old.

AVORY: What is your business?

ATKINS: I have been a billiard-marker.[125]

AVORY: You are doing nothing now?

ATKINS: No.

AVORY: Who introduced you to Wilde?

ATKINS: I was introduced to him by Schwabe in November 1892.

AVORY: Have you met Lord Alfred Douglas?

ATKINS: I have. I dined with him and Wilde at the Florence.

AVORY: What happened at dinner?[126]

ATKINS: Oscar Wilde kissed the waiter.

AVORY: Did he ask you to go to Paris with him?

ATKINS: Yes. We were seated at the table, and he put his arm around me and said he liked me. I arranged to meet him afterwards at Victoria Station, and went to Paris with him as his private secretary. We stayed at 29 Boulevard des Capucines. We had two rooms there—a bed-sitting room and a bedroom, one leading from the other. The day after we got to Paris, I did some writing for him. Afterwards, I lunched at the Café Julien with him. We went for a drive in the afternoon. Next day we went to a hairdressers, and I had my hair cut.

AVORY: Did you tell him to curl it?

ATKINS: No. He did it on his own account.

AVORY: Wilde was there?

ATKINS: Yes. He was having his hair cut, and was talking to the man in French all the time. After dinner on the second day we were in Paris, I went to the

Moulin Rouge. Mr. Wilde told me not to go, but I went. I had to pay to go in. I had some money Mr. Wilde had given me.

AVORY: You told Wilde on occasion while in Paris that you had spent the previous night with a woman?[127]

ATKINS: No. I had arranged to meet a girl at the Moulin Rouge, and Wilde told me not to go. However, I did go, but the woman was not there.

JUSTICE CHARLES: Mr. Wilde told him not to go to see those women, as women were the ruin of young fellows. Mr. Wilde spoke several times about the same subject, and always to the same effect.

As he continued with his testimony, Atkins stated that he returned to the rooms very late, and Wilde was in bed. Atkins went into Wilde's room and had something to drink. Schwabe, the person who introduced Atkins to Wilde, was in bed with Wilde. Atkins went to bed by himself. Before he got out of bed in the morning, Wilde came into Atkins's room. It was about 9.00 a.m. Atkins talked about the Moulin Rouge, and he told Wilde that he had enjoyed himself. Wilde said: "Shall I come into bed with you?" Atkins replied that it was time to get up. Wilde did not get into bed with him. A waiter came into the room with breakfast, and after drinking a cup of coffee Atkins got up. Schwabe, the man he saw in bed with Wilde, was about twenty-two years of age.

AVORY: You returned to London with Wilde?[128]

ATKINS: Yes.

AVORY: Did he give you money?

ATKINS: He gave me a cigarette case.

AVORY: You were then the best of friends?

ATKINS: He called me "Fred," and I addressed him as "Oscar." We liked each other, but there was no harm in it.

AVORY: Did you visit Wilde on your return?

ATKINS: Yes, at Tite Street. Wilde also called upon me at Osnaburgh Street. On the latter occasion, one of the Parkers was present.[129] I also went once to St. James's Place to see Wilde.[130]

AVORY: You know most of these youths. Did you know Sydney Mavor?

ATKINS: Only by sight. I had heard him called "Jenny" Mavor.[131]

Sir Edward Clarke began his cross-examination of the witness.[132]

CLARKE: Were you ill at Osnaburgh Street?

ATKINS: Yes, I had smallpox and was removed to the hospital ship.[133] Before I went, I wrote to Parker asking him to write to Wilde and request him to come and see me, and he did so.[134]

CLARKE: Where did you last see Mr. Wilde?

ATKINS: At the St. James's Theatre when he came forward at the end of a play.[135]

CLARKE: When did you first know the gentlemen whom you saw in Paris?

ATKINS: Early in 1892.

CLARKE: Had the gentleman promised to take you to Paris before you met Mr. Wilde?

ATKINS: Yes.

CLARKE: And he could not go at the appointed time?

ATKINS: Yes.

CLARKE: So, Mr. Wilde took you instead?

ATKINS: Yes.

CLARKE: You are sure you returned from Paris with Mr. Wilde?

ATKINS: Yes.

CLARKE: Did any impropriety ever take place between you and Wilde?

ATKINS: Never.

CLARKE: Have you ever lived with a man named Burton?

ATKINS: Yes. I lived with him for about three years at 124 Tachbrook Street.[136]

CLARKE: What was he?

ATKINS: A bookmaker.

Atkins added that he acted as clerk to Burton when they were at the races.[137] He also said that he appeared in the music-halls.

CLARKE: Have you and this Burton been engaged in the business of blackmailing?

ATKINS: I don't remember. (*Laughter in court.*)[138]

CLARKE: Has Burton not obtained money from persons on the ground that they have committed indecent acts with you?

ATKINS: No, sir.

CLARKE: Have you ever gone out into the streets in woman's dress?

ATKINS: No. (*The witness laughed.*) I swear I have not.

CLARKE: What names have you gone by?[139]

ATKINS: I have a professional name. I have sometimes called myself Denny.

CLARKE: Has this man Burton, to your knowledge, obtained money from gentlemen by accusing them or threatening to accuse them of certain offences?

ATKINS: Not to my knowledge.

CLARKE: Not in respect of a certain Birmingham gentleman?[140]

Reynolds's Newspaper also noted that at this point Clarke "wrote a name down."[141] The paper was passed to Atkins. Clarke asked if Atkins had seen or heard the name before.

ATKINS: No.

CLARKE: Where were you living on June 9th, 1891?

ATKINS: Lennox Gardens, Chelsea.[142]

CLARKE: That being your answer, I must particularize. On 9 June 1891, did you and Burton obtain a large sum of money from a Birmingham gentleman?

ATKINS: Certainly not.

CLARKE: Then I ask you if in June '91, did not Burton take rooms at 124 Tachbrook Street?

ATKINS: Yes. He lived with me there.

CLARKE: Do you swear that you never took the gentleman whose name I wrote down home with you from the Criterion? Did you take people home there?[143]

ATKINS: Not for the purposes of blackmail. Only friends for a game of cards.[144]

CLARKE: Well, for indecent purposes.

ATKINS: No.

CLARKE: Give me the names of two or three people whom you have taken home to Tachbrook Street?

ATKINS: I cannot. I forget them.

CLARKE: Now I am going to ask you a direct question, and I ask you to be careful in your reply. Were you and Burton ever taken to Rochester Row Police Station?[145]

ATKINS: Not that I know of.

CLARKE: Well, was Burton?

ATKINS: I think not—at least, he was not, to my knowledge.

CLARKE: Did you take the gentleman home?[146]

ATKINS: Never.

CLARKE: Did you, when dressed as a woman, take a gentleman home to 35 Alderney Street, Pimlico, in August 1892?[147] Did Burton come in and threaten him? Did you take the gentleman's watch and chain? And were you the following night taken to the police station, and did you there give the things up?

ATKINS: No. I never dressed as a woman in my life.[148]

CLARKE: Did the Birmingham gentleman give to Burton a cheque drawn for £200 drawn in the name of St. Denis or Denny, which he supposed to be your own name?

ATKINS: Not to my knowledge.

CLARKE: Where does Burton live now?

ATKINS: I don't think he lives anywhere now. I haven't seen him for six months.

CLARKE: Have you ever been to the Victoria Hotel in Northumberland Avenue?[149]

ATKINS: I have never been inside it.

CLARKE: About two years ago, did you and somebody else go there with two American gentlemen?

ATKINS: No. I did not. Never.

CLARKE: I think you did. Be careful in your replies. Did Burton extort money from these gentlemen?

ATKINS: I have never been there at all.

CLARKE: Have you ever been to Anderton's Hotel, Fleet Street, and stayed the night with a gentleman, whom you threatened the next morning with exposure?[150]

ATKINS: I have not.

CLARKE: When did you go abroad with Burton?

ATKINS: I think in February 1892.

CLARKE: When did you last go with him abroad?

ATKINS: Last spring.

CLARKE: How long were you away?

ATKINS: Oh! About a month.

CLARKE: Where did you stay?

ATKINS: We went to Nice and stayed at Gaze's Hotel.[151] We went to Monte Carlo in the afternoon.[152]

CLARKE: You were having a holiday?

ATKINS: Yes.

CLARKE: During which you continued with your business in the usual way?

Atkins did not reply.

CLARKE: What were you and Burton doing at Nice?

ATKINS: Simply enjoying ourselves.

CLARKE: During that visit of enjoyment, you and Burton fell out, I think.

ATKINS: Oh, dear no!

CLARKE: You separated from this Burton after that visit?

ATKINS: I gave up being a bookmaker's clerk.

CLARKE: What name did Burton use in the betting ring?

ATKINS: Watson was his betting name.

CLARKE: Did you blackmail a gentleman at Gaze's Hotel, Nice?

ATKINS: No.

CLARKE: Are you sure there was no quarrel between you and Burton at Nice?

ATKINS: There may have been a little one, but I don't remember anything of the kind.

Grain proceeded with his cross-examination.

GRAIN: Did you go to Scarborough about a year ago?[153]

ATKINS: Yes.

GRAIN: Did Burton go with you?

ATKINS: Yes.

GRAIN: What was your business there?

ATKINS: I was engaged professionally. I sang at the Aquarium there.[154]

GRAIN: Did you get acquainted while there with a foreign gentleman? A count?[155]

ATKINS: Not acquainted.

At this point, Grain wrote a name on a piece of paper and handed it up to the witness, who read it.

GRAIN: Do you know that gentleman?

ATKINS: No. I heard his name mentioned at Scarborough. He had a big yacht lying out in the bay.[156]

GRAIN: Then you never spoke to him?

ATKINS: No.

GRAIN: Was not a large sum—about £500—paid to you or Burton by that gentleman, about this time last year?

ATKINS: No.

GRAIN: Had you any engagement at the Scarborough Aquarium?

ATKINS: Yes.

GRAIN: How much did you receive a week?

ATKINS: I was paid four pounds ten shillings.

GRAIN: How long were you there?

ATKINS: Three weeks.

GRAIN: Have you ever lived in Buckingham Palace Road?[157]

ATKINS: In 1892.

GRAIN: Do you remember being introduced to an elderly man in the City?[158]

ATKINS: No.

GRAIN: Did you take him to your room, permit him to commit sodomy with and upon you, rob him of his pocketbook, and threaten him with exposure if he complained?

ATKINS: No.

GRAIN: Did you threaten to extort money from him because he agreed to accompany you home for a foul purpose?

ATKINS: No.

GRAIN: Did you ever stay at a place in the suburbs on the South Western Railway with Burton?[159]

ATKINS: No.

Clarke then redirected the cross-examination.

CLARKE: Did you ever meet a man named Driver?[160]

ATKINS: Yes, on the racecourse. He was a mere acquaintance. He never accompanied me on any of my singing tours.

The next witness was Mary Applegate, who since the start of the proceedings had been promoted to the position of housekeeper at Osnaburgh Street, where Atkins had formerly lodged until leaving about a month previously. As we see in *The Trial of Oscar Wilde*, she stated that Wilde had visited Atkins on two occasions.[161] Wilde, she said under examination, came at five and left at seven. Applegate pointed out that one of the housemaids came to her and complained about the state of the bedsheets in which Atkins slept after Wilde's first visit. The sheets were stained in a peculiar way.

Sydney Arthur Mavor of 66 St. Helen's Gardens, North Kensington, was the next witness.[162] He was examined for the prosecution on the strength of a statement that he was alleged to have made to the Marquess of Queensberry's solicitors. Mavor described himself as "something in the City in partnership with a friend."[163] In 1892, he became acquainted with Taylor at the Gaiety Theatre.[164] Taylor invited Mavor to Little College Street. Taylor, Mavor observed, was very civil and friendly, introducing Mavor to different people. Mavor did not think at the time that Taylor had any ulterior designs. One day, however, Taylor said to Mavor: "I know a man, in an influential position who could be of great use to you. He likes young men when they're modest and nice in manners and appearance. I'll introduce you." It was arranged that they should dine at Kettner's restaurant the following evening. Mavor called for Taylor, who said: "I am glad you've made yourself pretty. Mr. Wilde likes nice clean boys." This was, Mavor recalled, the first time Wilde's name was mentioned. Once they arrived at the restaurant, they were shown into a private room. Schwabe, Wilde, and another gentleman joined them later. Mavor believed that the third gentleman was Lord Alfred Douglas. Mavor thought the conversation at dinner was peculiar. Yet, since he knew that Wilde was an unconventional, bohemian man, he did not think the talk strange. Mavor said he was placed next to Wilde, who used occasionally to pull Mavor's ear or chuck him under the chin, but did nothing that was objectionable. At this lively dinner, Wilde remarked to Taylor about Mavor: "Our little lad has pleasing manners; we must see more of him." Wilde took Mavor's address. Soon after, Mavor received a silver cigarette case inscribed: "Sydney, from O. W., October 1892." "It was," Mavor stated, "quite a surprise to me!" The cigarette case was produced.[165] It was smaller than the others.[166] The judge looked at it and inquired how the inscription was done, and it was passed around the jury box, each juryman examining it with the most acute interest. Mavor meanwhile wiped his brow, as though he perspired.

In the same month, Mavor received a letter inviting him to the Albemarle Hotel, where he went to stay the night with Wilde, whom he had already seen at the Little College Street tea parties. He got there after eight, and he and Wilde had supper in a private sitting room, with two bedrooms opening out of it. He stayed the night. Mavor added that he and Wilde called each other "Oscar" and "Sydney." Mavor noted that he was never called by any nickname; he did not know that he had one. Thereafter, he asserted that nothing improper had ever taken place between himself and Wilde. Wilde, he observed, had never given him money; he was always glad of Wilde's friendship. Finally, Mavor explained to the prosecution that after he had seen Mr. Charles Russell, the solicitor, on 30 March 1895, he did not visit Taylor again, nor did he receive a letter from Taylor.[167]

Counsel for the defense cross-examined Mavor, and then counsel for the prosecution redirected the examination of the same witness.[168]

CLARKE: With regard to a certain dinner at which you were present: Was the gentleman who gave the dinner of some social position?[169]

MAVOR: Yes.

GRAIN: Taylor sent or gave you some cheques, I believe.

MAVOR: He did.

GRAIN: They were in payment of money you had advanced to him, merely?

MAVOR: Yes.

GILL: The "gentleman of position" who gave you the dinner was quite a young man, was he not?

MAVOR: Yes.

GILL: In fact, it was their first meeting, was it not?

MAVOR: So I understand.

Edward Shelley was called to testify. *Reynolds's Newspaper* remarked: "Shelley . . . formed a strange contrast with Mavor. Mavor has very thin lips, and only allowed the thinnest possible amount of voice to escape through them. Shelley speaks in a loud voice, and evidently with considerable pain. He was dressed in a long overcoat and a silk hat in his hand."[170] On being sworn, Shelley gave his age as twenty-one, and he said that in 1891 a firm of publishers in Vigo Street employed him.[171] He stated that, at that time, the company issued Wilde's books. Shelley recalled that Wilde was in the habit of coming to the firm's place of business. Wilde seemed to take note of Shelley and spoke to him for a few moments. One day, when Wilde was leaving Vigo Street, he invited Shelley to dine with him at the Albemarle Hotel. Shelley recalled that he kept the appointment (he said he was proud of the invitation), and that the two of them dined together in a public room. He stated that he had champagne with his dinner, and afterward whisky and soda and cigarettes in Wilde's sitting room.[172]

When the prosecution asked Shelley what happened next, the witness said he did not like to say, and he suggested that his depositions should be read over.

> SHELLEY (*continuing*): Mr. Wilde's conversation was principally about books and myself. Wilde said: "Will you come into my bedroom?" I did not know what he meant, and as I went into the room, he kissed me. I got into bed and Oscar undressed and I did likewise. Wilde was in bed with me all night.

Shelley then described a sexual act and added: "I had been drinking a lot of wine." He recollected that Wilde saw him the next day and again kissed him, and there was "a repetition of the previous night's performance." Wilde, Shelley remarked, was very kind and attentive, and pressed him to enjoy a drink. Then Wilde said told Shelley that he could assist in advancing the young man's career, and finally invited Shelley to accompany him to Brighton, Cromer, and Paris.[173] Moreover, Wilde gave Shelley a set of his writings, including *The Picture of Dorian Gray*. In the presentation copies, Wilde wrote a dedication: "To one I like well," or something to that effect. The witness noted that he later removed the pages bearing these inscriptions after the decision in the Queensberry case. Shelley stated that he was ashamed of Wilde's inscriptions because he felt that they were open to misconception. Further, Shelley remarked that his father objected to the friendship with Wilde. At first, Shelley said, he thought that Wilde was a kind of philanthropist, fond of youth and eager to be of assistance to young men of any promise. Wilde, however, made various speeches and engaged in behaviors that caused Shelley to change his opinion. Under cross-examination, Shelley was pressed to explain the nature of Wilde's actions that troubled him. Shelley declared that Wilde had kissed him and put his arms around him, and he emphasized that he objected vigorously to Wilde's advances. Later, Shelley observed, Wilde apologized for having drunk too much wine. About two years ago, Shelley maintained, he wrote Wilde a letter, in which he said that he could not have anything further to do with so immoral a man, and that he would not see him again.[174]

Justice Charles asked whether the letter could be produced. Since the letter was not forthcoming, the judge doubted whether the statement could be taken as evidence. The court then adjourned for half an hour for luncheon.

In the afternoon, Clarke cross-examined Shelley.[175]

> CLARKE: On what subject did you write to Mr. Wilde?
> SHELLEY: It was to break off the acquaintance.
> CLARKE: How did the letter begin?

SHELLEY: It began "Sir."
CLARKE: Give me the gist of it.
SHELLEY: I believe I said: "I have suffered more from my acquaintance with you than you are ever likely to know of." I further said that he was an immoral man, and that I would never, if I could help it, see him again.
CLARKE: Did you ever see him again after that?
SHELLEY: I did.
CLARKE: Why did you go and dine with Mr. Wilde a second time?
SHELLEY: I suppose I was a young fool. I tried to think the best of him.
CLARKE: Did it occur to you that it was a sin after the second occasion?[176]
SHELLEY: Yes, it did occur to me that it was a sin I was committing.
CLARKE: You seem to have put the worst possible construction on his liking for you. Did your friendly relations with Mr. Wilde remain unbroken until the time you wrote that letter in March 1893?
SHELLEY: Yes.
CLARKE: Have you seen Mr. Wilde since then?
SHELLEY: Yes.
CLARKE: After that letter?
SHELLEY: Yes.
CLARKE: Where did you see him?
SHELLEY: I went to see him in Tite Street.

At this juncture, *Reynolds's Newspaper* observed:

> Some discussion took place relative to the admission in evidence of the transcript of the shorthand notes taken in the case of Wilde v. Queensberry. The difficulty was overcome by Mr. C. F. Gill consenting to Sir Edward Clarke reading what portion of the notes he wished . . . relative to the evidence of Mr. Wilde at that trial with reference to certain letters of the witness to Mr. Wilde. Sir Edward Clarke read one letter in which the witness expressed his admiration of a new play, which had just been produced, of which Mr. Wilde was the author, and said that he intended to invite Mr. Wilde to dine with him. Sometime later, after the commission of the alleged acts by Mr. Wilde, [Shelley] was writing[:] "Dear Oscar . . . I can never forget your kindness, and am conscious that I can never sufficiently express my thankfulness to you" &c.[177]

In the course of his replies, Shelley stated that he had formed the opinion that "Wilde was very sorry for what he had done."[178]

CLARKE: What do you mean by "what he had done"?
SHELLEY: His improper behavior with young men.
CLARKE: Yet you say he never practised any actual improprieties upon you?

SHELLEY: Because he saw that I would never allow anything of the kind. He did not disguise from me what he wanted, or what his usual customs with young men were.

CLARKE: Yet you wrote him grateful letters breathing apparent friendship?

SHELLEY: For the reason I have given.

CLARKE: Was there present in your mind at the time you wrote this that Mr. Wilde had insulted you when you had had too much to drink?[179]

SHELLEY: Certainly, I could not forget such a thing.

CLARKE: Were you then under the painful sense of having committed sin?

SHELLEY: I tried to forget it. I wanted to think some good of the man.

Reynolds's Newspaper continued its commentary on Clarke's cross-examination of Shelley: "In another letter the witness said, referring to his late employer, Mr. Lane: 'I detest him.' Mr. Lane had offered him money in an hour of distress, yet he called [Lane] a 'viper.' The only explanation [Shelley] could give was that his mind had been overstrained through hard study."[180]

CLARKE: Were you in your sound mind when you wrote that?[181]

SHELLEY: My mind must have been disordered. I cannot remember any reason for calling John Lane a viper.

CLARKE: Now, tell me, why did you leave the Vigo Street firm of publishers?[182]

SHELLEY: Because it got to be known that I was friendly with Oscar Wilde.

CLARKE: Did you leave the firm of your own accord?

SHELLEY: Yes.

CLARKE: Why?

SHELLEY: People employed there—my fellow-clerks—chaffed me about my acquaintance with Wilde.

CLARKE: In what way?

SHELLEY: They implied scandalous things. They called me "Mrs. Wilde" and "Miss Oscar."

CLARKE: So, you left?

SHELLEY: I resolved to put an end to an intolerable position.

Reynolds's Newspaper commented on the next stage of Clarke's cross-examination: "Counsel read a number of other letters, couched in a pleading and religious strain, from [Shelley] to Mr. Wilde."[183] Shelley claimed to have been unwell when he wrote this correspondence.

CLARKE: You mean that your head was untrustworthy?

SHELLEY: Yes. (*Laughter in court.*)

CLARKE: You were in bad odour at home too, I think?[184]

SHELLEY: Yes, a little.

CLARKE: I put it to you that your father requested you to leave his house.

SHELLEY: Yes. He strongly objected to my friendship with Wilde.

CLARKE: You were uneasy in your mind as to Wilde's object?

SHELLEY: That is so.

CLARKE: When did your mental balance, if I can put it so, recover itself?

SHELLEY: About October or November last.

CLARKE: And you have remained well ever since?

SHELLEY: I think so.

CLARKE: Yet I find that in January this year you were in serious trouble.

SHELLEY: In what way?

CLARKE: You were arrested for an assault upon your father?

SHELLEY: Yes, I was.

CLARKE: Were you quite in your sound mind when you assaulted your father?[185]

SHELLEY: No, I couldn't have been.[186]

CLARKE: Where were you taken?

SHELLEY: To the Fulham Police Station.[187]

CLARKE: You were offered bail?

SHELLEY: Yes.

CLARKE: Did you send to Wilde and ask him to bail you out?

SHELLEY: Yes.

CLARKE: What happened?

CLARKE: In an hour, my father went to the station and I was liberated.

At this point, once Shelley was released from further cross-examination, Atkins was recalled.[188] The next stage of the proceedings caused a sensation. During the lunch break, Robert Humphreys, Wilde's solicitor, had been busy. Not satisfied with Atkins's replies under cross-examination, Humphreys had searched the records at Scotland Yard and Rochester Row. As a result, Humphreys made some startling discoveries. A folded document was handed up to Justice Charles, who at once assumed his sternest expression. The document was understood to be a copy of a record from Rochester Row. Atkins, looking very uncomfortable, reentered the witness box for further cross-examination by the defense.

CLARKE: Now, I warn you to attend and to be very careful. I am going to ask you a question. Think before you reply.

JUSTICE CHARLES: Just be careful now, Atkins.

CLARKE: On June 10th, 1891, you were living at Tachbrook Street?

ATKINS: Yes.

CLARKE: In Pimlico?

ATKINS: Yes.

CLARKE: James Dennis Burton was living there with you?

ATKINS: He was.

CLARKE: Were you both taken by two constables, 396A and 500A—you may have forgotten the officers' numbers—to Rochester Row Police Station and charged with demanding money from a gentleman with menaces?[189]

ATKINS (*huskily*): I was not charged with that.

CLARKE: Were you taken to the police station?

ATKINS: Yes.

CLARKE: You and Burton?

ATKINS: Yes.

CLARKE: What were you charged with?

ATKINS: With striking a gentleman.

CLARKE: In what place was it alleged this happened?

ATKINS: At the card table.

CLARKE: In your own room at Tachbrook Street?

ATKINS: Yes.

After consulting with his junior counsel Mathews, Clarke proceeded.

CLARKE: What was the name of the gentleman?

ATKINS: I don't know.

CLARKE: How long had you known him?

ATKINS: Only that night.

CLARKE: Where had you met him?

ATKINS: At the Alhambra.[190]

CLARKE: Had you seen him before that time?

ATKINS: Not to speak to.

CLARKE: Meeting him at the Alhambra, did he go with you to Tachbrook Street?

ATKINS: Yes, to play cards.

CLARKE: Not to accuse him, when there, of attempting to indecently handle you?

ATKINS: No.

CLARKE: Was Burton there?

ATKINS: Yes.

CLARKE: Anyone else?

ATKINS: I don't think so.

CLARKE: Eh?

ATKINS: No.

CLARKE: Was the gentleman sober?

ATKINS: Oh, yes.

CLARKE: Sure of it?

ATKINS: Yes.

CLARKE: What room did you go into?

ATKINS: The sitting room.

CLARKE: Who called the police?

ATKINS: I don't know.

CLARKE: The landlady, perhaps?

ATKINS: I believe she did.

CLARKE: Did the landlady give you and Burton into custody?

ATKINS: No. Nobody did.

CLARKE: Some person must have done. Who did?

ATKINS: All I can say is, I did not hear anybody.

CLARKE: At any rate, you were taken into Rochester Row, and the gentleman went with you?

ATKINS: Yes.

Police Constable 360A was called into court and took up a position close to the witness box. The constable gazed at Atkins.

CLARKE: Now, I ask you, in the presence of this officer, was the statement made at the police station that you and the gentleman had been in bed together?

ATKINS: I don't think so.

CLARKE: Think before you speak. It will be better for you. Did not the landlady actually come into the room and see you and the gentleman naked on or in the bed together?

ATKINS: I don't remember that she did.

CLARKE: You may as well tell us all about it, you know. Was that statement made?

ATKINS: Well, yes it was.

CLARKE: You had endeavored to force money out of this gentleman?

ATKINS: I asked him for some money.

CLARKE: At the police station, the gentleman refused to prosecute?

ATKINS: Yes.

CLARKE: So, you and Burton were liberated?

ATKINS: Yes.

CLARKE: About two hours ago, Atkins, I asked you these very questions and you swore upon your oath that you had not been in custody at all and had never been taken to Rochester Row police station. How came you to tell me those lies?

ATKINS: I did not remember it.

"Atkins," the *Illustrated Police Budget* remarked, "looked very abashed, and yet some of his former impudence still gleamed upon his now scarlet face."[191]

JUSTICE CHARLES (*to Atkins, pointing with his pencil to the doorway*): Leave the court.

Before the proceedings for the day drew to a conclusion, *Reynolds's Newspaper* noted that the court heard "[e]vidence of a formal character . . . with regard to the purchase by Mr. Wilde of certain small articles, which were given away by Mr. Wilde, also as to the apartments which [Wilde] occupied at hotels."[192] The publisher Charles Elkin Mathews gave evidence. He stated that it was brought to his attention that Wilde was communicating with Shelley.[193] Aloys Louis Vogel, proprietor of the Albemarle Hotel, said that he took steps to lose Wilde's custom after learning about the nature of his visitors. A representative from Walter Thornhill and Co., silversmiths, provided evidence of the supply of silver cigarette cases and other small items to Wilde. Charles Robinson, a bookkeeper at the Savoy Hotel, specified the rooms that Wilde had occupied there.

At 4.00 p.m., the trial was adjourned until Monday morning.[194] There were no applications for bail. The prisoners were taken back separately to H.M. Prison Holloway.

THIRD DAY: MONDAY, 29 APRIL 1895

The trial of Oscar Wilde and Alfred Taylor resumed at 11.00 a.m. on Monday, 29 April, before Mr. Justice Charles.[195] The large crowd that assembled in the street awaiting the opening of the doors again showed the interest that this trial was creating. There was a rush when the doors were unlocked, but as the public gallery was of limited capacity only comparatively few of those anxious to gain admission were allowed to enter. The police had orders to prevent the crowd from blocking the entrance and staircase leading into the court, and they carried out their task in a determined manner.

Mr. C. F. Gill, Mr. Horace Avory, and Mr. A. Gill appeared for the prosecution; Sir Edward Clarke, Mr. Charles Mathews, and Mr. Travers Humphreys for the prisoner Wilde; and Mr. J. P. Grain and Mr. Paul Taylor for the prisoner Taylor. Mr. Leonard Kershaw watched the case on behalf of the witness Sydney Mavor. Mr. Justice Charles took his seat on the bench at 11.30 a.m. The prisoners immediately entered the dock. "Wilde," the *Sun* observed, "promptly sat himself, and at once took up what is apparently his favourite position, his elbow on the corner of the dock rail and his heads resting on his palm or on his knuckles."[196] Meanwhile, Taylor "gazed around the court before sitting down, and seemed looking for someone. Then he spoke to his solicitor, and took his chair, smiling of course—he still is always smiling."[197] Even though Wilde's appearance looked better than before, he still seemed "ill and terribly aged by the events of the past three weeks."[198]

Grain, addressing Justice Charles, stated that at Bow Street Magistrates' Court Shelley had said that Taylor was a stranger to him. Grain added that he did not think that Shelley had made that claim in the evidence he gave on Saturday, and therefore Grain, with his lordship's permission, wanted to ask Shelley about his knowledge of Taylor.

GILL: Certainly, there is no evidence that the prisoner Taylor ever knew Shelley.[199]

JUSTICE CHARLES: I ought not strictly to add it, because it has not been sworn here. But did he say so before the magistrate?

GRAIN: He did, my lord.

JUSTICE CHARLES: Very well.

The foreman intimated that the members of the jury were under the impression that Taylor did not know Shelley. Justice Charles then quoted from his notes on Shelley's evidence: "Taylor is quite a stranger to me." John William Lehmann and Ebenezer Howard, the two shorthand writers, were called to produce their official records of *Regina (Wilde) v. Queensberry*.

The first witnesses to be called were Antonio Migge (a professional masseur), Jane Margaret Cotter (a chambermaid), and Annie Perkins (a former housekeeper), who repeated the evidence about Wilde's stay at the Savoy Hotel in March 1893 that they had already given at Bow Street Magistrates' Court. Clarke began his cross-examination of the masseur. Migge said that in March 1893, when Wilde was staying at the hotel, he massaged this client occasionally. One morning, between 16 and 20 March, Migge called and went into Wilde's rooms. The masseur saw someone in bed. At first, he thought it was a young lady, but afterward he realized that the person was a young man.

CLARKE: You had gone to the room at the usual time for massage, had you not?

MIGGE: Yes.

CLARKE: And when you opened the door Mr. Wilde was dressing?

MIGGE: Yes.

CLARKE: In what part of the room was he?

MIGGE: At the washstand.

According to Sherard, on entering the court to give evidence, the next witness, Cotter, met Wilde's gaze and dropped a "prolonged curtsey, eloquent, of deference, honour and esteem for a man pilloried as monster"; he found the florid gesture peculiar, since "she might have been expected, if truly convinced of such guilt, to entreating nothing but a feeling of entire repulsion."[200] Cotter's behavior, he recalled, "was multiple in its effect on the court": "It heartened the prisoner, it provoked hilarity amongst the Boeotians [i.e., the ignorant majority]."[201] Under Clarke's cross-examination, she recollected what she had seen in the rooms that Wilde occupied. Further, Cotter said she had reason to speak to the housekeeper about seeing a young man in Wilde's room (no. 362). Lord Alfred Douglas, she noted, occupied an adjoining bedroom (no. 361). Cotter remarked that Wilde stayed at the hotel for almost a month, and that she had never witnessed him at the hotel before that occasion. Thereafter, Perkins confirmed Cotter's statement regarding the communications that Cotter had made to her about Wilde's room.[202]

The next witness was Detective Sergeant William Harris. The police officer stated, in response to Clarke's questions, that in May 1893 he gained access to Taylor's rooms in 13 Little College Street. The windows were darkened with muslin and tapestries. At the bedroom windows, there were two large fans. Harris said that he kept observation on the property for three weeks. The whole of the place was draped, both ceilings and walls, and was darkened. Harris proceeded to say that he had received instructions to keep observation on 25 Denbigh Street, and on the morning of 6 April 1895 he saw Taylor coming out of the house. Harris took Taylor into custody on the charge of committing a sexual act with another man. Taylor told Harris: "Very well. I expected you last night. What are you going to do with me?" Harris stated he had informed Taylor that he would be taken to Bow Street Magistrates' Court. In addition, Harris found on Taylor a subpoena that referred to *Regina (Wilde) v. Queensberry*.

In response to Grain's cross-examination, Harris stated that he was not present at the Old Bailey during *Regina (Wilde) v. Queensberry*. Grain suggested that Taylor had heard a warrant had been taken out against him and that Taylor was on his way to give himself up to the police. Harris replied by stating that Taylor did not say on his arrest that he was on his way to surrender himself. Grain commented that the darkening of Taylor's windows was only the drapery used in continental cities and modern flats. Harris replied that he could not express an opinion about continental cities, but he had never seen blinds like those in Little College Street. Under further cross-examination, Harris stated that he had obtained access to Taylor's rooms by saying that he was a friend of Taylor's.

Two other police officers gave evidence. Detective Inspector Charles Richards once more described Wilde's arrest at the Cadogan Hotel on the evening of

5 April 1895, after the collapse of Wilde's case against the Marquess of Queensberry. Richards informed Wilde: "We are police officers and hold a warrant for your arrest." Wilde replied: "Yes. Where shall I be taken?" Richards replied: "To Scotland Yard and then to Bow Street." "Can I have bail?," Wilde asked. "No, I don't think you can," Richards said. On 6 April, Richards searched Taylor's rooms at Denbigh Street. There, he found seven pairs of trousers with the seams of the pockets cut open on one side. He also found a brooch, which he produced.[203] Detective Inspector Thomas Brockwell confirmed that he received Wilde into custody at Scotland Yard and conveyed him to Bow Street Magistrates' Court, where Wilde was searched.[204] Wilde said of the warrant: "Let me read it." Brockwell refused and added: "I cannot do that. If there is anything you cannot understand I will read it to you again." Brockwell stated that when he read the warrant to Taylor, he received this response: "Is that the only charge?"

Among other items that were found upon Wilde were miscellaneous writs and a slip of paper in Taylor's handwriting.[205] The police also found on Wilde a letter from Taylor, stating that Taylor had left the above note at his rooms for Sydney Mavor, in case Mavor should call. On arriving home, however, Taylor learned that a police officer had called and been admitted to Taylor's rooms for the purpose of writing a letter. Taylor's letter had been opened, and Taylor found a note stating that Detective Chief Inspector Littlechild of the London Metropolitan Police, who had visited his rooms, wanted to see Taylor and would keep an eye out for him at the Old Bailey the following morning.[206] Littlechild left the note on 4 April.

Under cross-examination, the police witnesses stated that Taylor attended Wilde's libel case against Queensberry at the Old Bailey. Littlechild, they said, was working for Queensberry. Gill then submitted as evidence the original documents that former detective sergeant Fred Kerley had found in Taylor's hatbox. Most of these documents had already been published.[207] Among them were assorted cheques—one that Taylor had drawn in favor of Wood (which Wood said he had not received), and the others in favor of Mavor for 30s. and £2 2s., respectively.[208] There was also a telegram from "Oscar" asking Taylor to call at the Savoy Hotel, and another from The Cottage, Goring-on-Thames, stating that Wilde could not change the dinner. Among the new exhibits was a New Year's card from Mavor to Taylor, which contained the following verse:

Always a bob in your pocket to spend,
Always a good and trusty friend,
Wishing you these, I add one more,
A happy and prosperous '94.[209]

CLARKE: There was a document found on Mr. Wilde when he was arrested that I should like to have read.

The letter in question may have been from the minor poet Robert W. Buchanan, who had recently submitted a number of items of correspondence to the *Star* in order to defend Wilde against adverse public opinion that might judge him guilty before the jury reached its verdict. In Buchanan's view, Wilde "may be all that public opinion avers him to be; indeed, he stands convicted already, out of his own mouth, of the utmost recklessness and folly; but let us bear in mind that his case still remains sub judice, that he is not yet legally condemned."[210] "This affair," Buchanan added, "is not yet ended, but already more than one piece of 'tainted' evidence has gone to pieces."[211]

GILL: Several letters were found upon the prisoner Wilde, which, subject to your lordship's view, I submit have nothing to do with this case. If your lordship will look at the letter, and thinks it desirable that it should be read, I will not press my objection.

CLARKE: I will hand your lordship a copy of the letter. All I suggest is that certain letters have been referred to, and the possible inference to be drawn from these letters is, of course, a matter that your lordship appreciates. If your lordship will look at this letter, which was found upon Mr. Wilde, I think you will say it is only fair that I should be allowed to read it.

JUSTICE CHARLES (*after inspecting the letter*): It amounts, Sir Edward, to a sympathetic letter from a friend of the defendant, written to him. I do not quite see what bearing it has upon this matter.

CLARKE: Simply this, my lord. The inference that is to be drawn in any case from the contents of documents found upon persons charged is a difficult thing to define. It varies in different cases. My view is that as certain other documents and letters found upon Mr. Wilde have been put in for the purpose, no doubt, of producing some impression relevant to the question of the minds of the jury, I ought to be allowed to read, for the same purpose, another letter found upon him at the same time. I will, however, defer to your lordship's opinion about it.

JUSTICE CHARLES: It comes to absolutely nothing. Supposing a letter had been found upon him written in a contrary sense by a person taking a different view, you might say it would be very wrong to read it to the jury, because it might prejudice them.

CLARKE: I quite appreciate your lordship's point, and if you think my request unreasonable, I will not insist.

JUSTICE CHARLES: I must leave it to Mr. Gill. I do not feel myself called upon to invite him to put it in.

CLARKE: I will not call upon my learned friend to read it on the ground that I have a grievance.

JUSTICE CHARLES: It will be sufficient, probably, that I have made the statement that it is a letter from a sympathetic friend.[212]

CLARKE: A distinguished man of letters.

JUSTICE CHARLES: A letter from a literary friend, and I think it is right I should say that in it he expressed the strongest feeling as to the charges under which the defendant Wilde is living.

The matter was then dropped, and Justice Charles inquired whether there was anyone to prove that the prisoner Taylor had attended the trial of the Marquess of Queensberry.

GILL: I think Kerley can prove that his attendance was secured here.

JUSTICE CHARLES: Then the jury may take it that Taylor was subpoenaed and was in attendance on the day named.

GILL: He was certainly in the neighborhood of the court.

Henry Avory Read, the clerk of arraigns, produced the indictment on the trial of John Sholto Douglas, 9th Marquess of Queensberry, for alleged libel on Oscar Wilde.[213] The alleged libel was contained on a card addressed: "For Oscar Wilde, Posing as Somdomite [*sic*]."[214] Justification was pleaded. The prosecution withdrew, and a verdict of "Not guilty" was taken. All of the persons called, except William Parker, Read said, were mentioned in the plea of justification.[215]

Gill intimated that he did not intend to call any more witnesses.

JUSTICE CHARLES: Of course, Mr. Gill, you know that up to the present I have not had the examination, the cross-examination, and re-examination of the defendant Wilde in the former trial.

GILL: No, my lord.

JUSTICE CHARLES: Do not think that I consider you in any way bound to put that in. You are not bound, assuredly, to call all the evidence you adduced before the magistrate, but I understood you to say on Friday that you desired to take the course I have suggested.[216]

GILL: Sir Edward Clarke having expressed a wish that the evidence of Mr. Wilde should be read, I consented to the whole of it being put in—examination, cross-examination, and re-examination; but, of course, I could not consent to any selected portions being read.

CLARKE: The whole of it being read will meet with no objection on my part, but I would suggest for your consideration that it is clear that there is a great deal in that evidence which has nothing whatever to do with the case, especially with regard to literary discussion and with reference to persons whose names have never been mentioned in this case. I submit this point for my learned friend's consideration. Of course, I was then appearing for the prosecution, Mr. Wilde being the prosecutor, and the whole of his evidence in chief had no reference whatever to matters which are now in issue before the jury, because I had not entered into the question of the plea of justification which was brought out in the cross-examination of Mr. Wilde, so that the whole of the statements made by him with regard to any matters now before the jury, and relevant to this case, were made in answer to his cross-examination. However, if desired, the whole of it can be read; but it will very soon be seen that it has reference to matters of literary controversy and criticism with which I do not think we have anything whatever to do.

Justice Charles then stated that the question before them was whether to read to the jury the evidence that Wilde gave during the Marquess of Queensberry's trial. Clarke objected that only the cross-examination that foreshadowed Queensberry's plea of justification had any bearing on the present charges, to which there was no reference in Mr. Wilde's examination-in-chief.[217] Gill, in response, contended that the following questions and answers of the examination-in-chief during the libel proceedings were pertinent, and he quoted from the transcript of the shorthand record of *Regina (Wilde) v. Queensberry*:

GILL (*reading aloud*):

CLARKE (*to Wilde*): Your attention has been called to the statements which are made in the pleadings referring to different persons and impugning your conduct with them?

WILDE: Yes.

CLARKE: Is there any truth in these accusations?

WILDE: There is no truth whatever in any one of them.[218]

GILL (*continuing*): My position with regard to this will, I think, be clearly understood by your lordship. At the end of the examination-in-chief, instead of being examined as to each particular charge in the plea of justification, Wilde was asked only these two questions.

JUSTICE CHARLES: Then what do you propose doing?

GILL: Having put that denial in these general terms, I propose, my lord, to read to the jury the whole of the cross-examination which has a bearing on what the value of that denial is, because, of course, it is simply a denial, without the matter being gone into in any way. Therefore, I propose to read the whole cross-examination, but not in reference to other persons, because I do not desire to introduce any matter which was outside the question at issue. At that time the question at issue was whether the prosecutor was such a person as described by the prisoner, and I wish to know what the value of the prosecutor's denial was by reading his cross-examination.

CLARKE: I am agreed, my lord, subject to the suggestion that I have already made—that it will be found that the first thirty pages of the cross-examination have reference to literary subjects. However, if my learned friend insists upon reading that, I will withdraw my objection.

GILL: It is the cross-examination on a question which is very important here.

CLARKE: I should not have thought it was relevant; but my learned friend appears to desire it, and your lordship will see what the character of that cross-examination is.

Gill proceeded to read aloud the questions that Mr. Edward Carson, Q.C., had addressed to Wilde, together with Wilde's replies about his literary publications such as *The Picture of Dorian Gray* and "Phrases and Philosophies for the Use of the Young," as well as the anonymously published story, "The Priest and the Acolyte," which appeared in the *Chameleon*.[219] As we have seen above (126–28), Carson's objective was to elicit the degree to which Wilde himself identified with the principles that Carson noted in these writings. The press reported some of Wilde's aphorisms in a rather condensed and distorted way that probably confused readers who were not acquainted with the writer's wit. The *Western Mail*, for example, summarized this part of the proceedings in brisk fashion: "The result embodied Wilde's views upon 'art' as distinct from 'morality.' In 'Phrases and Philosophies,' Wilde said there is no such thing as wickedness. It is a word invented by silly people to account for the curious attractiveness of others."[220] The *Western Mail* also recalled Gill's reading of Carson's question about "The Priest and the Acolyte," in which a priest expresses passion for an altar boy: "'Is [it] an immoral book?' Carson had asked. 'It is worse,' was Wilde's reply, 'it is badly written.'"[221] By comparison, the *Star* synopsized the effect of Gill's reading by alluding to Wilde's memorable witty apothegms:

> For the first time, Wilde began to show uneasiness as counsel rapidly, and with a minimum of expression, ran through the wonderful series of Oscarisms which made up a day and a half of cross-examination unparalleled in the history of the Old Bailey. There was not an intolerable irony in such flippancies and paradoxes as made amusing reading when Wilde was in the witness-box. As a refuge from the ghosts of his own intellectual fireworks, Wilde took to playing with a quill pen. He is grown perceptibly thinner since his incarceration. Taylor seemed profoundly bored and rested his arm on the ledge of the dock and his mouth in his hand in an attitude peculiar to himself.

> Events have already thrown a lurid new light on such Oscarisms as "Wickedness is a myth invented by good people to account for the curious attractiveness of others."
>
> "Pleasure is the only thing one should live for. Nothing ages like happiness."
>
> "A condition of perfection is idleness."
>
> "Adoration is a thing I reserve for myself."
>
> "I love scandals about other people. Scandals about myself don't interest me."
>
> "Sin is a thing that writes itself across a man's face."
>
> "There are no such things as secret vices. If a man has a vice it shows itself in the lines of his mouth." And a hundred other replies to Mr. Carson's questions of quotations by Mr. Carson from the prisoner's works.[222]

The *Star* added: "When the court adjourned for lunch, Mr. C. F. Gill had only got through the literary side of the cross-examination."[223]

Once the proceedings resumed after luncheon, Mr. A. Gill began reading aloud the shorthand notes where Mr. C. F. Gill had left off.[224] The longwinded recital began where Carson had questioned Wilde about a letter Wilde wrote to Alfred Douglas. This was the letter that opened "My Own Boy," and ended "Always, with undying love, Yours, Oscar." (The full text is reproduced at 77–78 above.) Of this letter, the *Star* noted: "Mr. A. Gill, who went on with the reading, ma[de] an even worse hash of the passages about the slim-gilt soul, and the 'rose-red lips, made no less for the music of song than for the madness of kissing.'"[225] Subsequently, A. Gill read out Wilde's answer to Carson's suggestions about the nature of Wilde's friendships with various young men who had been cross-examined in the present case.[226] At 2.30 p.m., A. Gill reached the seventy-third folio, and then C. F. Gill read aloud once more from the voluminous foolscap. Throughout, Justice Charles followed the records of Wilde's libel case closely, and he occasionally took notes.

Clarke interrupted C. F. Gill when the transcript of the libel proceedings approached the case of Alphonse Conway, the young man from Worthing. Clarke observed that he fully understood that his learned friend had given an understanding that no part of the cross-examination would be read aloud that did not refer directly to the persons called in the present prosecution. C. F. Gill demurred to this view by stating that his intention at the outset was to read all of Wilde's answers that had a bearing upon the question of his credibility. Accordingly, the prosecution continued with the deposition.

During C. F. Gill's reading from the transcript of the libel case, Wilde's account of Taylor prompted an objection from Grain. The prosecution read out the description of Taylor that Wilde had given in response to Carson's cross-examination: "I would not call him an intimate friend. He was a friend of mine."[227] At this juncture, Grain objected that Wilde's cross-examination in another case should not be made into evidence that counted against his client Taylor. Justice Charles stated that he could not exclude this part of Wilde's cross-examination on such grounds. He pointed out that it was evidence against Wilde, and for this reason it was legal to have it read in court. Moreover, Justice Charles observed that the question of whether Wilde's comments about Taylor were also evidence against Taylor depended on considerations, ones that he, as the justice, would take care not to lose sight of.

The ordinary time for adjourning the day's proceedings arrived, and still the reading went drearily on.[228] Horace Avory took the place of C. F. Gill, and his dry utterance did not come any closer to recalling the sparkle of the original performance. It was a welcome change when Clarke rose at 4.15 p.m. to begin his part of business by reading aloud the transcript of the libel case. Clarke read much more animatedly and had the opportunity of reading out Wilde's letters to the *Scots Observer*, referring to that journal's hostile review of *Dorian Gray*. In these letters, Wilde wrote: "I do not suppose that the criminal and illiterate classes ever read anything except newspapers. They are certainly not likely to be able to understand anything of mine."[229] And Wilde added: "As for the mob, I have no desire to be a popular novelist. It is far too easy."[230] The *Western Mail* commented on Wilde's letters to this magazine: "Wilde said virtue and vice were to the artist only as colours upon his palette. It was perhaps natural that Caliban, of the 'St James's Gazette,' should have written of the book as he had done, but he expressed his surprise that 'Thersites' of the 'Scots Observer' should have 'made [mows].'"[231]

At 4.40 p.m., C. F. Gill finished reading the last folio, and he announced that the prosecution was now closed.[232]

GILL: That is the case for the Crown, my lord.

JUSTICE CHARLES: I do not think it desirable to proceed any further this afternoon.

After the prisoners left the dock, Clarke handed Justice Charles a written statement of the objection that Clarke had taken at the opening of the case. This statement addressed the charges under the Criminal Law Amendment Act and those of conspiracy against the accused being joined in one indictment.

Clarke also handed up a formal objection to Justice Charles's decision that the prisoners were properly called upon to plea to the conjoint counts of the indictment, which charged them with:

(1) conspiracy;
(2) offenses under the Criminal Law Amendment Act 1885, section 11, under which the accused could themselves be competent witnesses.

Clarke's point was that, if the accused offered their testimony under the second head, they practically laid themselves open to cross-examination under both counts in the indictment. His contention was that the counts of the indictment had been joined in a way that prejudiced the prisoners as to their right to give evidence. At the same time, Clarke professed his readiness to agree to the form that Justice Charles might think best for stating the case.

Justice Charles stated he was under the impression that if there was anything substantial in the point, it should be raised by a case stated for the Court of Crown Cases Reserved.[233] He would, however, take time to consider the matter, and he promised to give his decision on the following morning. The court was adjourned at 4.45 p.m.[234]

FOURTH DAY: TUESDAY, 30 APRIL 1895

Before Mr. Justice Charles, sitting at the Central Criminal Court, the trial of Oscar Wilde and Alfred Taylor resumed.[235] Mr. C. F. Gill, Mr. Horace Avory, and Mr. A. Gill (instructed by Mr. Angus Lewis and Mr. Frayling of the Treasury) appeared for the public prosecutor. Wilde was defended by Sir Edward Clarke, Mr. Charles Mathews, and Mr. Travers Humphreys, while Taylor was represented by Mr. J. P. Grain and Mr. Paul Taylor. Once Justice Charles took his seat, C. F. Gill was the first to speak.

GILL: My lord, I have taken an opportunity of considering the indictment since the case for the prosecution was closed, and, in consultation with my friends Mr. Avory and Mr. [A.] Gill, I have come to the determination of not asking for a verdict on counts of the indictment charging conspiracy. Of course, I do that having in my mind that no evidence has been given here at all which was not directly material to the other charges.

CLARKE: Of course, if this had been done in the first instance, I should have applied that the prisoners be charged separately. My learned friend, I agree, is entitled to tell your lordship that he does not suggest that there is evidence of conspiracy. That is all he can do.

JUSTICE CHARLES: After the evidence was given, it occurred to my own mind that the counts of conspiracy were really unnecessary.

GILL: That was the conclusion arrived at on going through the evidence.

CLARKE: It is not a matter on which I have anything to say at the moment. Mr. Gill is entitled at any part of the case to say that he does not intend to ask the jury to say there is evidence before them on the charge of conspiracy, and I understand that to be the position.

GILL: That is not exactly the position.

CLARKE: I don't want to be pertinacious, but I wish to know what the position is, and whether he asks your lordship now to strike out these counts from the indictment.

GILL: I am taking the course of not asking for a verdict on those counts because it has been suggested that there would be a difficulty with regard to calling the prisoners by reason of these counts being in the indictment, and that I might take advantage of these counts to cross-examine upon matters outside the specific charges in the indictment. For that reason, I desired to take this course to avoid any difficulty being placed in the way of either of the prisoners, Wilde or Taylor, giving evidence.

JUSTICE CHARLES: You are entitled to take that course, Mr. Gill, and I understand, therefore, that you do not ask the jury to give a verdict of guilty upon the counts of conspiracy.

CLARKE: Then I ask that the verdict of the jury of not guilty on these counts shall be at once taken.

JUSTICE CHARLES: I cannot assent to that course.

CLARKE: Of course, my lord, I am entitled to a verdict at some time hereafter, because the prisoners have been given in charge—

JUSTICE CHARLES (*interrupting Clarke*): I think at the present stage of the trial all I can do is to say that I felt it my duty to accede to Mr. Gill's application.

CLARKE: All I can say at this moment is that, at some time of the case, I shall claim that a verdict of not guilty be entered on these counts.

JUSTICE CHARLES: Have you anything more to say, Sir Edward?

CLARKE: No, my lord. I was about to address the jury. The announcement that has just been made is one upon the importance and significance of which I will probably find it my duty to comment at a later stage of the proceedings. This is a remarkable incident in a remarkable trial. I was going to call Mr. Oscar Wilde before you as a witness, but I did not arrive at that decision in consequence of the statement made by Mr. Gill. Certainly, however, I feel strengthened in that resolution by the fact that such a tardy withdrawal of the charges has been made. These were charges which, if it had not been intended to proceed with them, ought not to have been put into the indictment. By taking the course I am adopting, my learned friend is entitled to reply on behalf of the Crown, but I have never during my professional life attached nearly as much importance to what is called the last word as some great advocates who taught me my calling.[236] Certainly, Mr. Wilde is entitled to go into the witness box and again to repeat his absolute and unqualified denial of the charges which are brought against him.

In relation to the observations that have focused on the "literary" part of the case, Mr. Gill urged upon the jury to dismiss from their minds all that they heard elsewhere with regard to this matter. Among the other remarkable aspects of this case is that it has been the occasion for conduct on the part of certain sections of the press, which is disgraceful, which imperils the administration of justice, and is to the highest degree injurious to the client for whom I am pleading. It is not fair to judge a man even by his own books. Coleridge said long ago: "Judge no man by his books, the man is more and greater than his books."[237] In this case, the strange unfairness is that an attempt has been made not to judge Mr. Wilde by his own books, but by books he did not write, and to judge him by an article which he himself has repudiated as horrible and disgusting. With regard to *The Picture of Dorian Gray*, the work was published in the American *Lippincott's Magazine*—one of the highest class of American periodical literature—and it was afterwards published in England, when Mr. Wilde, yielding to the suggestion of one of the most accomplished critics of our age, Mr. Walter Pater, altered one particular passage that bore an unpleasant interpretation.[238] If the jury were a committee sitting to consider whether the book would be approved, I would not have the smallest hesitation in defending it before them. And yet that work has been assailed in cross-examination with the aim of showing that its author must be an immoral man. Could anything be more unfair? When cross-examination was directed for the purpose of biasing the minds of a jury, when they came to consider matters of fact and evidence, I did not hesitate to denounce the attempt as most unfair to Mr. Wilde, and as violating every canon of fairness that ought to be applied to justice. What was it that Mr. Gill had to warn the jury against? Partly, I contend, against the effect produced by cross-examination, upon which I ask you to exercise your firm and honest judgment, as men who want to deal fairly by your fellows. With regard to the publication called the *Chameleon*, let me point out that the defendant was not acquainted with the editor, who wrote to him, as a distinguished man of letters, to contribute something to its columns.[239] Since Mr. Wilde was busy at the time, he sent some "Phrases and Philosophies for the Use of the Young," which he had used in some of his plays, and were of a paradoxical nature, and which, I submit, were innocent and harmless. In that publication, Mr. Wilde saw an article called "The Priest and the Acolyte," which was disgraceful, and Mr. Wilde was so indignant that he communicated with the editor on the subject, as he felt himself insulted by having his name on the title page of that publication. And, although he stated on oath his disapproval of that article, Mr. Wilde was cross-examined on it, and it was sought to attach stigma to him in that connection. Has the jury ever asked themselves: How is it that Mr. Wilde is now being charged for wrongdoing that is said to have been committed eighteen months ago? The reason is this: Mr. Wilde insisted on having the accusation brought against him investigated before the public. It was his act, and his alone, which brought the matter before the public, and has now placed him in the peril in which he stands. The defendant has for some time been a friend of Lady Queensberry and her sons. Lord Queensberry has been divorced by his wife.[240]

GILL: I submit this is in no way material to the present case. Sir Edward had the opportunity at the last trial of saying everything that ought to have been said on the subject, and he consented to the verdict of acquittal being taken by the jury. I now protest, therefore, against any attack being made against Lord Queensberry, who is not present.

JUSTICE CHARLES: Were the letters that have been referred to put in during the examination?[241]

CLARKE: Yes, my lord.

JUSTICE CHARLES: But they are not relevant?

GILL: Certainly not.

CLARKE: My friend rebuking me for irrelevance is rather amusing. (*Laughter in court.*)

GILL: It is not intended to be.

CLARKE: It is merely necessary to show how it was that Lord Queensberry was writing to members of his family, and that is why I have mentioned the divorce. As long as Lord Queensberry's letters were written only to his family, it is obvious why Mr. Wilde took no steps in the matter. But the moment that Lord Queensberry left that objectionable card at Mr. Wilde's club, the defendant applied for a warrant and had Lord Queensberry arrested. It was upon the advice of myself, Mr. Mathews, and Mr. Humphreys that Mr. Wilde took the course of withdrawing the prosecution, the reason being that it was perfectly obvious that the jury would not convict Lord Queensberry of a criminal offence. Mr. Wilde's counsel were responsible for the advice given to him, and it is principally because I have been responsible that I am here to meet, on Mr. Wilde's behalf, the accusation which could not properly have been tried before, but could be properly tried now. Has my client shrunk from the investigation? Not at all. If he was a guilty man, did the jury think that he would have made the charge against Lord Queensberry, and provoked all that investigation? Nor was this all. A few days before the first trial notice, Mr. Wilde was given notice of certain charges made against him, with names and dates. On March 30, Mr. Wilde knew the catalogue of accusations. Does the jury believe that if Mr. Wilde were guilty, he would have stayed in England and faced these accusations? Insane would hardly be the word for it, if Mr. Wilde really had been guilty and faced it with that investigation. I maintain that a guilty man would have listened to the evidence called in support of the plea of justification before going, as Mr. Wilde did, frankly into the witness box to answer the accusations preferred in the plea. Now I have the advantage of showing that Mr. Wilde will say in the witness box what has already been stated in the previous trial, before any evidence is called against him. This is most significant. I hope that if any doubt remains in the minds of the jury as to whether it is possible for you to convict the defendant upon such evidence as you have heard, that doubt will at once be removed when you hear his denial of these charges upon oath.

At this juncture, Grain intimated that he would call Taylor when the time arrived.

Clarke proceeded to call out Wilde's name, and the defendant stepped out from the dock and entered the witness box, where his presence soon led to the overcrowding of the court. In response to Clarke's examination, Wilde provided the following responses.

WILDE: I am forty years of age, and am the son of Sir William Wilde, surgeon-oculist to the Queen in Dublin. My mother is still living. I was student at Trinity College Dublin, and there obtained the classical scholarship and the Gold Medal for Greek. Afterwards, I went to Magdalen College, Oxford, and took the classical scholarship and the Newdigate Prize for English verse. In 1878, I took my degree, and then came down from Oxford. Since then, I have devoted myself to literary work and have been on lecturing tours in America and in England. Recently, I have devoted myself especially to dramatic literature. My first play, *Lady Windermere's Fan*, was produced on February 20, 1892, and since then three of my plays have been produced in London. During that time, I have also written *Salomé*, a tragedy in French.

CLARKE: I believe that in 1884 you married Miss Lloyd.

WILDE: Yes, I had that pleasure.

CLARKE: And you have two sons, Mr. Wilde?

WILDE: Yes.

CLARKE: And have your wife and sons been living with you at 16 Tite Street?

WILDE: Always, ever since we were married.

CLARKE: Besides having your house at Tite Street, did you for some time have rooms at St. James's Place?

WILDE: Yes, between October 1893 and April 1894. They were taken for literary work entirely. My home—if I may make a statement—being very small, and my sons not being at school, I always found it most convenient to do my work outside my own house, so as not to be disturbed. It was entirely and solely for that purpose, and it was there that I wrote my plays.

CLARKE: Was the evidence you gave upon the libel action absolutely and in all respects true evidence?

WILDE: Entirely true evidence.

CLARKE: You have heard the evidence given in this case. Is there any truth in any one of the allegations against you?

WILDE: There is no truth whatsoever in any of these allegations—no truth whatsoever.

Gill proceeded with his cross-examination. According to *The Trial of Oscar Wilde*, at this moment "Wilde seemed perfectly calm and did not change his attitude, or tone of polite deprecation."[242]

GILL: You are acquainted with a publication title the *Chameleon*.

WILDE: Very well indeed.

GILL: Contributors to that journal are friends of yours?

WILDE: That is so.

GILL: I believe that Lord Alfred Douglas was a frequent contributor?[243]

WILDE: Hardly that, I think. He wrote some verses occasionally for the *Chameleon* and, indeed, for other papers.

GILL: The poems in question were somewhat peculiar?

WILDE: They were certainly not the commonplaces like so much that is labelled poetry.

GILL: The tone of them met with your critical approval?

WILDE: It was not for me to approve or disapprove. I leave that to the reviews.

GILL: At the trial of Queensberry and Wilde, you described them as "beautiful poems"?[244]

WILDE: I said something tantamount to that. The verses were original in theme and construction, and I admired them.

GILL: The first one was "In Praise of Shame"?

CLARKE: I do not want to make any difficulty again, but I understood my learned friend to say that he was going to confine his cross-examination to the specific charges made here.

GILL: This is cross-examination to credit.[245]

JUSTICE CHARLES: I don't see how I can interfere. Questions which the learned counsel thinks should go to credit, he is entitled to put.

GILL: Listen, Mr. Wilde. I shall only keep you a very short time in the witness box.

Gill proceeded to read from Douglas's sonnet, "In Praise of Shame," which had appeared in the *Chameleon*:

Last night unto my bed methought there came
  Our Lady of strange dreams, and from an urn
  She poured live fire, so that mine eyes did burn
At sight of it. Anon the floating flame
Took many shapes, and one cried: "I am Shame
  That walks with Love, I am most wise to turn
  Cold lips and limbs to fire; therefore discern
And see my loveliness, and praise my name."

And afterward, in radiant garments dressed,
With sound of flutes and laughing of glad lips,
  A pomp of all the passions passed along,
All the night through; till the white phantom ships
  Of dawn sailed in. Whereat I said this song,
"Of all sweet passions Shame is loveliest."[246]

GILL: Is that one of the beautiful poems?

CLARKE: That is not one of Mr. Wilde's.[247]

GILL: I am not aware that I said it was.

CLARKE: I thought you would be glad to say that it was not.

JUSTICE CHARLES: I understand that was a poem by Lord Alfred Douglas.

GILL: Yes, my lord, and one which the witness described as a beautiful poem. The other beautiful poem is one that follows immediately and precedes "The Priest and the Acolyte."

WILDE: Might I be allowed—?

GILL: Kindly listen to me.

WILDE: Certainly.

JUSTICE CHARLES: You are at liberty to make any explanation you like afterwards.

GILL: In one of the sonnets by Lord Alfred Douglas a peculiar use is made of the word "shame"?

WILDE: I have noticed the line you refer to.

GILL: What significance would you attach to the use of that word in connection with the idea of the poem?

WILDE: I will merely say this, my lord: it is not for me to explain the work of anybody else. It does not belong to me.

GILL: You were remarkably friendly with the author. Perhaps he vouchsafed you an explanation?

WILDE: On one occasion, he did.

GILL: I should like to hear it.

WILDE: Lord Alfred explained that the word "shame" used in that poem is a word used in the sense of "modesty." I mean that I was anxious to point out that "shame turns cold lips"—I forget the line exactly—"to fire" is a quickened sense of modesty.

GILL: Your view, Mr. Wilde, is that the "shame" mentioned there is that shame which is a sense of modesty.

WILDE: That was the explanation given to me by the person who wrote it. The sonnet seems to me obscure.

GILL: During 1893 and 1894 you were a good deal in the company of Lord Alfred Douglas?

WILDE: Oh, yes.

GILL: Did he read that poem to you?

WILDE: Yes.

GILL: You can perhaps understand that such verses as these would not be acceptable to the reader with an ordinarily balanced state of mind?

WILDE: I am not prepared to say. It appears to me to be a question of taste, temperament, and individuality. I should say that one man's poetry is another man's poison! (*Laughter in court.*)

GILL: I daresay. There is another poem, described as "Two Loves." It contains these lines:

> "Sweet youth,
> Tell me why, sad and sighing, dost thou rove
> These pleasant realms? I pray thee tell me sooth,
> What is thy name?" He said, "My name is Love."
> Then straight the first did turn himself to me,
> And cried: "He lieth, for his name is Shame.
> But I am Love, and I was wont to be
> Alone in this fair garden, till he came
> Unasked by night; I am true Love, I fill
> The hearts of boy and girl with mutual flame."
> Then sighing said the other, "Have thy will.
> I am the love that dare not speak its name."

Was that poem explained to you?

WILDE: I think that is clear.

GILL: There is no question as to what it means?

WILDE: Most certainly not.

GILL: Is it not clear that the love described relates to natural love and unnatural love?

WILDE: No.

GILL: What construction can be put on the line: "I am the love that dare not speak its name"?

WILDE: I think the writer's meaning in quite unambiguous. "The love that dare not speak its name" in this century is such great affection of an elder for a younger man as there was between David and Jonathan, such as Plato made the very basis of his philosophy, and such as you find in the sonnets of Michelangelo and Shakespeare. It is that deep spiritual affection that is as pure as it is perfect. It dictates and pervades great works of art like those of Shakespeare and Michelangelo, and those two letters of mine, such as they are.[248] It is in this century misunderstood, so much misunderstood that it may be described as "the love that dare not speak its name," and on account of it I am placed where I am now. It is beautiful, it is fine, it is the noblest form of affection. There is nothing unnatural about it. It is intellectual, and it repeatedly exists between an elder and a younger man, when the elder man has intellect, and the younger man has all the joy, hope, and glamour of life before him. That it should be so the world does not understand. The world mocks at it, and sometimes puts one in the pillory for it.[249]

Wilde's speech created a sensation. As he stopped speaking, there was loud applause, mingled with some hisses, in the public gallery. The judge called the court to order.

JUSTICE CHARLES: If there is the slightest manifestation of feeling, I shall have the court cleared. There must be complete silence.

GILL: Then there is no reason why it should be called "shame"?[250]

WILDE: Ah, that, you see, is the mockery of the other love—love which is jealous of friendship and says to it: "You should not interfere."

The examination then turned to various events in Wilde's life that had occurred over two years previously.

GILL: You were staying at the Savoy Hotel at the beginning of March 1893?

WILDE: Yes.

GILL: And after that he [Douglas] went into rooms?[251]

WILDE: Yes.

GILL: I understand you to say that the evidence given in this case by the witnesses called in support of the prosecution is absolutely untrue.

WILDE: Entirely.

GILL: Entirely untrue?

WILDE: Yes.

GILL: Did you hear the evidence of the servant from the Savoy?

WILDE: It is absolutely untrue.

GILL: Had you a little quarrel with Lord Alfred Douglas in that week?

WILDE: No, we never did quarrel—perhaps a little difference. Sometimes he said things that pained me, and sometimes I said things that pained him.

GILL: Had he that week said unkind things?

WILDE: I always make a point of forgetting when he ever says anything unkind.

GILL: I wish to call your attention to the style of your correspondence with Lord Alfred Douglas.[252]

WILDE: I am ready. I am never ashamed of the style of my writings.

GILL: You are fortunate—or shall I say shameless? I refer to passages in two letters in particular.

Gill proceeded to read aloud a letter that Wilde wrote to Douglas from the Savoy Hotel in March 1893, which begins "Dearest of all Boys—Your letter was delightful," and concludes "Ever your own Oscar." (The full text is reproduced at 78 above.)

GILL: Do you think this is a perfectly harmless letter?

WILDE: There is nothing in it of which I am ashamed. It is full of deep feeling and sentiment.

Gill then quoted from another letter that Wilde had sent to Douglas from Babbacombe, Devon, in early 1893. Like the previous item of correspondence, this document had been subject to Carson's cross-examination of Wilde during the libel trial. This is the letter that begins "My Own Boy" and ends "Always, with undying love, yours Oscar." (See 77–78 above.)

WILDE: The letter is really a sort of prose poem in answer to an acknowledgement of one I had received from Lord Alfred.

GILL: Do you think that an ordinarily constituted being would address such expressions to a younger man?

WILDE: I am not, happily, an ordinarily constituted being.

GILL: It is agreeable to be able to agree with you, Mr. Wilde. (*Laughter in court.*)

WILDE: There is, I assure you, nothing in either letter of which I need be ashamed.

GILL: You have heard the evidence of the lad Charles Parker?

WILDE: Yes.

GILL: Of Atkins?

WILDE: Yes.

GILL: Of Shelley?

WILDE: Yes.

GILL: And these witnesses have, you say, lied throughout?

WILDE: Their evidence as to my association with them, as to the dinners taking place and the small presents that I gave them, is mostly true. But there is not a particle of truth in that part of the evidence which alleged improper behavior.

GILL: Why did you take up with these youths?

WILDE: I am a lover of youth. (*Laughter in court.*)

GILL: You exalt youth as a sort of God?

WILDE: I like to study the young in everything. There is something fascinating in youthfulness.

GILL: So, you would prefer puppies to dogs, and kittens to cats. (*Laughter in court.*)

WILDE: I think so. I should enjoy, for instance, the society of a beardless, briefless, barrister quite as much as that of the most accomplished Q.C. (*Loud laughter in court.*)

GILL: I hope the former, whom I represent in large numbers, will appreciate the compliment. (*More laughter in court.*) These youths were much inferior to you in station?

WILDE: I never inquired, nor did I care, what station they occupied. I found them, for the most part, bright and entertaining. I found their conversation a change. It acted as a kind of mental tonic.

GILL: You never suspected the relations that might exist between Taylor and his young friends?

WILDE: I had no need to suspect anything. Taylor's friends appeared to me to be quite normal.

GILL: You have attended to the evidence of the witness Mavor?

WILDE: I have.

GILL: Is it true or false?

WILDE: It is mainly true, but false inferences have been made from most of the evidence. Truth may be found, I believe, at the bottom of a well.[253] It is, apparently, difficult to find it in a court of law. (*Laughter in court.*)

GILL: Nevertheless, we endeavor to extract it. Did the witness Mavor write to you expressing a wish to break off the acquaintance?

WILDE: I received a rather unaccountable and impertinent letter from him, for which he afterwards expressed great regret.

GILL: Why should he have written it, if your conduct had been blameless?

WILDE: I do not profess to be able to explain the motives of most of the witnesses. Mavor may have been told some falsehood about me. His father was greatly incensed at his conduct at this time, and, I believe, attributed his son's erratic courses to his friendship with me. I do not think Mavor altogether to blame. Pressure was brought to bear upon him, and he was not quite right in his mind.

GILL: You made handsome presents to these young fellows?

WILDE: Pardon me. I differ. I gave two or three of them a cigarette case. Boys of that class smoke a good deal of cigarettes. I have a weakness for presenting my acquaintances with cigarette cases.

GILL: Rather an indiscriminate habit if indulged in indiscriminately.

WILDE: Less extravagant than giving jeweled garters to ladies. (*Laughter in court.*)[254]

Thereafter, Gill focused on the part of the evidence that the staff of the Savoy Hotel had given. On this matter, the press chose not to be explicit. Still, it appears that Gill pressured Wilde to respond to the staff members' observations about the soiled nature of the bed linens in Wilde's rooms and the presence of an unnamed young man in Wilde's bed. The *Daily Telegraph* reported that Wilde replied to this line of questioning "hotly."[255]

WILDE: How can I answer the statements of servants two years after I left the hotel? It is childish. I am not responsible for hotel servants. I have stayed at the hotel and been there constantly since.[256]

GILL: There is no possibility of mistake? There was no woman with you?

WILDE: Certainly not.

GILL: You saw the plea of justification in the Queensberry case, and you saw the different names?

WILDE: Yes.

GILL: At the hearing of that case before Mr. Justice Henn Collins, except the hall porter of your club and yourself, no other witness was called?

WILDE: No.

GILL: You had seen Taylor within a few days of the trial?

WILDE: Yes.

GILL: He was not called?

WILDE: No. He was subpoenaed by the other side. I knew that he was there.

CLARKE: And you knew that while the counsel for Queensberry was addressing the jury, the case was interrupted, a verdict of not guilty was agreed to, and the jury found that the justification was proved and the libel published for the public benefit?

WILDE: I was not in court.[257]

GILL: But you knew it?

WILDE: No, I did not. I knew my counsel had considered it would be impossible to get a verdict on the question as far as the literature went, and it was not for me to dispute their superior wisdom. I was not in court, nor have I ever read any account of that trial.

GILL: What is there untrue in the evidence of Shelley?

WILDE: I say his account of what happened is entirely untrue. It is true that he came to the Independent Theatre with me, but it was in a box with some friends.[258] His accusations of impropriety are equally untrue.

GILL: Do you see no impropriety in kissing a boy?

WILDE: In kissing a young boy, a child, of course not; but I certainly do not think one should kiss a young man of eighteen.

GILL: Then as to Shelley's letters. There was a line in a later one, which says: "God forgive the past; do your best for me now."[259] Do you know the meaning of that?

WILDE: Yes. Shelley was in the habit of writing many morbid, very morbid, letters to me, which I tore up. In them, he said he was a sinner and anxious to be in closer communion with religion. I always tore them up.

GILL: Charles Parker—What part of his evidence is untrue?

WILDE: Where he says that he came to the Savoy and that I committed acts of indecency with him. He never came to the Savoy with me to supper. It is true that he dined with me and that he came to St. James's Place to tea. The rest is untrue.

GILL: Anything else?

WILDE: I do not know.

GILL: Then, Atkins—What do you say is not true?

WILDE: It is not true when he says that he came into my room and saw me committing acts of indecency. The circumstances as to his going to Paris are wrong. It is true, however, that I met him at a dinner, met him again a day or two afterwards, and that within a few days more I went with him via a club train to Paris; also, that I gave him a cigarette case. Schwabe was, as Atkins said, in Paris, and it is true that Atkins slept in the room he described next to mine.

GILL: Did Atkins ever try to blackmail you?

WILDE: Oh, no. Never. I found him bright and amusing. I invited him to go to Paris because I did not care to travel alone. He has given a grotesque and monstrous account of the dinner party at the London restaurant.

GILL: In fact, was not Atkins an agreeable companion?

WILDE: He was amusing, pleasant. It was better than being alone.

GILL: And except that he says he saw Schwabe in bed with you, and that you wanted to get into his bed, his evidence is practically true?

WILDE: Well, I say that his account of the dinner party and his description of how and why he met me were quite wrong. I was busy in Paris and left Schwabe and Atkins to go about together.

GILL: Who introduced you to Wood?

WILDE: Lord Alfred Douglas.

GILL: Did you ever take Wood to Tite Street with you?

WILDE: It is entirely untrue that he ever went to Tite Street with me at all.

GILL: Apart from the suggestions of indecency, Atkins's statements are, in the main, true?

WILDE: Yes.

GILL: And the same remark applies to the evidence of Wood?

WILDE: Yes.

GILL: You have no complaint to make in regard to Burton?

WILDE: No. I do not know him.

GILL: Who introduced you to Taylor?

WILDE: Mr. Schwabe.

GILL: Why did you go to Taylor's rooms?

WILDE: Because I used to meet actors and singers of many kinds there.

GILL: Rather a curious establishment, was it not?

CLARKE: (*To Justice Charles.*) Is this on the conspiracy, my lord?

GILL: Those counts were withdrawn. This is evidence to credit.

JUSTICE CHARLES: The evidence is relevant upon the points that remain?

GILL: Certainly, my lord. (*To Wilde.*) Did it strike you that the place was at all peculiar?

WILDE: Not at all. I thought it Bohemian.

GILL: Did you notice that no one could see in through the windows?

WILDE: No. That I didn't notice.

GILL: He burned incense, did he not?

WILDE: Pastilles, I think.[260]

GILL: Incense, I suggest.

WILDE: I think not. Pastilles, I should think, in those little Japanese things that run along rods.

GILL: Did it strike you that this place was at all peculiar?

WILDE: Not at all.

GILL: Not a sort of street you would usually visit in. You had no other friends there?

WILDE: No. This was merely a bachelor's place.

GILL: Rather a rough neighborhood?

WILDE: That I don't know. It was near the Houses of Parliament. I went there to amuse myself by smoking some cigarettes, singing, chatting, and nonsense of that kind, to while an hour away.

GILL: Why did you ask Sydney Mavor to stay all night with you at the Albemarle Hotel?

WILDE: As company for me and as a compliment to himself.

GILL: Did you know what he was?

WILDE: No.
GILL: No occupation?
WILDE: I don't know.
GILL: Wood?
WILDE: No.
GILL: Parker?
WILDE: No.
GILL: Scarfe?
WILDE: No.
GILL: Taylor?
WILDE: I understood he had private means.
GILL: You never saw anything to create suspicion?
WILDE: No.
GILL: And up to the last trial nothing had shaken your faith in Taylor?
WILDE: Nothing.
GILL: After the case of Lord Queensberry was committed for trial, did you not see at Calais a boy named Tankard?[261] That was before the plea was put in.
WILDE: Oh, no.
GILL: Think!
WILDE: Do you mean after the plea of justification was issued?
GILL: You were at Calais about that time?
WILDE: Yes. I remember I saw Tankard. That was before the plea was put in.
GILL: Tankard was employed at the Calais Hotel, and you were going abroad with Lord Alfred Douglas?[262]
WILDE: Yes.
GILL: Did you know last year of Taylor's arrest?
WILDE: Yes. I saw that the charge was dismissed by the magistrate.
GILL: That satisfied you?
WILDE: What satisfied me was that I did not see on what grounds the police went there at all.
GILL: I may take it, Mr. Wilde, that you see no reason why the police should keep observation at Little College Street.
WILDE: No.

Gill then cross-examined Wilde about Alphonse Conway. Wilde, as he had stated before, met this young man at Worthing. He replied that Conway was such a bright, happy boy that it was a pleasure to talk to him. And he said that he bought Conway a walking stick, a suit of clothes, and a hat with a bright ribbon, though he was not responsible for the ribbon.

GILL: With regard to your friendship towards the persons I have mentioned, may I take it, Mr. Wilde, that it was as you describe, the deep affection of an elder man for a younger?

WILDE: Certainly not. One feels that once in one's life, and once only, towards anybody.

Clarke then quickly reexamined Wilde about Tankard.

WILDE: It was when I was passing through Calais that I recognized Tankard, who was doorkeeper at the buffet of the hotel. I asked him how he was getting on, and he told me he was learning French. At the time, I knew nothing about the plea of justification.

Clarke then asked about the letters of Wilde's that Wood had taken from Douglas's clothing at Oxford.

WILDE: I became aware at one time that Wood had some letters of mine, and I communicated with Sir George Lewis. Taylor arranged a meeting at his rooms.

CLARKE: Wood returned them?

WILDE: He gave me three letters back. They were not what I would call matters of great consequence, but no one likes their private letters read. They contained some slighting allusions to other people which I should not have liked made public. Then I received an anonymous letter saying that Wood had other letters and intended to try and extort money by means of them. I did not give any money for them at all, but I gave Wood some money to enable him to go to America.

Clarke inquired if Wilde had anything to do with the publication of Douglas's two poems in the *Chameleon*. Wilde denied that he had.

At this point of the morning, Clarke's examination of Wilde came to an end, and Wilde left the witness box. Since Clarke called no further witnesses, Gill called "Alfred Taylor," who—as the *Star* observed—"changed places with Wilde, nervously struggling to get off his right glove for the purpose of being sworn."[263]

GILL: What is your age now?[264]

TAYLOR: Thirty-three.

GILL: You were educated up to the age of sixteen or seventeen at Marlborough?[265]

TAYLOR: Yes. I spent a year at Preston, near Brighton, and then went into the militia.[266]

GILL: Did your father die in 1883?
TAYLOR: In 1874. My uncle died in 1883.

Gill asked if Taylor had been given to sodomy since early youth.[267] Was it, Gill inquired, not the case that Taylor had been expelled from Marlborough College because he had been caught in a compromising situation with a small boy in a lavatory? Moreover, Gill questioned Taylor about the witness's source of income since the bankruptcy. Had Taylor, Gill wished to know, made money by procuring lads and young men for rich gentlemen whom he knew were given to this behavior? Had Taylor, Gill continued, not extracted large sums of money from wealthy men by threatening to accuse them of indecencies? To each of these questions, Taylor returned the direct answer: "No." In reference to the charges of misconduct that Gill then put to Taylor one by one, the *Daily Telegraph* reported: "He absolutely denied the allegations made against him. They were entirely untrue."[268]

Gill then proceeded to ask whether Taylor used to have young men in the same bed with him.[269]

TAYLOR: It was true that I used to have a number of young men living in my rooms and sleeping in the same bed.
GILL: Was it true that you ever went through a mock marriage with Mason?
TAYLOR: Absolutely untrue.
GILL: Had you a woman's costume in your rooms?
TAYLOR: An Eastern costume.[270]
GILL: A woman's dress?
TAYLOR: Yes.
GILL: A woman's wig?
TAYLOR: I will explain. It was—
GILL: A wig?
TAYLOR: Yes.
GILL: Had you women's stockings?
TAYLOR: Yes.
GILL: At the time you were living in Chapel Street, were you in serious money difficulties?
TAYLOR: I had just gone through the Bankruptcy Court.
GILL: You made the acquaintance of the Parkers in the St. James's restaurant?
TAYLOR: It was outside, and I was introduced to them by a friend.
GILL: What did you give them your address for?
TAYLOR: Well, when one makes an acquaintance and you think you will like one another—
GILL: Are you in the habit of speaking to young men in Piccadilly?

TAYLOR: I know what you mean. No.
GILL: You go into Piccadilly?
TAYLOR: Yes, always.
GILL: St. James's?
TAYLOR: Yes.
GILL: Have you ever accosted men at the Alhambra or the Empire?[271]
TAYLOR: Never.
GILL: Did you know Mr. Wilde well?
TAYLOR: Yes.
GILL: Did you tell certain lads that he was fond of boys?
TAYLOR: No. Never.
GILL: Do you know that he is?
TAYLOR: I believe he is fond of young people.

Gill proceeded to question Taylor on the young men he had introduced to Wilde.

GILL: Did you meet the Parkers at the St. James's restaurant?[272]
TAYLOR: No. It is absolutely untrue.
GILL: When was it that you met them?
TAYLOR: Some month or more before I dined with Mr. Wilde.
GILL: Did you invite other young men?
TAYLOR: Several young men used to visit me.
GILL: Did you meet them in Piccadilly?
TAYLOR: Some of them.
GILL: In March 1893, you were in communication with Wilde?
TAYLOR: Yes.
GILL: Who introduced you to Wilde?
TAYLOR: Schwabe.
GILL: Haven't you discovered what these young men were?
TAYLOR (*smiling*): I have learnt from you.
GILL: But you didn't before?
TAYLOR: No.
GILL: Why did you introduce Charles Parker to Wilde?
TAYLOR: I introduced Charles Parker to Mr. Wilde because I thought the latter might use his influence to obtain for Parker some work on the stage.
GILL: Why did you bring Charles Parker to dinner at Kettner's restaurant?[273]
TAYLOR: The dinner was to celebrate my birthday. Wilde invited me to the dinner, and he told me to bring any friends I liked.
GILL: Do you know a man named Marling who was concerned with the Fitzroy Street raid?[274]

TAYLOR: I have heard a good deal.

GILL: Did you know Scarfe?[275]

TAYLOR: Yes. I took Scarfe to see Mr. Wilde at St. James's Place.[276]

GILL: Were you not arrested with Charles Parker in the Fitzroy Street raid?[277]

TAYLOR: Charles Parker and myself were arrested, but we were discharged from custody.

GILL: Did you know how Charles Parker made his living?

TAYLOR: No.

GILL: You continued on friendly terms with Wood?

TAYLOR: Oh, yes.

GILL: Where did you make Mavor's acquaintance?

TAYLOR: At the Prince of Wales's Theatre.[278]

GILL: Were you present at a dinner with Mavor when Wilde was there?

TAYLOR: Yes. Mavor and I were introduced to Wilde at the same time.

GILL: Did you arrange any dinners?

TAYLOR: Never.

GILL: Who was it?

TAYLOR: Mr. Wilde. I never gave any dinners. I was always present as a guest, either of Mr. Wilde or Schwabe.

The *Star* observed: "Taylor described with candor the way in which he made the acquaintance of the various lads who had given evidence in the case, and the tea parties in which they indulged at Little College Street. The cross-examination did not materially advance the case or evoke any kind of damaging admission."[279]

Grain then proceeded with his questions for Taylor. He asked about the nature of the woman's dress in Taylor's rooms.[280]

TAYLOR: The dress was an Oriental costume, which I brought from Constantinople for the purpose of going to a fancy-dress ball at Covent Garden.

Thereafter, Grain wanted to know whether Taylor had any awareness of the Parker brothers' background.

GRAIN: Did the Parkers tell you what they were?

TAYLOR: They said their father had something to do with horses.

GRAIN: At Fitzroy Square, how were you dressed?

TAYLOR: Almost as I am now.

The court adjourned for lunch.

After the court resumed its business, Clarke addressed the jury on behalf of Wilde.

CLARKE: That the counsel for the Crown introduced and then withdrew the conspiracy charges has placed me in great difficulty.[281] There is now no longer any joint charge. What is evidence against Taylor is not evidence against Wilde. Has the prosecution evidence which made them put that count upon the indictment? If they have not, why was the count of conspiracy put upon record, and why were the counsel for the defence placed for three days under the embarrassment of meeting an indictment with regard to part of which they call evidence, and with regard to another part of which they could not? The counsel for the Crown ought to have made up their minds on this point at the outset. A cruel hardship has been inflicted on Mr. Wilde. With whatever anxiety you might separate the evidence in your minds, you are hardly able to do so. The evidence of literature which was called against Wilde is not evidence against Taylor. Nor is the case of Shelley. At the same time, the character of the young men who frequented Taylor's rooms is no evidence against Mr. Wilde. In disentangling the evidence, you will be in a terrible position of responsibility. When we turn to the literature, we must consider its use in the cross-examination as to credit. I cannot help expressing astonishment after having protested in my former speech against the way in which public feeling has been excited and fanned against Mr. Wilde by the quotation of passages of literature for which he is not responsible. My learned friend should not have devoted the whole of that part of the cross-examination which dealt with literary questions to interrogating Mr. Wilde regarding two poems of which he was not the author. The questions Mr. Gill asked were not as to anything Mr. Wilde has written. The two poems were written by Lord Alfred Douglas, and with them Mr. Wilde had no more to do than myself or yourselves. What can be said of the morality of any of our poets if we are to measure it by the writings, not of themselves, but of others? A poet is no more responsible for what others have said than an artist is guilty when he paints a picture depicting the murder of Rizzio at the feet of Mary, Queen of Scots.[282]

As to the affection which Mr. Wilde has expressed in the letters that have been put in: He has himself described it as a pure and true affection, absolutely unconnected with, alien to, irreconcilable with, the filthy practices which this band of blackmailers has been narrating. Had Mr. Wilde been guilty, if he had not been innocent in this matter, would he have not recoiled from going into the witness box, which he has entered fearless as to what might be produced against him? And as for the letters about which so much has been said, Mr. Wilde produced in court the first of the two letters that have been used against him. Mr. Wilde is no ordinary man. He is a man who has written poetry and prose, brilliant dramas and charming essays—a man who from his youth upwards has been trained in the literatures of the world—not of this England of ours alone, but of those empires whose glories are to us only now a name. You must bear in mind, therefore, that he wrote letters in a tone which might to others seem high-flown, exaggerated, and absurd. But he is not ashamed or afraid to produce those letters. He goes into the box and says they speak of pure love, and when he says so, is he not to be believed?

I spoke to you before about the cowardice of guilt. I reminded you that these men—the Woods, the Parkers, the Atkinses, the whole tribe of them—flourish in so frightful a trade, because a man who has been tempted into any sort of guilt would rather give his whole fortune, rather exile himself from his country, than allow the thing to be suggested against him. When you are judging the evidence, contrast this shrinking of the guilty, upon which these bands of blackmailers live, with the openness with which Mr. Wilde has sought to have these charges investigated, the courage that brought him into the witness box in this court to face, once and for all, and, as he hopes and I hope, to dispose of the accusations which were being made against him. When a man comes forward and says, "I do not shrink from the judgment of the world upon these productions," you cannot not say that such a man was not to be believed. Has the defendant in this case not given the jury the best proof of his innocence? Innocence has courage and faith in the ultimate judgment of mankind. All of Mr. Wilde's moves have been open.

The evidence in the case of Edward Shelley is entirely different from the others. In it you will have to judge between Mr. Wilde and the young man. In cross-examining Mr. Wilde, the counsel for the Crown persisted in using the term "office boy," perhaps for the purpose of annoying Mr. Wilde, as it did, certainly for showing that such was the difference between the two men, there could be no reasonable explanation of their going about together. The real position is that Mr. Shelley is a young man who was making deep studies of literature, and who expressed his deep admiration for Mr. Wilde's own works. No man is insensible to the frank and honest admiration of a young man for any work of his, whether poem or speech. Mr. Wilde wished to return his kindness, and he gave Shelley a ticket for his play, and so on. Was there any one instance in which there has been the slightest attempt at secrecy?

Shelley says that Mr. Wilde took him into the bedroom, kissed him, and insulted him. But notice, as no doubt you have done, the conduct of that young man in the witness box. He could scarcely be held. He had been "insulted, degraded," he shouted; he did not know the character of the man, he said; and he made out that whilst under the influence of drink Mr. Wilde had offered him an insufferable insult. Yet, though Shelley showed what he thought of what he says occurred, he admitted that he went the next night with Mr. Wilde to the theatre. Mr. Wilde denies the story emphatically. Would you, even were there nothing to support that denial, commit a man to the suffering and degradation which their verdict might mean in this case? But there is much to support the denial. Fortunately, Mr. Wilde has kept letters that Shelley wrote to him; and those letters not only make it seem impossible that the incident ever took place, but, with the admissions of the young man himself, show that there were times when Shelley's intellect was affected.

Now let me address the Savoy Hotel evidence, which is next in importance against Mr. Wilde. What remarkable evidence this is. The chambermaid, though a woman whom Mr. Wilde did not know at all, would have one believe that Mr. Wilde rang for her and allowed her to go into the room to light his fire, whilst there was lying in bed a boy with whom he had an improper relation. Then as to the bed linen: How is it that not one scrap of similar evidence could be obtained from any of the other hotels at which Mr. Wilde had stayed? Why is it that none of the detectives for the prosecution could find any such evidence even as to the rooms Taylor occupied, where in the course of twelve months there must have been some linen sent to the laundry? Migge's story was of the most amazing character. He even admits that Wilde was expecting him. Yet Migge says that he opened the door of the room, saw Mr. Wilde dressing on one side of the chamber and a boy in the bed on the other side of the room. How was it that no one could be found who ever saw those boys either go into or come out from the hotel?

As to Parker, Wood, and Atkins: It does not need the experience those three young men had in blackmailing to teach them that they must make use of circumstances which actually occurred in order to suggest others. And having dealt with what they have suggested, the eloquent advocate, with thrilling accents, revived the scene of the previous Saturday, when Atkins made his notorious denials and his even more notorious retractions of those denials. Those three witnesses—Charles Parker, Wood, and Atkins, witnesses for the Crown—have admitted their participation in such practices as ought to disentitle their evidence to the slightest credence. You will never forget, for few juries have ever seen such, the scene that happened in the witness box on Saturday. You will have noticed how Atkins met those questions of mine with steady and stolid denial. Did the police know who Atkins was, and his shameful history? Was it the Public Prosecutor alone who was ignorant of Atkins's character? And if he were not, if he knew of these incidents in the shameful record of Burton and Atkins, what was the meaning of the Crown calling Atkins into the witness box for his evidence to be accepted as if it were untainted? Those who conduct criminal prosecutions have a duty towards the defendant as well as to the Crown and the public. It deepens one's horror that Mr. Wilde is at peril of these persons, to think that had the trial been finishing that day the denials made by Atkins might have had their effect upon the jury.

It is through detailed information, which I have received through anonymous letters, that I was able to convict the witness Atkins on Saturday of the attempted extortion which he so persistently denied until confronted with the police officers who had taken him into custody. It was, I think, strange that the Public Prosecutor, if he knew of this witness's real character, should have permitted Mr. Gill to tender his evidence against the accused. Wood, Parker, and Atkins, too, have shared the profits from blackmailing, and I protested that it should not have been accepted, on the uncorroborated evidence of men like them, that before 1892 they were uncorrupted.

I submit that the evidence that has been called for the prosecution is not reliable testimony. The principal witnesses for the prosecution, whose evidence has been wholly uncorroborated, belong to a wretched gang of blackmailers. Shelley has admitted that his mind was disordered at the time he wrote some of the letters that have been produced. I know with what extreme difficulty it is that juries are able to efface from their recollections things that bias their judgment, and to address themselves only to that evidence which is sound and true. Before you deal with this case, therefore, I implore you to make that effort, and only allow your judgment to be affected by those witnesses with regard to whom you can say with a clear conscience that you, as honorable and right-judging men, are entitled to be guided by true, and honest, and honorable testimony. Fix your minds firmly on the tests that ought to be applied to evidence, before you condemn a fellow man on a charge like this. If you guard yourselves from these prejudices which have floated about, and which have been dissipated to some extent by the incidents of the last few days, but from which it is impossible that this atmosphere should be absolutely clear, then I trust the result of your deliberations will be to gratify those thousands of hopes which hang on your decision, and will clear from this fearful imputation one of our most renowned and accomplished men of letters of today, and in clearing him, will clear society from a stain.

Reynolds's Newspaper observed: "An outburst of applause followed the conclusion of Clarke's speech, which had occupied two hours, but the demonstration was at once silenced. Wilde, who was visibly affected, wrote a brief note, which was handed down to the learned counsel."[283] Meanwhile, the *Star* noted Wilde's unease during Clarke's closing of the case for the defense: "Under the strain of these last hours of his trial, Wilde's remarkable phlegm is rapidly breaking down. During the afternoon he restlessly changed his position, scribbled repeatedly with a quill pen on a piece of blotting-paper, but was always haggardly regarding the counsel who was so brilliantly pleading his case, or the jury who were absorbed in Sir Edward Clarke's advocacy."[284] In *The Trial of Oscar Wilde*, the commentary remarks: "Wilde had paid great attention to the speech on his behalf and on one or two occasions had pressed his hands to his eyes as if expressing some not unnatural emotion."[285]

Grain then rose to address the jury on Taylor's behalf.[286] He submitted that there was really no case against his client. An endeavor, he observed, had been made to prove that Taylor was in the habit of introducing to Wilde youths whom he knew to be amenable to the practices of the latter, and Taylor was paid for this degrading work. The two young men named Parker, Grain remarked, were the only witnesses who claimed that Taylor introduced them to Wilde. All of the resources of the Crown, and of the eminent solicitors whom Lord Queensberry employed, had been unable to produce any corroboration of the Parkers' story of misconduct. The attempt to establish this association between Taylor and Wilde, Grain contended, had completely broken down. Taylor was, it is true, acquainted with Parker, Wood, and Atkins. Taylor had seen these young men constantly in restaurants and music-halls, and they had at first forced themselves upon his notice and thus became acquainted with a man whom they designed for blackmail. How, then, Grain asked, had Taylor got his livelihood? Grain said that he was perfectly prepared to answer that question. Taylor, he remarked, having run through his own large fortune, was living at Little College Street on an allowance from his father's firm. If Wilde had employed Taylor, Grain inquired, where was the proof of any kind of payment? Not a farthing piece, he stated, in money or value, had been shown to have passed between the two men.[287] Was it in the least degree likely that such scenes as the witnesses described, with such apparent candor and such wealth of filthy detail, could have taken place in Taylor's own apartments? It was incredible, Grain said, that a man could thus risk almost certain discovery. In conclusion, he stated that he confidently looked for the acquittal of his client, who was guilty of nothing more than having made imprudent acquaintances and having trusted too much to the descriptions of themselves given by others.

Gill replied for the prosecution in a carefully reasoned speech, which occupied two hours in delivery and created an enormous impression in the crowded court.[288] It had been argued, Gill said, that no man conscious of guilt would have dared to set the criminal law in motion against Lord Queensberry. As to that, he commented, the jury could not tell what was upon the prisoner Wilde's mind, or how far he was misled by the expectation that the case would take an entirely different course. The fact remained, Gill stated, that from the outset Lord Queensberry undertook to justify his attack. The charges now made against the defendants formed only a part of the allegations contained in the plea of justification. The reason was that some of the charges alleged were not within the jurisdiction of Bow Street Police Court. Sir Edward Clarke, Gill continued, had made a courageous and brilliant defense, and, incidentally, had made an admission (one that Gill now took full advantage of), that Clarke himself was in part responsible for the course taken on Mr. Wilde's behalf in the previous trial. And it was at least due to that circumstance that Clarke was now again appearing on behalf of the accused. As far as the conditional charge originally made by Lord Queensberry went, Gill had not found it necessary to cross-examine Mr. Wilde. The defendant's own counsel had admitted that the justification was proved and that it was for the public benefit that the libel was published.

Then Gill commented at great length upon the evidence. He contended that in a case of this description corroboration was of comparatively minor importance, for it was not likely that acts of the kind alleged would be practiced before a third party who might afterward swear to the facts. Therefore, when the witnesses described what had transpired when they and the prisoners were alone, he did not think that corroboration could conceivably be given. There was not, Gill observed, going to be an eyewitness to the events. But with respect to many things, Gill declared, the evidence was corroborated. Whatever the character of these youths might be, they had given evidence as to certain facts, and no cross-examination, however adroit, however vigorous, had shaken their testimony, or caused them to waver about that which was evidently firmly implanted in their memories. A man might conceivably come forward and commit perjury. But these youths were accusing themselves, in accusing another, of shameful and infamous acts, and this they would hardly do if it were not the truth. Wilde, Gill went on, had made presents to these youths, and it was noticeable that the gifts were invariably made after he had been alone, at some rooms or other, with one or another of the lads. In the circumstances, even a silver cigarette case was corroboration. His learned friend, Gill stated, had protested that no evil construction should be placed upon these gifts; but in the name of commonsense, what other construction was possible? When they heard of a man like Wilde, presumably of refined and cultured tastes, who might—if he wished—enjoy the society of the best and most cultivated men and women in

London, having, in company at Nice and other places on the Continent, uninformed, unintellectual, and vulgar ill-bred youths of the type of Charles Parker, then, in heaven's name, what were they to think?[289] All those visits, all those dinners, all those gifts, were corroboration. They served to confirm the truth of the statements made by the youths who confessed to the commission of acts for which the things he had quoted were positive and actual payment.

As to the letters to Lord Alfred Douglas: it seemed to Gill that they breathed an unholy passion. Against the respectability and credibility of Edward Shelley, nothing could be possibly said. Shelley stood entirely apart from the others. Was it suggested, Gill asked, that out of some horrible wickedness, or in some sort of dream, Shelley had come to perjure himself against Mr. Oscar Wilde, who, apart from those charges, had done him nothing but kindness? In the case of Sydney Mavor, Gill noted, it was evident that Wilde had, in some way, continued to disgust this youth. Some acts of Wilde, either toward himself, or toward others, had offended him. Was not the letter, Gill suggested, which Mavor had addressed to Wilde, desiring the cessation of their friendship, corroboration? At this moment, Justice Charles interposed, and said that although Mavor's evidence was clearly of importance, Mavor had denied that he had been guilty of any impropriety. Justice Charles therefore did not think that the two counts in reference to Mavor could stand. After a short discussion, these counts were struck from the indictment.

Before he reached his conclusion, Gill proceeded to deal with the statements that the witnesses had made on behalf of the prosecution. He stated that there was nothing to support Clarke's suggestion that Shelley, who had shown himself to be an absolutely respectable and trustworthy witness, was in a disordered state of mind. Meanwhile, as to those witnesses who had been described as blackmailers, they could have no conceivable object in bringing the allegations against the accused unless the charges they made were true in substance and in fact. At the close of the case for the prosecution, Gill stated that he should not ask for a verdict on the counts for conspiracy. He concluded his address at 7.00 p.m. Justice Charles announced that the court would adjourn and that he would begin his summing-up the following morning.[290]

FIFTH DAY: WEDNESDAY, 1 MAY 1895

The *Star* observed of the final day of the proceedings:

> The fifth and positively last day of the protracted trial of Wilde and Taylor. It is long since any Old Bailey trial has lasted five days, and longer since there has been so much uncertainty as to the issue of a case of equal importance with

> this. For the last time Wilde and Taylor were brought down from Holloway in the prison van, and their counsel betrayed the nervous tension in which four days' hard fighting has left them by attending unusually early. Simultaneously, with three loud raps upon the door, which announced the approach of the judge, the prisoners were brought into the dock. Wilde is grown positively grey in the face and can no longer keep out of his eyes the haggard consciousness of his terrible position. Taylor has changed less. He still wore a weakly amiable smile.[291]

Mr. C. F. Gill, Mr. Horace Avory, and Mr. A. Gill (instructed by Mr. Angus Lewis and Mr. Frayling of the Treasury) appeared for the public prosecutor; Wilde was defended by Sir Edward Clarke, Q.C., Mr. Charles Mathews, and Mr. Travers Humphreys; while the prisoner Taylor was represented by Mr. J. P. Grain and Mr. Paul Taylor.

At 10.35 a.m., twenty-five minutes later than expected, the usually punctual Mr. Justice Charles took his seat on the bench. He at once proceeded to his summing-up of the case to the jury. Before dealing with the actual charges preferred in the indictment, he reminded the jury of the indictment that had been originally agreed upon at the start of the trial. The *Sun* remarked that the judge's summing-up marked a departure from his conventional practice: "Mr. Justice Charles is known as an exceedingly exact man, a judge of almost singular punctiliousness, and it is very rarely indeed that he takes, as many judges do, any 'view' of the case he has to try. In avoiding that, his habit is to go minutely into the evidence—so minutely sometimes that in the end it often stands before the jury a maze of greater confusion even than before."[292]

On this occasion, Justice Charles took pains to direct the jury toward what he believed was the proper verdict.[293]

JUSTICE CHARLES: Originally this indictment contained counts against the two men for conspiring and agreeing together, but at the close of the case for the prosecution the learned counsel who conducted it informed me that he did not propose, having regard to the evidence that had been given, to insist upon these charges. I think that he took a wise course, inasmuch as it relieved the Court from a position which might have been embarrassing, for so long as those counts stood in the indictment together with the other counts this singular state of things resulted from the present condition of the law—that the defendants were competent witnesses on the one set of counts, and incompetent upon so much of the indictment which charged them with conspiracy. And the result would have been, had the learned counsel not adopted that course, that when the defendants were called yesterday, they would have been able to give evidence as to the one set of charges, and unable to testify as to the allegation of having agreed together. Having listened to the evidence, I think it right to add that I am sure I don't know why the charges of conspiracy were ever inserted in the indictment at all. It was a highly inconvenient course to adopt, but when Sir Edward Clarke invited me at once to deal with the matter, I did not feel at liberty to do so for the reasons I then stated. The defendants are entitled to be acquitted of that charge, and I shall direct a verdict of acquittal on it with regard to both of the prisoners, as well as with reference to Taylor upon two other counts, upon which no evidence proper for your consideration has been given. I must now ask you to apply your minds only to the evidence to which you have listened on this matter.

For weeks past, one has scarcely been able to open a newspaper without seeing some remark or other with reference to the conduct of the two defendants, and more especially to the conduct of the accused Wilde. I hope that none of you formed any opinion of any sort or kind whatever before you entered the jury box to try this case, and any preconceived notions which may have been entertained by any of you I do beg of you to place on one side. I know that I do not ask this in vain, for gentlemen like yourselves know well the solemnity of all the responsibility which rests upon a jury in all criminal cases, and certainly in this criminal case, because you are trying charges against two persons, both of them of education, and one of them with high intellectual gifts.

One word now with reference to the witnesses who have been called on the part of the prosecution: In a case of this kind, where the witnesses have been a party to the alleged offences, they are accomplices, and by—I cannot say the law of England—but by the wholesome practice of our courts for certainly 200 years, no defendant can be convicted by a jury upon the uncorroborated testimony of the accomplices in a crime. I recollect, on one occasion, how this was laid down by one of the greatest of our judges, the late Lord Bramwell.[294] Now, what a wise rule of practice that is. For if it were otherwise, to what terrible dangers might innocent people be exposed by designing or spiteful adversaries? In this case, therefore, had there been no corroboration of the testimony of the young men who have been called, it would have been my duty at once to have told you that you ought to acquit the prisoners at the bar. Now I am clearly of the opinion that there is corroboration in this case of all the witnesses, in the sense that the law requires. It would be idle to expect the corroboration of eyewitnesses, but there is corroboration as to the acquaintanceship of the defendants with these witnesses, and as to many other particulars of the narrative they have given you, which would render it quite impossible for me to withdraw this serious and anxious case from your consideration. But, before dealing with the evidence which has been adduced, let me add with regard to the witnesses that they are not only accomplices, but in three cases at least—those of [Charles] Parker, Wood, and Atkins—they have been properly described by Sir Edward Clarke, in the eloquent speech he addressed to you on behalf of Wilde, as persons who levied blackmail. While with regard to Atkins, he himself, in your hearing, was out of his mouth convicted of having told the grossest and most deliberate falsehoods. Therefore, as to these young men, they are not only accomplices, but when you come to consider the details of their evidence, you cannot overlook the fact that they are young men of the character which they themselves have admitted.

Regarding the oral evidence you have heard read, the examination and cross-examination of the defendant Wilde, which was given at the Queensberry trial, you must remember that Mr. Wilde then gave that evidence under oath, and therefore, in order to thoroughly appreciate what Wilde said yesterday, you must also keep in mind what he stated upon the previous occasion. The verdict on that occasion, I need hardly tell you, is in no way binding upon you, not in the slightest degree, because it was a verdict upon this libel, and delivered at the instance of Sir Edward Clarke for the reasons explained to you yesterday, without any evidence being called in support of the plea of justification.

With regard to what Sir Edward Clarke has called the "literary" part of the case: On behalf of the defendant, it is asserted that it was attempted to show by the cross-examination of Wilde as to the writings which he has published, and especially having regard to the book called *Dorian Gray*, that he was a man of a most unprincipled character. With regard to the magazine called the *Chameleon*, published in the autumn of last year, it was alleged that Wilde had given the sanction of his name to most abominable doctrines. You have not read *Dorian Gray*—I am assuming you have not, although it is possible that some of you may have done so—but the book has not been read to you during this trial, although extracts have been, and you have been placed by Sir Edward Clarke in possession of the general story of the book. You were told that it is a story of a youth who is addicted to all sorts of vices, which are left purposely veiled and undescribed, and whose own countenance does not reveal the abysses of iniquity into which he has fallen, but whose picture, which has been painted by an artist, does reveal something of these abysses. At the end of the story, Dorian Gray—so we were informed yesterday—stabs the picture, it being his real counterfeit presentment, and then he falls dead, when, upon his face—as I understand the narrative as given by Sir Edward Clarke—are all the signs which heretofore had been upon the picture only.

Now I own, gentlemen, that I think it is my duty to say at once that I do not consider that in a criminal case you ought to base any unfavorable inference upon the fact that Wilde is the author of *Dorian Gray*. A great writer, you were told yesterday, once said: "Judge no man by his books." I would rather say: "Judge no man, confound no man, with the persons he creates." If an imaginative writer puts into his novel or his play a consummate villain and puts into the mouth of that man sentiments revolting to humanity, you may criticize, if you please, the work. But it would never do, if the author of the work was charged with crime, to say: "Oh, you created that monster in your last novel, and you put into his mouth sentiments abhorrent to common humanity." That would not be fair because it is unfortunately true that while some of the greatest writers have passed long years in writing nothing but the most wholesome literature—literature of the highest genius, and which everybody can read, such as the literature of Sir Walter Scott and Charles Dickens—it is also true that there are other great writers, more especially in the eighteenth century, perfectly noble-minded men themselves, who, somehow or other, have permitted themselves to pen volumes which it is painful for any person of ordinary modesty to read. That is a literary truth capable of easy verification. A long cross-examination was also addressed to Wilde about the *Chameleon*, Wilde's only connection with that magazine being that it was prefaced by two pages of "Phrases and Philosophies for the Use of the Young," which I do not suppose you wish me to read.

FOREMAN OF THE JURY: No, my lord.

JUSTICE CHARLES: It will be sufficient to say of them that they are some of them amusing, some of them cynical, and some of them—if I may be allowed to criticize them—silly; but wicked in the sense that you ought to draw from them the inference that Wilde was capable of these crimes, no. But in Lord Queensberry's case, a long cross-examination took place with reference to the article called "The Priest and the Acolyte," with which Wilde had nothing to do, and of which the author ought to be thoroughly ashamed. To impute anything to the defendant that is in that story is quite absurd, and to judge a man by another's work, which he has never seen, would be highly unjust as well as absurd. With regard to the two poems contained in the *Chameleon*, the one a sonnet "In Praise of Shame," and the other some verses entitled "Two Loves," both of them by Lord Alfred Douglas: It was said that upon receiving that sonnet Wilde wrote the letter to the author which had been produced.

CLARKE: It was not upon receiving that sonnet that the letter was written.

JUSTICE CHARLES: There is no date to it. Oh, I beg your pardon, I am quite wrong. The letter was written before he had seen the sonnet.

CLARKE: Long before, my lord.

JUSTICE CHARLES: It must be so. The other letter, dated from the Savoy Hotel, and which was got back from Allen, must have been written in March 1893. These two letters were the subject of an elaborate cross-examination by Mr. Carson, and now Mr. Gill had insisted upon it by his questions that they were communications of an improper character and invited the jury to say so. Well, what had Oscar Wilde himself said about it? He affirmed that he was not ashamed, in any sense, of either of those two letters, that to him—although they breathed the language of affection and of passion, they did not breathe the language of an impure affection; and he said, with regard to the first of them, that it was a sort of prose sonnet. Further, he had stated that the affection mentioned in "Two Loves" was, to his mind, a love like that of David to Jonathan, like that spoken in the sonnets of Shakespeare, and such a love as Plato, the Greek philosopher, might have called the beginning of wisdom.[295] This was a part of the case upon which the jury must exercise their own judgment, but there was this to be said about that letter of sufficient importance to be undoubtedly well worthy of their attention. It was produced by Wilde himself at the trial which took place last sessions, and so it was said on his behalf by his counsel: "Give him credit for not being ashamed of it." I understood that the other letter, the one written from the Savoy Hotel, was produced during the defendant's cross-examination.

GILL: That is so, my lord.

JUSTICE CHARLES: With regard to Shelley, a most anxious task has devolved upon the jury. That witness, notwithstanding what might be said as to his having been in a state of intoxication on the occasion spoken of, was in the position of an accomplice, but his evidence has been corroborated quite sufficiently for you to consider it. At the same time, it is only fair to Shelley to point out that he is not of the same sort of conduct with which Wood, Atkins, and Charles Parker are discredited, and, in that sense, he is an untainted witness. Certainly, Shelley has conveyed the impression—although it is for the jury to say this—that when in the witness box, that what he has alleged had taken place against his will, but with this it is difficult to reconcile the fact that he afterwards allowed himself on several occasions to be in Mr. Wilde's company. The defendant has given a positive denial to the whole of Shelley's story with regard to one part of it. But, on behalf of the prosecution, it had properly been asked why the young man should have invented a tale which it must have been unpleasant to present in the witness box. With regard to the contention that Shelley's mind was disordered, I would invite the jury to say that, although there was in his correspondence which has been read evidence of excitability, to talk of him as a young man who did not know what he was saying is to exaggerate the effect of those letters.

With regard to the case of Atkins, I would characterize him as a most reckless witness, and probably the jury will be of the opinion that if he was the only person to have spoken in these matters, it would be totally unsafe to rely upon him at all, because he had the impudence in cross-examination to say that, although he knew a man named Burton, he had never been taken to Rochester Row Police Station with him in his life. The suggestion was a gross case of blackmailing, but the witness denied everything. Yet within a few hours it was proved that he had told the grossest falsehood—a falsehood so gross that the jury would be justified, if they thought fit, in declining to act upon any part of his testimony.

Justice Charles then reviewed the cases of the Parkers and Wood, and explained to what extent the charges affected Taylor. A man of good education, Taylor—even though he had inherited a considerable fortune—was in 1894 adjudicated bankrupt. Justice Charles reminded the jury that the evidence of the witness Mavor, as to whom no charge arose, had little or no value upon the issues now presented, except insofar as the jury learned from him how he, Wilde, and Taylor had become acquainted. Mavor's evidence, the judge went on to observe, was rather in favor of the prisoner Wilde than against him, for with regard to that particular witness the prosecution was unable to substantiate any charge whatsoever.

Justice Charles then concluded his summing-up.

JUSTICE CHARLES: This is a very important case to the community at large. It is very important that if the charges are proved, you should say so, and say so clearly. On the other hand, it is most important that innocent people should not be convicted, and I commit the case to you in the utmost confidence that you will do justice as between the public, on the one hand, and the two defendants, on the other. They have a right—and especially the defendant Wilde has a right—to ask you to remember that he is a man of great intellectual gifts, a man of high education, and a man whom one would suppose was incapable of the sort of acts with which he is charged in this indictment. So, with regard to Taylor, although nothing has been proved regarding his capabilities, he belongs to a class of people of whom it might be said that it is difficult to suppose that they would be guilty of such

> charges. But still, you must deal with the evidence fairly, remembering the two defendants' position, on the one hand, and your duty to the public, on the other. If you feel that you ought not to act upon the evidence of any of these witnesses, then say so, and acquit the prisoners. If, however, you are constrained to come to the conclusion either that all or some of these charges are proved against the prisoners, or either of them, then it will be your painful duty to return a verdict accordingly.

Reynolds's Newspaper recorded the four questions that Justice Charles then put to the jury:

> (1) Do you think that Wilde committed indecent acts with Edward Shelley and Alfred Wood, and met a person or persons unknown at the Savoy hotel, or with Charles Parker?
> (2) Whether Taylor procured or attempted to procure the commission of these acts, or any of them?
> (3) Did Wilde or Taylor, or either of them, attempt to get Atkins to commit indecencies?
> (4) Did Taylor commit indecent acts with Charles Parker or with William Parker?[296]

At the conclusion of Justice Charles's address, which had occupied three hours, the foreman of the jury asked: "May we retire, my lord?" to which Justice Charles replied "Certainly, gentlemen."

The *Star* commented on the lengthy deliberations that followed:

> The jury retired at twenty-five minutes to two. The prisoners were at once removed from the dock, Wilde striding down the stairs without glancing right or left. Taylor, as usual, looked intently into every corner of the court and gallery before diving down the stairs to the cells. His lordship for some time kept his seat, although he did not expect the jury to be long absent. The popular idea was that they would have considerable difficulty in arriving at a verdict, and Mr. C. F. Gill was so far of this opinion that he left the court for some time.
>
> An hour passed without any sign from the jury. An hour and a quarter, and no tinkle of the bell that announced their return. Then, at three o'clock, there came a message, written on a piece of blue foolscap, which was handed to the clerk of the court and carefully perused. The clerk vanished in search of the judge, and the weary and hungry crowd speculated freely on the nature of the crisis. It presently transpired—no one could have quite told how—that the jury had merely addressed to his lordship a request that some lunch might be sent in to them. This looked so unlike an early verdict that the counsel engaged in the case went out in search of sustenance. Even Sir Edward Clarke,

who has practically conducted the defence of Wilde single-handed, temporarily disappeared.

At 4.15 p.m., the judge sent for the Clerk of Arraigns (Mr. Henry Kemp Avory), who proceeded to his lordship's private room.

At 4.35 p.m., the jury had been locked up for three hours, and there was nothing to suggest that they had any idea of coming back.[297]

The *Daily Telegraph* observed the reappearance of the jury later that afternoon:

Remaining absent for three hours and forty minutes, the jury returned into court at 5.15 p.m. Mr. Justice Charles having then resumed his seat on the bench, the clerk, addressing the warders, said, "Bring the prisoners up," and Oscar Wilde and Alfred Taylor accordingly reappeared in the dock, where they stood, the first-named betraying no sign of either hope or anxiety, and the other accused smiling complacently.

JUSTICE CHARLES: I have received a communication from you to the effect that, with the exception of a minor question which I put to you with reference to the witness Atkins, you are unable to arrive at an agreement.

FOREMAN OF THE JURY: That is so, my lord. (*Sensation in court.*)

JUSTICE CHARLES: You are not agreed, I find, with regard to any of the other questions which I have put to you.

FOREMAN OF THE JURY: That is so, my lord.

JUSTICE CHARLES: Is there anything which you desire to ask me in reference to the other cases that you think may assist you in arriving at a verdict?

FOREMAN OF THE JURY: I have put the question to my fellow jurymen, and I do not think we can agree upon three questions out of the four.

JUSTICE CHARLES: I find from the entry which is written against the various sub-divisions of No. 1 that you cannot agree as to any of those sub-divisions.

FOREMAN OF THE JURY: That is so, my lord.

JUSTICE CHARLES: Is that in regard to No. 4?[298]

FOREMAN OF THE JURY: Yes, and also as to No. 4.

JUSTICE CHARLES: Now is there any prospect, gentlemen, if you retire to your room again? Of course, I hope that you have not been inconvenienced in any way by this deliberation. I ordered that to be done which you had asked for.

FOREMAN OF THE JURY: Thank you very much. We have not been inconvenienced.

JUSTICE CHARLES: Well, as I was going to say, is there any prospect if you proceed with your deliberation a little longer, that you will come to an agreement with regard to some of these questions?

FOREMAN OF THE JURY: I have put that question to my fellow jurors, and they say that there is no prospect. We have considered this matter for three hours now, and this is the only result we can agree to.

JUSTICE CHARLES (*having spoken privately with the clerk of arraigns*): I am very unwilling at any time to do anything that would look like compelling a jury to deliver a verdict. You have been very long in deliberating over this matter; and no doubt, gentlemen, you have done your very best to arrive at an agreement upon the questions.

FOREMAN OF THE JURY: We have, my lord.

JUSTICE CHARLES: On the other hand, the inconveniences of another trial are very great, and if you think that by deliberating for a reasonable time you can arrive at a conclusion upon any of the points, I would ask you to do so.

FOREMAN OF THE JURY (*after consulting with the jurors*): We fully considered the matter, my lord, before we came to court, and I don't think there is a chance of our agreeing at all. (*Pause.*) We have gone over it and considered it again and again.

JUSTICE CHARLES: Well, gentlemen, if you tell me that, I don't think I should be justified in detaining you in consultation any longer.

CLARKE: Before our lordship discharges the jury, I will ask you to direct them to return a verdict of not guilty upon the counts on which no evidence has been taken.

JUSTICE CHARLES: I thought I had already taken the necessary steps for that to be done, Sir Edward, when I informed the jury in the course of this morning that I should direct an acquittal upon the counts upon which no evidence has been offered. These were the counts of conspiracy and those which charged Taylor with certain acts.

GILL: If the jury is discharged, I will ask your lordship to discharge them without a verdict of any kind in the matter.

CLARKE: That cannot be done, my lord. I am entitled to a verdict upon the counts on which no evidence has been given before the jury. I need hardly point out to your lordship on the ground of convenience, as well as of right, that verdict ought to be entered.

GILL: Sir Edward is not quite right in saying that no evidence was given on these counts.

JUSTICE CHARLES: I directed this morning a verdict of acquittal upon the conspiracy counts.

CLARKE: I wish to have that entered.

JUSTICE CHARLES: And also, upon the two counts upon which no evidence proper to the consideration of the jury was given, and unless you can satisfy me that I ought not to do it, I think that the proper course would be to enter that verdict upon the record.

CLARKE: We are entitled to it.

GILL: I think there is a misapprehension as to the course taken with regard to these conspiracy counts. It was not that evidence was not offered upon them. Evidence was given which would have had a bearing on those counts in the course of the case, and of course they had a direct bearing with respect to the other charges. All that I said was that I did not desire a verdict on those counts.

JUSTICE CHARLES: I am quite aware of the way you have put it, Mr. Gill. You said at the close of the prosecution that you elected to ask the jury to answer questions limited to other counts, but that election having been made at the time when the defendants were given in charge of the jury, it seems to me that entitled them to have the verdict of not guilty entered upon the record. I do not think it is a matter of substantial importance, but subject to what was said to me as to the criminal practice, it seems to me that that is the right course. And I should say the same thing with regard to the two counts on which Taylor is charged to which I have alluded, the counts 16 and 20. The general matters which have occupied the court for so many days are matters upon which the jury are unable to come to an agreement, and upon these matters, therefore, and the counts which are concerned in them, I must discharge the jury from giving a verdict. I must further, before I do that, direct that the same course be taken with regard to the conspiracy counts, and the counts as to Mavor and Wood. The jury being of the opinion that Wilde and Taylor did not attempt to get Atkins to commit an offence with Wilde, I shall order the same course to be taken with regard to that count as with regard to the conspiracy counts and the others, upon which there has been no evidence.

CLARKE: It is only a matter of form; but it is not unimportant. And, as the whole indictment has been given in charge of the jury, I ask that your lordship will direct the jury to deliver a verdict of not guilty upon the conspiracy counts.

JUSTICE CHARLES (*to the jury*): You understood me this morning, gentlemen, to direct a verdict upon the counts I explained, and also upon the counts to which I have just made allusion.

Henry Kemp Avory, the clerk of arraigns, then took a formal verdict from the jury, in accordance with Justice Charles's direction.

HENRY KEMP AVORY: Upon the counts of conspiracy, you find the prisoners not guilty?

FOREMAN OF THE JURY: Not guilty.

HENRY KEMP AVORY: To the rest of the indictment, you are unable to agree?

FOREMAN OF THE JURY: That is so.

JUSTICE CHARLES (*to the jury*): As the matters which have kept you in court so long remain undecided, you are discharged, gentlemen.

CLARKE: I now make application that the defendant, Mr. Oscar Wilde, be admitted to bail. I need not say to your lordship, after what has taken place, that the Crown will make no objection to that application.

Mr. William Clarke Hall, in the absence of Grain, applied for bail on behalf of Alfred Taylor.

GILL: With regard to the question of bail, it will depend upon what course your lordship thinks desirable. With regard to the fresh trial: If it is to take place immediately, the question of bail would not be important to the defendants. But, if it is to go to the next sessions, I shall say nothing upon the matter. All the facts of the case are before your lordship, and I will say nothing to influence your lordship's judgment on the matter.

JUSTICE CHARLES: I do not feel able to accede to the application.

CLARKE: May we renew the application upon other material to your lordship in Chambers?

JUSTICE CHARLES: I think if it is to be renewed, the application had better be made in the usual way to the judge in Chambers.

CLARKE: If your lordship pleases. In regard to the retrial, I think you will not consider it right that it should take place immediately. The burden upon those engaged in this case is, I need hardly say, somewhat heavy. And I think it is only right that the Treasury should have an opportunity between this and another session of considering the mode in which the case should be presented, if at all.

GILL: The case will certainly be tried again. Whether it is tried at once or in the next session will be a matter of convenience. Probably the more desirable course will be for the case to go to the next sessions. That is the usual course.

JUSTICE CHARLES: If that be the usual course, let it be so.

GILL: All the witnesses will be bound over, and their recognizances enlarged?

JUSTICE CHARLES: Certainly.

The *Star* commented: "The prisoners had stood in the front of the dock leaning on the rail all this time with considerable unconcern. Taylor's thin lips had moved something like the ghost of a smile when the counts as to Atkins were dismissed, but when they left the dock both prisoners seemed perfectly self-possessed."[299] The *Globe* noted: "Mr. Wilde had listened to the result without any show of feeling."[300] The proceedings then terminated, and the accused were removed to the cells. The *Daily Telegraph* observed: "The May sessions of the Central Criminal Court opens the 20th of this month."[301]

Beerbohm, who had been deeply impressed in court by Wilde's oration on "the love that dare not speak its name," informed Reggie Turner that Wilde "looked most leoline and sphinx-like" when hearing the verdict.[302] He recalled, however, the unruly behavior in which several of the Crown's leading witnesses indulged outside the Old Bailey: "It was horrible leaving the court day after day and having to pass through a knot of renters (the younger Parker wearing Her Majesty's uniform—another form of female attire) who were allowed to hang around after giving their evidence and to wink at likely persons."[303] As we have seen from a press report in the *Sun* when the pretrial hearing was in progress (194), Beerbohm was not entirely exaggerating in his recollections of the Parker brothers' disrespectful antics once the proceedings had finished. Charles Parker, it appears, attracted attention in his military outfit, in ways that suggested that he would not decline performing sexual favors for queer male passersby. To Beerbohm, this appalling spectacle demonstrated the absurdity of the prosecution, where those reprobates who had delivered inculpating testimony against Wilde continued to flout the harsh 1885 law under which he was tried.

On the Saturday after the prosecution had resulted in a hung jury, the front cover of the *Illustrated Police News* featured a montage of images containing scenes that reminded readers of Wilde's past career and his current disgrace (fig. 22). In the top-left-hand corner, a young Wilde appears in the aesthetic costume, immortalized through Napoleon Sarony's studio photographs, that he wore while lecturing to American audiences in 1882. To the right, there is a contrasting portrait of the middle-aged writer enduring his pretrial hearing at Bow Street. Beneath the main drawing, which features a throng of bewigged lawyers, there is an illustration of the recent sale of Wilde's household goods.

To some eyes, the relishing of such scandal reeked of hypocrisy. A day later, the Irish writer George Egerton (Mary Chavelita Dunne Bright) found it hard to stifle her anger toward the sexual bigotry that was evident throughout the proceedings, in the press, and among Wilde's former associates. In a letter to her publisher, John Lane, who had recently withdrawn copies of Wilde's books from sale, Egerton contends that an appalling sexual double standard is in play regarding the pervasive antipathy toward her compatriot. Much of her ire is focused on the presumed inability of a lower-middle-class jury to judge Wilde's case intelligently:

> I think Oscar has been unfairly treated and that the English are the biggest hypocrites in the world—Everyone knew of it for years, and no one cut Oscar, yet when he is down they all held briefs for virtue[,] pretended astonished indignation, howled like old women and kicked the man like cads when he was down—I disliked him all through—but if I continued to know him whilst

"HOMOCEA"

POLICE NEWS

LAW COURTS AND WEEKLY RECORD

No. 1625 SATURDAY, MAY 4, 1895. Price One Penny

CLOSING SCENE AT THE OLD BAILEY.

TRIAL OF OSCAR WILDE

JURY

SALE OF OSCAR WILDES EFFECTS

IMPROVED AND ENLARGED.

Fig. 22. "Closing Scene at the Old Bailey: Trial of Oscar Wilde," *Illustrated Police News*, 4 May 1895: 1.

I knew the unacknowledged fact, I wouldn't cut him when it became /a\ known one—Shell[e]y is simply a bitter unlicked cur—As to the jury, it is a farce to call a nonconformist greengrocer, or a Methodist cheesemonger the Peer of a literary man like Oscar—We all know that a jury composed of say Rosebery, Leighton, the late Walter Pater or John Addington Symonds would look at a question of the kind from a different standpoint—All genius is more or less abnormal and from my point of view—the seduction of a girl leaving her with a child of no social standing is a much bigger crime—Enough.[304]

Even though the interest of the press in Wilde's affairs quietened down during the weeks that followed, one or two newspapers sought to capitalize on the controversy. The conservative-minded *Morning*, which prided itself on its maverick reportage, committed a serious indiscretion: the paper revealed that it had learned the secrets of the votes that the jury made in the retiring room:

> We are enabled this morning to draw aside the veil which has hitherto shrouded the proceedings of the jury of the Wilde case during their retirement, and to supply an authentic record on the voting of the four points submitted for their consideration. The following are the questions, and the result of the voting on them:—
>
> 1. Did Wilde commit indecent acts with Shelley? 10 for, 2 against; with Wood—8 for, 4 against; two persons at Savoy—10 for, 2 against; Charles Parker—10 for, 2 against.
> 2. Did Taylor procure, or attempt to procure, the commission of the acts, or any of them—10 for, 2 against.
> 3. Did Wilde or Taylor, or either of them, attempt to get Atkins to commit indecency with Wilde? Agreed, not guilty.
> 4. Did Taylor commit indecent acts, first, with Charles Parker; secondly, with W. Parker?—2 for, 10 against.[305]

In his detailed discussion of the trials, Millard comments that this was "[p]erhaps the grossest and most unfair" of the many hostile reports that appeared in the press: "Probably the figures were entirely fictitious, but the glaring injustice of publishing them is none the less obvious."[306]

5

THE SECOND CRIMINAL TRIAL: *REGINA* v. *TAYLOR*, *REGINA* v. *WILDE*, CENTRAL CRIMINAL COURT (OLD BAILEY)

The disagreement of the jury after the first trial left Oscar, after his agonising ordeal, free for the time. But all the hotels, clubs and even a large number of private friends who had been almost fighting with each other a few weeks, even days, ago to flatter and make much of him now refused point-blank to receive him at all. He was like a hunted stag, with no place to find refuge. He could not even take a room at an hotel.

And this was not that the hotels, clubs and private friends condemned him in any way at present. The question was in abeyance, everything entirely depending on what the result of the next trial might be. From place to place he went, refused everywhere, with extreme politeness certainly, for he might at any moment be reinstated and be the hero, martyr and lion of the day. But they would not take the risk.

I do not mean that he had not many loyal and devoted friends. But these were not in a position to offer him hospitality.

—*Ada Leverson, "Reminiscences: Afterwards" (1930)*

In her evocative reminiscences of Oscar Wilde, his loyal friend Ada Leverson provides the sharpest account of the harsh reality that he faced when Mr. Charles Edward ("Baron") Pollock granted him bail. Even though the first criminal trial against Wilde had concluded on Wednesday, 1 May 1895, it took the best part of another week before he was released from custody. Now that Wilde was charged solely with the misdemeanor of gross indecency, it was unreasonable for the judiciary, given the lesser nature of the crime, to deny him his freedom during the interim before the retrial. The technical matter that had to be agreed upon was the sum involved. As Wilde's attorneys knew, they would have to propose a hefty amount to convince Baron Pollock to grant bail, since the judge could decline an application if the amount appeared incommensurable with the charges. The lawyers had to ensure that their client was relieved from a further period of detention in H.M. Prison Holloway. Meanwhile, Wilde's hope was that once bail was granted, he would be able to settle into a hotel and enjoy some rest before his case reopened at the Old Bailey. As Leverson reminds us, this was not—given the scandal attached to Wilde's name—a possibility.

On Friday, 3 May 1895, Mr. Charles ("Willie") Mathews appeared at Baron Pollock's chambers to submit an application for Wilde's bail. As the *Evening Standard* observed, Mathews "cited a number of cases which tended to show that in a case of misdemeanour a judge has no discretion in the matter, but is bound under an act of Charles II to admit the Prisoner to bail."[1] When the judge asked for the amounts that Mathews was prepared to offer, Wilde's counsel said that he could promise two sureties of £1,000 each. Another day passed before Baron Pollock reviewed the depositions and came to a conclusion about the sums that should be posted. The *Illustrated Police News* commented:

> Baron Pollock, sitting in Chambers, decided on Saturday [4 May 1895] to allow Oscar Wilde out on bail. He stated that Wilde himself would need security of £2,500, and have two other sureties of £1,250 each. The judge, in the interval that had elapsed since Friday afternoon, read through the whole of the depositions, and consulted with Mr. Justice Charles. Mr. Mathews intimated that there might be some difficulty in obtaining two sureties for the amount fixed, though one surety could be obtained for a much larger sum. Baron Pollock said that in that event a further application should be made to him on Monday evening.
>
> It was stated on Saturday afternoon by a member of the firm of Messrs. Humphreys and Son, of Holborn Viaduct, the solicitors to Mr. Oscar Wilde, that there is no possibility of Mr. Wilde being released from Holloway until Tuesday, as it would take until then to arrange the preliminaries as to bail. Two sureties, he added, had come forward; but at present it would be inadvisable to mention their names. Mr. Wilde is being attended by the medical officer attached to the prison. Although his state of health is not such as to give cause for any particular anxiety, Mr. Wilde is reported to be suffering from an attack of nervous prostration.
>
> The Press Association understands that the Marquess of Queensberry paid an unexpected visit to Holloway Gaol on Saturday morning. The object of the visit of the marquess to Holloway had not transpired, but he had an interview

with the chief prison officials. Oscar Wilde and Taylor apparently knew nothing of the visit of his lordship, who did not remain at the prison long.[2]

The sums involved were heavy. If we compare the predicament of Edward de Cobain, MP, who in 1891 had fled to America after a magistrate issued a warrant for his arrest on counts of gross indecency, we can tell that Wilde's case involved considerable costs. Once the Belfast police finally apprehended de Cobain almost two years later, the magistrates determined that the defendant should be remanded for eight days, with bail set at £500 on the accused's own recognizances, with two sureties of £500 each. Since the sureties were not forthcoming, de Cobain languished in custody. Other crimes, admittedly, were costlier affairs. For offenses involving forgery and fraud, just to give one example, bail tended to be set much higher. In March 1893, for instance, Sir John Bridge required Charles Wells, who was accused of receiving substantial sums on a fraudulent patent, "to take bail in sureties of £5,000 each and Wells himself in £10,000."[3]

At Bow Street on Tuesday, 7 May 1895, Mr. Travers Humphreys, Mr. Angus Lewis (of the Treasury), and Detective Inspector Brockwell (of Scotland Yard) were in attendance with reference to the proposed bail of Mr. Oscar Wilde.[4] Addressing Mr. James Vaughan, the presiding magistrate, Humphreys explained that Baron Pollock had fixed the amount of bail at two sureties (each in the sum of £1,250) and Wilde himself (the sum of £2,500). Two gentlemen were present and willing to enter into sureties that guaranteed they would produce Mr. Oscar Wilde at the next sessions. Exactly how Wilde could claim he had access to £2,500 in assets looks somewhat mysterious, since his household belongings had been auctioned at his former home on Tite Street on 24 April 1895, in order to settle debts with a string of creditors. As we noted in chapter 2, Wilde withdrew the libel suit against Queensberry, which meant that he owed £677 in costs, a heavy sum that he has was unable to pay. There were, though, other sums available to him, including the £1,000 gift that Adela Schuster made available at this time. Schuster, who had entertained Wilde and his family at her imposing residence, Cannizaro House, Wimbledon, was a philanthropist and patron of the arts. The other amount was one that Ada Leverson's husband, Ernest Leverson, a diamond broker in the City of London, had previously made.[5]

Before Wilde was ordered to come from H.M. Prison Holloway in the police van, the magistrate wished to know the identities of the individuals who were offering the two sureties.

MR. JAMES VAUGHAN: Who are they?

MR. TRAVERS HUMPHREYS: They are the Revd. Stewart Headlam of 31 Upper Bedford Place, and Lord Douglas of Hawick and Tibbers.[6]

VAUGHAN: Is there any objection on the part of the Treasury?
MR. ANGUS LEWIS: No, sir.
VAUGHAN: Let them appear.

Headlam then stepped into the witness box and was sworn.

VAUGHAN: Are you worth £1,250 after all your just debts are paid?
STEWART HEADLAM: I am.
VAUGHAN: Are you willing to become bail for the appearance of Oscar Wilde?
HEADLAM: I am.

Then Percy Sholto Douglas, Lord Douglas of Hawick, was sworn. He gave his address as Chalcot House, Long Ditton, Surrey, and he was confident that he was worth £1,250 after all of his just debts were paid. He was also willing to become bail.

VAUGHAN: Have you any other name?[7]
PERCY SHOLTO DOUGLAS: Yes, Percy Sholto Douglas.
VAUGHAN: Let these gentlemen go into the office and enter their recognizances. Some officer must go with my order to the gaol, so that the defendant may be brought here in a cab at once.

Sergeant White, the Bow Street jailer, at once traveled to H.M. Prison Holloway in a cab with Percy Douglas, Stewart Headlam, and one of Messrs. Humphreys's clerks.[8] Although Percy Douglas had been closely engaged with Wilde's affairs ever since the libel trial against Queensberry began on 3 April 1895, Stewart Headlam was little more than a passing acquaintance. A radical Anglican clergyman of independent means, Headlam had developed a controversial reputation for his Anglo-Catholic interest in ritualism, his support for the working-class appeal of the music-halls, and his Christian socialism. He articulated his views forcefully in the *Church Reformer*, a journal he had founded in 1884. It is possible that Headlam and Wilde exchanged hellos at the Crown public house in Cranbourn Street. (This was the venue for bohemian types that evoked such humor in Max Beerbohm [see 68].) It appears that someone (possibly Ernest Leverson) had first approached Headlam's friend, the artist and designer Selwyn Image, who was central to the artistic group known as the Century Guild, to serve as one of Wilde's sureties.[9] Image, who co-edited the remarkable *Century Guild Hobby Horse*, a finely produced periodical dedicated to the unity of the arts, had delivered a series of lectures in 1887 that elicited Wilde's praise. In 1886, the *Hobby Horse* had published Wilde's short essay "Keats's Sonnet on Blue." Headlam, who believed that the press had done much to prejudge Wilde before any verdict had come down, declared in the *Church*

Reformer: "I was a surety not to his character but for his appearance in court to stand the trial. I had very little personal knowledge of him at the time."[10] He later informed his biographer that he "consented to act as his did because . . . 'a third party came to Selwyn Image, who was unable to take on the responsibility, and so I agreed to do so.'"[11] There is evidence that Headlam's decision to support Wilde resulted in an attempt to expel the churchman from the National Liberal Club. Compton Mackenzie recalls that not only did "intelligent Liberal journalists" such as Henry Norman and H. W. Massingham break ties with Headlam; it was also the case that several prominent clerics in the High Church (Father Jimmy Adderley, the Revd. C. L. Marson, and the Revd. Cecil Sharp) "behaved without charity" toward Headlam because of the "prevailing hysteria" surrounding Wilde's trials.[12]

Both Stewart Headlam and Percy Douglas returned to Bow Street at 1.45 p.m., for the purpose of receiving Wilde.[13] Three officials then returned with Wilde at 2.20 p.m. The news that was expected spread quickly, and a large crowd awaited his arrival. As the cab passed rapidly through the gates into the courtyard at Bow Street, it was possible to see that on the back seat were Wilde and White, while Inspector Brockwell, who originally had the prisoner in charge, sat with the jailer. Wilde was dressed in a dark frock coat and silk hat. The *Star* observed: "When Wilde alighted on the station yard, he walked with all the old air of being superior to, and untouched by, circumstances."[14] The newspaper, however, added: "Wilde if anything looked better and less haggard than during the trial at the Old Bailey, but is very much thinner and paler than when first taken into custody."[15] By comparison, *Reynolds's Newspaper* remarked: "Wilde looked far more cheerful than when he last appeared at Bow Street, but there was a wearied expression about his features strongly indicative of sleepless nights, and it could be plainly seen that he was in anything but robust health."[16]

On entering the police station, Wilde found Stewart Headlam and Percy Douglas awaiting his arrival. He was brought into the court building through a door leading to the private office of Mr. John Alexander, the chief clerk, where his recognizances of £2,500 were taken. This was a purely formal procedure where Wilde entered his obligations into what is commonly known as the bail book. The usual course in such cases, however, was not to take the recognizances of the sureties publicly at the police court. Instead, it was conventionally left to Lieutenant Colonel Everard Milman, the governor of H.M. Prison Holloway, to take the prisoner's recognizances, since as governor he was authorized to perform this task under the Summary Jurisdiction Rules 1886.[17] When Vaughan took the unexpected step of ordering that the prisoner should be brought to the police court, observers assumed that Wilde would be publicly interrogated as to his means. Vaughan, however, did not follow this course.

A considerable number of press representatives assembled at Bow Street, where they lined the passage. They saw nothing but the action of a zealous inspector, who told them that they must wait outside the building. Once in the street, they glimpsed Wilde and his sureties quietly depart through the magistrate's private door in Broad Court. A four-wheeler pulled up. Wilde, Headlam, and Douglas entered it, and they drove off in the direction of Drury Lane. The vehicle traveled to the Midland Grand Hotel at St. Pancras, which it reached at about 3.00 p.m.[18] Percy Douglas provided the rooms. Apparently, Wilde and his sureties undertook a consultation, because, by 4.00 p.m., Headlam had left the hotel by the main entrance. Later in the afternoon, Wilde received a visit from a gentleman, and they were also busily engaged for a considerable time discussing private affairs and the pending new trial.[19] The *Star* noted: "The Express Telegraph Company states that Mr. Oscar Wilde visited the Royal Courts of Justice this afternoon in order to have a consultation with Sir E. Clarke in his private room. Mr. Wilde's solicitors, at their client's own request, promised the authorities that they would keep them fully informed as to Mr. Wilde's movements and precise whereabouts until the time of the next trial. Mr. Wilde would in due course give himself up to the police."[20]

The next few hours, however, made it impossible for Wilde to gain the rest that he needed. On the evening of Tuesday, 7 May 1895, the management at the Midland Grand Hotel asked him to leave the premises. Robert Harborough Sherard elaborated on Wilde's predicament once the management at the Midland instructed him to leave:

> On leaving Holloway Prison, Wilde drove to a hotel where rooms had been engaged for him. As he was sitting down to dinner in his private room the manager of the hotel came in, shouted out that he knew who he was, and ordered him to leave the house at once. From thence Wilde drove to another hotel. Here he secured a room, and dinnerless, for he had no appetite left, was about to go to bed, when again he was driven forth into the streets. Some men, it appeared, had followed him from the gates of Holloway Prison—at whose instigation we need not inquire—and had determined that he should nowhere find shelter that night. They had threatened the manager of the second hotel that if he did not turn Oscar Wilde away they would wreck his house.
>
> He appears to have been refused admission, having been recognised, at other London hostelries that night. In the end he turned his thoughts towards his mother's home. Long past midnight his brother Willy [*sic*] heard a knock

> at the door of the house in Oakley Street.[21] When he had opened the door, Oscar Wilde, pale as death, dishevelled, unnerved, staggered into the narrow hall, and sinking exhausted on to a chair cried out: "Willy, give me a shelter or I shall die in the streets." Willy Wilde frequently related the incident afterwards, but with a mixing of metaphors which sufficiently indicates the condition into which he was passing.
>
> "He came," he used to say, "tapping with his beak against the window-pane, and fell down on my threshold like a wounded stag." To the horrors of that period of waiting the touch of the grotesque was not to be wanting.[22]

Wilde tried to settle into Oakley Street, but the only place he could sleep—as Sherard recalls from making visits there—was "a small camp-bedstead between the fireplace and the wall."[23] Several friends advised Wilde to leave England in order to escape the next trial. Even Percy Douglas, who had gone bail for him, offered such advice. Wilde's mother, however, resisted this prospect. According to the Irish poet W. B. Yeats, who visited Wilde at this time, Lady Wilde told her son: "If you stay, even if you go to prison, you will always be my son, it will make no difference to my affection, but if you go, I will never speak to you again.[24] Yeats gathered letters of support from his Irish compatriots, which he left with Wilde's mother and brother.

Still, Wilde desired to move to a place where he could relax more easily. As early as 8 May 1895, he wrote to his close friend Ada Leverson: "Can I call this evening?"[25] Slightly later, he once more contacted Leverson, who had already fulfilled Wilde's request for a supply of books—including Robert Louis Stevenson's novels *Kidnapped* (1886) and *The Master of Ballantrae* (1889)—while he languished in jail. "I have," he said, "no words to thank you for all you do for me."[26] Implicitly, he was responding to her offer of hospitality. As Wilde acknowledged, the Leversons, who bought three of his prized artworks during the Tite Street sale, expressed considerable support toward him at this difficult time: "Your kindness and Ernest's make things better for me."[27] His correspondence with her from Oakley Street shows that he was suffering exhaustion: "I have nervous prostration."[28] By 18 or 19 May, Ada Leverson collected Wilde at midday in a brougham from Oakley Street and took him to her finely appointed home at 2 Courtfield Gardens, Kensington. As Robert Ross recollected many years later, by welcoming Wilde into their residence the Leversons "faced the chance of social ostracism."[29]

Ada Leverson made Wilde comfortable in a room ordinarily used as a nursery, where he stayed during the day before coming down to the drawing room at 6.00 p.m., where he spent two hours in her company before dinner. During this period, she reveals, Wilde's hairdresser arrived each day to shave his face and wave his hair. He was, she says, always "most carefully dressed . . . there was a flower in his buttonhole."[30] At the same time, Wilde's solicitor, C. O. Humphreys, visited him, as did friends, who joined him for an evening meal. Leverson also records that during this period Wilde received a two-hour visit from his spouse, Constance: "I found afterwards that she had come with an urgent message from her lawyer imploring him to go away without fail before the next trial which would undoubtedly be his ruin."[31] Once she had witnessed Constance's distress, Ada Leverson sent a note up to the nursery begging Wilde to flee the country. "This is not like you, Sphinx," Wilde said to her later, using the nickname he had devised for her inscrutable wit; he then turned her attention to discussing books.[32] By the time the second criminal trial began on Monday, 20 May 1895, Wilde had moved back into his mother's home on Oakley Street. Headlam, who also counseled Wilde to skip bail, accompanied him as he traveled to and from the Old Bailey on each day of the trial. On occasion, Percy Douglas was also with him.

As the reconstruction of the proceedings that follows clearly reveals, the trial—even if it now focused solely on the the misdemeanor of gross indecency—was beset with various problems regarding the interpretation of evidence, the lead prosecutor's bullying style, the Crown's fabrication of the truth regarding the suborned witnesses, and the capricious outbursts of Justice Alfred Wills (fig. 23). Moreover, the visible discomfiture that the judge exhibited while presiding over the case made it more than apparent that he harbored deep-seated prejudices against the accused. No matter how strongly Sir Edward Clarke tried to advance his client's interests, he enjoyed no success in convincing Wills about the order in which the two defendants should be tried. Since, Clarke maintained, "Mr. Wilde's name stands first upon the indictment, and the first count concerns him, his case [should] be taken first" (316).[33] Clarke could tell that Taylor's unarguable involvement in the criminal side of London's queer subculture would bias the jury against Wilde.

Once Wills decreed that Taylor should be tried first, Wilde left the courtroom. When the proceedings began, the aggressive prosecutorial jousting of the solicitor general, Sir Frank Lockwood (fig. 24), captured attention in the press. Even the *Morning*, which expressed antagonism to Wilde's plight, observed: "there is no denying that [Lockwood] has departed widely from the traditional method of conducting a Crown prosecution."[34] The *Pall Mall Gazette*, which reported with noticeable economy on Wilde's appearances in court, concentrated on Sir Edward Clarke's pointed criticisms of Lockwood's bullish behavior. Clarke, the newspaper noted, sought "to induce Sir Frank Lockwood to remember what

Fig. 23. "Spy" [Leslie Ward], cartoon of Justice Alfred Wills,
Vanity Fair, 25 June 1896.

Fig. 24. "Spy" [Leslie Ward], cartoon of Sir Frank Lockwood, *Vanity Fair*, 20 August 1887.

seemed for a moment yesterday [i.e., Thursday, 23 May 1895] to forget—that he was not here to try to get a verdict by any means he could get it; but that he was here to get at the real facts of the case, in order that the jury might be the judge of them."[35] These were sage words of caution from a colleague who had at one time held the position of solicitor general for six years, longer than that of any other previous postholder. Such advice, however, hardly shifted Lockwood's rugged determination to secure the conviction of both Taylor and Wilde.

In this hostile atmosphere, not only Sir Edward Clarke but also Taylor's lead counsel, John Peter ("J. P.") Grain, sought to demonstrate the degree to which the young blackmailers testifying against the accused were disingenuous about their criminal pasts. Grain, when cross-examining Charles Parker, had unearthed inculpating information about the onetime valet's collaboration with another young reprobate, John Dernbach. The two troublemakers had extorted funds from an unidentified gentleman simply known as Clarke. Exactly where Grain had gained his knowledge of this case, which appears not to have resulted in a prosecution, remains obscure. Meanwhile, as the proceedings unfolded, Taylor was subjected to Wills's questioning about his personal life. Once Wills had acknowledged that Taylor had attended the distinguished private school Marlborough College, he expostulated: "Was it not repugnant to your public school [i.e., private school] ideas, this habit of sleeping with men?" (335). All Taylor could do was reply: "Not to me. Where there is no harm done" (335). Whenever Grain petitioned the judge with the idea that Taylor's supposed crimes had nothing to do with any activity at the Savoy Hotel, Wills turned around and declared that the testimony of one of the chambermaids, Jane Margaret Cotter, provided support for Charles Parker's claims. Much of Taylor's trial pivoted on the problematic concept of corroboration. Lockwood pushed so hard on what constituted corroboration that he even advanced the idea that a social gathering at a restaurant supported the belief that Wilde and Taylor had perpetrated the alleged misdemeanors. "For what honest purpose, Lockwood asked, could the ill-assorted dinner parties at Kettner's have been brought together?" (336). Somehow, Lockwood maintained that a lively repast at a well-known Soho dining establishment was tantamount to a sexual conspiracy.

As these absurd exchanges enlivened the courtroom, there was another episode relating to the retrial that occurred a few miles away in the West End. Once Taylor's case began to draw to a close, a bout of fighting occurred between the Marquess of Queensberry and his son Percy in Piccadilly. This fracas, which left Percy Douglas with a bruise on one eye, became a distraction in the press. The reason for the eruption of the conflict became public when, on 22 May 1895 at Great Marlborough Street Magistrates' Court, "the Marquis [*sic*] said . . . that it was the fault of his son, who had bailed Wilde, and today had followed the Marquis about, and struck him in Piccadilly."[36] "The son," the press added, "said it was all through his father writing letters of a most improper character to his wife."[37]

In the meantime, Wilde's trial began on Wednesday, 22 May 1895. The proceedings once again involved Clarke's interrogating Charles Parker and Alfred Wood about their blackmailing activities. Clarke revisited a criminal episode that he had discussed with these two young extortionists during the previous trial. He reiterated the great success that the seasoned scoundrel William Allen, who was not in court, had in extorting no less than £400 from an unidentified gentleman in August 1894. Wood freely admitted that he had received his handsome share of £175 from this heist. When pressed to divulge what the payment was for, Wood grudgingly conceded: "I suppose it was blackmailing, but I did not know then" (350). (The court was no doubt left wondering what other purpose Wood might have thought the money was for.) Grain, for his part, pressed Charles Parker on his role in this affair. He drew attention to the idea that the £30 that the witness has received from this blackmailing was "hush money" (319): a point that elicited a blunt denial.

It appears that Wood's and Parker's respective evidence was in peril of striking the jury as too contaminated to be taken seriously. For this reason, the Crown prosecution looked to other sources of support. Lockwood and his colleagues clearly sensed that it was in their interest to garner further testimony from additional members of the Savoy Hotel staff. They recruited further witnesses, including (in the *Star*'s description) "the dark, handsome waiter" Emile Becker, who claimed to have seen young men in Wilde's rooms, only to prove himself unable to recognize Charles Parker.[38] To advance its claims, the prosecution decided that the best way of elaborating Wilde's intimacies with Charles Parker, Edward Shelley, Alfred Taylor, and Alfred Wood would come through reading aloud relevant sections of the transcripts of the shorthand record that two court reporters had taken during the libel trial. This procedure largely repeated the recitation of the document that had occupied many hours in the first criminal trial. Once Clarke started reading from this long transcript, many who were in attendance cleared the Old Bailey because of the tedious lengths to which Lockwood had gone in trying to substantiate his claims.

Other cracks in the prosecution's case against Wilde soon began to show. In principle, the Crown prosecution had a potentially dependable witness in Edward Shelley: the former clerk at the publishing firm of The Bodley Head, Vigo Street, where he first met Wilde in 1892. Shelley, who came from a respectable working-class background and expressed literary aspirations, had no ties with the likes of the Parker brothers and Wood. In both the pretrial hearing and first criminal trial, Shelley had spoken openly about his sexual intimacy with Wilde at the Albemarle Hotel. There were, however, enduring difficulties with Shelley's testimony. As Clarke was the first to see, Shelley admitted that his various quarrels and rows with not only Wilde but also his former employer, the publisher John Lane, stemmed from mental instability. "Was your mental health," Clarke inquired, "getting worse and worse?" (348). Further disclosures revealed that Shelley had been arrested after he assaulted his father. Wills, who seems to have either forgotten or repressed the disclosures Shelley had made in the earlier proceedings about the onetime clerk's sexual intimacy with Wilde, appeared at his most erratic when he concurred with Clarke that the evidence of this young man, who by all accounts suffered from delusions, could not be corroborated. The memory of Shelley's admission, which caused him severe distress previously in court, that he had slept in the same bed with Wilde at the Albemarle Hotel, had no lasting impact on the judge. Wills declared that there was nothing dishonorable in the relationship: "it would be a terrible thing for society at large, if it were considered unnatural for a man to ask a younger man of good character to dine with him at his club or house and then thought to be evidence of guilt" (360). On these grounds, the justice concluded that "it was his duty to withdraw Shelley's case from the jury" (361).

As for Wilde himself, the ordeal, which involved the tiresome rehashing of evidence that had already been scrutinized before, took a toll on his performance. Lockwood persisted in trying to ensure that Wilde might let slip, as he had done during the libel trial, that the sole reason for spending time with the likes of Parker and Wood was his sexual attraction to them. Lockwood sarcastically inquired: "Was the conversation of these young men literary?" "I admit," Wilde replied, "that I am enormously fond of praise and admiration, and that I like to be made much of by my inferiors—inferiors socially. It pleases me very much" (371). By this point, Wilde's witty posturing, from what we can tell, was no longer amusing the court. "I liked their society," he told Lockwood, "simply because I like to be lionized" (371)—a verb he used more than once. As he pressed further on Wilde's social interactions with these youths, Lockwood asked the defendant about his acquaintance with Ernest Scarfe: "Did he call you Oscar?" (374). In response, Wilde responded affirmatively: "I have a passion for being called by my Christian name. It pleases me" (374). At this stage, such theatrical displays of boastfulness probably sounded more pitiful than pithy.

There were other befuddling details that clouded the courtroom's view of Wilde. One of the most taxing aspects of Lockwood's cross-examination touched upon the fecal stains that the Savoy staff claimed to have witnessed on Wilde's bedsheets. "Were the stains there, sir?," Lockwood queried. "If they were," Wilde declared, "they were not caused in the way the prosecution so filthily suggests" (378). Other equally puzzling moments occurred during Lockwood's interrogation, which involved his production of two scarfpins.[39] The solicitor general intimated that these items were highly suspicious gifts that Wilde had bestowed upon his young male admirers. "Did you give a pin to Harrington?," Lockwood asked. "I did not," Wilde stated, only to be interrupted by the prosecutor's indignation (375). The elusive identity of Harrington, a music clerk who never stepped forth to give testimony but identified himself to the court, pointed to an aspect of Wilde's social life that appeared abstruse in these exchanges. The jurors were most likely perplexed.

In any case, there were many questions surrounding the leading witnesses' evidence and the corroboration of that evidence. As he addressed the members of the jury, Clarke commented incisively on the blackmailers' unreliable testimony. "I can only say," Clarke stated, "that if these blackmailers are to be listened to in court against a defendant who was prepared on oath to give a denial to their story, the profession of blackmailing might become a more deadly mischief than it has been before" (380). Still, even if this eloquent attorney stated unequivocally that "this trial seems to be operating as an act of indemnity of all blackmailers in London" (380), it failed to gain the traction that the defense wanted to secure with the evidently overwhelmed jurors.

On the final day, Lockwood spun a bogus argument about the causal relations between sodomy and blackmail. In an astonishing address to the jury, the doughty solicitor general urged the jurors to believe that, without the perpetration of gross indecency, it was inconceivable that homosexual extortion could ever have existed. To round off his misleading observations, Lockwood insisted—in what was a flagrant lie—that "[i]t is not suggested that their evidence has been bought, or that they have been improperly influenced in any way" (388). This remark contradicted Clarke's earlier assertion, which he had made the day before, that "[t]hese men who have been the pests of London come smoothly and smilingly into court in the clothes that Lord Queensberry has bought for them, and we hear they are lodged and fed under the sympathetic care of the detective officers who have been provided them" (380). In principle, Lockwood was accurate in maintaining that these witnesses were not blackmailing Wilde on false claims or through extortion. He was, however, not telling the truth when he denied that their evidence "had been bought."

Faced with these untruths, the courtroom witnessed the proceedings stumble to a close. Once the time came for Justice Wills to present his summing-up to the jury, more confusion ensued. In the available summary of the judge's comments, he experienced some nervousness when even mentioning Alfred Douglas's role in the various sexual encounters that had involved Parker, Taylor, and Wood. "[H]e was," we learn, "anxious not to say anything that might blast the career of this young man who was on the threshold of life" (391). Even though Wills expressed disdain for the "offensive expression" that Queensberry left on a club card for Wilde (391), the impassioned letters that Wilde had sent to Douglas were sure signs of the danger that the young Scottish lord found himself in. On these grounds, the marquess was considerered to be an exemplary father—regardless of the estrangement that he had experienced from his son—who wished to ensure that his child was protected from an implicitly exploitative older male lover: "What father," Wills opined, "would not try to save his son from the associations suggested by the two letters from the prisoner Wilde to Lord Alfred Douglas?" (391). This perspective, however, seemed to baffle the jurors. At this juncture, the foreman wished to settle a matter that had crossed his colleagues' minds: "In view of the intimacy between Lord Alfred Douglas and Wilde, was a warrant ever issued for the apprehension of Lord Alfred Douglas?" (392). Wills, it seems, was close to losing his temper when he declared: "I should think not" (392). Pushed harder on the foreman's suggestion that "any guilt from these letters . . . applies as much to Lord Alfred Douglas as to the defendant," the judge reiterated the view that "anything that can be said for or against Lord Alfred Douglas must not be allowed to prejudice the prisoner" (393). Even if this legal point was technically true, it raised the suspicion that the refusal to countenance Bosie's immersion in this sexual underworld made it seem as though the judge had erected a smokescreen.

In his erratic assessment of the evidence, Justice Wills became confused about the testimony of the hotel staff. On the one hand, he conceded that the lapse of two years was so long that their evidence "must not be entirely relied upon" (395). At the same time, even though he concluded that the masseur Antonio Migge's recollections were unreliable, he was nonetheless struck by their "remarkable" substance (395). On the other hand, the judge expressed dismay that the housekeeper Annie Perkins appeared to be an accomplice in concealing a crime that was evident through the horrific stains that she had found on Wilde's bed linens. The judge was not, under any circumstances, persuaded by what he scornfully termed "the diarrhea line of defence" (394). Once he had wrapped up these contorted lines of reasoning, Wills ended by telling the jurors that they had to decide "whether there was evidence of guilt or of suspicion only" (395). It took the jury the better part of two hours to reach its verdict. After the foreman had finished reciting "Guilty" six times over, many who had been present in the courtroom gasped in astonishment that such a disorderly trial could have led to Wilde's conviction. It was left to the more sympathetic sections of the press, such as the *Star*, to ask questions about the many details regarding names, places, and publications that the trials—all the way from 3 April to 25 May 1895—had obfuscated (see 409–10 below).

THE TRIAL OF ALFRED TAYLOR

First Day: Monday, 20 May 1895

The May Sessions of the Central Criminal Court were opened this morning at 10.00 a.m. at the Old Bailey by the lord mayor (Sir Joseph Renals), as the chief commissioner, who took his seat in the chair of honor under the City sword.[40] The opening of the sessions was a most ceremonial affair. On his lordship's right was the recorder, Sir Charles Hall, Q.C., and on his left sat aldermen Sir Reginald Hanson, Bart., MP; Sir Stuart Knill, Bart.; Sir Robert Tyler, Bart.; Sir J. V. Moore; and Vaughan Morgan; with Mr. Sherriff Hand. Each carried an exquisite bouquet, and the bench was strewn with fragrant herbs. Journalists stated that this gesture was reminiscent of the time when it was necessary to take precautions against jail fever or typhus.[41] For a quarter of an hour, the dignitaries assembled on the bench presented a brave array of color from end to end, but one by one the aldermen glided silently from the court, and by the time the recorder had commenced his charge to the grand jury the civic array had thinned down to the lord mayor, Mr. J. V. Moore, Mr. Sherriff Hand, the chaplain, and the city marshal. The last-named official was Sir Simeon Stuart, Bart., whose baronetcy dated from the time of James I.

As a general rule, Her Majesty's judges did not visit the Old Bailey until two days after the opening of the sessions. It was by special arrangement that Mr. Justice Wills attended the Central Criminal Court on Monday, 20 May 1895 to begin the second trial of Oscar Wilde and Alfred Taylor on the charges of gross indecency and offenses against the eleventh section of the Criminal Law Amendment Act 1885, with regard to which the jury at the last sessions disagreed. Since no fresh indictment was presented, it was not necessary to send the case for a second time to the grand jury. The recorder read the charge, which made no reference to Taylor and Wilde, since the bill found against them at the previous trial still stood. At 11.00 a.m., once the recorder exited the court, Mr. Justice Wills took his seat.

The solicitor general, Sir Frank Lockwood, Q.C., MP, with Mr. Charles Frederick ("C. F.") Gill, Mr. Horace Avory, and Mr. H. Sutton (instructed by Mr. Angus Lewis and Mr. Frayling of the Treasury), appeared on behalf of the prosecution. Wilde was represented by Sir Edward Clarke, Q.C., MP; Mr. Charles ("Willie") Mathews; and Mr. Travers Humphreys. Mr. J. P. Grain, and Mr. Sydney Knox represented Taylor. Wilde had been released on bail during the past fortnight, while Taylor languished in Holloway Prison. Taylor was brought to the Old Bailey with other prisoners in a police van. After Wilde arrived in court, he approached the solicitors' table and conferred with Mathews. When the clerk of arraigns called on him to surrender to his bail, he stepped into the dock and made a slight bow toward the bench. Immediately afterward, Taylor joined Wilde.

The court then heard the indictment. It described Wilde as a forty-year-old author, charged with committing acts of gross indecency with Edward Shelley, Alfred Wood, and Charles Parker, as well as committing acts with unknown persons. Taylor was charged with attempting to commit an "abominable crime" with William Parker and Charles Parker, with procuring and attempting the commission of certain acts of gross indecency with Alfred Wood, with attempting to procure the commission of those acts with Sydney Mavor, and with committing those acts with William Parker and Charles Parker.

The *Sun* noted that at this point, after fourteen jurymen had filed into the box, "a singular incident" took place: "Their names were read over, and two of them stepped out, objected to—when, why, or by whom, did not appear."[42] In other words, no reason was given for the exclusion of the two jurors. Before the jury had been sworn, Sir Edward Clarke stated that he wished to make an application for a motion so that the defendants should be tried separately.

MR. JUSTICE WILLS: Unless the solicitor general has anything to say—
SIR FRANK LOCKWOOD: I have, my lord.

Clarke said that the grounds of his motion were that the prisoners had the right to be tried separately. At the last trial, he observed, there was an indictment against the defendants that contained twenty-five counts. Clarke did not know whether Justice Wills was in possession of an abstract of these charges. To make matters clear, Clarke stated that on many of these counts a verdict of not guilty was entered, and there now remained a certain number of counts, but not ones of conspiracy. He pointed out that only eight of those counts affected Wilde, and in none of them was there any allegation made against Taylor. The other counts, as Clarke noted, were against Taylor, and in none of them was there any charge against Wilde. In other words, there was no single count still included in the indictment on which both Wilde and Taylor could be convicted. Subsequently, Clarke reminded Justice Wills that in a very remarkable case, which his lordship had tried in the same court a decade previously, two persons were put on trial for murder.[43] There was not in that case any such division upon the indictment as there now was between the interests of the defendants. Clarke mentioned that his learned friend, the solicitor general, Sir Frank Lockwood, who appeared in that trial for one of the prisoners, made the same application that Clarke was now submitting. In the trial to which Clarke alluded, the attorney general at the time did not oppose the application, and there was every reason to believe that it would have been granted had the case against the defendant not been withdrawn. Grain, on behalf of Taylor, concurred with the application.

In response, Lockwood said that he did not propose dealing with the indictment in relation to the precedent to which Clarke had referred, since in that previous case his lordship had been relieved of any necessity of deciding which should be adopted. Moreover, Lockwood noted that in that earlier trial there was a charge of felony, which made it very different from the present case. Thus, Lockwood opposed Clarke's application. He stated that if the defendants were to be tried separately, it would be necessary to hear the case against Taylor first.

CLARKE: My lord, I should object to that.

LOCKWOOD: The sequence of events would necessitate that being done. Then, that course being taken, what would be the nature of the inquiry? It would be an inquiry into the conduct of one person on his trial, and necessarily evidence would have to be given of the conduct of another person who would not be upon his trial. In these conditions, it appears that those responsible for the indictment, rightly appreciating the situation, felt that it would be a hardship upon the other prisoner that any consideration of his conduct should arise upon a trial at which he was not represented. With regard to the course the Crown would take as to the order of the trial: that was a matter that must be left to the discretion of those responsible for the prosecution, and I hope his lordship will not allow my learned friend to dictate to the Crown as to the order in which the cases should be heard. Your lordship will be able to see that the two cases are so bound up that it is impossible to inquire into the one without necessarily inquiring into the other. In these circumstances, the fairest course would be for the two defendants to be tried together.

CLARKE: The chief ground on which my learned friend has opposed the separate trial of the defendants is that such a course would involve injustice to them. The best judges of that matter are those who have the responsibility of advising and representing the defendants, and we are of the opinion that it would involve injustice to both if the prisoners were put upon their trial together. Therefore, I respectfully urge upon your lordship, it being clear that there is no one count in the indictment upon which both of the defendants can be convicted, that, in these circumstances, they are entitled to be tried separately.

JUSTICE WILLS: I need hardly say that this is a matter which has been present to my consideration before I came here, because I do not affect to be entirely ignorant of what has taken place before, as I anticipated that this application would be made. Therefore, I may say I have considered it carefully with regard to the evidence that has been given, and in view of that evidence my opinion is that the two defendants should be tried separately.

LOCKWOOD: As your lordship pleases. In that case, I propose, my lord, to take the case of Taylor first.

Clarke immediately objected on behalf of Wilde, on the ground that Wilde would be prejudiced in the eyes of the jury by having the case against Taylor heard first.

CLARKE: Then I apply that the case against Wilde should be taken first. His name stands first upon this indictment, and the first count is directed against him. There are reasons present, I am sure, to your lordship's mind, why it would be unjust to Mr. Wilde that his case should be tried after, and immediately after, the trial of the other defendant.

Lockwood again raised an objection, stating that the prosecution could do as it pleased in the matter.

JUSTICE WILLS: It ought not to make any difference, Sir Edward. Certainly, I—and I am sure the jury—will do our very best to take care that the last trial shall have no influence upon the present.

CLARKE: I am sure the jury will try and do their duty. But there never was a time and a case in which that duty is more difficult to discharge, and I respectfully ask that as Mr. Wilde's name stands first upon the indictment, and the first count concerns him, his case be taken first.

JUSTICE WILLS: I don't see how I can very well interfere with the discretion of the prosecution or with their rights. I certainly think the matter is within their rights. It has always been recognized as such.

CLARKE: If your lordship pleases. But I will make now an application which I shall certainly renew at a later stage of the proceedings, that the trial of Mr. Wilde shall stand over until the next sessions, and I am prepared to urge that upon your lordship.

JUSTICE WILLS: Don't you think that, Sir Edward, such an application had better be made when we see the result of this trial? If it should be an acquittal, so much the better for the other prisoner.

Clarke suggested that there would be no objection to allowing Wilde out on the same bail as before.

JUSTICE WILLS: Certainly, if the bail are here.

Since Lockwood offered no objection, Justice Wills repeated that there was no reason for refusing the application, if the bail were present. If they were not present, Clarke stated, the sureties could be sent for. While the court waited for Percy Douglas and Stewart Headlam to return to the building, Wilde was taken down to the cells. Headlam came back to the court fairly promptly. It did, however, take until 2.45 p.m. before Percy Douglas appeared. At that point, Wilde was at liberty to leave the Old Bailey.

Sir Frank Lockwood, on behalf of the prosecution, began by stating the nature of the charges that were brought against the accused, and he pointed out that to prove the case against Taylor it would be necessary that the conduct of other persons should form a matter of investigation.[44] Briefly, the solicitor general explained Taylor's career and connections with "a person named Oscar Wilde." Taylor was a young man from a good family, who had attended a large public school.[45] He had entered the militia. On reaching his majority, he had come into a fortune, although these funds were exhausted some time before the events that would be presented before the jury. Since losing his fortune, Taylor had no occupation. Lockwood then opened the case against Taylor, stating that he would join with Grain to obtain the fairest and most impartial trials for the prisoner in the dock.

Lockwood went on to relate the manner in which Charles Parker and William Parker had met the prisoner at the St. James's restaurant in March 1893. Moreover, the solicitor general described the Parker brothers as men of a humble background and no education, who could have had no legitimate attraction for a man of intellect. Taylor, Lockwood said, had offered to introduce the Parkers to Wilde, and Taylor invited them to his rooms at 13 Little College Street. When they called on Taylor, he told them that he had arranged to introduce them to Wilde at a restaurant—either Kettner's or the Solferino—that evening.[46] The former groom and former valet joined Wilde for dinner, though neither of them had ever met him before. The Parker brothers and Taylor dined with Wilde in a private room. Lockwood then repeated the conversation that took place at the conclusion of the dinner, and he recounted the subsequent visit that Charles Parker allegedly made to the Savoy Hotel, where Wilde had rooms. After mentioning the acts of indecency that had allegedly occurred at the hotel, Lockwood explained that when Charles Parker had stayed there for two hours, Wilde gave the young man £2. Charles Parker had afterward visited

Wilde at the Savoy and received £3. On other occasions, Wilde had given him a cigarette case and a gold chain-ring. Lockwood regretted the necessity under which he found himself going into detail about the conduct of a man who was now not on trial—Oscar Wilde. He noted that Wilde was a man of some literary distinction, who had attained a measure of eminence as a dramatist. At the time, Wilde lived in Tite Street, Chelsea; in addition, Lockwood observed that Wilde had occupied rooms not only at the Savoy but also at 10 and 11 St. James's Place, which Charles Parker had also visited. Wilde, Lockwood informed the jurors, had taken Charles Parker to the Crystal Palace and to other places of amusement, and had visited the young man's lodgings at Park Walk, Chelsea. Lockwood stated that if the last visit were true, it would demonstrate that Taylor had procured Charles Parker for the purpose mentioned in the indictment.

With regard to Alfred Wood, Lockwood contended that Taylor had procured Wood for Wilde, in the same way and with the same motives that he had for introducing Charles Parker to the dramatist. Wood, the solicitor general maintained, was a clerk, in a humble position in life, who had no occupation when he met Taylor. Lockwood said that Wood had no ostensible means of getting his living. He mentioned that Wood met Wilde at an appointed time through a telegram. The person who introduced Wood to Taylor sent this communication. Up to the point of Wood's visit to the Café Royal in Regent Street, the solicitor general noted, Wood had no acquaintance with Wilde. Afterward, Wilde gave Wood dinner at the Florence restaurant, and then took him to Tite Street, where indecencies occurred. This visit was repeated. Lockwood stated that Wilde had given Wood money and presents from time to time, ultimately parting with enough funds to finance Wood's passage to America.

The first witness to be called was Charles Parker. The *Star* remarked that the young man was "a fresh-colored lad with a face that would attract rather than repel a stranger"; he was, the paper noted, "[n]eatly dressed in blue serge."[47] Soon after C. F. Gill had begun his examination, Justice Wills interjected to point out that the counsel was posing leading questions. In response to Gill's inquiries, Charles Parker mostly replied "Yes" or "No." The witness repeated the account of his meeting with Taylor at the St. James's restaurant, his subsequent introduction to Wilde, the dinner at the Florence, the visits to the Savoy Hotel, and the several weeks that he and his brother spent at Taylor's rooms at 13 Little College Street. During their time at Taylor's rooms, the brothers witnessed their host dressing as a woman and enacting a mock-marriage ceremony with Charles Spurrier Mason. Charles Parker denied that he had ever known Wilde before Taylor introduced them at the restaurant, where the four of them enjoyed dinner with champagne, liqueurs, and cigarettes. Before the witness completed his evidence, he recalled his arrest with Taylor in 1894: the time when he decided to leave London and enlist.

JUSTICE WILLS: His arrest? On what charge?

Gill appeared uncomfortable at the question, and—since Charles Parker hesitated in giving an answer—the judge followed up with a further question.

JUSTICE WILLS: I only want to know, you know. You leave the impression that there is something mysterious. What were you arrested for?

CHARLES PARKER: For being in a house in Fitzroy Street.[48]

GILL: Really for being there with a felonious purpose. There were men there dressed as women.

JUSTICE WILLS: Then I suppose they were charged with consorting together to commit acts of indecency. Much better to have the whole thing out.

GRAIN: In that case, then, better to have it out that both Taylor and Parker were discharged by the magistrate.

Once Grain had explained that the charges against Alfred Taylor and Charles Parker had been dropped, Gill resumed his examination. Charles Parker described in further detail the places he had visited with Wilde and the gifts that Wilde had presented to him. Grain then proceeded with his cross-examination. Charles Parker admitted to Grain that he knew a man named Harrington, whose acquaintance he had also made at the bar of the St. James's restaurant.[49] Charles Parker added that Harrington did not introduce him to Taylor, nor did anyone introduce him to Harrington.

GRAIN: Have you ever received hush money?[50]

CHARLES PARKER: No.

GRAIN: Have you ever threatened to charge people with offences unless they paid you money?

CHARLES PARKER: No.

GRAIN: You know Wood and Allen?

CHARLES PARKER: Yes.

GRAIN: Be careful. You have been in that box before. Have you not already admitted receiving £30?

CHARLES PARKER: They did not tell me it was hush money. They gave it to me.

GRAIN: That was just before you enlisted?

CHARLES PARKER: Yes.

GRAIN: Did either Allen or Wood tell you how they got it?

CHARLES PARKER: Yes. They said they got it out of a gentleman.[51]

GRAIN: A gentleman with whom you had committed acts of indecency?

CHARLES PARKER: Yes.

GRAIN: Did you know a person of the name of Macklin?[52]

CHARLES PARKER: No. But I have heard the name before. I have heard Taylor speak of him.

GRAIN: Did he not come to your rooms at Camera Square about May 1894?

CHARLES PARKER: I never knew his name. At least, it did not sound like that. I know the man you mean.

GRAIN: Do you know a person named Clarke?[53]

CHARLES PARKER: Yes.

GRAIN: When he hung up his coat in your room, did you not take those letters out of his pocket?

CHARLES PARKER: No.

GRAIN: Do you swear that?

CHARLES PARKER: Yes.

GRAIN: Did he not accuse you the next day of having stolen his letters?

CHARLES PARKER: No. He gave me one of the letters.

GRAIN: One of Clarke's letters?

CHARLES PARKER: Yes.

GRAIN: What did you want with one of Clarke's letters?

CHARLES PARKER: I didn't want it. I gave it back.

GRAIN: Did you not go in June 1894, about Whitsuntide, to Mr. Clarke and ask him for £10?[54]

CHARLES PARKER: Yes.

GRAIN: Had you the letters with you?

CHARLES PARKER: No.

GRAIN: A letter?

CHARLES PARKER: No.

GRAIN: What did you want £10 for?

CHARLES PARKER: To go to America.

GRAIN: Where is Mr. Clarke now?

CHARLES PARKER: I don't know.

GRAIN: But why should Clarke give you £10?

CHARLES PARKER: He was the only friend I had in London. I had known him for three years.

JUSTICE WILLS: What is he?

CHARLES PARKER: He was a silver-broker or something in the silver trade. He lived at 3 Northumberland Mansions.[55] At that time he worked for his brother-in-law in Bond Street, but he is now out of the country.

GRAIN: Did you not at that interview take Clarke's watch out of his pocket?

CHARLES PARKER: No.

GRAIN: What? Was not a constable sent for?

CHARLES PARKER: I don't think a constable was sent for.

GRAIN: Did he threaten to charge you?

CHARLES PARKER: Not for that.

GRAIN: What do you mean by that?

CHARLES PARKER: Clarke said his brother was coming, and that if I did not be off, he would send for a constable.

GRAIN: You swear that you did not take his watch and chain, and that when the constable came you gave it up?

CHARLES PARKER: I do swear it.

GRAIN: Did he not threaten to charge you with stealing his gold watch and chain?

CHARLES PARKER: No.

GRAIN: Did not Clarke introduce you to a man named Dernbach?[56]

CHARLES PARKER: No. I knew Dernbach. Taylor introduced me to him. I introduced Dernbach to Clarke.

GRAIN: Did you ever threaten Clarke about letters he had written to Dernbach?

CHARLES PARKER: No.

GRAIN: Did you ever demand money from Dernbach?

CHARLES PARKER: Never.

GRAIN: Did you know Dernbach's occupation?

CHARLES PARKER: No.

Parker finished his responses to Grain's question by stating that he told Taylor that his father was a horse-dealer at Datchet: "At least he trained horses, that sort of thing."[57] Grain completed his cross-examination. Lockwood then reexamined Charles Parker. Millard comments: "Throughout his occupancy of the box, the wretched witness stood with a grin and a smirk upon his face. When he was asked about his arrest in Fitzroy Street, one would have thought from looking at him that the reminiscence was a most pleasant one, and similarly with many other of the incidents he related. As the case went on, astonishment and wonder grew how it was possible for the Crown to demean itself by relying on the evidence of such creatures."[58]

The next witness was Charles Parker's older brother, William Parker. The *Star* observed that he was a "coarser copy of the last witness."[59] Avory examined him.[60] William Parker once again recalled his introduction to Wilde and the dinner at the Soho restaurant where Wilde stated that Charles Parker was "the boy for me."[61] The witness also testified that he had committed indecencies with Taylor. Under cross-examination from Grain, William Parker said that he had been unemployed for about two weeks before he met Taylor. At this juncture, Lockwood asked Justice Wills whether it might be possible to finish the case that day. The judge responded that, since he wished to conclude the proceedings promptly, the interval for luncheon would be curtailed.

After luncheon, the next witness, Alfred Wood, was called. Lockwood examined him. Of Wood's self-presentation, the *Star* reported that he appeared "a smooth-tongued fellow with a deliberate, non-committal manner of speech"; Wood's demeanor did "not make him seem any the more ingenuous."[62] Wood described his acquaintance with Taylor. It was not certain, however, that Taylor was responsible, at least directly, for Wood's introduction to Wilde. The contact between Wood and Wilde came through a third party, whose name was not mentioned at this point of the proceedings. As observers of the first criminal trial were aware, it was Alfred Douglas who sent a telegram from Salisbury to Wood about meeting Wilde at the Café Royal at an appointed time. Grain, objecting that it was not Taylor who had made this introduction, prevented the witness from stating what had taken place between himself and Wilde. The *Star* reminded its readers that William Allen had obtained from Wood the two stolen "'red rose-leaf lips' and 'red and yellow wine' letters" that Wilde had sent to Alfred Douglas, and that Allen had used this correspondence in an attempt to extort funds from Wilde.[63] At the same time, the newspaper noted, Wood came to Wilde for assistance in order to seek employment in America.

LOCKWOOD: Why did you go to Mr. Wilde?

WOOD: I was not quite fit to mix with people in that position of life, with plenty of money, and I wanted to get away abroad and into a situation.

JUSTICE WILLS: I suppose the purport of this evidence is that Wilde was anxious to get Wood out of the way?

LOCKWOOD: Yes, and that he paid money for it.

Wood recounted that Wilde gave him £20 so that he could go to America. He would not admit that he had bartered with Wilde. Wood stated that on the following day he had lunch with Wilde, who had given him another £5. Then Wood recalled the letter he had sent to Taylor from New York in which he referred to "telling Oscar to send" him "a draft for an Easter egg if he liked."[64] Justice Wills requested that the solicitor general clarify how Wood became acquainted with Wilde.

LOCKWOOD: From whom came the telegram in consequence of which you went to the Café Royal?

WOOD: From Lord Alfred Douglas.

JUSTICE WILLS: Had you any acquaintance with Lord Alfred Douglas at the time when you met Wilde?
WOOD: Yes.
LOCKWOOD: Where had you met Lord Alfred Douglas?
WOOD: At Taylor's rooms in Little College Street.
LOCKWOOD: Who introduced you to him?
WOOD: No one. He was in the room, and he shook hands with me.

Here Justice Wills remarked that the evidence of procuration against Taylor appeared no stronger than it might against three or four other persons. Since Douglas, not Taylor, had made the introduction, evidence about Wilde's conduct could not be used as evidence against Taylor. The judge pointed out that there had to be direct evidence, if any, of a criminal motive on Wilde's part. Grain attached so little importance to Wood's evidence that he did not proceed to cross-examine the witness. Wood was asked to step down. Justice Wills then pointed out that the evidence that Jane Margaret Cotter, a chambermaid at the Savoy Hotel, had given at the first criminal trial could not be taken as evidence against Taylor.

Several other witnesses were then called. The first was Ellen Grant, a caretaker at 13 Little College Street, where Taylor was resident from January 1892 to August 1893. She once again described the oriental stuffiness of Taylor's rooms, the draperies covering the windows, the perfumes, and midday oil. She remarked that she was aware that Taylor's room had been put to improper use.[65] She added that she informed her husband that care should be taken to make sure that whatever went on in Taylor's rooms should be hidden from other people's eyes and ears. Grant noted that young men used to visit Taylor and spend some time there. Wilde, she remarked, was a frequent visitor. Under Grain's cross-examination, Grant stated that she did not tell Taylor that the police had been to make inquiries about him. The *Illustrated Police Budget* recorded that another witness, Mrs. Brown, a lodger at 13 Little College Street, "settled one point as to Taylor's burning incense in his room, saying he burnt scent 'in a thing swung about on the end of chains'"; under cross-examination, the witness "said the ladies' silk stockings, wigs, brooches, and French shoes were used by Taylor for fancy-dress balls."[66]

Thereafter, Cotter, the chambermaid from the Savoy, was permitted to repeat her evidence about Wilde's stay at the hotel in March 1893. She stated that she had complained to the hotel management about the state of the bed linens and the utensils in Wilde's room.[67] When pressed for particulars, Cotter hesitated. After stating that she refused to make the bed or empty the chamber pot, she handed in her notice, though her employer prevailed upon her to withdraw it.[68] Through a series of questions, counsel extracted further information. The bed linens, Cotter said, were stained. The color was brown. The towels were similarly discolored. One of the pillows was marked with face powder. There was excrement in one of the utensils in the bathroom. Wilde, Cotter recalled, handed her a half sovereign for her services. But when she saw the state of the room, she gave the coin to the management. Grain interjected to say that Taylor had nothing to do with anything that might or might not have taken place at the hotel at that time. Lockwood responded by stating that Cotter's evidence provided some corroboration of Charles Parker's testimony. Justice Wills agreed.

The next witness to be called had not previously given evidence. Emile Becker, a waiter at the Savoy, testified that Wilde and Douglas had stayed at the hotel in March 1893.[69] Becker remarked that once Douglas left the hotel, other young men visited Wilde. Thomas Price, who followed Becker, gave similar evidence with regard to Wilde's rooms at the private hotel in St. James's Place. Price was able to identify Taylor as one of Wilde's callers. Sophia Gray, the landlady at 3 Chapel Street, deposed that Taylor stayed in her house from August 1893 to the end of the year. She stated that Charles Parker used to visit Taylor, and she confirmed that Charles Parker stayed with Taylor for three weeks. Wilde, she noted, visited once. Fred Kerley, the retired police inspector, deposed that he had received from Sophia Gray a hatbox full of papers that Taylor had left at her house. Among the documents, he found a slip of paper bearing Charles Parker's address, together with two telegrams from Wilde to Taylor putting off appointments with young men. The next witness, Lucy Rumsby, deposed that Charles Parker lodged for two weeks in her house at 50 Park Walk, Chelsea. Margery Bancroft, a tenant in the same property, swore that she had seen Wilde come to 50 Park Walk in a cab. Three further witnesses were called: Mr. Robinson, the bookkeeper at the Savoy; Detective Sergeant William Harris, the officer who had kept observation on 13 Little College Street and arrested Taylor; and Inspector Charles Richards, who charged Taylor. These witnesses concluded the case for the prosecution. Since the witnesses' evidence had taken up so much time during the afternoon, it was not possible to complete the case that day.

Grain proceeded to open his case for the defense, on the understanding that the hearing would be thereafter adjourned. He urged that, so far as the case against Taylor went, there was an almost entire absence of corroboration. Grain contended that the counts charging Taylor with procuring should be struck out altogether. Furthermore, he observed that regarding the charges of committing indecencies with the Parker brothers, there was once more absolutely no corroboration of the stories of these young men, who must themselves have been consenting parties had these acts taken place. In response, Lockwood maintained that there was ample corroboration to go to the jury. Justice Wills stated that there was sufficient corroborative evidence to overcome any technical difficulty, and he thought it better that there should be a verdict, for reasons that would appear in his summing-up.

At this juncture, Grain addressed the jury, opening the case for the prisoner.[70] He asked the jury to believe that it was impossible for a young man of such education and background to have committed the offenses with which Taylor was charged—unless the prisoner was out of his mind. The evidence that the Parker brothers had given, Grain observed, could not be accepted, since both of these witnesses were accomplices in the acts. He noted that a man could not be convicted of such offenses on the uncorroborated evidence of accomplices. Moreover, he pointed out that the law established that one accomplice could not corroborate another accomplice. There was, in his view, really no independent corroborative evidence, and when he called on his client, who would deny all of the allegations, he would call on the jury to acquit the accused. Grain then remarked on the emphasis that had been placed on the manner in which Taylor furnished and decorated his rooms. Taylor's rooms were decorated only as a young man of style might be expected to furnish his bachelor apartments.

No doubt, Grain commented, Taylor had been unwise, but it did not follow that Taylor was a criminal. The prisoner was the son of a man of property with a high commercial position, whose business was still carried on successfully through a limited company. Taylor had been educated at Marlborough College and then by private tutors, and he had done his best to secure a commission in the army through the militia. Unfortunately, Taylor had succeeded too early to the uncontrolled possession of a large fortune that his father and uncle had left him. Since he was led into habits of idleness and extravagance, and into what Grain at once admitted was a more or less vicious mode of life, Taylor soon spent the whole of his fortune and a great deal more. The result was that he found himself in the bankruptcy court. Yet Grain insisted that it was incredible to think that a man who began his life under such favorable circumstances should be guilty of these unmentionable acts. Counsel stressed that there was no suggestion that Taylor had reaped a single penny of advantage from anyone. Instead, the evidence against him was the tainted evidence of young men who, on their own admission, might have been put in the dock in place of Taylor, or by his side. At the worst, the case for the Crown rested solely on suspicion, and they had failed absolutely to substantiate the allegations in a manner that could justify conviction.[71] The Crown ought not act, he argued, out of mere suspicion but on positive proof. Under all of the circumstances, Grain submitted, his client was entitled to an acquittal. At this point, Grain stated that he would put his client in the witness box on the following day.

At the conclusion of Grain's speech, Justice Wills decided to adjourn the hearing until the next morning. Before leaving at 5.10 p.m., the judge asked the jury to keep their minds open, and urged them not to discuss the case with anybody.[72]

Second Day: Tuesday, 21 May 1895

On this morning, the trial of Alfred Taylor, in connection with the charges against Oscar Wilde, resumed before Mr. Justice Wills.[73] *Lloyd's Weekly Newspaper* reported that, outside the Old Bailey, Fred Kerley approached Wilde in order to serve him "with a notice from the Court of Bankruptcy arising from [Wilde's] failure to meet the expenses incurred by the Marquis [*sic*] of Queensberry in his defence to Wilde's libel action."[74] Inside the court, the solicitor general Sir Frank Lockwood, Mr. C. F. Gill, Mr. Horace Avory, and Mr. Sutton appeared for the prosecution, and Mr. J. G. Grain and Mr. W. Clarke Hall for the defense. Sir Frank Lockwood arrived (as the *Galignani Messenger* put it) "breezy and burly, before half past 10."[75] Mr. C. F. Gill and Mr. Horace Avory were already in their places, arranging with the Treasury solicitors—Mr. Cuffe (the public prosecutor), Mr. Angus Lewis, and Mr. F. G. Frayling—the last stages of their case. Wilde did not put in an appearance today. Sir Edward Clarke was present. Even though Clarke's presence was not essential, since he was not engaged in Taylor's trial, he watched the case closely on his client's behalf. The court was crowded. No sooner had Justice Wills taken his seat on the bench than Grain called Taylor, who quickly entered the witness box, where he was sworn.

GRAIN: What is your age?[76]

TAYLOR: I am thirty-three.

GRAIN: You are the son of the late Henry Taylor, who was a manufacturer of an article of food in large demand?

TAYLOR: I am.

GRAIN: You were at Marlborough School?

TAYLOR: Until I was seventeen.

Taylor stated that he was then tutored privately at Preston, near Brighton. In 1882, he joined the militia regiment with a view to seeking a commission in the army. The following year, he came of age, when he abandoned his military ambitions.

GRAIN: You inherited £45,000 I believe?
TAYLOR: Yes.
GRAIN: And spent it?
TAYLOR: It went.
GRAIN: Since then, you have had no occupation?
TAYLOR: I have lived upon an allowance made to me.
GRAIN: Is there any truth in the evidence of Charles Parker that you misconducted yourself with him?
TAYLOR: Not the slightest.

Taylor added that he did not procure either of the Parker brothers to commit indecencies with Wilde.

GRAIN: What rooms had you at Little College Street?
TAYLOR: One bedroom, but it was subdivided and I believe there was generally a bed in each division.[77]
GRAIN: You had a good many visitors?
TAYLOR: Oh, yes.

The *Galignani Messenger* took note of Taylor's attitude throughout the examination: "All this he said in a clear, composed voice, standing with his hands on his hips, in an easy unconcerned attitude. He did not change his position when Sir Frank Lockwood rose to cross-examine, but his utterance became more nervous and staccato, and he rocked uneasily from one foot to the other."[78]

LOCKWOOD: Since you left the militia, have you had any fixed occupation?[79]
TAYLOR: No. I do nothing but spend my money.
LOCKWOOD: How long did you live at Little College Street?
TAYLOR: Mrs. Grant would tell you the exact date. I fancy it was about a year and a half.
LOCKWOOD: There was only one bed in your rooms there?
TAYLOR: Yes.
LOCKWOOD: And from time to time, young men calling upon you?
TAYLOR: Eighteen to twenty-one, if you call those boys.
LOCKWOOD: Boys of sixteen?
TAYLOR: I don't remember anyone as young as sixteen, except Mrs. Grant's children, who brought up my milk in the morning.
LOCKWOOD: Did Charles Mason stay with you?
TAYLOR: Yes, about a week, when I first went there, in 1892.
LOCKWOOD: What is his age?
TAYLOR: He is now about twenty-six or twenty-seven.

LOCKWOOD: Did he sleep in the same bed with you?

TAYLOR: Yes.

LOCKWOOD: Were you on terms of affection with him?

TAYLOR: I don't understand your question. If you mean, did I commit acts of indecency with him, I did not.

LOCKWOOD: How did you address him?

TAYLOR: As "Dear Charlie."

LOCKWOOD: In writing to him, did you send him your love?

TAYLOR: Yes. I generally do.

LOCKWOOD: When you are writing to a young man?

TAYLOR: If he is a great friend of mine, I might say "with love," "Yours affectionately," or something of that kind.

LOCKWOOD: And that is how Mason would address you?

TAYLOR: I suppose so.

LOCKWOOD: Do you remember going through a form of marriage with Mason?

TAYLOR: No. Never.

LOCKWOOD: Did you not tell Parker that you had?

TAYLOR: No. Nothing.

LOCKWOOD: No burlesque ceremony?[80]

TAYLOR: No. Nothing.

LOCKWOOD: Had you articles of women's dress there?

TAYLOR: Only an Eastern costume.

LOCKWOOD: A woman's costume?

TAYLOR: It was made for a woman. I wore it.

LOCKWOOD: On what occasions?

TAYLOR: At fancy dress balls, at carnivals at Olympia, at Covent Garden, and at the Queen's Gate Hall.[81]

LOCKWOOD: You dressed as a woman?

TAYLOR: Hardly that. I wore knickerbockers and stockings under a long open cloak.

LOCKWOOD: And a woman's wig?

TAYLOR: No. The wig was made for a ball to which I went dressed as Dick Whittington.[82]

LOCKWOOD: Women's stockings?

TAYLOR: Yes.

LOCKWOOD: How many different men have shared your bedroom?

TAYLOR: Must I give all of my friends' names?

LOCKWOOD: Yes, sir, you must.

TAYLOR (*to Justice Wills*): May I not write them down on a piece of paper?

JUSTICE WILLS: No. We will have no names held back.

TAYLOR: I would rather write them down.

JUSTICE WILLS: If you write it, I shall read it out. I don't approve of mystery in cases of this kind. It is something done good-naturedly, and great mischief is caused. It is supposed that there is some kind of mystery, and that judge and everybody else are in a kind of conspiracy. We will have nothing of that kind.

Taylor then produced the names of Charles Mason, the Parker brothers, and Sydney Mavor. Pressed further, Taylor added Harrington's name. Lockwood urged Taylor to disclose more names.

TAYLOR: Must I mention my friend's name?

The witness mentioned the name of Ernest Macklin, whom he had met at his mother's house.

LOCKWOOD: Where was that?

TAYLOR: Must I say?

LOCKWOOD: No. Never mind. I will spare your mother that. Did Macklin ever sleep with you at Little College Street?

TAYLOR: No. Never.

LOCKWOOD: Can't you remember any others?

TAYLOR: I'm trying to think. Perhaps you can help me if you have the names.

LOCKWOOD: You say that you did not accost the Parkers, but that Harrington introduced you to them?

TAYLOR. Yes.

LOCKWOOD: Did you offer the Parkers a drink at that first meeting?

TAYLOR: They stood a drink and I retaliated.[83]

LOCKWOOD: After Harrington had introduced them?

TAYLOR: He was living with them. Harrington and the Parkers came up to the bar at the same time as I did.

LOCKWOOD: What were you doing there?

TAYLOR: I was having a drink after the theatre.

LOCKWOOD: Following your usual custom of doing nothing?

TAYLOR: Yes, if that is what you call doing nothing.

LOCKWOOD: Did you not give your address to the Parkers on the occasion of your first meeting at the St. James's bar?

TAYLOR: No.

LOCKWOOD: Where is Harrington now?

TAYLOR: I do not know.

LOCKWOOD: Here?

TAYLOR: Probably, probably for all I know.

The press commented on Lockwood's next move: "'Call him,' commanded the solicitor general with his finest brigadier-general air, and the shouts of the ushers promptly evoked a dark, good-looking young fellow with crisp black hair and a small moustache. Yes, that was Harrington, said the witness, who seemed more surprised than pleased at seeing him. He first met Harrington at the house of a man named Court in July 1892."[84]

LOCKWOOD: Who was Court?

TAYLOR: He was a schoolmaster.

LOCKWOOD: What was the attraction about Harrington?

TAYLOR: I don't know what his attraction was.

LOCKWOOD: Did you take Harrington to the Tivoli?[85]

TAYLOR: No.

LOCKWOOD: Why did he stay with you on Saturday and Sunday?

TAYLOR: Oh, I asked him.

LOCKWOOD: Did you take him the same night to a restaurant in Victoria Street?[86]

TAYLOR: Not the same night. I never took him at all. It was my friend.

LOCKWOOD: Who was your friend?

TAYLOR: Must I mention his name?

LOCKWOOD: Yes, you must.

TAYLOR: Schwabe.[87]

LOCKWOOD: That is the person you say introduced Wilde to you?

TAYLOR: Yes.

LOCKWOOD: Was it not a man named Harold Henry?[88]

TAYLOR: I think you are right. It was. I have dined with Schwabe and Harrington, but it was on another occasion.

LOCKWOOD: Who is Henry?

TAYLOR: A musician; a clerk in a music publishers at Putney.

LOCKWOOD: Have you slept with him?

TAYLOR: Yes. He was staying with me at the time.

LOCKWOOD: He was in your bedroom?

TAYLOR: Yes. Whenever my friends came to see me, they always saw all the rooms because they were rather interested in them.

Taylor denied that he had been guilty of any impropriety with Harrington. Grain objected that Lockwood had raised a question about a man who had not been called in the case. In response, Justice Wills stated that the question was relevant regarding the cross-examination of the witness's character.

The witness adhered to the story that Harrington introduced the Parker brothers to him at the St. James's bar.

LOCKWOOD: Did you know that Charles Parker had been a gentleman's servant?

TAYLOR: I knew it afterwards, but I did not know at the time.

LOCKWOOD: When did you hear that William Parker had been a groom?

TAYLOR: Not until the trial.

LOCKWOOD: On the occasion of leaving the Parkers at the St. James's restaurant, did you invite them to visit you at Little College Street?

TAYLOR: I cannot remember.

LOCKWOOD: What was the attraction about them?

TAYLOR: They were very nice.

LOCKWOOD: In what way "very nice"? Nice looking?

TAYLOR: No. Pleasant spoken.

LOCKWOOD: Anything else?

TAYLOR: Amusing.

LOCKWOOD: How came it about that those two young fellows went to your house on the first occasion?

TAYLOR: They came to see me. They came in the morning. They were staying with me at the time of the dinner. They came to me when they left Hunter Street, Brunswick Square.[89] They asked me if I could put them up for a week, and I did so. Ultimately, I persuaded William Parker to go home to his father. Charles Parker determined to remain in London. After a few weeks, he went away to Paris with a gentleman, and stayed in Paris about five months. I saw him only once after that.

LOCKWOOD: At this time, were you in communication with Oscar Wilde?

TAYLOR: I used to go see him at the Savoy. I told him the Parkers were staying with me when he asked me to dinner.

LOCKWOOD: Did you receive the telegram dated March 7th, 1893: "Could you call at six o'clock Savoy, Oscar"?

TAYLOR: Yes.

LOCKWOOD: And this one: "Obliged to see Tree at five o'clock, so don't come to Savoy. Let me know at once about Fred"?

TAYLOR: Yes.

LOCKWOOD: I suppose "Fred" means Fred Atkins?

TAYLOR: Yes.

LOCKWOOD: Did you take the Parkers to dine with Wilde at a restaurant?

TAYLOR: Yes.

LOCKWOOD: When you first met them, did you not mention the name of Oscar Wilde?

TAYLOR: No, not on that occasion.

LOCKWOOD: Did you say that Oscar Wilde had lots of money?

TAYLOR: Not then.

LOCKWOOD: When?

TAYLOR: Not at any time, because I don't think he had.

LOCKWOOD: Did you say he was fond of boys?

TAYLOR: I may have said he was fond of young people—that he liked their society. I did not put it in the way you mean.

LOCKWOOD: Where were you in the habit of meeting the Parkers?[90]

TAYLOR: At the Alhambra, the Empire, the Pavilion, and the St. James's restaurant.[91]

LOCKWOOD: Who paid? These are not free institutions.

TAYLOR: We all paid for ourselves. I was not in a position to pay for other people.

At this stage of the proceedings, the Marquess of Queensberry came into court for the first time since his acquittal on 5 April. He was given a seat in the pew reserved for Friends of the Corporation.[92]

LOCKWOOD: Did you use to meet them in Piccadilly?

TAYLOR: No, no.

LOCKWOOD: They walked along Piccadilly?

TAYLOR: I know what you are insinuating.

LOCKWOOD: I am insinuating that you walked along Piccadilly.

TAYLOR: I frequently walked through Piccadilly.

LOCKWOOD: Why did you take the Parkers to dinner with Mr. Wilde?

TAYLOR: Mr. Wilde asked me to dinner, as it was my birthday. The Parkers happened to be staying with me. I said so, and Mr. Wilde told me to bring them along with me.

LOCKWOOD: There were four of you at table: Oscar Wilde, yourself, the ex-groom, and the ex-valet?[93]

TAYLOR: Yes.

LOCKWOOD: Why did you take them?

TAYLOR: They were my friends. Charlie Parker wanted to go on the stage. I thought Mr. Oscar Wilde would be a useful man to help them.

LOCKWOOD: Your friends of a fortnight?

TAYLOR: You might say three weeks. The party was of a convivial nature. We all laughed a good deal.

LOCKWOOD: At the humours of the Parkers?

TAYLOR: No, at the humours of Oscar Wilde.

LOCKWOOD: Oh, so it was Wilde who was amusing, not the Parkers?

TAYLOR: Yes. I supposed it amused him to amuse us.

LOCKWOOD: Did you hear him say that Charles Parker was the boy for him?

TAYLOR: No. I did not.

LOCKWOOD: Did Charles Parker leave the restaurant with Wilde?

TAYLOR: No.

LOCKWOOD: Up to that point, the story of the Parkers is true?

TAYLOR: Yes, up to that point.

LOCKWOOD: And from that point?

TAYLOR: The Parkers went with me into the St. James's and had drinks, and then both went with me to Westminster and slept at my place. After that date, William Parker went to Datchet, and Charles went to Paris with someone whose name has not been mentioned in this case.[94]

LOCKWOOD: You say that distinctly?

TAYLOR: I do.

LOCKWOOD: How do you suppose Charles Parker was getting his living?[95]

TAYLOR: At that time, I understood that he had an allowance from his father.

LOCKWOOD: Then why were you keeping him at your house?

TAYLOR: Oh, his father wouldn't give him any money then.

LOCKWOOD: You did not know that he was penniless?

TAYLOR: No.

LOCKWOOD: Except for what he got from the gentlemen he met?

TAYLOR: Ah, I didn't know of that.

LOCKWOOD: Where was Parker living at the time of the arrest at Fitzroy Square?

TAYLOR: At 72 Regent Street, Chelsea.[96]

LOCKWOOD: With Wood?

TAYLOR: I think so.

LOCKWOOD: How came you to go to Fitzroy Square?[97]

TAYLOR: It was by Parker's invitation. He had two tickets. I supposed it was a sort of nightclub, and that a ball was on.

LOCKWOOD: Did you see there, men dressed as women?

TAYLOR: No.

LOCKWOOD: Did you see them outside the house?

TAYLOR: No.

LOCKWOOD: After the arrests, did you see Marling at the police station?[98]

TAYLOR: Yes.

LOCKWOOD: Who was Marling?

TAYLOR: I understood that he was a betting man.[99]

LOCKWOOD: Did you introduce Scarfe to Wilde?[100]

TAYLOR: Yes.

LOCKWOOD: Who was Scarfe?

TAYLOR: He was a young man who had just come back from the gold diggings.

LOCKWOOD: When did you make the acquaintance of Alfred Wood?

TAYLOR: In May 1892, at Atkins's rooms in Alderney Street.

LOCKWOOD: What was he?

TAYLOR: I thought he was a gentleman. I understood he had money. I was lunching one day at the Florence, when Schwabe, Wood, and Wilde came down from a private room. I have never dined or lunched with Wood and Wilde together.

Taylor also recalled that Wilde gave Wood money to go to America, but he did not think that it was blackmail or that the money was for the return of Wilde's letters—"which were of no value," he added.

LOCKWOOD: What is Mavor?

TAYLOR: A gentleman. I dined with him the night I was introduced to Mr. Wilde.

LOCKWOOD: What is your definition of a gentleman?

TAYLOR: He had private means.

LOCKWOOD: What is Mason?

TAYLOR: He is also a gentleman in that sense. He is connected with a newspaper, and is a very busy man.

LOCKWOOD: That is a rather vague description.

TAYLOR: Well, he possesses a number of shares in a newspaper. I have known him and Macklin for many years. He was a very old friend of mine. I have known him since boyhood.

Lockwood then proceeded to question Taylor about his links with Charles Spurrier Mason. Among the papers that the former police inspector, Fred Kerley, found in the hatbox left at 3 Chapel Street, where Taylor had rooms from August 1893 until the end of the year was the following letter from Mason, which Lockwood read aloud:

My dear Alfred,

As soon as you can afford it do let me have some money and I shall be pleased and obliged. I would not ask you if I could get any myself, but you know the business is not so easy. There is a lot of trouble attached to it. I have not met any one yet. Come home soon, dear, and let us go out sometimes together. Have very little news. Going to a dance on Monday and to the theatre to-night.

With much love,
Yours always, Charlie

The *Star* observed that the solicitor general proceeded with his cross-examination in "truculent tones."[101]

LOCKWOOD: What is the explanation of those words, "Come home soon, dear," used between two men?

TAYLOR: I don't see anything in it. Anyhow, I am not responsible for the expressions of another. It's the way you read it.

LOCKWOOD: Then read it yourself, sir, and tell me if that is the kind of language you exchange with the men who were on such terms with you that they slept in your bed?

TAYLOR (*laughing nervously*): I did not see anything in that.

CLARKE (*interrupting*): My lord—

LOCKWOOD (*turning around to Clarke, and stating emphatically*): *You* are not engaged in this case.[102] (*To Taylor*): Do you call it a proper letter, sir?

TAYLOR: I think it is a perfectly proper letter, seeing the very long friendship that has existed between us. But, remember, I did not write the letter.

JUSTICE WILLS: In this letter written to you by Mason, how do you explain the passages, "I have not met anyone yet"?

TAYLOR: He had been expecting someone to help him get work.

JUSTICE WILLS: You are an old public-school boy. Was it not repugnant to your public-school ideas, this habit of sleeping with men?

TAYLOR: Not to me. Where there is no harm done, I see nothing repugnant in it.

Grain then reexamined Taylor. He remarked that since Taylor's bankruptcy one of his brothers had been making him a small allowance. "A very small sum," Taylor said.

At 12.15 p.m., Taylor left the witness box and returned to the dock. He had given evidence for an hour and three-quarters. In his address to the jury for the defense, Grain said that he believed his client had emerged almost triumphantly from this ordeal. The jury, he observed, would have no further doubt in finding Taylor not guilty of the counts on which he was charged, since the counts were supported through the tainted evidence of men, every one of whom had left the witness box a self-confessed criminal. There was, Grain stated, not the slightest corroboration of any kind in the Parker brothers' statements, and thus the jury should not convict on these witnesses' statements alone, since these were tainted witnesses. With regard to the charge of procuring: Grain submitted that the prosecution had altogether failed to make its case. He maintained that when a man or woman took to the abominable business of procuring young persons for immoral persons, they did so for gain. But in this case, there had never been any suggestion that Taylor had received money from Oscar Wilde. Not one penny had been extracted from anyone with respect to the crimes that had been imputed to Taylor.

Grain proceeded to acknowledge that the introduction of Harrington into the proceedings was nothing other than a dramatic tactic that had no possible object except to imply that the offenses had been committed by Harrington and Taylor, and thus to discredit Taylor's evidence in the minds of the jury. Grain pointed out that Taylor had ample reason during the past two years to know that he was under suspicion, and that the police were watching him. Taylor, Grain noted, had nothing to keep him in England, and he could not, had he gone abroad, have been extradited on any of the charges that were now brought against him. Instead of doing that, however, Taylor had preferred to await his trial. Taylor had elected to go into the witness box, and to submit to the searching cross-examination of the counsel for the Crown. Grain added that Taylor's demeanor was incompatible with that of a guilty man. In conclusion, Grain begged the jury to clear their minds of all preconceived notions, and to give the accused the benefit of every reasonable doubt.

Lockwood then reviewed the whole case for the prosecution. He referred to Grain's contention that there was a complete absence of corroboration. Lockwood pointed out that corroboration in a matter of this kind could not possibly be of a direct nature, and, quite short of that, there was sufficient corroboration to support the evidence. If stronger corroboration were needed for a conviction, he argued, this terrible vice would rear its head in our midst unchecked. How, he asked, could there be direct independent corroboration? Of its very nature, this vice was carried out secretly. Lockwood treated it as an accepted fact that Taylor's rooms in Little College Street were "a place taken in this secluded street as a place where persons who had these filthy appetites might meet and gratify them." [103] For what honest purpose, Lockwood asked, could the ill-assorted dinner parties at Kettner's have been brought together? The court adjourned for luncheon at 1.30 p.m.

The *Star* observed about the resumption of the court's business: "Refreshed by a slight luncheon, Sir Frank Lockwood concluded his address at twenty minutes past two with a scathing denunciation of unnatural affections, and a strong appeal to the jury to make an example of the prisoner."[104] Lockwood's comments began by focusing on the corroboration of evidence. He remarked that he had not alluded to what was alleged to have taken place between Wilde and Parker at St. James's Place.[105] A waiter from the private hotel in St. James's Place, Lockwood commented, had corroborated Parker's evidence on that point. If it were not corroboration, he asked, then in the name of commonsense, what was corroboration?

At this point, Grain raised an objection stating that it was not possible for him, as Taylor's counsel, to call Wilde to give evidence for Taylor, since Wilde was himself awaiting trial at the moment. In response to Grain's objection, Justice Wills remarked: "You could not be expected to call Mr. Oscar Wilde. I shall tell the jury that." Lockwood commented that he was not attempting to state that Wilde could or should be called.

Lockwood continued by stating that he agreed with Grain about the grave nature of the charge and the responsibility he had in establishing the charges that had been made. He had, however, listened patiently to evidence. What kind of corroboration did Grain expect to have been produced? If, Lockwood contended, the prosecution was bound to produce direct evidence, they would be powerless to check this vice. He noted that Grain had asked the jury not to believe Charles Parker because this young man had been mixed up in blackmailing. But, the solicitor general asked, was there ever a word to suggest that Charles Parker had attempted to blackmail Mr. Wilde? What, Lockwood inquired, had Charles Parker to gain, and how much had he to lose, through the story he told? Although Charles Parker and William Parker would be shunned and loathed, they had not gained a penny or had any object in coming to court.

The solicitor general proceeded to observe that on these matters Charles Parker's evidence was as fully corroborated as possible. With regard to Wood, Lockwood admitted that this witness was a man who had fallen low enough to be a blackmailer and the associate of blackmailers. Yet Wood, he noted, was also a friend of Taylor's, and Wood had stayed at Taylor's rooms without any inappropriate activity taking place. After speaking for twenty minutes, Lockwood completed his speech for the prosecution. He concluded by telling the jury that if they believed the story of the Parkers to be true, they must not shrink from returning a verdict of guilty.

The *Star* noted that the mood of the court changed once the judge commenced his summing-up: "It was like a lull in a storm when Mr. Justice Wills, in a still small voice, began a dispassionate review of the evidence."[106] He concentrated on the necessity of insisting on independent corroboration of charges of this dreadful character.

> JUSTICE WILLS: There would be a great terror added to life if that rule were not observed. If I had not thought that in respect of all these charges there was corroborative evidence fit to be submitted to you in respect of each one of these, which did not depend upon the testimony of these accomplices, I should most undoubtedly have stopped the case. The weight of such corroboration is entirely a question for you, gentlemen of the jury.

Justice Wills then laid before the jury a distinction between the various charges upon which Taylor was being tried. He emphasized that a prisoner was never convicted on the uncorroborated evidence of persons who were his accomplices in the crime with which he was charged. The judge proceeded to note that the greater part of the evidence, up to the point where indecency was alleged, was admitted. This was evidence that showed an association between men of education and position with uneducated men-servants, which was certainly remarkable. The Parker brothers, he observed, had declared that improper conduct had taken place, and in his lordship's opinion there was sufficient corroboration to warrant the case going to the jury. It was for the jury to decide whether, in their opinion, there was corroboration that should weigh with them. It might very well be the case that, although there was evidence proper to be left to the jury, they might not think it sufficient to justify conviction. There could be no doubt, he said, that the Parkers were introduced to Wilde by Taylor; but as to the charge of procuration, the question divided itself under two heads: the introduction and the object of it. But unless the jury thought that Taylor's introduction of Wilde to the Parkers led to the alleged consequences, it was nothing, and if it led to such consequences without Taylor's knowledge, it was also nothing. And unless the jury was satisfied as to the subsequent stories that Charles Parker had told, then the introduction amounted to nothing. God forbid, he stated, that he as the justice should for a moment entertain the thought that for one man to give another supper—no matter how greatly such men were removed socially—was sufficient ground for suspicion, not even though the one gave money to the other.

If, Justice Wills maintained, Wilde knew that the Parkers were sharing the same bed with Taylor, it was a strange thing that a man of Wilde's education should have admitted them, or even Taylor, to his intimacy. Since the jurors knew about the life and manners of this country, Justice Wills asked them whether the giving of such a dinner to these young men was sufficient foundation for the story that had been told. Yet Taylor had denied the suspicious part of the incident. Thus, it was for the jury to decide for themselves whether they should believe either the Parker brothers or Taylor.

After analyzing all of the evidence, Justice Wills stated that there was a strong line of demarcation between his duty and the jury's duty. It would, he noted, be an ill day for the administration of justice when juries did not act and think for themselves. He would say that he was absolutely impartial, having no thought but to strive to do his duty. He reminded the jury that anything that he had said that might seem either for one side or the other they must discard. The jury, he stated, must judge for themselves whether the evidence was conclusive.

Justice Wills then moved to the specific counts upon which the jury would have to give a verdict. In the charge of procuration regarding Wood, there had not been corroboration, and, on that charge, he advised the jury to find a verdict of not guilty. The second charge against Taylor, Justice Wills continued, involved the commission of deeds that were revolting to human nature. He noted that Taylor, under examination, had given corroborative evidence as far as corroborative evidence could go in the direction of proving such an act. It was apparent from Taylor's statements, the judge commented, that the prisoner had sunk much lower than the social level that he had maintained when a public schoolboy. The description of Taylor's rooms, Wills observed, pointed to what he called an unhealthy effeminacy, which in itself alone might be nothing, but in connection with the visits of the young men of questionable character to those rooms, this was something that the jury could not overlook. In conclusion, the judge remarked that he did not remember a case that had given him more trouble and anxious care. If the jury had any reasonable doubt as to the prisoner's guilt, the prisoner was entitled to the benefit of the doubt. If, however, they believed that the charges had been satisfactorily proved, they had but one duty—though it was a sad one—to perform.

The *Galignani Messenger* expressed hesitancy about the manner in which Justice Wills put forward his arguments in relation to the second charge against Taylor:

> [T]his was a very different charge from that made by Mr. Justice Charles. Throughout, his lordship seemed to be going directly in support of a verdict of guilty, not only against Taylor, but also, by very broad complication, against Wilde. He frequently contrasted sharply "the scholar and the gentleman" with "that ex-valet whom you have seen, and with whom you can tell how far you would yourselves like to consort." In speaking of Taylor's admissions, too, that he had allowed the Parkers to share his bed, he described them as "living as three decent people ought not to live, especially people in Taylor's position of life." Frequently, he referred to Taylor's bringing up, and the feeling of repugnance [Taylor] ought to have felt; but then it was evident that he had sunk much lower than he was when he came into that fortune which was his ruin. [Justice Wills] had never tried a case which gave him so much pain; but if they felt that the story of the prosecution was proved they must give their verdict fearlessly. If they fell short of that, then the defendant was entitled to acquittal.[107]

The jury retired at 3.25 p.m. to consider their verdict. At 3.55 p.m., the jury sent in a note to Justice Wills, who at once returned to the bench. His lordship called upon Taylor to stand. The jury then came in, and, in answer to the usual question, the foreman announced that they disagreed on the charge of procuring the commission of offenses by Parker and Wilde. Then the foreman stated that the members of the jury were not agreed as to the wording of the counts that the judge had placed before them.

In response, Justice Wills said that he thought the best thing to do was to write down for the jurors the exact wording of the particular counts of the indictment to which the foreman had referred. When the judge had done this, he inquired whether the jury was agreed upon the other counts. The foreman stated that the jurors were agreed upon the other counts. Justice Wills thought that he need not trouble the jury with respect to the wording of the other counts, but he asked whether the solicitor general was in attendance. The clerk of arraigns duly reported.

HENRY KEMP AVORY: I have sent for him, my lord.

JUSTICE WILLS: I cannot see any earthly reason for dealing with the other counts, but I will wait and see what the solicitor general has to say.

Immediately, Lockwood came into court, and after consulting with Gill, he said that as far as the prosecution was concerned, they would accept the verdict of the jury upon two counts. Grain, on behalf of Taylor, offered no objection.

Justice Wills ruled that the jury could be discharged regarding the second and third counts—those of procuring.

The foreman then stated that they found a verdict of guilty on the count alleging indecency against Taylor with Charles Parker, and also upon the count of charging Taylor of indecency with William Parker.

At the direction of Justice Wills, the jury delivered a verdict of not guilty on the count charging Taylor with procuring Wood. The jury was discharged from giving a verdict on the counts for procuring Charles Parker and William Parker.

Justice Wills announced that he would postpone sentencing until after the charges against Wilde had been heard. At this point, Taylor was removed to the cells. Clarke began to make an application on Wilde's behalf.

CLARKE: With regard to the case of the other defendant: Mr. Wilde is here in attendance, of course; but it is getting late, and perhaps, after a second jury has disagreed on this matter—

LOCKWOOD (*angrily*): My lord, I must protest against my learned friend making these little speeches.

JUSTICE WILLS: You can hardly call it a disagreement, Sir Edward. If it is material to go at once with the case, I should not for a moment think of discharging the jury, and should have kept them here for two or three hours more.

LOCKWOOD: It was merely the expectation that some such use might be attempted to be made of the decision that caused me, even for a moment, to hesitate to take the verdict, but I was perfectly satisfied that the verdict should be entered.

JUSTICE WILLS (*to Clarke*): Do you say you prefer it should be taken tomorrow morning?

CLARKE: I am quite content to proceed now if the Crown is going on—but with a different jury, of course.

LOCKWOOD: I think, perhaps, my lord, it would be better that we should commence it tomorrow morning.

JUSTICE WILLS (*to the jury*): Very well. I may repeat what I said yesterday, that I was most anxious to keep these two cases separate, and in these circumstances you, gentlemen, having heard the evidence in this case, I think it is most proper, in the interest of securing a fair trial, that you should not try the next case, and that it should be heard by a jury from the next court who have heard nothing of this case at all.

It was agreed that Wilde's case should begin on the following morning, and that another jury should be empaneled to try it.

THE TRIAL OF OSCAR WILDE

Third Day: Wednesday, 22 May 1895

The *Star* opened its commentary on the third day of the proceedings by drawing attention to the exceptional circumstances in which Oscar Wilde found himself at the Central Criminal Court:

> It does not often happen to anyone to make three appearances at the Old Bailey at three consecutive sessions, before three different judges. It was, therefore, quite in accordance with Mr. Oscar Wilde's boast of not posing as being ordinary that he should achieve this extraordinary distinction. He first appeared before Mr. Justice Henn Collins to prosecute his charges of libel against the Marquess of Queensberry, who was found not guilty. Wilde was thereupon arrested on the motion of the public Prosecutor, and tried at the last sessions before Mr. Justice Charles on charges of gross indecency, with regard to which the jury disagreed. This morning he surrendered to his bail for retrial before Mr. Justice Wills and a new jury. Since he was first arrested, the charges against him have been somewhat modified and reduced. On the other hand, the man Taylor, who was first charged as his accomplice, has been found guilty of "attempting to commit the abominable crime" with William Parker and Charles Parker, and it remains to be seen how far this may

> prejudice Wilde. It is in [Wilde's] favour again that the counts of conspiracy with Taylor to procure the commission of immoral acts were withdrawn at the last trial, and that the jury yesterday could not agree as to the count charging Taylor with procuring for Wilde.
>
> The jury empanelled this morning is a dozen of potent, grave, and reverend signors. There are three courts sitting, and the juries are frequently changed. Jurors are sometimes in waiting for a week before being called at all. They are called in the order of their names on the list, and never know till they are called what case they will have to hear.[108]

The press recorded that Wilde arrived early at the Old Bailey, and it commented on his haggard appearance, as well as the disordered nature of his hair.[109] Initially, Wilde sat on the usher's bench below the jury box, opposite his leading counsel, Sir Edward Clarke. Counsel for the prosecution—the solicitor general Sir Frank Lockwood, Mr. C. F. Gill, and Mr. Horace Avory—were in attendance when Mr. Justice Wills took his seat upon the bench at 10.30 a.m. Once he was called upon to surrender, Wilde stepped into the dock, where he sat down at the farthest distance from the jury. The *Star* noted: "He anxiously gnawed his fingers, or played nervously with his suede gloves."[110] After the clerk of arraigns instructed the usher to swear the jury for a misdemeanor, he read out the indictment. The indictment was now straightforward, since the charge of conspiracy had been removed. It alleged that the prisoner unlawfully committed certain acts with Charles Parker, Alfred Wood, certain persons unknown, and Edward Shelley. "To this indictment," the clerk added, "the prisoner pleads not guilty."

The solicitor general proceeded to present the case to the jury. The defendant was charged, he said, with offenses against the Criminal Law Amendment Act 1885, between 20 February 1892 and 22 October 1893. Lockwood stated that he would deal with these charges in chronological order. The *Star* remarked: "[I]t was observed that by adopting this course [the solicitor general] played his trump card first by putting forward the case of Shelley, his only principal witness who had not been more or less discredited by admissions of complicity in blackmailing."[111] Lockwood recalled the circumstances under which Wilde met Shelley, who was a lad of eighteen or nineteen, employed in the office of Wilde's publishers, Mathews and Lane, at The Bodley Head in Vigo Street. Wilde invited Shelley to dine at the Albemarle Hotel.[112] Shelley accepted Wilde's invitation, and dined with his host in the public room. Afterward, also at Wilde's invitation, they adjourned to a private room, and eventually went to bed together, where indecent acts were committed. There was, the solicitor general continued, independent corroboration of Shelley's story, though such corroboration did not go to the length of describing the details of the offenses. Acts such as these, he pointed out, were not committed in the light of day, but—as far as possible—with the strictest secrecy and concealment.

Lockwood then stated that in January 1893 Wilde made the acquaintance of Alfred Wood: a young clerk out of employment who at that time was living at 13 Little College Street ("'a house,' the *Star* recalls the solicitor general as saying, 'occupied by a man of the name of Taylor' . . . the assumption [was] that the jury had never heard of Taylor before").[113] He described Wood's curious introduction to Wilde. A telegram from Lord Alfred Douglas summoned Wood to meet Wilde at the Café Royal. Once Wilde had met Wood at the Café, he escorted the young man to a luncheon at Kettner's restaurant in Rupert Street. Subsequently, Wilde took Wood to his home at Tite Street, Chelsea, where the offenses charged in the indictment were alleged to have taken place. Lockwood mentioned that Wilde gave Wood two £10 and two £5 notes, and Wood gave Wilde certain letters in return. As Millard remarks: "It was not difficult to see what that transaction meant."[114] In January 1893, Wilde provided Wood with funds to travel to America, where Wood hoped to establish a career. After giving Wood these funds, Wilde stayed on good terms with the young man, entertaining him at luncheon in a luxurious manner.

The next part of the indictment, Lockwood observed, related to offenses committed with persons unknown at the Savoy Hotel in March 1893, when Wilde and Douglas occupied rooms 361 and 362, respectively, which were adjoined. Of the occurrences that took place there, he maintained, there was the valuable corroborative evidence of the hotel servants. The evidence he was prepared to offer, the solicitor general stated, was very direct. He said he would call a chambermaid, who would state that on going into the room in the morning she saw a boy in Oscar Wilde's bed. She would also, he noted, be able to give other evidence of a convincing nature. A masseur, who attended Wilde, would give similar evidence.

The last section of the case, Lockwood stated, was that in which Wilde was charged with misconduct at the Savoy Hotel and at rooms that he had occupied at 10 and 11 St. James's Place, with Charles Parker, whom Taylor had introduced to Wilde. The solicitor general spoke of the dinner that the Parker brothers had enjoyed with Wilde, and he maintained that Charles Parker's evidence would be corroborated in very material particulars.[115] On one occasion, he commented, Wilde visited Parker at the young man's lodgings in Park Walk, and a woman in the same house would tell that she heard Parker come in with someone, and that she saw Wilde leave the house. As a consequence of a statement that this lodger had made to the landlady, Parker left his rooms the next day.

LOCKWOOD: Gentlemen, I have endeavoured to limit myself to a plain and simple statement of the class of testimony which the prosecution is in a position to call before you. In conclusion, I can only invite your very earnest and careful attention, for, indeed, it is upon this evidence that the defendant must be judged, and not upon any statements made by counsel.

Mr. C. F. Gill then called for Edward Shelley, and "the gaunt young bookseller" (as the *Star* styled him) "stalked into the witness box."[116] "The reproof administered at the last trial by Mr. Justice Charles," the newspaper observed, "had taken its effect, for the witness comported himself more quietly, and with fewer airs of a blighted genius and a Christian martyr."[117] Shelley deposed that he was only seventeen when he was hired to work as a clerk at The Bodley Head publishers in Vigo Street, and his young age at the time accounted for his modest amount of pay, which initially was only 15s. a week. Shelley stated that he first dined with Wilde at the Albemarle Hotel, in a public room. Afterward, Wilde asked him to stay all night at the hotel, and he shared Wilde's bed.

While Shelley was giving his evidence, the Marquess of Queensberry arrived from Great Marlborough Street Magistrates' Court.[118] He was, the *Star* commented, "flushed with haste—or victory—and was allowed to take a seat at the end of the judicial bench":

> As [Queensberry] stared across at the prisoner, he smiled broadly, as though he realized and relished the change of positions since Wilde was in the witness-box and himself in the dock. The court was full of curiosity to know what had happened at Marlborough Street. But no information was for the time forthcoming. Wilde at first seemed quite oblivious of Lord Queensberry's presence. He passed the morning in an attitude of fixed dejection, hardly ever changing his position, except to exchange a few words with his solicitor across the front of the dock. There was little enough in the proceedings to rouse his attention.[119]

At noon, Clarke rose to cross-examine Shelley. He elicited replies that showed that Wilde's intimacy with Shelley lasted only three months and terminated nine or ten months before Shelley left his position at the publishers Mathews and Lane. In March 1893, Shelley went to see Wilde at the Savoy Hotel, where they quarreled, and after that incident Shelley wrote to Wilde that he would not see him again. Clarke pointed out that Wilde had replied to the effect that if it had been the case that Shelley had written that letter a few months earlier, it would have stung Wilde. But since, as Clarke noted, the letter arrived when it did, Wilde—since he was enjoying the success of *A Woman of No Importance*—did not feel so upset. The *Star* reported that at the pretrial hearing in Bow Street Magistrates' Court, Shelley had said that it was toward the end of

1893 or in early 1894 that he quarreled with Wilde.[120] Under Clarke's present cross-examination, however, Shelley could not remember whether he did not say that impropriety took place only on one occasion. Today, he spoke of two such incidents. On the first occasion, Shelley stated, he was not quite sober. He was, he added, excited, but drunk. If, he went on to say, he had realized what was going to happen, he would have resented it.

CLARKE: Then why did you go there again?
SHELLEY: I was weak, of course.
CLARKE: Within what space of time did these two incidents take place?
SHELLEY: Within a week?
CLARKE: Did you think Mr. Wilde also had too much to drink?
SHELLEY: No.
CLARKE: Then did it seem to you an accidental occurrence?
SHELLEY: No. I was entrapped. He knew I admired him very much, and he took advantage of me—of my admiration, and of—I won't say innocence—I don't know what to call it.
CLARKE: Has Wilde ever given you money?
SHELLEY: Yes, long afterwards.
CLARKE: Not as the price of consenting to this?
SHELLEY: No.
CLARKE: Have you ever published any works of your own?[121]
SHELLEY: I have written some, but have never published anything.
CLARKE: Did you ever show them to Mr. Wilde?
SHELLEY: No.
CLARKE: Despite what you allege, did your friendship for Mr. Wilde continue up to the spring of 1893?
SHELLEY: Yes.
CLARKE: Had your mental health begun to fail in October 1892, Mr. Shelley?[122]
SHELLEY: I don't think so.
CLARKE: But it had failed in March 1893?
SHELLEY: Yes. I had overworked myself.
CLARKE: You say, though, that in October you were in a great state of mental worry brought on by insomnia?
SHELLEY: Yes.
CLARKE: And I suppose that from October '92 to March the next year you gradually grew worse?
SHELLEY: Yes.

At this point, Clarke's cross-examination turned to Shelley's correspondence with Wilde. The letters revealed that Shelley had held Wilde in high esteem at the start of their acquaintance. Clarke asked Shelley to read out each letter:

Sunday Evening, 21 February 1892

Dear Mr. Oscar Wilde,—

I must again thank you for *The House of Pomegranates* [a book of stories that the witness parenthetically explained were "not fit for children"] and the theatre ticket. It was very good of you to send them to me, and I shall never forget your kindness. What a triumph was yours last night [the first night of *Lady Windermere's Fan*]. The play is the best I have seen on stage, with such beauty of form and wit that it adds a new phase of pleasure to existence. Could Lady Blessington live anew, the conversations would make her jealous. George Meredith might have signed it. How miserable everything seems beside it! Except, of course, your books. But then your books are part of yourself.[123]

Eight months later, the witness wrote the following letter to Wilde:

27 October 1892

Dear Mr. Oscar Wilde—

Will you be at home Sunday evening next? I am most anxious to see you. I would have called this evening, but I am suffering from nervousness, the result of insomnia, and am obliged to remain at home. I have longed to see you all through the week. I have much to tell you. Do not think me forgetful in not coming before, because I shall never forget your kindness, and am conscious that I can never sufficiently express my thankfulness to you.[124]

CLARKE: Now, Mr. Shelley, do you mean to tell the jury that, having in your mind that this man had behaved disgracefully towards you, you wrote this letter?

SHELLEY: Yes, because after these two occurrences he treated me very well. He seemed really sorry for what he had done. He introduced me to his wife. I dined with them twice, and he seemed to take a real interest in me.

As the *Galignani Messenger* observed, Shelley's revelation about the hospitality he received at the Wilde family's Tite Street home "created a deep sensation" in the court.[125]

The witness then disclosed that Wilde offered him £100 to go away and study, but Shelley refused it. He stated that John Lane, the publisher, had also tried to assist him, and the court learned that in his "hysterical letters" to Wilde (as the *Star* characterized them) Shelley wrote about "the brutal insults of Vigo Street."[126] Shelley's correspondence revealed that he had written to Wilde about leaving the "harsh horrible existence of The Bodley Head" for a clerkship in the City of London.[127] Besides speaking of his plans to resign from Mathews and

Lane, Shelley informed Wilde that he was contemplating moving to Chelsea, where he could "read with a coach in the evening."[128] Shelley stated that his parents had accused him of idleness, which was the reason that he had written of "eating the bitter food of charity and contempt."[129] Shelley revealed that he had left his employment in the City of London before the libel trial, and he maintained that the only money that Wilde had ever given him was the 10s. that he had received at Kettner's restaurant.

Clarke drew the jury's attention to another of Shelley's letters:

> Oscar:—
>
> I want to go away and rest somewhere—I think to Cornwall for two weeks. I am determined to live a truly Christian life, and I accept poverty as part of my religion. But I must have health. I have so much to do for my mother.[130]

CLARKE: What did you have to do for your mother?[131]

SHELLEY: I pay for my keep. (*Some laughter in court.*)

CLARKE: That is surely more like doing something for yourself? Have you a brother who is permanently unwell?

SHELLEY: Yes.

CLARKE: Is his mind disordered?

SHELLEY: Yes.

Clarke alluded to further statements from the same letter that Shelley had sent to Wilde:

CLARKE (*reading aloud*): "I am an artist. I know that I am. Will you see if you can lend me £10 until Christmas. I can repay it by that time. I must have rest. I am weak and ill. I am so thin they think me strange."

The court learned that after Wilde did not lend the desired £10, Shelley made a further appeal for assistance in finding a place at either a publisher's or newspaper's office.[132] In reference to his old employer, John Lane, Shelley informed Wilde: "I would accept nothing from that viper. He hurt me too much. I despise him, but I cannot forget."[133] In response to Clarke's question about Shelley's motive for characterizing Lane as a viper, the witness could not suggest any intelligent reason.

CLARKE: If Wilde were the sort of person you should not know, why were you not grateful to Mr. Lane for trying to save you?

SHELLEY: Human nature—a failing of human nature.

Clarke focused attention on another letter that Shelley dispatched to Wilde: "You have deadly enemies in London. Hence the *Daily News* article."[134] Once these lines had been read aloud, Clarke questioned Shelley about the ways these letters revealed the witness's state of mind at the time.

CLARKE: Was your mental health getting worse and worse?
SHELLEY: I had made myself ill with studying at it. There is nothing the matter with me now.
CLARKE: Are you sure of that?
SHELLEY: Quite sure.

The court then discovered that Shelley had swallowed his pride and approached Lane for employment. By the next post, however, Shelley wrote once more to Lane stating that he would not take any offer from the publisher. And in yet another letter Shelley told Wilde: "I am afraid sometimes I am not very sane, I feel so nervous and ill."[135]

CLARKE: In January last, you committed an assault on your father?[136]
SHELLEY: Yes. I lost my temper.
CLARKE: And were you locked up?
SHELLEY: Yes.
CLARKE: And when you were arrested, you asked that a messenger should go for Mr. Wilde?
SHELLEY: Yes.
CLARKE: At that time was your mind deranged?
SHELLEY: I think I must have been out of my mind to assault my father.
CLARKE: In 1894, Shelley, was your mental health getting worse?[137]
SHELLEY: I won't say worse, but I was very ill, through over-study.
CLARKE: Were you worse than you are today?
SHELLEY: There is nothing the matter with me now. (*Laughter in court.*)
CLARKE: Are you quite sure?
SHELLEY: Oh, I am quite sure of that. (*More laughter in court.*)

At this juncture, the solicitor general reexamined Shelley. He pointed out that at the time Shelley was employed at The Bodley Head in Vigo Street, he was contented and happy. At the pretrial hearing, Lockwood noted, Shelley had not been asked to talk about the two occasions when Wilde committed indecencies with him. This evidence, the solicitor general went on to say, had not been heard at Bow Street because Sir Edward Clarke had made an express request that those proceedings should be taken very briefly. "Really, I—," Clarke interrupted. "I have every confidence in Mr. Gill," the solicitor general retaliated, noting that this was the suggestion he had taken from Gill. The *Galignani Messenger* observed: "Sir Edward lowered his eyebrows. In deep rage, he burst out: 'Indeed, Mr. solicitor, that is not the sort of remark you should make to me!'"[138]

"For a moment," the newspaper added, "there was intense excitement, as with deepening colour the two great lawyers glared at one another. But they saw in time that it would be only a mere personal squabble of cross feeling and not fine argument."[139] Lockwood recovered his temper, but he remarked that there was sufficient ground for Gill's observation about the pretrial hearing.

Before lunch, two further witnesses were called. Charles Elkin Mathews, who had recently been in the publishing partnership with John Lane at The Bodley Head, stated that he was aware of the intimacy that had developed between Shelley and Wilde. Thereafter, Aloys Louis Vogel, proprietor of the Albemarle Hotel, repeated the evidence that he had given at both the pretrial hearing and the first criminal trial.

Once the court resumed after lunch, Alfred Wood went into the witness box. Under Clarke's cross-examination, Wood repeated his evidence about Alfred Douglas's telegram, which summoned him to meet with Wilde at the Café Royal. Wood recalled that he had encountered Douglas at Taylor's rooms at 13 Little College Street. After he had greeted Wilde for the first time at the Café Royal, Wood accompanied him to the Florence restaurant in Rupert Street. As the press observed, Wood had disclosed all of this information as recently as the past Monday in the case against Taylor.

The *Galignani Messenger* took careful note of Wood's behavior:

> [H]e cast an anxious eye upon Sir Edward Clarke. But the confessed blackmailer soon regained his wonted impertinence as Sir Frank dealt with him in kindly tones. In the intervals of answering questions which revealed the story previously told, he turned calmly around towards the jury-box, and took almost as lengthy a view of the jury as they took of him. Wilde meantime sat scratching geometric designs with a quill pen on a scrap of blue paper.
>
> Neither Sir Edward, the judge, nor the foreman could get him to say when he was last honestly employed.[140]

CLARKE: Since you met Taylor, have you earned a single shilling—honestly?[141]

Wood replied that he had been working for his brother, but could not say when.[142] He had not, he said, wanted to work since he came back from America.

CLARKE: When did you work for your brother?
WOOD: I hesitate, because I do not want to drag his or anyone's name into it.
CLARKE: What is your brother?
WOOD: A commission agent.
JUSTICE WILLS: A turf agent?[143]
WOOD: Yes, my lord, but in a very small way.
CLARKE: How much did you earn from him?

WOOD: Oh, it varied.[144]
CLARKE: Where are you living now?
WOOD: Bromley Terrace, Greenwich.
CLARKE: Are you lodging there?
WOOD: I am living with a detective. (*Laughter in court.*)
CLARKE: A Crown detective?
WOOD: Yes.
CLARKE: In August last year was £400 or £500 paid to Allen by a gentleman?
WOOD: Yes.
CLARKE: And you received £175?
WOOD: Yes.
CLARKE: For what?
WOOD: I suppose it was blackmailing, but I did not know it then.
CLARKE: Where was that?
WOOD: At a house in Regent Street.[145]
CLARKE: What was the number?
WOOD: I do not remember.
CLARKE: Who lived there?
WOOD: I did.
CLARKE: Who was the young man concerned?
WOOD: Charles Parker.
CLARKE: Where was the money paid?
WOOD: Near the station at Charing Cross.

The *Star* clarified what was involved in the blackmailing incident that had taken place in August 1894: "the means of making the gentleman pay was a charge of indecency with Charles Parker at a corner house in Regent Street."[146] "The sensation this sort of thing caused," the *Galignani Messenger* remarked, "can easily be imagined."[147] The newspaper reported that Wood admitted that he had seen the gentlemen "writing something," with Parker and Allen present; the document was probably a cheque.

The remainder of Clarke's cross-examination involved various questions that sought to test the reliability of the witness's testimony.

CLARKE: Did you give Parker any money?
WOOD: Allen did.
CLARKE: How much?
WOOD: £30.
CLARKE: How long had you known Allen?
WOOD: From March or April 1893.
CLARKE: On what date did you go to America?

WOOD: I arrived on 1 April 1893.
CLARKE: Did you say at the police court that on a certain occasion you were drunk?
WOOD: I was not drunk, but I had too much to drink. I knew what I was doing.
CLARKE: Was there anybody else besides you and Allen and Charles Parker in the distribution of the money?
WOOD: No one else.
CLARKE: Have you had other transactions of the same kind?
WOOD: No.
CLARKE: How long had you been back from America?
WOOD: I came back in May.

Clarke then pressed Wood to talk about the money that this young man's father had left him. Wood stated that the amount was about £100. Wood could not tell where he got it, or what the solicitor paid him. After a time, however, when Justice Wills stated that Wood should name the solicitor, the witness said that it was "Tidy, Sackville Street."[148]

CLARKE: So, you say Mr. Tidy paid you £100?
WOOD: About that. It was £88 2s. 10d.

The cross-examination then moved to Wilde's private correspondence that Wood had appropriated from Alfred Douglas's clothing.

CLARKE: You have met Lord Alfred Douglas?[149]
WOOD: Yes, at his rooms at the "Varsity."[150]
CLARKE: He was kind to you?
WOOD: Yes. He gave me a suit of clothes while I was there.
CLARKE: And you found two letters in one of the pockets?[151]
WOOD: Yes.
CLARKE: From whom?
WOOD: From Mr. Wilde to Lord Alfred.
CLARKE: How did they begin?
WOOD: One was addressed "Dear Alfred," the other to "Dear Bosie.'"[152]

Wood admitted that William Allen had taken these letters from him, and that Allen, on returning the letters to Wood, kept one of them back. At the time, Allen told Wood: "I don't want any more. This one is quite hot enough."

CLARKE: Did you know what Allen meant?
WOOD: I did not. (*Laughter in court*.)
CLARKE: But had you read the letters?
WOOD: No. Not to my knowledge.

CLARKE: Had you?
WOOD: I do not remember. I think not.
CLARKE: Then how did you know they began "Dear Alfred" and "Dear Bosie"?
WOOD: I can't swear I read them. I may have glanced through them.

Clarke's cross-examination then moved to Wood's travel to America, which Wilde had funded. "I wanted," Wood said, "to get away from these people and the life."

CLARKE: What life?
WOOD: Eating these dinners.
CLARKE: What people?
WOOD: Wilde and Lord Alfred Douglas.
CLARKE: And though, at your request, Mr. Wilde gave you money to help you to go to America to begin life anew honestly, as you say, you came back, and in August got again with Allen, and had that £175.
WOOD: Yes.

The solicitor general then reexamined Wood.

LOCKWOOD: When did you first meet Lord Alfred?[153]
WOOD: At Taylor's rooms in Little College Street.
LOCKWOOD: Then you visited him at the university?
WOOD: Yes.

After Lockwood concluded his reexamination of Wood, Shelley was recalled at the request of Justice Wills, who wanted to know when Shelley first addressed Wilde as "Oscar." It began, Shelley said, at Wilde's request when the two of them dined together.

Charles Parker was the next witness. C. F. Gill began the examination. The witness repeated the evidence that he had previously given during the pretrial hearing, the first criminal trial, and the recent trial of Taylor. Charles Parker noted again that he had formerly been a valet and that he had enlisted in the Royal Artillery on 3 October 1894, where he had been a gunner. Subsequently, he recalled in great detail the meeting that he and his brother William had with Taylor at the St. James's bar. He mentioned the dinner that he and his brother enjoyed with Wilde and Taylor at a Soho restaurant. And then he recalled his experience in Wilde's rooms at the Savoy Hotel. On this occasion, however, as *The Trial of Oscar Wilde* observes, the witness's descriptions of the intimacy that he experienced with Wilde were more graphic than before. Charles Parker "relat[ed] the most disgusting facts in a perfectly serene manner": "He said that Wilde invariably began his 'campaign' before arriving at the final nameless act—with indecencies. He used to require the witness to do what is vulgarly known as 'tossing him off,' explained Parker quite unabashed, 'and he would often do the same to me. He suggested two of three times that I should permit him to insert "it" in my mouth, but I never allowed that.' He gave other details equally shocking."[154]

Clarke then opened his cross-examination. His questions focused on the blackmailing incident, to which he had referred in his cross-examination of Wood.

> CLARKE: Are you the Charles Parker who, in August 1894, received £30, part of money got by blackmail?
>
> CHARLES PARKER: I am.
>
> CLARKE: Where did the practices in respect of which that money was paid take place?
>
> CHARLES PARKER: At 7 Camera Square.

The press noted that Wood had sworn that the incident occurred at 72 Regent Street, Chelsea, although Parker swore that he was quite sure the blackmail took place in his lodgings at 7 Camera Square.

Clarke then asked Charles Parker for clarification about the indecencies that were alleged to have taken place at the Savoy.[155] Beforehand, in response to Gill's questions, the witness stated that Wilde had locked the sitting room door at the hotel.

> CLARKE: Are you sure?
>
> CHARLES PARKER: Yes.
>
> CLARKE: You have a clear recollection?
>
> CHARLES PARKER: Yes.

For further elucidation of this point, Clarke read out Charles Parker's reply at the previous trial, in which the witness declared that Wilde did not lock the door. Charles Parker responded to Clarke by remarking that he must have made a mistake in the earlier proceedings. It was, the witness noted, the bedroom door that had been locked. Clarke further established that since the first criminal trial Charles Parker had been maintained at the expense of the prosecution.[156] For the first time, Charles Parker admitted that he was currently living at Chiswick with his brother William, where both of them were under the care of the police, who had given them board and lodging.[157] Charles Parker added that he had not undertaken any military service since March 1895.

The case was adjourned at 4.45 p.m. until the next morning.[158] Wilde was again admitted to bail. Justice Wills advised the jury not to speak to anyone about the case.

Fourth Day: Thursday, 23 May 1895

The court at the Old Bailey was crowded when the trial against Oscar Wilde resumed on this morning. Once again, Wilde surrendered to his bail so that he could answer the charges aganst him under the eleventh section of the Criminal Law Amendment Act. Sir Frank Lockwood, Mr. C. F. Gill, and Mr. Horace Avory conducted the prosecution on behalf of the public prosecutor. Sir Edward Clarke, Mr. Charles Mathews, and Mr. Travers Humphreys defended Wilde. The press noted that among the individuals who arrived during the proceedings were the Marquess of Queensberry and his son Lord Douglas of Hawick, whose street fight near Piccadilly had been the subject of a hearing at Great Marlborough Street Magistrates' Court the previous day.

The first witness to be called was William Parker, the older brother of Charles Parker. The *Star* stated that he was "a dull-looking fellow in a brown tweed suit."[159] In his cross-examination, Clarke asked questions that tried to elicit previously unheard information about the Parker brothers' encounter with Alfred Taylor before they joined him for dinner with Wilde at a Soho restaurant.

CLARKE: Did you know that your brother was going to the Savoy for an indecent purpose?

WILLIAM PARKER: That is what Taylor gave us to understand.

CLARKE: Did you hear such a proposal made to your brother and not interfere to prevent it?

WILLIAM PARKER: No, I didn't then.

CLARKE: Had you intended to do the same sort of thing yourself?

WILLIAM PARKER: Yes, perhaps.

CLARKE: You were perfectly sober?

WILLIAM PARKER: Yes.

Lockwood then rose to reexamine William Parker and asked the following question: "What had Taylor said to you?" Clarke objected, stating that the question was irregular. Justice Wills sustained the objection, stating that Lockwood's question went a little too far. Lockwood resumed his seat.

"Then," the *Star* observed, "came a branch of the case on which the prosecution seem[ed] inclined to rely largely."[160] Several witnesses from the Savoy Hotel were called. Gill called on Charles Robinson, bookkeeper at the hotel, to produce the records of Wilde's stay there during March 1893. Jane Margaret Cotter, a chambermaid, gave evidence that she had seen a boy in Wilde's room. She deposed that Wilde occupied room number 362, while Lord Alfred Douglas stayed in room number 361, which had an adjoining chamber. Cotter remarked that she had to call the attention of the housekeeper Mrs. Perkins to the state of Wilde's bed. On the third morning of Wilde's stay, she continued, he rang the housemaid's bell at around 11.00 a.m. She met him in the door of room 361, and he told her that he wanted a fire in his room. It was then that Cotter saw in 362 a boy of eighteen or nineteen years of age, with dark, close-cropped hair and a sallow complexion. One or two days later, she recalled, Douglas left the hotel, and Wilde moved into rooms at the front of the premises. "Sir Edward," the *Star* noted, "then perpetrated a very neat bit of cross-examination."[161]

CLARKE: Why do you wear eyeglasses?
COTTER (*bashfully*): Because I am shortsighted.[162]
CLARKE: You always wear them when you are about your work?
COTTER (*snatching off her pince-nez*): Oh dear, no. I have only worn them today because I thought I might have to recognize somebody.
CLARKE: Then you did not wear them when you saw the boy in Wilde's room, since you had to put them on when you needed to recognize anybody?
COTTER: Yes, that's about the size of it.

Under Gill's reexamination, Cotter said she had distinctly seen what she alleged in the examination-in-chief. The next witness was Alice Saunders, another chambermaid from the Savoy Hotel, who corroborated Cotter's evidence. She said that she had been asked to give evidence the previous Friday. As Saunders was testifying, Percy Douglas came into court. He looked, according to *Reynolds's Newspaper*, "rather puffy about the eyes, and stood for some minutes in front of the dock talking with a representative of Wilde's solicitors": a sign that that he was still recovering from the punch-up with his father that had taken place in Piccadilly Circus two days before.[163] Thereafter, Antonio Migge, the freelance masseur who offered his services to guests at the Savoy Hotel, repeated for Gill the evidence that he, too, had witnessed a boy in Wilde's rooms. Migge stated that he went to Wilde's room to offer massage at the usual hour. He knocked on the door and entered. Wilde told Migge that there was no need for massage that morning.

Under Clarke's cross-examination, Migge was asked whether the bedroom door was locked or unlocked. "No," Migge stated, "the door was not locked." As Clarke posed further questions to the masseur, he discovered that Migge could not recall whether the boy was fair or dark. This part of the cross-examination was significant. "Sir Edward," Millard observes, "had again succeeded in shaking the credibility of a witness, and that, too, in a part of the case on which the prosecution very largely relied."[164]

Emile Becker, the waiter from the Savoy Hotel who had first been called the previous Monday in the case against Taylor, repeated under Gill's examination the evidence that he had seen young men in Wilde's rooms. Becker stated that he had seen five or so young men in total. The waiter recalled that he had taken champagne and whiskies and sodas to Wilde's room and had seen young men there. Becker stated that when Wilde had the sitting room at the front of the hotel, he had served a supper of cold fowl and champagne to Wilde and a young man.

Clarke, in his cross-examination, set out to show that Becker's recollections might have been due to his knowledge of press reports about the previous trial against Taylor.

CLARKE: I suppose you read the accounts of the previous trial?[165]

EMILE BECKER: Oh, yes.

CLARKE: You saw it stated that Charles Parker said he had chicken and champagne?

BECKER: I think I saw it on Monday.

JUSTICE WILLS: Had you not seen it before?

BECKER: No.

CLARKE: It was a matter of considerable interest to everybody at the Savoy Hotel?

BECKER: Yes, it was.

CLARKE: Did you read in the papers that Charles Parker said: "We had chicken and champagne for supper"?

BECKER: I don't know. I don't remember seeing it in the paper.

CLARKE: How many rooms had you to look after?

BECKER: Seven sitting rooms.

CLARKE: Plenty of suppers in such a busy place?

BECKER: Not many upstairs.

CLARKE: Have you seen Charles Parker?

BECKER: Yes, he was pointed out to me.

CLARKE: You did not recognize him?

BECKER: No.

Under reexamination, Becker stated that he had met with a police inspector at the Savoy Hotel on Friday, 17 May 1895.

Once Becker stepped out of the witness box, Annie Perkins—who now resided at Southsea, Hampshire—testified that she had been a housekeeper at the Savoy in 1893. Perkins stated under examination that her attention had been drawn to the condition of Wilde's room. To substantiate further the intimacy between Wilde and Charles Parker, the prosecution called Margery Bancroft, who was lodging at 50 Park Walk, Chelsea, when Charles Parker had rooms at that address in spring 1893. She testified that she saw Wilde come to Parker's lodgings one night, and she witnessed Wilde and Taylor depart from the residence together. Taylor, the court learned, lived nearby at 3 Chapel Street. Bancroft remarked that Taylor was constantly in and out of Charles Parker's lodgings. Under Clarke's cross-examination, however, Bancroft became less confident about her allegation that Charles Parker left 50 Park Walk with Wilde. She said that she saw the prisoner get into the cab, though she knew that her neighbor did not return to the house. Asked how she knew that Charles Parker did not reenter the house, Bancroft recalled that her dog would have barked if he had. Bancroft also asserted that she knew Wilde by sight; she said that he had been pointed out to her at the Royal Academy by two ladies, but she had never seen Wilde at 50 Park Walk. Bancroft added that she knew that Charles Parker's weekly rent was 5s., since she prepared the bills for the landlady. In response to the prosecution's reexamination, Bancroft stated that the cab in which Wilde drove away had three lights on it.

Just after 12 noon, the Marquess of Queensberry arrived. He had a yellow rose in his buttonhole and carried a silk hat on the head of his umbrella. Upon entering the court, he nodded familiarly to acquaintances in the reserved enclosure, making himself—in the words of *Reynolds's Newspaper*—"the cynosure of all eyes."[166] "Judge and stewards," the paper continued, "took no notice, and, after one indifferent stare, Wilde returned to his languid contemplation of the witness."[167] Once Bancroft completed giving her evidence, Lucy Rumsby, the landlady at 50 Park Walk, testified under examination, as did Sophia Gray, the landlady at 3 Chapel Street, where Taylor had lodged from August 1893 until the end of the year.

The next witness was the former police detective Fred Kerley. He, too, repeated evidence that he had given at both the pretrial hearing and the previous trial. In response to questions from the prosecution, Kerley spoke about the papers (telegrams, cheques, and tradesmen's bills) that he had discovered in the leather hatbox the landlady, Sophia Gray, had withheld from Taylor when he moved out of 3 Chapel Street. Subsequently, Thomas Price, a staff member at Geneux's private hotel at 10 and 11 St. James's Place, recounted once more his evidence that during Wilde's tenancy he slept there only a dozen times. The prosecution then called on Inspector Charles Richards and Inspector Thomas Brockwell. The police officers gave evidence about their arrest of Oscar Wilde at the Cadogan Hotel, 75 Sloane Street. Thereafter, the two court shorthand writers—John William Lehmann and Ebenezer Howard—testified about the notes they had taken on Wilde's libel suit against Queensberry in early April 1895. Lockwood then put in these shorthand notes as evidence, and he declared that he intended to read only those portions that referred to Wilde's relations with Charles Parker, Edward Shelley, Alfred Taylor, and Alfred Wood.

Clarke at once stated that he wished to read aloud the examination-in-chief from these notes on *Regina (Wilde) v. Queensberry*.

> JUSTICE WILLS: It won't be necessary to read the whole, I hope. (*Laughter in court.*)[168]

Clarke replied that he did not wish to read the whole document. Yet the moment he proceeded to read sections of the transcript aloud, a few people in the courtroom expressed their displeasure. "Sir Edward began," the *Star* noted, "to an accompaniment of thunderclaps, the reading of Wilde's evidence-in-chief, in the prosecution of Lord Queensberry for libel. This rapidly cleared the court."[169] In the meantime, as the tedious reading of the libel proceedings began, Wilde—as the *Sun* recorded—"amused himself once more with scratching sketches on a slip of paper with a quill pen": "By moving, he chanced to knock his papers over the top of the dock, and they fell among some of the young counsel standing near, to whom they gave no little amusement. But Wilde quickly leant over, and, tapping him on the shoulder who was holding the slips, repossessed himself of his papers, in the meantime looking severely and reprovingly at the limb of the law. He then tore them up into very small pieces and scattered them on the floor of the dock."[170]

Once Clarke finished his reading of the examination-in-chief, Lockwood started reading out loud the section of Carson's cross-examination that addressed Wilde's correspondence with Douglas. Lockwood passed lightly over a passage where Wilde complained about the unfair manner in which Carson read out these letters to Douglas, which put the worst construction possible upon the correspondence. Lockwood drew attention to certain phrases in the second of Wilde's letters that Wood had stolen from a suit of Douglas's clothes: "I would sooner," Wilde had informed Douglas in this correspondence, "be rented all day than have you bitter, unjust, and horrible." During the libel proceedings, Wilde had explained that "rent" was a slang term for blackmail. Lockwood then dwelt on another passage in which Wilde had written: "Why are you not here, my dear, my wonderful boy? I fear I must leave—no money, no credit, and a heart of lead."[171] Gill relieved Lockwood of the reading of the notes until the court adjourned for lunch at 1.30 p.m.

As the *Star* observed, there were various strategic issues that emerged for Wilde's counsel when Lockwood read out selected excerpts of the proceedings:

> Sir Frank Lockwood had promised that his reading should be confined to passages which relate to Wood, Shelley, Parker, and Taylor. But he first read,

> sonorously and appreciatively, the sparring between Wilde and Mr. Carson about the prisoner's correspondence with Lord Alfred Douglas. It was suggested that if Sir Edward Clarke were permitted to read Wilde's examination-in-chief at the last trial, he would not call him to give evidence again. It is, of course, to the interest of the prosecution to refuse to read the notes of the last trial, so as to get Wilde into the witness-box, subject to the cross-examination of the solicitor general. The situation had therefore become critical, and during the luncheon interval both Mr. C. Mathews and Mr. Travers Humphreys went down to the cells to confer with Wilde.[172]

By 2.15 p.m., when the court resumed its business, Avory—who took up the next segment of reading—had only made his way to the start of the second day of the proceedings in the libel trial against Queensberry. It took until 3.00 p.m. before the court heard the last of the prosecution's evidence from *Regina (Wilde) v. Queensberry*.

Before proceeding any further, Clarke submitted that there was no case to go to the jury upon the counts alleging indecent practices at the Savoy Hotel. Charles Parker, Clarke said, had sworn that he left the hotel on both occasions soon after midnight, and so he could not therefore be identified with the boy whom the hotel staff claimed they saw during the mornings.

Justice Wills, however, said that various things had been put together to prove something else, which was a process that he would do his best to point out to the jury. The condition of the rooms, the judge maintained, presented a certain amount of corroboration of the charges. The very fact, he said, that a man in such a position of life as Wilde was found with a boy in his bed seemed so utterly unusual that very little additional evidence would make a case to go to the jury. Then again, Justice Wills remarked that although two witnesses had sworn that whatever had occurred in Wilde's rooms had been reported to the housekeeper, it was very strange to think that she should have done nothing at the time. The judge said that he did not know what sort of person she could have been not to take steps in the matter at once.

> CLARKE: That being so, I hope your lordship will relieve me from the necessity of dealing with it.[173]

Lockwood contended it might be that the Savoy's management was reluctant to publicize a scandal that would be prejudicial to the hotel. He could not say whether that was or was not a high motive, but it was one that would obviously operate in such a matter.[174]

Meanwhile, Clarke submitted that there was no evidence that Wilde and the boy were in bed together. On this point, Justice Wills agreed. He said that the fact that Wilde had rung for the chambermaid to come into the room made it difficult to accept the story in its entirety. From the point of view of evidence, the judge stated that the masseur Migge's testimony was even more slender. It would not, Justice Wills commented, be fair to an individual charged like Wilde that a number of nothings should make up a something. The judge, however, thought that it would be wiser to leave the whole matter to the jury, since the responsibility for assessing the evidence was ultimately theirs. At the same time, he felt that the question of this evidence was so uncertain that he would reserve it for the Court of Criminal Appeal, if the prosecution so desired.[175] Lockwood asked for the whole of the charges to be left to the jury; he maintained that the jurors could weigh the worth of the evidence.

At this juncture, Clarke submitted the significant point that there was no corroboration regarding Edward Shelley, and thus it was the case that Shelley's evidence should be withdrawn from the jury. Lockwood, in turn, asked what the relations were between these two men—Wilde and Shelley—who were of such unequal ages. The solicitor general declared that he would invite the jury to understand that Shelley was a young man who was fascinated by Wilde's literary culture, and who was brought through his companionship under Wilde's control and domination—that Shelley was, as he put it, "entrapped," and that Shelley was thus not so much an accomplice as a victim. There was, Lockwood contended, a certain amount of corroboration—evidence of opportunity.

Justice Wills remarked that he had to confess that in the case of Shelley there was an important difference from the others.[176] In Shelley's case, the judge continued, there were traces of disturbed intellectual and actual delusions.[177] Moreover, the judge stated that Shelley's manner in the witness box conveyed that this young man was stamped with a particular excitation, which was a common accompaniment of mental disturbance. There was, too, Justice Wills observed, mental derangement in the Shelley family, since the witness had a brother who was incapacitated. Moreover, the judge noted that Shelley did not stand on the same footing as the other men. No one, he said, who had read Shelley's letters could claim that they were written for money. Then again, Justice Wills could not see any corroboration in Shelley's statements. At this point, the judge noted (as Justice Charles had before him) that it would be a terrible thing for society at large, if it were considered unnatural for a man to ask a younger man of good character to dine with him at his club or house and then thought to be evidence of guilt.

Lockwood called attention to the evidence, and he claimed that there was ample corroboration. He reminded Justice Wills of the letter in which Shelley said: "Let God judge the past." Lockwood then pursued a complex argument to support his view. He stated that, in light of the very grave importance of the case to the defendant, and regarding the difficulty of producing direct corroboration, even though it was the case that Shelley was not an accomplice, Shelley's story was nonetheless corroborated. For this reason, the case ought to be left with the jury.[178]

In response, Clarke submitted that he had no intention of following his learned friend but wished to keep instead to the legal points. Clarke noted that, according to Shelley's own evidence, the witness was an accomplice. It had, he said, been stated over and over again that the corroboration should relate to certain facts about the truth or falsehood that proved or disproved the offense, and such substantiation in this instance remained entirely absent. In Clarke's view, the corroboration stopped at the very point where the innocence stopped.

Justice Wills then made a judgment. He said that he had entertained a very clear view in regard to the case, and thus he arrived at a decision without hesitation. In the first place, he argued, Shelley must be treated as an accomplice. It was, he remarked, a rule of law that, when an offense was proved by the evidence of an accomplice, there was no case to go to the jury unless the evidence of the accomplice was corroborated in some particular or other that rendered it highly probable that the offense was committed. Justice Wills could see nothing—apart from what Shelley himself had said—in the admitted facts that was inconsistent with a perfectly honorable relationship with Wilde, and he added that the letters from Shelley that Wilde had put in as evidence ran against the notion that there was anything dishonorable between the two men. As a result, the judge said that it was his duty to withdraw Shelley's case from the jury.

Clarke then asked the judge to adopt the same perspective in the case of Wood. He pointed out that there was no corroboration of any sort that Wood had been to Wilde's family home at Tite Street, Chelsea. Lockwood responded by stating once more that there was ample corroboration. He protested against having these cases withdrawn from the jury. There was, he noted, corroboration in the payment that Wilde made to enable Wood to travel to America. The solicitor general quoted letters to show that, although Justice Wills had rightly stated the rule of practice, it was not a rule of law, and that it was the duty of a judge to tell the members of the jury that they might—if they pleased—act on the unconfirmed testimony of an accomplice.

Clarke instantly rose to his feet to cite other authorities that made points to the contrary, and he remarked that the contention that "the wholesome practice of our Courts for certainly 200 years" was really an inflexible rule.[179] It was, he said, cruel to suggest that the generous action of a man such as Wilde, who gave Wood the means of getting away from bad companions to begin a new life in another country, was corroboration of his own misconduct. "For the first time in the course of this case," the *Star* noted, "applause was heard in various parts of the court at this point."[180] Justice Wills decided that he must leave the case of Wood to the jury.

In the meantime, Clarke did not extend his contention about the lack of corroboration to the case of Charles Parker. By then, it was nearly 4.00 p.m., and Clarke had to elect either to call Wilde or to allow Lockwood to begin the presentation of the prosecution's case to the jury. Clarke indicated his intention of putting Wilde in the witness box by appealing to the judge.

CLARKE: I presume your lordship will not ask me to go on now?[181]
JUSTICE WILLS: No, tomorrow morning.

The court was adjourned at 4.00 p.m.[182]

The *Star* reflected on the day's proceedings:

> Excitement in court was intense when his lordship intimated his intention of withdrawing from the jury the Shelley case, which has been universally regarded as the strongest against the prisoner. Wilde for the first time sat up erect. Counsel for the Crown were obviously taken by surprise, and turned in confusion to their law books. The solicitor general for the moment lost his temper, and held towards the judge the same truculent attitude that he has throughout adopted with Sir Edward Clarke. His lordship wore a very worried look, and seemed much relieved when Sir Edward Clarke proposed an adjournment. Wilde was again released on bail, and left the court with his sureties.[183]

Fifth Day: Friday, 24 May 1895

As the *Star* pointed out, once the trial against Oscar Wilde resumed at the Old Bailey on Friday, 24 May 1895, "[t]here was a simmer of excitement . . . when it became known that Wilde was to give evidence in his own behalf."[184] His counsel awaited him when he arrived with his sureties, Stewart Headlam and Percy Douglas, at 10.00 a.m. On arriving at court, Wilde spoke for a few minutes with his junior counsel Mr. Travers Humphreys at one end of the same bench. Sir Frank Lockwood and Mr. C. F. Gill were in consultation over their briefs at the other end of the bench. Once Wilde finished his conversation with Humphreys, he spoke with his sureties while facing the witness box. At 10.30 a.m., when Justice Wills arrived, Wilde was called upon to surrender his bail. Wilde then took a seat at the corner of the dock, where—as the newspaper observed—"he began to amuse himself with a pen and a piece of paper." When Sir Edward Clarke arrived, the solicitor general rose in order to reopen the controversy about Justice Wills's decision to withdraw Shelley's evidence from the jury. On the previous day, Lockwood had cited miscellaneous cases in support of not withdrawing Shelley's evidence. This morning he quoted a more recent case, *Regina v. Meunier*, in which Mr. Justice Cave had said that no doubt it was the practice to warn a jury that they should not convict unless they thought the evidence of an accomplice was corroborated.[185] At the same time, the judge admitted that he knew of no power to withdraw the case from the jury for want of corroborative evidence. In response to Lockwood's argument, Justice Wills stated that he preferred to adhere to the course of action he had taken as the result of careful deliberation. He did, however, say that he was willing to put to one side the question for the consideration of the Court of Crown Cases Reserved.[186]

Clarke then opened the case for the defense. He "embarked," the *Star* noted, "on one of the finest of the many admirable orations which have been heard from him in this court."[187]

CLARKE: I shall call Mr. Wilde into the witness box again to state on his oath for the third time in this court that there is no truth whatever in those accusations which are made against him, and to face for the third time in this court, and now with a new assailant, that cross-examination which may be administered to him in regard to these accusations.[188] When he has given that evidence and when he has been cross-examined, the case will be complete, and it will be my duty then to address you upon the character of the evidence with which you are asked to deal.

But first I have to say a few words about my learned friend Sir Frank Lockwood's conduct of the prosecution. I had the honour to hold the office of solicitor general, which Sir Frank Lockwood now holds, for a longer period than any man has held it during the last 100 years. And having been solicitor general for six years, it is not likely that I, at any place or time, will speak lightly of the responsibilities of that office. But I always look upon the responsibility of a Crown counsel, and especially upon the responsibility of a law officer of the Crown, as a public rather than a private interest or responsibility. He is a minister of justice, with a responsibility more like the responsibility of a judge than like that of a counsel retained for a particular combatant in the forensic fray. I learned my work in this court from the best example I ever saw of a law officer conducting criminal cases: that great advocate, Sir John Holker, who twenty years ago was conducting great cases in this court with a determined fairness which I admired, and at the time I trusted I might be able to emulate.[189] While, therefore, I say these things without the least unfriendliness of feeling towards the solicitor general, I say them in the hope that it might do something to induce my learned friend to remember what I feared for a moment yesterday that he had forgotten: that he was here to lay before the jury for their judgment the facts on which they would be asked to come to a very serious consideration. I have now to answer but the remnant of a charge.

Some weeks ago, the indictment contained twenty-five counts, some of which were counts for conspiracy, and on which indictment there was a point reserved which could be argued if necessary.[190] Suddenly, the counts for conspiracy were withdrawn, and as to the other counts the jury were discharged because they could not agree upon a verdict. Then came this trial. When the case was more important than it is now, it was not thought necessary to have a law officer of the Crown to conduct the prosecution, but it was left to the practised and competent hands of Mr. Gill. I did not have to remonstrate with Mr. Gill on any point of his address. But now came down a law officer. There is a strange and invidious distinction belonging to the law officers of the Crown. Why they enjoy it, I do not know. I never availed myself of it when I was a law officer, and I would not do so if it were my fate to fill the position again. It was the privilege of the attorney general and the solicitor general, when they came down to prosecute, that if the defendant had called no witnesses at all, the law officer had the last word. That was an important change. Mr. Wilde had twice given a denial to these charges, but he was kept in prison without bail contrary to practice and, as he believed, contrary to law. Now, broken as he is—and no one who saw him when he came into the court for the first time can fail to see what has happened to the man—broken as he is by the anxiety of these successive trials, I might have spared him the indignity of having to go into the witness box, to go through the ordeal of repeating his denial on oath.[191] But if I did not call him, I knew what the reply of the solicitor general would be. A further hardship was thus inflicted upon Mr. Wilde.

I made an application that these persons [i.e., Wilde and Taylor] be tried separately, and it was decided that they should be tried separately. I was here representing Mr. Wilde, who was the first person mentioned in the indictment, and I claimed that he should be tried first. I cannot imagine any reason or logic or fairness which might be suggested for the course which was adopted for trying the other defendant first. In Taylor's case, the jury were unable to agree as to the issue referring to Mr. Wilde, and were discharged without giving a verdict as to that issue. Practically, this was the third time that this issue has been placed before a jury. There can be no cause for complaint against me, if I feel a little soreness at the treatment which Mr. Wilde has sustained. I ask the jury to remember that it was Mr. Wilde's own action in preferring the charge of libel against the Marquess of Queensberry that has brought about this inquiry. I cannot leave one observation unmade. In the evidence given by Mr. Wilde at the hearing of the charge of libel against the Marquess of Queensberry, there was only one statement that was contradicted by an independent witness. Mr. Wilde had never been to Park Walk, and a woman had been called on the part of the prosecution who stated that she had seen a gentleman—a gentleman, she said, who was Mr. Wilde—drive away in a hansom cab from Park Walk. She was the only independent witness who contradicted any statement made by Mr. Wilde.

I ask the jury to remember these things in relation to the question with which you have to deal. What I have to say as to the character of the witnesses on whose evidence you are asked to reply are observations that I will make hereafter. I submit that, on the evidence set before you, you cannot come to any other conclusion than that it is your duty to acquit Mr. Wilde.

Wilde was called at 11.10 a.m., and at Clarke's request he took a seat in the witness box. The prisoner's "voice," according to the press, which had been "so full and confident" at the first trial, "had become hollow and husky, and he seemed glad to lean over the front of the witness-box."[192] Clarke began his examination by asking general questions about Wilde's friendship with Lady Sibyl and her sons, Percy and Alfred. He then asked Wilde about the marquess's libelous visiting card. Wilde provided details about the production of his various plays, and he stated that it was for convenience of composing his literary work that he took rooms at the private hotel at 10 and 11 St. James's Place.

WILDE: Most literary men like to work out of their own house. It is quieter—and better.

Clarke proceeded to observe that in the course of Wilde's evidence during the libel case Wilde was asked certain questions regarding Charles Parker and Alfred Wood, in answer to which Wilde made certain statements.[193]

CLARKE: Were all of those statements absolutely true?

WILDE: Entirely.

CLARKE: Have you any qualification or alteration to make in regard to those statements?

WILDE: No. I have no observation to make.

CLARKE: Is there any truth whatever in the accusations made against you in the indictment?

WILDE: None, whatever.

"The reply," the press noted, "came with emphasis, and with something of the old rotundity."[194]

Once Lockwood rose in order to begin his cross-examination, Wilde also rose.

LOCKWOOD: Don't rise, please, unless you wish.
WILDE: I can hear better.

After a few minutes, however, Wilde sat down. The solicitor general began by asking about the beginning of Wilde's acquaintance with Alfred Douglas.[195]

LOCKWOOD: When did you first know Lord Alfred Douglas?
WILDE: At the beginning of 1892.
LOCKWOOD: And when did the Marquess of Queensberry first object to your intimacy with Lord Alfred Douglas?
WILDE: In March 1893.
LOCKWOOD: Are you sure?
WILDE: I am very bad about dates. It must have been last year, 1894.
LOCKWOOD: Where is Lord Alfred Douglas now?
WILDE: Abroad.
LOCKWOOD: Where?
WILDE: He is in Paris, at the Hôtel des Deux Mondes.[196]
LOCKWOOD: When did he go?
WILDE: About three weeks ago.
LOCKWOOD: Did he leave after the first trial?
WILDE: No, he stayed for a while after the Queensberry trial.
LOCKWOOD: Did he stay until your first trial as defendant?
WILDE: No. He went away to France at my own wish.
LOCKWOOD: Of course, you have been in communication with him?
WILDE: Certainly. These charges are founded on sand. Our friendship is founded on a rock. There has been no need to cancel our acquaintance.[197]
LOCKWOOD: What did you do when you learned that the Marquess of Queensberry objected to your friendship for his son?
WILDE: I said I was perfectly ready to cease the acquaintance if it would make peace between him and his father. But he preferred to do otherwise.
LOCKWOOD: And the intervention of the father had no effect?
WILDE: No.

The solicitor general then read aloud from the two items of correspondence that Wilde had sent to Douglas, which had been used as evidence on several previous occasions: the libel trial, the pretrial hearing, and the first criminal trial. (The full texts of these letters appear on 77–78 above.)

LOCKWOOD: Are these a sample of the style in which you addressed Lord Alfred Douglas?

WILDE: No. I do not think I should say a sample. No! The letter written from Torquay was intended to be a kind of prose poem in answer to a poem he had written to me in verse. It was written under the circumstance of great feeling.

LOCKWOOD (*reading*): "My Own Boy": Is that the way you usually addressed him?[198]

WILDE: I do not say usually, but often. He was much younger than I was. It was a fantastic, extravagant way of writing to a young man. As I said at the first trial, it does not seem to me to be a question of whether a thing is right or proper, but of literary expression. It is a little like a sonnet of Shakespeare.

LOCKWOOD: I did not use the word proper or right. Was it decent?

WILDE: Oh, decent? Of course. There is nothing indecent in it.

LOCKWOOD (*emphatically*): You understand the meaning of the word, sir?

WILDE (*quietly*): Yes.

LOCKWOOD (*reading*): "Your sonnet is quite lovely. It is a marvel that those red rose-leaf lips of yours should be made no less for the music of song than for the madness of kissing." Now, I ask you this, Mr. Wilde, do you consider that was a decent way of addressing a youth? Do you think that was a decent way for man of your age to address a man of his?

WILDE: It was a beautiful way for an artist to address a young man of culture and charm. Decency does not enter into it.

LOCKWOOD: Then I ask you whether you consider it a decent mode of addressing a young man?

WILDE: I can only give you the same answer. It was a literary mode of writing to another, intended to be a prose poem.

LOCKWOOD: Do you consider it decent phraseology?

WILDE: Oh, yes. Yes.

LOCKWOOD (*reading*): "Your slim gilt soul walks between passion and poetry . . . Hyacinthus, whom Apollo loved so madly, was you in Greek days." You were speaking of love between men?

WILDE: What I meant by the phrase was that he was a poet, and Hyacinthus was a poet, and—. (*Wilde's voice became inaudible.*)

LOCKWOOD (*reading*): "Always, with undying love"?

WILDE: It was not a sensual love.

LOCKWOOD: Is that again poetic expression or an expression of your feelings?

WILDE: That is an expression of my feelings. (*Wilde smiled and bowed to Clarke.*)

The solicitor general proceeded to read from the second letter, which begins "Dearest of All Boys" and concludes "Ever Your Own Oscar" (see 78). This is the document where Wilde regrets how Bosie, who is "so Greek and gracious," had said "hideous things to him." Millard notes that Lockwood took pains to read this document in a manner "in which even the most innocent expressions of friendship, and of harmless humour could be constructed into a bad meaning."[199]

LOCKWOOD: That, I suppose, is true—that is, not poetic?

WILDE: Oh, no, no. That was prose of the most sordid kind. (*Suppressed laughter in court.*)

LOCKWOOD (*continuing to read*): "I have also got a new sitting-room over the Thames—but you, why are you not here, my dear, my wonderful boy—? I fear I must leave; no money, no credit, and a heart of lead—Ever your own Oscar." He came and stayed with you at the Savoy?

WILDE: Yes, in the month of February.

LOCKWOOD: Did he come to you in response to that appeal?

WILDE: He came shortly afterwards on his way to Germany.[200]

LOCKWOOD: How often did he stay with you at the Savoy Hotel?

WILDE: Three times.

LOCKWOOD: You were alone, you two?

WILDE: Oh, yes.

LOCKWOOD: The approach to your room was through his?

WILDE: Yes.

LOCKWOOD: Were you aware of his father objecting to your acquaintance?

WILDE: Oh, no.

LOCKWOOD: What was the charge which Lord Queensberry made against you?

The press noted that, in response to this question, Wilde hedged a little with Lockwood, presumably because the defendant was reluctant to utter in court the words that Queensberry had written on the visiting card.[201] But Wilde eventually articulated the offensive message: "posing as a sodomite."

LOCKWOOD: Between Lord Queensberry's committal and his trial, did you and Lord Alfred Douglas go abroad?

WILDE: Yes. We were abroad about a week, and I returned to appear as prosecutor.

LOCKWOOD: Before the trial, did you see Lord Queensberry's plea of justification?

WILDE: Yes.

LOCKWOOD: That plea alleged all the misconduct of which evidence has since been given, besides making charges which have not been heard because they refer to occurrences in Paris?

WILDE: Yes.

LOCKWOOD: Did you abandon the prosecution?

WILDE: It was abandoned by the advice of my counsel.

LOCKWOOD: With your consent?

WILDE: Yes. I admit that it was with my consent. But none of those matters has been entered into. It was entirely about literature, and it was represented to me that I could not get a verdict because of the two letters you have read.

LOCKWOOD: Was Taylor present?

WILDE: I did not see him during the trial, but he sent me a letter.

LOCKWOOD: Were you not cross-examined as to your knowledge of Taylor and his character?

WILDE: Yes.

LOCKWOOD: And as to the establishment he maintained at 13 Little College Street?

WILDE: Yes.

LOCKWOOD: How long had you known Taylor?

WILDE: I met him first in September 1892.

LOCKWOOD: How many times have you been in the College Street "snuggery" of the man Taylor?[202]

WILDE: Yes, I paid visits to his rooms, but I have not been there more than five or six times in my life.

LOCKWOOD: Was there any but male society there?

WILDE: On, no. Entirely male.

LOCKWOOD: Youths?

WILDE: Oh, young men.

LOCKWOOD: What were their names?

WILDE: I met Mavor and Schwabe there. I only went to tea parties lasting half an hour or so, and I cannot after a lapse of three years remember who I met. You ask me to remember whom I met at a tea party three years ago. It is childish. How can I?

LOCKWOOD: Did you meet Charles Mason there?

WILDE: No. I met him at a dinner.

LOCKWOOD: The boys Wood, Mavor, and Parker—what was their occupation?

WILDE: One doesn't ask people their occupations at a tea party.

LOCKWOOD: Did Taylor strike you as being a very pleasant companion?

WILDE: Yes. I thought him very bright.

LOCKWOOD: Did you know what his occupation was?

WILDE: No. I understood that he had none.

LOCKWOOD: Had any of these young men any occupation?

WILDE: Oh, there were young men—singers—I did not ask.

LOCKWOOD: Did you see anything remarkable in the furnishing of Taylor's rooms?

WILDE: No. Nothing.

LOCKWOOD: The windows were curtained?

WILDE. Yes, but not obscured.

LOCKWOOD: Did you know that Taylor's male friends stayed with him and shared his bed?

WILDE: No. I know it now.

LOCKWOOD: Does that alter your opinion of Taylor?

WILDE: No. I don't think so. I don't think it is necessary to conclude that there was anything criminal. It was unusual. I don't believe anything criminal took place between Taylor and these boys. And if they were poor and he shared his bed with them, it may have been charity.

LOCKWOOD: Did it shock that he should have done it?

WILDE: No. I saw no necessity for being shocked.

LOCKWOOD: I must press you. Do you approve of his conduct?

WILDE: I don't think I am called upon to express approval or disapproval of any person's conduct.

LOCKWOOD: Would the knowledge that they habitually shared his bed alter your opinion of Taylor?

WILDE: No.

Clarke objected that the prisoner should be asked for his opinion of another person's conduct. Justice Wills sustained the objection, though he added that it came too late. At this point, Lockwood focused on the gifts that Wilde had made to the young men he had met through Taylor. Wilde objected to the general character of Lockwood's inquiry. Still, he disclosed the information about each of the presents he had made. Wilde recalled giving Sydney Mavor a cigarette case, which cost £4.

LOCKWOOD: Did you give one [i.e., a cigarette case] to Charles Parker?

WILDE: Yes, but I am afraid that only cost £1.

LOCKWOOD: Silver?

WILDE: Well, yes. I have a great fancy for giving cigarette cases.

LOCKWOOD: To young men?

WILDE: Yes.

LOCKWOOD: How many have you given?

WILDE: I might have given seven or eight in 1892 and 1893.

Justice Wills observed that a cigarette case did not convey any impression unless one knew what Lockwood meant. Lockwood tried another tack.

LOCKWOOD: Was the conversation of these young men literary?

WILDE: No. But the fact that I had written a play which was a success was to them very wonderful, and I was gratified at their admiration.

LOCKWOOD: The admiration of these boys?

WILDE: Yes. I was fond of praise. I liked to be lionized and made much of.[203]

LOCKWOOD: By these boys?

WILDE: Yes.

LOCKWOOD: Whose very names you don't remember?

WILDE: Yes. I admit that I am enormously fond of praise and admiration, and that I like to be made much of by my inferiors—inferiors socially. It pleases me very much.

The press noted that Wilde "resumed the languid, affected drawl of the Queensberry cross-examination."[204]

LOCKWOOD: What pleasure could you find in the society of boys much beneath you in social position?

WILDE: I make no social distinctions.

LOCKWOOD: What did you do with them?

WILDE: I read to them. I read one of my plays to them.

LOCKWOOD: Did it not strike you that in your position you could exercise a considerable influence over these lads for good or ill?

WILDE: No. I am bound to say that I don't think it did. The only influence I could exercise on anybody would be a literary influence. Of course, in the case of these young men that would be out of the question. Otherwise, I don't see what capacity I have for influencing people.

LOCKWOOD: I did not mean literary influence.

WILDE: I like to be liked. I liked their society simply because I like to be lionized.

LOCKWOOD: You, a successful literary man, wished to obtain praise from these boys?

WILDE: Praise from anyone is very delightful. Praise from literary people is usually tainted with criticism.

LOCKWOOD: You had not known Taylor many months when you invited him to dine on the occasion of his birthday, and gave him carte blanche to bring his friends?

WILDE: That is so.

LOCKWOOD: Did you limit the number?

WILDE: Oh dear, no.

LOCKWOOD: As many as he liked?

WILDE: Well, I did not ask him to bring a crowd.

LOCKWOOD: Then it was a pure coincidence that the table was laid for four, and that he brought the two Parkers?

WILDE: No. I think he ordered dinner for himself. I told him to go to Kettner's because I have been in the habit for years of dining there.[205]

LOCKWOOD: Did you know at the time that the Parkers were a valet and groom respectively?

WILDE: No, and had I known it, I should not have cared.

LOCKWOOD: You have no sense at all of social differences?

WILDE: No.

LOCKWOOD: You preferred Charles?

WILDE: I make no preference.

LOCKWOOD: You like bright boys?

WILDE: I like bright boys. Charles Parker was bright. I liked him.

LOCKWOOD: Did you not pause to consider whether it should be of the slightest service to lads in their position to be entertained in such a style by a man in your position?

WILDE: No. They enjoyed it as schoolboys would enjoy a treat. It was something they did not get every day. I don't suppose they would have cared to be entertained to a chop and a pint of ale. They were used to that.

LOCKWOOD: You looked on them as schoolboys?

WILDE: They were amused by the little luxuries of Kettner's, the pink lampshades and so forth.

LOCKWOOD: Did you give them wine?

WILDE: Yes, I certainly should not stint a guest.

LOCKWOOD: You would let them drink as much as they liked?

WILDE: I should not limit their consumption. But I should consider it extremely vulgar for anyone to take too much wine at table.

LOCKWOOD: After dinner, what did you do?

WILDE: I bade the Parkers goodbye, and they went away with Taylor.

LOCKWOOD: Did you not take Charles Parker to the Savoy Hotel?

WILDE: No. Certainly not.

LOCKWOOD: Was Taylor charming?

WILDE: Charming is not the word I would apply to him. I found him bright and pleasant.

LOCKWOOD: Intellectual?

WILDE: Not intellectual. Clever, decidedly.

LOCKWOOD: Artistic?

WILDE: Yes.

LOCKWOOD: Very good taste with his scents and—?

WILDE: I think it good taste to use perfumes. I thought his rooms were done up with considerable taste. I think he had very pleasant taste. His rooms were cheerful.

LOCKWOOD: Not a very cheerful street, Little College Street?[206]

WILDE: Few streets are cheerful. I have known artists who have lived quite close to there.

LOCKWOOD: Did you like the situation?

WILDE: I thought it a particularly nice one—close to Westminster Abbey. (*Laughter in court.*[207])

LOCKWOOD: Is it true that when you met Parker in Trafalgar Square, you said: "You are looking as pretty as ever"?

WILDE: No. I don't think I used those words.

LOCKWOOD: Would you consider such words right to use to a youth?

WILDE: Oh, no. It would be frivolous.

LOCKWOOD: You don't object to being frivolous?

WILDE: Oh, I—

Clarke objected to the cross-examination pursuing subjects that were not connected with the charges. Justice Wills, however, thought that Clarke was not justified in raising an objection.

LOCKWOOD: Did you ever sup alone with any young man at the Savoy Hotel at that time?

WILDE: I could not remember. You are asking me of three years ago. Lord Alfred Douglas may have been with me.

LOCKWOOD: But he would have been perfectly well known to the waiters at the Savoy?

WILDE: Oh, yes.

LOCKWOOD: Wherever you are well known, he would be?

WILDE: I don't know that.

LOCKWOOD: You have stayed together at the Savoy, at the Albemarle, at the Avondale, at St. James's Place, at the Metropole in Brighton, at Cromer, and Goring, at the Albion at Worthing, and at Torquay?

WILDE: Yes. He has not stayed with me at St. James's Place, but I have lent him my rooms there.

LOCKWOOD: Did Charles Parker ever visit you?

WILDE: He might have visited me seven or eight times at St. James's Place, and on one occasion he dined with me at Kettner's, and we afterwards went to the Pavilion.

LOCKWOOD: When did you last see him?

WILDE: In December last, in the street.

LOCKWOOD: Did you receive this letter from him?

7 Camera Square

Dear Oscar:

Am I to have the pleasure of dining with you this evening? If so, kindly reply by messenger or wire to the above address. I trust you can, and we can spend a pleasant evening. With kind regards and apologies,

Yours faithfully,
Chas. Parker

WILDE: Yes. I remember receiving that letter.

LOCKWOOD: Did you respond to the invitation?

WILDE: No. I don't think so.

LOCKWOOD: Did you ever go to see Parker at his Chelsea lodgings?

WILDE: No. I am certain I didn't.

LOCKWOOD: How much money have you given Charles Parker in cash?

WILDE: Four or five pounds.

LOCKWOOD: Why?

WILDE: Oh, I give young men money with pleasure.

LOCKWOOD: Do you remember a young man named Scarfe?

WILDE: Yes. Taylor brought him to see me. Scarfe represented himself as a young man who had made money in Australia.

LOCKWOOD: Why was he brought to you?

WILDE: Because many people at the time had great pleasure and interest in seeing me.

LOCKWOOD: Did he call you Oscar?

WILDE: Yes.

LOCKWOOD: At once?

WILDE: I had to ask him to. I have a passion for being called by my Christian name. It pleases me.

LOCKWOOD: Did you give him a cigarette case?

WILDE: Yes.

LOCKWOOD: Has he dined with you alone?

WILDE: Yes.

LOCKWOOD: Do you remember Alphonse Conway?

WILDE: Yes. I met him on the beach at Worthing last year in August. He was seventeen years old. He had an ambition to go to sea.

LOCKWOOD: Of what station in life is he?

WILDE: Of no particular station.

LOCKWOOD: Did he not sell papers on the pier?

WILDE: Oh, never when I was there.
LOCKWOOD: What was his mother?
WILDE: She was a widow, and let lodgings.
LOCKWOOD: Did you buy him a suit?
WILDE: Yes, of blue serge.
LOCKWOOD: And a stick?
WILDE: Yes.
LOCKWOOD: And took him to Brighton?
WILDE: Yes, we had a twenty-four hours' trip to Brighton. That was a month afterwards.
LOCKWOOD: What rooms had you at Brighton?
WILDE: Two bedrooms and a sitting room. We slept in adjoining rooms.
LOCKWOOD: When did you see Conway last?
WILDE: Outside the court two days ago.

The press noted that, at this point of Lockwood's cross-examination, when he was asking Wilde about the "moral effects of the trip on [Alphonse], there was time to observe that today Lord Queensberry could not get a seat, but had to stand at the back of the reserved enclosure, where he sucked on the brim of his hat and stared across at the witness with twinkling beady eyes."[208] Moreover, journalists also reported that "the witness . . . had constantly to sip at the frequently replenished glass at his side."[209]

LOCKWOOD: Do you know Harrington?
WILDE: Yes. I met him in the company of Schwabe at the Café Royal.

At this point, Lockwood produced two scarfpins.

LOCKWOOD: Did you give a pin to Harrington?[210]
WILDE: I did not.
LOCKWOOD: What—?

Since there appeared to be some confusion about the scarfpins that Lockwood believed had been a gift from Wilde to Harrngton, the judge interposed.

JUSTICE WILLS (*to the jury*): Of course, gentlemen, you must take that denial. There is no right to contradict it.

At this juncture, Lockwood pursued his cross-examination by turning to Wilde's knowledge of Alfred Wood.

LOCKWOOD: Did you ever meet Wood by appointment at the Café Royal?
WILDE: Yes. I had been asked to assist him, and took him to supper at the Florence. I had already had supper myself.

LOCKWOOD: Then why not give him five shillings to go and get his supper?

WILDE: Ah, that would be treating him like a beggar. He was sent to me by Lord Alfred Douglas.

LOCKWOOD: Did you know that he came from 13 Little College Street?

WILDE: No. I did not know that. He told me he was a clerk out of employment, and was anxious to find employment. I could not do that, but I gave him money.

LOCKWOOD: Why should he be sent to you for money?

WILDE: The money was not really from me, but was from Lord Alfred Douglas, who was at Salisbury.

LOCKWOOD: There are such things as postal orders, I believe?

WILDE: Yes.

LOCKWOOD: Did you tell him that your people were away from home at the time?

WILDE: Yes.

LOCKWOOD: Why?

WILDE: It occurred to me in the course of conversation.

LOCKWOOD: When did you see Wood next?

WILDE: About two days afterwards, by appointment, at the Café Royal.

LOCKWOOD: Why should you meet him again?

WILDE: I had been asked to interest myself in him.

LOCKWOOD: You have heard since that Wood was staying at Taylor's?

WILDE: No.

LOCKWOOD: Did you not know that at the time Lord Alfred Douglas had met him at Taylor's?

WILDE: No.

LOCKWOOD: Who told you first that Wood was anxious to leave the country?

WILDE: Taylor.

The press commented on Lockwood's next move as follows:

> The solicitor general passed rapidly forward to the time at which Taylor told Wilde that Wood wished to go to America, and Wilde learned through an anonymous letter that he was to be blackmailed because of his stolen correspondence with Alfred Douglas. Wilde went to Sir George Lewis, and then Taylor came to him with a story that Wood was very much distressed and concerned, and arranged the meeting at Little College Street. The witness stated that Wood gave him the letters as soon as he entered the room. They were, he said, letters of no importance.[211]

LOCKWOOD: Where are they?

WILDE: I tore them up. They were of no importance.

LOCKWOOD: But you gave Wood money for them?

WILDE: I then gave Wood £15, but it was not as the price of the letters. I had gone prepared to bargain for them if they were worth buying back.

LOCKWOOD: To bargain for what?

WILDE: For those letters.

LOCKWOOD: And you took money with you for the purpose?

WILDE: Yes.

LOCKWOOD: Do you mean on your oath to say that the payment had nothing to do with the delivery of those letters?

WILDE: None whatever.

LOCKWOOD: And you got the letters?

WILDE: Yes.

LOCKWOOD: And gave him luncheon and an additional sum of £5 on the following day?

WILDE: Yes.

LOCKWOOD: And he went to America?

WILDE: Yes.

LOCKWOOD: From that time did you hear from him or of him till you saw his name in the plea of justification?

WILDE: No.

LOCKWOOD: Do you know a boy named Walter Grainger?

WILDE: He was a servant in Lord Alfred Douglas's lodgings at Oxford. He asked me if I could get him a place in London.

LOCKWOOD: Did you find him a place?

WILDE: Yes.

LOCKWOOD: Where?

WILDE: In my own house at Goring.

LOCKWOOD: When did he come?

WILDE: I should think it was in July 1893. He remained in my service until I left Goring in October.

LOCKWOOD: You have seen him here, I dare say?

WILDE: Yes.

LOCKWOOD: When you stayed at the Savoy, had you young men there to see you?

WILDE: The great majority of my friends were young.

LOCKWOOD: Were you ill at the Savoy?

WILDE: Yes.

LOCKWOOD: You were attended by a masseur?

WILDE: Yes.

LOCKWOOD: Did the masseur come to see you when you were occupying rooms 343 and 346?

WILDE: Yes.

LOCKWOOD: In reference to the Savoy Hotel evidence, is it true that the masseur and the chambermaid saw boys in your room?

WILDE: Entirely untrue. No one was there.

LOCKWOOD: There was no one there, man or woman?

WILDE: No.

LOCKWOOD: You answer also that the chambermaid's statement is untrue?

WILDE: Absolutely.

LOCKWOOD: You deny that the bed linen was marked in the way described?[212]

WILDE: I do not examine bed linen when I arise. I am not a housemaid.

LOCKWOOD: Were the stains there, sir?

WILDE: If they were, they were not caused in the way the prosecution so filthily suggests.

The solicitor general concluded his cross-examination at 1.30 p.m., when the court adjourned for luncheon. From the *Sun*'s perspective, it was surprising that Lockwood ended his inquiries at this point: "There were several who thought he was only just beginning."[213] During the lunch period, the paper also noted, Queensberry left the court, walked down the Old Bailey, and then found himself surrounded by so many people that he took a hansom in order to escape their attentions.

Reynolds's Newspaper observed that, after the adjournment, Wilde "returned to the dock obviously feeling that he had gone through a troublesome experience with less annoyance than he had anticipated."[214] The *Galignani Messenger* concurred about Wilde's demeanor. Once the court resumed its business, the paper remarked that the "experiences of the morning had, indeed, been an ordeal"; Wilde, the report continued, "looked thoroughly shaken."[215] As Wilde answered his counsel's next round of questions, the *Star* noted that his spirit appeared to be increasingly broken: "Wilde stood, his foot on a seat, his elbow on his knee, his chin in his hand. When free to return to the dock, he dragged his feet heavily across the court, and seemed both ill and exhausted."[216]

Clarke opened his reexamination with various questions about Wilde's libel case against the Marquess of Queensberry.

CLARKE: On the cross-examination of yourself in the Queensberry trial, a name was written on paper as the name of the person who introduced Taylor to you. Was that person whose name was then suppressed Mr. Schwabe?[217]

WILDE: Yes.

CLARKE: Is Mr. Schwabe a gentleman of wealth and position?

WILDE: Yes.

CLARKE: Taylor was well educated, and a clever musician?

WILDE: A very clever musician. He used to sing and play a great deal in his rooms.

CLARKE: Had you any idea at the time of your acquaintance that Taylor was addicted to improper practices?

WILDE: I had no conception whatever—no conception whatever of anything of the kind.

In answer to Clarke's further questions, Wilde added that he was perfectly well known at both Kettner's and the Florence restaurant. He told the court that he had been in the habit of going to Kettner's ever since he left Oxford in 1879.

CLARKE: Had you any interest in Wood beyond the fact of Lord Alfred Douglas knowing him?

WILDE: None, except that Lord Alfred asked me to take an interest in the young man and be kind to him.

CLARKE: When Wood brought the letters to you, did he attempt to get money from you for them?

WILDE: No. He at once handed me the letters and said he highly regretted I should have thought him capable of trying to blackmail me.

CLARKE: Is it then positively untrue that you gave Wood £15 for the letters?

WILDE: I would not have given him fifteen pence for them. They were of no importance.

CLARKE: Was there anything that you would object to have known?

WILDE: There may be people who would regard some of the words of the letter as frivolous, but then there was nothing in the letters. They were of no importance.

Reynolds's Newspaper noted that, as Wilde made this reply, he "waved his gloves to-and-fro with a gesture of disregard for the people there may be."[218] Wilde's response concluded Clarke's reexamination, and Wilde returned to the dock.

Clarke then presented to the jury his case for the defense.

CLARKE: Having in my mind the observations which, under some stress of feeling, I made in the early part of the day, I may state at the outset that I recognize the admirable fairness with which the solicitor general cross-examined Mr. Wilde.[219] And if earlier in the day I was moved by what I am glad to think I then described as the momentary forgetfulness of my learned friend yesterday to expressions which sounded hostile in regard to him, he will let me say at once, in the frankest manner, that the way in which he has cross-examined absolutely destroys any suggestion which might have lain in my words. Mr. Wilde had for the third time given evidence under circumstances more arduous and difficult than perhaps evidence was ever given by a witness before. You will realize how strong a pledge, how powerful an assertion of innocence it is that he should come to take his place in the box to challenge the investigation not limited to matters contained in the indictments, but free to range over the whole history of the associations of his life. Was there a single point of the cross-examination at which he had fenced or shrunk from a question? Was there not rather a promptness, a fullness of expression, which could not but satisfy you that he was honestly telling what was on his mind? A man like this, assailed by tainted evidence, is entitled to be believed and to have his word accepted against a horde of blackmailers such as you have seen. And is it upon their testimony that he (*pointing swiftly to the bending figure in the dock*) is to be convicted?[220] I can only say that if these blackmailers are to be listened to in court against a defendant who was prepared on oath to give a denial to their story, the profession of blackmailing might become a more deadly mischief than it has been before. These men who have been the pests of London come smoothly and smilingly into court in the clothes that Lord Queensberry has bought for them, and we hear they are lodged and fed under the sympathetic care of the detective officers who have been provided them.

Why, this trial seems to be operating as an act of indemnity of all blackmailers in London. Wood and Parker, in giving evidence, have established for themselves a sort of statute of limitations. In testifying on behalf of the Crown, they have secured immunity for past rogueries and indecencies. It is on the basis of Parker and Wood that you are asked to condemn Mr. Wilde. Mr. Wilde knew nothing of these men's characters. They were introduced to him, and it was his love of admiration that caused him to like to be in their society. The positions should be changed—since it is these men who ought to be the accused, not accusers.

I see no necessity in explaining away Mr. Wilde's friendship with Taylor, the young man of fortune and accomplishments, who had been to a public school, and whose pleasantly furnished rooms were the resort of young men, among whom Oscar Wilde, the dramatist, the poet, would be an honored visitor, a man who might talk at his ease, to whom they would listen with admiration, and who might drink his fill of the uncritical adoration which he has admitted was very sweet to him.

The prosecution has adduced in support of the credibility of Wood and Parker that these young men never tried to make any charge against Mr. Wilde before the plea of justification in the libel case. The very observation that they have not made any charge against the prisoner seems to me a cogent proof that these young men, who have confessed to the fruits of blackmailing, have not been able to "rent" Wilde, and that there is no truth in their accusation at all. Would Parker have gone into the army or Wood to America, if they had an assured provision in the fears of Oscar Wilde? If Charles Parker and Wood thought they had material for making a charge against Mr. Wilde, do you think they would not have made it? Do you think they would have remained year after year without trying to get something from him? It is not surprising that Mr. Wilde wished to get his letters back because you say things in letters about other people, and especially about your own relations, which you would not like to have published.

The *Star* noted that, among Clarke's most eloquent and memorable *obiter dicta* during this impressive speech, were observations that related to the interpretation of certain details that had arisen during the proceedings about the dinner Wilde enjoyed with Alfred Taylor, Charles Parker, and William Parker in Kettner's restaurant sometime in February or March 1893.[221] In Clarke's view, the jury needed to understand that the prosecution's suggestion that the venue was supposedly peculiar should be dismissed from their minds. Clarke focused the jurors' minds that the conventions in this kind of restaurant might initially appear strange. There was, however, nothing amiss in the fact that a *table d'hôte* dinner was served as well as the fact that shades covered the candle flames:

CLARKE: This is a foreign restaurant, where dinner is served at a fixed price, where no waiter would think of putting a candle on the table without one of the shades, which are treated as such momentous matters in a Crown prosecution, where scarcely anyone would dine without having black coffee, liqueurs, and cigarettes afterwards. Can't you realize that Mr. Wilde probably talked all the time? That Taylor probably appreciated? That the others were content to enjoy the good entertainment and admire? And that there Mr. Wilde was quite satisfied with the entertainment himself?

"On a masterly analysis of the evidence," the *Star* observed, "Sir Edward Clarke claimed for Wilde a verdict of acquittal."[222] "Then," the paper continued, "in a peroration which was heard with breathless attention by a court crowded to suffocation," Clarke made his final address to the jury.[223]

CLARKE: If, on examination of this evidence, you see that it is your duty to say that this charge has not been proved, I am sure you will be glad that that brilliant promise which has been clouded by these accusations, that light of reputation, which was nearly quenched in the torrents of prejudice which a few weeks ago were sweeping through—I will not say our courts, but through at all events our press—you will be glad that your verdict has saved

> that reputation from absolute ruin, and has left him a distinguished man of letters, a brilliant Irishman, to live among us a life of honor and repute, and to give, in the maturity of his genius, gifts to our literature of which we have only the promise of his brilliant past.

"Sir Edward Clarke," the *Western Mail* noted, "then resumed his seat amid an outburst of applause, which was, however, promptly subdued."[224]

The solicitor general then rose and began his reply for the prosecution.[225] He denied that the prosecution had behaved with any unfairness toward Wilde. He thought that the counsel conducting the prosecution were right in thinking that a law officer should be instructed to appear for the prosecution. Regarding the right of reply, which belonged to law officers such as himself, and regarding Clarke's observation that Clarke never availed himself of this right when solicitor general, Lockwood noted that his learned friend had no right to lay down a rule that could not affect others who filled that office.[226]

Lockwood then proceeded to observe, as he opened his presentation of the case for the prosecution, that it was natural that the jury's every instinct made them shrink from condemning a fellow man of a crime such as that with which the defendant was charged. But they had to remember that it was only upon the evidence that they should condemn him. They could not, Lockwood remarked, appreciate that evidence unless they knew the manner of man they were dealing with. Mr. Wilde was said to be a man of culture and literary scholarship, and they would expect to find him associating with his equals in thought and literature, not these illiterate boys.[227] But they found him at 13 Little College Street, surrounded by these youths, whose admiration was so gratifying to him. In regard to the letters the prisoner obtained from Wood, Lockwood maintained, he should ask the jury to come to the conclusion that Wilde met Wood in order to buy those letters of which the jury had seen a sample. Wilde, Lockwood stated, dreaded that such letters should get into circulation, since he knew that any honorable man—he meant really a man—would detect in this correspondence the breadth of an unnatural passion, which among Christian men could not be named without horror and dismay.[228]

Lockwood had not concluded his speech when, at Justice Wills's bidding, the court rose. At 4.00 p.m., the hearing of the case was adjourned until the next morning.[229] Wilde was admitted to the same bail.

Sixth Day: Saturday, 25 May 1895

As before, the solicitor general Sir Frank Lockwood, Mr. C. F. Gill, and Mr. Horace Avory prosecuted on behalf of the public prosecutor; and Sir Edward Clarke, Mr. Charles Mathews, and Mr. Travers Humphreys defended. The *Star* began its characteristically thorough report on the final day of Oscar Wilde's second criminal trial with reflections on the reputation that Sir Frank Lockwood had established for himself since his appointment as solicitor general in the summer of 1894:

> The fourth, and presumably the last, day of Wilde's second trial at the Old Bailey opened with cool breezes and a court less crowded and oppressive than it was yesterday, when the prisoner's cross-examination attracted the sensation-hunters. The solicitor general, whose speech to the jury on behalf of conviction, was cut short in the middle by the adjournment last night, was the first of the counsel in the case to reach the court, where he occupied himself in a last hasty glance through the pages of his brief. It is interesting to recall that the present is the second case in which Sir Frank Lockwood has been brought into a cause célèbre to exert against a prisoner the enormous influence of the "last word." In November last, when all England was waiting with breathless interest for the issue of the trial of Read for the murder of Florrie Dennis, [which] the newly-appointed solicitor general went down to Chelmsford to prosecute, he had the last word with the jury, and Read was hanged. In that case, too, it was Mr. C. F. Gill who was superseded in the conduct of the Crown case.
>
> At half-past ten, Mr. Justice Wills arrived. A second case, a charge of wilful murder against one Jane White, had been placed in the list for the day, and his lordship carried with his paper the black cap. But this prisoner, who was brought first into the dock, was committed only to the coroner's warrant, the Treasury had concluded to offer no evidence against her, and a verdict of not guilty was taken. So, it happened that when Oscar Wilde, poet and dramatist, was called upon to surrender, he became involved in the door of the dock with the discharged.[230]

Meanwhile, *Reynolds's Newspaper* drew attention to Wilde's dispirited demeanor as he entered the dock: "his appearance fully justified the words used by Sir Edward Clarke the previous day—'broken as he is, worn as he is.'"[231] Wilde had passed into the court with his sureties, Percy Sholto Douglas, who sat at the solicitors' table, and the Revd. Stewart Headlam. Queensberry occupied a seat near the bench. In the court were some of Wilde's literary associates, including Robert Harborough Sherard, the poet and novelist Ernest Dowson, and the travel writer Harry de Windt.

Once Lockwood resumed his presentation of the case for the prosecution, which had been abruptly curtailed mid-speech during the previous afternoon, he informed the jury that he thought that no one could believe Wilde's answers to the charges. It was difficult, Lockwood maintained, to fail to interpret the prisoner's conduct as that of a guilty man, and it was their duty to say so in their verdict. The solicitor general dwelt on Clarke's observation that it was Wilde himself who initially courted inquiry into the matter through a lawsuit against the Marquess of Queensberry for libel. In Lockwood's opinion, it was necessary for him to remind the jury of the respective positions in *Regina (Wilde) v. Queensberry*. Clarke, Lockwood observed, had maintained that the marquess's libels referred to events from two years before, and Clarke had also stated that, in the lapse of time, witnesses for Mr. Wilde could no longer be contacted. But what witness, Lockwood asked, had been lost sight of? The solicitor general suggested that it was the fact that Wilde had seen nothing of Charles Parker, and could rely implicitly on his friend Taylor's discretion, that encouraged him to prosecute the marquess for libel.

CLARKE (*interrupting*): I must rise to object to the solicitor general's rhetorical description of what has never been proved in evidence, in asserting that an intimate friendship existed between Mr. Wilde and Taylor.

LOCKWOOD: Gentlemen, it is not rhetoric; it is a plain statement of fact. What are the indications of an intimate friendship? They call one another by their Christian names. Does he not say to Taylor: "Bring your friends; they are my friends; I will not inquire too closely whether they come from the stable or the kitchen"? No doubt my learned friend desires not to disconnect them. He wishes as a result of this trial that the one should be condemned and the other left to continue his grand literary career.

CLARKE: I protest.

LOCKWOOD: It appears that the counsel for the defence desires now that one man should go down and the other be saved because of a false glamour upon art.[232]

CLARKE: My lord, I protest. I must distinctly protest against this sort of appeal to the jury—this suggestion to the jury that it is my desire now that one man should go down and the other be saved because of a false glamour upon art.

LOCKWOOD: Oh, you may protest.

JUSTICE WILLS: So far, no mention has been made of the verdict in the other case.

CLARKE: All of this is as far removed from the evidence as anything ever heard in this court.

LOCKWOOD: I am alluding, my lord, and I maintain that I am right in alluding, to my learned friend's last appeal to the jury as to the literary position of his client; and I am dealing, in connection with that, with his connection to the man Taylor, and I say that these men must be judged equally.

CLARKE: They ought to have been fairly tried in the proper order.

LOCKWOOD (*passionately*): Oh, my lord, these interruptions shall avail my friend nothing.

JUSTICE WILLS: The solicitor general is perfectly within his rights. The only objection is to allusions to the result of the trial of Taylor.

Lockwood proceeded to discuss the history of blackmailing. He stated that extortion had been made possible because of the letters that Wilde had written to Douglas. In reference to Wilde's letter that contained the phrase "madness of kisses," the solicitor general offered the following observations:

LOCKWOOD: I contend that such a letter found in the possession of a woman, from a man, would be open to but one interpretation. How much worse was the inference to be drawn when such a letter was written by one man to another! It had been attempted to show that this was a prose poem, a sonnet, a lovely thing, which I suppose we are too low to appreciate. Gentlemen (*in thundering tones*), let us thank God, if it is so, that we do not appreciate things of this sort, save at their proper value, and that is somewhat lower than the beasts. If that letter had been seen by any right-minded man, it would have been looked upon as evidence of a guilty passion. And you—men of pride, reason, and honor—are supposed to be put off with this story of the prose poem, of the sonnet, of the lovely thing.

Lockwood pointed to one or two phrases in Wilde's letter, and he commented specifically on the classical reference to Apollo and Hyacinthus.[233] He declared that this allusion sufficiently showed what was in the prisoner's mind when Wilde wrote the letter to Douglas.

At this juncture, Clarke interposed and protested Lockwood's remarks. He objected to the insinuation that he previously attempted to characterize the prose poem as a "lovely thing."

CLARKE: Sir Frank is saying something I have said, words that I declare I never used. I have not said anything to influence the cross-examination of my learned friend.[234]

LOCKWOOD: No! No! I never suggested that he was so candid.

When the solicitor general referred to Clarke's "cand[or]," it provoked a laugh in the public gallery. He added that he had no sympathy with such demonstrations of opinion. At this juncture, Justice Wills expressed his displeasure at such outbursts. According to the *Star*, the judge, who was "taking the case on bare nerves, almost tearfully admonished the crowd."[235]

JUSTICE WILLS: These interruptions are offensive to me beyond anything that can be described. To have to try a case of this kind, to keep the scales even, but to be pestered with the applause of expressions of feeling of senseless

> people who have no business to be here at all except for the gratification of morbid curiosity is too much. I fear that no further interruption of this kind will be heard throughout the rest of the trial. If there is anything of this kind again, I shall clear the court.

Once silence had been restored, Lockwood drew the jury's attention to important circumstances about Wilde's libel suit against Queensberry. He pointed out that Wilde did not know, until after the marquess had been committed for trial and when it was too late for the prosecution to retire, that certain past chapters in his life would be opened and read. And Lockwood added that it was only when Carson subjected Wilde to cross-examination (which drew attention to those past chapters) that the libel case was abruptly terminated. At that point, he noted, it was incontestable that Queensberry's plea of justification was both proven and published in the public interest. Lockwood went on to observe that had the criminal court been able to deal with offenses alleged to have taken place outside that court's jurisdiction, there would have been additional counts in the indictment.

This observation enabled Lockwood to speak about cases—ones not mentioned in the indictment—that had been discussed during his cross-examination of the defendant. He contended that he had pursued this line of questioning because he wanted the jury to have every opportunity of ascertaining for themselves the kind of man Wilde was. Wilde, he said, made very large claims on his own behalf, by reason of his social position and his literary distinction. Yet in the case of Alphonse Conway, it was revealed how little the defendant valued that position. Furthermore, it was a commonsense conclusion that Wilde had bargained with Wood and bought the letters. If what Wilde said was true with regard to his first meeting with Wood, all that he had to do was hand over the money to Wood. Lockwood commented that Wood had no motive for deceiving the jury on the present occasion. From this point onward, as the *Star* observed, Lockwood "settled down to a wordy and somewhat disconnected survey of the evidence finding everywhere corroboration, which he submitted to the jury as fatal to the prisoner."[236]

The solicitor general's attention then turned to Charles Parker's testimony. He said that the fact that Wilde had never seen William Parker since the dinner at Kettner's restaurant corroborated the Parker brothers' evidence about the conversation that took place at that dinner. In Charles Parker's case, as in Wood's, Wilde's evidence contained admission upon admission, until it came to the point that admission should cease and confession begin. Lockwood pointed to the evidence from the waiter at the Savoy Hotel, who corroborated what Charles Parker had said. The waiter had testified that a supper was served to Mr. Wilde and a young man in a private room. Charles Parker had described the supper, and Wilde could give no explanation about his guest. All Wilde could say was that his guest was not Charles Parker. Moreover, Margery Bancroft, who said that she knew Wilde perfectly well by sight, also gave corroborative evidence. Mrs. Bancroft, Lockwood noted, had been so much troubled by what she had seen that she complained to Charles Parker's landlady. As a consequence, the landlady asked Parker to leave his lodgings. With regard to the charges about the Savoy Hotel, the solicitor general asked why it was that Lord Alfred Douglas, who slept in the next room, had not been called to deny the chambermaid's statements. There was, Lockwood stated, no reason that Wilde should not be cross-examined with reference to other offenses. He reiterated that the jury was entitled, in the interests of justice, to put a commonsense interpretation upon the conditions and circumstances under which the young men outside the present case were found. In this respect, the case of Conway was highly significant. What possible benefit, Lockwood asked, could it be to a boy in Conway's position to be taken from Worthing to Brighton and allowed to stay in a hotel all night?

The next stage in Lockwood's address to the jury concentrated on both Charles Parker's and Alfred Wood's respective roles as blackmailers. He wished to remind the jury of the conditions that might lead a man to sink so low that such an individual—even though he was willing to state in court that he had committed such acts—would still not hesitate to commit them. Lockwood answered this apparent puzzle through recourse to an intricate argument.

LOCKWOOD: My learned friend has said that these witnesses are blackmailers, and has warned you against giving a verdict which should enable this detestable trade to rear its head unblushingly in this city. Gentlemen, I should have as much right to ask you to take care lest by your verdict you should enable another vice, as detestable, as abominable, to raise its head with unblushing effrontery in this city. The genesis of the blackmailer is the man who has committed these acts of indecency with him. And the genesis of the man who commits these foul acts is the man who is willing to pay for their commission. Were it not that there are men willing to purchase vice in this most hideous and detestable form, there would be no market for such crime, and no opening for these blackmailers to ply their calling. But where was the motive? It is not suggested that either of these men blackmailed Wilde. They have had much to lose and nothing to gain by giving evidence here. It is not suggested that their evidence has been bought, or that they have been improperly influenced in any way.

Lockwood proceeded to discuss the relations that had undoubtedly existed among Wilde, Taylor, Wood, and Charles Parker, and he said that he thought it remarkable that Wilde should have two acquaintances, one after another, both of whom were friends of Taylor, and both of whom were in a different social position from Wilde's own. The solicitor general further urged that there was distinct corroboration of evidence in Wood's case, and that no motive had been put forward that the jury could reasonably consider what might have prompted the witnesses to come and give false evidence. Lockwood then addressed Wilde's relations with Taylor, whom during the libel trial Mr. Carson had charged with procuration on Wilde's behalf. The solicitor general pointed out that Taylor had been at the Old Bailey during the libel proceedings, though he had not been called into the witness box. Why not? Lockwood inquired.

One would have thought, the solicitor general said, that after the incident with Wood, Taylor would have been asked to be careful in the selection of the friends whom he introduced to Wilde. But no, Lockwood stated, that was not the case. Taylor, he noted, had carte blanche to bring any friends he pleased, and it was manifest that Taylor's intimacy with Charles Parker was not a matter of ordinary friendship. Lockwood repelled the suggestion that Mr. Russell, the Marquess of Queensberry's solicitor, or any representative of the Crown, had given a fee or reward to the young men who had given evidence. All that the prosecution had done, he maintained, was to take precautions in order to prevent tampering with those witnesses, and to ensure their attendance in court. Naturally, Lockwood said, the witnesses had been removed secretly from place to place, and he made no apology for the course the Crown had taken in this matter. Charles Parker, the solicitor general claimed, could not have any sinister motive in telling a story that involved his own shame, and to an extent his own condemnation. It had never been shown, he said, that Parker—whatever his past conduct might have been—had attempted to extort money from Wilde.

Lockwood contended that Wilde's own admissions—ones that agreed up to a certain point with Wood's evidence—proved Wood's story to be true. What necessity was there, he asked, for Wilde to give Wood supper in a private room or to tell Wood that Wilde's family was out of town? Wilde's subsequent story about Wood was most extraordinary. The transaction regarding the letters, Lockwood observed, was capable of one construction only. Wilde knew, he said, that these were letters that he should recover; thus, he bought them and tore them to pieces. Lockwood noted, however, that Wilde kept the one that he received from William Allen, since Wilde knew that Mr. Beerbohm Tree had a copy of it, which meant that it was useless to destroy the original. If, then, the jury came to the conclusion that Wilde had purchased these letters, it shed light upon his conduct. It showed, in the solicitor general's view, that Wilde knew the class of men with whom he had been intimate, and with whom he continued to be intimate. Lockwood went on to say that Sir Edward Clarke had unintentionally exaggerated what Mr. Justice Wills had said regarding the two cases of the person or persons unknown. His learned friend, Lockwood stated, made it appear as though the evidence in these cases was exceedingly slender. But, as a matter of fact, he said, his lordship left that part of the case unreservedly to the jury. Lockwood argued that there was ample evidence as to these particular charges. The defendant, he claimed, had given no explanation of the discoveries that the hotel's employees had made. It was no conclusive answer, Lockwood said, to contend that Wilde did everything openly. If crime, he reasoned, was always cautious, it would always go unpunished, and thus it was in moments of carelessness that crime was detected. The witnesses from the Savoy Hotel, Lockwood said, could have no possible objective in patching together a bogus case.

> LOCKWOOD: Now, gentlemen, I have been through the whole of this case. I have pointed out to you its strength, and I have asked you to do your duty in regard to it. I have already dealt with that (as I think) unfortunate appeal, which my learned friend made as to the literary past or literary future of Oscar Wilde. With that we have in this case nothing whatever to do. He has a right to be acquitted if you believe him to be an innocent man, be his lot high or low. But if, gentlemen, in your consciences you believe that he is guilty of these charges—well, then you have only one consideration, and that is to follow closely the obligation of the oath which has been imposed upon you.

The solicitor general concluded his speech at 12.25 p.m. The *Star* observed that throughout Lockwood's presentation, "Wilde listened impassively from his corner of the dock, but all through the morning he carried frequently to his nose a small vinaigrette of cut glass."[237]

Justice Wills then began his summing-up for the jury. He pointed out that the jurors' duty was "the cold, calm, resolute administration of justice," and he said that he would himself rather try the most shocking murder case that it had fallen to his lot to try than be engaged in any case like this one. It might, he said, be thought that the difficulty and distress of dealing with the case would be increased by the position and education of the person accused. His lordship could not say that his own difficulty or sense of responsibility was increased by that consideration. Whatever might be the guilt or innocence of the accused, the defendant's conduct, he said, had nonetheless been such—particularly regarding Lord Alfred Douglas—that it would be impossible for twelve intelligent, impartial, and honest gentlemen to say there was no good ground for an indignant father to charge Wilde with having "posed," as the Marquess of Queensberry had suggested.

Thereafter, Justice Wills continued by stating that in his opinion the conspiracy charges should never have been introduced in the previous trial, and he acknowledged that the joining of the charges against the two prisoners justified the disagreement of the jury in that earlier trial. As to the present trial, his lordship stated that he would have preferred to have the prisoners tried in a different order, but he did not think that the defendant had suffered because of the course that the solicitor general had chosen to take. In his opinion, the fact that Taylor's case had been heard first had not in any way prejudiced Wilde's case.

In turning to the evidence, Justice Wills said that there were three—or, substantially, four—charges in the indictment. There were, he noted, charges of improper conduct with Wood and Parker, and two charges regarding persons at the Savoy Hotel. The judge stated that he could never bring himself to make a colorless summing-up, which was no good to anybody. Still, he called upon the jury to look upon his opinions not as views that they were expected to adopt but as matters for their criticism.

Justice Wills proceeded to observe that the passing of section 20 of the Criminal Law Amendment Act 1885, which made a defendant a competent but not compellable witness, was never intended to alter or to infringe upon a sacred old principle of English law: namely, that the prosecution must make out the charge against the accused.[238] Had that act not been passed, many innocent persons might have been convicted and many guilty persons might have escaped. The judge confirmed that he had become a convert to the beneficial nature of this Act of Parliament after ten years' experience of its working.

Speaking generally, the judge noted, he had to admit (and it was for the jury to say whether he was unduly stretching the remark in favor of the defendant) that it was exceedingly difficult, if not impossible, for a man to remember exactly where he was or with whom he was two years ago. Justice Wills believed that this fact was in favor of the accused, so far as it went. It would, he said, be a bad day for the administration of justice in England either when juries ceased to take their directions from the judge, or when they surrendered to any judge in the land—no matter what his learning, experience, or ability—their own independent judgment on the facts that were before them. It was the province of the jury, he said, to decide upon the facts.

It was impossible, he stated, in dealing with Wood's case, to avoid dealing also with Lord Alfred Douglas. Lord Alfred, the judge remarked, was not present in the court, and it must be remembered in Lord Alfred's favor that if neither side called him, he could not volunteer as a witness. (The *Western Mail* recorded that at this point a juror piped up about Douglas: "He could be here."[239]) Justice Wills proceeded to say that he was anxious not to comment on anything that might blast the career of this young man who was on the threshold of life. Undeniably, he noted, Lord Alfred's family seemed a house divided against itself. But he went on to comment, even if there was no filial love or parental affection, even if there was nothing but hatred between father and son, one question remained: What father would not try to save his son from the associations suggested by the two letters from the prisoner Wilde to Lord Alfred Douglas? The judge stated that he would avoid saying whether those letters appeared to point to actual criminal conduct. Yet he asked the jury to suppose that these letters were prose poems, to suppose that they were things that only persons of high culture could appreciate. Were these letters the less poisonous for a young man? It was strange, the judge remarked, that it should not occur to a gentleman capable of writing such letters that any young man to whom they were addressed must suffer in the estimation of everyone if the correspondence became public knowledge. The Marquess of Queensberry, Justice Wills noted, had taken a method of interfering, which one would have thought no gentleman would have taken, in leaving at the defendant's club a card containing a most offensive expression. It was, he said, a message that left the defendant no alternative but to prosecute or be branded as a man who could not deny a foul charge. At this point, the *Star* reported, "Lord Queensberry found some of these expressions so little to his taste that he presently got up and left the court."[240]

Justice Wills proceeded to speak of the ill-assorted friendship between Lord Alfred Douglas and Alfred Wood, whom Lord Alfred had introduced to Wilde, and to whom Lord Alfred gave a suit of clothes containing the "madness of kissing" letter. The judge found it more understandable that a lad such as Wood should be given cast-off clothes than a silver cigarette case. His lordship had no doubt that the "red rose-leaf lips" letter was the worst of the bundle that fell into the blackmailers' hands, but he regarded it as highly unfortunate that the other letters should have been destroyed. If, he argued, these letters were indeed harmless, as the defendant had said they were, they would have been an answer to this charge. Justice Wills further pointed out that Charles Parker and Alfred Wood had been introduced to the accused for certain assistance a long time ago, and although both of these young men had been industrious blackmailers during the interval, they had neither seen Wilde again nor attempted to make any charge against him until now. That, his lordship admitted, was a "most remarkable fact," one "of overwhelming influence."

Once more, Justice Wills said, there was truth in the aphorism that a man should be judged by the company he keeps. The jury had seen the Parker brothers, just as they had seen Wood, and the same question must arise in their minds: Were those the kind of young men with whom they would care to sit down and dine? Were these young men the sort of persons one expected to find in the company of people of education? It was a very long time ago for a waiter to remember having served a supper at the Savoy Hotel, and the sums that appeared on the bill were high for such a supper. He said he knew nothing of the Savoy, though he thought "chicken and salad for two, 16s." very high. The judge was reluctant to say that he would never have supper at the hotel himself.

Regarding Wood's story about his visit to Tite Street, Justice Wills noted that it was remarkable for a man such as Wilde even to meet with a man of Wood's social position. Nonetheless, the judge remarked, Wilde himself said he was an exceptional person, one who disregarded social distinctions. At the same time, it was only fair to observe that Wilde had never professed any liking for Wood. Wilde stated that he had taken interest in Wood simply because he had been asked to. If, the judge argued, Wood's story about the visit to Tite Street was true, it might have been possible to obtain corroboration. But counsel for the prosecution had not been able to obtain it. Justice Wills said that he thought if Wood had really been in Wilde's home, Wood would have been able to give a more detailed description of his visit than he had done in the course of his evidence. On the question of corroboration, the judge pointed out that the jury was not expected—since corroboration in cases of this kind was difficult to obtain—to be satisfied with less corroboration than if it were easy to obtain. Justice Wills commented, however, that regarding Wood, unless the jury believed that Wood's evidence was corroborated, they must not act on it. The reason, he said, was that Wood was a blackmailer—a person belonging to the vilest type of man that great cities produce.

At this point, the foreman of the jury interposed with several questions.

FOREMAN OF THE JURY: In view of the intimacy between Lord Alfred Douglas and Wilde, was a warrant ever issued for the apprehension of Lord Alfred Douglas?

JUSTICE WILLS: I should think not. We have not heard of it.

FOREMAN OF THE JURY: Was it ever contemplated?

JUSTICE WILLS: Not to my knowledge. A warrant would in any case not be issued without evidence of some fact, of something more than intimacy.

I cannot tell, nor need we discuss that, because Lord Alfred Douglas may yet have to answer a charge. He was not called. There may be a thousand considerations of which we may know nothing that might prevent his appearance in the witness box. I think you should deal with the matter upon the evidence before you.

FOREMAN OF THE JURY: But it seems to us that if we are to consider these letters as evidence of guilt, and if we adduce any guilt from these letters, it applies as much to Lord Alfred Douglas as to the defendant.

JUSTICE WILLS: Quite so. But how does that relieve the defendant? Our present inquiry is whether guilt is brought home to the man in the dock. We have got the testimony of his guilt to deal with now. I believe that to be the recipient of such letters and to continue the intimacy is as fatal to the reputation of the recipient as to the sender, but you have really nothing to do with that at present.

The judge had not concluded his summing-up when the court adjourned for lunch.

Once the court resumed its business, Justice Wills refocused attention on the case of Lord Alfred Douglas.

JUSTICE WILLS: There is a natural disposition to ask: Why should this man stand in the dock, and not Lord Alfred Douglas? But the supposition that Lord Alfred Douglas will be spared because he is Lord Alfred Douglas is one of the wildest injustice—the thing is utterly and hopelessly impossible. I must remind you that anything that can be said for or against Lord Alfred Douglas must not be allowed to prejudice the prisoner; and you must remember that no prosecution would be possible on the mere production of Wilde's letters to Lord Alfred Douglas. Lord Alfred Douglas, as you all know, went to Paris at the request of the defendant, and there he has stayed, and I know absolutely nothing more about him. I am as ignorant in this respect as you are. It may be that there is no evidence against Lord Alfred Douglas—but even about that I know nothing. It is a thing we cannot discuss, and to entertain any such consideration as I have mentioned would be a prejudice of the worst possible kind.

The judge then reviewed other aspects of the evidence that had been heard during the trial. He turned first of all to Charles Parker's testimony. He stated that some of his previous remarks about Wood applied here, though there were differences between the two cases. Parker, Justice Wills observed, seemed to have been introduced to Wilde by Taylor, and there could be no doubt that Taylor was a friend of Wilde's. But, he noted, the amount of intercourse between

Wilde and Taylor that the prosecution had proved was not very great. The admissions that Wilde made about the innocent nature of his acquaintance with Parker were undoubtedly remarkable, and it was for the jury to decide whether the explanations were satisfactory. If, he contended, the jury thought that Wilde's visit to Park Walk was made up, it was a very strange thing, and there was nothing to be said against the person who confirmed that part of the case—Margery Bancroft. If anything could have been found, he said, against this witness, it would have been found by the defense. The jury, the judge went on to say, must therefore recognize that the witness was neither a streetwalker not a disreputable woman, and that she had for years been in employment. This witness's evidence, Justice Wills maintained, was good because it was difficult to see any wrong motive that she could have in coming forward to blast the reputation of the defendant. At this point, his lordship commented that he was confronted with a difficulty—namely, a rule of law that prevents a witness from telling what he or she had heard from someone else.[241] It had not, he said, transpired what was the full extent of the complaint that Mrs. Bancroft had made to the landlady at Park Walk. The jury, he observed, would have to draw their own inferences from her evidence, and also put what construction they thought most reasonable on Charles Parker's story generally, taken in conjunction with surrounding circumstances.

Nor, Justice Wills proceeded to note, must it be presumed that the mere fact of two men sleeping together should be punished. Poverty and misery, he admitted, frequently compelled this to happen, and it might even compel men and women to sleep together promiscuously. God forbid, he exclaimed, that sleeping together for such reasons should be considered a crime. But when, he observed, the jurors discovered a man who was spending £40 to £50 a week, it seemed astonishing that the defendant should not get at least the whole of his bed for his money, and it was natural to ask why Wilde did not offer another room to his guest.

Justice Wills went on to express his wish that medical evidence should have been called. It was, he stated, a loathsome subject, but he made a point of never shrinking from details that were absolutely necessary. Medical evidence, he contended, would have shed light on what had been alluded to as marks of grease or Vaseline smears.[242] Then, with reference to the condition of the bed, there was—he added—the diarrhea line of defense.[243] That was a story, his lordship noted, that he was not able to appreciate. The judge stated that he had tried many other similar cases, but he had never heard that defense before. It struck him as possible, he said, but, more than anything else, it impressed him with the importance of having medical evidence in such a case, which unfortunately the jury had not had. The worst state of the sheets, Justice Wills recalled, was not alleged on the night that the chambermaid said that she had seen the boy in the bed. There was, he noted, the same sort of thing, but not so bad.[244]

At the same time, Justice Wills argued, the evidence of the Savoy Hotel's members of staff—given the long lapse of time since these events occurred—must not be entirely relied upon. If, he said, an employee at the hotel noticed anything wrong and said nothing about it for two years, he could not consider that person's testimony as evidence on which we would "hang a dog."[245] It was, his lordship thought, a strange thing that this matter should not have become the subject of inquiry until two years afterward. Then again, he observed, the masseur Migge's evidence was remarkable, though it was not safe to rely upon it. The evidence of the chambermaid was no less extraordinary, he stated, no matter from what point one viewed it. The thing that struck Justice Wills as most remarkable about the story was that, though the housekeeper Annie Perkins was acquainted with what her staff had seen, absolutely no notice was taken of the circumstance. For this reason, the judge argued, the housekeeper became an accomplice in the whole affair, and—without saying that she was as bad as any of them—he claimed there was a very great breach in Perkins's sense of duty in these matters. Justice Wills pointed out that Perkins had admitted that the chambermaid, Jane Margaret Cotter, had communicated with her. He considered that, if Cotter had informed Perkins of the condition of the room, and if Perkins had taken no steps to prevent such a thing in the future, she would be liable to become an accessory before the fact in the event of its being repeated. It was, the judge stated, a condition of things that one shuddered to contemplate in a first-class hotel. Once he had considered all of the evidence, Justice Wills concluded that the question was whether there was evidence of guilt or of suspicion only, and it was this question that the jury would have to answer. He then thanked the jurors for the patience they had displayed throughout the prolonged hearing.

At 3.35 p.m., the jury retired to consider their verdict. The *Star* noted the atmosphere in the court: "The judge also retired, and Wilde, as at the last trial, was taken down to the cells. A great buzz of excited conjecture filled the court. Counsel showed in their faces the strain and anxiety of the case, and gradually drifted out into the cooler corridors. The general opinion in court was that the jury would again disagree."[246] The press reported that while the court was filled with the hum of conversation, Percy Douglas and Stewart Headlam left the courtroom at the same time that Wilde descended the steps. It was understood that the young men who had given evidence stood waiting outside the court. Almost an hour and a half elapsed before the court heard anything from the jury. Their ninety-minute adjournment prompted speculation among the prosecution and the defense. Millard reports that Lockwood is supposed to have stated to Clarke: "You'll dine your man in Paris to-morrow."[247] At 5.00 p.m., the jury requested some water, and again, at 5.20 p.m., some ink and paper. The request caused one of the barristers to observe audibly: "They have used all their ink." At 5.25 p.m., the jury sent a note to the judge, who returned to court at once. The jury also came in, and Wilde came to the front of the dock and leaned forward upon the woodwork in front of him. It appeared to reporters that at this point the jury wanted Justice Wills to read over to them once more the notes about the waiter, Thomas Price, from the private hotel at 10 and 11 St. James's Place. The evidence was to the effect that Alfred Taylor had visited that address once, that Charles Parker had been there five or six times, and that Thomas Price had served the men tea.

FOREMAN OF THE JURY: Is there any evidence of Charles Parker having stayed there?

JUSTICE WILLS: No.

Reynolds's Newspaper commented on the tension that followed Justice Wills's response to the foreman's inquiry:

> It seemed at first as if the jury intended to declare their verdict at once. They stood in a group, craning their necks in order to speak to one another. But, after a few minutes, the foreman said: "My lord, you will excuse us for a moment." The jury then left again, and Wilde disappeared.
>
> The jury came back, however, after an interval of a short duration, and the foreman stood up to declare the verdict. There was perfect silence throughout the building. Wilde was standing up for the first time during the day; his appearance was one of great dejection, though there was not the slightest sign of any animation in his face.[248]

The *Illustrated Police Budget* observed: "Immediately the jury returned, Wilde rose from his seat in the dock and leant over the front eagerly scanning the faces of the twelve good men and fine, seemingly trying to read in their physiognomies his fate. On this morning, Wilde's face was as white as a miller's apron, and he raised that face to hear the decision of the jury."[249]

THE CLERK OF ARRAIGNS: Gentlemen, have you agreed upon your verdict?

FOREMAN OF THE JURY: We have.

CLERK OF ARRAIGNS: Do you find the prisoner at the bar guilty of an act of gross indecency with Charles Parker at the Savoy Hotel on the night of his first introduction to him?

FOREMAN OF THE JURY: Guilty.

CLERK OF ARRAIGNS: Do you find him guilty of a similar offence a week later?

FOREMAN OF THE JURY: Guilty.

CLERK OF ARRAIGNS: Do you find him guilty of the offence at St. James's Place?

FOREMAN OF THE JURY: Guilty.

CLERK OF ARRAIGNS: Do you find him guilty of this offence at about the same period?

FOREMAN OF THE JURY: Guilty.

CLERK OF ARRAIGNS: Do you find him guilty of a similar offence with Alfred Wood at Tite Street?

FOREMAN OF THE JURY: Guilty.

CLERK OF ARRAIGNS: Do you find him guilty of the offence in Room no. 346 of the Savoy Hotel?

FOREMAN OF THE JURY: Guilty.

CLERK OF ARRAIGNS: Do you find him guilty of all counts in the indictment except that relating to Edward Shelley?

FOREMAN OF THE JURY: Yes. Not guilty on that count.

"The people," the *Star* remarked, "looked at the face of the prisoner, and it was like the face of a corpse."[250]

Once Taylor had been placed next to Wilde in the dock, the court assumed that the judge would pass sentence. The moment that Taylor appeared, however, Clarke rose:

CLARKE: I have to suggest to your lordship that you will not pass sentence until the next sessions. There is a demurrer on record, which has to be argued, and I submit that it would be well to postpone passing sentence in order that that argument may be considered.

GRAIN: I do not know how far that will affect the case of Mr. Taylor, but I think it would affect him equally. Therefore, if I may re-echo the observation of Sir Edward Clarke, I would make the same application.

LOCKWOOD: I oppose the application. The matter has been argued and decided. It relates to certain counts not included in the indictment. And passing sentence now can in no way affect any argument that may be raised at any future time.

CLARKE: The conspiracy counts are contained in the indictment.

JUSTICE WILLS: But there is a verdict of not guilty on them. What is the contention?

CLARKE: That the indictment was bad, there being a different mode of trial. In a case of conspiracy, the defendants are not capable of being witnesses, but in the other they are capable of giving evidence, and they plead to that indictment alone. The demurrer is just as arguable, whatever has taken place since.

GILL: That question was argued before Justice Charles, and he held the indictment to be perfectly good.

LOCKWOOD: Sentence can be passed without prejudicing the argument before the Court of Crown Cases Reserved.[251]

JUSTICE WILLS: Of the correctness of the indictment, I have myself no doubt. But, in any case, my passing sentence will not interfere with the arguing of the point raised, and I think it my duty to pass sentence at once. It is not a matter about which I entertain any doubt. And to pass sentence now will in no way prejudice the result of the inquiry. I think it may be well to complete the proceedings here on other counts.

The *Star* commented on the way in which Justice Wills proceeded to pass sentence: "Here came another dramatic surprise. The studied fairness of the summing-up had not prepared anybody for the burning, scathing words in which his lordship passed sentence. Seldom have such terms been heard at the Old Bailey, never perhaps addressed to a man of Wilde's antecedents."[252]

JUSTICE WILLS: Oscar Wilde and Alfred Taylor, it has never been my lot to try a case of this kind so bad. One has to put a certain constraint upon oneself to prevent one from describing in language I would rather not use, the sentiments which must arise in the breast of every man who has any spark of decent feeling left in him, and who has heard the details of these two terrible trials. That the jury have arrived at a correct verdict, I cannot persuade myself to entertain a shadow of a doubt; and I hope that at all events those who sometimes imagine that a judge is half-hearted in cases of indecency and immorality because he takes care that no prejudice shall enter into them may see that that is consistent at least with the utmost sense of indignation at the horrible crimes brought home to both of you. It is no use of my addressing you. People who do these things must be dead to every sense of shame, and one cannot hope to produce any effect upon them. It is the worst case I ever tried. That you, Taylor, kept a kind of male brothel it is impossible to doubt,[253] and that you, Wilde, have been at the centre of a circle of extensive corruption of young men of the most hideous kind it is equally impossible to doubt. I shall, under such circumstances, be ex-

> pected to pass the severest sentence which the law allows. In my judgment, it is utterly inadequate for such cases. The sentence upon each of you is imprisonment with hard labour for two years. (*Sensation.*)[254]

The *Star* recorded Wilde's unsuccessful attempt at responding to the sentence:

> As his lordship finished, Wilde rose to his full height. He held by the front of the dock—seeming to need its support—and his lips, which were of the same livid color as his face, moved. Those nearest the dock say he cried: "May I not speak, my lord?" But the only words audible were two deeply articulated words, astonishing in such a connection, the words "Shame! Shame!" which came from the back of the public gallery, and were instantly drowned in the ushers' strident cries of "Silence! Silence!" Taylor was already leaving the dock, with the light cat-like tread habitual to him. But Wilde seemed to have lost control of his limbs. When at last he turned away, between the two warders, he trailed his feet like a man smitten with paralysis, and descended with obvious difficulty the step leading to the cells. Already the voices of the newsboys could be heard crying "Wilde Verdict" in the sunny street, and the facile cheers of the ever-virtuous British crowd had been audible throughout the judge's address. The Old Bailey was filled with a Saturday afternoon crowd, which applauded and made jokes upon the result indifferently.[255]

In his unpublished memoir "Ultima Verba," Sherard commented on Justice Wills's refusal to listen to Wilde's "piteous appeal" to speak aloud: "I, who was seated just below the dock and exactly before Clarke and Lockwood, was impelled to my feet with no other purpose than to say: 'I'll say it for you, Oscar,' but I was pulled down by [Ernest] Dowson, saying, 'You'll do no good and only get sent to gaol'; and before I had time to recover, poor Oscar had disappeared into the bottomless pit."[256]

The actor Seymour Hicks, who came to know Wilde through Ada Leverson, similarly recalled witnessing Wilde's despair at the verdict. As he sat between George R. Sims, on the one side, and Max Beerbohm, on the other side, Hicks observed Wilde's terror when he came up from the cells to hear the jury's recitation of "Guilty": "He had visibly changed. His hair, naturally straight, though generally waved in ordinary times, lay straggling and damp upon a forehead covered with sweat, his lips were purple, and his face, distressed and anxious, gave him the appearance of a massive bull in the agony of death. He hardly glanced at the jury, but his gaze wandered round the court and for a second fell on me. I hope he saw in my eyes the sorrow I felt for him, for I was thinking of the Mr. Wilde I knew, and all that the world of literature was losing, not the other Wilde for whose blood the crowd were justly clamouring. He had no sign of recognition."[257] Like Sherard, Hicks noticed that Wilde struggled to make his voice heard: "Wilde, who had stood at the edge of the dock in front of him, leaned forward and gripped it more tightly and made an attempt to speak. He seemed incapable of doing so, however, and, in answer to a whispered command from the warder at his side, turned heavily towards the stairs which led to the gateway of a greater hell than even he with all his vision could ever have imagined."[258]

As we see in chapter 6 of *Oscar Wilde on Trial*, the press provided glimpses of the two-year ordeal that Wilde had begun. On occasion, the reporters relished his suffering. But at the same time several observers expressed skepticism about many aspects of the trial. To some of these dissenting voices, it was not at all clear that justice had been done.

Part III

AFTER THE TRIALS

6

IMPRISONMENT: PENTONVILLE, WANDSWORTH, READING

It is a relief to have done with the Wilde and Taylor case; and the general feeling will be that the sentence of two years' hard labour passed upon the prisoners is a substantial measure of justice. Possibly the compassion that is always excited by the spectacle of a hunted animal brought to bay may operate with some in the case of Wilde, who in connection with these charges has stood twice in the dock, but the sentiment, never quite logical at the best will be dispelled by the stern language of the judge who declares that he has never tried a worse case than this, and that he has not the shadow of a doubt as to the man's guilt. If anything could add to the gravity of the verdict of the jury, who found Wilde guilty of all counts of the amended indictment, it is such words as these.

—*[Anon.,] "The Wilde Case," Morning, 27 May 1895*

[T]he imprisonment of Oscar Wilde is an outrage that shows how thoroughly the doctrine of liberty is misconceived. A man who has done nothing in the least degree invasive of any one; a man whose entire life, so far as is known or charged, has been one of strict conformity with idea of equal liberty; a man whose sole offence is that he has done something which most of the rest of us (at least such is the presumption) prefer not to do,—is condemned to spend two years of cruel imprisonment at hard labor.

—*[Anon.], "The Criminal Jailers of Oscar Wilde," Liberty, 15 June 1895*

The moment Oscar Wilde was escorted down the stairs beneath the Old Bailey and led into the cells of nearby Newgate Prison, responses to his plight ran across the whole gamut of opinion. On the conservative side, the Tory *Morning*, which had caused such outrage by reporting on the jury's votes after the first criminal trial, condemned him outright. This newspaper maintained that there was really no support for any fainthearted compassion when one recalled Justice Wills's assertion that he had never tried a worse case. On the radical side, there was the sharp commentary in Benjamin Tucker's American anarchist journal, *Liberty*, which included the writings of several well-known British Individualists, including William Donisthorpe, whose thinking resonates in sections of Wilde's polemical essay "The Soul of Man under Socialism" (1891).[1] For Tucker's readers, Wilde's sexual behaviors had harmed nobody at all. Tucker was not alone in upholding this view, although those who sympathized with the view of Wilde's treatment as unjust tended to articulate their outlook in private. For example, the gifted author John Davidson, who moved in literary circles that overlapped with Wilde's, confided to a friend that "what the law has to do" with the "crime, so-called" of which Wilde had been accused was hard for him to fathom: "as long as there is no rape," there could not, as Davidson saw it, be any grounds upon which the law should condemn a man's sexuality.[2] Such open-mindedness was not entirely rare at the time. To be sure, the hostile commentaries in the press, such as we have seen in the *Morning*, outnumbered those that proved sympathetic toward Wilde's suffering. Still, dissenting voices spoke firmly about the wrongfulness of the conviction, and such figures expressed these sentiments, as Tucker did, in print.

This chapter begins by exploring the opportunities that various critics and journalists took to comment, in divergent respects, on the early stages of Wilde's imprisonment before the memory of his trials began to recede. The sections that follow then examine the ways in which Wilde weathered his two-year sentence, which went through a series of marked shifts. During the first fourteen months, his jail term inflicted untold damage upon his physical and mental health. By late summer 1896, however, his fortunes took a gradual turn for the better, especially after the home secretary, Sir Matthew White Ridley, granted him access to a broader supply of books, as well as the pen and paper that enabled him to return to the practice of writing. In the end, this practice, which inspired him to develop the long document known much later as *De Profundis*, meant that he could, at least to some degree, emotionally transcend the rigors of incarceration.

"A RIGHTEOUS VERDICT"? RESPONSES TO THE TRIALS

No sooner had Justice Wills meted out Wilde's sentence than vulgar merrymaking took place among the boisterous crowds that had gathered in the street outside the Old Bailey. In 1902, Robert Harborough Sherard conjured a sensational picture of this unseemly sight: "men and women joined hands and danced an ungainly farandole, where ragged petticoats and yawning boots flung up the London mud in *feu de joie*, and the hideous faces were distorted with savage triumph. I stood and watched this dance of death for a few minutes, regretting that [the Russian painter Vasily] Veretschagin [*sic*] was not by my side."[3] The *Illustrated Police Budget* went so far as to feature a coarsely drawn sketch of two female prostitutes cavorting on the pavement.[4] H. Montgomery Hyde has suggested that one of the streetwalkers bawled in Cockney: "'E'll 'ave 'is 'air cut regular now."[5]

Various editorials gloated at the verdict. There was no surprise when the *News of the World*, which had already expressed misgivings about the "public harm" that resulted from reporting the proceedings, appealed to its readers' prejudices.[6] The report reveals how long-lasting an impression Wilde's onetime image as an iconic aesthete remained in the popular imagination. The paper recalled his debut in the late 1870s as a fashionable man who had sported outré boutonnières at artistic events, such as the opening of the Grosvenor Gallery: "The æsthetic cult, in the nasty form, is over, and its idol has fallen from its pedestal. Oscar Wilde, the wearer of the lily and the worshipper of the sunflower, has been convicted of the foulest crime that man can commit—a crime so foul that to call the criminal a beast is to insult the animal creation—and for the next two years will be busy with the honest if arduous labour imposed on convicts in Her Majesty's prisons."[7]

For its part, the conservative *Daily Telegraph* aired similar views: "No sterner rebuke," it intoned, "could well have been inflicted on some of the artistic tendencies of the time than the condemnation on Saturday of OSCAR WILDE at the Central Criminal Court."[8] Especially welcome, according to this editor, was the warning that the conviction had sent to those "novelists who have sought to imitate the style of paradox and unreality, poets who have lisped the language of nerveless and effeminate libertinage."[9] On this account, Wilde's "considerable intellectual powers and unbounded assurance" meant that he had for years held dangerous sway over "those who had neither experience nor knowledge of the principles which he travestied."[10] As we can tell, this wholehearted attack also conceded grudging respect for a man whose supreme abilities were as great, one might think, as those of any major political figure.

Just as easy to anticipate were the unforgiving remarks that Henry ("Labby") Labouchere, MP, made in his polemical journal *Truth*. He not only championed Wilde's conviction as a "righteous verdict"; he also went out of his way to condemn Alfred Douglas "as an exceptional young scoundrel," one who might "have given evidence, which, if believed, would have told in regard to one of the indictments for Wilde."[11] In Labouchere's view, the cowardly Douglas chose "to put the Channel between himself and British jurisdiction, leaving his associate in the lurch."[12] Further, Labouchere was quick to remind his audience of the pride that he took in having devised the amendment to the 1885 law that sent Wilde to jail:

> The verdict of the jury was amply justified by the evidence set before it. On the first jury there were, I understand, ten for a verdict of guilty and two for an acquittal. One of the two was a gentleman who, having returned a verdict on a court-martial which he subsequently thought wrong, declared that he never would incur this risk again, and he was consequently impervious to all argument. Wilde and Taylor were tried on a clause in the Criminal Law Amendment Act which I had inserted in order to render it possible for the law to take cognisance of proceedings like theirs. I took the clause *mutatis mutandis* from the French code. As I drafted it, the maximum sentence was seven years. The then Home Secretary and Attorney-General, both most experienced men, however, suggested to me that, in such cases, convictions are always difficult, and that it would be better were the maximum to be two years. Hence the insufficiency that the law allows, which, as Mr. Justice Wills observed, is totally inadequate to the offence.[13]

Parts of this self-satisfied commentary suffer from distortion. There is no truth in the assertion that Labouchere adapted the wording of his amendment to the Criminal Law Amendment Bill from French legislation. The Revolutionary Penal Code that France implemented in August and September 1791 did away with the nation's harsh anti-sodomy laws. Additionally, France upheld the principle of not criminalizing homosexual intimacy in private through the new criminal code enacted under Napoléon in 1810.

Set against these hostile commentaries, a handful of noteworthy voices expressed their dissent. Lockwood's abuses of protocol, in particular, caught the attention of the legal press. The *Scottish Law Review* produced an outspoken commentary on the solicitor general's prosecutorial style: "Sir Frank Lockwood is a *nisi prius* [i.e., assizes] advocate, with whom it has become a second nature to look upon winning a verdict as a piece of successful professional rivalry with a competing brother advocate."[14] Expressly objectionable, this journalist maintains, was Lockwood's exploitation of the privilege to seize upon the last word with the jury, a behavior that infuriated Clarke. Never once had Clarke, who previously held the same position as Lockwood for six years, "claimed the right" to address the jury in this manner.[15] Lockwood's haughty attitude, this reporter also notes, was perilous because "there was a very marked tendency to a sympathy with Wilde which had not shown itself before, and a feeling that, on the whole, an acquittal was more likely than not to be the result."[16] The assumption was that, if Lockwood had not been so bullish, Wilde would have been exonerated. Meanwhile, this commentator reserves several lingering criticisms for the judge.[17] Of Justice Wills, we learn, it is clear that "[h]e has not had even much of the ordinary experience of crime . . . . And after all his years on the bench, there still remains a naivete of manner and expression which one would hardly expect in an old gentleman in that position."[18]

To some observers, however, there was more to Wilde's conviction than the solicitor general's harangues and the justice's naïveté. The fact that both Wilde and Lockwood belonged to the Eighty Club, which advanced the causes of the Liberal Party, and that the two men were social acquaintances, had also raised suspicions that the Liberal government under Lord Archibald Primrose, 5th Earl of Rosebery, had strong motivation to protect itself from any further association with the disgraced Irish writer. Among members of Wilde's close circle, his conviction inspired the belief that Rosebery's administration had sought to make an example of him in order to divert suspicion away from the party's high-ranking members, including the prime minister himself. Douglas, in a substantial article that he drafted for the Parisian periodical *Mercure de France* a few months after Wilde began his sentence, held this opinion:

> I may perhaps be allowed to advance a theory here. I give it for what it is worth, but I can say that it is not merely a hypothesis. I did not invent it; I have heard it on good authority that the Government was intimidated. Mr. Wilde's enemies and the Queensberry faction threatened to make new revelations incriminating senior members of the ruling party if Mr. Wilde would not be condemned. I know *for an absolute fact* that the London police have on their books the names of more than 4,000 persons, many of whom occupy the most exalted places in politics, in art and society, who are known as habitual pæderasts, and yet none of them are prosecuted. Mere moral indignation cannot, therefore, account for the ferocity of this attack against a single man, and I venture to think that my explanation is the right one: *Mr. Wilde was sacrificed to save the reputation of a party.*[19]

Similarly, More Adey, who became one of Wilde's staunchest supporters after the conviction, agreed. In a long letter that he prepared for the French press—one that, on reflection, he chose not to mail—Adey declares: "It has long been reported that a person—indeed several persons—but one in particular, in very high authority, has been involved in unisexual [i.e., homosexual] practices which are in England illegal . . . I am certain that the Treasury [the office that appointed attorneys on behalf of the Crown] were forced by a body of private persons[,] some of whose names I know, headed by the infamous Lord Queensberry to obtain a conviction by some means or other against Mr. Wilde. These individuals, I believe, blackmailed the Treasury, holding over the Treasury the threat that, if Wilde were not convicted, damning evidence ~~should~~ would be produced against important and exalted persons."[20]

In any case, Lockwood's headstrong determination to condemn Wilde struck one or two contemporaries as extreme. In 1932, Edward Marjoribanks claimed—without providing any source of authority—that even Carson was startled by Lockwood's tenacity. "Cannot you let up on the fellow now?" Carson asked Lockwood.[21] "He has," Carson added, "suffered a great deal."[22] Lockwood's defensive response suggests that there was much more at stake in the Crown prosecution than Wilde's culpable sexual behavior: "'I would,' Lockwood said, 'but we cannot: we dare not: it would at once be said, both in England and abroad, that owing to the names mentioned in Queensberry's letters we were forced to abandon it.'"[23] To this day, we do know which "names" were vulnerable to exposure. Douglas's, Adey's, and (courtesy of Marjoribanks) Lockwood's respective observations are polemical ones that raise the specter of a wholesale government conspiracy.

Even to those who voiced no suspicions about the government's motivation in hastening the retrial, there were serious doubts about the ethics of the whole affair. W. T. Stead, even though he deplored the prisoner's "dirty tricks of indecent familiarity with boys and men," focused on the moral hypocrisy in the court's treatment of Wilde.[24] In Stead's opinion, it was clear that the law operated on a double standard when it came to the sexual exploitation of girls and women: "If Oscar Wilde . . . had ruined the lives of half a dozen simpletons of girls, or had broken up the home of his friend by corrupting the friend's wife, no one could have laid a finger on him. The male is sacro-sanct: the female is fair game. To have burdened society with a dozen bastards, to have destroyed a happy home by his lawless lust—of these things the criminal law takes no account."[25]

Stead's incisive observations spurred similarly pointed responses. Edward Carpenter, the homophile socialist who had taken a strong interest in Wilde's plight, sent Stead a letter, in which he enclosed a copy of his *Homogenic Love, and Its Place in a Free Society* (1894): "I have long thought that the tendency [i.e., of male homosexual desire], which in the case of Wilde has been so fatally mis-developed, is really capable under proper direction of being cultivated into an ennobling love. The feeling has, in one form or other, been a factor in human life in all times & countries—and that would be a reason for supposing that it requires wise guidance to its proper expression rather than blind

~~persecution~~ /extinction\."[26] Douglas, for his part, was more forthright in his reaction to Stead's *Review of Reviews*. In a long missive, he informed Stead: "Why on earth in the name of liberty and common sense a man cannot be allowed to love a boy rather than a woman when his nature and his instinct tell him to do so, and when he has before him the example of such a number of noble and gifted men who have had similar tastes, (such as Shakespeare, Marlowe, Michael Angelo, Frederick the Great and a host of others) is another question and one to which I should like to hear a satisfactory answer."[27]

Meanwhile, the *Star* focused on problems with procedural technicalities. In a column titled "Some Mysteries of the Wilde Case," the reporter provided "a list of blanks that were left unfilled at the first two trials," in tones that were at times sarcastic.[28] The article, since it contains such thoughtful speculation on details that were at the time unresolved, warrants quoting in its entirety:

> One curious change of policy was observed during the trial of the Queensberry, Wilde, and Taylor scandals. In the early stages of these cases, everybody seemed agreed that no names should be mentioned unnecessarily, and the evidence became a patchwork of noughts and crosses, dotted with X, Y, and Z, where proper names should have been. The blanks were at first numerous, and a full score of little pieces of paper, with mysterious names written upon them were handed to the various judges and magistrates who have had a hand in this unsavory stew. Then on Wednesday last [i.e., 22 May 1895] Taylor was called into the box, and being pressed for the name of one of his associates at Little College Street, asked, "Must I mention my friend's name? I would rather write it down." "No," roared the Solicitor-general, "we will have no names kept back!" and Mr. Justice Wills quietly added, "If you write it, I shall read it out. I do not approve of mystery in cases of this kind. It is sometimes done good-naturedly, and great mischief is caused. It is supposed that there is some kind of mystery, and that the judge and everybody else are concerned in a kind of conspiracy. We will have nothing of that kind."
>
> Now, if this is good rule for one, it is a good rule for all, and the public may be excused for trying to fill up some of the blanks which remain. For example, it would be interesting to know:—
>
> 1. Who is the Oxford undergraduate who created "The Chameleon," and seduced the unsuspecting Wilde and the innocent Lord Alfred Douglas into contributing to its pages?
> 2. Who wrote the story of "The Priest and the Acolyte," which so polluted the said pages, that even Wilde—he says himself—protested?
> 3. Who was the "friend of Lady Queensberry" who first took Lord Alfred Douglas to Tite Street, and introduced him to Wilde in 1891?

4. Who was the friend of the Marquess of Queensberry who accompanied him on his visit to Tite Street in 1894, when he threatened Wilde with condign punishment if he did not cease to associate with Lord Alfred? Wilde applied to this friend his perpetually recurring phrase, remarking that "his name was of no importance."
5. Who was the "gentleman" who lived at Margaret Street, Regent Street, in whose house Wilde first met Atkins and Mavor? (It may have been Schwabe, whose name was in the early stages of the case treated as a profound mystery.)
6. Who was the gentleman "whose name it is not necessary to mention" in whose company Charles Parker on one occasion called on Wilde at the Albemarle Hotel?
7. Who is the gentleman who was blackmailed of £500 by Allen and Wood at their den in Regent Street, on accusations of misconduct with Charles Parker?
8. Who was the musical composer with whom Charles Parker went to Paris for a month—according to himself as valet—six months after he first met Taylor?
9. Who is the "Birmingham gentleman" whose name was handed to Atkins on a piece of paper with the suggestion that he tried to blackmail him at 124 Tachbrook Street, on the occasion when he and Burton were taken to Rochester Row police station?
10. Who is the gentleman the same scoundrels are accused of having blackmailed of £200 at 35 Alderney Street, in August 1892?
11. Who are the "two American gentlemen" they are accused of having tried to blackmail at the Hotel Victoria in Northumberland Avenue in 1893?
12. Who is the "foreign nobleman" whose yacht lay off Scarborough, whom they are accused of blackmailing of £500?
13. Who is the "elderly City man" they are accused of blackmailing by picking his pocket of his papers at their lodging in Buckingham Palace Road, afterwards going to his office and threatening to expose him?[29]

In a similar spirit, *Reynolds's* remarked in a front-page article titled "Male Prostitution" that it was astonishing to see that Wilde's conviction rested largely on the basis of supposedly corroborated evidence from men who admitted their sexual involvement with him. The most prominent of these witnesses made their living by threatening to expose vulnerable gentlemen for their homosexual misdeeds. "Are the male strumpets who have given evidence in this case," *Reynolds's* had inquired the day after Wilde's conviction, "to go unpunished?" "We are not," the reporter adds, "going to gloat over the ruin of the unhappy man who has been convicted and sentenced to two years' hard labour at the Central Criminal Court."[30] Although the article states that Wilde's behavior was an outrage to society, the commentary shifts focus to the ways that the trials belonged to a series of public scandals about male prostitution, from the time of the Boulton and Park cross-dressing debacle in 1870–71 through the Dublin Castle controversy to the more recent case of Edward de Cobain.[31] "Wilde's crime," *Reynolds's* observes, "would have been infinitely greater, had it been proved that he seduced any of the prostitutes upon whose evidence he has been convicted. But with the dismissal of Shelley's case, the prosecution were obliged surely [i.e., compelled], for the most part, upon the testimony of notorious harlots and blackmailers. But that evidence has satisfied the jury."[32] Even though the reporter cannot fathom the reason that led a man like Wilde to associate himself with these reprobates, the more pressing question concerned the fate of the criminals who had testified against him. "Has the Crown bribed them to give evidence by the promise of a pardon? And is no notice to be taken of the Judge's remarks with reference to Lord Alfred Douglas?"[33] If, the paper comments, the "beastly witnesses" were "not brought to justice," there would be the "suspicion in the public mind that the prosecution" had secured "a conviction that does not square with an Englishman's sense of justice and fair play."[34]

Equally trenchant was the pamphlet *Apologia pro Oscar Wilde*, which the thirty-year-old musician Dalhousie Young completed within a week of Wilde's conviction. Besides offering an interpretation of Wilde's writings that differs "materially from that which was put upon them by the prosecution," Young boldly advances the idea that the crime that Wilde had perpetrated should hardly be classified as a crime at all: "Not only did the ancients, the civilized Greeks and the organized Romans, think that it was not a matter in which the state should interfere, but the Code de Napoléon takes no notice of it whatever."[35] Young's distinctly modern view is that the law has no business interfering in the private sexual behaviors of consenting adults. "For the act we are considering," he says, "is one done by mutual consent of two men, an act which does not in any way render them unable to fulfil the duties of citizenship and which does not affect directly or indirectly, for good or for ill, any other person."[36]

"I LONGED TO DIE": H.M. PRISON PENTONVILLE AND H.M. PRISON WANDSWORTH

Young's heartening words appeared in the early weeks of what turned into the next phase of Wilde's distressing experience: the difficult month-and-a-half that he endured in H.M. Prison Pentonville.[37] Modern jails such as Pentonville operated on the insufferable principles of the "separate system" laid down by the Prisons Act 1865; the ensuing Prisons Act 1877, masterminded by Edmund Du Cane, extended this model—one that minimized communication between inmates—to jails across the country. Hard labor, which was not abolished until the Criminal Justice Act 1948 (11 & 12 Geo. 6 c. 58), was central to the methods of punishment. The 1865 law defined hard labor as "work at the tread wheel, shot drill, crank, capstan, stonebreaking, or such other like description of hard bodily labour" (28 & 29 Vict. c. 126 s. 19). Within decades, the meaninglessness of such brutality became apparent to the prison commissioners. In the same year that Wilde received his sentence, the voluminous report that the Liberal Member of Parliament and Privy Councillor Herbert Gladstone submitted to the home secretary, H. H. Asquith, confirmed that these laws had made English jails intolerable. Gladstone's *Minutes of Evidence Taken of the Departmental Committee of Prisons* (1895) emphasizes from the start that hard labor has little purpose other than to demoralize prisoners. "Recommendations," it states, "have been made to us in favour of the increase in workshop labour, the abolition of the crank and the treadwheel, the abolition of the rules of dark cells in convict prisons, the prevention of crowding in chapel, the improvement of prison food, and the instruction of prison officers."[38] Such comments alert us to the fact that Wilde began his sentence at a time when the English prison system had reached a point of crisis.

For a short amount of time, the press kept its readers up to date with the harsh circumstances in which Wilde transmogrified from a finely accoutered aesthete into a common prisoner. The *Daily Telegraph*, for example, carried a solemn report from the Press Association about Wilde's humbling experience:

> On removal, both men were suffering from nervousness and betrayed their mental anxiety. When handed over to the governor of Pentonville the prisoners were taken into the reception ward. Each had to give details of his identity and religion and submit to a medical examination, after which they passed through the hands of the prison bathroom attendants and barber, and they exchanged their own clothes for those provided by the prison authorities, subsequently being handed over to the care of the prison chaplain. Yesterday they attended the prison chapel with the other occupants of the gaol, and with the exception of exercise they were confined to their cells, where they will in future be kept unless their health becomes such as to entitle them to infirmary treatment, in which event the prison doctor will decide the nature of the labour they must perform. By the terms of their sentences they will be isolated from their friends, except upon four occasions a year, and even this privilege may be forfeited by indifferent conduct.[39]

By comparison, the *Illustrated Police Budget* made much of the physical humiliation that Wilde underwent once he entered Pentonville. The journalist was especially preoccupied by the fact that Wilde's seemingly lavish coiffure had to be brought in line with prison regulations: "It must have taken Mr. Wilde years to train and grow his hair as it stood early on Saturday; it took the prison barber just two minutes to cut all the locks off. When the hair was reduced to an ordinary length by the aid of a pair of scissors, the barber got to work with his cropping machine, and in less than fifteen minutes had reduced Mr. Wilde's hair to so fine a point that even a man with long nails could not get hold of it. Oscar looked a poor picture when all his locks were gone. Probably when his whiskers grow, he may present a better appearance; but at the moment he looks an awful sight."[40] The report proceeds to itemize what it believes is Wilde's new prison regime: a meager diet of beans, bacon, and potatoes; a plank bed raised a few inches from the floor; and the brutality of hard labor on the treadmill ("six hours daily making an ascent of 6,000ft.," with varying periods of rest).[41] The truth was that the prison governor had determined that the tasks best suited to the six-foot Irishman weighing 190 pounds were sewing mailsacks and picking oakum (that is, shredding with one's fingers lengths of tarry rope that were used for caulking the hulls of ships).

It was perhaps because of the infamous conditions in Pentonville that reports began to circulate about Wilde's deterioration. Ten days after his conviction, several dailies contained short reports stating that he had already declined into insanity. Wilde also appeared to be suffering physically. On 6 June 1895, the *Morning* stated that he had weathered an attack of diarrhea: a condition that became acute in the coming months. "This was followed," the newspaper added, "by mental prostration and melancholy," which had been exacerbated by doses of "potassium of bromide."[42] So severe, on this account, was Wilde's reaction that he was said to have been sent to the prison infirmary. Such alarming commentaries prompted Wilde's older brother, Willie, to make inquiries. Immediately, the governor of Pentonville said that the reports were "cruel fabrications."[43] "Prisoner," he added confidently, "is going on very well."[44]

At the same time, there were concerted efforts to challenge Wilde's conviction. The *Pall Mall Gazette* observed that Sir Edward Clarke had approached Sir Robert Reid, the attorney general, with an application for Reid's "fiat to issue for writ of error in respect of a point of law . . . as the framing of the indictment."[45] Clarke's intention, it appears, was to argue that the criminal proceedings against Wilde had been irregular, since the original indictment joined charges of conspiracy (a felony) with those of gross indecency (a misdemeanor). Nothing, it appears, came from Clarke's application. Within the next two weeks, C. O. Humphreys submitted, also to no avail, a petition for the remission of Wilde's sentence.

In the meantime, at the Home Office Sir Evelyn Ruggles-Brise, who had been a contemporary of Wilde's at Oxford, stood at the helm of the prison commission. He reviewed requests from Wilde's friends and associates, family members, and various attorneys for permission to visit him. The most significant visitor in these early weeks was the Liberal politician Richard Burdon Haldane, MP. Haldane, who had been passed over as solicitor general when Lockwood took the appointment in 1894, was troubled by the thought of Wilde's weakening condition. During Haldane's interview with Wilde on 12 June 1895, he could tell that the inmate needed more reading matter than such standard fare as John Bunyan's *Pilgrim's Progress* (1678). As Haldane recollected, once they had agreed that Gustave Flaubert's works might not be admitted, he and Wilde "hit upon St. Augustine's Works and on [Theodor] Mommsen's History of Rome."[46] Haldane's list of fifteen requested volumes, which he submitted on 28 June 1895, also included Blaise Pascal's *Pensées* (1670), Walter Pater's *Renaissance: Studies in Art and Poetry* (first published in 1873), and four titles by John Henry Newman.[47]

Haldane presumably made further arrangements that he believed would improve Wilde's lot. Two weeks later, the document authorizing his transfer to another jail was submitted, and on 4 July 1895 he was moved across London to H.M. Prison Wandsworth.[48] Few individuals knew about Wilde's removal from Pentonville to Wandsworth. Haldane may have labored under the mistaken assumption that Wandsworth would provide a more suitable environment for Wilde, since the Revd. William Douglas Morrison—a vocal critic of the separate system—served as a chaplain there. In an 1894 essay on recidivism, for instance, Morrison had posed pressing questions about the principles upon which prison discipline was based: "How can we expect a man to do better when we are doing our utmost to make him worse?"[49] Wandsworth, however, as Morrison's despairing observations might suggest, eventually proved even more deleterious to Wilde's health than his brief stay in Pentonville. Besides diarrhea, he suffered from bouts of sleeplessness and hunger. "While I was in Wandsworth Prison," Wilde recalled, "I longed to die."[50] As he told André Gide after his release, there was one thing that prevented him from taking his own life: "what kept me from doing so was looking at *the others*, and seeing that they were as unhappy as I was, and feeling sorry for them."[51]

As J. Robert Maguire has pointed out: "Under the prison regulations, Wilde was entitled to send and receive a letter and have two visitors upon completion of three months of sentence."[52] This routine was repeated at quarterly intervals.

The first regular visitor was Robert Harborough Sherard, who enjoyed a twenty-minute interview with Wilde on 25 August 1895. Sherard, a well-meaning individual whose meddling in Wilde's personal affairs eventually dissolved their friendship, told the press that the "convict appeared well" but needed more reading material than a single book a week.[53] "The prisoner," he said, "has lately been reading Pater and Newman."[54] Still, although Sherard notified the *Daily Chronicle* that he was "much struck by [Wilde's] courage and resignation," he later remarked (in different publications) that the prisoner's hands were disfigured, and that his nails were broken and bleeding."[55] The injuries came from hard labor.

At this point, Sherard had taken it upon himself to bring about a détente between Constance and Oscar. Since the start of Wilde's sentence, Constance had remained the sole individual with the privilege of receiving a letter from him. Wilde's correspondence with Constance, which has gone missing, appears to have persuaded her to exercise caution in pursuing a divorce. On 13 September 1895, she requested permission to see her spouse. "My husband, I have reason to know," she wrote, "is apprehensive of my obtaining a divorce from him within a short time. As my mind is not however definitely made up to this step but is dependent on questions which can only be properly discussed between him and me personally, I am most anxious to be allowed to talk over matters with him."[56] The letter closes with a comment on her frail health (she had been experiencing difficulties with her mobility for the past six years), and she mentions that she has found someone who will escort her to the jail toward the end of the following week. Eight days later, after Constance had made the journey from Switzerland to speak with Wilde at Wandsworth, she told Sherard that her husband had "been mad /the last 3 years\."[57] She also reported, in words that reveal how disillusioned Wilde had become regarding his affair with Bosie, that if he "saw Alfred Douglas he would kill him." Her interview with her spouse, as she made clear, was "indeed awful."[58]

By the second week of September, rumors were abroad that Wilde's health had gone into serious decline. Morrison confided to Haldane that he was in a troubling state. The chaplain convinced himself that Wilde's poor health had its roots in the prisoner's unbridled desires: "I fear from what I hear and see that perverse sexual practices are again getting the mastery over him."[59] Masturbation, as far as Morrison could tell, was driving the prisoner to distraction. Especially disturbing as well was the stench inside Wilde's cell, which the chaplain mistakenly believed must have transpired from self-abuse: "The odour of his cell is now so bad that the officer in charge of him has to use carbolic in it every other day."[60] Ruggles-Brise was disturbed to learn that Morrison had reported this to Haldane; there was, he insisted in a letter to the Member of Parliament, no validity to Morrison's bizarre claims. At the same time, Ruggles-Brise tactfully admitted: "I do not for a moment believe that Mr. Morrison made [these allegations] otherwise than in perfect good faith and out of a sincere anxiety for the welfare of the prisoner."[61] This communication was markedly different from the note that Ruggles-Brise, in rather hurried handwriting, had already put into the official record: "It is the fact that the [warder] told Mr. Morrison that he suspected Wilde of masturbation on account of the odour of his cell."[62] Aghast at this suggestion, Ruggles-Brise referred to an enclosed doctor's report, which stated that Wilde's cell smelled because the inmate was unused to scrubbing the floor; for this reason, Wilde had been given Jeyes Fluid to disinfect the water.[63] Still, Ruggles-Brise feared that Morrison was concocting a story for the press: "I am afraid Mr. Morrison is a dangerous man, who is trying to make of Wilde a peg whereon to hang his theories of the brutality of our prison system."[64]

In government circles, the discussion of Wilde's plight had become a source of great sensitivity. Leakage of unwelcome information about the prisoner's failing health aroused increasing concerns at the Home Office. Toward the end of September, the authorities took note of two short articles that had appeared in Massingham's *Chronicle*. The first, which mentions that Wilde had lost 22 pounds in weight since entering jail, comments on the ways his weakened condition shows how "our prison system destroys the mind and enfeebles the body of its victims."[65] (Morrison in all probability relayed this intelligence.) The second, which states that it has received confirmation of the earlier report from "a well-known literary man," observes that Wilde is "suffering greatly from sheer want of nourishment."[66] Sherard, the "literary man" in question, had pulled strings to secure a second interview in September (on this occasion, he used his birth name, R. S. Kennedy).[67] The authorities were immediately suspicious of Sherard's intrusiveness. By 16 October 1895, a warder submitted a report that he had overheard Sherard communicating to Wilde "that something could be done, by means of the Daily Chronicle, to call attention to his case."[68]

As his mental and physical ordeal intensified, Wilde had also been suffering strain from his disordered finances. Within weeks of his imprisonment, the press made its readers aware of the bankruptcy proceedings that had opened against him. In the later part of June, Queensberry initiated an action against him, and on 2 July 1895, two days before his transfer to Wandsworth, Fred Kerley served Wilde a copy of the marquess's receiving order.[69] In the following month, the court issued the order, which revealed that Wilde's debts amounted to a staggering £3,591.[70] Constance's attorneys, Hargrove and Co., had been taking steps to see if bankruptcy could be avoided. By 4 September 1895, C. O.

Humphreys told More Adey that Hargrove planned to make a bid on the life interest on the marriage settlement. (The settlement had been agreed on 10 January 1884.)

The trust funds were considerable. There were £3,336 in debentures (secured corporate bonds) with the Canadian Pacific Railway alone. The other investments, which included mortgage bonds, stocks, and shares, amounted to just over £22,250, with interest rates varying between 4 percent and 10 percent.[71] Hargrove wished to secure a deal. If Wilde surrendered his life interest for a token £5 and permitted a charge on the royalties from his literary rights, the claim on both the £1,000 loan that Wilde had taken out on the marriage settlement and the compound interest would be defrayed. In principle, such an arrangement would make it easier, through subscriptions from friends and associates, to discharge the remaining debts that were owed to Wilde's creditors. This proposal, which proved unacceptable to Wilde's counsel, counted as the first in a series of attempts to resolve the question whether he should comply with Constance's wish to hand over the life interest entirely to her. Since his legal advisers repeatedly obstructed this request, the dispute over this source of income continued throughout Wilde's sentence. Constance needed sufficient funds to maintain her family, while Wilde required an adequate allowance on which to subsist after his release. Furthermore, Constance also felt that her husband should be removed as the natural guardian of their sons, especially given her fears that she might predecease him. She wanted sole custody. On 12 August 1895, Adey's lawyer, Henry Martin Holman, stated that, should Constance make any such application, Wilde must have access to his children. Besides, the document opined that it was premature to reach an agreement about the matter of custody until he was released.

By 24 September 1895, Wilde arrived for the public examination of his finances, although he did not appear before the registrar. His counsel, John Peter ("J. P.") Grain, since he had studied Hargrove's plan, asked for the proceedings to be adjourned. The court learned that, although Wilde had no immediate assets, there was the probability of future royalties from his books and plays; moreover, a subscription fund had already raised £1,000.[72] With his hair uncut, he looked the shadow of his former self. Wilde's disheveled appearance shocked his old friend Arthur Clifton, who attended the hearing. Clifton was there because he served as a co-trustee of the marriage settlement, to which Wilde owed the largest sum. Since Clifton held this responsibility, he gained permission to speak privately with Wilde: "He was," Clifton told a mutual friend Carlos Blacker, "terribly despondent and said several times that he did not think he w[oul]d be able to last the punishment out."[73] "The trial," Clifton went on, "was a mere travesty of justice. I am going to do my best to get the punishment reduced."[74] Like a number of other observers at the time, Clifton suspected that Wilde's homosexual life had "been enormously exaggerated so as to shield others."[75] Ross was also present, and he, too, managed to speak for half an hour with Wilde. Adey was at the hearing as well.

In the weeks that immediately followed, Wilde's health underwent severe ups and downs. On 20 September 1895, a prison doctor reported to the Home Office that Wilde was "in good mental & bodily health": "he is in thoroughly good hands."[76] By mid-October, however, the inmate—no doubt because of his chronic diarrhea—languished in Wandsworth's infirmary. Frank Harris reveals the terrible impact that this period during the fall of 1895 had upon his friend: "'I died,' [Wilde] said quietly, 'and came to life again, as a patient . . . What with the purgings and the semi-starvation and sleeplessness and, worst of all, the incessant torturing self-reproaches, I got weaker and weaker; I could scarcely move.'"[77] Even though he informed the warder that he was too weak to rise from his bed, he was scolded for malingering (namely, feigning illness in order to escape his duties), fell over while getting up, bruised himself, and then struggled to reach the chapel. During the service, he fainted. "I fell on my ear," Wilde informed Harris, "and I must have burst the drum of it, or injured it some way."[78] Most likely, the ruptured tympanum exacerbated preexisting problems in Wilde's middle ear that eventually led to the meningoencephalitis that killed him five years later.

Toward the end of October 1895, Wilde's condition had worsened to such a degree that a further medical report was commissioned. On this occasion, two doctors from Broadmoor Criminal Lunatic Asylum, Berkshire, produced a twelve-page inquiry that found little amiss with Wilde's mental and physical wellbeing. These physicians observed that, since entering Wandsworth, Wilde had gained 6 pounds in weight. Moreover, they noted that his daily life in the prison hospital had lifted his spirits: "He expressed himself as being quite satisfied with his present treatment and as being comparatively happy in the associated Infirmary Ward, signifying his intense dislike of the thought of having to return to his prison cell."[79] They recommended, however, changes in Wilde's diet, since they believed the daily rations of watered-down oatmeal (known as skilly) and brown bread might have been responsible for his sickness. Wilde's condition, though, did not improve. During the early part of November, the authorities placed him under round-the-clock watch.

By 12 November 1895, Wilde had recuperated enough to present himself for the public examination of his debts at the court in Carey Street. The time had arrived when he would be declared bankrupt, since Percy Douglas had not come through with a promised £500, and further hopes of another £400 from a different source had been dashed. Wilde was visibly ailing. To *Reynolds's*, Wilde's demeanor was almost unrecognizable: "He looked dreadfully pale and worn and ill. His face has shrunk and the skin hangs down from the cheek-bones, making ugly wrinkles on either side of his nose. They have cut his hair in a shocking way and parted it down the side, and he wears a short, scrubby, unkempt beard, such as afflicts the denizens of doss-houses. He leaned on the ledge of the witness-box, but the position was not a languid pose. It was the attitude of a man without strength or energy to stand upon his feet."[80] Elsewhere, the press chose to focus not on his health but on his history of extravagance. The *Daily News*, for example, noted that, although he maintained no accounts of his own, in 1893 alone Wilde's "liabilities exceeded his assets by almost £1,450."[81]

Given the displeasure that Morrison's and Sherard's leaks had caused, Ruggles-Brise took steps to remove Wilde from Wandsworth. Already, on 17 October 1895, the prison governor, Captain A. P. H. Helby, had informed the commissioners that Sherard appeared intent on making "the prisoner the subject of newspaper agitation."[82] Perhaps wishing to be spared the nuisance of prying journalists, the governor wanted Wilde out of his custody: "I would suggest whether it may not be advisable that the prisoner should be transferred to a country prison, where he would be less accessible to such influences."[83] A few days afterward, the lengthy report from the two doctors based at Broadmoor stated: "with careful treatment and, shortly, removal to a prison in the country, with different work and a greater range of reading there is nothing to indicate that prison will prejudicially affect him."[84] The hope was that a larger cell, better air, and more engaging tasks, such as bookbinding and gardening, would sustain Wilde through the rest of his sentence.

"*THEY TREAT ME CRUELLY*": H.M. PRISON READING UNDER HENRY B. ISAACSON

The day after the bankruptcy proceedings had terminated (he signed his statement on 19 November), Wilde was promptly transferred to H.M. Prison Reading, a smaller prison located thirty miles west of London.[85] The transfer, however, involved a short but harrowing exposure before the public that became deeply ingrained in Wilde's memory. In the long prison letter known as *De Profundis*, Wilde recalled his anguish at the ways an amassing crowd mocked him while he waited for half an hour on a railway platform for the connection that would take him to Reading:

> From two o'clock till half-past two that day I had to stand on the centre platform of Clapham Junction in convict dress and handcuffed, for the world to look at. I had been taken out of the Hospital Ward without a moment's notice being given to me. Of all possible objects I was the most grotesque. When people saw me they laughed. Each train as it came up swelled the audience. Nothing could exceed their amusement. That was of course before they knew who I was. As soon as they had been informed, they laughed still more. For half an hour I stood there in the grey November rain surrounded by a jeering mob. For a year after that was done to me I wept every day at the same hour and for the same space of time.[86]

This was the first public sighting of Wilde outside the courts since the start of his sentence. In memory of the brutal humiliation that he should never have suffered, on 23 July 2019 a permanent rainbow plaque was unveiled on the platform at Clapham Junction to remind the public of the homophobic abuse that Wilde had endured. On his arrival at Reading, he was placed in cell C.3.3. In the prison, this designation—which referred to the gallery, the landing, and the cell number—became synonymous with his identity.

H.M. Prison Reading initially offered small improvements upon the deadening environment of Wandsworth. The Home Office informed the governor, Lieutenant Colonel Henry B. Isaacson, a former marine, that Wilde should undergo a full medical examination. Isaacson was also told that the prisoner would receive further books. The list that Wilde had submitted contained miscellaneous reference works, including a copy of H. G. Liddell and R. Scott's *Greek–English Lexicon*. These titles were paid for by Adela Schuster, who worked closely with Adey to see if there were any means by which Wilde's sentence could be remitted. Adey, who was likely Wilde's first visitor at Reading, arranged for the volumes to be sent to the jail. Even if Wilde had access to wider reading, he soon exhausted the available supply in the prison library. To be sure, he acquired new skills. On 23 January 1896, Haldane optimistically informed Adey: "Wilde is well—working in the garden & at bookbinding."[87] (Wilde was industrious. On his release, a journalist reported that Wilde had "bound four Bibles" and "rebound no end of hymn-books used by the prisoners."[88]) Still, even with these extra tasks to preoccupy him, the tedium was extreme.

Under Isaacson's strict regimen, the additional reading materials hardly alleviated Wilde's dispiriting plight. As he told Gide in June 1897, it took some time before he grasped how to breach the ban on communicating with other inmates during the sole hour of exercise in the prison yard each day. "I had already been in prison six weeks," Wilde divulged to the French writer, "and I had not spoken to anyone—not a soul."[89] Even so, his fellow inmates soon determined who he was. A prisoner who was following him said sotto voce: "Oscar Wilde, I pity you, because you must suffer more than we do."[90] "No, my friend," Wilde said as discreetly as he could, "we all suffer alike."[91] Wilde recalled that had he learned to speak without moving his lips he and the other man would most probably not have been called out of line. "You will both," the warder said, "have to go before the Governor."[92] At the end of their interrogation by Isaacson, who wanted to know who had spoken first, the two men were given fifteen days' confinement.

These inconspicuous conversations, though, were not sufficient to secure Wilde's mental stability. In February 1896, Constance, who became distressed by the hardship that her husband was suffering, traveled once more from Europe in order to make a further visit, this time breaking the heartrending news that his beloved mother had died earlier in the month. This was, she acknowledged, a delicate task. "I believe it will half kill him," she stated to her sister-in-law.[93] "Poor Oscar has been bitterly punished for breaking the laws of his country[.] I am not so strong but I could bear the journey better if I thought that such a terrible thing would not be told him roughly."[94] During this visit, on 19 February, Constance spoke with Wilde about their family affairs in a private room, and she was able to kiss him. Meanwhile, Adey drafted a letter for Wilde that emphasized the recent success of the French production of *Salomé*, under the direction of Aurélien Lugné-Poe, by the Théâtre de l'Œuvre in Paris. He also mentioned the provincial productions of *An Ideal Husband* in Newcastle upon Tyne and Brighton.[95] But even if such a cheering epistle had reached Wilde, it is unlikely that it would have elevated his mood.

Toward the end of May 1896, Ross and Sherard visited their friend—a day earlier, it appears, than Wilde had expected. The interview, perhaps owing to the fact that Wilde had been caught off guard, turned into a nerve-racking experience. In a moving letter to Adey, Ross explained that he and Sherard were shaken by Wilde's appearance—so much so that Sherard "was nearly breaking down all the time & shewed himself fearfully nervous."[96] Wilde was too tearful to make coherent conversation. He simply spouted "odd disconnected remarks," although at one point he was alert enough to inquire "whether any of the present Government [under the Marquess of Salisbury] would be favorably disposed towards him," in hopes of an early release.[97] "He cried the whole time," Ross said, "& when we asked him to talk more he said he had nothing to say & wanted to hear us talk."[98] Wilde, however, began to ramble, and Ross took careful note of the prisoner's main complaints: "He is not allowed paper and pencil . . . The Doctor very unkind to him . . . Could only read a little."[99] Moreover, he expressed his grief at the lack of reading materials: "Had read everything else in Library several times."[100] Wilde then requested copies of Walter

Pater's latest book (*Gaston de Latour* [1896]), Geoffrey Chaucer's works, and a prose translation of Dante Alighieri. "Asked how he felt generally," Ross states, "he said in a half aside low voice, 'They treat me cruelly.'"[101]

Even though it was apparent to Ross that Wilde was suffering from both anemia and gout, he had much greater concern about Wilde's "wandering remarks" and the prisoner's questions as to whether they thought "his brain seemed all right."[102] As Ross knew, it was in the interests of officials to set aside the evident symptoms of the mental breakdown that Wilde was facing. "Each person," Ross told Adey, "has his view as to what constitutes a decayed mind, but if I were asked about Oscar before a commission, I should say that 'Confinement apart from all labour or treatment had made him temporarily silly.'"[103] To be sure, Ross feared that he might sound as if he was exaggerating. But the truth was shattering: "If asked whether he was going to die. It seems quite ~~probable~~ / possible \ within the next few months, even if his constitution remained unimpaired."[104] On his way out, Ross managed to secure a few minutes with Isaacson to express his grave concerns about Wilde's welfare. The governor replied dismissively that Wilde "was doing as well as could be expected."[105] In all probability, Adey or Ross communicated their concerns to Ruggles-Brise, since on 13 June 1896 the prison commissioner asked Isaacson to "[b]e good enough to report on the present mental condition of the prisoner Oscar Wilde."[106]

The day after this troubling visit, Wilde regained a measure of equilibrium, as we can tell from a cogent letter that he sent to Ross. In this item of correspondence, he turns to his exasperation with Douglas, which had been deepening during the past year. By this juncture, Douglas had been unable to communicate with Wilde. Douglas, who had resided on the Continent since 24 April 1895, was disappointed not to have exchanged correspondence with Wilde. As he said to Ada Leverson, the governor of Wandsworth told him "that Oscar had the power to correspond but that he deliberately preferred not to."[107] "Can you," he asked, "throw any light on this question?"[108] "It seems to me quite inconceivable that he should prefer to correspond with his 'family' than with me."[109] Over time, Douglas's puzzlement about Wilde's brush-off transformed into indignation, since he had begun to see that Adey and Ross had deemed that only harm might arise if Wilde started communicating with him. Despite everything, Douglas hardly kept silent in protesting the injustice done to his onetime lover. We have already noted his letter to Stead. At roughly the same moment, Douglas submitted a long petition to Her Majesty the Queen pressing her for a prerogative of mercy (i.e., a pardon granted at the recommendation of the home secretary): "Will you not save this man, who even if he be guilty has already been punished more, a thousand times more cruelly than he deserves?"[110]

Bosie had also been speaking out against Wilde's imprisonment with editors from the French press. During his second visit to Wandsworth, Sherard—who spent much of his time in France—disclosed Douglas's intention to publish an article in the *Mercure de France* about his intimate friendship with Wilde. In July 1895, the journal had already published a highly sympathetic essay, "Défense d'Oscar Wilde," by Hughes Rebell, the French translator of the Irish author's *Intentions* (1891, revised 1894). Eloquently, Rebell put Justice Wills's condemnation of Wilde's sexual life into critical perspective: "On se demande quel crime a pu commettre Oscar Wilde pour être traité de la sorte, s'il a trahi l'Angleterre, tenté d'assassiner la reine ou de faire sauter le Parlement. On reste étonné quand on apprend qu'Oscar Wilde n'a commis aucun crime, q'il n'a même probablement pas commis la faute contre nature dont on l'accuse,—du moins sa culpabilité n'est-elle pas encore démontrée" (One wonders what crime Oscar Wilde may have committed to be treated in this way, whether he betrayed England, attempted to assassinate the queen, or to blow up Parliament. We are astounded when we learn that Oscar Wilde did not commit any crime, that he probably did not even commit the crime against nature of which he is accused,—at least his guilt has not yet been demonstrated).[111] The prisoner, however, was agitated by the prospect of suffering further uninvited attention in the periodicals, and he insisted that Sherard caution Bosie about making additional approaches to the *Mercure de France*. Sherard obliged.

By summer 1896, Douglas was gaining the distinct impression that Wilde had spurned him altogether. In the autobiography that he published in the late 1920s, which is colored by the feud that he had conducted with Ross during the preceding decade, Douglas states that he never did anything "dishonorable or cowardly . . . to abandon" Wilde.[112] By the time Wilde had spent several months in Reading, Douglas says, the prisoner forbade him to send any letters whatsoever: "I was told by Ross that Oscar has 'turned against' me, and in fact he stated categorically that I was on no account to write to him and that I was to hand over any letters of his I had to Ross."[113]

Douglas, as far as Wilde was concerned, needed to keep quiet. Wilde was horrified to discover that Bosie planned to dedicate his dual-language volume *Poems/Poèmes* (1896) to him. (This collection reprints both "In Praise of Shame" and "Two Loves," the two poems from the *Chameleon* that had been discussed in court regarding Douglas's defense of male homoerotic desire. The volume also contains "In Sarum Close" and a number of Douglas's early homoerotic lyrics.[114]) More pressing, however, was the thought that Douglas still had in his possession letters from Wilde: "In case I die here you will destroy them. In case I survive I will destroy them myself."[115] The same was true of all other gifts he had made to Bosie, since they held too many shameful liabilities for

Wilde's "unfortunate children": "I cannot," he admitted, "of course get rid of the revolting memories of the two years I was unlucky enough to have him with me, or of the mode by which he thrust me into the abyss of ruin and disgrace to gratify his hatred of his father and other ignoble passions."[116] Wilde instructed Ross to communicate these demands to Bosie. In turn, Douglas found it impossible to fathom Wilde's violent change of heart toward him. Two days later, in defiance of Wilde's express wishes, Douglas published an outspoken defense of homosexual desire and his intimacy with Wilde. The piece appeared in an art magazine, the *Revue blanche*. "M. Oscar Wilde," Douglas wrote, "est maintenant torturé pour avoir été un uraniste, un hellenique, un homosexuel, comme vous voudrez" (Mr. Oscar Wilde is now tortured for being a Uranist, a Hellenist, a homosexual, whatever you will).[117] This protest amounted to just the kind of publicity Wilde could not, by this time, withstand. On receiving news of Wilde's wishes from Ross, Douglas uttered his despair: "If Oscar asks me to kill myself I will do so, and he shall have back the letters when I am dead."[118]

Wilde's level of distress remained intense. Both Adey and Ross turned to Harris to see if this friend, who enjoyed influence with the government, might secure a special visit. Even if Harris had a tendency to overdramatize his involvement in Wilde's career, the interview that he had with the prisoner on 16 June 1896 at Reading deeply troubled him. Harris had already communicated his concern for Wilde's welfare to Ruggles-Brise, and he expressed admiration for the prison commissioner's humane disposition. The head of the prison commission, we learn, confided his misgivings about the harshness of Wilde's sentence: "It was a great pity that Wilde ever got into prison, a great pity."[119] During Harris's visit, the emaciated prisoner—who at first found it difficult to talk—unraveled a catalogue of grievances against Isaacson's regime. "I am," Wilde informed Harris, "perpetually being punished for nothing; this governor loves to punish, and he punishes by taking my books from me."[120] Harris recalled Wilde's chilling words about the conditions in which he had to live out the brutal sentence: "Everybody knows that you are purged and starved to death. That's what two years' hard labour means. It's not the labour that's hard. It's the conditions of life that make it impossibly hard; they break you down body and soul."[121] The only heartening aspect to Wilde's daily existence emerged in the kind words that he addressed to the guard who was present, though out of earshot, throughout the interview. "'I have been telling my friend,' said Oscar to the warder, 'how good you have been to me.'"[122] Before he departed, Harris tried to leave a banknote under a piece of blotting paper for the guard. But the warder, whose identity is unknown, declined the gratuity. Harris, who returned the bill to his pocket, exited the room assured that the guard was "an honest, good man, full of the milk of human kindness."[123] Nonetheless, even though Wilde truly appreciated the warder's benevolence, his plight looked bleak.

There was, however, a suggestion that Harris made to Wilde that most likely assisted in bringing about a positive change in his friend's fortunes. Harris contended that Wilde should request not only a greater supply of books but also regular access to pen and paper. "You shall have writing materials and your books, Oscar. Force yourself to write. You should give a record of this life as far as you can, and of all its influences on you."[124] Just over two weeks later, Wilde submitted a long and eloquent petition to the Home Office on blue prison foolscap paper (the large-size paper used for official documents). Wilde asked Ridley to understand that solitary confinement deprives the mind of "healthy intellectual activity, such as books, writing materials, companionship."[125] Wilde framed his plea by claiming that "the terrible offences of which he was rightly found guilty" were ones that other European countries treated as "diseases to be cured by a physician" and not "crimes to be punished by a judge."[126] To strengthen his case, he referred to the fact that both Cesare Lombroso and Max Nordau, two modern leading theorists of degeneration, had identified a link between the "sexual madness" from which he suffered and "the literary and artistic temperament."[127] Such insanity, Wilde asserted, would spread from his previous "monstrous sexual perversion" to his "entire nature and intellect."[128] Without books, pen and paper, and sociability, he said, he would be prey to "morbid passions, and obscene fancies, and thoughts that defile, desecrate, and destroy."[129] He concluded by commenting that his bodily as well as his mental health were imperiled. Particularly distressing was the loss of "hearing of the right ear through an abscess that has caused a perforation of the drum."[130]

Isaacson passed Wilde's document to the prison commissioners with a brief report from the physician at Reading, Oliver Calley Maurice. The doctor declared that since entering the jail Wilde had "gained flesh." "I have never been able," Maurice added, "to see any evidence of insanity or approaching insanity." He also dismissed "any deficit" in Wilde's vision, though he noted that the prisoner had "a slight perforation of the drum in the right ear."[131] These views were confirmed by the visiting committee of five inspectors, who reported on 10 July 1896 that Wilde had put on 8 pounds in weight, been relieved of picking oakum, and permitted more books and exercise than before. They observed, however, that it would be wise to conduct an "expert medical inquiry" on Wilde's sight and hearing.[132]

On receiving these documents, Ruggles-Brise also accepted a further visit from Harris, who reported on his recent interview with Wilde. Taken together, Wilde's petition and Harris's communications made their way to the home secretary. Ridley, who wanted Isaacson to pay close attention to Wilde's health, concluded that no one less than the pioneering psychiatrist Henry Maudsley should examine the well-known prisoner. It transpired that toward the end of the month, it was not Maudsley but David Nicholson—one of the doctors from Broadmoor who had previously visited Wilde at Wandsworth—who concluded that there was "no indication of insanity."[133] Wilde's eloquent petition, though, was sufficiently stirring to convince Ridley to make two significant concessions. First, he sent instructions to Isaacson that Wilde should "be provided with foolscap paper, ink, and pen, for use in his leisure moments in his cell."[134] There were nonetheless provisos. The writing materials had to be withdrawn every night after the cells were locked up. It was also vital that Wilde's writing activities should not interfere with his regular duties. Secondly, Ridley told Isaacson "to ask the prisoner to name any work or set of works with which he desires to be provided."[135] These two privileges were to transform Wilde's situation.

Still, soon after the petition had been submitted to Ridley, Isaacson presided over the event that left one of the deepest scars on Wilde's prison experience. This was the execution of the homicide Charles Thomas Wooldridge: a trooper who had slit the throat of his spouse, Laura Ellen Wooldridge, in a jealous fit of rage.[136] Wooldridge's hanging, which took place on the gallows housed inside a shed in the exercise yard, occurred on 7 July 1896. As Wilde later informed one of the warders, the execution unnerved him: "it was horrible, horrible!"[137] The taking of Wooldridge's life forms the basis of the poem that Wilde composed not long after his release, *The Ballad of Reading Gaol* (1898), which recalls the ominous "Governor all in shiny black, / With the yellow face of Doom."[138] In truth, as Wilde confided to his publisher Leonard Smithers, Isaacson's complexion was rubicund: "a great red-faced, bloated Jew who always looked as if he drank."[139] This anti-Semitic outburst, however, also contained its own inaccuracy. Isaacson, contrary to Wilde's belief, was not Jewish.[140] At the time that Wilde's infuriation with the governor had reached its peak, welcome changes were afoot. Soon after the state execution of Wooldridge, Isaacson received a promotion, which led to his departure for H.M. Prison Lewes, Sussex, before the end of the month.

"THE MERE HANDLING OF PEN AND INK HELPS ME": H.M. PRISON READING UNDER JAMES OSMOND NELSON

The individual who succeeded Isaacson was the thirty-five-year-old James Osmond Nelson. Wilde found Nelson to be a "very charming man" and "the most Christ-like man I ever met."[141] There is no question that Nelson treated

Wilde, with whom he held regular fifteen-minute interviews, both compassionately and respectfully. "Wilde," he recalled, "was certainly the most amazing and brilliant talker I have ever met."[142] It was Nelson who responded to the recent dispatches from the Home Office. He thoughtfully suggested that it would be best for Wilde to write in "a manuscript book strongly but coarsely bound" that "could be issued and withdrawn without arousing any comments amongst other prisoners."[143] He also submitted Wilde's long list of requests for books. In turn, the prison commission's office stated that, provided that Nelson specified the particulars of each title and ensured the budget did not exceed £10, the books would be acquired.

Wilde's list of volumes included several of his cherished works of English and European literature, along with titles in modern history and philosophy that he had most likely first encountered when studying for his degree in Literæ Humaniores at Oxford twenty years before. To be sure, he noted that there were no inexpensive sets of Charles Dickens's and William Makepeace Thackeray's works for the inmates. Still, his choices related mainly to his own literary and scholarly interests. At the very top was "A Greek Testament." Apart from editions of Christopher Marlowe's works, Edmund Spenser's verse, and Thomas Percy's *Reliques of English Poetry* (1765), his requests were largely for nineteenth-century writings such as Thomas Carlyle's *Sartor Resartus* (1836) and *History of Friedrich II of Prussia* (1858–65), along with Ralph Waldo Emerson's essays. Some of the titles addressed Christianity. These volumes included Henry Hart Milman's *History of the Jews* (1829), Leopold von Ranke's *Popes of Rome* (1834–36), W. E. H. Lecky's *History of Rationalism* (1855), and Henry Thomas Buckle's *History of Civilization in England* (1857). The other religious studies that he listed encompassed Ernest Renan's controversial *Vie de Jésus* (1863), which treats Christ as a historical personage. (Wilde assured the authorities that the chaplain had no objection to Renan's *Vie* because the edition would be in the original French. In other words, it was unlikely that any other inmate would be able to read it.) The bulk of these titles made their way into Wilde's hands. As one of his warders noted, Wilde "had a quite a library in his cell."[144] Access to this collection was clearly satisfying. Of the poetic works he desired, the most significant appears to have been Dante's *Divine Comedy*. "I read Dante every day, in Italian," he later told Gide, "and all through, but neither the *Purgatorio* nor the *Paradiso* seemed written for me. It was *Inferno* above all that I read."[145]

By September 1896, the privileges that the home secretary had granted Wilde were beginning to alleviate his dismay. Although he complained to Adey about "days that are endless in their dull monotony of apathy or despair," he admitted that the "mere handling of pen and ink helps me."[146] "I cling to my notebook: it helps me," he said; "before I had it," he went on, "my brain was going in very evil circles."[147] Since he had not received any reply to his previous petition, he wrote directly to Ridley pleading for "the expiration of his term of eighteen months' confinement, or at any rate before Christmas comes."[148] The request was ignored. Once it became apparent that he would have to withstand six further months in jail, Wilde's attitude turned to one of not only resignation but also resilience. "I am," he admitted to Ross, "dazed with a dull sense of pain."[149] Then again, he conceded that there were "kinder elements in this evil prison air than there were before: sympathies have been shown to me."[150] As he enjoyed more interaction with other inmates, his emotional life improved, and the renewal of his lifelong habit of reading and notetaking calmed his nerves: "I read Dante, and make excerpts and notes for the pleasure of using a pen and ink."[151] He was reading so voraciously that he exhausted his supply of books once again. As a consequence, Adey compiled a list of twenty-seven additional titles that he agreed to pay for.

Wilde spent hours devouring his books. On 10 March 1897, he submitted another list of desired titles; the sundry list featured English and Italian editions of Dante's *Vita nuova*, along with modern works of fiction including Thomas Hardy's *The Well-Beloved* (1897) and George Meredith's *Amazing Marriage* (1895). On 6 April 1897, he enclosed in a letter to Ross an additional list of requests for reading materials, this time itemizing French works he knew well, such as Charles Baudelaire's *Fleurs du mal* (1857, revised 1861), together with recent ones, including his former friend Pierre Louÿs's successful novel *Aphrodite* (1896). He also asked for a broad span of recent titles in English, such as W. B. Yeats's *Secret Rose* (1897). Importantly, he requested two of Morrison's studies of prison reform, which—perhaps because he feared offending the authorities—Ross penciled out.[152] In anticipation of his release, Wilde wanted travel guides to Europe, along with basic supplies of pen and paper, some silver brushes, and his dispatch box. As we can tell, he wished to be in step with contemporary writing, as well as adequately prepared for his departure in two months' time.

The steady progress of Wilde's mood impressed the warders. One of the guards recalls important details about his enhanced daily routine. "Wilde's reason was saved," we learn, because the "stringent regulations under which he had hitherto lived" were relaxed.[153] No longer did Wilde perform manual labor. Instead, his time was involved exercising up to four times in the yard and attending chapel. The kindly warder Thomas Martin, an Irishman who joined the prison in March 1897, noted that the sermons to which the inmates were subjected wearied Wilde. "In Church," Martin remembered in 1906, "the Poet seemed to suffer from *ennui*. He sat in a listless attitude with his elbow resting on the back of his chair, his legs crossed."[154] When he was not exercising or at prayer, Wilde devoted the spare hours to reading and writing. Martin stated that the prisoner, who "wrote mostly in the evenings," improvised by "plac[ing] his plank bed" on "two wooden trestles," which served—in Wilde's own words—as "a very good table."[155]

Martin, who smuggled in reading materials and treats for the inmate, preserved several of the notes that Wilde passed to him discreetly. On these scraps of paper, Wilde tells the guard that he is "looking better—and happier" for a good reason: "I have a good friend who gives me the *Chronicle*, and *promises* me ginger biscuits."[156] Later, Martin—who kept in touch with Sherard until the late 1930s—reported that he ran errands into town so that he could obtain "the weeklies that [Wilde] wanted"; Martin understandably grew "anxious that [his] absence might be noticed."[157] These memories resonate with those of the anonymous warder who recalled how he would use sheets of prison foolscap to direct questions at Wilde arising from his evening study. "In this way," the prison guard recalled, "I obtained his views on almost every conceivable subject, written, in his beautiful hand, on the other side of the sheet."[158] Before Wilde's release, this warder had accumulated no fewer than fifty such sheets in Wilde's graceful handwriting, which were regrettably lost during the warder's service in the second Anglo-Boer war.

Both Martin and his unnamed colleague also noted Wilde's "kindliness and self-sacrifice" toward other prisoners.[159] There was, it seems, competition among the convicts "as to who should get beside him on the exercise ring or in the prison chapel"; "no one," this anonymous warder recalled, "could have had daily intercourse with Oscar Wilde without growing to like him."[160] At one point, Wilde asked the guard to "oblige him by taking half his bread and giving it to a prisoner in the next cell."[161] Even though it was against the regulations to fulfil this request, the warder knew that "Wilde had a big heart": "he shed tears of blood when he thought of the sufferings of others."[162] Martin went so far as to say that "while in prison [Wilde] lived the life of a saint."[163]

There were, however, external events that continued to unsettle Wilde. To begin with, Adey received from Douglas one hectoring letter after another. These missives concentrated much more on Douglas's egotism than on any empathy he might have for the privations that Wilde had borne. Bosie stated that he remained puzzled that Adey should have suggested that a "reconciliation" between Douglas and Wilde might be possible: "I have never quarreled with Oscar," Bosie said. "The last time I saw him he kissed the end of my finger through an iron grating at Newgate, & he begged me to let nothing in the world alter my attitude & my conduct towards him."[164] The very idea that Wilde had uttered "cruel insults & . . . unmerited reproaches" against him struck Bosie as the work of an "evil & lying spirit which at present inhabits Oscar's body."[165] He was particularly aggrieved to hear from the French actor-manager Lugné-Poe that the Leversons had claimed that Douglas "prevented Oscar from going away when he was on bail."[166] Understandably, Douglas wished to be spared the name-calling. "Tell him that I know I have ruined his life, that everything is my fault, if that pleases him. I don't care. Doesn't he think that my life is just as much ruined as his and so much sooner?"[167] "Do work for me, More," Douglas insisted, "& even if you cut him to the heart & make him unhappy you will really be doing him good if only you can make him love me again & know that he is being martyred for my sake."[168] Adey, from what we can tell, chose wisely not to relay to Wilde what Douglas himself admitted was his "drivelling" self-pity.[169] In the meantime, Bosie's mother made it clear to Adey that her lawyer had insisted that it was inadvisable for her son to return to England or Scotland. Both Adey and Ross, who believed that they had Wilde's best interests at heart, did what they could to ensure that Bosie entertained himself at European resorts, including Capri, Naples, and Paris, during much of Wilde's jail term.

The reading and writing privileges that the Home Office granted Wilde enabled him to reflect carefully on his dispiriting history with Douglas. He began to articulate his downfall as a form of tragedy in which forces greater than himself had determined his fate. Moreover, he acknowledged that his calamity had to a large degree been and gone, since the degradation that he had suffered so publicly was now retreating into the past. But there was, he feared, worse to come for a man who had managed to survive such abasement. "*My* tragedy has lasted far too long: its climax is over," he informed Ross, "its end is mean."[170] The problem was that the prospect of his release from the adversities of prison would entail yet further anguish. "I am quite conscious of the fact when the end *does* come I shall return an unwelcome visitant to a world that does not want me."[171] This item of correspondence, together with various others from the later months of 1896, in many ways served as a prelude to the major literary work that he appears to have started composing the following January. This was the 50,000-word contemplative letter that he addressed to Douglas. Once he completed his draft, he informed Ross that the document should be thought of as an "Encyclical letter" and "may be spoken of as the *Epistola: In Carcere et Vinculis* [*Letter: In Prison and in Chains*]."[172] By this point, he had very firm ideas about the preparation of the letter in typescript, with copies ready to be sent to select friends. He also made a request through Nelson to see if he could mail the letter to Douglas. (Ruggles-Brise replied that "this correspondence cannot be allowed."[173]) It was left to Ross in 1905 to publish—under the title *De Profundis* (a title taken from Psalms)—those sections of the document that do not allude explicitly to the affair with Bosie.

Wilde's *Epistola*, which counts among the foremost Victorian prison memoirs, was for him a crucial achievement. "It is," he told Adey in February 1897, "the most important letter of my life, as it will deal ultimately with my future attitude towards life, with the ways in which I desire to meet the world again, with the development of my character: with what I have lost, what I have learned, and what I hope to arrive at."[174] Ross's abbreviated 1905 edition shows how beneficial the requested supply of books had been for Wilde's creativity. Many of the passages, which reached thousands of readers at the time, focus on the exemplarity of Jesus Christ and the joys of reading the New Testament in the original Greek. So inspiring was the ancient language that Wilde convinced himself it was "the *ipsissima verba* [the precise words] . . . used by Christ."[175] "It was always supposed," Wilde goes on to remark, "that Christ talked in Aramaic. Even Renan thought so. But now we know that the Galilean peasants, like the Irish peasants of our own day, were bilingual, and that Greek was the ordinary language of intercourse all over Palestine."[176] Elsewhere, he dwells philosophically upon the emotional travails resulting from his imprisonment. "I have passed," he says, "through every possible mood of suffering."[177]

As we have noted in previous chapters, the life events that largely motivated this powerful letter—ones that did not appear in 1905—record at length Wilde's disillusionment with Bosie. Just as noteworthy, however, are his deliberations on the legal system. With hindsight, Wilde convinced himself that he could have triumphed in his defense had he chosen to lay bare the fact that Queensberry had plotted against him, as the following substantial passage reveals:

> Had I so chosen, I could on either trial have saved myself at [Queensberry's] expense, not from shame indeed, but from imprisonment. Had I cared to show that the Crown witnesses—the three most important—had been carefully coached by your father and his solicitors, not in reticences merely, but in assertions, in the absolute transference, deliberate, plotted, and rehearsed, of the actions and doings of someone else on to me, I could have had each one of them dismissed from the box by the Judge, more summarily than even wretched perjured Atkins was. I could have walked out of Court with my tongue in my cheek, and my hands in my pocket, a free man. The strongest pressure was put on me to do so. I was earnestly advised, begged, entreated to do so by people whose sole interest was my welfare, and the welfare of my house. But I refused. I did not choose to do so. I have never regretted my

> decision for a single moment, even in the most bitter periods of my imprisonment. Such a course of action would have been beneath me.[178]

This excerpt shows that Wilde sought to reassure himself that he had been unwilling to contest the Crown's charges against him because doing so would have been inherently undignified. But the likelier truth, as we have already observed in *Oscar Wilde on Trial*, is that the hardships that he suffered during each phase of the Crown prosecution meant that he was too demoralized to speak up against his enemies. Wilde's contention that he could have vanquished the plot that John Sholto Douglas and Charles Russell had ingeniously devised looks infeasible. Instead, the evidence that these adversaries had collected overwhelmed him. He had not been able to predict the lengths to which his antagonists would go in order to unmask his sexual indiscretions. Later in *De Profundis*, however, Wilde is more candid about the decisions that he made. He confesses that he was misguided in turning to the law in order to expose the wrong that Queensberry had inflicted upon him. "The one disgraceful, unpardonable, and to all time contemptible action of my life," he informs Douglas, "was my allowing myself to be forced into appealing to Society for help and protection against your father."[179] Once Wilde admits that he seriously underestimated the political climate of the time, he draws attention to his apparent naïveté in believing that the judiciary might have ever looked sympathetically upon his plight: "I had put into motion the forces of Society . . . Society turned on me and said, 'Have you been living all this time in defiance of my laws, and do you now appeal to those laws for protection?'"[180] It is almost as if Wilde cannot believe that at the time of pursuing the libel case against the marquess he risked exposing himself as a criminal rather than appearing as an individual whose rights had been violated. Nonetheless, the more significant point that emerges from this long document is that he expresses no regrets about the lamentable tragedy that befell him. Even in the face of having lost so much, he still maintains great pride in his remarkable achievements: "I was a man who stood in symbolic relations to the art and culture of my age."[181]

At the point Wilde started on the letter that became *De Profundis*, much of his attention concentrated on the possible life that he might lead after his release. By the end of 1896, Adey—after paying substantial fees to C. O. Humphreys—disposed of the solicitor's services.[182] From this point onward until the summer of 1897, Wilde, as we can see from a letter he sent from Reading, authorized Stoker and Hansell, Gray's Inn Road, to act on his behalf. He was especially eager for Hansell to agree to his desire for his wife to have the life interest on the marriage settlement. As we can tell from a document signed on behalf of the official receiver on 13 April 1897, his largest debt was still the very substantial amount of £1,557 16s. 2d. to the settlement.[183] (The twenty or so other sums, apart from £60 17.s. 11d. owed to Hatchards booksellers, were altogether smaller.) Wilde's advisers, however, went against his wishes. In the same letter to Ross in which he discussed the *Epistola*, Wilde reiterated his wish to surrender everything to his spouse, who at this juncture still threatened divorce. He bore no hard feelings against Constance: "I am really very fond of my wife and very sorry for her."[184] "She could not understand me," he observed, "and I was bored to death with the married life."[185] In the final weeks of his sentence, the risk of divorce subsided. Had Constance petitioned for divorce, it would have led to a civil case that once again rehearsed Wilde's homosexual encounters. As Wilde informed Douglas in *De Profundis*, her solicitors had received a statement about his intimacies from Walter Grainger: the under-butler whom he hired at Goring-upon-Thames.[186] For Wilde, the prospect of facing this part of his personal history was chilling. As he pointed out to Ross, any divorce proceedings would involve a fresh prosecution "on appalling charges of a new and more infamous character" than before.[187] Were the case to come to court, there was every possibility that Wilde could be prosecuted for committing sodomy, which carried a sentence of up to ten years.

Wilde's tense affairs with his wife and family were mercifully resolved nine days before his release. Adey's attorney, Martin Holman, informed him that Constance's legal adviser, Sidney Hargrove, and Wilde's solicitor, Arthur Hansell, had attended a joint meeting where they managed to settle the life interest for £75, the guardianship of Cyril and Vyvyan, Wilde's annual allowance, and the strict terms attached to the dispensation of that sum. "[I]t is arranged," Holman noted, "that after Mrs. Wilde's death the £150 is to be paid to me for Mr. Wilde for his life unconditionally: during her life Mrs. Wilde will pay the same amount to me quarterly subject to Mr. Wilde doing nothing 'which would entitle his wife to a divorce or a decree for a judicial separation, or be guilty of any moral misconduct, or notoriously consort with evil or disreputable companions.'"[188] Constance's distant cousin and former neighbor Adrian Hope, in his role as guardian, attended the interview. Hope stated that he did not care what kind of life Wilde might choose to lead in the future, "provided he did not molest his wife and children, and provided he kept out of the newspapers."[189] There was a further caveat. Should there be "any public scandal in which Mr. Wilde was mixed up," Hope "would at once put the matter before Mr. Hansell and ask for his authority to stop the allowance.[190] As Holman recognized, it was essential to impress upon Wilde "how absolutely fatal any further intercourse with Lord Alfred Douglas" would be.[191] In any case, Queensberry was once again behaving like a bully. The marquess said, just as he had declared after the failed libel suit, that he would shoot Douglas and Wilde on the spot should they be found together again.

Such news made Wilde despair. His patience with the measures that Adey, in particular, had made on his behalf wore thin. Even though the specter of divorce proceedings had disappeared, Wilde grew disillusioned with the man who had done his utmost to protect him legally. In fairness, Wilde admitted to Ross that Adey was "cultivated . . . sympathetic . . . kind." But this well-meaning individual lacked business acumen: "He is a *stupid man*, in practical concerns."[192] These comments appear in a long letter where Wilde expresses his dismay at the lack of proper funds on which he needed to live in the coming months. Moreover, his recent visit from Adey and Ross, who were also accompanied by the artist Charles Ricketts, had exasperated him. (Ricketts, who said to Wilde that "he supposed time went very fast in prison," demonstrated "an entirely inartistic lack of sympathetic instinct."[193])

Since early April, Adey had been communicating his concerns to the prison commissioners that it was essential Wilde end his sentence inconspicuously. The authorities agreed. They recognized that it was time to consider "the best course to adopt to secure Oscar Wilde's discharge without publicity or interference."[194] As Adey explained to Ernest Flower, MP, a supporter of penal reform whom he hoped would speak to the home secretary on the matter, it was vital to avoid "the curiosity and interference of the Press" and "the persecution of certain disorderly persons."[195] The other fear was that Queensberry and his henchmen, who had harassed Wilde after bail was granted on 7 May 1895, would once more indulge in provocative behavior.

There was, however, one further experience that assailed Wilde's nerves during the final days before his release. As Peter Stoneley has confirmed from the visiting committee minutes, on Saturday, 15 May 1897, a prisoner—James Edward Prince, who occupied cell A.2.11—was sentenced to "24 strokes of the birch rod over malingering."[196] Soon after his release, Wilde told the *Daily Chronicle* that he heard a disturbance while he was polishing the tins that he used for dinner. "I thought," Wilde recalled, "some animal like a bull or a cow was being unskilfully slaughtered outside the prison walls."[197] It soon became clear, however, that the noise originated with a man who was suffering a flogging. Worse still, Wilde suspected that it might be A.2.11, whose anguished condition had already become visible to the other prisoners at chapel. A.2.11, Wilde recollected, had already been "continually punished" for his outbursts and his habit of making a "grin idiot-like" at his minders; the following day Wilde witnessed the distressed prisoner in the exercise yard, "his weak, ugly, wretched face bloated by tears and hysteria almost beyond recognition."[198] The man's agonized condition served as a forceful reminder of the violence of the separate system. We know from the anonymous warder's memoir that the brutal punishment of A.2.11 left Wilde in shock.

> On a certain Monday morning . . .
> . . . I entered his cell and
> found [Wilde] in a most wretched condition. His
> eyes were red like fire as though he had
> been crying all the night.
> "Whatever's the matter, Mr. Wilde?" I asked
> in alarm.
> "Oh!" he gasped, "a dreadful thing happened
> here on Saturday afternoon! (I hadn't been
> in the prison from twelve o'clock on that
> particular Saturday) They flogged that poor
> idiot, Prince! It was worse—a thousand
> times worse—than the hanging of the soldier![”][199]

On one of the scraps that Wilde passed to Martin, he had already begged to know Prince's name. He also wanted to discover "the names of the children who are in for [stealing] rabbits, and the amount of the fine"; his intention was to get these juveniles held in an adult jail "out tomorrow," very probably on the day of his release.[200]

During these concluding days, legal affairs also pressed upon Wilde's mind. Just forty-eight hours before the end of his jail term, Hansell visited him in order to ensure that he signed the deed of arrangement. According to an anonymous warder, Constance accompanied the lawyer, although she chose not to let her spouse know of her presence. "Let me," she said to the guard, "have one glimpse of my husband."[201] He obliged. Once she drew back, the warder witnessed her "laboring under deep emotion."[202] During this delicate interview, the solicitor also broke the news that the authorities had agreed that Wilde should leave Reading one day early. At 8.00 p.m. on Tuesday, 18 May 1897, Martin appeared before C.3.3 carrying the clothes with which Wilde had entered prison. He was to be taken to Pentonville. The inmate was escorted not to Reading Station but to the less populous Twyford, where he caught the 8.52 p.m. train. Thereafter, Wilde disembarked at the suburban Westbourne Grove. His final night was spent at the jail in which he had withstood hard labor two years before.

On the previous Saturday, Adey had been in touch with the Home Office to explain the arrangements that he would make for collecting Wilde from the gates of Pentonville. "The earliest possible hour on the morning of May the 19th," Adey wrote, "will suit me best."[203] There were other plans as well. As Adey later informed Schuster, the only individual he could find who was "both able and willing to accompany" him was the Revd. Stuart Headlam (the radical Anglican who had put up bail for Wilde on 7 May 1895).[204] Adey also confided to her that Wilde had no wish to be collected by Ernest Leverson (there were tensions about the funds that Leverson himself had dispensed on Wilde's behalf), and he also stated that Frank Harris had refused to be present. The idea was that after spending the morning at Headlam's finely decorated home at 31 Upper Bedford Place, Bloomsbury, Wilde and Adey would travel by cab and rail before boarding a ferry across the English Channel to Dieppe. Once word reached Wilde about this scheme, he voiced his unhappiness with the arrangements. Two days before his release, he told Reggie Turner that the thought of going to the home of someone whom he knew as remotely as Headlam was unappealing. Instead, he wanted to take rooms in a hotel somewhere close to the Euston Road. Turner replied that it was inconceivable that Wilde would be welcomed at any establishment in England. All the same, Turner did his best hearten Wilde: "Dear Oscar, we all believe that the greatest triumphs of your life have yet to come."[205]

Perhaps because he felt powerless in the face of the preparations that his friends had made, Wilde expressed his displeasure to Adey in the most direct terms. He repeated the resentment that he had already confided to Ross: "if you came abroad with me it would only distress us both." "I could," he told Adey, "talk to you about nothing but of the mode" in which Adey's actions, especially regarding the deed of arrangement, had proved so disadvantageous.[206] "It is," as Nicholas Frankel observes, "a mark of Adey's immense generosity of spirit and sensitivity to his friend's suffering that he was willing to overlook these recriminations and meet Wilde at the prison gates two days later."[207] Regardless, Adey understood that Wilde did not always mean the bitter words he at times unleashed. "Oscar," Adey told Schuster, "always writes charmingly after he has shown any petulance."[208] Moreover, Adey had done many other good deeds for the prisoner. In early May, Wilde had sent him a comprehensive list of all of the clothing items, accessories, and colognes that he wished to have on his release. No expense, it seems, was to be spared. These included a blue serge suit from Doré and Sons on Conduit Street, which Ross obtained, along with cosmetics such as Houbigant's soap, Pritchard's tooth powder, and a trademarked hair dye called Koko Maricopas. "I want, for psychological reasons," he said, "to feel entirely physically cleansed of the stain and soil of prison life."[209]

In the end, everything went according to plan. Certain sections of the press, even though they sought to discover what was afoot with Wilde's release, were outwitted. The *Morning* knew that Wilde had been "secretly removed" to London and understood that the train had arrived at Westbourne Park at 10.40 p.m.; it mistakenly assumed, however, that he would gain his freedom after a night in Holloway.[210] Still, the *Pall Mall Gazette*, which had been just as watchful, was more accurate in its reporting. Like the *Morning*, it tracked the prisoner to Twyford and concluded that Wilde "was looking remarkably well."[211] Moreover, he appeared to be sporting his "Byronic locks." The paper also noted that "the beard of the erstwhile prisoner has been allowed to grow." This journalist observed that Wilde "was conveyed in a closed carriage to Pentonville Prison." By the time this issue of the *Pall Mall Gazette* appeared, it claimed that a brougham had already at 9.00 a.m. drawn "in to the principal entrance of the Metropolitan House of Detention, [and] some five minutes later it left with Oscar Wilde—a free man."[212] The timing, however, was incorrect. The truth was that the carriage had been and gone not long after 6.00 a.m. The only detail on which the reporter admitted ignorance was the identity of the people who had come to collect Wilde.

As Adey, Headlam, and Wilde made their way through central London, they spotted "a newspaper placard" with "the anticipatory announcement 'Release of Oscar Wilde.'"[213] Once safely inside the house, Wilde "was given his first cup of coffee after two years."[214] An hour or so later, two more guests arrived. Ada Leverson recalled that she and her husband joined the party for breakfast, where they were a little apprehensive about the reunion. Wilde had already spruced himself up for their visit: "He came in, and at once put us at our ease. He came in with the dignity of a king returning from exile. He came in talking, smoking a cigarette, with waved hair and a flower in his button-hole, and he looked markedly better, slighter, and younger than he had two years previously. His first words were, 'Sphinx, how marvellous of you to know exactly the right hat to wear at seven o'clock in the morning to meet a friend who has been away! You can't have got up, you must have sat up.'"[215]

As they enjoyed this repartee, Wilde temporarily upset his friends' desire to whisk him away to the Continent. According to Ada Leverson, he dispatched a letter to a Catholic retreat (in hopes that it might accept him for a period of six months), though it appears more likely that he wished to meet personally with a Jesuit priest for religious counsel.[216] Within hours, he received a reply declining the request. "[H]e broke down," Leverson recalled, "and sobbed bitterly." Very soon, she and her spouse departed. Only later did she learn that Wilde eventually traveled "to Berneval with friends."[217]

Adey escorted Wilde from Headlam's residence sometime around noon. "Everything went off," Adey told Schuster, "without any unpleasantness. Oscar and I drove from Headlam's house to West Croydon."[218] Traveling to an outlying station avoided any journalists who might be lurking at London Victoria. By 6.25 p.m., Wilde dispatched a telegram informing Ross that he was on his way from Newhaven by the night boat. "More," he added, "has been such a good friend to me."[219] He signed himself, for the first time, by his incognito "Sebastian Melmoth" (his luggage, which Turner had given him, was duly embossed with the initials "S.M."). This well-considered name combined two identities resonating with personal meaning. Sebastian, a figure that several Victorian queer men embraced, was not only an early Christian martyr but also reputed in modern culture to be the lover of the Emperor Diocletian, whose forces clubbed the saint to death. Melmoth, meanwhile, is the protagonist of the Gothic romance *Melmoth the Wanderer* (1820). This was the great achievement of Wilde's maternal great-uncle Charles Maturin. The name, too, gestured toward the kindness of Wilde's loyal friends. Five years earlier, Adey and Ross had furnished a memoir of Maturin for a three-volume edition of the novel, which was issued by Richard Bentley.

After a rough crossing, the ferryboat *La Tamise* touched the French shore at 4.30 a.m. Wilde's loyal friends Ross and Turner were there to greet him. "As the steamer glided into the harbour," Ross recalled, "Wilde's tall figure, dominating the other passengers, was easily recognized . . . There was the usual irritating delay and then Wilde with that odd elephantine gait which I have never seen in anyone else stalked off the boat."[220] Ross and Turner at once conveyed Wilde and Adey to the Hôtel Sandwich, where the party of four enjoyed a light repast with red and white wine. This was the beginning of Wilde's exile. Never again would he return to the land that had imprisoned him.

CODA: RELEASE

I must remake my maimed life on my own lines.

—*Oscar Wilde, "To Carlos Blacker," 22 September 1897*

The wonderful way in which [Wilde] bore his imprisonment and his condition when he was released gave a false impression of the effect his trials and imprisonment really had on his health and general "morale."

—*More Adey, "To Adela Schuster," 12 March 1898*

"I MUST LOVE AND BE LOVED, WHATEVER PRICE I PAY FOR IT": BERNEVAL-SUR-MER AND POSILLIPO, 1897–1898

Soon after Oscar Wilde settled into his week-long stay at the Hôtel Sandwich, Dieppe, he drafted a detailed letter for the *Daily Chronicle* about the various hardships that he had witnessed during his two-year sentence. This powerful document, which contains many forceful observations about the need for prison reform, appeared in the 28 May 1897 issue of H. W. Massingham's activist newspaper under the headline "The Case of Warder Martin: Some Cruelties of Prison Life." The spur for its composition was the troubling news, which had recently appeared in the *Chronicle*, that the prison commissioners had dismissed Thomas Martin: the generous-hearted warder who befriended Wilde during the final three months of the sentence. Part of their friendship stemmed from Martin's willingness to break prison rules by running errands into Reading town, where he purchased copies of not only the *Chronicle* but also other journals that Wilde wished to read. The authorities discharged Martin because he had given sweet biscuits to a hungry child held on remand. That Martin should have been summarily removed from his post because he acted humanely toward a distressed juvenile motivated Wilde to voice sharp criticisms of a brutal prison system.

There is no doubt that Wilde had for some time intended to communicate with Massingham about his prison experience. Moreover, the newspaper counted among the dailies that the authorities hardly wanted convicts to peruse. Ada Leverson recalled that when she and her husband visited Wilde on the morning of his release, Wilde joked about the way that he defiantly read this particular newspaper on the train that took him to Westbourne Grove: "Do you know one of the punishments that happen to people who have been 'away' [i.e., in jail]? They are not allowed to read *The Daily Chronicle*! Coming along I begged to be allowed to read it in the train. 'No!' Then I suggested I might be allowed to read it upside down, and never enjoyed it so much. It's really the only way to read newspapers."[1] Besides remarking on the injustice of firing Martin from his post, Wilde was unambiguous when pointing to the terrible suffering that children endured in modern jails. "I saw the three children myself," Wilde notes, "on the Monday preceding my release. They had just been convicted."[2] "They were," he adds, "quite small children, the youngest—the one to whom the warder gave the biscuits—being a tiny little chap."[3] Wilde mentions that he could tell the child "was a very poor boy" because he was wearing prison socks and shoes.[4] The child's own shoes, if he had any, were most likely unwearable. Further, Wilde states that Martin would still have been employed had the child who ate the biscuits not disclosed the prison guard's kindheartedness to one of the discipline-wielding senior warders.

Still, Martin, as Wilde also acknowledged, took other risks as well. One of Martin's most generous gestures was to defy the regulations by emptying the slops of a newly incarcerated prisoner who was contending with the diarrhea that resulted from the indigestible diet of "badly-baked prison bread" and "coarse Indian meal stirabout" (a porridge made with maize).[5] It is, Wilde observes, inconceivable that such a horrifying regime, in which adults undergo such pain, should be inflicted upon minors. The moment, he says, has clearly come for parliament to spend half an hour debating the matter so that this unacceptable situation comes to an end: "Of course no child under fourteen years of age should be sent to prison at all."[6]

These words, which built on the findings of earlier critics such as Henry Mayhew and John Binny in 1862, urged penal reforms that Lord Salisbury's government was still not ready to implement. In 1895, Herbert Gladstone—the prominent Liberal Member of Parliament who became a privy councillor under Lord Rosebery's administration—had published his *Minutes of Evidence Taken by the Departmental Committee on Prisons*, which was the first major step toward restructuring an inflexible centralized prison system. Gladstone's voluminous report, whose recommendations influenced the Prisons Bill 1898, devotes a section to the treatment of minors in jail. In a bleak paragraph, Gladstone summarizes the consensus that his committee reached after its members interviewed numerous experts about the question of juvenile detention:

> Several witnesses were in favour of the total discontinuance of committing this class of offenders to prison. We do not think that this is practicable or desirable. For inquiry or on arrest children have to be detained. We strongly hold that it is most undesirable to commit them either to police cells or to workhouses. In many cases prisons are the only available places of detention. Further, we think that in the case of grave offences for which reformatories are not available, that imprisonment is necessary. At the same time children should be subjected to special treatment, and in every way be kept absolutely apart from other prisoners. But for the fact that the number of them is so small, the total number on March 21, 1894, being exactly 100, it would be desirable to keep them in parts of prisons specially reserved. It might be possible to do this in one of the London prisons. We think that the ordinary prison discipline and regulations should not be applied to juveniles, but that governors and the visiting committees should be made responsible for their treatment subject to general instructions which should be issued by the Secretary of State. The principle of these instructions should be that each child should be treated according to its own peculiarities of temperament; that the fact of imprisonment should be the main deterrent; and that treatment should be altogether of a reformatory character. We think that the age of 16, above referred to, should be raised to 17.[7]

The *Minutes*, which grudgingly acknowledges that the plight of juvenile offenders remains unsatisfactory, is never clear about the different ages of the 100 children who languished in the "separate system." To be sure, the report defines a juvenile as an individual under the age of sixteen. But when we notice in the *Minutes* that during 1893 there were 2,009 persons under the age of twelve in England and Wales convicted for indictable offenses, it raises the question of how many other small children besides the young inmates that Martin assisted at Reading suffered penal servitude of this kind.

In his inquiries into the records of Reading Prison, Peter Stoneley has found there is "no documentary trace" of the three boys who were accused of petty theft.[8] In the period preceding Wilde's conviction by two to three years, the prison register reveals that twenty-two juveniles served time for offenses such as "stealing a shirt" (fourteen days of hard labor), "stealing gravy soup" (ten days of hard labor and five years at a reformatory school), and "stealing sweets" (ten days of hard labor and four years at a reformatory school).[9] These particular inmates were in their early teens. The youngest juvenile, who was ten years old, received a sentence of three weeks of hard labor for killing a duck.

Two weeks after Wilde's letter appeared, the *Chronicle* dispatched a copy to the home secretary, Sir Matthew White Ridley. The document was then forwarded to the prison commissioners, who in their confidential notes expressed much greater uneasiness than Gladstone's official report allowed. "The Commissioners," they state, "are not responsible for small boys coming into prison and are unable to understand the action of the magistrate in sending them to prison instead of to a reformatory or Industrial School. It is a rare thing for children of this age (12) to be sentenced to imprisonment, and the sentence is, in our opinion, as foolish as it is inappropriate."[10] Still, if they agreed with Wilde about the foolhardiness of such sentencing, they recoiled from his claim that in prison a child is so terrified that they cannot eat or drink. "It is not the case," they stressed, "that children suffer from hunger," since the "powers of the Medical Officer are unlimited and carefully exercised."[11]

A further document in the same file shows that Wilde's comments caused additional agitation among the members of this official body. In a set of mostly typewritten notes, an unidentified commissioner regrets the evident "literary ability" displayed in Wilde's letter, since he says it is likely to give the sharp criticism of the system "more importance than it deserves." As this anonymous official sees it, everyone involved in the firing of the warder is to blame. Martin, this author writes, was a culprit: "an unsatisfactory officer," one who—"if he honestly believed the boy was suffering from hunger"—"should have reported this to the Governor." Just as culpable are the children who were locked up: "the two boys to whom Oscar Wilde refers, were no doubt left without the discipline which most boys require and which the fortunate boys get at home and at school." Evidently, "the JJ [i.e., Juvenile Justice] who sent them to prison might have done better." Even so, in the commissioner's view this was not a grave problem because the two children "were very bad boys: one had been whipped for stealing, another had been sent to a truant Industrial School." Wilde, he believed, had regretfully made "the very common mistake of judging boys of this kind by boys brought up in more luxurious surroundings." The message is clear. Even if it stands as an inadequate last resort, an adult prison is the only place in which these insubordinate twelve-year-old boys will suffer a punishment that will "make them good citizens in later life." But rather than dismiss Wilde's charges out of hand, the official concludes that it would be unwise to ignore such an ably argued letter. The government, we read in the memo, should conduct a question-and-answer session in the House of Commons in order to settle the inaccuracies of Wilde's claims.

Parliamentary questions had already been asked about Martin's case. The Irish Member of Parliament Michael Davitt, who had previously been sentenced to fourteen years of imprisonment for his Home Rule activism, posed two questions—the one on 25 May, the other on 27 May—to the home secretary. On the first occasion, Ridley stated that "the dismissal was fully justified," and on the second he flatly denied Davitt's query "whether the circumstances which induced [the home secretary] to dismiss a warder recently from Reading Prison included the giving of some bread to a youthful prisoner who was found crying from hunger in his cell."[12] Not long after, Wilde learned that Davitt also proposed to confront Ridley on the other controversial issue raised in "Some Cruelties of Prison Life"—the brutal flogging of A.2.11 (James Edward Prince). On 1 June 1897, Wilde wrote directly to Davitt on this matter, and he added a postscript—together with a letter from one of the warders—confirming that Prince had been flogged once again.

Such interventions were not the only ones that Wilde made on behalf of the men who had suffered alongside him. Now resident at the Hôtel de la Plage, Berneval-sur-Mer, five miles from Dieppe, Wilde began to disburse precious funds both to the inmates whom he had befriended and to the warders who had treated him humanely. As we can see from his account book, on 27 May 1897 he sent £5 to Martin, which may well have been the sum he wished to return for the amount the warder had been willing to lend him on his release.[13] Four days later, he listed the postal orders that Ross had mailed on his behalf to ten other individuals. These included two prison guards, Charles Fleet (£1 10s.) and George Groves (£3 10s.). (Groves was delighted. On 2 June 1897, he wrote appreciatively: "I hardly know how to thank you enough for your kindness."[14]) Other amounts went to Henry Bushell, a petty thief in his early twenties who—as Stoneley has discovered—was imprisoned no fewer than twenty-one times between June 1892 and October 1911. In Wilde's letter to the young man, which he sent through his lawyers in London, he declared, with more than a touch of condescension: "Don't, like a good little chap, get into trouble again."[15] Enclosed with the letter was the sum of £2, along with an additional 10s. that Wilde entrusted to Bushell to pass on to the "little dark-eyed chap" who was held in C.4.14.[16]

Around the same time, Wilde asked Ross to let Governor Nelson know that he was settled in Normandy. "Please . . . tell him," Nelson replied to Ross, "that I shall be only too glad to learn from him when he feels equal to writing a letter."[17] On 28 May 1897, Wilde obliged. He communicated to Nelson his "not merely sincere, but *affectionate* gratitude" for the "kindness and gentleness" that the governor had shown to him in prison.[18] Wilde stated, moreover, that it would have been awkward for him to broach with the governor the sensitive issues regarding the flogging of Prince, along with the suffering of the children held on remand in an adult jail. Then again, Wilde made it clear that neither of these terrible memories should obscure the fact that he maintained the deepest respect for Nelson's "humane spirit."[19] Nelson, Wilde added, expressed great compassion to everyone under his care. He was all the more grateful to Nelson because C.3.3 had "made more demands" than the other inmates. "I lacked," Wilde admitted, their "cheerful acquiescence." The letter concludes with Wilde's unapologetic stance on the time he served. "I am not," he insisted, "a scrap ashamed of the having been in prison." Instead, what aggrieved him was "the materialism of the life" that had led to his incarceration.[20]

On that note, Wilde had just about settled his correspondence with those members of the prison community whose humane deeds had touched him. He kept an eye on the men who were biding their time before they, too, would be released. As he said to Reggie Turner almost three weeks after he had left Reading: "I only know five chaps now in Reading Gaol. By the end of the year—on December 2 in fact—all my friends, thank God, will be free men, as I am."[21] Among the fellow prisoners who benefited from Wilde's largesse was the twenty-seven-year-old Arthur Cruttenden, a onetime soldier who had been sentenced to eighteen months for drunkenness in the harness room of the Royal Horse Artillery.[22] At the end of May, Wilde asked Ross to send a letter to this friend, together with £2 and a clipping of "Some Cruelties of Prison Life." Wilde's communication presumably contained an invitation to visit him in France. He followed up by asking Turner to do him a favor by lending him the substantial sum of £6 10s., which he wished Cruttenden to have. The request renewed Wilde's former habit of cadging funds from his closest acquaintances, whom he never repaid. "Arthur Cruttenden," Wilde remarked, "requires clothes—a blue-serge suit, a pair of brown leather boots, some shorts, and a hat."[23] Part of the sum covered Cruttenden's expenses so that the young man could make the journey to Berneval. Cruttenden took up the offer and stayed a few days during the middle of the month. Just in case Turner misunderstood the nature of the friendship, Wilde pointed out that it was not a physical one: "I had better say candidly that he is not a 'beautiful boy' . . . I am thankful and happy to be able to say that I have no feeling for him."[24] This was a telltale comment, since it showed that two years of solitary confinement had scarcely eradicated his homosexuality.

Besides doing right by his prison pals, Wilde had other pressing matters on his mind. A naturally sociable individual, he had to confront his "terrible position of isolation."[25] There was no question that there were days of brooding loneliness. The estrangement from his family wounded him. "I have," he told Ross two weeks after leaving jail, "heard from my wife. She sends me photographs of the boys—such lovely little fellows in Eton collars—but makes no promise to allow me to see them: she says *she* will see me, twice a year, but I want my boys."[26] The photographs of Cyril and Vyvyan, whom he never saw again, were with him at the time of his death. Still, he was hardly without company. Cruttenden counted among several visitors. The artist William Rothenstein visited Berneval with Edward Strangman, who had plans to translate *Lady Windermere's Fan* into French. The poet Ernest Dowson also visited Wilde on more than one occasion. Dowson, who had attended Wilde's final trial, relished Wilde's humor. "His gorgeous spirits," Dowson told a friend, "cheered me mightily."[27] Especially amusing, he thought, was the contradiction between Wilde's avowed "notions of economy" and his "perversely extravagant" behavior.[28] As Dowson knew, Wilde could not live within his means. More to the point, Dowson benefited from Wilde's generosity. It appears that Wilde advanced him "between £18 and £20."[29] At various other times, Wilde lent funds to friends when he could least afford to do so. Apart from these cronies, he received social calls from the young composer Dalhousie Young, who had contributed money to support Wilde, and the gifted painter Charles Conder, who borrowed money from him. On his jaunts to Dieppe, Wilde descended on the bohemian Café Tribunaux. There was, at any rate, a cultural life to be had.

In these early weeks, Wilde also spent time with André Gide, to whom he confided that prior to his arrest he always "knew that there would be a catastrophe, either that or something else."[30] When he showed Gide the cottage into which he moved in July that year, Wilde said that he had plans to write two biblical tragedies: "*Pharoah* first, and the one called *Ahab and Jezebel* (he pronounced it 'Isabelle'), which he related to me admirably."[31] In July, the theatre manager Charles Wyndham dropped by to suggest that Wilde adapt the French playwright Eugène Scribe's *Verre d'eau* (1840). Opportunities abounded. The time, it seems, had come for Wilde to restart his career. At Berneval, he began transforming his carceral experience into a major poem, *The Ballad of Reading Gaol* (1898).

After settling down in the seaside village, Wilde continued living for the best part of three-and-a-half more years: a busy time when he exulted in unconstrained sexual freedom and established new friendships in the French capital, while also suffering bouts of poverty, emotional distress, and eventually a fatal illness. This intense period of his life, which has been expertly documented by Nicholas Frankel and Matthew Sturgis, led within months to his reunion with Alfred Douglas.[32] At first, when Bosie's letters started to arrive Wilde admitted the hazards of renewing their friendship. "To be with him," he acknowledged to Ross on 28 May 1897, "would be return to the hell from which I do not think I have been released."[33] As Wilde understood well, Ross had taken responsibility for administering his allowance, which would be terminated if there was any reconciliation with Douglas. All the same, within a week Wilde had begun to sign off his letters to Bosie "with fondest love."[34] Soon, he was sending enraptured letters to Douglas every day. ("Of course," he said on 4 June 1897, "I love you more than anyone else."[35]) As the excitement grew, Wilde suggested that Bosie come to Berneval under a fanciful incognito: "Your name," Wilde wrote, "is to be Jonquil du Vallon."[36] On second thoughts, however, Wilde recognized that there were too many risks involved, no matter how much they sought to avoid detection. Scarcely a month after his release, he told his lover: "it is impossible for us to meet."[37] Wilde, not unreasonably, feared that "if Q[ueensberry] came over and made a scene and scandal it would utterly destroy" his future and alienate his friends.[38] Be that as it may, Wilde's unhappiness became so intense that on 28 August he met Douglas at Rouen. The tryst occurred, as Wilde conceded, against his better judgment. "Yes," he confessed to Ross, "I saw Bosie, and of course I love him as I always did, with a sense of tragedy and ruin."[39] By the middle of September 1897, he had hatched a plan to escape with Douglas. Strapped, as usual, for cash, he had only enough money to reach Paris. O'Sullivan generously furnished the rest of the fare. He rendezvoused with Bosie at the spa resort of Aix-les-Bains. Thereafter, he and Douglas traveled to Italy, where they made a home in Naples. Friends were obviously dismayed. But Wilde refused to apologize. "I cannot," he divulged to Ross, "live without the atmosphere of Love: I must love and be loved, whatever price I pay for it."[40] To underscore his point, Wilde sounded a histrionic note by speaking of the despair that he had suffered in Berneval. "I was so lonely," he declared, "that I was on the brink of killing myself."[41]

Love, as usual with Bosie, proved costly. At the beginning of their adventure, they stayed for two weeks at the Hotel Royal, where they ran up a bill of £68, which remained unpaid for a few months.[42] Just before he left these lodgings, Wilde granted an interview to the actor-manager and novelist Giuseppe Garibaldi Rocco. Together, they enjoyed beer and cognac at the Gran Caffé Gambrinus. Wilde was in a mordant mood. "I accomplished all that I set out to undertake in the world . . . now there is nothing left for me to do but wait for death."[43] Some days after Wilde "burst out laughing" at these unnerving remarks, he and Douglas moved into the Villa Giudice, Posillipo, where they resided for the best part of two months.[44] For the first time in two-and-a-half years, Wilde and Douglas were free to enjoy the partnership that they had tried to sustain before the trials. Wilde completed the *Ballad* there, and he also focused, as he informed Ross, on reconstructing *A Florentine Tragedy*: the blank verse drama on which he had been working from late 1893 until the time of his arrest. Moreover, at this time he collaborated (at least in principle) with Douglas on the libretto for Young's opera *Daphnis and Chloe*. Douglas promptly produced a few lyrics (now lost) for Young's commission. (The wealthy composer had parted with an advance of £100.) Wilde, however, even if he told Young that he planned to finish his work in six weeks, never got it done. Socially, the two men suffered some strain. An attaché from the British Embassy stopped by to communicate the unease that other expatriates felt at Wilde and Douglas's decision to reside on the Neapolitan coast. (Lord Rosebery maintained a home not far from their villa.) Still, they socialized with friends. Harry de Windt met Wilde at the Gambrinus, where he learned that the author had been offered a large sum to embark on a lecture tour of America to speak about his two-year sentence. The prospect was not tempting. "[N]othing," Wilde told de Windt, "can be worse than an English prison!"[45]

Despite these ups and downs, Wilde and Douglas tried to move ahead with their life together. As Douglas recollected: "Oscar and I were fairly happy at Naples, though we had several quarrels."[46] Their commitment to each other is apparent in a set of four photographs taken with a box camera, presumably at the villa. In fig. 25, a well-dressed Wilde—who dons a blazer that camouflages his increasing girth, a neatly pressed white shirt, and a summery straw boater—sits alfresco at a table where he has momentarily adjourned from a glass of red wine in order to acknowledge the camera. Meanwhile, a dapper Douglas sports a neat, dark jacket with contrasting white bowtie; he stands next to his forty-three-year-old boyfriend, gently placing his right hand on Wilde's left shoulder, while lifting his own glass as if to commemorate this moment. The overexposed picture nicely captures the intimacy between the two men.

But their companionship at Posillipo would not last. The quarrels turned into furious rows because of the financial pressure that they were under. Already, by late September Constance Wilde had learned from an old friend, Carlos Blacker, that Wilde and Bosie were together once more. She made it clear to her husband that she could not withstand his return to Douglas. Two months later, she cut off his modest allowance. At the time, Douglas's mother, Lady Sibyl, who passed along £25 per month to him, made a similar threat. In Wilde's opinion, these actions were completely unfair. "I had silence and solitude for two years," he resentfully informed Adey; "to condemn me now to silence and solitude would be barbarous."[47] It was an impossible situation. "How on earth," Wilde asked, "am I to live?"[48] Ultimately, it was money that came between him

Fig. 25. Photograph of Oscar Wilde and Alfred Douglas, Naples, *c*. October 1897, 9 cm × 9 cm.

and Bosie. As he explained to Ross, the moment he expected Douglas "to repay his own *share*" of the expenses they had run up, "he became terrible, unkind, mean, and penurious, except where his own pleasures were concerned."[49] The couple, it appears, had fallen back into patterns of hurtful behavior.

By 3 December 1897, Douglas deserted Wilde. In order to settle matters, Lady Sibyl arranged for Wilde to receive two substantial payments of £100, one in December and another after the New Year.[50] In return, Wilde pledged that he would never reconnect with her son. He tried to get on with his work. Around this time, Rocco, together with the poet Biagio Chiara, expressed a wish to complete an Italian translation of *Salomé*. Wilde hoped, too, that the distinguished actress Eleanora Duse might be persuaded to take the leading role, although she declined because of Wilde's sullied reputation. Even though Douglas had paid advance rent on the villa until the end of January 1898, Wilde could not concentrate. By the middle of December, he had traveled to Sicily. He remained unable, no matter how hard he had tried, to lead the life he truly yearned for. Even after his sojourn in Taormina, where he likely spent time with the homoerotic photographer Count Wilhelm von Gloeden, he felt restless. During these weeks, the essayist Logan Pearsall Smith spread deplorable rumors about Wilde's plight. "He is surrounded," Smith told Robert C. Trevelyan, "by the old low lot, makes money by writing obscenities for Smithers, and . . . all decent people have abandoned him."[51] Wilde forsook the villa, moved to Naples briefly, and resolved to decamp to Paris. As O'Sullivan saw it, Douglas's absence affected Wilde badly. The depression that Wilde endured was so troubling that at one point he yearned to be back in his "prisoner's cell picking oakum."[52] Wilde articulated his frustration at the way his friends had censured the interlude with his boyfriend. "It is," Wilde told Ross, "very unfair of people being horrid to me about Bosie and Naples."[53] "To have altered my life," he asserted, "would have been to have admitted that Uranian [i.e., homosexual] love is ignoble. I hold it to be noble—more noble than other forms."[54] If anything, from this point onward Wilde displayed greater determination than ever to realize his desires.

"I DO NOT ACKNOWLEDGE THAT I HAVE EVER BEEN WRONG": PARIS, 1898–1900

Paris offered such opportunities. On Sunday, 13 February 1898, Wilde settled into the Hôtel de Nice in the Latin Quarter, without much of the £200 that he had recently received. The same day, *The Ballad of Reading Gaol* appeared from Leonard Smithers. Based in London, Smithers was the somewhat notorious publisher who had become synonymous with English decadence. The previous summer, Wilde had for the first time met him through Dowson at Dieppe. Smithers had already brought the sensual poetry of Dowson, O'Sullivan, and Symons to public attention. He worked closely with Aubrey Beardsley and Arthur Symons on the short-lived decadent journal the *Savoy* (1896). An irrepressible maverick, Smithers stepped forward as the only publisher willing to support the resuscitation of Wilde's career. Once the *Ballad* was out, Wilde had copies sent to friends in England and France. His well-timed polemic urging prison reform came to public attention when forthright advocates such as the Revd. William Douglas Morrison spoke loudly about the need to dispense with solitary confinement. Morrison must have had Wilde in mind when he wrote in May 1898 about "a prisoner of considerable intellectual gifts" who at first bore up to the harsh conditions with "remarkable fortitude."[55] "But," Morrison observes, "at the end of a few weeks, it was easy for the experienced eye to see that this man would break down long before his sentence came to an end."[56]

This is exactly the harsh reality that the *Ballad* records. Nowhere does this finely crafted poem—which adapts the six-line stanzas of Thomas Hood's popular *Dream of Eugene Aram, the Murderer* (1829)—convey the gratitude that Wilde had expressed to Nelson. Neither is there much that relates to the warm camaraderie that he felt toward some of his fellow prisoners. Instead, Wilde's imagination focuses on the hanging of Charles Thomas Wooldridge, to whose memory the poem is dedicated. The trooper received the death sentence for slitting his spouse's throat three times. As we noted in chapter 6, the execution took place inside a shed within the exercise yard at H.M. Prison Reading.

Wilde chose to publish the *Ballad* under his cell number at Reading: C.3.3. This type of designation, as we also saw in the previous chapter, was the means by which inmates came to identify one another. Attributing authorship to C.3.3 was a significant gesture. Instead of drawing attention to the name that had scandalized the nation, the selfless cell number expressed solidarity with the "other souls in pain," who paced around the exercise yard in silence.[57] As Wilde's speaker notes, when the prisoners learned that one of their company was a "man who had to swing," the violence of the jail system shattered their nerves.[58] Such harrowing news frightened the speaker so much that the "very prison walls / Suddenly seemed to reel."[59] "We were," he writes, "as men who through a fen / Of filthy darkness grope."[60] Such lines, with their walloping internal rhymes and jolting catalexes, thump home their political message. Not a good word is spared for the prison guards: "The Warders strutted up and down / And kept their herd of brutes."[61] Their complicity in the state murder, which took place behind closed doors, is visible through "the quicklime on their boots."[62] (W. E. Henley, who had come to abhor Wilde well before the trials, considered such details suspect: "One may hazard the presumption quicklime, being fully as destructive of leather as it of flesh and bone, the warders, once their work was done, would have carefully wiped their boots."[63]) The description exposes the hypocrisy of a heartless institution that did not care to cover up its dirty work.

Not surprisingly, *Reynolds's Newspaper*, the radical weekly that had treated Wilde's trials with such broadmindedness, was bold in its praise. Hardly shy in divulging that the poem was by Oscar Wilde ("this brilliant and broken man of letters"), the reviewer berated the "horde of hypocritical wolves who would hound a man to death for a transgression for which he has been punished, thus acting in the face of the Bible in which they profess to believe, and of Christ, whom they have the impudence to say they follow."[64] Elsewhere, however, even among Wilde's friends, critical opinion varied. Nelson, who was doubtless stung by the negative depiction of the prison, confided to Ross that he found it "a terrible mixture of good[,] bad and indifferent."[65] Meanwhile, Edmund

Gosse stated that even if the work contained "hysterical and exaggerated passages," there were nonetheless "several stanzas of penetrating and convinced emotion."[66] (From what Gosse says, it appears that Ross himself proved unimpressed by the literary quality of the *Ballad*.) Still, the poem, whose composition began in late May 1897 and ended toward the end of the year, gained the public attention that Wilde hoped for. Without question, this widely noticed work had the potential to mark a new beginning in his career.

The *Ballad*, at least for a few months, enabled Wilde to recover some of his reputation and gain a measure of influence over a charged political issue. In the end, even if the royalties were modest (3d. a copy), the *Ballad* became the bestselling of the sixteen books that he published in his lifetime. Over 5,000 copies (far more than Smithers initially anticipated) were sold within the first four months of publication. During the passage of the Prison Reform Bill in Parliament, the poem had already enjoyed such an impact that the Irish nationalist T. P. O'Connor declared: "Everybody in this House has read the startling and striking poem written by a prisoner recently liberated, entitled 'The Ballad of Reading Gaol.'"[67] The attention that the *Ballad* garnered also prompted Wilde to intervene once more into the heated debate about penal reform; in a second, long letter to the *Chronicle*, he stated: "The necessary reforms are very simple. They concern the needs of the body and the needs of the mind."[68] Better food, proper sanitation, and a good supply of books were essential in a system where the time had come "to humanise the governors of the prisons, to civilise the warders and to Christianise the chaplains."[69] He signed himself, acknowledging his newfound reputation, "*THE AUTHOR OF THE BALLAD OF READING GAOL*."

Wilde's decision to restart his life in Paris promised much for him. It was a city that he knew well, and it was also where he had for the past fifteen years developed assorted literary contacts. As Frankel has demonstrated, Wilde "had always enjoyed a greater sense of intellectual freedom and recognition" in a great European capital that did not outlaw his desires.[70] Wilde hardly wasted time in beginning to enjoy the sexual opportunities on offer. Within days of reaching his hotel, he embarked on a romance with a doting but expensive former infantryman: the Anglo-French Maurice Gilbert, who later enjoyed affairs with Bosie, Ross, and Turner. (Ross informed Smithers that he had squandered a whole quarter's allowance on entertaining Gilbert; the blond-haired beauty was "a costly courtesan for those who admire him."[71]) By July, Wilde related to Ross the delight he took in smothering kisses on the lover both of them had shared. "Out of such a mouth," Wilde waxed poetical, "I would drink Lethe in this world and in the next ambrosia."[72]

Not everyone, however, was impressed by the new beau. In mid-March, Carlos Blacker, whom Wilde had known since the early 1880s, was initially under the impression that his old friend, now separated from Bosie, was living alone. He went, at Constance's prompting, to visit Wilde. Once Blacker learned of Gilbert's presence, he duly informed Constance of her husband's refusal to reform his ways. Blacker also mentioned that Wilde was so stretched for funds that he had lent his friend 150 francs. (This was one of the various smaller and larger sums that Wilde received from others.) The moment she heard this news, Constance's temper frayed. In a furious letter, while she writes to Blacker that "I do not wish him dead," she nevertheless comments pretty scornfully on the favor that she has asked Blacker to perform: "Oscar is so pathetic and such a born actor . . . You will say in the face of all this why did I ask you to go and see him in Paris? Well I thought you would have nothing to do with his money affairs, and I strongly advise you to leave them alone. I knew that you were in your own house, and therefore could not ask him to dinner, and I was silly enough to think that you would give him merely the intellectual stimulus he needed."[73] As Constance also told Blacker, she had already resumed her husband's allowance, although it was whittled down to £10 a month. Ross, as before, had been dispensing it. Her embittered tone may have been related to the medical problems that were impeding her mobility. Just over two weeks later, Constance perished through an incompetent surgical procedure.[74] She was forty years old.

Like many others, Constance—who read the *Ballad* with compassion—held out hope that her spouse might at last settle back into intellectual pursuits and sustain himself through writing. During the first weeks that he spent in Paris, Wilde at times suggested that he would like to continue his career. This was the impression that he made on the Irish journalist Chris Healy when they enjoyed conversing over lunch on the Boulevard St. Michel. "He talked lightly," Healy recalls, "about his trial, but his face lighted up when he spoke of his prison treatment."[75] No sooner had Wilde made witty pronouncements on certain contemporaries ("I invented Aubrey Beardsley," he quipped) than he "leaned back in his chair, lit a cigarette, and gazed reflectively on the beautiful scarab ring on his finger."[76] Wilde then declared: "I shall start working again, and trust to the generosity of the English people to judge it on its merits, and apart from their Philistine prejudices against myself. I do not acknowledge that I have ever been wrong . . . only society is stronger than I. Should the English people refuse my work, then I shall cross to America, a great country which has always treated me kindly."[77]

Such musings, though, were pipedreams. Assuredly, Wilde spent part of his time revisiting works that he had already completed. But he could not create anything new. In May 1898, he oversaw Henry-D. Davray's prose translation of the *Ballad*, which appeared in the *Mercure de France*. Moreover, he carefully revised *The Importance of Being Earnest* and *An Ideal Husband* for publication, both of which Smithers issued in 1899. (The press, noticeably, rebuffed these editions with blank silence. Neither volume carried Wilde's name. In any case, soon after their publication, Smithers went bankrupt.) Still, Wilde had already started to confide to friends—as he had already confided to Blacker—that the *Ballad* was his "*chant de cygne*" (swan song).[78]

Yet even if Wilde appeared bleak about his professional career, he revealed that he was fully engaged with the literary currents of the day. His lively interest in the cultural world emerges in the vivid memoir by the novelist Wilfred Hugh Chesson, who spent several hours with him in July 1898. Chesson explains the circumstances that gave rise to the meeting. After unearthing one or two of Wilde's books sold at the Tite Street sale in a nearby Chelsea bookstore, he decided to contact the author. "The find," he says, "was a happy one."[79] Chesson offered Wilde the annotated private copies of *Vera; or, The Nihilists* (1880) and *The Duchess of Padua* (1883) as gifts. They met when Wilde was staying with Douglas at an inn called l'Idée at Nogent-sur-Marne. Presumably, Chesson had no idea that Wilde had fled the Hôtel d'Alsace in the Latin Quarter because he had not settled his bill. As they exchanged views, one decisive matter arose from the conversation. Wilde stated that his days as a writer were pretty much over. "Of course I can write," he remarked "but I have lost the joy of writing."[80]

Chesson's memoir has additional significance because it reminds us that Wilde had been keeping controversial political company. "He told me," the novelist recalled, "that he knew Esterhazy."[81] For the past two years, the French officer Ferdinand Walsin-Esterhazy had been under suspicion as the traitor who divulged state secrets to the German enemy. In 1894, another officer, Alfred Dreyfus, was charged with the offense of selling 200 classified documents and sentenced to life imprisonment on Devil's Island, French Guiana. That Dreyfus was Jewish unleashed a spate of anti-Semitic riots in no fewer than twenty cities. Georges Picquart, the head of counter-espionage, however, determined that Dreyfus was innocent. By the time Wilde began socializing in Paris, the tide of opinion was turning against Esterhazy. On 13 January 1898, the French novelist Emile Zola published his letter "J'accuse . . . !," which explained how Dreyfus had been framed and why the case should be reopened. At this juncture, Wilde was spending his time drinking with Esterhazy and the military officer's staunch defender, the journalist Rowland Strong, along with Strong's assistant, Chris Healy. During the interview, Chesson learned that the robust dog that Wilde had with him was Strong's. The pet's name, Wilde quipped, was Dreyfus.

As we know from J. Robert Maguire's authoritative study of Wilde's entanglement in the Dreyfus Affair, by the time he met Chesson Wilde had already leaked precious information about Esterhazy's treason, which Blacker entrusted to him back in March 1898. Not long after Zola's "J'accuse . . . !," which led to the French writer's conviction for libel, Blacker had reconnected with Alessandro Panizzardi, the Italian military attaché whom he first met in the summer of 1895. Ever since the 1880s, Panizzardi had been sexually intimate with Maximilian von Schwartzkoppen, his counterpart in the German military, to whom Esterhazy had passed along the sensitive documents. Panizzardi, who fully understood the injustice against Dreyfus, told Blacker that he had facsimiles of materials Esterhazy had sent to Schwartzkoppen. The time had come to unleash the truth to the British press. Soon afterward, Blacker indiscreetly shared this intelligence with Wilde. Later, Wilde broke Blacker's confidence while carousing with Strong and Healy.

There were serious consequences. Healy, who connived with the Dreyfusards, relayed to them the precious secret, which resulted a few weeks later in an article in *Le Siècle* that declared Esterhazy's guilt. Eventually, all hell broke loose. In mid-June, Strong discredited Blacker in the *New York Times* by telling readers that this Dreyfusard had been involved in a "club incident connected with card playing which took place two or three years ago between Mr. Blacker and the Duke of Newcastle, resulting in the former being made bankrupt on the petition of the Duke for £10,000 money lent."[82] Strong was thus dragging up a painful incident involving the duke's slanderous remarks that Blacker had cheated him at cards. Blacker had sued. In the early stages of the case, which dragged on from 1894 until Blacker reached a settlement in early 1896, Wilde worked closely with Sir George Lewis in order to protect Blacker's reputation. Now, in the summer of 1898, Blacker—who suspected that Wilde had not only betrayed him but also attacked him in the press—fired off a moralistic letter to this very old friend. Not surprisingly, Wilde could not tolerate any more of the "hypocritical ass" who thought it "morally wrong" of him to have kept up with Bosie.[83] Once Wilde broke off relations with Blacker, he announced to Ross: "So Tartuffe goes out of my life."[84] Still, if that were not enough, Wilde could not—in the volatile context of the Dreyfus affair—resist drawing on his own reserve of anti-Semitic sentiment: "Of course the fact of his being a Jew on his father's side explains everything."[85] As a matter of fact, Blacker had no Jewish heritage. The only redeeming aspect to this story of bigotry and treachery is that Healy, who supported Dreyfus's cause, communicated what he had heard to Zola. This was a decisive moment. From this point on, Zola exerted such pressure on the authorities that by the end of August Colonel Hubert-Joseph Henry, who had forged evidence against Dreyfus, confessed to his crimes and took his own life. Henry's suicide, Healy observes, "caused a world-wide revulsion of feeling in favour of Dreyfus, and the renewed agitation" resulted in Dreyfus's release.[86] In Healy's view, "the successful agitation was all due to the information Oscar Wilde had given."[87] By 1 September 1898, Esterhazy had fled to England.

This episode points to the political unseemliness attached to some of Wilde's contacts in Paris. He was spending too much, drinking too heavily, and gossiping with abandon. These dubious habits too often made his existence in the French capital hard to bear. Even if Wilde enjoyed periods of time with Douglas again, they never renewed their relationship. He faced mounting debts. On occasion, he went without meals. He also alienated old friends. At his lowest point, he was not unknown to beg for money on the streets when he spotted an old acquaintance. The most infamous episode became known many years later. The Australian opera singer Nellie Melba recalled that she found herself confronted in Paris by "a tall shabby man": "'Madame Melba—don't you know who I am? I'm Oscar Wilde,' he said, 'and I'm going to do a terrible thing. I am going to ask you for money.'"[88] In response, Melba reached into her purse, found ten Louis coins, and watched him walk away with the cash. As Wilde's appearance visibly declined, people sometimes looked aghast at his condition. The American journalist George Barr Baker recalled glimpsing Wilde at the Café Deux Magots near the Latin Quarter. "Finishing his coffee," Baker remarked, "he slowly rose and left the place . . . [T]he fine shoulders looked aged and bent in the glare of the lamps."[89] Not surprisingly, after news of Wilde's death in November 1900 spread across town "[e]veryone remained convinced that [he] had resorted to suicide because he was utterly ruined and, more to the point, discouraged and disheartened."[90] "Paris killed him," O'Sullivan concluded; "in Italy he would have lived longer, and, I should think, happier."[91]

This depressing picture of Wilde's downward spiral into alcoholism, poverty, and despair tends to overlook the attractions that Paris continued to hold for him and the sociability that he was able, at least for a while, to sustain. Especially rewarding was the Calisaya, the American-style bar on the Boulevard des Italiens that had become his "literary resort" for his circle: "we all gather there at five o'clock—[Jean] Moréas, and [Ernest] La Jeunesse, and all the young poets."[92] Moreover, the charms of this café included various handsome young men: "One beautiful boy of bad character—of the name of Georges—goes there too, but his so like Antinous, and so smart, that he is allowed to talk to poets."[93] Moreover, when funds were available, Wilde took the initiative to travel, as he did (sometimes unhappily) in the company of a young gay Englishman, Harold Mellor. These jaunts also provided sexual opportunities. In Rome during spring 1900, for example, he exulted in his time with male prostitutes. With an impish sense of fun, he enjoyed elaborating these erotic encounters to titillate Ross. "How evil it is to buy Love," he exclaimed, "and how evil to sell it!"[94] "And yet," he added, while relishing such shameless pleasures, "what purple hours one can snatch from that grey slowly-moving thing we call Time! My mouth is twisted with kissing, and I feed on fevers."[95] On this account, his homosexuality—at whatever price it came—proved unconquerable.

At the same time, Wilde obsessed over his financial woes. His letters add up sums that he believes he is owed and monies that he needs. But it has to be said that Wilde's penury was intermittent, and the times when he was penniless were very much his own doing. Douglas, who in 1899 came into a large inheritance from Queensberry (it eventually totaled £15,000), hardly stinted in supplying his former lover with funds. In 1900, Bosie added to previous sums (perhaps as much as £1,000) by writing checks to the tune of £332—although Wilde pressed him to part with £1,500 or more.[96] Whatever income came Wilde's way rapidly slipped, as it had always done, through his hands. Whenever he could, he lived the high life.

Wilde also did not stint himself when buying books and periodicals. In 1904, Robert Harborough Sherard visited the Hôtel d'Alsace, where the manager, Jean Dupoirier, had not disturbed any of the belongings in the ground-floor room where Wilde had died, including the Pravaz syringe that Dupoirier used to administer shots of morphine to his guest. Wilde's property included "two large trunks" containing "three hundred odd volumes."[97] "He was a great reader," Dupoirier recalled. "One rarely saw him without a volume in his hand. He would sit for hours in the yard there sipping his *apéritif* and reading."[98] Sherard, however, noted that "the books showed little sign of usage"; many of the pages had not been cut.[99] Still, a few items caught Sherard's attention: "[Wilde] seems to have collected and read everything that he could lay his hands upon which treats of prison life in England—books and magazines. There were copies of the *Nineteenth Century*, with disquisitions by Du Cane, and there were popular sixpenny magazines, in which articles had appeared on the personal experiences of convicts. And amongst the books that had been read, I found a copy of the second edition of Howard on *Prisons*, with the corner of page 51 turned down, where the noble John pleads for 'more human treatment of prisoners in the articles of food, lodging, and the like.'"[100]

Wilde's waning health, though, kept him practically bedridden and dispirited for the final ten weeks of his life. The growing discomfort in his right ear incurred considerable expense. On 15 October 1900, when he required surgery to relieve the pain, friends raised 1,500 francs (about £60) to cover the fee. The hope was that he would experience a slow but sure recovery. By this point, it was left to others to sustain Wilde's career. As the patient rested in his insalubrious hotel room, Harris reaped "some hundreds of pounds a week" on the London stage with *Mr. and Mrs. Daventry*.[101] This daring play about adultery was based on a scenario that Wilde had unscrupulously sold several times to different people who believed that the drama he promised to develop for them would be profitable. (Harris took care to pay off those who saw nothing in return for their advances.) Even though Wilde's name did not appear anywhere in the publicity, when the production opened on 25 October 1900 it became obvious that he had a hand in it. George Bernard Shaw recalled: "Before the curtain went up George Moore informed me that I should see at a glance that the whole play was by Oscar Wilde."[102] *Mr. and Mrs. Daventry*, which featured Stella Campbell in the leading role, ran for 116 performances.[103] Just over a month into the production, the forty-six-year-old Wilde was dead.

Two of Wilde's most loyal friends, Reggie Turner and Robert Ross, attended him in the final hours, when meningoencephalitis swiftly took his life. Not long before Wilde expired, Ross, himself a Catholic, called upon an Irish Passionist priest, Fr. Cuthbert Dunne, to hurry to Wilde's deathbed. Dunne was asked not only to perform the last rites; he also received a barely conscious Wilde into the Church of Rome. Dunne kept detailed notes on this experience. Among the priest's papers is a touching letter from Wilde's youngest son, Vyvyan Holland, who had been sent by his guardian to Stonyhurst College, the Jesuit school near Clitheroe, Lancashire. (Holland had become a Catholic two years earlier when he was a pupil in Monaco.) Through the good offices of his head teacher, Holland asked Dunne to extend his gratitude to everyone who had made Wilde's conversion possible. "I beg you," Holland wrote on 14 December 1900, "to thank Mr. Robert Ross for all he did. I have never heard of him but from all accounts he must have been a very good man."[104] Ross and Turner had found the funds for a discreet service at Saint-Germain-des-Prés and a burial at the suburban Bagneux Cemetery, which took place on 3 December 1900. Douglas was the chief mourner.

Most of the press reports on Wilde's decease were discouraging. "The verdict that a jury passed upon his conduct at the Old Bailey in 1895," the *Pall Mall Gazette* commented, "destroyed for ever his reputation, and condemned him . . . to ignoble obscurity for the remainder of his days."[105] But here and there some critics noted the considerable loss to literature. As Max Beerbohm acknowledged in the *Saturday Review*: "His conventional comedies were as superior to the conventional comedies of other men as was 'The Importance of Being Earnest' to the everyday farces whose scheme was so frankly accepted in it."[106] "His death," the *Athenæum* observed, "further reduces the number of Englishmen capable of writing comedy."[107] Meanwhile, a small number of voices protested Wilde's severe mistreatment. The homophile campaigner and advocate of penal reform George Ives, for example, published a prescient poem in *Reynolds's*, which had always shown more sympathy than other papers with Wilde's plight: "Some day on history's page / Shall his mournful fate be told."[108]

In Ross's eyes, Wilde's death, if unexpectedly quick, nonetheless came at the right moment. A week after Wilde's funeral, he shared his thoughts with Louis Umfreville Wilkinson, the Radley schoolboy who had struck up a charming correspondence with the exile in Paris: "Though his death has been a great shock to those who knew him as well as I did, it was in many ways for the best. He was very unhappy, and would become more unhappy as time went on."[109] In later years, good friends were sometimes pressed to share their thoughts on what might have become of Wilde had he lived beyond the nineteenth century. To Charles Ricketts, the gay artist who furnished designs for such books as *A House of Pomegranates* (1891), *The Picture of Dorian Gray* (1891), and *Poems* (1892), there was no question that the trials and imprisonment that had befallen Wilde eventually overwhelmed one of the greatest talents of the age: "He was at once summarized by a period, in all its faults, but was also the *enfant terrible* of that period. His fall was an accident, a miscalculation, and the result of a conspiracy. He impressed me as at once the kindliest and most generous of men I ever met and the most richly endowed in intellect."[110] "What would Wilde have been?" Ricketts went on to ask.[111] "Would he have been a great critic, would he have revived the art of artificial comedy—by that I mean criticism of manners and character instead of our modern comedy of adultery and brutal pathos? I am unable to say!"[112]

Certainly, in the years leading up to World War I, commentators found it difficult to entertain how Wilde might have fared had he survived the decades to come. Still, with Ross's remarkable initiatives at that time—especially his editions of *De Profundis* (1905) and the triumphant fourteen-volume *Collected Works* (1908)—the moment had arrived to resurrect Wilde's reputation. Since then, the Irish writer's brilliance and defiance have attracted ever-increasing amounts of critical praise. In 1923, the gay artist and writer Laurence Housman—in his sensitive reconstruction of a conversation that took place with

Wilde in 1899—emphasized that "whatever else might be said for or against the life of promiscuous indulgence he appears to have led," there was one point that stood out in Wilde's "great service to humanity": "it made the 'unmentionable' mentionable."[113] Over sixty years later, Richard Ellmann, in the best-selling biography that did so much to refocus scholarly attention on Wilde's extraordinary life, adopted a similar perspective when he asserted: "Wilde is one of us."[114] This illustrious writer's exultant modernity, which has placed him at the forefront of internationally respected authors, ensures that his unique legacy—his exceptional writings followed by the undeserved sentence that he bravely endured—continues to resound to this day.

In light of the considerable wrong that was done to Oscar Wilde from the moment that he was arrested to his two unjustifiable years of imprisonment, the time has come to petition the British government for a retrospective royal prerogative of mercy—a pardon recommended to the Crown by the home secretary—that explicitly exonerates him in name. Such pardons are rare. There have nevertheless been welcome advances in this area of justice. In Wilde's distressing case, especially when we evaluate the serious missteps of the trials, a prerogative of mercy is assuredly warranted. This point was already clear to legal commentators in the mid-twentieth century. In 1933, Albert Crew looked back upon the "barbarity and severity" of the sentence that Justice Wills passed upon Wilde: "It is suggested that had the Criminal Court of Appeal [1907–66] been then in existence it is probable that his conviction, owing to the circumstances of the trial . . . would not have stood."[115] Twenty-one years later, Earl Winterton, in a parliamentary session focused on homosexual crime, remarked that "the conviction of, and sentence upon, Oscar Wilde . . . were regarded at the time, and are still regarded to-day by some learned in the law, as having been harsh and unfair."[116] As we have seen in *Oscar Wilde on Trial*, Wilde was given the maximum punishment under the 1885 law on the basis of questionable evidence whose corroboration appeared equally dubious.

Of the five prerogatives of mercy that have been granted since World War II, the one that has drawn greatest attention occurred in 2014 when it was given to the computing genius Alan Turing. In March 1952, Turing was charged for enjoying sexual intimacy with the nineteen-year-old Arnold Murray under the same law that sent Wilde to jail. At his trial, Turing was offered the choice of a prison sentence or probation. In choosing the latter, he received shots of what was known at the time as stilboestrol: a synthetic estrogen that rendered him impotent and resulted in gynecomastia (a condition where men develop breasts). Two years later, Turing appears to have taken his life through ingesting cyanide, although the precise circumstances of his demise are still uncertain. In summer 2012, after a concerted campaign led by John Leech, MP, Lord Sharkey sponsored a bill that was submitted to the House of Lords in order to grant Turing a statutory pardon for offenses under section 11 of the Criminal Law Amendment 1885. With the support of the prime minister David Cameron, the government proceeded under the royal prerogative of mercy. On 24 December 2013, Queen Elizabeth II signed a pardon; and in 2014, Her Majesty officially announced that Turing was pardoned. An additional honor in Turing's memory was the use of his portrait, together with images connected with his career including the mathematical table and formulas from his pathbreaking 1936 paper "On Computable Numbers," on the new £50 note issued by the Bank of England on 23 June 2021.

By late 2016, a parliamentary move toward implementing what was commonly called "Turing's Law" received wide press coverage. The Policing and Crime Act 2017 provides a posthumous pardon for the 50,000 or so individuals (including Oscar Wilde) who were convicted of offenses that were removed from statutory law through the Sexual Offences Act 2003. Among the previous legislation for which the 2017 Act specifies "[p]osthumous pardons" is "an offence under section 11 of the Criminal Law Amendment Act 1885" (Policing and Crime Act 2017 (c. 3), section 164 (3) (c)). In creating this posthumous pardon, the 2017 Act does not name any of individuals who were sentenced. In Scotland, by comparison, the Historical Sexual Offences (Pardons and Disregards) Act 2018 extends pardons to those surviving individuals who were convicted of acts of gross indecency under previous legislation. Now that more than 120 years have passed since Oscar Wilde died in such trying circumstances—ones that had much to do with the trials that he endured and the sentence that he suffered—the case for the Crown to make an explicit pardon for the acts of gross indecency that he was deemed to have committed remains more pressing and more urgent than ever before.

NOTES

INTRODUCTION

Epigraphs: *Regina v. Oscar Wilde and Alfred Taylor* (398); *The Complete Letters of Oscar Wilde*, ed. Merlin Holland and Rupert Hart-Davis (London: Fourth Estate, 2000), 1044; and Ada Leverson, *Letters to the Sphinx from Oscar Wilde, with Reminiscences of the Author* (London: Duckworth, 1930), 23–24.

1. The clerk of arraigns "has to discharge for the judge sitting on the crown side (i.e., in criminal cases) the duties which are discharged for him on the civil side; taxation of costs, allowances to witnesses, the business connected with jurors, their excuses and fines, the custody of documents, the duty of recording verdicts and making out warrants after sentence, are, in addition to advising the court upon points of criminal procedure, among the duties of the clerk of arraigns" (*Second Report of the Legal Departments Commission, Command Papers*, col. 1107 [1874]: 22–23).

2. *Regina v. Oscar Wilde and Alfred Taylor*, 396–97. Subsequent page references to the reconstruction of the proceedings of the Crown prosecution, which follows in part II of the present volume, appear in parentheses.

3. See [W. T. Stead], "The Maiden Tribute of Modern Babylon," *Pall Mall Gazette*, 6 July 1885: 1–6; 7 July 1885: 1–6; 8 July 1885: 1–6; 10 July 1885: 1–6. The *Pall Mall Gazette*, an afternoon daily paper that appealed to members of gentlemen's clubs, ran a feature that acknowledged the widespread press reaction to Stead's exposé, "The Press on 'The Maiden Tribute,'" 20 July 1885: 11. Modern studies of the controversy include Deborah Gorham, "The 'Maiden Tribute of Modern Babylon' Re-Examined: Child Prostitution and the Idea of Childhood in Late-Victorian England," *Victorian Studies* 21, no. 3 (1978): 353–79; Judith R. Walkowitz, *City of Dreadful Delight: Narratives of Sexual Danger in Late-Victorian London* (Chicago: University of Chicago Press, 1992), 81–134; and Gretchen Soderlund, *Sex Trafficking, Scandal, and Transformation of Journalism, 1885–1917* (Chicago: University of Chicago Press, 2013), 24–66.

4. J. E. C. Welldon, "Abnormality and Crime," *Saturday Review*, 17 December 1921: 687. Welldon adds that the passing of the 1885 law "was secured by some very question-

able methods of journalism" (687); his comment arises from the disruptive attempt, in 1921, to pass a "still more drastic Bill" that "was only defeated owing to the proposition that both sexes should be brought within the four corners of the 11th section of the Act in 1885" (687). Welldon, who was dean of Durham, was remarking on the first effort to criminalize lesbianism in English law; the 1921 amendment, which sought to spoil the bill, was worded by the proposer F. A. Maquisten as follows: "Any act of gross indecency between female persons shall be a misdemeanour in the same manner as any such act committed by male persons under section eleven of the Criminal Law Amendment Act 1885." When it was discussed in Parliament on 15 August 1921, the Lord Chancellor, F. E. Smith, 1st Baron Birkenhead, declared: "Lord Desart has pointed out with unanswerable force and with great truth, as I think, that the overwhelming majority of the women of this country have never heard of this thing at all. If you except a sophisticated society in a sophisticated city, I would be bold enough to say that of every thousand women, taken as a whole, 999 have never even heard a whisper of these practices" (*Hansard's Parliamentary Debates*, 5th series, vol. 43, col. 575 [https://api.parliament.uk/historic-hansard/lords/1921/aug/15/commons-amendment-2]). On the context of this proposed amendment, see Caroline Derry, "Lesbianism and Feminist Legislation in 1921: The Age of Consent and 'Gross Indecency between Women,'" *History Workshop Journal* 86 (2018): 245–67.

5. See [anon.], "Mr. Justice Wills on the Criminal Law Amendment Act," *Pall Mall Gazette*, 29 May 1886: 14. Those convicted included a tailor who had assaulted a twelve-year-old boy, and a laborer who had "attempted to have carnal knowledge with his step-daughter, aged fifteen."

6. Floyer Sydenham, "Advertisement," in Plato, *The Banquet: A Dialogue Concerning Love—The Second Part*, ed. and trans. Sydenham (London: W. Sandby, 1767), 247.

7. Adam Smith, *An Inquiry into the Nature and Causes of the Wealth of Nations*, 2 vols. (London: W. Strahan and T. Cadell, 1776), 2:382.

8. During the opening decades of the nineteenth century, the phrase was applied to unacceptable behaviors in many different parts of Britain. The *Public Ledger and Daily Advertiser* noted a so-called "May Fair," where vendors erected booths on Lisson Green in West London, and made local residents feel "in danger of their lives and property; no female could come to their houses but was insulted" ([anon.], "Paddington Fair Countermanded," *Public Ledger and Daily Advertiser*, 3 May 1817: 3). In Barnes, near London, the villagers were annoyed that someone had dug up the corpse of a murderer "to gratify the horrible curiosity of some idle people" (*London Courier*, 27 July 1812: 3). The *Hull Packet* reported a case in which a servant claimed, in a case brought by a husband aggrieved by his wife's infidelity, that "she had witnessed such gross indecency on the part of the plaintiff, as to have seen him in bed with his wife and his wife's sister at the same time" ([anon.], "Court of King's Bench: Thursday, December 7," *Hull Packet*, 19 December 1809: 4). In an early study of searchable nineteenth-century British newspapers, Charles Upchurch observes: "'Gross indecency' referred more often than not . . . to incidents of heterosexual sex, or the 'gross indecency' of a suicide, theater performance, or an art exhibition. Of the sixty-one hits for 'gross indecency' between 1800 and 1870 in the *Times Digital Archive* only three related to sex between men" ("Full-Text Databases and Historical Research: Cautionary Notes from a Ten-Year Study," *Journal of Social History* 46, no. 1 [2012]: 96).

9. "[I]t may be asked if whether [*sic*] it is not too ridiculous to style any work an oratorio which contains such gross indecency as that of the scene in which the corruption of the 'pure' fool, Parsifal, is attempted by Klingsor's 'she-demons,' transformed into 'flower-maidens,' and subsequently by the witch, Kundry" ([anon.], "Wagner's Parsifal," *Illustrated Sporting and Dramatic News*, 22 November 1884: 12). In 1884, the *Illustrated London News* spoke of "the French writer's occasional gross indecency" ([anon.], "New Books," 8 March 1884: 23). The plumber John Hilder was told at the police court that "it was a gross indecency to go about in a woman's dress in a public place" ([anon.], "Summary of This Morning's News," *Pall Mall Gazette*, 5 March 1881: 6).

10. [Anon.], "Immorality," *South Wales Daily News*, 21 February 1879: 2. This widely reported libel case, which had its origins in accusations of indecency that Barnwell communicated to a nephew of Chamberlaine's in October 1877, came before the Queen's Bench in February 1879, received a verdict in favor of the plaintiff, and—in light of the damages awarded to him—went through subsequent unsuccessful appeals. Chamberlaine was ultimately awarded £3,000 in damages, although the justices who reviewed the case under further appeal in July 1881 recommended a reduction to £800. For more on this case, see "The Keevil Libel Case, 1879," in Rictor Norton, *Homosexuality in Nineteenth-Century England: A Sourcebook Compiled by Rictor Norton* (http://rictornorton.co.uk/eighteen/1879keev.htm).

11. [Anon.], "Extraordinary Action for Libel," *Bristol Mercury*, 20 February 1879: 3. References to the term "sodomy" in the press at this time were infrequent. On the legal history of prohibiting sodomy in England and the increasing difficulty in articulating the word in nineteenth-century journalism, see 5–8.

12. [Anon.], "Verdict of the Jury—Acquittal of Mr. Ford," *Western Times*, 23 November 1878: 3. Ford was tried on ten counts of indecent assault. For more on this case, see "The Exeter Scandal, 1878," in Norton, *Homosexuality in Nineteenth-Century England* (http://rictornorton.co.uk/eighteen/1878exet.htm).

13. [Anon.], "The Raid on a 'Fancy Dress' Ball," *Liverpool Echo*, 30 September 1880: 4.

14. [Anon.], "The Raid on a 'Fancy Dress' Ball," 4. The phrase "nameless offence" served as a euphemism for sodomy in the press at this time.

15. Labouchere's motivation for inserting this clause into the bill has been debated by F. E. Smith, who contends that the politician's wording aimed to support those Members of Parliament, such as Charles Henry Hopwood, who had misgivings about this legislation because of "its threats to personal liberty and its engendering of blackmail"; Smith maintains that Labouchere's clause was "an extravagant motion designed to overturn the Bill—but one that got away" (F. E. Smith, "Labouchere's Amendment to the Criminal Law Amendment Bill," *Historical Studies* 17 [1976]: 169). The records of the debate in the House of Commons on 6 August 1885 show that Labouchere's clause received only passing attention (see *Hansard*, 3rd series, vol. 8, cols. 1397–98 [https://api.parliament.uk/historic-hansard/commons/1885/aug/06/consideration]).

16. Havelock Ellis and John Addington Symonds, *Sexual Inversion* (London: Wilson and Macmillan, 1897), 153. The main text is primarily by Ellis. The volume was controversial. On the circumstances that led to the publication of this volume and the reasons that led to its seizure by the police, see Joseph Bristow, "Symonds's History, Ellis's Heredity:

Sexual Inversion," in *Sexology in Culture: Labeling Bodies and Desires*, ed. Lucy Bland and Laura Doan (Chicago: University of Chicago Press, 1998), 79–99.

17. Ellis and Symonds, *Sexual Inversion*, 153.

18. See Wayne R. Dynes, "Buggery," in *Encyclopedia of Homosexuality*, ed. Dynes, 2 vols. (New York: Garland, 1990), 1:172; and Edward Coke, *The Third Part of the Institutes of the Laws of England: Concerning High Treason; and Other Pleas of the Crown, and Criminal Causes* (London: M. Flesher, W. Lee, and D. Pakeman, 1644), 58.

19. [Anon.], *The Arraignment and Conviction of Mervin Lord Audley, Earle of Castlehaven* (London: T. Thomas, 1642), 11. Castlehaven was beheaded.

20. Thomas Blount, "Buggery," in *A Law-Dictionary and Glossary*, 3rd ed. (London: E. Nutt and R. Gosling, 1717), n.p.

21. William Blackstone, *Of Public Wrongs*, ed. Ruth Paley, in *Commentaries on the Laws of England*, 4 vols. (Oxford: Clarendon Press, 2016), 4:142.

22. Blackstone, *Of Public Wrongs*, 143.

23. Paul Johnson, "Buggery and Parliament, 1533–2017," *Parliamentary History* 38, no. 3 (2019): 330.

24. It is important to note that after the execution of Pratt and Smith there were many cases where men were found guilty of committing sodomy; their convictions are often listed as "death recorded," which means that the judge did not articulate the death penalty in court. The phrase "death recorded" emerged in the Judgement of Death Act 1823 (4 Geo. 4 c. 48), which enabled judges to abstain from meting out a death sentence. The final notation of "death recorded" relates to John Spencer, a Catholic priest who was indicted on several counts for sexually assaulting boys placed in his care. Spencer was found guilty of buggery in two cases (www.oldbaileyonline.org, version 8.0, 25 June 2021) (*OPBO*) JOHN SPENCER (60) (t18600709-612). (The record inserts hyphens between the first and last letters of the word "buggery.")

25. Charles Upchurch, *Before Wilde: Sex between Men in Britain's Age of Reform* (Berkeley, CA: University of California Press, 2009), 93–94.

26. Upchurch, *Before Wilde*, 94. The incident was reported in the *Weekly Dispatch*, 25 September 1842: 459.

27. On the Old Bailey Online website, a search for men found guilty of gross indecency between 1890 and 1899 reveals over 150 cases.

28. Just to give one example: James Jelley was convicted of committing sodomy on 8 January 1894; he was sentenced to ten years' penal servitude, though he was discharged as a habitual criminal on 11 October 1897. See *The Proceedings of the Old Bailey: London's Criminal Court, 1674 to 1913* (www.oldbaileyonline.org, version 8.0, 15 March 2019) (*OBPO*), JAMES JELLEY (27) (t18940108-208). The official record replaces the word "sodomy" with asterisks.

29. This was a period when observers, such as C. H. Norman, noted that "this offence is being punished with great ferocity by certain judges." Norman implies that the charge of sodomy had led to recent sentences that had "ranged from four years' penal servitude up to thirteen years' penal servitude" ("Oscar Wilde," *Tribune*, 23 July 1948: 13).

30. Two months after Wilde's conviction, at a local court in Kent "Solomon Banfield, 16, labourer, was indicted with attempting to commit an unnatural offence with a mare,

at Ash, on June 1st." Since Lord Medway pointed out that "there was no corroborative evidence, a very necessary thing in such cases," the "prisoner was acquitted" ([anon.], "West Kent Quarter Sessions," *Maidstone Journal and Kentish Advertiser*, 4 July 1895: 8). It should be clear that gross indecency, unlike sodomy, restricted its definition to sexual acts between males.

31. Depending on the methods used for searching the phrase "gross indecency" at *OBPO*, the results for the period January 1886–May 1895 suggest there were roughly 130 trials involving the crime of gross indecency. These records indicate that Wilde was tried on a greater number of counts for breaking the eleventh section of the 1885 law than in any preceding case.

32. [Anon.], "Central Criminal Court—May 23," *Daily Telegraph*, 24 May 1895: 8.

33. The original legal meaning of blackmail existed in Scottish law, during both the seventeenth and eighteenth centuries, to refer to rental payments that were made in kind through such means as cattle, labor, or coin rather than silver. The modern concept of blackmail as funds extorted through threats and pressure becomes increasingly familiar in usage from the early 1880s onward.

34. John H. Langbein, *The Origins of Adversary Criminal Trial* (Oxford: Oxford University Press, 2005), 203.

35. The law formalized this rule in order to protect witnesses from perjuring themselves through the Perjury Act 1911: "A person shall not be liable to be convicted of any offence against this Act, or of any offence declared by any other Act to be perjury or subornation of perjury, or to be punishable as perjury or subornation of perjury, solely upon the evidence of one witness as to the falsity of any statement alleged to be false" (1 & 2 Geo. 5 c. 6 s. 13).

36. In court proceedings, a demurrer is a response made where a defendant's counsel does not dispute the truth of the allegation but claims it does not have sufficient grounds to justify a legal action.

37. The official change of name from Wilde to Holland eventually took place through a Petition for a Royal Licence in 1903. See the copy of Justice Kekewich's note, British Library, Add. MS 81754 A–F. Wilde's younger son, Vyvyan Holland, recalls the struggles that he and his brother, Cyril, had after fleeing to the Continent, in eradicating any vestige of the name Wilde from their belongings, including their cricket flannels: "to have to deny [our father] and to lock up all knowledge of him in our hearts was a terrible burden for children to bear" (*Son of Oscar Wilde*, 2nd ed. [New York: Carroll & Graf, 1999], 95). The first edition of Vyvyan Holland's memoir appeared in 1954.

38. *OBPO*, April 1895, trial of OSCAR FINGAL O'FFLAHARTIE WILLS WILDE (40) ALFRED TAYLOR (33) (t18950422-397); May 1895, trial of OSCAR FINGAL O'FFLAHARTIE WILLS WILDE (40) ALFRED WATERHOUSE SOMERSET TAYLOR (33) (t18950520-425).

39. Figure 1 shows that Queensberry's scrawl is fairly difficult to make out, though the spelling error in "Somdomite" is evident. The most noteworthy aspect of the card, however, lies in the marquess's choice of the word "Posing," which emerged as a point of discussion on several occasions during the trials (see, for example, 14 and 368). The document contains a handwritten letter "A" in the bottom left-hand corner, which indicates that it was the first exhibit in Wilde's prosecution against Queensberry for libel. Figure 2—

the envelope in which Sidney Wright, hall porter at the Albemarle Club, placed the card—featured as Exhibit "B" in the proceedings (The National Archives, CRIM 1/41/6, fo. 2). Commentators have sometimes construed the wording on the card as "For Oscar Wilde, Posing as a Somdomite," under the suspicion that these were the phrases that Queensberry wanted to inscribe. This was Wright's interpretation when Queensberry appeared at Great Marlborough Street Magistrates' Court on 2 March 1895; Queensberry interposed and stated that the words were "posing as sodomite." See Merlin Holland, *Irish Peacock and Scarlet Marquess: The Real Trial of Oscar Wilde* (London: Fourth Estate, 2003), 4. (The American edition of this volume is titled *The Real Trial of Oscar Wilde: The First Uncensored Transcript of the Trial of Oscar Wilde vs. John Douglas (Marquess of Queensberry), 1895* [New York: HarperCollins, 2003].)

40. John Sholto Douglas, 9th Marquess of Queensberry, "To Minnie Douglas," 4 March 1895, in [Francis Archibald Kelhead Douglas], the Marquess of Queensberry and Percy Colson, *Oscar Wilde and the Black Douglas* (London: Hutchinson, 1949), 58.

41. Marc-André Raffalovich, "L'Affaire Oscar Wilde," *Archives de l'anthropologie criminelle* 10 (1895): 456. The English translation is adapted from Marc-André Raffalovich, *Uranism and Unisexuality: A Study of Different Manifestations of Sexual Instinct*, trans. Nancy Erber and William A. Peniston, ed. Philip Healy with Frederick S. Roden (Basingstoke: Palgrave Macmillan, 2016), 208.

42. Wilde, "To Robert Ross," [28 February 1895], in *The Complete Letters*, 634–35.

43. Wilde, "To Robert Ross," [28 February 1895], 634.

44. *OBPO*, March 1895, trial of JOHN SHOLTO DOUGLAS, MARQUESS OF QUEENSBERRY (t18950325-336).

45. *OBPO*, March 1895, MARQUESS OF QUEENSBERRY (t18950325-336).

46. Charles Tattersall, "Genius on Trial: Key Sources Relating to Oscar Wilde at The National Archives," podcast, 3 July 2009, https://media.nationalarchives.gov.uk. Tattersall does not provide a reference for the basis of this observation.

47. John Addington Symonds, "To Charles Kains-Jackson," 18 December 1892, in *The Letters of John Addington Symonds*, ed. Herbert M. Schueller and Robert L. Peters, 3 vols. (Detroit, MI: Wayne State University Press, 1969), 3:791. Kains-Jackson was an editor and lawyer known to both Wilde and Douglas (see 93). The previous year, in a letter to the sexologist Havelock Ellis, Symonds had commented on "Labby's inexpansible legislation" (July 1891, *Letters*, 3:587).

48. [Anon.], "Blackmailing a City Merchant," *Reynolds's Newspaper*, 3 February 1895: 3.

49. [Anon.], "Blackmailing a City Merchant," 3. It is not clear under which law Turner was tried. The legal provisions against this type of extortion are discussed in [anon.], "Blackmail," *Justice of the Peace*, 12 February 1895: 99.

50. *OBPO*, 17 June 1895, trial of JOHN SHEPHERD, GEORGE MOODY, GEORGE WILTON (t18950617-519).

51. The Wolfenden Report (as it was generally known) concluded: "the evidence put before us has not established to our satisfaction the proposition that homosexuality is a disease" (*Report of the Committee on Homosexual Offences and Prostitution* [London: Her Majesty's Stationery Office, 1957], 15). The report was issued a year after section 13 of the

Sexual Offences Act 1956 stated: "It is an offence for a man to commit an act of gross indecency with another man, whether in public or private"; the penalty was two years' imprisonment (4 & 5 Eliz. 2 c. 69). On the research into male homosexuality that the committee led by Jack Wolfenden undertook in the mid-1950s, see Frank Mort, *Capital Offences: London and the Making of the Permissive Society* (New Haven, CT: Yale University Press, 2010), 139–96. Matt Houlbrook discusses the blackmailing of queer men during the interwar and postwar periods through 1957 in *Queer London: Perils and Pleasures in the Sexual Metropolis, 1918–1957* (Chicago: University of Chicago Press, 2005), especially 235–42, 276–86, and 333–43.

52. Historians identify *R v. Jones* (1776) as the earliest criminal case of homosexual extortion in England, though there were earlier episodes involving blackmailers and blackmailing rings in the eighteenth century; of the 1776 case, W. H. D. Winder remarks that it "established that a threat to accuse of sodomitical practices is a sufficient foundation for robbery," and that the judges concluded that it was necessary to show that a "sufficient degree of force had been made use of" ("The Development of Blackmail," *Modern Law Review* 5, no. 1 [1941]: 26). Upchurch discusses the early nineteenth-century legislation, especially the Threatening Letters Act 1825 (6 Geo. 4 c. 19), that addressed homosexual extortion and attempted sodomy (see *Before Wilde*, 94–100). He reveals that the criminal courts in London heard only thirty-three cases involving extortion through threats of accusation of an unnatural offense; the conviction rate, however, was high, with three-quarters of the defendants receiving sentences of ten years or more (*Before Wilde*, 100).

53. H. G. Cocks, *Nameless Offences: Homosexual Desire in the Nineteenth Century* (London: I.B. Tauris, 2003), 17.

54. I. Playfair [J. H. Wilson], *Gentle Criticisms on British Justice* (Newcastle upon Tyne: privately printed, 1895). 3. Wilde's closest supporters, especially More Adey, persuaded Wilson to suppress this document. The correspondence between Adey and Wilson is held at the Clark Library, MS Wilde, Box 83, Folder 8. W749L A233 (1895). Comparatively little is known about Wilson's identity. John Stokes has pointed out that Wilson wrote two volumes of poetry, *"Zalmoxis" and Other Poems* (1892) and *Iscariot's Bitter Love* (1912), both of which demonstrate the poet's erudition in classical and European literature. Stokes states that Wilson's poetry "reflects a view of the world in which sexual alignments are intimately connected with, yet secondary to, expressions of love, grief, outrage" (John Stokes, *Oscar Wilde: Myths, Miracles, and Imitations* [Cambridge: Cambridge University Press, 1996], 49). Wilson had connections with the social reformers Robert Spence Wilson and Elizabeth Spence Wilson in Newcastle upon Tyne.

55. [Wilson], *Gentle Criticisms*, 3.

56. Edward Carpenter, *The Intermediate Sex: A Study of Some Transitional Types of Men and Women* (London: George Allen and Unwin, 1908), 79.

57. The Dublin Castle scandal erupted on 25 August 1883, when the Irish MP Tim Healy insinuated in William O'Brien's nationalist newspaper *United Ireland* that a senior officer in the Royal Irish Constabulary, James Ellis French, was homosexual. French, most probably at the urging of senior administrators at Dublin Castle, claimed £5,000

damages. O'Brien responded by hiring a private detective, John Meiklejohn, who had disgraced himself in the 1870s when serving as an inspector for Scotland Yard. Meiklejohn's task was to uncover French's involvement in Dublin's homosexual networks. Meiklejohn's sleuthing uncovered the same-sex intimacies of Gustavus Charles Cornwall, the Secretary to the General Post Office. On 10 May 1884, *United Ireland* launched an attack of Cornwall's reputation. Cornwall took out a libel suit demanding £10,000 damages. The exposure of French and Cornwall led to different outcomes. From July to December 1884, the Crown took out actions against each man, with Cornwall (although charged with committing and conspiring to commit acts of sodomy) eventually exonerated, on the one hand, and French, after three trials, sent down for two years with hard labor, on the other hand. Several other men became entangled in the proceedings, which resulted in the conviction of three middle-aged individuals who were discovered to have been running male brothels in Dublin. Cornwall continued to pursue his libel case against O'Brien through 23 February 1885, when the Queen's Bench refused the trial. There is, to date, no definitive study of the controversy.

58. Richard Ellmann, *Oscar Wilde* (New York: Knopf, 1988), opposite 429. The first British edition, which has different pagination, appeared from Hamish Hamilton in 1987. This is one of numerous smaller and larger errors that appear in Ellmann's biography. The mistakes are listed in Horst Schroeder, *Additions and Corrections to Richard Ellmann's "Oscar Wilde,"* 2nd ed. (Braunschweig: privately printed, 2002).

59. In 1992, John Stokes observed that in the Viollet library the photograph "is filed with another picture, obviously of the same person and taken at the same session, labelled *Leonora Sengera dans le rôle de Salomé à Leipzig*; it's undated though the photographer is identified as Carl Bellach of Leipzig." Stokes adds: "The photo seems to have come to the library from the collection of the late Guillot de Saix" (John Stokes, "Wilde Shot," *London Review of Books*, 27 February 1992). Merlin Holland revealed that the photograph depicted Guszalewicz ("Wilde as Salomé?," *Times Literary Supplement*, 24 July 1994: 14). The image, which first appeared in an article in the German periodical *Bühne und Welt* 9 (1907): 439–47, was initially identified by Horst Schroeder.

60. Perhaps the best-known reaffirmation that the photograph represents "Oscar Wilde in the costume of Salome," together with the observation that Wilde "looks like a Burne-Jones in drag," appears in Marjorie Garber, *Vested Interests: Cross-Dressing and Cultural Anxiety* (New York: Routledge, 1997), 339. See also Elaine Showalter, *Sexual Anarchy: Gender and Culture at the Fin de Siècle* (New York: Viking, 1990), 156–57. Showalter responded to Holland's "Wilde as Salomé?" with an essay, "It's Still Salome," *Times Literary Supplement*, 2 September 1994: 13–14.

61. The original documents on which Holland bases his edition are catalogued as "Transcripts (Taken from the Original Shorthand Notes) and Other Material Relating to Oscar Wilde's Prosecution of the Marquess of Queensberry for Criminal Libel in April 1895" (British Library, Western Manuscripts, Loan MS 122). These documents, which came into the hands of the British Library in the early twenty-first century, remain there on permanent loan. Nothing is publicly known about the hands into which they fell after Wilde's conviction.

62. Holland, *Irish Peacock*, 78.

63. The phrasing recurs in "Plea of Justification Filed by the Defendant in *Regina (Wilde) v Queensberry*," National Archives CRIM/4/1118, in Holland, *Irish Peacock*, 287–90. The term "sodomy" is repeated eleven times, and the term "gross indecency" twenty-four times in Queensberry's plea.

64. Matthew Sturgis, *Oscar: A Life* (London: Head of Zeus, 2018), 546.

65. "Plea of Justification," in Holland, *Irish Peacock*, 291. The phrase "sodomitical practices" recurs with some frequency in legal writings of the later eighteenth and early nineteenth century.

66. See Holland, *Irish Peacock*, 81 and 80.

67. The grand jury found true bills of twenty-five counts against the two defendants. There was discussion during the first criminal trial against Wilde and Taylor about the way that Queensberry's plea of justification served as the basis of the counts against the two men. See chapter 4 (200–2).

68. On the estimated number of men who were convicted for homosexual offenses, see Kate McCann, "Turing's Law: Oscar Wilde among 50,000 Convicted Gay Men Granted Posthumous Pardons," *Daily Telegraph*, 31 January 2017.

CHAPTER ONE

Epigraph: Hesketh Pearson, *The Life of Oscar Wilde* (London: Methuen, 1946), 116.

1. Oscar Wilde, "To Lord Alfred Douglas," [January–March 1897], in *The Complete Letters of Oscar Wilde*, ed. Merlin Holland and Rupert Hart-Davis (London: Fourth Estate, 2000), 759. The particular individuals whom Wilde has in mind here are the seasoned blackmailer Robert Cliburn and the prostitute, extortionist, and comic performer Frederick Atkins.

2. Oscar Wilde, "The New Helen," "Portia," and "Phêdre," in Wilde, *Poems and Poems in Prose*, ed. Bobby Fong and Karl Beckson, in *The Complete Works of Oscar Wilde*, 11 vols. to date (Oxford: Oxford University Press, 2000–), 1:106-9, 121, and 116.

3. W. P. Frith, *My Autobiography and Reminiscences*, 3 vols. (London: Richard Bentley, 1887–88), 2:256.

4. Frith, *My Autobiography*, 2:256.

5. For further information on Graves's print, see Martin Beisly, Mark Bills, and Rosie Jarvie, *William Powell Frith, R.A. (1819–1909): The Private View at the Royal Academy, 1881* (London: Martin Beisly, 2019), 35–39.

6. Oscar Wilde, "To Florence Balcombe," [? 30 November 1878], in *The Complete Letters*, 71.

7. Violet Hunt, *I Have This to Say: The Story of My Flurried Years* (New York: Boni and Liveright, 1926), 173.

8. [Anon.], "Swinburne and Water," *Punch*, 23 July 1881: 26.

9. The verse is quoted in both Robert Harborough Sherard, *The Real Oscar Wilde: To Be Used as a Supplement to, and Illustration of "The Life of Oscar Wilde"* (London: T. Werner Laurie, 1916), 48, and Richard Ellmann, *Oscar Wilde* (New York: Knopf, 1988), 233. The verse probably appeared in the 23 May 1883 issue of Edmund Yates's *World: A Journal for Men and Women*. I have been unable to trace the original.

10. Constance Lloyd, "To Otho Holland Lloyd," 26 November 1883, in Wilde, *The Complete Letters*, 222.

11. The figure was confirmed at Wilde's bankruptcy hearing on 12 November 1895; see the transcript of the hearing in Donald Mead, "Heading for Disaster—Oscar's Finances," *Wildean* 46 (2015): 100.

12. In a letter dated 17 April 1884, Levy presented a check for £25 to Wilde before the wedding (Clark Library, MS Wilde, L66L W6721, Box 39, Folder 3).

13. Oscar Wilde, "To Lillie Langtry," [*c*. 22 January 1884], in *The Complete Letters*, 224.

14. Oscar Wilde, "To Waldo Story," [postmark 22 January 1884], in *The Complete Letters*, 225.

15. Wilde, "To Waldo Story," [postmark 22 January 1884], 225.

16. Wilde, "To Waldo Story," [postmark 22 January 1884], 225.

17. Constance Lloyd, "To Oscar Wilde," [*c*. April 1884], British Library, Eccles Bequest, 81690, quoted in Franny Moyle, *Constance: The Tragic and Scandalous Life of Mrs. Oscar Wilde* (London: John Murray, 2011), 78.

18. Oscar Wilde, "To Norman Forbes-Robertson," [early June 1885], in *The Complete Letters*, 262.

19. Wilde, "To Norman Forbes-Robertson," [early June 1885], 262.

20. Moyle, *Constance*, 79.

21. Moyle, *Constance* 5.

22. Anon., "Mrs. Humphry," "Social Echoes," *London Society* 53 (1888): 667.

23. [Anon.], "Women's Dress: Rational or Fashionable?" *Pall Mall Gazette*, 26 March 1886: 11.

24. Adrian Hope, "To Laura Troubridge," 25 April 1885, in Hope and Laura Troubridge, *Letters of Engagement, 1884–1888: The Love Letters of Adrian Hope and Laura Troubridge*, ed. Marie-Jacqueline Lancaster (London: Tite Street Press, 2002), 115. After Constance Wilde died in April 1898, Hope became the guardian of Wilde's sons.

25. Hope, "To Laura Troubridge," 25 April 1885, 115.

26. Oscar Wilde, "To More Adey," 8 March 1897, in *The Complete Letters*, 681.

27. Vyvyan Holland, *Son of Oscar Wilde*, 2nd ed., ed. Merlin Holland (New York: Carroll and Graf, 1999), 52.

28. Holland, *Son of Oscar Wilde*, 50.

29. See Mrs. [Florence] Fenwick-Miller, "The Ladies' Column," *Illustrated London News*, 29 April 1893: 534.

30. [Anon.], "The Eighty Club," in *The Eighty Club: 1895* (London: privately printed, 1895), 3–4. This wording appeared in each of the club's annual reports.

31. Thomas Wright, "Party Political Animal," *Times Literary Supplement*, 4 June 2014: 14.

32. [Oscar Wilde], "Mr. Froude's Blue-Book," *Pall Mall Gazette*, 13 April 1889: 3, in *Journalism II*, ed. John Stokes and Mark W. Turner, in Wilde, *Complete Works*, 7:206.

33. [Oscar Wilde], "Mr. Symonds's History of the Renaissance," *Pall Mall Gazette*, 10 November 1886: 5; "Mr. Morris's Odyssey," *Pall Mall Gazette*, 26 April 1887: 5; and "Mr. Pater's Imaginary Portraits," *Pall Mall Gazette*, 11 June 1887: 2–3, in *Journalism I*, ed. John Stokes and Mark W. Turner, in Wilde, *Complete Works*, 6:105, 156, and 180.

34. [Oscar Wilde], "Primavera," *Pall Mall Gazette*, 24 May 1890: 3, in Wilde, *Complete Works*, 7:249.

35. Constance Wilde, "Children's Dress in this Century," *Woman's World* 1 (1888): 417.

36. "A. B. W." [A. B. Walkley], "The Drama: *Lady Windermere's Fan*," *Speaker*, 27 February 1892: 257.

37. William Archer, review of *A Woman of No Importance*, *World*, 26 April 1893, reprinted in *Oscar Wilde: The Critical Heritage*, ed. Karl Beckson (London: Routledge and Kegan Paul, 1970), 144.

38. Archer, review of *A Woman of No Importance*, 144–45.

39. Wilde, *Two Society Comedies: "A Woman of No Importance" and "An Ideal Husband,"* ed. Ian Small and Russell Jackson (New York: W. W. Norton, 1983), 75.

40. Nellie Melba, *Melodies and Memories* (New York: George H. Doran, 1926), 79.

41. Alfred Douglas, *The Autobiography of Lord Alfred Douglas*, 2nd ed. (London: Martin Secker, 1931), 59.

42. Douglas, *Autobiography*, 59–60.

43. Moyle, *Constance*, 183.

44. Frank Harris, *Oscar Wilde: His Life and Confessions*, 2 vols. (New York: privately printed, 1916), 2:486.

45. Constance Wilde, "To Lady Mount-Temple," undated letter, University of Southampton, Broadlands Archive, 57/14/93, quoted in Antony Edmonds, *Oscar Wilde's Scandalous Summer: The 1894 Worthing Holiday and the Aftermath* (Stroud: Amberley, 2014), 22.

46. This part of Gertrude Simmonds's witness statement appears in Neil McKenna, *The Secret Life of Oscar Wilde* (London: Century, 2003), 241.

47. Herbert Vivian, "The Reminiscences of a Short Life," *Sun*, 17 November 1889: 4.

48. Vivian, "The Reminiscences of a Short Life," 4.

49. Vivian, "The Reminiscences of a Short Life," 4.

50. Wilde, "To Herbert Vivian," [postmark 20 May 1890,] in *The Complete Letters*, 427.

51. André Raffalovich, *A Willing Exile: A Novel*, 2 vols. (London: F. V. White, 1890), 1:56.

52. Raffalovich, *A Willing Exile*, 1:79.

53. Constance Wilde, "To Arthur Humphreys," 1 August 1894, British Library, Eccles Bequest 81732, quoted in Moyle, *Constance*, 243, and Edmonds, *Oscar Wilde's Scandalous Summer*, 91. Humphreys also issued editions of Wilde's essay "The Soul of Man under Socialism" (*Fortnightly Review* 49 [1891]: 292–319), as *The Soul of Man* from 1895 through 1919.

54. Wilde, "To Lord Alfred Douglas," [January–March 1897], 688.

55. J. Robert Maguire, *Ceremonies of Bravery: Oscar Wilde, Carlos Blacker, and the Dreyfus Affair* (Oxford: Oxford University Press, 2013), 65.

56. Donald Mead, "Earnings from Journalism," *Wildean* 45 (July 2014): 73.

57. Account Book for Channon's Stores, Grocery and Provisions, Wines, Spirits and Bottled Beers [1892–95], British Library, Add. MS 81761.

58. Ada Leverson, *Letters to the Sphinx from Oscar Wilde, with Reminiscences of the Author* (London: Duckworth, 1930), 44.

59. I provide details about each of these venues in the reconstruction of the proceedings in part II below.

60. Jeremy Reed, *The Dilly: A Secret History of Piccadilly Rent Boys* (London: Peter Owen, 2014), 14. For the later history of the "Dilly Boys" during the mid-twentieth century, see Matt Houlbrook, *Queer London: Perils and Pleasures in the Sexual Metropolis, 1918–1957* (Chicago: University of Chicago Press, 2005), 58–74.

61. Oscar Wilde, *The Picture of Dorian Gray: The 1890 and 1891 Texts*, ed. Joseph Bristow, in Wilde, *Complete Works*, 3:38 and 3:211.

62. J. P. Mahaffy, *Social Life in Greece from Homer to Menander* (London: Macmillan, 1874), viii.

63. Mahaffy, *Social Life in Greece*, 238.

64. Mahaffy, *Social Life in Greece*, 239.

65. Mahaffy, *Social Life in Greece*, 239.

66. Mahaffy, *Social Life in Greece*, 239.

67. Mahaffy, *Social Life in Greece*, 311.

68. Mahaffy, *Social Life in Greece*, 308.

69. Mahaffy, *Social Life in Greece*, 308.

70. J. P. Mahaffy, *Social Life in Greece from Homer to Menander*, 2nd ed. (London: Macmillan, 1875), x.

71. Lawrence Danson, "Oscar Wilde, W. H., and the Unspoken Name of Love," *ELH* 58, no. 4 (1991): 991.

72. Linda Dowling, *Hellenism and Homosexuality in Victorian Oxford* (Ithaca, NY: Cornell University Press, 1994), 64.

73. Walter H. Pater, *Studies in the History of the Renaissance* (London: Macmillan, 1873), xi. Pater revised and retitled this study as *The Renaissance: Studies in Art and Poetry* in successive editions published in 1877, 1888, and 1893.

74. Pater, *Studies in the History of the Renaissance*, 213.

75. Pater, *Studies in the History of the Renaissance*, 161. Pater's chapter first appeared as "Winckelmann," *Westminster Review*, n.s. 31 (1867): 80–110.

76. Pater, *Studies in the History of the Renaissance*, 161.

77. Wilde, *Complete Works*, 3:25 and 3:187.

78. Vincent O'Sullivan, *Aspects of Wilde* (London: Constable, 1936), 68. Wilde's comment, though not Wilde's name, was mentioned in O'Sullivan's anonymous tribute, "Walter Pater: By an Undergraduate," *Pall Mall Gazette*, 2 August 1894: 3. Lionel Johnson, who also attended Pater's lecture on Wordsworth at Toynbee Hall, recorded the same anecdote in "To Campbell Dodgson," 5 February 1891, quoted in "Some Letters of Lionel Johnson," ed. Raymond Roseliep, unpublished doctoral dissertation, University of Notre Dame, 1953, 110.

79. Merlin Holland, *Irish Peacock and Scarlet Marquess: The Real Trial of Oscar Wilde* (London: Fourth Estate, 2003), 78.

80. Holland, *Irish Peacock*, 78.

81. Oscar Wilde, "The Grave of Keats," in *Complete Works*, 1:36.

82. Wilde, "The Grave of Keats," 1:36.

83. Oscar Wilde, "The Tomb of Keats," *Irish Monthly* 5 (1877): 476–78, in *Complete Works*, 6:12.

84. Wilde, "The Tomb of Keats," 6:12.

85. Oscar Wilde, "Charmides," in *Complete Works*, 1:70 and 73.

86. Rupert Croft-Cooke, *Bosie: The Story of Lord Alfred Douglas, His Friends and Enemies* (London: W. H. Allen, 1963), 42.

87. McKenna, *The Secret Life of Oscar Wilde*, 12.

88. Whittington-Egan, *Frank Miles and Oscar Wilde: "Such White Lilies"* (High Wycombe: Rivendale Press, 2008), 36.

89. Whittington-Egan, *Frank Miles and Oscar Wilde*, 36.

90. I discuss this event in relation to the broader context of Wilde's friendship with Gower in "Oscar Wilde, Ronald Gower, and the Shakespeare Memorial," *Etudes anglaises* 69, no. 1 (2016): 7–22.

91. Whittington-Egan, *Frank Miles and Oscar Wilde*, 42.

92. Whittington-Egan, *Frank Miles and Oscar Wilde*, 42.

93. Oscar Wilde, "The Grosvenor Gallery," *Dublin University Magazine* 90 (1877): 118–26, reprinted in *Complete Works*, 6:3.

94. This report in *The Man of the World* is quoted in [anon.], "Criminal Investigation against a Newspaper," *Reynolds's Weekly*, 22 December 1878: 5. I have not been able to trace the original.

95. [Anon.], "Criminal Investigation against a Newspaper," 5.

96. Roger Fry, "To Basil Williams," [May 1891], in *The Letters of Roger Fry*, ed. Denys Sutton, 2 vols. (London: Chatto and Windus, 1972), 1:146.

97. Canon Robert Miles, "To Oscar Wilde," 21 August 1881, quoted in Whittington-Egan, *Frank Miles and Oscar Wilde*, 74. Canon Miles's correspondence with Wilde is held in the Clark Library, MS Wilde, Box 43, Folder 17.

98. Rennell Rodd, *Social and Diplomatic Memories*, 3 vols. (London: Edward Arnold, 1922–25), 1:9.

99. Rodd, *Social and Diplomatic Memories*, 1:22.

100. Rodd, *Social and Diplomatic Memories*, 1:25.

101. Oscar Wilde, "To J. M. Stoddart," 7 August 1882, in *The Complete Letters*, 178.

102. Oscar Wilde, "*L'Envoi*," in Rennell Rodd, *Rose Leaf and Apple Leaf* (Philadelphia, PA: J. M. Stoddart, 1882), 13 and 27–28.

103. Rodd, *Rose Leaf and Apple Leaf*, 33. The quoted words in the dedication are from Rodd, "By the South Sea," in *Rose Leaf and Apple Leaf*, 50.

104. Algernon Charles Swinburne, "To Theodore Watts," 8 November 1882, in *The Swinburne Letters*, ed. Cecil Y. Lang, 6 vols. (New Haven, CT: Yale University Press, 1960), 4:312.

105. Thomas Mosher, "Bibliographical Note," in Rodd, *Rose Leaf and Apple Leaf* (Portland, ME: Thomas B. Mosher, 1906), 97–98.

106. [Anon.], "The New Renaissance," *Saturday Review*, 4 November 1882: 597.

107. Rodd, *Social and Diplomatic Memories*, 1:25.

108. Oscar Wilde, "To Robert Harborough Sherard," [early April 1883], in *The Complete Letters*, 205.

109. Oscar Wilde, "To H. C. Marillier," [postmark 5 November 1885], in *The Complete Letters*, 266.

110. Wilde, "To H. C. Marillier," [postmark 5 November 1885], 266.

111. Oscar Wilde, "To H. C. Marillier," [postmark 8 November 1885], in *The Complete Letters*, 267.

112. Oscar Wilde, "To H. C. Marillier," [postmark 14 November 1885], in *The Complete Letters*, 268.

113. Oscar Wilde, "To H. C. Marillier," [postmark 12 December 1885], in *The Complete Letters*, 272.

114. Horst Schroeder identifies Wilde's derivation of the term *l'amour de l'impossible* in "The Critic as Artist" from Symonds's *Studies of the Greek Poets* (1873); see "Ερος τον αδυνατον—*L'Amour de l'impossible*: A Graeco-French Collocation in 'The Critic as Artist,'" *Notes and Queries* 40, no. 1 (1993): 52–53.

115. Wilde, "To H. C. Marillier," [postmark 12 December 1885], 272.

116. Jonathan Fryer, *Robbie Ross: Oscar Wilde's Devoted Friend* (London: Constable, 2000), 18.

117. See Croft-Cooke, *Bosie*, 49.

118. Fryer, *Robbie Ross*, 21. Wilde slept with men at the family residence. Douglas confirmed that they spent the night together at Tite Street. Wilde was found gulty of committing an act of gross indecency with Alfred Wood at the Tite Street home. (See 397.)

119. William Shakespeare, "Sonnet 20," in *Shakespeare's Sonnets*, ed. Katherine Duncan-Jones, The Arden Shakespeare, 3rd series (London: Thomas Nelson, 1997), 151. On Edmond Malone's elaboration of Thomas Tyrwhitt's theory that the dedicatee of Shakespeare's *Sonnets* was a boy-player known as Willie Hughes, see Joseph Bristow and Rebecca N. Mitchell, *Oscar Wilde's Chatterton: Literary History, Romanticism, and the Art of Forgery* (New Haven, CT: Yale University Press, 2015), 251–56.

120. Oscar Wilde, "The Portrait of Mr. W. H.," *Blackwood's Edinburgh Magazine* 146 (1889): 15.

121. Wilde, "The Portrait of Mr. W. H.," 7.

122. Oscar Wilde, "To Robert Ross," [early July 1889], in *The Complete Letters*, 407–8.

123. Wilde, "To Robert Ross," [early July 1889], 408.

124. Oscar Wilde, "To J. M. Stoddart," [received 17 December 1889], in *The Complete Letters*, 416.

125. Wilde, *Complete Works*, 3:12, 3:4, 3:176, and 3:169.

126. Wilde, *Complete Works*, 3:4 and 3:169.

127. Wilde, *Complete Works*, 3:12. Wilde deleted part of this passage in the 1891 edition; see 3:176. Some of Wilde's revisions to the 1890 text were the subject of Carson's cross-examination during the libel trial; see 127–28 and 134.

128. Wilde, *Complete Works*, 3:20 and 3:183.

129. Wilde, *Complete Works*, 3:21 and 3:183.

130. Wilde, *Complete Works*, 3:25. The text of the 1891 edition contains some revisions; see 3:186.

131. Wilde, *Complete Works*, 3:25 and 3:187.

132. Wilde, *Complete Works*, 3:90. Wilde revised the text slightly in the 1891 edition; see 3:264.

133. Wilde, *Complete Works*, 3:90.
134. Wilde, *Complete Works*, 3:135 and 3:298.
135. Wilde, *Complete Works*, 3:135 and 3:298.
136. Wilde, *Complete Works*, 3:135. The text in the 1891 edition is slightly different; see 3:299.
137. Wilde, *Complete Works*, 3:162 and 3:356.
138. Wilde, *Complete Works*, 3:164 and 3:357.
139. Wilde, *Complete Works*, 3:164 and 3:357.
140. Wilde, *Complete Works*, 3:164 and 3:357.
141. Robert Ross, "To Oscar Wilde," [June 1890], quoted in Fryer, *Robbie Ross*, 51.
142. Ross, "To Oscar Wilde," [June 1890], 51.
143. [Sidney Henry Jeyes], "A Study in Puppydom," *St. James's Gazette*, 20 June 1890: 3, reprinted in Beckson, ed., *Oscar Wilde: The Critical Heritage*, 68.
144. [Anon.], review of Oscar Wilde, *The Picture of Dorian Gray*, *Daily Chronicle*, 30 June 1890: 7, reprinted in Beckson, *Oscar Wilde: The Critical Heritage*, 72.
145. [Charles Whibley?], review of Oscar Wilde, *The Picture of Dorian Gray*, *Scots Observer*, 5 July 1890: 181, reprinted in Beckson, ed., *Oscar Wilde: The Critical Heritage*, 75.
146. [Whibley?], review of Wilde, *The Picture of Dorian Gray*, reprinted in Beckson, ed., *Oscar Wilde: The Critical Heritage*, 75.
147. The charge, which includes the felonies of conspiracy and sodomy, is quoted in H. Montgomery Hyde, *The Cleveland Street Scandal* (London: W. H. Allen, 1976), 24.
148. Quoted in Hyde, *The Cleveland Street Scandal*, 108.
149. [Anon.], "The Terrible Scandals in 'High Life,'" *Reynolds's Newspaper*, 1 December 1889: 4. Several months later, the same newspaper referred to "the Cleveland Street gang of aristocratic sodomites" ([anon.], "Salisbury, the Shuffler," *Reynolds's Newspaper*, 9 March 1890: 4). References to "sodomite" and "sodomites" were rare in journalism at this time.
150. [Anon.], "The Terrible Scandals in 'High Life,'" 4. The tone that *Reynolds's* adopted during Wilde's trials did not sound such a harsh note.
151. Quoted in Hyde, *The Cleveland Street Scandal*, 146.
152. Hyde, *The Cleveland Street Scandal*, 146.
153. Hyde, *The Cleveland Street Scandal*, 146.
154. Hyde, *The Cleveland Street Scandal*, 146.
155. [Henry Labouchere], "Entre nous," *Truth*, 23 January 1890: 156.
156. [Labouchere], "Entre Nous," *Truth*, 2 January 1890: 8.
157. [Labouchere], "Entre nous," 23 January 1890: 157.
158. Quoted in Hyde, *The Cleveland Street Scandal*, 145.
159. [Anon.], "The Government and Mr. Labouchere," *Pall Mall Gazette*, 1 March 1890: 7.
160. [Anon.], "Lord Euston's Case," *Reynolds's Newspaper*, 19 January 1890: 4.
161. [Anon.], "Lord Euston's Case," 4.
162. [Anon.], "The Cleveland Street Scandals," *Reynolds's Newspaper*, 25 May 1890: 3. In defending Somerset, Newton served six weeks' imprisonment for perverting the course of justice. On his release, he surprisingly resumed his practice; on this matter, see Martin

Dockray, "The Cleveland Street Scandal 1889–1890," *Journal of Legal History* 17, no. 1 (1996): 1–16. Douglas hired Newton to defend Taylor during the first Crown prosecution against Taylor and Wilde (see 171).

163. Oscar Wilde, "To the Editor of the *Scots Observer*," [23 July 1890], in *The Complete Letters*, 441. This was one of several letters that Wilde sent in defense of his novel (see, for example, *The Complete Letters*, 446–49). The *Scots Observer* continued the discussion about Wilde's novel through 6 September 1890. For a detailed account of the debate, see Stuart Mason [Christopher Sclater Millard], *Oscar Wilde: Art and Morality—A Record of the Discussion which Followed the Publication of "Dorian Gray,"* 2nd ed. (London: Frank Palmer, 1912).

164. Oscar Wilde, "A Preface to 'Dorian Gray,'" *Fortnightly Review* 49 (1891): 480; cf. Wilde, *The Picture of Dorian Gray* in *Complete Works*, 3:167.

165. Wilde, "A Preface to 'Dorian Gray,'" 480; cf. Wilde, *Complete Works*, 3:167.

166. Wilde, "A Preface to 'Dorian Gray,'" 481; cf. Wilde, *Complete Works*, 3:168.

167. Blunt Papers, Fitzwilliam Museum Cambridge, quoted in Elizabeth Longford, *A Pilgrimage of Passion: The Life of Wilfrid Scawen Blunt* (London: Weidenfeld and Nicolson, 1979), 289–90.

168. Quoted in Longford, *A Pilgrimage of Passion*, 289–90.

169. In the British Library copy of *Poetry of the Crabbet Club* (n.p.: privately printed, 1892), the names of the authors of the anonymous contents have been penciled in. Wilde is said to be the author of "Crabbet Club Song" (3–4) and "An Ode of Invitation" (17–18). The copy belonged to the English politician Athelstan Rendall. British Library, Eccles Bequest 408.

170. Journal entry, 25 April 1895, in Harcourt Lewis, *Loulou: Selected Extracts from the Journals of Lewis Harcourt (1880–1895)*, ed. Patrick Jackson (Madison and Teaneck, NJ: Fairleigh Dickinson University Press, 2006), 259.

171. [Anon.], *The Political Libel Actions of Gatty v. Farquharson and Gatty v. the Western Gazette and Pulman's Weekly News Company, Limited: Verbatim Evidence from Official Shorthand Notes* (London: Penny and Hull, 1894), 3.

172. [Anon.], *The Political Libel Actions*, 4.

173. [Anon.], *The Political Libel Actions*, 4.

174. [Anon.], *The Political Libel Actions*, 5.

175. [Anon.], *The Political Libel Actions*, 32.

176. [Anon.], *The Political Libel Actions*, 57.

177. Max Beerbohm, "To Reggie Turner," [postmark 29 September 1893], in *Letters to Reggie Turner*, ed. Rupert Hart-Davis (London: Rupert Hart-Davis, 1964), 71–72. In 1932, the publisher Grant Richards, who had come to prominence in the mid-1890s, recalled that the Crown, which "was the meeting-place of all the young 'daycadongs' in letters and painting in the 'nineties is no more" (*Memories of a Misspent Youth* [London: W. Heinemann, 1932], 337).

178. Frederick Althaus, "To Oscar Wilde," 12 November 1888, Clark Library, MS Wilde, A467L W6721, Box 2, Folder 13.

179. Frederick Althaus, "To Oscar Wilde," 4 June 1889, Clark Library, MS Wilde, A567L W6721, Box 2, Folder 13.

180. Frederick Althaus, "To Oscar Wilde," 29 September 1892, Clark Library, MS Wilde, A567L W6721, Box 2, Folder 13.

181. This information is given in Ellmann, *Oscar Wilde*, 283; McKenna, *The Secret Life of Oscar Wilde*, 89; and Matthew Sturgis, *Oscar: A Life* (London: Head of Zeus, 2018), 370. Wilde continued to make hyperbolic gestures in his correspondence with Le Gallienne; on receiving a copy of the young writer's *George Meredith: Some Characteristics* (1890), he wrote: "I hope so much to see you . . . I hope your laurels are not too thick across your brow for me to kiss your eyelids" (*The Complete Letters*, 457).

182. The poem, which is in manuscript, appears in *The Complete Letters*, 367.

183. Sturgis, *Oscar*, 370–71.

184. Clyde Fitch, "To Oscar Wilde," *c*. 1889, Clark Library, MS Wilde, F544L W6721, Box 26, Folder 41.

185. Oscar Wilde, "To the Editor of the *Daily Telegraph*," 10 February 1892, in *The Complete Letters*, 520.

186. The report, which appeared in the *Star* (6 February 1892: 1), is quoted in Jerusha Hull McCormack, *John Gray: Poet, Dandy, Priest* (Waltham, MA: Brandeis University Press, 1991), 82.

187. *Star*, 15 February 1892: 1, quoted in McCormack, *John Gray*, 83.

188. Max Beerbohm, "Oscar Wilde: By [Max Beerbohm Masquerading as] an American," *Anglo-American Times*, 25 March 1893, reprinted in Beerbohm, *Letters to Reggie Turner*, 290.

189. Holland, *Irish Peacock*, 143.

190. Oscar Wilde, "To Alfred Douglas,' [January–March 1897], in *The Complete Letters*, 730.

191. Alfred Douglas, *Without Apology* (London: Martin Secker, 1938), 41.

192. Alfred Douglas, "To Frank Harris," 20 March 1925, Harry Ransom Center, University of Texas, quoted in H. Montgomery Hyde, *Lord Alfred Douglas: A Biography* (London: Methuen, 1984), 27.

193. Quoted in Hyde, *Lord Alfred Douglas*, 27.

194. Quoted in Hyde, *Lord Alfred Douglas*, 28.

195. Quoted in Hyde, *Lord Alfred Douglas*, 28.

196. Oscar Wilde, *Salomé: Drame en un acte*, in *Plays I*, ed. Joseph Donohue, in Wilde, *Complete Works*, 5:526.

197. Wilde, *Complete Works*, 5:553.

198. Pigott-Smyth's remark, which he confided to Spencer Ponsonby, is quoted in John Russell Stephens, *The Censorship of English Drama, 1824–1901* (Cambridge: Cambridge University Press, 1980), 112.

199. [Anon.], "The Censure and 'Salomé': An Interview with Mr. Oscar Wilde," *Pall Mall Gazette*, 29 June 1892: 2.

200. [Anon.], "The Censure and 'Salomé,'" 2.

201. Douglas, *Autobiography*, 119.

202. [Anon.], "Oscar Wilde: Brought Up at Bow-St This Morning," *Star*, 11 April 1895: 3.

203. See journal entry, 25 April 1895, in Harcourt, *Loulou*, 259.

204. [Anon.], "Blackmailing: By W. E. Allen (A Convicted Blackmailer)," *Reynolds's Newspaper*, 18 December 1898: 8. Allen had recently been released from jail after serving an eighteen-month sentence for extorting £5 from the author and composer Cotsford Dick, in return for some pawnbrokers' tickets. The tickets related to the belongings that had been stripped from Dick's person when he was assaulted on the Thames Embankment in December 1896.

205. Alfred Douglas, "In Sarum Close," in *Collected Poems* (London: Martin Secker, 1919), 21. The poem appears in Alfred Douglas, *Poems/Poèmes* (Paris: Mercure de France, 1896), 24.

206. Douglas, "In Sarum Close," 21.

207. Douglas, "In Sarum Close," 21.

208. Oscar Wilde, "To Alfred Douglas," [? January 1895], in *The Complete Letters*, 544. Holland and Hart-Davis suggest that Wilde's letter was written from Babbacombe sometime in January 1893. Douglas's poem "In Sarum Close" uses the old name of the city of Salisbury, famous for its thirteenth-century cathedral, one of the finest examples of early English Gothic. At the time, Douglas's mother (Lady Sibyl) resided in St. Ann's Gate, Salisbury, which is close to the cathedral. The octave of Douglas's poem contains the following lines: "I thought to cool my burning hands / In this calm twilight of gray Gothic things." The sestet, however, turns to address the object of love (implicitly Wilde) through the metaphor of a bejeweled crown: "thou, my love, my jewel, set / In a fair setting." In the concluding line, Douglas's poetic voice expands the metaphor to the idea that he and his beloved shine brightly together as "Two neighbour jewels in Love's coronet'" (*Collected Poems*, 21).

Wilde's letter contains allusions to both his own and Douglas's works. His reference to "red rose-leaf lips" resembles Lord Henry Wotton's comments on Dorian Gray's "rose-red youth" in *The Picture of Dorian Gray* (Wilde, *Complete Works*, 3:21 and 3:184). In Greek myth, the beautiful youth Hyacinthus was the lover of the god Apollo. Douglas published his homoerotic lyric "Hyacinthus," which Wilde had likely read, in the *Artist and Journal of Home Culture*, 1 April 1893; the poetic voice declares: "thy godlike shape / Is, to a woman's coarser curve, / As the trod live-blood of the grape / Unto dull water" (99). During the libel case, a transcription of Wilde's letter, which had come through blackmailers into the hands of Queensberry's defense, was a frequent point of reference.

The letter, which remained out of Douglas's hands, was later kept on file by Sir George Lewis, who released it on behalf of the prosecution when the dancer Maud Allan took out a suit for obscene and crmininal libel against Noel Pemberton Billing, MP, in 1918. Billing had made the ludicrous claim that Allan's leading role in a private performance of Wilde's *Salomé* appealed to "the cult of the clitoris": an alleged "cult" of homosexual perverts holding high office that German enemy agents had manipulated, with threats of exposure, in order to triumph during World War I. The letter was read aloud in order to discredit Douglas as a witness for Billing's defense, at a time when Douglas persisted in denouncing his personal involvement with Wilde. Douglas was so infuriated that Justice Darling threatened to eject him from the Old Bailey. "It is," Douglas protested, "a rotten sodomitically inclined letter written by a diabolical scoundrel to a wretched silly youth" (Michael Kettle, *Salome's Last Veil: The Libel Case of the Century* [London: Hart-Davis, MacGibbon, 1977], 180).

209. Croft-Cooke, *Bosie*, 73.

210. Oscar Wilde, "To Alfred Douglas," [March 1893], in *The Complete Letters*, 559–60.

211. Holland, *Irish Peacock*, 51.

212. Holland, *Irish Peacock*, 123.

213. Wood used this phrase in his testimony during the second Crown trial against Wilde (see 351); see [Christopher Sclater Millard], *Oscar Wilde: Three Times Tried*, Famous Old Bailey Trials of the XIX Century (London: Ferrestone Press, 1912), 393.

214. Holland, *Irish Peacock*, 52.

215. Holland, *Irish Peacock*, 53.

216. Holland, *Irish Peacock*, 53.

217. Holland, *Irish Peacock*, 55.

218. Wilde, "To Lord Alfred Douglas," [January–March 1897], 758.

219. Wilde rented rooms at Geneux's private hotel, 10 and 11 St. James's Place, from October 1893 until the end of March 1894; he wrote much of *An Ideal Husband* (1895) there; see Wilde, *The Complete Letters*, 573. Geneux's private hotel was an elite establishment; the Rajah of Sarawak stayed there in September 1893. The artist Aubrey Beardsley had rooms there in late 1895 and early 1896. In the proceedings below, Geneux's is referred to only by its street address. Born in Switzerland, the proprietor Edouard Geneux became a naturalized British subject in 1882.

220. McKenna, *The Secret Life of Oscar Wilde*, 240.

221. In his closing speech for the Crown prosecution during the first trial, C. F. Gill remarked: "The charges now made against the defendants formed only a part of the allegations contained in the plea of justification. The reason was that some of the charges alleged were not within the jurisdiction of Bow Street Police Court" (282). Lockwood made a similar observation about the jurisdiction of the court in Wilde's libel case (see 386). Wilde's alleged sexual involvement with Grainger took place at Goring-on-Thames, and that with Conway at Worthing and Brighton.

222. Oscar Wilde, "To Sydney Barraclough," [December 1892], in *The Complete Letters*, 539.

223. There are different accounts of the reasons that Douglas's involvement with a youth led to his move to Egypt. Ian Small observes that commentators have identified the individual as either "Philip Danney" or "Alfred Lambart," as well as Charles Dansey. See Small, "Commentary," in "*De Profundis*"; "*Epistola: In Carcere et Vinculis*," ed. Small, in Wilde, *Complete Works*, 2:212–13. Neil McKenna presents materials that suggest that "[t]he boy is question was probably Claude Dansey" (*The Secret Life of Oscar Wilde*, 264). McKenna adduces evidence indicating that Dansey's outraged father, who eventually learned of Ross's sexual intimacy with his son in October 1893, wanted to retrieve all of the correspondence between the lovers, whose affair had begun six months before. Based on the available accounts, it appears that Lieutenant-Colonel Dansey also wished to pursue a legal case against Ross but desisted once he learned that, even though

Ross might be incarcerated for two years (presumably on charges of gross indecency), Claude himself would likely receive six months' imprisonment as an accomplice. Sturgis, who endorses McKenna's interpretation of the litigious episode, which absorbed much of October that year, states that the "drama . . . played out a further strain on Wilde's relations with Douglas" (*Oscar*, 492). Ross, it seems, had also enjoyed intimacy with Philip Wortham, one of the sons of the Revd. Biscoe Hale Wortham, headmaster of the English College, Bruges, where Dansey was a student. Meanwhile, Ross, for his part in the affair, had been dispatched by his family to Davos, Switzerland, so that the heated controversy could cool down.

The abbreviation MI5 stands for Military Intelligence, Section 5; its origins go back to the Secret Service Bureau, established in 1909.

224. Edmonds, *Oscar Wilde's Scandalous Summer*, 69.

225. Edmonds, *Oscar Wilde's Scandalous Summer*, 85.

226. Quoted in McKenna, *The Secret Life of Oscar Wilde*, 298.

227. Quoted in McKenna, *The Secret Life of Oscar Wilde*, 299.

228. Edmonds, *Oscar Wilde's Scandalous Summer*, 84. Edmonds, who has conducted detailed research on Conway, states that he was born on 10 July 1878 ("An Ideal Boy?," *Wildean* 45 [2014], 98).

229. Edmonds has gone to great lengths to unearth information that might illuminate what happened to Conway after the trials; he claims that "a strong possibility must be that Sarah [Conway's single mother] and Alphonse . . . emigrated to Australia in 1895 or soon after, which would be one reason—a change of name would be another—for their disappearance from the English archival records" (Antony Edmonds, "Family Matters Relating to Alphonse Conway," *Wildean* 43 [2013], 98).

230. Leverson, *Letters to the Sphinx*, 24.

CHAPTER TWO

Epigraph: Oscar Wilde, *Lady Windermere's Fan: A Play about a Good Woman*, ed. Ian Small, 2nd ed. (London: Ernest Benn; New York: W.W. Norton, 1999), 63.

1. Frank Harris, *Oscar Wilde: His Life and Confessions*, 2 vols. (New York: privately printed, 1916), 1:150–51.

2. Harris, *Oscar Wilde*, 1:202.

3. Harris, *Oscar Wilde*, 1:239.

4. Harris, *Oscar Wilde*, 2:575.

5. Page numbers in parentheses refer to the reconstruction of the Crown prosecution against Wilde in part II of the present volume, unless otherwise noted.

6. The full text of this letter appears on 77–78.

7. Alfred Douglas, *The Autobiography of Lord Alfred Douglas*, 2nd ed. (London: Martin Secker, 1931), 138. Douglas's autobiography first appeared in 1929.

8. Douglas, *Autobiography*, 139.

9. Douglas, *Autobiography*, 139.

10. Douglas, *Autobiography*, 139.

11. Nicholas Frankel, *Oscar Wilde: The Unrepentant Years* (Cambridge, MA: Harvard University Press, 2017), 14.

12. Oscar Wilde, "To Lord Alfred Douglas," [January–March 1897], in *The Complete Letters of Oscar Wilde*, ed. Merlin Holland and Rupert Hart-Davis (London: Fourth Estate, 2000), 689.

13. Ian Small, "Introduction," in "*De Profundis*"; "*Epistola: In carcere et vinculis*," ed. Ian Small, in Oscar Wilde, *The Complete Works of Oscar Wilde*, 11 vols. to date (Oxford: Oxford University Press, 2000–), 2:3.

14. Oscar Wilde, "To Robert Ross," 1 April 1897, in *The Complete Letters*, 781.

15. Rupert Croft-Cooke, *Bosie: The Story of Lord Alfred Douglas, His Friends and Enemies* (London: W. H. Allen 1963), 82.

16. Wilde, "To Lord Alfred Douglas," [January–March 1897], 730.

17. Wilde, "To Lord Alfred Douglas," 631.

18. Wilde, "To Lord Alfred Douglas," 774–75.

19. Wilde, "To Lord Alfred Douglas," 755.

20. Wilde, "To Lord Alfred Douglas," 755.

21. It has not been possible to discover information about the circumstances that inspired the visit to the studio of Campbell Gray (A. J. Campbell and C. E. Gray). These two photographic portraits of Wilde and Douglas were presumably taken for personal use. Many of this company's images were used for cabinet cards promoting theatrical and music-hall performances.

22. Alfred Douglas, "Oscar Wilde," in *Oscar Wilde: A Plea and a Reminiscence*," ed. Caspar Wintermans (Woubrugge: Avalon Press, 2002), 33.

23. Douglas, "Oscar Wilde," 33. The phrase "the beginning of wisdom" is arguably more biblical than Platonic ("The fear of the Lord is the beginning of wisdom" [Proverbs 9:10]), although there are passages in *Phaedrus* where Socrates speaks of the "φιλόσοφον" (philosopher) as, literally, a "lover of wisdom" (Plato, *Euthyphro, Apology, Crito, Phaedo, Phaedrus*, trans. Harold North Fowler [1914; repr., Cambridge, MA: Harvard University Press, 1990], 574, 575).

24. Douglas published an enthusiastic review of the French-language edition of *Salomé* in his journal the *Spirit Lamp*, in which he attacks the English moralizers who speak out against the play's morbid treatment of sexuality in biblical times: "It is probably morbid and unhealthy, for there is no representation of quiet domestic life, nobody slaps anybody else on the back all through the play, and there is not a single reference to roast beef from one end of the dialogue to the other" (Alfred Douglas, "*Salomé*: A Critical Review," *Spirit Lamp*, 4, no. 1 [1893]: 27).

25. Douglas, "*Salomé*: A Critical Review," 27.

26. See H. Montgomery Hyde, *Lord Alfred Douglas: A Biography* (London: Methuen, 1984), 43. Hyde comments that this was "an enormous sum for those days, when food and drink and servants were relatively cheap" (43). The rental was £200.

27. Harris, *Oscar Wilde: His Life and Confessions*, 1:178.

28. Wilde, "To Lord Alfred Douglas," [January–March 1897], in *The Complete Letters*, 692.

29. Wilde, "To Lord Alfred Douglas," [January–March 1897], 692. There were some blunders in the translation.

30. Oscar Wilde, "To Charles Kains-Jackson," 6 November 1893, in *The Complete Letters*, 574.

31. Alfred Douglas, "To John Lane," 30 September 1893, quoted in Wilde, *The Complete Letters*, 574.

32. Aubrey Beardsley, "To Robert Ross," [late] November [1893], in *The Letters of Aubrey Beardsley*, ed. Henry Maas, J. L. Duncan, and W. G. Good (London: Cassell, 1970), 58. For an illuminating discussion of the controversies around Beardsley's drawings for *Salomé*, see Stephen Calloway, *Aubrey Beardsley* (London: V&A Publications, 1998), 70–83.

33. Oscar Wilde, "To Mrs. Patrick Campbell," [March 1894], in *The Complete Letters*, 587.

34. Robert Ross, "To Roger Fry," undated, in Roger Fry, *The Letters of Roger Fry*, ed. Denys Sutton, 2 vols. (London: Chatto and Windus, 1972), 1:21.

35. Jean Paul Raymond and Charles Ricketts, *Oscar Wilde: Recollections* (London: Nonesuch Press, 1932), 52. This study largely constitutes a series of fictional letters that Ricketts pretends to have written to an imaginary friend, Raymond.

36. Oscar Wilde, "To Lady Queensberry," [8 November 1893], in *The Complete Letters*, 575.

37. Alfred Douglas, "To George Cecil Ives," 11 November 1894, Clark Library, MS Douglas, D733L I95, Box 20, Folder 2. Comparatively little is known about the Order of Chaeronea, its membership, and its longevity. It was a secret society that developed a series of rituals, passwords, and seals. Ives, it seems, was not able to persuade Douglas and Wilde to join the society (see Neil McKenna, *The Secret Life of Oscar Wilde* [London: Century, 2003], 269–70). Ives's papers, which contain materials relating to the society, are held at the Harry Ransom Center, University of Texas.

38. Douglas, "To George Cecil Ives," 11 November 1894.

39. [Anon.], "The Assizes," *The Times*, 17 July 1891: 10. On Fyffe's career, court case, and death, see Robert Darwall-Smith, "Charles Alan Fyffe: A Victorian Tragedy," *University College Record* 23, no. 1 (2001): 72–84.

40. Alfred Douglas, "To Charles Kains-Jackson," 29 November 1893, Clark Library, MS Douglas, D733L K135, Box 20, Folder 3. It is not clear which case Douglas has in mind.

41. Douglas, "To Charles Kains-Jackson," 29 November 1894. It has not been possible to trace this case. The actor Roy Horniman, who was in his mid-twenties at the time, later became known for his anti-Semitic novel *Israel Rank: The Autobiography of a Criminal* (1907).

42. Douglas, "To Charles Kains-Jackson," 29 November 1894.

43. Oscar Wilde, "To Alfred Douglas," [*c*. 20 December 1893], in *The Complete Letters*, 577.

44. Evelyn Baring, 1st Earl of Cromer, "To Venetia Pollington," 6 January 1894, quoted in Roger Owen, *Lord Cromer: Victorian Imperialist, Edwardian Proconsul* (Oxford: Oxford University Press, 2004), 253.

45. Wilde, "To Lord Alfred Douglas," [January–March 1897], in *The Complete Letters*, 695.

46. Hyde, *Lord Alfred Douglas*, 52.
47. Wilde, "To Lord Alfred Douglas," [January–March 1897], 696.
48. Wilde, "To Lord Alfred Douglas," [January–March 1897], 696
49. Wilde, "To Lord Alfred Douglas," [January–March 1897], 696
50. Douglas, *Autobiography*, 21.
51. John Sholto Douglas, 9th Marquess of Queensberry, "To Alfred Douglas," 1 April 1894, quoted in Merlin Holland, *Irish Peacock and Scarlet Marquess: The Real Trial of Oscar Wilde* (London: Fourth Estate, 2003), 214.
52. Queensberry, "To Alfred Douglas," 1 April 1894, 214.
53. Lord Alfred Douglas, "To the Marquess of Queensberry," [*c*. 2 April 1894], quoted in Holland, *Irish Peacock*, 215.
54. John Sholto Douglas, 9th Marquess of Queensberry, "To Alfred Montgomery," 6 July 1894, in Holland, *Irish Peacock*, 216.
55. The Tenth Marquess of Queensberry [Francis Archibald Kelhead Douglas], *The Sporting Queensberrys* (London: Hutchinson, 1942), 123.
56. Queensberry, "To Alfred Montgomery," 6 July 1894, in Holland, *Irish Peacock*, 216.
57. Holland, *Irish Peacock*, 57.
58. Wilde, "To Lord Alfred Douglas," [January–March 1897], 699.
59. Holland, *Irish Peacock*, 58.
60. Holland, *Irish Peacock*, 58.
61. Quoted in Richard Ellmann, *Oscar Wilde*, 420.
62. Quoted in Ellmann, *Oscar Wilde*, 420.
63. Wilde, "To Lord Alfred Douglas," [January–March 1897], 708.
64. See Linda Stratmann, *The Marquess of Queensberry: Wilde's Nemesis* (New Haven, CT: Yale University Press, 2013), 187.
65. The Albemarle Club (founded in 1874) was open to men and women; Wilde's spouse, Constance, was also a member. The club, which critics saw as radical for not only mixing male and female members but also mixing them in equal numbers, was located at 13 Albemarle Street, off Piccadilly, in Central London. Karl Baedeker notes that in 1896 it had 750 members (*London and Its Environs: Handbook for Travellers*, 10th ed. [Leipsic: Karl Baedeker, 1896], 100). At the time, Queensberry had been staying at the nearby Carter's Hotel, 14 and 15 Albemarle Street.
66. Quoted in Stratmann, *The Marquess of Queensberry*, 169.
67. Stratmann, *The Marquess of Queensberry*, 195.
68. Douglas, "In Memoriam: Francis Archibald Douglas, Viscount Drumlanrig, Killed by the Accidental Explosion of His Gun, October XVIII, MDCCCXCIV," in Alfred Douglas, *Poems/Poèmes* (Paris: Mercure de France, 1896), 116.
69. Stratmann, *The Marquess of Queensberry*, 198.
70. Edmund Trelawny Backhouse, "The Dead Past," Oxford, Bodleian Library, MSS Eng. Misc. d. 1223–26, fo. 165, in Edmund Trelawny Backhouse, *The Dead Past*, ed. Peter Jordaan (n.p.: Alchemie Books, 2017), 203. The typescript, which dates from 1943, contains a "Preface" in which Backhouse declares: "my papers . . . are faithful records of my friendships with these eminent persons [i.e., Paul Verlaine, Stéphane Mallarmé, Aubrey Beardsley, and Walter Pater], not one syllable being added nor invented" (fo. i). The manuscript

and typescript of Backhouse's Chinese memoirs have been published as *Décadence Mandchoue: The China Memoirs of Sir Edmund Trelawny Backhouse*, ed. Derek Sandhaus (Hong Kong: Earnshaw Books, 2011).

71. Backhouse, "The Dead Past," fo. 166, in *The Dead Past*, 204.

72. Backhouse, "The Dead Past," fos. 165–66, in *The Dead Past*, 203–4.

73. Backhouse, "The Dead Past," fo. 174, in *The Dead Past*, 212–13.

74. Backhouse, "The Dead Past," fo. 174, in *The Dead Past*, 213. Backhouse claims that the detectives gleaned evidence from "two maid servants at the inn" who divulged "concrete proofs" about the "condition of the drapery of the bed linen on which the two lovers had passed their night" (213).

75. Backhouse, "The Dead Past," fo. 174, in *The Dead Past*, 213.

76. Hugh Trevor-Roper, *A Hidden Life: The Enigma of Sir Edmund Backhouse* (London: Macmillan, 1976), 242. Trevor-Roper expresses antipathy to Backhouse's sexual tastes: "Both volumes [of memoirs] are grossly, grotesquely, obsessively obscene. Backhouse presents himself as a compulsive pathic homosexual who found in China opportunities for indulgence which, in England, owing to repressive laws and Victorian hypocrisy, could only be dangerously and furtively enjoyed" (243). In his introduction to *Décadence Mandchoue*, Sandhaus rebuts several of Trevor-Roper's claims that Backhouse's records of his sexual activities are far-fetched (see, in particular, xv–xx).

77. McKenna, *The Secret Life of Oscar Wilde*, 316.

78. T. M. Healy, *Letters and Leaders of My Day*, 2 vols. (London: T. Butterworth, 1928), 2:416. In the original text, Rosebery's name is omitted and a long dash appears in its place. Ellmann inserts Rosebery's name in *Oscar Wilde* (465). Healy adds: "I asked Lockwood not to prosecute [Lady Wilde's] son again because I wished the mother should be spared further agony" (2:417).

79. Lord Durham's letter is reproduced in Matthew Sturgis, *Oscar: A Life* (London: Head of Zeus, 2018), 556. On Regy Brett's intimate connections with his queer male friends, see Morris B. Kaplan, *Sodom on the Thames: Sex, Love, and Scandal in Wilde Times* (Ithaca, NY: Cornell University Press, 2005), 113–65.

80. Leo McKinstry, *Rosebery: Statesman in Turmoil* (London: John Murray, 2005), 365.

81. Journal entry, 1 October 1894, in Lewis Harcourt, *Loulou: Selected Extracts from the Journals of Lewis Harcourt (1880–1895)*, ed. Patrick Jackson (Madison, NJ: Fairleigh Dickinson University Press, 2006), 238. Cf. McKinstry, *Rosebery*, 363.

82. McKinstry, *Rosebery*, 363.

83. Wilde, "To Lord Alfred Douglas," [January–March 1897], 697.

84. Oscar Wilde, "To George Alexander," [*c*. 25 October 1894], in *The Complete Letters*, 620.

85. Wilde, "To Lord Alfred Douglas," [January–March 1897], 697.

86. Wilde, "To Lord Alfred Douglas," [January–March 1897], 698.

87. Wilde, "To Lord Alfred Douglas," [January–March 1897], 698.

88. [Anon.], "An Essay in Burlesque," *Globe*, 28 September 1894: 3.

89. On the information about the ways in which Wilde's homosexual coterie sported green carnations, see 102.

90. [Robert Hichens], *The Green Carnation* (London: William Heinemann, 1894), 3.

91. [Hichens], *The Green Carnation*, 4. A hansom-cab was a fast and light horse-drawn carriage, patented in 1834, which maneuvered well in London's traffic.

92. [Hichens], *The Green Carnation*, 4.

93. [Hichens], *The Green Carnation*, 22–23.

94. [Hichens], *The Green Carnation*, 25.

95. [Anon.], "Satire à la mode," *Pall Mall Gazette*, 27 September 1894: 4. The reviewer concludes with this observation: "A man may certainly burlesque himself if he like; in fact, it would be a clever thing to do. Has Mr. Wilde done it?"

96. Oscar Wilde, "To the Editor of the *Pall Mall Gazette*," 1 October 1894, in *The Complete Letters*, 617. The reviewer responded by stating that the suggestion that Wilde wrote the novel was "made . . . to amuse him" (*Pall Mall Gazette*, 3 October 1894: 11).

97. [Anon.], "Mr. Hichens," *Nottingham Evening Post*, 9 November 1894: 2. E. F. Benson enjoyed considerable success with *Dodo* (1893), a fictional satire on fashionable society, which features "an outrageously unconventional heroine"; [anon.], "New Novels," *Graphic*, 15 July 1893: 11. The protagonist was said to have been based on Margot Tennant, who later married the politician H. H. Asquith.

98. [Anon.], "The Decadent Guys (A Colour-Study in Green Carnations)," *Punch*, 10 November 1894: 225. In 1891, Wilde added the subtitle "A Study in Green" to his essay "Pen, Pencil and Poison," which had first appeared in 1889.

99. [Anon.], "The Decadent Guys," 225.

100. [Anon.], "The Decadent Guys," 225.

101. [Anon.], "Notes," *National Observer*, 6 April 1895: 547.

102. Franny Moyle, *Constance: The Tragic and Scandalous Life of Mrs. Oscar Wilde* (London: John Murray, 2011), 251.

103. [Anon.], "Mrs. Oscar Wilde at Home," *To-Day*, 24 November 1894: 94.

104. [Jerome K. Jerome], Editorial, *To-Day*, 29 December 1894: 241.

105. Jerome, Editorial, 241.

106. Oscar Wilde, "Phrases and Philosophies for the Use of the Young," in *The Collected Works of Oscar Wilde*, ed. Robert Ross, 14 vols. (London: Methuen, 1908), 8:178. The text is italicized in Oscar Wilde, "Phrases and Philosophies for the Use of the Young," *Chameleon* 1, no. 1 (1894): 3.

107. Wilde, "Phrases and Philosophies," in *The Collected Works*, 8:178.

108. Oscar Wilde, "A Few Maxims for the Instruction of the Over-Educated," *Saturday Review*, 17 November 1894: 533. This list of aphorisms is omitted from the 1908 edition of *The Collected Works*.

109. Alfred Douglas, "In Praise of Shame," *Chameleon* 1, no. 1 (1894): 25.

110. Alfred Douglas, "Two Loves," *Chameleon* 1, no. 1 (1894): 27.

111. Douglas, "Two Loves," 27.

112. Douglas, "Two Loves," 27.

113. Douglas, "Two Loves," 27–28.

114. Douglas, "Two Loves," 27-28.

115. Douglas, "Two Loves," 28.

116. Douglas, "Two Loves," 28.

117. Douglas, "Two Loves," 28.

118. John Sholto Douglas, "To Minnie Douglas," 11 March 1895, in Francis Archibald Kelhead Douglas and Percy Colson, *Oscar Wilde and the Black Douglas* (London: Hutchinson, 1949), 59.

119. [John Francis Bloxam], "The Priest and the Acolyte," *Chameleon* 1, no. 1 (1894): 47.

120. [Anon.], "The Week," *Athenæum*, 12 January 1895: 57.

121. Oscar Wilde, *Two Society Comedies: "A Woman of No Importance" and "An Ideal Husband,"* ed. Ian Small and Russell Jackson (New York: W. W. Norton, 1983), 160.

122. Wilde, *Two Society Comedies*, 157.

123. Wilde, *Two Society Comedies*, 161.

124. [Anon.], "London Theatres," *Stage*, 10 January 1895: 15.

125. Wilde, *Two Society Comedies*, 213.

126. William Archer, review of Wilde, *An Ideal Husband*, reprinted in William Archer, *The Theatrical "World" of 1895* (London: Walter Scott, 1896), 19.

127. Quoted in Moyle, *Constance*, 8.

128. Gilbert Burgess, "'An Ideal Husband' at the Haymarket Theatre: A Talk with Mr. Oscar Wilde," *Sketch*, 9 January 1895: 495.

129. Burgess, "'An Ideal Husband' at the Haymarket Theatre," 495.

130. [Anon.], "Mr. Wilde on Mr. Oscar Wilde: An Interview," *St. James's Gazette*, 18 January 1895: 4.

131. [Anon.], "Mr. Wilde on Mr. Oscar Wilde," 5.

132. [Anon.], "Mr. Wilde on Mr. Oscar Wilde," 5.

133. Oscar Wilde, "To Robert Ross," [*c*. 25 January 1895], in *The Complete Letters*, 629.

134. Wilde, "To Robert Ross," [*c*. 25 January 1895], 629.

135. André Gide, *Si le grain ne meurt* (Paris: Gallimard, 1955), 290. Gide's title (*If the Grain Does Not Die*) derives from John 12:24; it has been translated into English, on the basis of the King James Version, as *If It Die*.

136. Gide, *Si le grain ne meurt*, 293.

137. Gide, *Si le grain ne meurt*, 295.

138. [Anon.], "'Guy Domville' at the St. James," *Sketch*, 9 January 1895: 2.

139. According to Baedeker, the Hotel Avondale was "new and well furnished" (*London and Its Environs*, 10th ed., 8). In its advertising, the Avondale made a point of stating that it was "a fashionable hotel . . . furnished in a truly sumptuous manner," with "[c]uisine under the management of celebrated French chefs": "Luncheons 3/6, from 12.30 to 3, Dinners Table d'hôte, 7/6, or à la carte, at separate tables"; advertisement for the Hotel Avondale, *Truth* 37 (1895): 930. Kennion later became a successful art dealer in London.

140. Oscar Wilde, "To Arthur L. Humphreys," [*c*. 12 February 1895], in *The Complete Letters*, 630.

141. Oscar Wilde, "To R. V. Shone," [13 February 1895], in *The Complete Letters*, 632.

142. Wilde, "To R. V. Shone," [13 February 1895], 632.

143. Robert Harborough Sherard, *Oscar Wilde: Twice Defended from André Gide's Wicked Lies and Frank Harris's Cruel Libels* (Chicago: Argus Book Shop, 1934), 13.

144. C. O. Humphreys, Son, and Kershaw, "To Oscar Wilde," 28 February 1895, in Wilde, *The Complete Letters*, 635.

145. A. E. W. Mason, *Sir George Alexander and the St. James's Theatre* (London: Macmillan, 1935), 79.

146. Wilde, *The Importance of Being Earnest: A Trivial Comedy for Serious People, in Three Acts*, ed. Joseph Donohue, in Wilde, *Complete Works*, 10:768.

147. Wilde, *Complete Works*, 10:768.

148. Wilde, *Complete Works*, 10:769.

149. Wilde, *Complete Works*, 10:770.

150. Wilde, *Complete Works*, 10:851.

151. "A. B. W." [A. B. Walkley], "The Drama: *The Importance of Being Earnest*," *Speaker*, 23 February 1895: 213.

152. [Anon.], "The Importance of Being Oscar," *Sketch*, 20 February 1895: 213.

153. Quoted in Stratmann, *The Marquess of Queensberry*, 211.

154. The card is reproduced in fig. 1 (13); the debate about the wording is discussed above (465–66).

155. Stratmann, *The Marquess of Queensberry*, 211.

156. Stratmann, *The Marquess of Queensberry*, 211.

157. Wilde, "To Lord Alfred Douglas," [January–March 1897], 703.

158. Oscar Wilde, "To Robert Ross," [28 February 1895], in *The Complete Letters*, 634. The reference to the tower of ivory comes from Song of Solomon 7:4.

159. Sir Edward Clarke, "To Robert Ross," 24 March 1897, in Robert Ross, *Robert Ross, Friend of Friends: Letters to Robert Ross, Art Critic and Writer, Together with Extracts from His Published Articles*, ed. Margery Ross (London: Jonathan Cape, 1952), 46.

160. Pearson, *The Life of Oscar Wilde*, 285.

161. Pearson, *The Life of Oscar Wilde*, 285.

162. Ellmann, *Oscar Wilde*, 440.

163. Ellmann, *Oscar Wilde*, 440.

164. Ellmann, *Oscar Wilde*, 439.

165. Edward Hamilton, *The Destruction of Lord Rosebery: From the Diary of Sir Edward Hamilton, 1894–1895*, ed. David Brooks (London: The Historians' Press, 1986), 236.

166. Holland, *Irish Peacock*, 3.

167. Holland, *Irish Peacock*, 5.

168. Holland, *Irish Peacock*, 5.

169. John Juxon, *Lewis and Lewis* (London: Collins, 1983), 274.

170. Quoted in Edward Marjoribanks [with Ian Colvin], *The Life of Lord Carson*, 3 vols. (London: Victor Gollancz, 1932–36), 1:157. Marjoribanks took his own life before the first volume appeared in 1932; the remaining two volumes were completed by Ian Colvin.

171. Marjoribanks, *The Life of Lord Carson*. 1:175.

172. Marjoribanks, *The Life of Lord Carson*, 1:171.

173. Marjoribanks, *The Life of Lord Carson*, 1:172.

174. H. Montgomery Hyde, *Carson: The Life of Edward Carson, Lord Carson of Duncairn* (London: Heinemann, 1953), 129.

175. John George Littlechild, *The Reminiscences of Chief-Inspector Littlechild*, 2nd ed. (London: Leadenhall Press, 1894), 12.

176. Marjoribanks, *The Life of Lord Carson*, 1:201.

177. [Anon.], "Charge of Libelling Oscar Wilde," *Lloyd's Weekly Newspaper*, 17 March 1895: 5.

178. [Anon.], "Queensberry Case," *Reynolds's Newspaper*, 10 March 1895: 1.

179. Holland, *Irish Peacock*, 18.

180. Holland, *Irish Peacock*, 18–19.

181. Holland, *Irish Peacock*, 19.

182. [Anon.], "The Wilde Libel Case," *Pall Mall Gazette*, 9 March 1895: 7.

183. [Anon.], "The Queensberry–Wilde Case," *Globe*, 28 March 1895: 5.

184. [Anon.], "The Queensberry–Wilde Case," *Globe*, 5.

185. Holland, *Irish Peacock*, 290.

186. Holland, *Irish Peacock*, 290.

187. Alfred Douglas, "Oscar Wilde," in *Oscar Wilde: A Plea and A Reminiscence*, 25.

188. Douglas, "Oscar Wilde," 25.

189. I. Playfair [J. H. Wilson], *Gentle Criticisms on British Justice* (Newcastle upon Tyne: privately printed, 1895), 5, 6. I discuss other aspects of this important pamphlet above (19).

190. On the sums that these witnesses were paid, see 179 and 504.

191. Travers Humphreys, *A Book of Trials* (London: William Heinemann, 1953), 38.

192. Humphreys, *A Book of Trials*, 38.

193. Caspar Wintermans, *Alfred Douglas: A Poet's Life and His Finest Work* (London: Peter Owen, 2007), 52.

194. Sturgis, *Oscar*, 547.

195. Harris, *Oscar Wilde: His Life and Confessions*, 1:197.

196. Harris, *Oscar Wilde: His Life and Confessions*: 1:199.

197. George Bernard Shaw, "Preface" to *The Dark Lady of the Sonnets* (1910), reprinted in *Selected Short Plays: Definitive Text*, ed. Dan H. Laurence (London: Penguin, 1987), 103.

198. Harris, *Oscar Wilde: His Life and Confessions*, 1:200.

199. Robert Harborough Sherard, *The Life of Oscar Wilde* (London: T. Werner Laurie, 1906), 353. A brougham was a light, four-wheeled horse-drawn carriage, built from the late 1830s onward, which could seat up to four people and had good maneuverability in traffic.

200. Sherard, *The Life of Oscar Wilde*, 353.

201. [Anon.], "Oscar Wilde Libel Case," *Pall Mall Gazette*, 3 April 1895: 7.

202. [Anon.], "Oscar Wilde Libel," *News of the World*, 7 April 1895: 7.

203. [Anon.], "Oscar Wilde: Defends Himself at the Old Bailey," *Star*, 3 April 1895: 3.

204. [Anon.], "Oscar Wilde Libel Case," 7. By comparison, in Paris the *Galignani Messenger* noted as follows the words that Queensberry had written on the card: "'To Oscar Wilde, posing as — —' (an expression which we are unable to print)"; [anon.], "The Society Scandal," 4 April 1895: 1.

205. [Anon.], "Miscellaneous Notes," *United Ireland*, 13 April 1895: 1.

206. Holland, *Irish Peacock*, 42.

207. Holland, *Irish Peacock*, 62. Carson asked no fewer than seven times if Wilde found the story "blasphemous" (70–71). Wilde refused to be drawn: "The word blasphemous is not my word" (71). The belief that Wilde was the author of the story appears to owe much to Queensberry. On 11 March 1895, the marquess told Minnie Douglas: "The story by Wilde is of a priest and a boy and of their unnatural and hideous love as they call it" (Douglas and Colson, *Oscar Wilde and the Black Douglas*, 59).

208. Holland, *Irish Peacock*, 64.

209. Holland, *Irish Peacock*, 69.

210. Holland, *Irish Peacock*, 75.

211. Marco Wan, "A Matter of Style: On Reading the Oscar Wilde Trials as Literature," *Oxford Journal of Legal Studies* 31, no. 4 (2011): 724–25.

212. Holland, *Irish Peacock*, 103.

213. Wilde, *The Picture of Dorian Gray: The 1890 and 1891 Texts*, ed. Joseph Bristow, in Wilde, *Complete Works*, 3:90.

214. Holland, *Irish Peacock*, 90.

215. Wilde, "To Alfred Douglas," [? January 1895], in *The Complete Letters*, 544, quoted in Holland, *Irish Peacock*, 106. The complete letter is quoted above at 77–78.

216. Holland, *Irish Peacock*, 107.

217. Holland, *Irish Peacock*, 108.

218. On the first morning of the libel trial, Clarke pointed out that Wilde's letter to Douglas was part of a literary exchange: "a sort of prose sonnet, an answer written to a piece of poetry written to Lord Alfred Douglas, a piece of poetry which is transcribed in the sonnet in this *Spirit Lamp* which I now hold in my hand" (Holland, *Irish Peacock*, 34). On 4 May 1893, the *Spirit Lamp*—an Oxford literary journal that Douglas edited—had published "Sonnet" by Pierre Louÿs, which translates a line from Wilde's letter into French poetry ("HYACINTHE! ô mon cœur! jeune dieu doux et blond!" [HYACINTH! oh my sweetheart! young, gentle, and fair-haired god!]). The poem carries a note: "*A letter written in prose poetry by Mr. Oscar Wilde to a friend, and translated into rhymed poetry by a poet of no importance*" (Pierre Louÿs, "Sonnet," *Spirit Lamp*, 4, no.1 [4 May 1893]: 1). The note, which alludes to Wilde's recent drama *A Woman of No Importance*, presumably aimed to assure readers that the twenty-two-year-old Louÿs, who was not yet a known quantity outside France, had no intimate involvement with Wilde.

219. Holland, *Irish Peacock*, 110.

220. Holland, *Irish Peacock*, 111.

221. Holland, *Irish Peacock*, 118.

222. Holland, *Irish Peacock*, 114.

223. Holland, *Irish Peacock*, 115.

224. Holland, *Irish Peacock*, 115, 116.

225. Holland, *Irish Peacock*, 129.

226. Holland, *Irish Peacock*, 133.

227. Holland, *Irish Peacock*, 134.

228. Holland, *Irish Peacock*, 138.

229. [Anon.], "Criminal Libel Action against Queensberry," *Morning*, 4 April 1895: 1. Christopher Sclater Millard notes that Carson produced the photograph, cigarette case,

novel, and "a silver-mounted crook-handled grape-vine stick"; *Oscar Wilde: Three Times Tried*, Famous Old Bailey Trials of the XIX Century (London: Ferrestone Press, 1912), 61. Neither Millard nor Holland mentions the "suit of blue serge" that Wilde stated he bought for Conway (together with the "straw hat"); both of these items also made an appearance. See Millard, *Oscar Wilde: Three Times Tried*, 61; and Holland, *Irish Peacock*, 149.

230. Holland, *Irish Peacock*, 151.

231. [Anon.], "Silk and Stuff," *Pall Mall Gazette*, 4 April 1895: 1.

232. [Anon.], "Oscar To-Day: A Startling Cross-Examination by Mr. Carson," *Evening News*, 4 April 1895: 3.

233. [Anon.], "Wilde v. Queensberry: The Great Libel Suit," *Daily Chronicle*, 4 April 1895: 6.

234. Holland, *Irish Peacock*, 155, 156, 163.

235. Holland, *Irish Peacock*, 163.

236. Holland, *Irish Peacock*, 164.

237. Holland, *Irish Peacock*, 169.

238. Holland, *Irish Peacock*, 210.

239. Holland, *Irish Peacock*, 207.

240. Holland, *Irish Peacock*, 208. Sturgis notes that at Goring-on-Thames "Wilde was sleeping regularly with Grainger" (*Oscar*, 487). Still, Wilde's slip at this point, which voices his repugnance, raises questions about the alleged intimacy between him and Grainger.

241. Holland, *Irish Peacock*, 196.

242. Holland, *Irish Peacock*, 185.

243. Holland, *Irish Peacock*, 189.

244. Gold prospecting in Australia promised lucrative financial rewards at the time. Percy Sholto Douglas sought to make his fortune in overseas trade. His first venture involved a journey to Ceylon in 1892, where he sought to establish himself as a tea grower. From there, he traveled to Kalgoorie, Western Australia, where he worked as a gold prospector and reputedly made about £20,000, though he dissipated his earnings through speculation. In 1892, Ernest Scarfe was probably twenty-three or twenty-four years old when he boarded the *RMS Ophir* for Melbourne, where he sought his fortune in the gold fields. It appears that Percy Douglas befriended Scarfe when the young man was returning to London from Australia in early 1893. On his return, Scarfe made contact with Alfred Taylor, Alfred Douglas, and Oscar Wilde (see, for example, 80–81, 133, 276, and 374 above).

245. Holland, *Irish Peacock*, 199.

246. Holland, *Irish Peacock*, 200.

247. Holland, *Irish Peacock*, 203. The use of the article "an" before "hotel" was common in British English until the mid-twentieth century.

248. Holland, *Irish Peacock*, 204.

249. Holland, *Irish Peacock*, 205.

250. Holland, *Irish Peacock*, 212.

251. Holland, *Irish Peacock*, 212.

252. Holland, *Irish Peacock*, 218.

253. Holland, *Irish Peacock*, 78.

254. Holland, *Irish Peacock*, 224.

255. Holland, *Irish Peacock*, 227. The *Daily Chronicle* was one of several newspapers that carried a report about the arrests; [anon.], "Police Raid on the West-End," *Daily Chronicle*, 14 August 1894: 8. John Watson Preston, the tenant who rented the apartment where the party was held, had issued tickets at 2s. 6d. to cover alcoholic beverages.

256. Holland, *Irish Peacock*, 226.

257. I discuss these arrests in "Homosexual Blackmail in the 1890s: The Fitzroy Street Raid, the Oscar Wilde Trials, and the Case of Cotsford Dick," *Australasian Journal of Victorian Studies* 22, no.1 (2017), https://openjournals.library.sydney.edu.au/index.php/AJVS (accessed 23 May 2021). The street was sometimes referred to as Fitzroy Square in the proceedings. See, for example, 169 and 179.

258. Holland, *Irish Peacock*, 181.

259. Holland, *Irish Peacock*, 227.

260. Edward Shelley, "To Oscar Wilde," 27 March 1893, quoted in Holland, *Irish Peacock*, 233.

261. Edward Shelley, "To Oscar Wilde," 14 June 1894, quoted in Holland, *Irish Peacock*, 235.

262. Edward Shelley, "To Oscar Wilde," 28 August 1894, quoted in Holland, *Irish Peacock*, 236.

263. Holland, *Irish Peacock*, 238.

264. Holland, *Irish Peacock*, 240.

265. Holland, *Irish Peacock*, 241.

266. Humphreys, Son, and Kershaw, "To the Marquess of Queensberry," 11 July 1894, quoted in Holland, *Irish Peacock*, 246.

267. Marquess of Queensberry, "To Humphreys, Son, and Kershaw," 18 July 1894, quoted in Holland, *Irish Peacock*, 247.

268. Holland, *Irish Peacock*, 247.

269. In a letter to Charles Kains-Jackson dating from November 1894, Bloxam mentions visiting George Ives at Ives's flat in The Albany, Piccadilly. "There," Bloxam states, "I had the good fortune to meet Oscar. We discussed the paper [i.e., the *Chameleon*] fully, and the name" (19 November 1894, Clark Library, Wilde B657L K13, Box 6, Folder 5). Bloxam, who signs himself "Jack" in this correspondence, mentions that during his discussion with Ives and Wilde, he discarded the earlier title for the magazine, which was the *Parrot Tulip*. In court, Wilde stated that he encountered the editor at a friend's home in The Albany (see Holland, *Irish Peacock*, 247–48). Bloxam's looks certainly captivated Wilde, who described the unnamed young man as "an undergraduate of strange beauty" to his friend Ada Leverson; Oscar Wilde, "To Ada Leverson," [? early December 1894], in *The Complete Letters*, 625. Wilde also informed Leverson that he found "The Priest and the Acolyte" "too direct: there is no nuance: it profanes a little by revelation": a view that confirms his response to Carson (625).

270. Holland, *Irish Peacock*, 248.

271. Holland, *Irish Peacock*, 248.

272. Holland, *Irish Peacock*, 251.

273. Holland, *Irish Peacock*, 253.
274. Holland, *Irish Peacock*, 255.
275. Wilde, *Complete Works*, 3:21; Holland, *Irish Peacock*, 259.
276. Holland, *Irish Peacock*, 261.
277. Holland, *Irish Peacock*, 271.
278. Oscar Wilde, "To Constance Wilde," [? 5 April 1895], in *The Complete Letters*, 637.
279. Holland, *Irish Peacock*, 278.
280. Holland, *Irish Peacock*, 278.
281. Holland, *Irish Peacock*, 278.
282. Holland, *Irish Peacock*, 279.
283. Douglas, "Oscar Wilde," 25.
284. Holland, *Irish Peacock*, 281.
285. Holland, *Irish Peacock*, 282.
286. Holland, *Irish Peacock*, 283.
287. Holland, *Irish Peacock*, 283.
288. [Anon.], "Queensberry–Wilde Libel Trial," *St. James's Gazette*, 5 April 1895: 8.
289. Richard Henn Collins, "To Edward Carson," 5 April 1895, British Library, Add. MS 81732; copy in RP3046[i]. The letter appears in Marjoribanks, *The Life of Lord Carson*, 1:229.
290. [Anon.], "Miscellaneous Notes," 1. Here, *United Ireland* also notes that soon after Carson had "turned the tables on great genius Oscar," he was congratulated on his triumph by leading Irish nationalists Tim Healy and J. G. Swift MacNeill; the report wryly observes that this gathering suggests Carson is perhaps "a friend of Ireland in disguise."
291. [Anon.], "Miscellaneous Notes," 1.
292. [Anon.], "Miscellaneous Notes," 1.
293. Edward Clarke, "Oscar Wilde," undated, British Library, Add. MS 81758.
294. Harris, *Oscar Wilde: His Life and Confessions*, 1:238.
295. Queensberry's letter was widely reported; see, for example, [anon.], "Queensberry–Wilde Case," *Daily Telegraph*, 6 April 1895: 3, and [anon.], "Wilde v. Queensberry," *Daily Chronicle*, 6 April 1895: 8.
296. [Anon.], "Queensberry Corrects," *Sun*, 6 April 1895: 3. As Colligan points out, Queensberry's lawyers probably advised him to make this retraction, since death threats were punishable under the Offences against the Person Act 1861; Colette Colligan, "Oscar Wilde's Sex Trials in Paris's Expatriate Press," *Textus* 28, no. 1 (2015): 71. Section 16 of the 1861 act stated: "Whosoever shall maliciously send, deliver, or utter, or directly or indirectly cause, knowing the contents thereof, any letter or writing threatening to kill or murder any person, shall be guilty of felony, and being convicted thereof shall be liable, at the discretion of the court, to be kept in penal servitude for any term not exceeding ten years and not less than three years,—or to be imprisoned for any term not exceeding two years, with or without hard labour, and with or without solitary confinement, and, if a male under the age of sixteen years, with or without whipping" (24 & 25 Vict. c. 100 s. 16).
297. See Stratmann, *The Marquess of Queensberry*, 235.

298. [Anon.], "Oscar Wilde's Arrest," *Illustrated Police Budget Supplement*, 13 April 1895: 7.

299. [Anon.], "Marquis and Oscar Wilde: Criminal Libel Action—Verdict," *Reynolds's Newspaper*, 7 April 1895: 4.

300. [Anon.], "Oscar Wilde: Arrested at Chelsea," *Echo*, 6 April 1895: 2.

301. The *Illustrated Police Budget* provided the time of Wilde's luncheon at the hotel; [anon.], "Oscar Wilde's Arrest," *Illustrated Police Budget Supplement*, 13 April 1895: 7. Sir George Lewis's offices were located at 10, 11, and 12 Ely Place, where he and his siblings were born and raised. Ely Place is located off Charterhouse Street, north of Holborn Viaduct. Several press reports state that Wilde was accompanied by "three other gentlemen," one of whom was a lawyer. This may suggest that Reggie Turner, who studied for the bar, was in their company (see, for example, [anon.], "Arrest of Oscar Wilde," *Manchester Evening News*, 6 April 1895: 3; cf. Sturgis, *Oscar*, 557, 845).

302. Max Beerbohm, "To Ada Leverson," 9 April 1895, in *Letters of Max Beerbohm, 1892–1956*, ed. Rupert Hart-Davis (New York: W. W. Norton, 1988), 8.

303. Holland, *Irish Peacock*, xxxi.

304. [Anon.], "Queensberry–Wilde Case," *Daily Telegraph*, 3.

305. [Anon.], "Marquis and Oscar Wilde: Criminal Libel Action—Verdict," 4.

306. [Anon.], "Marquis and Oscar Wilde: Criminal Libel Action—Verdict," 4.

307. Oscar Wilde, "To the Editor of the *Evening News*," 5 April 1895, in *The Complete Letters*, 637. H. Montgomery Hyde notes that Robert Ross jotted down this letter on the back of two envelopes, which Wilde signed after consulting his solicitor, C. O. Humphreys; H. Montgomery Hyde, *Oscar Wilde*, Famous Trials 7 (Harmondsworth: Penguin, 1962), 150. On Hyde's volume, see xx–xxi above.

308. Quoted in Hyde, *Oscar Wilde*, Famous Trials, 150–51.

309. Frank Harris states that Ross withdrew £200 and then "raced off to meet Oscar at the Cadogan Hotel" (*Oscar Wilde: His Life and Confessions*, 1:238). The head office of the London and Westminster Bank (1833–1909) was located at 1 St. James's Square in central London. Reginald Walter Brooks, a clerk from the bank, gave evidence about Wilde's account during the first criminal trial (see 195).

310. [Anon.], "Oscar Wilde: Arrested at Chelsea," 2. Hatton Garden is located between Clerkenwell Road and Holborn. Holborn Circus marks the convergence of Hatton Garden, Holborn, New Fetter Lane, and Charterhouse Street.

311. Harris, *Oscar Wilde: His Life and Confessions*, 1:238–39. Wilde went to what is now Room 118 in the Belmond Cadogan Hotel, which reopened, after a five-year period of refurbishment, in 2019.

312. Harris, *Oscar Wilde: His Life and Confessions*, 1:239. At the time of Wilde's arrest, Constance Wilde was at the home of her aunt Mary Napier, in Lower Seymour Street, Marylebone, in the West End of London. Franny Moyle confirms that Ross broke the news about Wilde's arrest to Constance (see *Constance*, 266).

313. This letter appeared in several newspapers, including the *Echo*; [anon.], "Oscar Wilde: Arrested at Chelsea," 2.

314. The *Illustrated Police Budget* gives the time that Sir John signed the warrant as "five minutes to five o'clock"; [anon.], "Oscar Wilde's Arrest," *Illustrated Police Budget Supplement*: 7.

315. Alfred Douglas, *Oscar Wilde and Myself* (London: John Long, 1914), 106–7. The reliability of this book, since it was written at a time when Douglas sought to defend his reputation, remains open to question. Harris tells a different story about Wyndham. He claims that at around 4.00 p.m. Wyndham visited the hotel, wishing to see him. Since Douglas was not available, Wyndham tried to communicate with Wilde, who was also reluctant to talk. In the end, Wyndham spoke with Ross, urging him "to get Oscar to leave the country at once to avoid scandal"; Harris, *Oscar Wilde: His Life and Confessions*, 1:239. According to Harris, Douglas "burst into the room" demanding to see Wyndham, and fifteen minutes later he "announced he was going out with Wyndham to see someone of importance" (1:240).

316. [Anon.], "Oscar Arrested," *Morning Leader*, 6 April 1895: 5.

317. [Anon.], "Oscar Wilde: Arrested at Chelsea," 2. A saddlebag chair was a fashionable one upholstered with the type of carpeting that was used in the saddlebags put on camels.

318. [Anon.], "Oscar Wilde's Arrest," *Illustrated Police Budget Supplement*, 8. The other identifiable newspaper cast onto the carpet is the *Pall Mall Gazette*.

319. See 251.

320. Oscar Wilde, "To Lord Alfred Douglas, [5 April 1895], in *The Complete Letters*, 637–38. Both George Alexander and Lewis Waller, who were centrally involved in the productions of Wilde's *Importance of Being Earnest* (St. James's Theatre) and *An Ideal Husband* (Theatre Royal Haymarket), respectively, refused to put up bail for Wilde. 41 Norfolk Square, close to Paddington Station, was Humphreys's private residence where he had lived since 1869.

321. Robert Ross, "Introductory Note," in Oscar Wilde, *A Florentine Tragedy: Opening Scene by T. Sturge Moore* (Boston, MA: John W. Luce, 1908), v–vi. (Ross's edition is based on the typescript and manuscript materials relating to the play that came into his hands in 1904.) On 9 April 1895, Wilde wrote to Adey asking him to tell Ross "to go to Tite Street and get a type-written manuscript, part of my blank-verse tragedy [i.e., *A Florentine Tragedy*], also a black book containing *La Sainte Courtisane* in bedroom" (*The Complete Letters*, 642).

322. Ross, "Introductory Note," vi.

323. This report appeared in several newspapers; see the *Echo* ([anon.], "Oscar Wilde: Arrested at Chelsea," 2).

324. [Anon.], "Oscar Wilde's Arrest," *Illustrated Police Budget Supplement*, 7.

325. [Anon.], "Mr. Oscar Wilde in a Cell at Bow Street," *Paris Herald*, 6 April 1895: 1. By the time of Wilde's arrest, five issues of the *Yellow Book* (1894–97)—a quarterly, hardbound journal of art and literature—had appeared. Edited by the American writer Henry Harland and the artist Aubrey Beardsley, the periodical, which Elkin Mathews and John Lane initially issued under their Bodley Head imprint, gained some notoriety when its opening number featured controversial contributions from the satirist Max Beerbohm, the poet and critic Arthur Symons, and Beardsley. Even though some of the contributions

were traditionalist writings not tinged with eroticism, the *Yellow Book*—which took its title from sensational yellow-backed French novels—became a byword for avant-garde Decadence. Lane and Mathews published several of Wilde's books (see 506 below), though at Beardsley's bidding Wilde remained excluded from contributing to the *Yellow Book*.

326. J. Lewis May explains that Lane decided to withdraw Wilde's books in response to the controversy that arose after a Sunday newspaper stated: "Arrest of Oscar Wilde, *Yellow Book* under His Arm." (May suggests that the *Yellow Book* was *Aphrodite: mœurs antiques* [*Aphrodite: Ancient Manners* (1896)], a bestselling, highly sexual novel by Wilde's one-time friend French author Pierre Louÿs. This is a mistaken claim. As David Charles Rose has pointed out, *Aphrodite* "was first printed on 20th March 1896 and placed for sale in the bookshops in Paris in the 28th"; *Oscar Wilde's Elegant Republic: Transformation, Dislocation and Fantasy in Fin-de-Siècle Paris* (Newcastle upon Tyne: Cambridge Scholars, 2015), 226. In response to this press report, people threw stones at the publishers' premises on Vigo Street "and clamoured for the head of Bodley on a charger"; J. Lewis May, *John Lane and the Nineties* (London: John Lane at The Bodley Head, 1936), 80. Wilde's arrest, Lane is supposed to have said, "killed *The Yellow Book*, and it nearly killed me." May comments: "six of the most prominent Bodley Head authors sent a cable to John Lane stating that unless he suppressed [Aubrey] Beardsley's work in volume V of *The Yellow Book* and omitted Oscar Wilde's name from his catalogue, they would withdraw their books" (May, *John Lane*, 80). Katherine Lyon Mix states that Lane's panicked business manager, Frederic Chapman, broke off the editorial relationship with Beardsley (*A Study in Yellow: "The Yellow Book" and Its Contributors* [Lawrence: University of Kansas Press, 1960], 144).

327. [Anon.], "Oscar Wilde's Arrest," *Illustrated Police Budget Supplement*, 7.

328. These two thoroughfares and parkland in southwest London mark the progress of the cab eastward to Scotland Yard. Hobart Place is located next to Lower Grosvenor Gardens. The section of Buckingham Palace Road that Wilde traveled leads into Birdcage Walk, which follows the southern perimeter of St. James's Park.

329. [Anon.], "Arrest of Oscar Wilde," *Western Mail*, 6 April 1895: 5. The *Daily Telegraph* noted different details in Wilde's dress; it noted that Wilde appeared in a "blue-black overcoat and dark striped trousers" and was "wearing brown Suède gloves" ([anon.], "The Charges against Oscar Wilde," 8 April 1895: 5).

330. [Anon.], "Oscar Wilde's Arrest," *Illustrated Police Budget Supplement*, 7.

331. [Anon.], "Arrest of Oscar Wilde," *Western Mail*, 5.

332. The name should have been recorded as Charles Parker, who gave evidence at the pretrial hearing and at both of the subsequent criminal trials.

333. [Anon.], 'The Queensberry–Wilde Case," 3; small changes have been made to punctuation. Ross brought a Gladstone bag filled with clothes for Wilde. After making several visits to Wilde's home at Tite Street, Ross (on his mother's advice) departed from London for Calais. "The decision to stay or go," Maureen Borland observes, "was the most difficult decision Robbie had ever made, but in the end he went to France, convinced that if he was free he would be able to fight the bigotry and intolerance that was destroying Wilde's life and that would, if not checked, destroy them all"; Maureen Borland, *Wilde's*

Devoted Friend: A Life of Robert Ross, 1869–1918 (Oxford: Lennard, 1990), 47. On the evening of 5 April 1895, Reggie Turner also left for Calais.

334. [Anon.], "The Queensberry–Wilde Case." The *Illustrated Police Budget* provided a somewhat different account of Wilde's belongings: "He was then searched, and twenty £5 notes found in his pocket-book, his cigarette-case and matches taken from him"; [Anon.], "Oscar Wilde's Arrest," *Illustrated Police Budget Supplement*, 7. The Tavistock Hotel, which opened in the 1850s, was located on the Piazza, Covent Garden; Baedeker referred to it as a hotel "for gentlemen only" that stocked "good wines" (*London and Its Environs*, 10th ed., 8).

335. [Anon.], "Oscar Wilde: Arrested at Chelsea," 2. The *News of the World* carried a similar report; [anon.], "The Wilde Case," 7 April 1895: 1.

336. [Anon.], "Oscar Wilde's Arrest," *Illustrated Police Budget Supplement*, 7.

337. Alfred Douglas, "To George Ives," [? 6 April 1895], Lord Alfred Douglas Collection 1890–1951, Clark Library, MS Douglas, D733L I95, Box 20, Folder 2.

338. [Anon.], "Arrest of Oscar Wilde," *Western Mail*: 6.

339. Advertisement, *Morning Post*, 27 April 1895: 4.

340. See, for example, [anon.], "St. James's," *St. James's Gazette*, 27 April 1895: 1. Various papers carried similar notices, including the *Pall Mall Gazette* ([anon.], "To-Night's Entertainments," 27 April 1895: 1).

341. Michael Seeney, *From Bow Street to the Ritz: Oscar Wilde's Theatrical Career from 1895 to 1908* (High Wycombe: Rivendale Press, 2015), 122–23.

342. [Anon.], "The Charges against Oscar Wilde: Another Arrest," *Daily Telegraph*, 8 April 1895: 5, quoted in [anon.], editorial, *Sketch*, 17 April 1895: 655.

343. Editorial, *Westminster Gazette*, quoted in editorial, *Sketch*, 17 April 1895, 655.

344. Editorial, *Sketch*, 17 April 1895, 655.

CHAPTER THREE

Epigraph: Lord Alfred Douglas, "Oscar Wilde," in *Oscar Wilde: A Plea and A Reminiscence*, ed. Caspar Wintermans (Woubrugge: Avalon Press, 2002), 25.

1. [Anon.], "The Wilde Case," *News of the World*, 7 April 1895: 1. As we can see from the discussion in chapter 2 (150–51), the *News of the World* was exaggerating about the extent to which Wilde's name was removed, at this early stage, from the publicity for these two comedies.

2. [Anon.], "The Wilde Case," *News of the World*, 7 April 1895, 1.

3. [Anon.], "Wilde the Man," *Morning*, 6 April 1895: 4.

4. Constance Wilde, "To Mrs. Robinson," 19 April 1895, in *The Complete Letters of Oscar Wilde*, ed. Merlin Holland and Rupert Hart-Davis (London: Fourth Estate, 2000), 642.

5. H.M. Prison Holloway, Parkhurst Road, north London, opened in 1852 as the Holloway House of Correction, and it remained a mixed prison (for men, women, and children) until 1903, when it became female-only. On 25 November 2015, George Osborne, the chancellor of the exchequer, announced that the prison would be closed and sold to property developers.

6. Constance Wilde, "To Mrs. Robinson," 642.

7. [Anon.], "Police Intelligence," *Standard*, 8 April 1895: 2.

8. James Fitzjames Stephen, *A History of the Criminal Law of England*, 3 vols. (London: Macmillan, 1883), 1:239.

9. The Bail Act 1898 did away with the need to demand sureties when there was no risk of the accused absconding (61 & 62 Vict. c. 7). The drafting of the Criminal Justice Bill 1967 coincided with several critical interventions in the need to reform the bail system; see, for example, Michael Zander, "Bail: A Re-Appraisal," *Criminal Law Review* (1967): 25–39, 100–110, 128–42; and A. K. Bottomley, "The Granting of Bail: Principles and Practice," *Modern Law Review* 31, no. 1 (1968): 40–54.

10. [Anon.], "The Charges against Wilde," *Daily Telegraph*, 8 April 1895: 5.

11. [Anon.], "Oscar and Taylor," *Reynolds's Newspaper*, 14 April 1895: 1; the subheading for this part of the report is "Wilde as 'B. 24.'"

12. [Anon.], "Oscar and Taylor," 1.

13. [Anon.], "Wilde Has Been Ill," *Reynolds's Newspaper*, 14 April 1895: 1. Established in 1872, the Exchange Telegraph Company originally used tickertape telegraph machines to distribute financial and business information from the London Stock Exchange and other markets to subscribers. Their information was communicated through tickertape machines located in banks, gentlemen's clubs, and offices. The company added a legal service in 1876 and a news service in 1879. Known from the 1950s onward as Extel, the company went through several mergers, and is now owned by Thomson Reuters.

14. [Anon.], "Oscar Wilde in Prison," *Star*, 8 April 1895: 3.

15. [Anon.], "At Holloway: How Wilde Fares in Prison," *Sun*, 8 April 1895: 3. The *Echo* also furnished a report that stated: "Oscar Wilde betrayed considerable emotion when he was on the point of leaving Bow Street Police Station for Holloway Jail on Saturday evening. He was understood to say that he would take his life if he had the opportunity, and, as a precaution, his scarf pin was taken away from him" ([anon.], "Oscar Wilde in Jail," *Echo*, 8 April 1895: 3).

16. [Anon.], "At Holloway," 3.

17. Alfred Douglas, *The Autobiography of Lord Alfred Douglas*, 2nd ed. (London: Martin Secker, 1931), 108.

18. [Anon], "Oscar Wilde in Prison," 3; a typographic error has been corrected.

19. Douglas, *Autobiography*, 108.

20. British Library, Add. MS 81758, quoted in Derek Walker-Smith and Edward Clarke, *The Life of Sir Edward Clarke* (London: Butterworth, 1939), 251. Clarke's decision to defend Wilde pro bono during the criminal trials met with some criticism in the legal press; see [anon.], "Obiter Dicta," *Law Journal*, 13 April 1895: 239.

21. In 1902, for example, the *Western Mail* observed that Clarke's "quiet earnestness and . . . scrupulous fairness . . . have earned Sir Edward the title 'the Bayard of the bar'"; [anon.], "The Stop-Day Action," *Western Mail*, 28 July 1902: 5. The medieval French knight the Chevalier de Bayard was renowned as "the knight without fear and beyond reproach."

22. Douglas, "Oscar Wilde," 25–26.

23. Douglas, *Autobiography*, 110. The Cleveland Street scandal, which focused on a male brothel, is discussed in chapter 1 (61–65).

24. Edward Maltby, *Secrets of a Solicitor* (London: John Long, 1929), 175.

25. Edward Marjoribanks [with Ian Colvin], *The Life of Lord Carson*, 3 vols. (London: Victor Gollancz, 1932–36), 1:230, 228.

26. Maltby, *Secrets of a Solicitor*, 175.

27. The commentary and exchanges that follow have been largely adapted from [anon.], "Oscar Wilde: Charged with Infamous Conduct," *Reynolds's Newspaper*, 7 April 1895: 1, unless otherwise noted.

28. [Anon.], "Oscar Wilde," *Echo*, 6 April 1895: 2.

29. [Anon.], "Oscar Wilde," *Echo*, 6 April 1895, 2.

30. [Anon.], "Examination of Saturday," *Illustrated Police News*, 13 April 1895: 3.

31. [Anon.], "Examination of Saturday," 3.

32. [Anon.], "Oscar Wilde's Arrest," *Illustrated Police Budget Supplement*, 13 April 1895: 7.

33. [Anon.], "Oscar Wilde," *Echo*, 6 April 1895, 2.

34. This statement appears in [anon.], "Oscar Wilde: Charged with Infamous Conduct," 1.

35. [Anon.], "Oscar Wilde: Charged with Infamous Conduct," 1. It is not known who the woman was, though there is some possibility that Wilde's close friend Ada Leverson, who offered considerable support to him during the trials, attended the pretrial hearing (see 304–5). The *Sun* observed: "She was not Mrs. Wilde, at all events"; [anon.], "In the Dock: Wilde and Taylor Together," 6 April 1895: 3.

36. [Anon.], "Oscar Wilde's Arrest," *Illustrated Police Budget Supplement*, 7.

37. [Anon.], "Oscar Wilde's Arrest," 7.

38. [Anon.], *The Trial of Oscar Wilde: From the Shorthand Reports* (Paris: privately printed, 1906), 16. On this source, see xix–xx above. Sir Augustus Harris's apparent rebuff is open to question. Amy Charlotte Bewicke Menzies ("Mrs. Stuart Menzies") recalls: "when Oscar Wilde was in trouble [Sir Augustus] was one of the first to appear to stand bail for his friend" (*Further Indiscretions by a Woman of No Importance* [New York: E. P. Dutton, 1918], 113).

39. [Anon.], "The Society Scandal," *Galignani Messenger*, 7 April 1895: 1.

40. [Anon.], "The Society Scandal," *Galignani Messenger*, 7 April 1895, 1.

41. [Anon.], "Oscar Wilde: Charged with Infamous Conduct," 1.

42. [Anon.], "Oscar Wilde at Bow Street," *Globe*, 6 April 1895: 5.

43. [Anon.], "Oscar Wilde's Arrest," *Illustrated Police Budget Supplement*, 7.

44. Located on the Strand, the Savoy Hotel opened on 6 August 1889. Built by the theatre impresario Richard D'Oyly Carte on the profits he made from managing Gilbert and Sullivan's comic operas, it was London's most opulent hotel, with electric elevators, speaking tubes, and private bathrooms.

45. Little College Street is located close to both the Houses of Parliament and Westminster Abbey; despite its proximity to Parliament, the street was regarded as insalubrious.

46. Kettner's, 28–31 Church Street (now Romilly Street), Soho, opened in 1867 on the premises of what had been four Georgian town houses; Auguste Kettner, chef to Louis Napoleon III, was the founder. (His name, which became a byword for fine dining, was

celebrated through *Kettner's Book of the Table: A Manual of Cookery, Practical, Theoretical, Historical* [London: Dulau, 1877], even though this was the work of gastronomist and literary critic Eneas Sweetland Dallas.)

47. Camera Square (now Chelsea Park Gardens) is located between Park Walk and Beaufort Street, Chelsea. Parker subsequently pawned both of these gifts from Wilde (see 170). In August 1894, Alfred Taylor lodged at 7 Camera Square. The property appears to have been maintained by Lucy Rumsby, who also acted as the landlady at 50 Park Walk, where Parker rented a room in spring 1893.

48. [Anon.], "Oscar Wilde: Charged with Infamous Conduct," 1.

49. [Anon.], "The Oscar Wilde Scandal," *Manchester Courier and Lancashire General Advertiser*, 8 April 1895: 8.

50. Parker's declaration that he was nineteen may have been inaccurate; in the pretrial hearing, the court learned that he was twenty-one years old (see [Christopher Sclater Millard], *Oscar Wilde: Three Times Tried*, Famous Old Bailey Trials of the XIX Century (London: Ferrestone Press, 1912), 163).

51. [Anon.], "The Wilde Prosecution," *Daily Chronicle*, 8 April 1895: 7.

52. [Anon.], "The Wilde Case," *Western Mail*, 8 April 1895: 8.

53. [Anon.], "The Wilde Prosecution," 7.

54. [Anon.], "Oscar Wilde," *Echo*, 6 April 1895, 3.

55. Denbigh Street is located between Warwick Way and Belgrave Road; part of it is almost parallel to Tachbrook Street, where the extortionists Frederick Atkins and James Dennis Burton lived in June 1891 (see 237).

56. [Anon.], "The Arrest of Taylor," *Illustrated Police News*, 13 April 1895: 3.

57. Gill's question appears in [anon.], "Oscar Wilde's Arrest," *Illustrated Police Budget Supplement*, 10.

58. This detail appears in several reports; see [anon.], "Oscar Wilde Arrested," *Cardiff Times*, 13 April 1895: 5.

59. This and the next exchange between Gill and Charles Parker appear in [anon.], "Oscar Wilde," *Echo*, 6 April 1895, 3.

60. I have supplied Gill's question.

61. The Hôtel de Solferino, 7 and 8 Rupert Street, Haymarket, had a small well-established Italian restaurant.

62. Opened in 1858, St. James's Hall—which occupied the "Nash Quadrant" between George Court, Regent Street, Piccadilly, and Vine Street—contained two restaurants; it was famous for musical concerts and for such noted events as Charles Dickens's 1868 "Farewell Readings." In the 1890s, the bar area was frequented by prostitutes, who conducted much of their business in nearby Piccadilly. The establishment was nicknamed Jimmie's. On 12 September 1893, the artist Aubrey Beardsley joked with the publisher John Lane: "I am going to Jimmie's dressed up as a tart and mean to have a regular spree"; *The Letters of Aubrey Beardsley*, ed. Henry Maas, J. L. Duncan, and W. G. Good (London: Cassell, 1970), 53. The building was demolished in 1905.

63. These details appear in [anon.], "Arrest of Oscar Wilde," *Lloyd's Weekly Newspaper*, 14 April 1895: 15; and [anon.], "Oscar Wilde," *Echo*, 6 April 1895, 3.

64. Charles Parker's reply and his next exchange with Gill have been adapted from [anon.], "Oscar Wilde's Arrest," *Illustrated Police Budget Supplement*, 10.

65. The Crystal Palace, the nickname given to the cast-iron and plate-glass Great Exhibition Hall, which opened at Hyde Park, London, in 1851, was disassembled and rebuilt at Sydenham, south London, in 1854, where it remained until it burned to the ground in 1936.

66. The London Pavilion, 1 Piccadilly Circus, opened in 1885; it was one of a new generation of finely furnished and decorated music-halls, with electric lighting, that hosted "variety theatre." The premises were no longer used for theatrical purposes after 1981.

67. Park Walk is located between Fulham Road and the King's Road, Chelsea.

68. The distance is roughly a mile, and it takes about twenty-five minutes to walk.

69. Not to be confused with the Albemarle Club (see 98 and 483 above), the Albemarle Hotel, 60–61 Piccadilly, was built in 1887–88. It advertised itself as "the most luxuriously and artistically fitted Hotel in Europe"; advertisement for the Albemarle Hotel, *Truth*, 27 February 1890: 444.

70. These last two sentences and the exchange that follows between C. F. Gill and Charles Parker have been adapted from [Millard], *Oscar Wilde: Three Times Tried*, 149.

71. Gill probably feared, once again, that the name of Alfred Douglas might emerge at this stage of the proceedings. On 19 April 1895, Gill wrote to Cuffe, the director of public prosecutions: "I have considered the question as to whether a prosecution ought to be instituted against Lord Alfred Douglas on account of his connection with the case of Oscar Wilde and Alfred Taylor, and in the result I have come to the conclusion that no proceedings should be taken on the evidence we have in the statements of different witnesses." Gill added that the only evidence of Wilde's intimacy with Douglas was based on "two remarkable letters to Douglas"; "[u]pon this sort of evidence," he observed, "it would not be possible to formulate any criminal charge and there is no proof of any act of indecency between them."

Gill also observed: "With reference to the evidence of the young men who have been called as witnesses against Wilde and Taylor only two of them Woods [*sic*] and Charles Parker suggest misconduct on the part of Douglas with them. These witnesses would clearly require corroboration and although there is ample as against Wilde even in his own cross examination of his relations with them, as regards Douglas there appears to be no corroboration whatsoever"; National Archives, DPP 1/96.

The next day, in a letter to Charles Murdoch, an undersecretary at the Home Office, Cuffe remarked: "From the best information we can obtain as to Lord A. Douglas we believe that he is a person of weak character," and that Douglas "never had the force of will or character to emancipate himself from his ~~dependency~~ /degrading\ submission to Wilde, whom, no doubt, he still regards with the utmost devotion and affection"; National Archives, HO 45/24516.

72. The detail about Trafalgar Square appears in several reports, including [anon.], "Oscar Wilde Arrested," *Cardiff Times*, 5. Trafalgar Square, which is located in central London, is a major landmark; it takes its name from the Battle of Trafalgar (21 October 1805).

73. This and the next two exchanges between Gill and Charles Parker appear in [anon.], "Oscar Wilde," *Echo*, 6 April 1895, 3.

74. Taylor had rooms at 3 Chapel Street, from August 1893 until the end of the year, where he paid £3 a month.

75. The arrest took place at the police raid on 46 Fitzroy Street on 12 August 1894 (see 319 and 333 above).

76. Charles Parker was not telling the truth when he claimed to have no knowledge of Alfred Wood. As he admitted in the first criminal trial, he had been involved in blackmailing activities with Wood, whom he appears to have met through Taylor's gatherings at 13 Little College Street (see 219).

77. Frederick ("Fred") Atkins (a.k.a. Fred Denny). Millard records that Charles Parker also stated that he did not know Sydney Mavor (*Oscar Wilde: Three Times Tried*, 149).

78. Charles Parker's response to the inquiry about Ernest Scarfe is somewhat cryptic; it is not entirely clear what the "woman's dress" signifies, although it may suggest that Scarfe cross-dressed. Both Atkins and Taylor at times wore women's clothing. Possibly, the available reports have omitted one of Gill's questions.

79. Officially known as the Central Criminal Court ("C.C.C.") since 1834, the Old Bailey was sometimes referred to as the Sessions house. The term "sessions" also referred to the periods in the year when the court was in operation, or "in session."

80. This and the next three exchanges between Gill and William Parker appear in [Anon.], "Oscar Wilde," *Echo*, 6 April 1895, 3.

81. [Anon.], "Oscar Wilde at Bow-St.," *Morning Leader*, 8 April 1895: 5.

82. Later during the first criminal trial (227), Fred Kerley, the retired detective inspector, said that among the documents that Taylor had left behind at his lodgings in 3 Chapel Street was a piece of paper on which Charles Parker, when he was at the St. James's bar, had written Taylor's address. As we can see here, William Parker stated that the handwriting was his own.

83. This and the next three exchanges between Gill and William Parker appear in [Anon.], "Oscar Wilde," *Echo*, 6 April 1895, 3.

84. This exchange and the two ensuing exchanges between Sir John Bridge and William Parker, and Gill and Taylor, have been adapted from [Millard], *Oscar Wilde: Three Times Tried*, 151.

85. According to *Reynolds's Newspaper*, William Parker stated: "It was some time in March"; [anon.], "Oscar Wilde: Charged with Infamous Conduct," 1.

86. In the first criminal trial, Grant stated that she was not the landlady of the property but that she had a portion of the house in which she let rooms to Taylor (see 226).

87. Fancy-dress balls and carnivals (often known as costume parties outside Britain) were regular features at large venues during this period.

88. [Anon.], "In the Dock: Wilde and Taylor Together," *Sun*, 6 April 1895: 3.

89. The *Sun* commented that Grant frequently heard Taylor talking to someone whom he "addressed as 'Hosker'" (the aspirate on "Oscar" signaling her working-class London accent); [anon.], "In the Dock: Wilde and Taylor Together," 3.

90. A brass plate on a door, with the name of an occupant engraved upon it, would have been the sign of a gentleman.

91. Founded by French wine merchant Daniel Nicholas Thévenon (1833–97), the Café Royal (1865–2008), 68 Regent Street, became one of London's most fashionable restaurants. Wilde frequently dined there.

92. The Hôtel de Florence, 57 Rupert Street, Haymarket, which contained an Italian restaurant, opened in 1889. It was one of Wilde's favorite places for dining; "table d'hôte 3s. lunch 1s. 6d."; Karl Baedeker, *London and Its Environs: Handbook for Travellers*, 10th ed. (Leipsic: Karl Baedeker, 1896), 15.

93. Wilde leased the beautifully decorated home of Lady Georgiana Mount-Temple (a distant cousin and confidante of Constance Wilde's) at Babbacombe Cliff, near Torquay, Devon, from probably mid-November 1892 to 1 March 1893 (see Wilde, *The Complete Letters*, 537). Constance and their two sons, Cyril Wilde (later Holland) and Vyvyan Wilde (later Holland), stayed at Babbacombe for part of this period. Wilde was there from time to time. Douglas joined Wilde and his family in mid-February 1893.

94. This wording, which I have supplied here, is not recorded in any of the press reports; *Reynolds's Newspaper* observed that Wood's evidence was "of course unreportable" ([anon.], "Oscar Wilde: Charged with Infamous Conduct," 1).

95. Langham Street, which intersects with Great Portland Street in the West End of London, is almost two miles and roughly forty minutes' walk from Little College Street. The details about Wood's lodgings appear in several reports, including [anon.], "The Prosecution of Oscar Wilde," *Huddersfield Chronicle*, 8 April 1895: 4.

96. Gill's comment implies that the letters belonged to someone other than Wilde; the recipient of the letters in question was Alfred Douglas, whose name, at this juncture, Gill was still eager to keep out of the pretrial hearing.

97. This sentence, together with the passages that follow to the end of the proceedings that took place on this day, has been adapted from [Millard], *Oscar Wilde: Three Times Tried*, 155–59.

98. [Anon.], "Oscar Wilde's Arrest," *Illustrated Police Budget Supplement*, 13 April 1895, 10.

99. Gill is referring to the witness statements that Day, Russell, and Co. collected in connection with Queensberry's defense in anticipation of Wilde's libel case. The manuscript, which contains a short statement from Mavor, remains in private hands. The document, which constitutes fifty handwritten pages, was exhibited as *Marquis* [*sic*] *of Queensberry vs. Oscar Wilde Working Papers* (Cat. 170) at *Oscar Wilde: L'impertinent absolu*, Petit Palais: Musée des Beaux-Arts de la Ville Paris, 28 September 2016–15 January 2017.

100. Reports diverge in their spelling of the masseur's name. *Lloyd's Weekly Newspaper*, for instance, records the name as "Antoin Maggi" ([anon.], "Arrest of Oscar Wilde," 14 April 1895, 15); the *Echo* states that it was "Anton Miggi" ([anon.], "Wilde and Taylor," 29 April 1895: 3); and [anon.], *The Trial of Oscar Wilde* refers to him (in a phonetic transcription from shorthand) as "Massur Mijji" (77). It has not been possible to find further information about Migge's employment at the Savoy or his career as a masseur.

101. Later, in the first criminal trial, Cotter's evidence suggested to the judge "that conduct of the grossest kind has been indulged in"; [anon.], *The Trial of Oscar Wilde*, 77. Wilde's brother, Willie, entered the courtroom when Cotter began giving evidence. Matthew Sturgis remarks that Migge and Cotter had confused "Wilde's room with the adjoin-

ing one belonging to Lord Alfred Douglas"; Wilde, he adds, was unwilling to correct the matter in order to defend Bosie (Matthew Sturgis, *Oscar: A Life* [London: Head of Zeus, 2018], 569). During the first criminal trial, Douglas apparently contacted his lawyers to set the record straight.

102. This sentence and the commentary that follows have been adapted from [anon.], "Arrest of Oscar Wilde," *Lloyd's Weekly Newspaper*, 15; [Millard], *Oscar Wilde: Three Times Tried*, 158–59; and [anon.], "The Queensberry–Wilde Case," *Illustrated Police News*, 13 April 1895: 3.

103. The last two sentences appear in [anon.], "The Charges against Wilde," *Daily Telegraph*, 8 April 1895: 5.

104. The friends presumably included Alfred Douglas.

105. [Anon.], "Oscar Wilde's Arrest," *Illustrated Police Budget Supplement*, 10; small changes have been made to punctuation. The previous year, *Reynolds's Newspaper* reported that an inquest was held at H.M. Prison Holloway into the death of William Henry Parkinson, a major in the 4th Battalion of the King's Liverpool Regiment. Parkinson wrote to a friend that he had been accused of "indecent behaviour to two boys"; he added: "I need not say it is a regular case of blackmail." The report also noted that, on the instructions of his solicitor, "the prisoner was next day put into a special cell, for which 6s. was charged. It was better furnished and more comfortable than the ordinary cells. The prisoner's food was sent in from the outside by his friends; [anon.], "Indecency and Suicide," *Reynolds's Newspaper*, 18 November 1894: 3. Parkinson, who was forty-nine, took his life by smashing the mirror and slitting his throat. The phrase "durance vile" refers to a long prison sentence.

106. [Anon.], "At Holloway," 3.

107. [Anon.], "Oscar Wilde in Prison," *Illustrated Police Budget*, 20 April 1895: 8; further quotations appear on this page.

108. [Anon.,] "Oscar Wilde in Prison," 8.

109. This description, together with the cross-examination and commentary that follow, has been adapted from [anon.], "Oscar and Taylor," *Reynolds's Newspaper*, 14 April 1895: 1, unless otherwise noted. The *Echo* reported: "Mr. Smythe, solicitor, watched the case for someone whose name did not transpire"; [anon.], "Wilde and Taylor," 19 April 1895: 2. The attorney was William Doveton Smyth, whose name often appeared as "Smythe" in the press. It is not known for whom Smyth held a watching brief (i.e., to act as an observer on a criminal case that might affect a client indirectly).

110. This detail appears in [anon.], "Oscar Wilde and Taylor at Bow Street," *Illustrated Police News*, 20 April 1895: 1–2.

111. [Anon.], "Oscar Wilde: Brought Up at Bow Street This Morning," *Star*, 11 April 1895: 3.

112. [Anon.], "Oscar Wilde: Brought Up at Bow Street This Morning," 3.

113. [Anon.], "Oscar Wilde and Taylor at Bow Street," 2.

114. This statement appears in [anon.], "Oscar Wilde and Taylor at Bow Street," 2.

115. The wording of Sir John Bridge's speech appears in [anon.], "The Oscar Wilde Case," *Western Mail*, 13 April 1895: 5.

116. [Anon.], "Oscar Wilde: Brought Up at Bow Street This Morning," 3.

117. More Adey, "To an Unknown Correspondent," [June 1895], Clark Library, Wilde, Box 1, Folders 2–8, A233L U58 1895. Adey did not send this letter.

118. C. H. Norman, "Letter: Wilde's 'De Profundis,'" *Times Literary Supplement*, 28 September 1928: 745. By this calculation, Parker and Wood received around £35 each from the time of Wilde's arrest on 5 April 1895 to his sentencing on 25 May 1895. Adey recorded similar sums. He claimed that Queensberry parted with "£21 for retaining the services of Shelley" ("To an Unknown Correspondent," [June 1895]). The scale of witness fees varied on class and profession. In 1879, Frederick H. Short noted that "Common labourers, journeymen, &c." received a term fee of 5s. if in the same town, and slightly more if needing to travel, while "Gentlemen, merchants, and bankers" along with "Professional men" received 21s.; *The Taxation of Costs in the Crown Office* (London: Stevens and Haynes, 1879), 24.

119. I. Playfair [J. H. Wilson], *Gentle Criticisms on British Justice* (Newcastle upon Tyne: privately printed, 1895), 13.

120. Ellmann, *Oscar Wilde*, 475, 615. Ellmann references Norman's correspondence with Hart-Davis.

121. This information, together with the details in the sentence that follows, appears in [anon.], "The Oscar Wilde Case," *Western Mail*, 13 April 1895, 5. The *Sun* claimed that Parker said he was nineteen years old and born in 1876; [anon.], "Wilde in Court," 11 April 1895: 3. On the record of Parker's age when he enlisted, see 516.

122. Edward Harrington, a music publisher's clerk, was present at the Old Bailey during the first and second criminal trials, but he was not called to give evidence; Harrington knew Maurice Salis Schwabe and Taylor.

123. The following exchanges between Newton and Charles Parker have been adapted from [anon.], "The Oscar Wilde Case," *Western Mail*, 13 April 1895, 5, unless otherwise noted.

124. This commentary appears in [anon.], "Oscar Wilde and Taylor at Bow Street," *Illustrated Police News*, 20 April 1895, 2.

125. Gill's comment and the exchange that follows with Newton appear in [anon.], "Oscar Wilde and Taylor at Bow Street," 2.

126. The identity of Charles Parker's former employer remains unknown.

127. A sovereign was a gold coin worth £1; it remained in circulation until World War I when Great Britain came off the gold standard.

128. The identity of the man from whom Charles Parker, together with Alfred Wood and William Allen (see 319), extorted funds remains unknown.

129. The next two exchanges between Newton and Charles Parker have been adapted from [anon.], "Oscar Wilde: Brought Up at Bow Street This Morning," *Star*, 11 April 1895. 3; and [anon.], "The Oscar Wilde Case," *Western Mail*, 13 April 1895, 5.

130. This exchange appears in [anon.], "Wilde and Taylor," *Echo*, 11 April 1895: 3.

131. [Anon.], "Oscar and Taylor," 1. The *Sun* was equally taken aback: "The quiet, assured tone in which the wretched creature announced his villainy literally stunned the court"; [anon.], "Wilde in Court," 3.

132. [Anon.], "Oscar Wilde: Brought Up at Bow Street This Morning," 3.

133. The *Star* and other newspapers record the meeting date as November 1893, when it should have been November 1892; this may have been a slip in the reporting or a failure of memory on Atkins's part, since he and Wilde arrived in Paris on 21 November 1892. *Reynolds's Newspaper* refers to the unidentified individual in Atkins's evidence as the "nameless man of the Old Bailey proceedings"; [anon.], "Oscar and Taylor," 1. The person who introduced Wilde to Taylor was Schwabe.

134. London Victoria Station, which continues to serve southern and southeast England, opened in 1860. The club train was a first-class rail service that departed from Victoria at 3.00 p.m.; the additional charge was 15s. ([William Pullam, ed.], *Handbook for Travellers on the Riviera: From Marseilles to Pisa*, [ed. the Revd. Henry William Pullen] [London: John Murray, 1892], 3).

135. The Boulevard des Capucines contained several hotels. Karl Baedeker describes number 29 as one of "two large *Maisons Meublées*"; *Paris and Its Environs*, 9th ed. [Leipsic: Karl Baedeker, 1896], 5. Wilde had resided at this private hotel before, in November–December 1891, when he enjoyed a period of rest after completing his one-act tragedy *Salomé* in French. Neil McKenna notes that the hotel "was run with absolute discretion by Madame Goly"; *The Secret Life of Oscar Wilde* (London: Century, 2003), 211.

136. [Anon.], "Oscar Wilde and Taylor at Bow Street," *Illustrated Police News*, 2.

137. The Café Julien was located at 3 Boulevard des Capucines, Paris. Built by the brothers Isaac Pereire and Emile Pereire, Le Grand Hôtel (12 Boulevard des Capucines) opened in 1861; it counted among the city's largest hotels.

138. The *Western Mail* records this detail; [anon.], "The Oscar Wilde Case," 13 April 1895: 5.

139. The last monarch to issue the Louis d'Or was Louis XVIII, when it was a 10-franc coin; a Louis, however, usually meant a 20-franc coin.

140. Opened in 1889, the Moulin Rouge, on the Place Blanche, remains one of the most famous cabarets in Paris, renowned for its outré performances. On 3 February 1893, it hosted the second costume ball of the Bal des Quat'z'Arts, which featured nude female models walking about as living artworks. Admission to the cabaret was between 2 and 3 francs.

141. The *Illustrated Police News* notes this response; [anon.], "Oscar Wilde and Taylor at Bow Street," 2.

142. [Anon.], "Oscar Wilde and Taylor at Bow Street," 2.

143. Atkins's reply was not reported in the press. I have supplied this remark for the same reasons as those that account for its insertion above in Wood's speech (174).

144. This and the following five exchanges between Gill and Atkins have been adapted from [anon.], "The Oscar Wilde Case," *Western Mail*, 13 April 1895: 5.

145. Wilde's letter to Atkins has not survived. Atkins's testimony suggests that Wilde wanted him to return the document so that it should be destroyed.

146. The information in Atkins's speech has been adapted from both [anon.], "Oscar and Taylor," *Reynolds's Newspaper*, 1; and [anon.], "Oscar Wilde and Taylor at Bow Street," 2. The hotel that Atkins mentioned was the Florence (see 182 above).

147. The following three exchanges between Gill and Atkins and between Newton and Atkins appear in [anon.], "Oscar Wilde and Taylor at Bow Street," 2.

148. This and the following eight exchanges between Newton and Atkins have been adapted from [anon.], "The Oscar Wilde Case," *Western Mail*, 13 April 1895: 5. The unnamed gentleman was Schwabe.

149. The gentleman in question was Alfred Taylor.

150. This exchange between Sir John Bridge and Atkins, and the next exchange between Gill and Atkins, appear in [anon.], "The Oscar Wilde Case," *Western Mail*, 13 April 1895: 5.

151. Together, Elkin Mathews and John Lane published five of Wilde's volumes: *Poems* (1892), which was a reissue of remaining copies of *Poems* (London: David Bogue, 1881), with fresh binding and title page by Charles Ricketts; the French edition of *Salomé: Drame en un acte* (co-published with the Librairie de l'Art Indépendant, Paris); *Lady Windermere's Fan* (1893); Douglas's English translation of *Salomé*, with designs by Aubrey Beardsley; and *The Sphinx* (1894), also with designs by Ricketts. Their partnership, under the Sign of The Bodley Head, lasted until 1894. The premises of this publisher and bookseller were on Vigo Street, which is located between Regent Street and the intersection of Burlington Gardens and Savile Row. After 1894, both Lane and Mathews continued to publish from this address. In 1894, Lane issued *A Woman of No Importance*. Later, one further work, a revised and lengthened version of *The Portrait of Mr. W. H.* (which originally appeared in shorter form in *Blackwood's Edinburgh Magazine* [1889]), remained under contract. Lane informed Wilde, however, that Mathews would not publish Wilde's *Portrait* "'at any price,' but he wants the plays" (7 September 1894, in Wilde, *The Complete Letters*, 607).

152. [Anon.], "Oscar Wilde: Brought Up at Bow Street This Morning," *Star*, 11 April 1895, 3. A reefer is a thick overcoat.

153. This and the next three exchanges between Gill and Shelley have been adapted from [anon.], "The Oscar Wilde Case," *Western Mail*, 13 April 1895: 5.

154. The Independent Theatre Society (1891–97) was funded by private subscriptions supporting the production of dramas that would otherwise find it impossible to pass through the Examiner of Plays in the Lord Chamberlain's office. The theatre impresario J. T. ("Jack") Grein arranged the society's program; the first production was an English translation of *Ghosts* (1882) by the controversial Norwegian dramatist Henrik Ibsen. Ibsen became well known among British theatregoers with the June 1889 production of his play *A Doll's House* (1879) at the Novelty Theatre, London. The drama, which explores a woman's decision to leave her husband and family, marked a decisive shift in the kinds of subject matter that could be addressed on the London stage. The *Musical World*, for example, observed: "It is probable that the history of the drama records no controversy so keen as that which has waged, and is still waging in our midst, around . . . 'A Doll's House'"; [anon.], "A Doll's House," *Musical World*, 22 June 1889: 398. There is a strong possibility that Shelley accompanied Wilde to the Royalty Theatre on 4 March 1892, where the Independent Theatre Society presented a bill of three dramas: John Gray's *The Kiss*, an English translation of *Le Baiser* (1887), by the French author Théodore de Banville; *The Minister's Call* (1892) by Arthur Symons; and *A Visit*, an English translation by William Archer of *Et Besøg* (1882), by the Danish writer Edward Brandes. In the first criminal trial, Wilde stated that Shelley had joined him at the theatre with a party of friends (see 270). The event was

associated with members of Wilde's male homosexual coterie, who reportedly donned green carnations as a token of their attraction to men.

155. Members of the Prince of Wales's Club, Coventry Street, in the West End of London, included literary men such as Robert W. Buchanan and William Le Queux.

156. The large paper (foolscap quarto) edition of Wilde's *Picture of Dorian Gray* appeared on 1 July 1891 in an exclusive run of 250 copies, printed on Dutch handmade paper and in a more elaborate design than that of the crown octavo edition of 1,000 copies, which had been published several months earlier. For a bibliographical description of these editions, see Oscar Wilde, *The Picture of Dorian Gray: The 1890 and 1891 Texts*, ed. Joseph Bristow, in *The Complete Works of Oscar Wilde*, 11 vols. to date (Oxford: Oxford University Press, 2000–), 3:lxxi–lxxii.

157. This exchange between Newton and Shelley appears in [anon.], "Oscar Wilde: Brought Up at Bow Street This Morning," *Star*, 11 April 1895, 3; and [anon.], "The Oscar Wilde Case," *Western Mail*, 13 April 1895: 5.

158. A rattan cane, made from a pliable species of palm most commonly associated with the port of Malacca in Malaysia, is a gentlemen's walking stick.

159. [Anon.], "Wilde in Court," *Sun*, 11 April 1895, 3.

160. This detail appears in [anon.], "Oscar Wilde: Brought Up at Bow Street This Morning," 3.

161. The British Library copy of this page of *Reynolds's Newspaper* has suffered damage at this point. The commentary on Mrs. Gray that follows has been adapted from [anon.], "Oscar Wilde: Brought Up at Bow Street This Morning," 3.

162. Some of the details about Gray's testimony have been adapted from [anon.], "The Oscar Wilde Case," *Western Mail*, 13 April 1895: 5.

163. The *Sun* mentions this detail; [anon.], "Wilde in Court," 3.

164. The *Sun* mentions this detail; [anon.], "Wilde in Court," 3.

165. The information about Mary Applegate has been adapted from [anon.], "Oscar Wilde and Taylor at Bow Street," 2; and [anon.], "The Oscar Wilde Case," *Western Mail*, 13 April 1895: 5.

166. As Atkins pointed out in the first criminal trial, he had been living at 28 Osnaburgh Street, which is located between Euston Road and Longford Road in the West End of London.

167. In the first criminal trial, Thomas Price from Geneux's stated that Harry Barford called six or seven times at the private hotel for Wilde (see 233). Barford was a jobbing actor working on the London stage and in regional theatre.

168. [Anon.], "Oscar and Taylor," 1.

169. Most of Aloys Louis Vogel's speech that follows has been adapted from [anon], "Oscar and Taylor," 1.

170. Several details in Vogel's testimony have been adapted from [anon.], "Oscar Wilde and Taylor at Bow Street," 2; and [anon.], "The Oscar Wilde Case," *Western Mail*, 13 April 1895: 5.

171. Southsea is a suburb of Portsmouth, Hampshire; in the Victorian era, it developed as a seaside resort known for its respectable middle-class neighborhoods.

172. The excrement that one of the chambermaids, Jane Margaret Cotter, found on the bed-sheets was disclosed in the first and then discussed at greater length in the second criminal trial (see 323–24 and 378).

173. Millard presents Mathews's response differently: "Witness saw that Mr. Wilde was writing to Shelley, and Shelley was requested to leave the firm's employ"; *Oscar Wilde: Three Times Tried*, 172. The *Western Mail* stated: "After that a communication was made to Mr. Lane, and Shelley left their employ"; [anon.], "The Oscar Wilde Case," 13 April 1895, 5. Mathews had also recently gone into print dissociating himself from Wilde. He informed *The Times*: "You mention in your report that the young man Shelley was introduced to Mr. Oscar Wilde by one of the partners of the publishing firm of Mathews and Lane, Vigo Street. Allow me to say that I know nothing of Mr. Oscar Wilde except in a business capacity by publishing his 'Lady Windermere's Fan,' etc., and never introduced Shelley or any person to him in my life" (Elkin Mathews, "Mr. Elkin Mathews Writes to Us from Vigo-Street," *The Times*, 8 April 1895: 13).

174. The detail about the use of the gold brooch appears in [Millard], *Oscar Wilde: Three Times Tried*, 173.

175. It is not clear who Harry Bartlett was. This may be an erroneous transcription of the name "Barford" (see 187 and 233).

176. The details in Harris's testimony have been adapted from [anon.], "The Oscar Wilde Scandal," *Manchester Courier and Lancashire General Advertiser*, 8; and [anon.], "The Oscar Wilde Case," *Western Mail*, 13 April 1895: 5.

177. The information about Wood and his exchanges with Gill has been adapted from [anon], "The Oscar Wilde Case," *Western Mail*, 5.

178. In relation to Wood's communication, [anon.], *The Trial of Oscar Wilde* observes: "It would be left for the jury to consider what would have been the inner meaning of these and other transactions" (78). Wood's letter indicates that he thought Wilde would be easy to exploit for financial purposes. The reference to an "Easter egg" may have had some specific sexual connotation. By this time, Easter eggs—which could take the form of jewelry caskets or painted decorations on eggshells for the holy season—were associated with luxurious confectionery.

179. Walter Thornhill and Co., cutlers and silversmiths, had premises at 144–45 New Bond Street from 1878 to 1895. The business continued to trade until 1912.

180. Sir John Bridge's speech appears in [Millard], *Oscar Wilde: Three Times Tried*, 175.

181. In 1863, the Liberal MP William Saunders (1823–95) and Edward Spender (dates unknown) established the Central Press Agency (later called the Central News Limited), 5 New Bridge Street, London, which gained a reputation for embellished and unreliable reporting.

182. [Anon.], "The Oscar Wilde Case," *Western Mail*, 5.

183. John Lane, "To George Egerton," 21 April 1895, in George Egerton, *A Leaf from the "Yellow Book": The Correspondence of George Egerton*, ed. Terence De Vere White (London: Richards Press, 1958), 38.

184. W. E. Henley, "To Charles Whibley," 13 April 1895, in *The Selected Letters of W. E. Henley*, ed. Damian Atkinson (Aldershot: Ashgate, 2000), 245. Atkinson observes that the

phrase "Bugger at Bay" was coined at this time by Henley's friend the Edinburgh lawyer Charles Baxter; the phrase refers to Edwin Landseer's famous painting *The Stag at Bay* (1846).

185. The account of the third day of the arraignment and committal that follows has been adapted from [anon.], "The Oscar Wilde Scandal," *Supplement to the Manchester Courier*, 20 April 1895: 8; and [anon.], "Wilde and Taylor," *Reynolds's Newspaper*, 21 April 1895: 5. Neither of these reports quotes the examinations and cross-examinations at any length.

186. [Anon.], "Wilde and Taylor," *Sun*, 19 April 1895: 3. The description implies that many homosexual men were taking a strong interest in the proceedings.

187. [Anon.], "Oscar Wilde," *Illustrated Police Budget*, 27 April 1895: 8.

188. [Anon.], "Wilde and Taylor," *Sun*, 19 April 1895: 3.

189. [Anon.], "Wilde and Taylor," *Sun*, 19 April 1895: 3.

190. [Anon.], "Wilde and Taylor," *Sun*, 19 April 1895: 3.

191. Wilde maintained a friendship with Mason. "I hope," Wilde wrote in a letter to him in August 1894, "marriage has not made you too serious"; *The Complete Letters*, 603. Although this may be an allusion to Mason's ceremony with Taylor (described later in the paragraph), it probably refers to his marriage in 1894 to Katherine Charlotte Walker.

192. William Parker's question is recorded in [Millard], *Oscar Wilde: Three Times Tried*, 179.

193. [Anon.], "Wilde and Taylor," *Reynolds's Newspaper*, 21 April 1895: 5. Once again, it is reasonable to assume that William Parker uttered the word "sodomy."

194. [Anon.], "Wilde Case," *Star*, 19 April 1895: 3.

195. On Francis Frederick ("Fred") Kerley, see 118–19 above. Press reports often misspell his name as "Kearley."

196. Tree's name was omitted from the report in *Reynolds's Newspaper*; [anon.], "Wilde and Taylor," 21 April 1895, 5.

197. The information about Wilde's change of rooms at the Savoy appears in [Millard], *Oscar Wilde: Three Times Tried*, 180.

198. The complete transcript of Lehmann and Howard's record was read out in the first criminal trial and in excerpts during the second criminal trial (see 255–57 and 358–59). Their shorthand reports remain missing from public records (see "Introduction," 14). The longhand transcripts of the shorthand reports held in the British Library (Western Manuscripts, Loan MS 122), which form the basis of Holland's *Irish Peacock*, are not those that Lehmann and Howard took. Holland's volume is based on the notes of "Messrs. Cherer, Bennett, and David, 8 New Court, Care Street, WC," whose services the Marquess of Queensberry commissioned.

199. This and the next sentence appear in [Millard], *Oscar Wilde: Three Times Tried*, 183.

200. [Anon.], "Oscar Wilde," *Illustrated Police Budget*, 20 April 1895, 8.

201. This and the next four exchanges between Newton, Travers Humphreys, and Sir John Bridge appear in [anon.], "Wilde and Taylor," *Echo*, 19 April 1895: 2. The graver charge was presumably conspiracy.

202. Sir John Bridge's speech appears in [Millard], *Oscar Wilde: Three Times Tried*, 184. In the same volume, Millard observes: "one would have thought rape, robbery with violence, and willful murder were much more serious" than this misdemeanor (185).

203. [Anon.], "Wilde and Taylor," *Reynolds's Newspaper*, 21 April 1895, 5.

204. [Anon.], "Oscar Wilde's Trial," *Morning*, 20 April 1895: 5. The individual in question in this speculative report was rumored to be Alfred Douglas.

205. [Anon.], "Oscar Wilde's Trial," *Morning*: 5. The identity of this potential witness is not known.

206. Douglas, *Autobiography*, 110.

207. Douglas, *Autobiography*, 110.

CHAPTER FOUR

Epigraph: [anon.], "Wilde and Taylor at the Old Bailey," *Sun*, 26 April 1895: 3.

1. Information about this stage of the trial appeared in various newspapers, including [anon.], "The Oscar Wilde Case," *Manchester Courier, and Lancashire General Advertiser*, 24 April 1895: 8. The counts in the indictment are recorded on 210. The members of the grand jury were as follows (National Archives, CRIM/19):

1. Walter Vernet Charrington	2. James William Denton	3. Thomas Wright
4. James Shotter	5. Edward John Drew	6. John Percy Day
7. Thomas Day	8. Arthur Bray	9. Charles Dunch, Jr.
10. George Downing	11. Walter Bowen	12. Samuel Abrahams
13. Ernest Drew	14. Frederick George Anstey	15. Frank Ansdell
16. Frank Crawshay	17. William Bull	18. Clement Dawbarry
19. William Askwell	20. Frank Wilson	21. George Evans Plater
22. John Frederick Adair	23. George Booth	

A high percentage of the jurors, in all three of the trials that Wilde endured, were men who did not belong to the professional class. (On occasion, their Cockney origins were a source of wisecracks in the press. The *Daily Chronicle*, to take one example, noted that when the jury members were sworn in during the libel trial "[h]alf of them said 'Here' to their names, and half of them said ''Ere'"; [anon.], "Wilde v. Queensberry: The Great Libel Suit," *Daily Chronicle*, 4 April 1895: 6.) Their residential addresses were frequently located in nearby areas of north and east London, including Bow, Hackney, Hoxton, Islington, and Stamford Hill. On the provisions of the Jury Act 1826 (6 Geo. 4 c. 50) and the Juries Act 1870 (33 & 34 Vict. c. 77), which specified who could serve as jurors (namely, men between twenty-one and sixty years of age who met a property qualification) and who remained exempt from jury service, see Seymour F. Harris, *Principles of the Criminal Law: A Concise Exposition of the Nature of Crime, the Various Offences Punishable by the English Law, the Law of Criminal Procedure, and the Law of Summary Convictions*, 4th ed. (London: Stevens and Haynes, 1886), 411–20.

2. Founded in 1868 by a group of regional newspaper proprietors, the Press Association was established to provide a London-based news collection and reporting service. Its first

telegram was transmitted from the offices it occupied in Wine Office Court, off Fleet Street (the hub of the national newspaper industry in Britain). In 2005, the company changed its name to PA Group.

3. The commentary that follows in this section has been adapted from [anon.], "Wilde Case: Mr. Charles Mathews Applies for Postponement," *Star*, 24 April 1895: 3.

4. The cramped "Old Court" was built in 1774; it had a notoriously narrow corridor leading to a compact courtroom. The "New Court" was completed fifty years later. "In order to accommodate the growing number of trials, a second courtroom was added in 1824 by converting a neighbouring building. Reflecting the still increasing role of lawyers, the new courtroom had seating for attorneys, counsel [i.e., for the prosecution and defense], and law students. There were also seats for spectators, jurors in waiting, prosecutors and witnesses, and officers of the court" (Clive Emsley, Tim Hitchcock, and Robert Shoemaker, "Historical Background—History of the Old Bailey Courthouse," *Old Bailey Proceedings Online* [November 2019], https://www.oldbaileyonline.org/static/The-old-bailey.jsp).

5. The plea of justification, which John Sholto Douglas, 9th Marquess of Queensberry, submitted in support of his criminal libel against Wilde, is discussed on 21–22 above; the full document is reproduced in Merlin Holland, *Irish Peacock and Scarlet Marquess: The Real Trial of Oscar Wilde* (London: Fourth Estate, 2003), 286–91. That the plea could serve as an indictment relates to the provisions of the Libel Act 1843 (6 & 7 Vict. c. 96 s. 6).

6. [Anon.,] "Wilde Case: Mr. Charles Mathews Applies for Postponement," 3.

7. [Anon.], "The Charge against Wilde," *Daily Chronicle*, 25 April 1895: 7.

8. The phrasing (as we see on 22 above) recurs in "Plea of Justification Filed by the Defendant in Regina (Wilde) v Queensberry," National Archives, CRIM/4/1118, in Holland, *Irish Peacock*, 287–90.

9. [Anon.], "Oscar Wilde," *Illustrated Police Budget*, 27 April 1895: 9. The paper added, somewhat cryptically: "It is stated that one gentleman, who would give important evidence against Wilde and Taylor, has left England for the 'benefit of his health.' He has, it is added, left no address behind" (9). The identity of this rumored individual is unknown.

10. [Anon.], "Sale of Oscar Wilde's Effects," *Daily Chronicle*, 25 April 1895: 7. Max Beerbohm, who was close to Alfred Douglas, informed their mutual friend Reggie Turner that Ada Leverson and Ernest Leverson, both of whom gave Wilde immense support during the trials, had acquired several major artworks from the sale: "The Leversons have got the full-length portrait of Hoscar [by Harper Pennington (fig. 7, 37)] and Rothenstein's pastel of Bosie and also of him a larger nude picture by [Charles] Ricketts." (Beerbohm enjoyed rendering Wilde's first name with a Cockney aspirate.) As Rupert Hart-Davis points out, the nude was by Ricketts's personal and professional partner, Charles Haslewood Shannon (Max Beerbohm, "To Reggie Turner, 3 May 1895, in *Letters to Reggie Turner*, ed. Rupert Hart-Davis, [London: Rupert Hart-Davis, 1964], 103).

11. Donald Mead, "Oscar's Finances: The Pillage of the House Beautiful," *Wildean* 47 (2015): 50.

12. "The Central News is requested by Lord Alfred Douglas to state that in response to an urgent telegram from his mother he started yesterday for Italy to see her, but hoped to return to London in a few days. A Dalziel's cablegram says that Lord Alfred Douglas crossed yesterday from Dover to Calais, and remained at the latter place"; [anon.], "The

Oscar Wilde Case," *Portsmouth Evening News*, 27 April 1895: 3. Davison Alexander Dalziel, 1st and last Baron Dalziel of Wooler, founded Dalziel's Cable News Agency. The company, which had a branch in New York, was established in London in 1889.

13. The 1898 law specified that an individual who is accused and who chooses to give evidence at their trials cannot be asked by the prosecution or be compelled to answer "any question tending to show that he has committed or been convicted of or been charged with any offence other than that wherewith he is then charged, or is of bad character" (61 & 62 Vict. c. 36 s. 1[f]). (There were, however, three provisions listed in subparagraphs of this section that identified specific circumstances where the accused could be cross-examined by the prosecution.) The legal shift was in part motivated by a belief in fair play; the concern was that those charged with criminal offenses should be able to defend their respectable reputations by rebutting scandalous accusations. On the consequences of this change in law, especially regarding adultery cases, see Wendie Ellen Schneider, *Engines of Truth: Producing Veracity in the Victorian Courtroom* (New Haven, CT: Yale University Press, 2015), 181–209; and, regarding the problems that arose when there were misleading assumptions about good and bad character, see R. J. C. Munday, "Reflections on the Criminal Evidence Act 1898," *Cambridge Law Journal* 44, no. 1 (1985): 62–86.

14. On Bernard Abrahams's shadowy role in negotiating settlements between extortionists and their victims, see 138 above.

15. Beerbohm, [postmark 3 May 1895], *Letters to Reggie Turner*, 102.

16. The commentary and cross-examination that follow in this section have been adapted from [anon.], "Wilde–Taylor at the Old Bailey," *Reynolds's Newspaper*, 28 April 1895: 1; and [anon.], "Wilde and Taylor at the Old Bailey," unless otherwise noted.

17. [Anon.], "Wilde and Taylor at the Old Bailey": 3. The members of the jury for the trial were recorded as follows (National Archives, CRIM 6/19):

1. Thomas Rouse	2. Francis Augustus Dodd	3. Samuel James Dommett
4. George Robertson	5. Henry Goldacy Rees	6. Gilbert Lambirth
7. George Thomas Dodswell	8. William Reeves	9. Wm Walter Reeson
10. Thomas Richard Ross	11. Walter Kendall	12. Joseph Peachey

18. This and the next statement have been adapted from [anon.], "Oscar Wilde: Last Scene of the Sensational Trial," *Star*, 26 April 1895: 3.

19. This commentary has been adapted from [anon.], "The Oscar Wilde Trial: Case for the Prosecution," *Manchester Courier, and Lancashire General Advertiser*, 27 April 1895: 9.

20. [Anon.], "Oscar Wilde Prosecution: Committal," *Illustrated Police News*, 27 April 1895: 6.

21. It is not clear which volume Wilde brought into court, since none of his volumes featured a blue binding.

22. [Anon.], "Central Criminal Court. [Before Charles, J.]. 25, 20 April; 1 May. Reg. v. Wilde and Taylor," *Justice of the Peace* 59, no. 19 (11 May 1895): 296. This is the most detailed list of the counts that I have located. The exchanges between Clarke, Gill, and Justice Charles that follow, together with the commentary on case law, have been adapted

from this source, unless otherwise noted. Punctuation has been modified in several places. As R. S. Wright points out in his 1873 survey of the development of the law of conspiracy, this broad area of the criminal law could be implemented in the name of protecting public morals and decency; he mentions an 1864 case involving the procuration of an unmarried girl of seventeen years of age to become a prostitute (*The Law of Criminal Conspiracies and Agreements* [London: Butterworths, 1873], 32). The background to the law of conspiracy on sexual matters is discussed in chapter 2 (119 and 157).

23. The commentary in this sentence has been adapted from [anon.], "Oscar Wilde: Last Scene of the Sensational Trial," 3.

24. Clarke's demurral and Gill's subsequent response have been adapted from *Justice of the Peace* 59, no. 19 (11 May 1895), 296.

25. Section 20 of the 1885 Act reads as follows: "*Person charged and his wife to be competent witnesses.* Every person charged with an offence under this Act, and under section forty-eight (*a*) and sections fifty-two and fifty-five (*b*), both inclusive, of the Act of the session of the twenty-fourth and twenty-fifth years of the reign of Her Majesty, chapter one hundred, or any of such sections, and the husband or wife (*c*) of the person so charged, shall be competent but not compellable (*d*) witnesses on every hearing at every stage of such charge, except an inquiry before a grand jury" (48 & 49 Vict. c. 69 s. 20).

26. In the late nineteenth century, *Regina v. Payne and Others, L. R. 1 C. C. R.* 349 (1872) was cited in relation to the general rule of common law, where any person who was interested in the result of the proceedings was not competent to testify; as William Wills put it, a party could not "give evidence for or against any co-plaintiff or co-defendant when their cases were tried together" (*The Theory and Practice of the Law of Evidence* [London: Stevens and Sons, 1894], 83).

27. The legal press took note of Clarke's point of argument. See, for example, [anon.], "The Legal Point Raised in the Wilde Case," *Law Journal*, 4 May 1895: 285.

28. As Hyde observes: "This indictment presented an immediate difficulty. Before the year 1885, as the law then stood in England, no accused person could go into the witness box and give evidence on his own behalf. However, the Act of 1885 laid down that any person charged with an offence under that Act could give such evidence if he so wished, although he could not be compelled to do so. In regard of all other offences, both felonies and misdemeanours, *including conspiracy*, the law remained unchanged" (H. Montgomery Hyde, *Oscar Wilde*, Famous Trials 7 [Harmondsworth: Penguin, 1962], 167; emphasis in original).

29. *Regina v. Owen* (1888), in which the defendant was prosecuted on a count of indecent assault, and on a further count of common assault, was tried under section 20 of the Criminal Law Amendment Act 1885, which covered rape, indecent assault, and the forcible abduction of girls and women. The jury convicted the defendant of a common assault. The question for the Court of Crown Cases Reserved (see 514) was whether a defendant called as a witness for the defense under section 20 of the 1885 act could be legally convicted of a common assault. The conviction was affirmed.

30. *Regina v. Wealand* (1888) was widely cited in relation to an anomaly in the provisions of the 1885 Act. Arthur Reginald Butterworth explained the case, which was tried at the Old Bailey before Mr. Justice Hawkins, and the conviction was referred to the Court

of Crown Cases Reserved (see n. 33 below) for further legal opinion; see *The Criminal Evidence Act 1898* (London: Sweet and Maxwell, 1898), 40–41.

31. The commentary in this and the next paragraph has been adapted from [anon.], "Oscar Wilde," *Star*, 26 April 1895: 3.

32. Justice Charles's speech appears in *Justice of the Peace* 59, no. 19 (11 May 1895): 296.

33. Established in 1848, the Court of Crown Cases Reserved considered questions of law that emerged from the conviction of a person for treason, felony, or misdemeanor and that were reserved by the trial judge or justices to be put forward to this court. The Court of Crown Cases Reserved, in which at least five High Court judges sat together, did not permit retrial, only a judgment on a point of law.

34. In later editions of *A Digest of the Law of Evidence*, James Fitzjames Stephen (1829–94) recorded that John Duke Coleridge, 1st Baron Coleridge, found the outcome of *Regina v. Wealand* "an anomaly," one that showed "an unsatisfactory state of the law"; James Fitzjames Stephen, *A Digest of the Law of Evidence*, 9th ed. (London: Macmillan, 1919), 202.

35. [Anon.], "Oscar Wilde at the Old Bailey: Scene in Court," *Illustrated Police Budget*, 4 May 1895: 8.

36. This commentary appears in [anon.], "The Wilde–Taylor Case: Trial at the Old Bailey," *Illustrated Police News*, 4 May 1895: 3.

37. Each of the cases that Clarke cited (dating from 1871, 1864, and 1837, respectively) pointed to the problems involved in trying Wilde and Taylor jointly on counts of conspiracy (a felony) and gross indecency (a misdemeanor).

38. [Anon.], "Oscar Wilde: Last Scene of the Sensational Trial," 3.

39. Justice Charles's speech appears in [anon.], "Oscar Wilde: Last Scene of the Sensational Trial," 3.

40. This commentary appears in [anon.], "Oscar Wilde: Last Scene of the Sensational Trial," 3.

41. This and the next two sentences appear in [anon.], *The Trial of Oscar Wilde: From the Shorthand Reports* (Paris: privately printed, 1906), 17–18.

42. This sentence appears in [anon.], "Oscar Wilde: Last Scene of the Sensational Trial," 3.

43. This and the next sentence have been adapted from [anon.], *The Trial of Oscar Wilde*, 18.

44. The commentary in this and the next sentence has been adapted from [anon.], "The Oscar Wilde Trial: Case for the Prosecution," 9.

45. The commentary in the remainder of this paragraph and in all of the next two paragraphs has been adapted from [anon.], *The Trial of Oscar Wilde*, 18–20.

46. This handwritten document, which was quoted in the pretrial hearing (see chapter 2, 188), was presumably the draft of a telegram that Taylor sent to Mavor.

47. Gill was manipulating the truth. At the time of the proceedings, Wilde was forty and Mavor twenty-eight years of age.

48. The commentary in this and the next two sentences has been adapted from [anon.], "Oscar Wilde: Last Scene of the Sensational Trial," 3.

49. [Anon.], "Wilde–Taylor at the Old Bailey," 1. The same wording appears in [anon.], "Wilde and Taylor at the Old Bailey," 3.

50. [Anon.], "The Wilde–Taylor Case: Trial at the Old Bailey," 3. The same wording appears in [anon.], "Trial of Oscar Wilde: Evidence for the Prosecution," *Morning*, 27 April 1895: 1.

51. [Anon.], "The Wilde–Taylor Case," 9. The same wording appears in [anon.], "Trial of Oscar Wilde: Evidence for the Prosecution," 1.

52. The commentary in the remainder of this paragraph, together with the following six exchanges, has been adapted from [anon.], *The Trial of Oscar Wilde*, 21–22.

53. It is noticeable that the name of the restaurant where the Parker brothers dined with Wilde has changed at this point from Kettner's to the Solferino. In the ensuing examination, it remained unclear in which of the two restaurants the Parker brothers had dined with Wilde and Taylor, although later testimony from Alfred Taylor revealed that the initial meeting occurred at Kettner's.

54. This exchange between Gill and Charles Parker, followed by Gill's question, appears in [anon.], *The Trial of Oscar Wilde*, 23.

55. This and the following exchange between Gill and Charles Parker appear in [anon.], *The Trial of Oscar Wilde*, 23. At this point in its report, *Reynolds's Newspaper* remarks in square parentheses: "[Witness here described certain acts of indecency which took place in the apartment]"; [anon.], "Wilde–Taylor at the Old Bailey," 1. The *Morning* made the identical observation; [anon.], "Trial of Oscar Wilde: Evidence for the Prosecution," 2.

56. At this point in its report, *Reynolds's Newspaper* inserted the following paraphrase of Charles Parker's testimony in square parentheses: "[Witness here related proposals made by Taylor for the commission of indecencies, but to which Parker would not assent. He gave evidence as to the actual commission of gross acts at Taylor's rooms in Chapel Street]"; [anon.], "Wilde–Taylor at the Old Bailey," 1. The *Morning* provided a similar comment in [anon.], "Trial of Oscar Wilde: Evidence for the Prosecution," 2.

57. This and the next four sentences in Charles Parker's reply have been adapted from [anon.], *The Trial of Oscar Wilde*, 23–24.

58. This part of Charles Parker's reply appears in [anon.], *The Trial of Oscar Wilde*, 24.

59. This and the next two exchanges between Gill and Charles Parker appear in [anon.], *The Trial of Oscar Wilde*, 24.

60. I have supplied Gill's question.

61. At this juncture, *Reynolds's Newspaper* inserted the following paraphrase of Charles Parker's testimony in square parentheses: "[Witness described a revolting act of indecency with Wilde, which took place on one of these occasions]"; [anon.], "Wilde–Taylor at the Old Bailey," 1. The same wording appeared in the *Morning*; [anon.], "Trial of Oscar Wilde: Evidence for the Prosecution," 2. It is probable that this was a further occasion on which Charles Parker used the word "sodomy."

62. [Anon.], "Oscar Wilde: Last Scene of the Sensational Trial," 3.

63. [Anon.], "Oscar Wilde: Last Scene of the Sensational Trial," 3. A version of this remark appears in [Christopher Sclater Millard], *Oscar Wilde: Three Times Tried*, Famous

Old Bailey Trials of the XIX Century (London: Ferrestone Press, 1912), 200. The precise content of Gill's discovery is obscure.

64. This and the next exchange appear in [Millard], *Oscar Wilde: Three Times Tried*, 200–201.

65. [Anon.], "Oscar Wilde: Last Scene of the Sensational Trial," 3.

66. This commentary appears in [Millard], *Oscar Wilde: Three Times Tried*, 201.

67. This and the next two sentences have been adapted from [anon.], "Oscar Wilde: Last Scene of the Sensational Trial," 3.

68. The official record shows that Parker enlisted in the Royal Artillery on 3 October 1894. At the time, he claimed that his age was nineteen years and five months. Charles Parker served as a gunner. He was discharged shortly after Wilde's sentence.

69. This and the next exchange, together with the opening of Charles Parker's speech that follows, have been adapted from [anon.], *The Trial of Oscar Wilde*, 26.

70. William Allen was a seasoned blackmailer. His real name, according to his solicitor, Bernard Abrahams (see 138 above), was William Pea ("Proceedings of the Central Criminal Court, 25 October 1897, page 118," *Old Bailey Proceedings Online*, version 8.0, https://www.oldbaileyonline.org/images.jsp?doc=189710250118), although some newspapers recorded it as "Kea"; see, for instance, [anon.], "The Alleged West-End Blackmailing: Disclosures by Convicts," *Daily News*, 20 January 1898: 3. It appears that he was subpoenaed during the libel trial, as was his partner in crime Robert Henry Cliburn; both men absconded to Broadstairs, Kent, to escape the reach of the law. This information emerged in relation to the evidence that Allen gave in connection to the eighteen-month prison sentence he received in 1897 for receiving stolen goods from the assault on Cotsford Dick that took place in December 1896 (see 478).

71. I have supplied Gill's question.

72. Crawford Street is located between Seymour Place and North Audley Street in the West End of London. Arthur Marling, whose name crops up at certain points in the libel trial, pretrial hearing, and the two criminal trials, lived at 8 Crawford Street in 1894.

73. This part of Charles Parker's reply appears in [Millard], *Oscar Wilde: Three Times Tried*, 203. In the second criminal trial, Wood disclosed that during the proceedings he was living in Greenwich, in southeast London, under the supervision of a detective whom the Crown employed (see 350).

74. This and part of the next exchange between Clarke and Charles Parker appear in [anon.], *The Trial of Oscar Wilde*, 27.

75. In [anon.], *The Trial of Oscar Wilde* (27), Charles Parker is said to have replied: "Cranford Street" (a location in Limehouse, East London). It appears much likelier that Charles Parker resided close to, if not with, Wood and Allen in Crawford Street.

76. This and the next two exchanges between Clarke and Charles Parker appear in [anon.], *The Trial of Oscar Wilde*, 27.

77. This commentary and the next five exchanges have been adapted from [Millard], *Oscar Wilde: Three Times Tried*, 203. There was clearly some sensitivity about the employer's name, whose identity was never disclosed.

78. A "character" was "[a] testimonial, especially one given by a previous employer" (*OED*); usage was common in the eighteenth and nineteenth centuries.

79. D'Oyley Street, a fashionable thoroughfare off Sloane Street, is located close to Chelsea; it is not clear why Clarke mentioned this location.

80. The *Sun* recorded the name as Burr; [anon.], "Wilde and Taylor at the Old Bailey," 3. The identity of the individual remains unknown. The names Thurr and Thur are very rare in official records.

81. This commentary appears in [anon.], "Oscar Wilde: Last Scene of the Sensational Trial," 3.

82. A different exchange appears in [anon.], *The Trial of Oscar Wilde* (28):

CLARKE: Was the door locked during the time you describe?

CHARLES PARKER: I do not think so. It was late and the prisoner told the waiter not to come up again.

83. Part of this exchange between Clarke and Charles Parker appears in [Millard], *Oscar Wilde: Three Times Tried*, 205.

84. Robert Henry Cliburn (who also went by the name of Robert Henry Harris) was an experienced blackmailer, who received a sentence of seven years' imprisonment on 7 March 1898 for extorting funds from the composer and writer Cotsford Dick, and for acting as an accessory to William Allen (also William Pea, or Kea) in this crime. The main perpetrator was a bricklayer, Harry Saunders, who assaulted Dick on the Thames Embankment on 19 December 1896. Saunders stripped Dick of an Astrakhan-lined topcoat, a scarf-pin, a pocketbook, and other valuables. Another accessory, Arthur Marling, pawned these items. Like Cliburn, Allen, Saunders, and Marling served jail time for their involvement in this crime (see 478 and 516).

85. This and the next four exchanges between Clarke and Charles Parker appear in [Millard], *Oscar Wilde: Three Times Tried*, 205.

86. This commentary has been adapted from [anon.], "Oscar Wilde: Last Scene of the Sensational Trial," 3.

87. This and the next five exchanges between Grain and Charles Parker have been adapted from [Millard], *Oscar Wilde: Three Times Tried*, 206. On Harrington, see 504.

88. The roller-skating rink in Knightsbridge was a popular meeting-place for young homosexual men; Matt Cook, *London and the Culture of Homosexuality, 1885–1914* (Cambridge: Cambridge University Press, 2003), 25. Roller-skating had become a craze at the time.

89. The identity of the composer remains unknown, although there is some possibility that it may have been Cotsford Dick, on whom Allen and Cliburn attempted blackmail in 1896.

90. A guinea amounted to 21s. (i.e., £1 1s.); the last guinea coin was issued in 1816, when—after the "Great Recoinage"—it was replaced by the sovereign (worth £1). Even after the sovereign replaced the guinea coin, luxury goods and furnishings, bespoke clothing, attorneys' fees, and other professional services were paid for in guineas, since the name guinea sounded classier than the ordinary pound.

91. This exchange appears in [Millard], *Oscar Wilde: Three Times Tried*, 207.

92. This and the next sentence, together with the exchange that follows between Gill and Charles Parker, appears in [Millard], *Oscar Wilde: Three Times Tried*, 207.

93. This and the next two exchanges between Gill and Charles Parker, together with the commentary and the subsequent exchange between Justice Charles and the witness, have been adapted from [anon.], "The Oscar Wilde Trial: Case for the Prosecution," 9.

94. This commentary has been adapted from [anon.], "Wilde and Taylor at the Old Bailey," 3.

95. The commentary in this paragraph has been partly adapted from [Millard], *Oscar Wilde: Three Times Tried*, 207–8, since the page in the British Library copy of *Reynolds's Newspaper* has suffered damage at this point. As noted above, the name of the restaurant where the Parker brothers dined with Wilde and Taylor varies from Kettner's to the Solferino throughout the proceedings.

96. The commentary in this paragraph has been adapted from [anon.], *The Trial of Oscar Wilde*, 28.

97. I have supplied Clarke's question.

98. The names of both of the restaurants are recorded in [anon.], "Wilde and Taylor at the Old Bailey," 3.

99. In the second criminal trial, Taylor stated that he had known Ernest Macklin for many years (see 334).

100. This and the next sentence appear in [anon.], "The Oscar Wilde Trial: Case for the Prosecution," 9.

101. I have supplied Clarke's question.

102. Grant's reply, together with the subsequent exchange, appears in [Millard], *Oscar Wilde: Three Times Tried*, 209.

103. In [Millard], *Oscar Wilde: Three Times Tried*, Grant makes the following reply to Gill at this point: "The house, 13 Little College Street, is a very old-fashioned one. The ground floor was originally a baker's shop" (209). It is not clear what Gill had asked her, though the remark about the building may have to do with the fact that some of the rooms had been subdivided (see Taylor's comment on 327).

104. The unspecified "something" that Rumsby claimed to have heard may have been too indecent to report.

105. [Anon.], "Oscar Wilde at the Old Bailey: Scene in Court," 9. The same wording appears in the *Morning*; [anon.], "Trial of Oscar Wilde: Evidence for the Prosecution," 1.

106. Hock and seltzer (a mixture of German Hochheimer Riesling and carbonated mineral water, originally from the German spa town of Selters) was Wilde's favorite aperitif.

107. *Reynolds's Newspaper* glosses this act by using the phrase "an act of indecency" in square parentheses; it is likely that Wood made reference to sodomy ([anon.], "Wilde–Taylor at the Old Bailey," 1). The *Morning* recorded Wood's evidence as follows: "[Witness then admitted having committed an act of gross indecency with Wilde]"; [anon.], "Trial of Oscar Wilde: Evidence for the Prosecution," 2.

108. *Reynolds's Newspaper* incorrectly records the address as Langham Place; "Wilde–Taylor at the Old Bailey," 28 April 1895: 1.

109. This commentary has been adapted from [anon.], "Society Scandal: Trial of Oscar Wilde," *Western Mail*, 27 April 1895: 5. Douglas was devoted to horseracing, and in later life he owned racehorses. (In 1900, Douglas spent his inheritance from Queensberry on

a racing stable at Chantilly, in northern France.) It is not clear which horseracing event he attended with Burton. Aintree Racecourse, Liverpool, is famous for hosting the Grand National, a preeminent handicap steeplechase event, which began in 1839. On Wood's joke about the Easter egg, see 508 above.

110. The time of adjournment is given in the court records; National Archives, CRIM 9/16, n.p.

111. [Anon.], "Wilde–Taylor at the Old Bailey," 1. A "briefless barrister" was an attorney without a brief (i.e., he was unemployed). The term became the source of a joke on Wilde's part later in the first criminal trial (see 268).

112. The commentary that follows has been adapted from [anon.], "Second Scene of the Last Phase of the Trial," *Star*, 27 April 1895: 3.

113. During the second criminal trial, the court learned that Wood had left for America on 1 April 1893 and returned in May that year (see 351).

114. [Anon.], *The Trial of Oscar Wilde*, 29.

115. [Anon.], "Oscar Wilde's Trial: Further Evidence for the Prosecution," *Morning*, 29 April 1895: 5.

116. This commentary has been adapted from [anon.], "Wilde–Taylor at the Old Bailey," 1.

117. This exchange between Clarke and Wood appears in [anon.], "Oscar Wilde: Second Scene of the Last Phase of the Trial," 3.

118. In the libel trial, Carson asked Wilde: "And had you got Sir George Lewis to write a letter to Wood?" Wilde replied: "Yes." "And Wood," Carson continued, "had refused to go near Sir George Lewis?" Wilde responded by saying that he did not know; Holland, *Irish Peacock*, 113.

119. The proceedings of Wilde's libel trial suggest that Allen, who appropriated one of Wilde's letters from Wood, had transcribed the correspondence and sent the copy to Sir Herbert Beerbohm Tree (see 79 above). Tree returned the document to Wilde on 23 April 1893; see Holland, *Irish Peacock*, 51–52.

120. The following nine exchanges between Gill and Wood, the two exchanges between Grain and Wood, and Justice Charles's speech have been adapted from [Millard], *Oscar Wilde: Three Times Tried*, 224–25.

121. During the second criminal trial, Wood was more explicit about the circumstances in which he found the four letters. He had been invited to visit Alfred Douglas in his rooms at 34 High Street, which Douglas later stated were "over the Loder[']s Club"; Alfred Douglas, *The Autobiography of Lord Alfred Douglas*, 2nd ed. (London: Martin Secker, 1931), 86. Douglas gave Wood a set of clothes (presumably so that Wood could join his host for dinner), and Wood found Wilde and Douglas's correspondence inside the clothing. The incident occurred in March or April 1893.

122. [Anon.], "Oscar Wilde's Trial: Further Evidence for the Prosecution," 5.

123. The first exchange between Avory and Atkins has been adapted from [anon.], *The Trial of Oscar Wilde*, 31; the volume claims to represent this examination "in full." (*The Trial of Oscar Wilde*, however, mistakenly refers to the witness as "Frank Atkins" [31].)

124. [Anon.], "Oscar Wilde's Trial: Further Evidence for the Prosecution," 5. A Newmarket coat was a fashionable formal morning coat (with a cutaway front and a split back)

that had originally been designed in the eighteenth century for horseriding. In September 1894, Atkins—under the name Frederick Denny—brought a case against a young married couple at Clerkenwell Magistrates' Court. Denny claimed that the eighteen-year-old Frances Cecil had stolen from him a gold hunter watch and chain, a silver cigarette case, an old gold coin, three gold rings, and a purse containing £5 5s., which had a total value of £40. Denny had met Frances Cecil for a champagne dinner at the Café Monico, Shaftesbury Avenue, and afterward retired to a private hotel on the Euston Road. She handed these goods to her spouse, Eustace Clarence Cecil. A pawnbroker gave evidence that he had pawned the gold coin. The hearing revealed that Eustace Cecil, who came from a distinguished family, had inherited £2,000, which he had squandered. At the trial that followed in November 1894, the court learned that when Denny confronted Eustace Cecil about the theft, Cecil stated that if Denny pursued the matter through the law, he would be named as the co-respondent in a divorce case. The judge decided that there were many "extenuating circumstances" in the case, and it was agreed that the prisoners should be sent, at the expense of their friends, to New Zealand, under the terms of the Probation of First Time Offenders Act 1891 ([anon.], "Alleged Robbery by a Salesman," *Illustrated Police News*, 10 November 1894: 3).

125. A billiard-marker kept the scores in the popular game of billiards, which was played in numerous venues, including public houses and men's clubs; the job was usually undertaken by teenage boys.

126. This exchange between Avory and Atkins appears in [Millard], *Oscar Wilde: Three Times Tried*, 226–27.

127. This exchange between Avory and Atkins, together with Justice Charles's subsequent observation and the commentary that follows in the next paragraph, appears in [anon.], *The Trial of Oscar Wilde*, 31–32.

128. This and the following exchanges between Avory and Atkins have been adapted from [anon.], *The Trial of Oscar Wilde*, 32, unless otherwise noted.

129. In [Millard], *Oscar Wilde: Three Times Tried*, Atkins mentioned a different man: "On the latter occasion there was also present a young man named Harry Barford" (227).

130. This part of Atkins's reply has been adapted from [Millard], *Oscar Wilde: Three Times Tried*, 227.

131. This part of Atkins's reply has been adapted from [Millard], *Oscar Wilde: Three Times Tried*, 227.

132. The cross-examination of Atkins by Clarke that follows has been adapted from [anon.], *The Trial of Oscar Wilde*, 32–39, unless otherwise noted.

133. After the smallpox epidemic of 1886, which exerted pressure on the number of hospital beds in London, the Metropolitan Asylum Board chartered three vessels so that they could be transformed into hospital ships. At the time of Atkins's sickness, they were moored at London Reach, seventeen miles from London Bridge. They were decommissioned in 1903.

134. In [Millard], *Oscar Wilde: Three Times Tried*, the name is "Barford," not "Parker" (227); it is hard to know which is correct.

135. Atkins is presumably referring to George Alexander's production of *The Importance of Being Earnest*, which premiered at the St. James's Theatre on 14 February 1895; at the

time, however, Wilde refused to take a bow at the end of the opening performance because he had learned that the Marquess of Queensberry threatened to throw vegetables at him. It remains unclear if Wilde stepped forward to take a bow at the end of a later performance.

136. This part of Atkins's reply has been adapted from [Millard], *Oscar Wilde: Three Times Tried*, 228.

137. The commentary in this paragraph has been adapted from [Millard], *Oscar Wilde: Three Times Tried*, 228.

138. Atkins's reply, together with the next two exchanges between Clarke and Atkins, appears in [anon.], "Oscar Wilde: Second Scene of the Last Phase of the Trial," 3.

139. This speech appears in [Millard], *Oscar Wilde: Three Times Tried*, 229.

140. The identity of the "Birmingham gentleman" remains unknown.

141. [Anon.], "Wilde–Taylor at the Old Bailey," 1.

142. Lennox Gardens was a relatively new housing development completed in 1886.

143. This part of Atkins's reply appears in [anon.], "Wilde–Taylor at the Old Bailey," 1.

144. This part of Atkins's reply appears in [anon.], "Wilde–Taylor at the Old Bailey," 1.

145. The London Metropolitan Police station on Rochester Row, Westminster, which intersects with Vauxhall Bridge Road, was in operation from 1846 to 1993; the building has since been converted into flats.

146. This and the next exchange between Clarke and Atkins have been adapted from [anon.], "Wilde–Taylor at the Old Bailey," 1.

147. 35 Alderney Street is located between Warwick Way and Clarendon Street, south of Victoria Station.

148. This speech, together with several details in the next two exchanges between Clarke and Atkins, have been adapted from [Millard], *Oscar Wilde: Three Times Tried*, 230.

149. Opened in 1887, the luxury Victoria Hotel had 500 bedrooms; it formed part of a complex of three hotels originally developed in 1882 by the Northumberland Avenue Hotel Company.

150. Anderton's Hotel, 162 Fleet Street: "a favorite resort of many dining clubs and masonic lodges"; Karl Baedeker, *London and Its Environs: Handbook for Travellers*, 10th ed. (Leipsic: Baedeker, 1896), 11.

151. [Anon.], *The Trial of Oscar Wilde*, 35. There was no Gaze's Hotel in Nice, on the French Riviera. Atkins meant a hotel that took Gaze's hotel coupons, which were sold by the tour operator Messrs. H. Gaze and Son, 142 the Strand, London. According to Henry Gaze and Sons (Ltd.), *Gaze's Tourist Gazette* 10 (1897), 55, there were two hotels in Nice—the Grand Hotel Metropole and the Hotel Westminster—that accepted the company's coupons.

152. Atkins's reply appears in [anon.], "Wilde–Taylor at the Old Bailey," 1.

153. In the closing decades of the nineteenth century, Scarborough, North Yorkshire, became one of England's leading seaside resorts; it was famous for the 365-bedroom Grand Hotel, which opened in 1867, and at the time counted among the largest hotels in the world.

154. Opened in 1877, the People's Palace and Aquarium, Scarborough, was a two-and-a-quarter acre complex that included a concert hall, reading room, dining area, and fernery; at the time, the aquarium had the largest tank in the world.

155. The identity of the "foreign gentleman . . . a count," remains unknown. Rupert Croft-Cooke speculates whether this foreign nobleman could have been Marc-André Raffalovich, a wealthy Russian who had been educated in France and England; in 1893, Raffalovich became the life partner of the Catholic poet and priest John Gray, with whom he wrote a play, *The Blackmailers*, which was produced for a single performance at the Prince of Wales's Theatre on 7 June 1894. Rupert Croft-Cooke, *Feasting with Panthers: A New Consideration of Some Late Victorian Writers* (London: W. H. Allen, 1967), 276. On Raffalovich's criticisms of Wilde, see 14 and 45.

156. This part of Atkins's reply appears in [Millard], *Oscar Wilde: Three Times Tried*, 231. Croft-Cooke states, regarding Atkins's time in Scarborough, that Raffalovich "had a yacht at this time"; *Feasting with Panthers*, 276.

157. Much of Buckingham Palace Road runs alongside Victoria Station.

158. The identity of this "elderly man in the City" remains unknown.

159. The London and South Western Railway opened in stages between 1838 and 1840, and was absorbed into the Southern Railway in 1923. The railway network had a branch line to Ascot, where Ascot Racecourse—home to the major horseracing events Royal Ascot and the Gold Cup—is located.

160. This exchange between Grain and Atkins appears in [Millard], *Oscar Wilde: Three Times Tried*, 232. The identity of Driver remains unknown.

161. This and the next sentence have been adapted from [anon.], *The Trial of Oscar Wilde*, 39.

162. This commentary has been adapted from [anon.], *The Trial of Oscar Wilde*, 40–41, unless otherwise noted. St. Helen's Gardens, North Kensington, is a suburban street featuring well-appointed townhouses; it was developed as part of the St. Quintin Estate between 1867 and 1890.

163. The information about Mavor's partnership was picked up in various news reports; see, for instance, [anon.] "Trial of Oscar Wilde," *Lincolnshire Echo*, 27 April 1895: 3. His exact line of business in the City of London, the location of the London Stock Exchange, was not clarified.

164. The Gaiety Theatre (1864–1903), Aldwych, was a large 2,000-seat theatre known for music-hall entertainment, operettas, burlesques, and pantomime.

165. The commentary in this paragraph and most of the next has been adapted from [anon.], "Wilde–Taylor at the Old Bailey," 1.

166. This commentary indicates that similar gifts made by Wilde to his young male friends were circulated among members of the jury during the proceedings.

167. This commentary has been adapted from [anon.], *The Trial of Oscar Wilde*, 41.

168. The cross-examinations between Clarke and Mavor, Grain and Mavor, and Gill and Mavor that follow have been adapted from [anon.], *The Trial of Oscar Wilde*, 41–42.

169. Clarke was referring to Alfred Douglas. There appears to have been a gentlemen's agreement between Clarke and Gill not to refer explicitly to Douglas at this point.

170. [Anon.], "Wilde–Taylor at the Old Bailey," 1.

171. The commentary has been adapted from [anon.], *The Trial of Oscar Wilde*, 42; it is not clear from the report whether Gill or Avory undertook the cross-examination for the prosecution.

172. The commentary in this and the next two sentences, together with Shelley's subsequent speech and the two sentences that follow thereafter, has been adapted from [anon.], "Wilde–Taylor at the Old Bailey," 1.

173. The commentary in this sentence and most of the remainder of this paragraph has been adapted from [anon.], *The Trial of Oscar Wilde*, 42–43. Wilde stayed at the Hotel Metropole, Brighton, Sussex, in March 1891; he also had rooms there with Douglas from 4 to 7 October 1894. Wilde and his family stayed at Grove Farm, Felbrigg, near Cromer, Norfolk during the later part of the summer (August–September) 1892.

174. The commentary in this and the next two sentences has been adapted from [anon.], "Wilde–Taylor at the Old Bailey," 1.

175. The exchanges between Clarke and Shelley that follow have been adapted from [anon.], *The Trial of Oscar Wilde*, 43–45, unless otherwise noted.

176. This exchange between Clarke and Shelley appears in [anon.], "Wilde–Taylor at the Old Bailey," 1.

177. [Anon.], "Wilde–Taylor at the Old Bailey," 1.

178. This commentary and the next three exchanges between Clarke and Shelley have been adapted from [anon.], *The Trial of Oscar Wilde*, 45.

179. This and the next exchange between Clarke and Shelley appear in [anon.], "Wilde–Taylor at the Old Bailey," 1. The letter (dated 14 June 1894), in which Shelley informed Wilde that Lane was a "viper," had been read aloud by Clarke during the libel trial, though at the time Clarke had suppressed Lane's name (Holland, *Irish Peacock*, 235).

180. [Anon.], "Wilde–Taylor at the Old Bailey," 1.

181. This exchange between Clarke and Shelley has been adapted from the *Star*; [anon.], "Oscar Wilde: Second Scene of the Last Phase of the Trial," 3.

182. This and the next four exchanges between Clarke and Shelley appear in [anon.], *The Trial of Oscar Wilde*, 45–46.

183. This commentary, the exchange between Clarke and Shelley that follows, and the subsequent commentary have been adapted from [anon.], "Wilde–Taylor at the Old Bailey," 1. Shelley's correspondence with Wilde has not survived.

184. This and the next seven exchanges between Clarke and Shelley have been adapted from [anon.], *The Trial of Oscar Wilde*, 46–47.

185. This exchange between Clarke and Shelley appears in [anon.], "Wilde–Taylor at the Old Bailey," 1.

186. This and the next three exchanges between Clarke and Shelley have been adapted from [anon.], *The Trial of Oscar Wilde*, 47.

187. Fulham Police Station, 520 Fulham Road, London, opened in 1863, and was extended during the 1890s before a new building was established, on adjoining Heckfield Place, in 1914. Further information can be found in Peter Kennison, *Discovering More behind the Blue Lamp: Policing Central and North and South West London* (London: Coppermill Press, 2004), 221–28. In 2016, the main building of Fulham Police Station closed; Fulham Boys' School now occupies the premises. The police station was located just over half a mile from Shelley's home in Hildyard Road.

188. The commentary in this paragraph, together with Justice Charles's comment and the exchanges between Clarke and Atkins that follow, has been adapted from [anon.],

"Wilde–Taylor at the Old Bailey," 1; and [anon.], *The Trial of Oscar Wilde*, 48–49. There are very close resemblances between the records in both of these sources.

189. The identity of the man from whom Atkins and Burton attempted to extort funds remains unknown.

190. Occupying a building erected in 1854 in Leicester Square in the West End of London, the Alhambra Theatre opened its doors in 1858 as a music-hall; the building was destroyed by fire in 1882, and a new building—featuring Moorish architecture—took its place the following year.

191. [Anon.], "Oscar Wilde at the Old Bailey: Scene in Court," 8; and [anon.], "Wilde: Second Day of the Wilde Trial," *Sun*, 27 April 1895: 3.

192. The commentary in this and the next paragraph has been adapted from [anon.], "Wilde–Taylor at the Old Bailey," 1.

193. The commentary in the remainder of this paragraph has been adapted from [Millard], *Oscar Wilde: Three Times Tried*, 243.

194. The time of adjournment appears in the court records; National Archives, CRIM 9/16, n.p.

195. The commentary in this and the two next paragraphs has been adapted from [anon.], "The Oscar Wilde Trial: Case for the Prosecution Closed," *Manchester Courier, and Lancashire General Advertiser*, 30 April 1895: 3.

196. [Anon.], "Wilde's Trial: The Two in the Dock," *Sun*, 29 April 1895: 3.

197. [Anon.], "Wilde's Trial: The Two in the Dock," 3.

198. [Anon.], "Wilde's Trial: The Two in the Dock," 3.

199. The cross-examinations and commentary that follow have been adapted from [Millard], *Oscar Wilde: Three Times Tried*, 244–57, unless otherwise noted.

200. Robert Harborough Sherard, "Ultima Verba: With Some Reflections on the Mischief Caused by Pernicious Amnesia—Being an Open Letter to George Bernard Shaw," British Library, Add. MS 81688, fo. 90.

201. Sherard, "Ultima Verba," fo. 90.

202. Perkins presumably commented on the presence of an unidentified young man in Wilde's room, as well as the excrement found on the bed linens. Harris claimed that, during his lunchtime meeting with Wilde after the first criminal trial, Wilde had concurred: "it was probably the chambermaids' testimony which had weighed most heavily against him" (Frank Harris, *Oscar Wilde: His Life and Confessions*, 2 vols. [New York: privately printed, 1916], 1:284).

203. This detail appears in [anon.], "The Oscar Wilde Trial: Case for the Prosecution Closed," 3. Taylor used this brooch to tie his nightgown; it came from his collection of jewelry (see 226 and 323 above). The item, which was presumably designed as a woman's accessory, was presented as evidence of Taylor's predilection for sexual indecency.

204. The commentary in this and the next four paragraphs has been adapted from [anon.], "Wilde–Taylor: Result of the Trial," *Reynolds's Newspaper*, 5 May 1895: 1.

205. The detail about the writs appears in [anon.], "The Oscar Wilde Case: Proceedings at the Old Bailey," *Western Mail*, 30 April 1895: 6. The "slip of paper" was the note from Alfred Taylor to Sydney Mavor (see 188).

206. There appears to have been an element of deception here, which the ensuing examination corrected. At the time, Littlechild was working as a private investigator for Queensberry's solicitor, Charles Russell.

207. References to these documents can be found above (189–90, 195, 251, and 334).

208. The details about the exhibits in this and the next sentence have been adapted from [anon.], "The Oscar Wilde Case: Proceedings at the Old Bailey," 6.

209. In British English, a "bob" was an everyday word for a shilling.

210. Robert Buchanan, "Camera Obscura," *Star*, 16 April 1895: 4. This letter sparked an exchange in the same newspaper between Buchanan, Alfred Douglas, and Queensberry. A few days later during the pretrial hearing, Buchanan insisted: "Personally, I would not condemn even a dog on the kind of tainted evidence which has been foreshadowed during the recent preliminary inquiry, but the case, as I said, is still only sub judice, and none of us yet know with any certainty whether or not a jury of Englishmen will pronounce Mr. Wilde guilty" (Robert Buchanan, "Oscar Wilde: To the Editor of the 'Star,'" *Star*, 20 April 1895: 3). Buchanan recognized that much of the evidence came from questionable witnesses.

211. Buchanan, "Camera Obscura," 4.

212. The literary author of the letter that Justice Charles refused to share with Clarke remains unknown. It seems likely to have been Buchanan, who proved highly critical of the pretrial hearing. Still, the judge may have been exercising discretion in order to protect the identity of another literary figure.

213. The commentary in this paragraph has been adapted from [anon.], "The Oscar Wilde Case: Proceedings at the Old Bailey," 6.

214. The *Western Mail* presents Read's rendition of Queensberry's message on the visiting card as "For Oscar Wilde, posing as a s———"; [anon.], "The Oscar Wilde Case: Proceedings at the Old Bailey," 6.

215. Read's comment about the witnesses who were called is not accurate. There were various males mentioned in Queensberry's plea of justification who did not give evidence in the pretrial hearing and criminal trials: Ernest Scarfe (whose name came up in the proceedings several times), Herbert Tankard (who had moved from London to Calais), Walter Grainger (who was seventeen when he was in Wilde's company at Goring-on-Thames from late June or early July through October 1893), and Alphonse Conway (the sixteen-year-old whom Wilde met on the beach at Worthing, Sussex, on 20 August 1894). Grainger was present at the libel trial. During the second criminal trial, Wilde informed Sir Frank Lockwood that he had seen Conway outside the Old Bailey, and Wilde confirmed that he had also seen Grainger near the courtroom (see 375 and 377). As Edmonds observes, "[w]hat Alphonse was doing there is a matter of conjecture," since there was no charge against Wilde in relation to Conway; it seems probable that Conway was in attendance at the Old Bailey because, as Antony Edmonds suggests, he was "still on [Queensberry's] payroll, in the [marquess's] hope of embarrassing and distressing Wilde and making a public display" (*Oscar Wilde's Scandalous Summer: The 1894 Worthing Holiday and the Aftermath* [Stroud: Amberley, 2014], 81). The same inferences can probably be made about Grainger's presence during the trials.

216. The available press reports do not refer to any discussion that took place on Friday, 26 April 1895 about the wish to submit the shorthand record of Wilde's libel suit against Queensberry as evidence that should be called upon in the Crown prosecution. It is probable that this conversation took place in private with Justice Charles.

217. Clarke's objection was that the record of only the two pretrial hearings before the libel case should be read aloud to the jury during the first criminal trial. These hearings, which took place at Great Marlborough Street Magistrates' Court on 2 and 9 March 1895, are reproduced in Holland, *Irish Peacock*, 3–22.

218. Clarke's cross-examination of Wilde during *Regina (Wilde) v. Queensberry* contains some small differences in Holland, *Irish Peacock* (64):

> CLARKE: Your attention has been called, I think, to the statements which are made in the plea here?
>
> WILDE: Yes.
>
> CLARKE: Referring to different persons and impugning your conduct with them?
>
> WILDE: Yes.
>
> CLARKE: Is there any truth whatever in either of those accusations?
>
> WILDE: There is no truth whatever in any one of them.

219. The commentary in this paragraph has been adapted from [anon.], "The Oscar Wilde Case: Proceedings at the Old Bailey," 6; small changes have been made to punctuation.

220. [Anon.], "The Oscar Wilde Case: Proceedings at the Old Bailey," 6. The aphorism should read: "Wickedness is a myth invented by good people to account for the curious attractiveness of others"; Oscar Wilde, "Phrases and Philosophies for the Use of the Young," *Chameleon* 1, no. 1 (1894): 1, reprinted in *The Collected Works of Oscar Wilde*, ed. Robert Ross, 14 vols. (London: Methuen, 1908), 14:176–78.

221. [Anon.], "The Oscar Wilde Case: Proceedings at the Old Bailey," 6. In Holland, *Irish Peacock* (6), the cross-examination during the libel trial runs as follows:

> CARSON: Then, I suppose I may take it that in your opinion the piece ["The Priest and the Acolyte"] was not immoral?
>
> WILDE: Worse, it was badly written. (*Laughter.*)

222. [Anon.], "Oscar Wilde: More Witnesses Are Called for the Prosecution," *Star*, 29 April 1895: 3. Of the "Oscarisms" mentioned in the *Star*'s report, the first three appear in "Phrases and Philosophies for the Use of the Young." (The third should read: "The condition of perfection is idleness.") The fourth—"Adoration is a thing I reserve for myself"—condenses Wilde's reply to the following question that Carson put to him: "Have you ever felt the feeling of adoring madly a beautiful male person many years younger than yourself?" Wilde responded: "'I have never given adoration to anybody except myself.' (*Loud laughter*)" (Holland, *Irish Peacock*, 91). This part of Carson's cross-examination of Wilde focused on a passage in the 1890 text of *The Picture of Dorian Gray* where Basil Hallward says to the protagonist: "I quite admit that I adored madly, extravagantly, absurdly" (Wilde, *Complete Works*, 3:90). The next three "Oscarisms" also come from the same passage in Wilde's novel, where Lord Henry Wotton speaks to Dorian Gray (3:128); Carson quoted

extensively from this part of the 1890 text and asked whether Wilde thought that "what [the characters] were talking about was a charge of sodomy." As Carson observed, Wilde excised this passage when the novel appeared in the expanded text, which Ward, Lock, and Co. published as a single volume in 1891. Carson went so far as to say that the lines in the 1890 text were "left out of the purged edition"; this was a description that Wilde denied (Holland, *Irish Peacock*, 101–2, 86).

223. [Anon.], "Oscar Wilde: More Witnesses Are Called for the Prosecution," 3.

224. This and the next sentence have been adapted from [anon.], "The Oscar Wilde Case: Proceedings at the Old Bailey," 6.

225. [Anon.], "Oscar Wilde: More Witnesses Are Called for the Prosecution," 3.

226. This and the next two sentences have been adapted from [anon.], "The Oscar Wilde Case: Proceedings at the Old Bailey," 6.

227. See Holland, *Irish Peacock*, 112.

228. This and the next seven sentences have been adapted from [Millard], *Oscar Wilde: Three Times Tried*, 255.

229. Oscar Wilde, "To the Editor of the *Scots Observer*," 9 July 1890, in *The Complete Letters of Oscar Wilde*, ed. Merlin Holland and Rupert Hart-Davis (London: Fourth Estate, 2000), 438.

230. Wilde, "To the Editor of the *Scots Observer*," 9 July 1890, 439.

231. [Anon.], "The Oscar Wilde Case: Proceedings at the Old Bailey," 6. The report garbles Wilde's letter, which reads: "An artist, sir, has no ethical sympathies at all. Virtue and wickedness are to him simply what the colours on his palette are to the painter . . . . That the editor of the *St. James's Gazette* should have employed Caliban as his art-critic was possibly natural. The editor of the *Scots Observer* should not have allowed Thersites to make mows in his review" (Wilde, "To the Editor of the *Scots Observer*," 9 July 1890, 439). The reviews to which Wilde alludes are [Samuel Henry Jeyes], "A Study in Puppydom," *St. James's Gazette*, 24 June 1890: 3–4; and [Charles Whibley?], unsigned notice, *Scots Observer*, 5 July 1890: 181, reprinted in *Oscar Wilde: The Critical Heritage*, ed. Karl Beckson (London: Routledge and Kegan Paul, 1970), 67–71 and 74. In Shakespeare's *The Tempest* (c. 1610–11), Caliban is a half-human, half-monstrous character, and in *Troilus and Cressida* (1602), Thersites, who takes his name from the violent Greek officer of the Trojan War, is an abusive comic servant. Both reviews were extremely hostile (see 60 above).

232. This sentence and the remaining commentary, together with both Clarke's and Justice Charles's comments, have been adapted from [Millard], *Oscar Wilde: Three Times Tried*, 255–57. The detail about the time of the adjournment appears in [anon.], "The Oscar Wilde Case: Proceedings at the Old Bailey," 6.

233. On the Court of Crown Cases Reserved, see 514 above.

234. The time of adjournment is given in the court records; National Archives, CRIM 9/16, n.p.

235. The commentary that follows has been largely adapted from [anon.], "Wilde–Taylor: Result of the Trial," 1; and [Millard], *Oscar Wilde: Three Times Tried*, 259–68.

236. The principle of whether the prosecution or the defense should take the "last word" in a criminal trial became a bone of contention in the second Crown proceedings against Wilde (see 364).

237. Clarke was mistaken. This quotation does not originate with Samuel Taylor Coleridge (1772–1831). In *Biographia Literaria* (1817), Coleridge espoused the opposite view: "The men of the greatest genius, as far as we can judge from their own works or from the accounts of their contemporaries, appear to have been of calm and tranquil temper in all that related to themselves. In the inward assurance of permanent fame, they seem to have been either indifferent or resigned with regard to immediate reputation. Through all the works of Chaucer there reigns a cheerfulness, a manly hilarity, which makes it almost impossible to doubt a correspondent habit of feeling in the author himself"; Samuel Taylor Coleridge, *Biographia Literaria; or, Biographical Sketches of My Literary Life and Opinions*, ed. James Engell and W. Jackson Bate, in *Collected Works of Samuel Taylor Coleridge*, 16 vols., Bollingen Series LXXV (Princeton: Princeton University Press, 1985), 7.1:33.

238. The English essayist, fiction writer, and classical scholar Walter Pater was arguably the most significant critical influence upon Wilde. In the libel proceedings, when Carson asked Wilde if the 1891 text of *The Picture of Dorian Gray* "was modified and purged a good deal" from the 1890 version in *Lippincott's*, Wilde replied that Pater had spoken to him about the novel one afternoon: "I say there were additions made in one case or two—in one case, certainly. It had been pointed out to me not by any newspaper criticism or anything, but by the only critic of this century I set high, Mr. Walter Pater, he had pointed out to me that a certain passage was liable to misconstruction" (Holland, *Irish Peacock*, 78). In 1891, Pater published a thoughtful review of *The Picture of Dorian Gray*, in which he claims that Wilde "carries on . . . the brilliant critical work of Matthew Arnold"; "A Novel by Mr. Oscar Wilde," *Bookman*, November 1891: 59.

239. During the libel trial, Wilde stated that he had met the unnamed Bloxam at the rooms of a friend at The Albany, Piccadilly, central London. See 136 and 491.

240. Lady Sibyl Montgomery, Marchioness of Queensberry's petition for divorce, on the grounds of adultery, was heard on 22 January 1887. Two of the marquess's former servants, Thomas Gill and William Hucking, deposed that in Queensberry's rooms at 24 St James's Street, London—a location that Lady Sibyl never visited—they witnessed an unnamed woman entering the premises on certain occasions in 1885 and 1886. *The Times* reported that Hucking "satisfied himself that his master and the lady were in the bedroom"; [anon.], "The Queensberry Divorce Case," *The Times*, 24 January 1887: 4.

241. The letters in question presumably include those between the Marquess of Queensberry and Alfred Douglas, which had been quoted at length during the libel proceedings. During the libel case, Clarke read a letter from Wilde's solicitors, Humphreys, Son, and Kershaw, in which they informed Queensberry that he had "most foully and infamously libelled" Wilde and Douglas; Holland, *Irish Peacock*, 245.

242. Gill's cross-examination of Wilde that follows has been adapted from [anon.], *The Trial of Oscar Wilde*, 56–58; and [anon.], "Wilde–Taylor Case: Evidence of the Prisoner," *Daily Telegraph*, 1 May 1895: 4.

243. Gill's question is slightly misleading, insofar as there was only one issue of the *Chameleon*, which appeared in December 1894 before the publisher, Gay and Bird, withdrew it from sale.

244. In the libel trial, Wilde referred to Douglas's "In Praise of Shame" and "Two Loves" as "exceedingly beautiful poems"; Holland, *Irish Peacock*, 67.

245. Cross-examination to credit (i.e., to test a witness's creditworthiness) is a technique that frequently aims to expose information about a defendant's private life that sullies the individual's reputation. There was a longstanding legal debate—one that came to attention in the press during the 1880s and 1890s—about the advisability of this method of investigating a defendant's character. For a critique of the practice, see [anon.], "The Abuse of Cross-Examination," *Saturday Review*, 12 December 1891: 657–58; and for a defense, see George Bramwell, 1st Baron Bramwell, "Cross-Examination," *Nineteenth Century* 31 (1892): 183–87. Schneider demonstrates the ways in which, during the later nineteenth century, "[e]veryone agreed that cross-examination as to character was necessary on some level"; still, "Victorian lawyers were also keenly sensitive to the importance of reputation and the dangers posed by the revelation of old misconduct in an age that treasured character above all else"; *Engines of Truth*, 82.

246. Alfred Douglas, "In Praise of Shame," *Chameleon* 1, no. 1 (1894): 25.

247. Clarke's comment, together with Gill's cross-examination of Wilde and Justice Charles's observations that follow, has been adapted from [Millard], *Oscar Wilde: Three Times Tried*, 269–72; and [anon.], *The Trial of Oscar Wilde*, 58.

248. The two letters that Wilde mentioned—the one from Babbacombe, Devon (January 1893), where he had been staying with his family, and the other from the Savoy Hotel (March 1893)—were quoted by Gill later in the proceedings (see 367–68).

249. This wording appears in [anon.], "Wilde–Taylor: Result of the Trial," 1. Wilde alludes to the love between David and Jonathan in the Bible: "I am distressed for thee, my brother Jonathan: very pleasant hast thou been unto me: thy love to me was wonderful, passing the love of women" (2 Samuel 1:26); to the dialogues of the Greek philosopher Plato (such as the *Phaedrus* and the *Symposium*); to the homoerotic elements in the sonnets of Italian artist Michelangelo (Michelangelo di Lodovico Buonarroti Simoni), which had become clear through the 1878 English translation of John Addington Symonds; and to the male poetic voice's desire for the "fair youth" (the mysterious "Mr. W. H.") of the *Sonnets* (1609) by William Shakespeare.

250. Gill's cross-examination of Wilde that follows has been adapted from [anon.], "Wilde–Taylor Case: Evidence of the Prisoner," 4, unless otherwise noted.

251. Gill's question about Douglas's going "into rooms" referred to taking rented accommodation.

252. From this point onward, Gill's cross-examination of Wilde has been adapted from [anon.], *The Trial of Oscar Wilde*, 59–63.

253. "Truth may be found at the bottom of a well" (old adage).

254. Wilde's joke appears to poke fun at Gill's reputation as either a flirtatious or a brazen man. In 1892, the American *Travelers Record* observed: "'Ta-ra-ra Boom-de-ay.' That's what Lottie Collins sings at the Gaiety; but you can hear it any day at the Law Courts. It is the song that all Mr. C. F. Gill's clients sing when he 'winks the other eye' at the jury and pulls the rockiest case out of the fire" ([anon.], "How It Would Work: For Professional Men to Compete by Advertising Methods," *Travelers Record*, July 1892: 8). Collins was a

celebrated music-hall entertainer. With its suggestive lyrics about a "queen of swell society," the song was accompanied by Collins with a risqué skirt dance, in which she made high kicks that displayed her thighs, stockings, and garters.

255. [Anon.], "Wilde–Taylor Case: Evidence of the Prisoner," 4.

256. Gill's cross-examination of Wilde that follows, together with Justice Charles's and Clarke's remarks, has been adapted from [Millard], *Oscar Wilde: Three Times Tried*, 274–79; and [anon.], "Wilde–Taylor Case: Evidence of the Prisoner," 4.

257. On Wilde's absence from the court after mid-morning on the final day of the libel trial, see 138 above.

258. It is not clear who else attended the Independent Theatre with Wilde and Shelley. On this event, see 185 above.

259. During the libel trial, Clarke read out passages from several of Shelley's letters to Wilde; none of them contained these words. Clarke also read aloud from Shelley's correspondence to Wilde during the second criminal trial (see 346–48).

260. Pastille burners, which enjoyed popularity especially in the 1820–50 period, were used to deodorize the air in English homes; most porcelain manufacturers produced them.

261. Queensberry's solicitor, Charles Russell, tracked Herbert Tankard—a former page-boy at the Savoy Hotel—to Calais, where Russell took a witness statement. Tankard claimed that Wilde had kissed him fondly, and regularly gave him a large tip of 2s. 6d.; Neil McKenna, *The Secret Life of Oscar Wilde* (London: Century: 2003), 221–12.

262. The *Star* observed that this was "the occasion of a flying visit to Monte Carlo"; [anon.], "Oscar Wilde: Fourth Day—Some Surprises," 30 April 1895: 3. Wilde and Douglas traveled together to Monte Carlo on 12 March, and they returned to London a week later. Their return was noted in the press (see, for example, [anon.], [untitled], *Morning Post*, 20 March 1895: 5). It is not clear at which hotel in Calais Tankard was employed.

263. [Anon.], "Oscar Wilde: Fourth Day—Some Surprises," 3.

264. This and the next two exchanges between Gill and Taylor appear in [anon.], "Wilde and Taylor: Conspiracy Charges Withdrawn," *Echo*, 30 April 1895: 3.

265. Marlborough College, a private secondary school located in Marlborough, Wiltshire, was founded in 1843 to educate sons of Church of England clergy; it became fully coeducational in 1989. Taylor was educated privately before attending Marlborough College for a year (1877–78). It has not been possible to verify why he left the school.

266. In 1880, Taylor entered the militia, going into the 4th Battalion of the Royal Fusiliers, City of London Regiment.

267. This and the next four sentences have been adapted from [anon.], *The Trial of Oscar Wilde*, 63–64.

268. [Anon.], "Wilde–Taylor Case: Evidence of the Prisoner," 4.

269. The exchanges between Gill and Taylor that follow have been adapted from [Millard], *Oscar Wilde: Three Times Tried*, 281–82, unless otherwise noted.

270. Since the early eighteenth century, Turkish dresses had been fashionable items to be worn at fancy-dress balls; in all probability, Taylor's garment was the type of so-called "harem costume" that features loosely fitting trousers under knee-length skirts.

271. Opened in 1884, the 2,000-seat Empire Theatre transformed three years later into a music-hall known as the Empire Theatre of Varieties; like the Alhambra (see 524 above), the theatre had a promenade around the auditorium, where open bars were located that became associated with prostitution. On 30 July 1894, the purity campaigner Laura Ormiston Chant visited the Empire with a friend in order to witness firsthand the female prostitutes soliciting clients on the promenade. Later that year, Chant led a well-publicized campaign to persuade the London County Council (LCC) to deny the renewal of the Empire's theatre license. George Joseph Edwardes, manager of the Empire, hired C. F. Gill as his defense attorney before the LCC's Theatre Committee. The dispute about the license led to the temporary closure of the theatre from 27 October to 2 November 1894. On reopening, the promenade had been cleared of sex workers and the open bars had dwindled in number. On Gill's defense of Edwardes, see Joseph Donohue, *Fantasies of Empire: The Empire Theatre of Varieties and the Licensing Controversy of 1894* (Iowa City: University of Iowa Press, 2005), 103–4.

272. This and the next eight exchanges between Gill and Taylor appear in [anon.], "Wilde and Taylor: Conspiracy Charges Withdrawn," 3.

273. I have supplied Gill's question.

274. For details about the police raid at Fitzroy Street, see above (134–35 and 333).

275. This and the next eight exchanges between Gill and Taylor have been adapted from the commentary in [anon.], "Wilde and Taylor: Conspiracy Charges Withdrawn," 3.

276. Rupert Croft-Cooke asserts, without providing documentation, that the female impersonator and receiver of stolen goods "Marling [see 134 and 333 above] . . . introduced Scarfe to Taylor"; Croft-Cooke, *Feasting with Panthers*, 277.

277. I have supplied Gill's question.

278. The Prince of Wales's Theatre, which is located on Coventry Street, near Leicester Square, central London, was opened in 1884, rebuilt in 1937, and refurbished in 2004. In the 1880s and early 1890s, the theatre was known for its popular productions.

279. [Anon.] "Oscar Wilde: Fourth Day—Some Surprises," 3.

280. Grain's examination of Taylor has been adapted from [anon.] "Oscar Wilde: Fourth Day—Some Surprises," 3; and [anon.], "Wilde and Taylor: Conspiracy Charges Withdrawn," *Echo*, 3.

281. Clarke's speech has been adapted from [anon.], "Wilde–Taylor Case: Evidence of the Prisoner," 4; and (in greater detail) from [Millard], *Oscar Wilde: Three Times Tried*, 283–91. Both the *Daily Telegraph*'s report and Millard's account are partly in indirect and partly in direct speech.

282. David Rizzio was the private secretary of Mary, Queen of Scots, who reigned as queen of Scotland from 1542 to 1567 and was queen consort of France from 1559 to 1560; her second husband, Henry, Lord Darnley, initiated the murder of Mary's secretary, David Rizzio, who was stabbed fifty-six times, on the suspicion that he had impregnated her. There are several well-known paintings of the brutal homicide, including *The Murder of David Rizzio* (1833) by Sir William Allan.

283. [Anon.], "Wilde–Taylor: Result of the Trial," 1. The note presumably contained Wilde's thanks for Clarke's impressive summing-up.

284. [Anon.], "Oscar Wilde: Fourth Day—Some Surprises," 3.

285. [Anon.], *The Trial of Oscar Wilde*, 68.

286. The commentary in this paragraph has been adapted from [anon.], *The Trial of Oscar Wilde*, 68–69; and [Millard], *Oscar Wilde: Three Times Tried*, 291–92.

287. In Britain, a farthing was a coin worth a quarter of a penny; it was minted from 1714 until 1960, when it ceased to be legal tender. Traditionally, a farthing was synonymous with the smallest denomination of value imaginable.

288. The commentary in this and the next six paragraphs has been adapted from [anon.], *The Trial of Oscar Wilde*, 69–70; and [Millard], *Oscar Wilde: Three Times Tried*, 292–94.

289. At this juncture, Gill's memory appears to be failing. There is no record that Wilde entertained any young man at Nice.

290. The court records confirm that the case was adjourned at 7.00 p.m.; National Archives, CRIM 9/16, n.p.

291. [Anon.], "Wilde: Impressive Summing Up by Mr. Justice Charles," *Star*, 1 May 1895: 3; some small changes have been made to punctuation.

292. [Anon.], "Wilde: The Last Scene in the Trial," *Sun*, 1 May 1895: 3.

293. The commentary on and reproduction of Justice Charles's summing-up that follow, together with the proceedings to the end of the first criminal trial, have been adapted from [anon.], "Wilde–Taylor Case: Summing-Up and Result," *Daily Telegraph*, 2 May 1895: 4. This report represents Justice Charles's summing-up through direct and indirect speech.

294. George Bramwell, 1st Baron Bramwell, remained vigilant about the principle of convicting the accused on uncorroborated evidence. In *A History of the Criminal Law in England*, James Fitzjames Stephen observes: "The principle that the uncorroborated evidence of an accomplice is not to be acted upon, which is now well established, though it cannot be said to have the force of a positive rule of law, seems to have been unknown, and was at all events systematically disregarded and even disavowed in the seventeenth century"; *A History of the Criminal Law in England*, 3 vols. (London: Macmillan, 1883), 3:401). Justice Charles's observation may also relate to Bramwell's comments on the practice of not permitting the accused to speak in one's defense. During the House of Lords' deliberation of the Law of Evidence Amendment Bill 1886, Bramwell remained concerned that, even though the provisions of the Explosives Act 1875 and Criminal Law Amendment Act 1885 granted accused individuals the right to give evidence in their defense, the law needed to be extended: "It must be a most grievous thing to an accused person that, when he could prove his innocence, he was not allowed to give evidence" (*Hansard's Parliamentary Debates*, 3rd series, vol. 303, 9 March 1886, col. 223 [https://api.parliament.uk/historic-hansard/lords/1886/mar/09/no-18-second-reading#column_223]).

295. "The fear of the Lord is the beginning of wisdom" (Proverbs 9:10; Psalms 111:10).

296. [Anon.], "Wilde–Taylor: Result of the Trial," 1. The list of questions also appeared elsewhere, such as [anon.], "Wilde: The Last Scene in the Trial," 3. These questions do not represent the subdivisions that became a matter of issue among the jurors.

297. [Anon.], "Wilde: Impressive Summing Up," 3; some minor changes in punctuation and wording have been inserted here.

298. This exchange between Justice Charles and the foreman of the jury appears in [anon.], "Oscar Wilde Case: Judge's Summing-Up," *Globe*, 1 May 1895: 5.

299. [Anon.], "Wilde: To Be Re-Tried at the Next Sessions," *Star*, 2 May 1895: 3.

300. [Anon.], "Oscar Wilde Case: Judge's Summing-Up," 5.

301. [Anon.], "Wilde–Taylor Case: Summing-Up and Result," 4.

302. Beerbohm, "To Reggie Turner," [postmark 3 May 1895], 103.

303. Beerbohm, "To Reggie Turner," [postmark 3 May 1895], 103. The term "renters" refers to male prostitutes ansd extortionists.

304. George Egerton, "To John Lane," 5 May 1895, Clark Library, MS Wilde, B855IL L265 1895., Box 7, Folder 63. Besides Lord Rosebery, the Liberal politician who remained prime minister until 21 June 1895, Egerton is referring to the noted painter Sir Frederic Leighton; the critic Walter Pater, whose aesthetic writings left a deep impression on Wilde's own works; and John Addington Symonds, the prolific homophile author whose research on the Italian Renaissance was an important resource for Wilde.

305. The report is supposed to have appeared in the *Morning*, 8 May 1895 (see [Millard], *Oscar Wilde: Three Times Tried*, 322), though it was not present in the microfilm of the edition I consulted. *Reynolds's Newspaper* commented on the "cruel, heartless, and reckless" reporting of this "Tory organ," pointing out that "Wilde has not been convicted of any crime" at this juncture; the paper added that the *Morning* should be taken to "the High Court for contempt" ([anon.], "Oscar Wilde's Trial," *Reynolds's Newspaper*, 12 May 1895: 1).

306. [Millard], *Oscar Wilde: Three Times Tried*, 322.

CHAPTER FIVE

Epigraph: Ada Leverson, *Letters to the Sphinx from Oscar Wilde, with Reminiscences of the Author* (London: Duckworth 1930), 36.

1. [Anon.], "Imperial Parliament," *Evening Standard*, 4 May 1895: 2. Mathews was presumably referring to the Habeas Corpus Act 1679 (31 Cha. 2 c. 2), which gave prisoners and their legal representatives the right to challenge their detention.

2. [Anon.], "Oscar Wilde: The Amount of Bail Fixed," *Illustrated Police News*, 11 May 1895: 4. The condition "nervous prostration," which appears in many medical books during the late nineteenth century, was a form of nervous debility, one that—like similar diseases such as neurasthenia and hysteria—doctors believed would lead to insanity.

3. [Anon.], "London, Wednesday, March 1, 1893," *Morning Post*, 1 March 1893: 6. Sir John Bridge determined the sums at Bow Street Magistrates' Court.

4. The commentary and exchanges that follow have been adapted from [anon.], "Wilde Released: Mr. Vaughan Accepts Bail This Morning," *Star*, 7 May 1895: 3; and [anon.], "Release of Oscar Wilde: His Bail and Sureties," *Reynolds's Newspaper*, 12 May 1895: 4, unless otherwise noted.

5. In March 1895, Ernest Leverson had lent Wilde £500 to assist in defraying the cost of engaging counsel for the libel trial. The complete sum was never repaid. In a letter dated 17 May 1897, just before Wilde was released from jail, Leverson states that he has arranged

for a further sum of £250 to be at Wilde's disposal, and assures him that he could offer him a "fresh loan"; Oscar Wilde, *The Complete Letters of Oscar Wilde*, ed. Merlin Holland and Rupert Hart-Davis (London: Fourth Estate, 2000), 828. Further, Wilde also handed over to Leverson the £1,000 that his friend Adela Schuster had given him during the period when he was out on bail.

6. Upper Bedford Place is located in the Bloomsbury district of central London. Headlam had been resident there since 1887.

7. The following exchange between Mr. James Vaughan and Percy Sholto Douglas, together with Vaughan's further comment, appears in [anon.], "Release of Oscar Wilde," *Lloyd's Weekly Newspaper*, 12 May 1895: 1.

8. Sergeant White was head jailer at Bow Street from 1882 to 1898. In 1899, Howard H. Birt explained the responsibilities of the sergeant jailer:

> On his entry into [the prisoners' waiting room] the prisoner passes under the control of the gaoler, and this official is responsible for him from the time when he is "sent to court"—to use the language of the charge sheet—until at the end of the day the black van arrives to transfer him to the prison. The duties of a gaoler are many and onerous. At a court with an average amount of work he may have as many as a hundred prisoners passing through his hands in one day, and it will be his task to see that each one, with the constable in charge, appears before the magistrate in the order fixed. (Howard H. Birt, "How a London Police Court Is Worked," *Leisure Hour*, January 1899: 193)

9. Richard Ellmann speculates that the diamond trader Ernest Leverson, since he "was debarred by the terms of his business partnership from going bail for anyone," approached Image; *Oscar Wilde* (New York: Knopf, 1988), 466.

10. Stewart Headlam, "Personal," *Church Reformer* 14, no. 6 (1895): 124. Headlam also remarked: "I became bail for Mr. Oscar Wilde on public grounds: I felt that the action of a large section of the Press, of the theatrical managers at whose houses his plays were running, and of his publisher, was calculated to prejudice his case before his trial had even begun."

11. F. G. Bettany, *Stewart Headlam: A Biography* (London: John Murray, 1926), 130.

12. Compton Mackenzie, *On Moral Courage* (London: Collins, 1962), 61–62. Alfred F. Havighurst notes that in 1968 the socialist journalist C. H. Norman informed him that the editor of the *Daily Chronicle*, H. W. Massingham, tried to collect signatures for expelling Wilde from the National Liberal Club in May 1895 (*Radical Journalist: H. W. Massingham [1860–1924]* [Cambridge: Cambridge University Press, 1974], 67).

13. This detail appears in [anon.], "Oscar Wilde—£5,000 Bail," *Illustrated Police News*, 18 May 1895: 8.

14. [Anon.], "Wilde Released," 3.

15. [Anon.], "Wilde Released," 3.

16. [Anon.], "Release of Oscar Wilde: His Bail and Sureties," 4.

17. Under section 13 of the Summary Jurisdiction Rules 1886, a prison governor could take recognizances from prisoners; William Paley, Walter Henry Macnamara, and Ralph

Neville, *Paley's Law and Practice of Summary Convictions under the Summary Jurisdiction Acts, 1848–1899*, 8th ed. (London: Sweet and Maxwell, 1904), 619.

18. Designed by George Gilbert Scott, the Midland Grand Hotel (1873–1935) occupied the front of St. Pancras Station, London. The building, which British Rail used as offices for many years, reopened in 2011; it now contains the St. Pancras Renaissance Hotel, managed by Marriott International, and apartments developed by the Manhattan Loft Corporation.

19. There is a possibility that the "old personal friend" was Frank Harris, who claimed to have met with Wilde on various occasions just before and after Wilde was granted bail. In his 1916 biography, Harris does not specify meeting Wilde at the Midland Hotel, though he states that he offered to go bail and that he considered the opportunity of hiring a yacht from Cowes on the Isle of Wight to enable Wilde to escape across the Channel (*Oscar Wilde: His Life and Confessions*, 2 vols. [New York: privately printed, 1916], 1:278–80).

20. [Anon.], "Wilde Released: Mr. Vaughan Accepts Bail This Morning," *Star*, 7 May 1895, Clark press cuttings, 91, Clark Library, Wildeiana, Box 17. (This paragraph does not appear in the British Library microfilm, which is presumably an earlier edition of the paper.)

21. The usual spelling of the familiar form of William Wilde is "Willie."

22. Robert Harborough Sherard, *The Life of Oscar Wilde* (London: T. Werner Laurie, 1906), 357–58. Sherard's insinuation is that the Marquess of Queensberry hired trouble-makers who followed Wilde wherever he went and harassed hotel managers, though there is no evidence to substantiate Sherard's claim. Matthew Sturgis states that Queensberry himself, together with Sir Claude de Crespigny, confronted Wilde at the Midland Grand: "Wilde hastily decamped across the road to the Great Northern Hotel, by King's Cross. But Queensberry followed him there. And it seems, this performance was repeated at several other hotels across London during the course of the evening"; *Oscar: A Life* (London: Head of Zeus, 2018), 577. See also Linda Stratmann, *The Marquess of Queensberry: Wilde's Nemesis* (New Haven, CT: Yale University Press, 2013), 243.

23. Robert Harborough Sherard, *Oscar Wilde: The Story of an Unhappy Friendship* (London: Hermes Press 1902), 163–64.

24. W. B. Yeats, "The Tragic Generation," in *Autobiographies*, Vol. 3 of *The Collected Works of W. B. Yeats*, ed. William H. O'Donnell and Douglas N. Archibald, 14 vols. (New York: Macmillan and Scribners, 1989–2015), 226.

25. Oscar Wilde, "To Ada Leverson," 8 May 1895, in *The Complete Letters*, 649.

26. Wilde, "To Ada Leverson," [early May 1895], in *The Complete Letters*, 650.

27. Wilde, "To Ada Leverson," 6 May 1895, in *The Complete Letters*, 648.

28. Wilde, "To Ada Leverson," [early May 1895], 649.

29. Press cutting from the *Star*, March 1911, in Robert Ross, scrapbook, British Library, Add. MS 81824, fo. 26.

30. Leverson, *Letters to the Sphinx*, 38.

31. Leverson, *Letters to the Sphinx*, 41.

32. Leverson, *Letters to the Sphinx*, 42.

33. Page numbers in parentheses refer to the reconstruction of the Crown prosecution against Wilde in part II of the present volume, unless otherwise noted.

34. [Anon.], "The Wilde Case," *Morning*, 27 May 1895: 4.

35. [Anon.], "Oscar Wilde at the Old Bailey: Case for the Defence," *Pall Mall Gazette*, 24 May 1895: 7.

36. [Anon.], "Lord Queensberry and His Son: The Affray in Piccadilly," *Pall Mall Gazette*, 22 May 1895: 7.

37. [Anon.], "Lord Queensberry and His Son," 7.

38. [Anon.], "Wilde: Weak, Ill, and Utterly Dejected in the Dock," *Star*, Special Edition, 23 May 1895: 3.

39. Scarfpins were worn by men and women; the ones marketed to men often featured sporting and nautical designs.

40. The commentary and exchanges that follow have been adapted from [anon.], "Central Criminal Court—May 23. (Before Mr. Justice Wills.) Prosecution of Oscar Wilde," *Daily Telegraph*, 24 May 1895: 8; [anon.], "The Society Scandal: Re-Opening of the Case," *Galignani Messenger*, 21 May 1895: 1; [anon.], "Wilde and Taylor: They Appear Again at the Old Bailey," *Echo*, 20 May 1895: 3; and [Christopher Sclater Millard], *Oscar Wilde: Three Times Tried*, Famous Old Bailey Trials of the XIX Century (London: Ferrestone Press, 1912), 329–35.

41. The eighteenth-century penal reformer John Howard wrote extensively about the "destruction of multitudes" through "*gaol-fever*" (typhus) and smallpox in English prisons; *The State of the Prisons in England and Wales* (Warrington: William Eyres, 1777), 2. Observers in court are likely to have known about the onetime practice of fumigating the court from Charles Dickens's novel, *A Tale of Two Cities* (1859), which is set in Revolutionary France; the narrative refers to a "court [that] was bestrewn with herbs and sprinkled with vinegar as a precaution against gaol air and gaol fever" (Charles Dickens, *A Tale of Two Cities* [London: Chapman and Hall, 1859], 41).

42. [Anon.], "Wilde Appears in the Dock," *Sun*, 20 May 1895: 3.

The members of the sworn jury were recorded as follows (National Archives, CRIM 9/16):

1. George Draper	5. Herbert Humphrey	9. James Phillips
2. Cha[s.] John Saunders	6. Charles Reeves	10. David Edwards
3. Beedoe Edmett	7. Louis Schonewald	11. David Howells
4. Christopher Edmondson	8. Cordeaux Rhys	12. Joseph Hovell

43. Clarke was alluding to the famous trial of the French-born Adelaide Blanche Bartlett (*née* de la Tremoille)—who may have been the illegitimate daughter of a member of Queen Victoria's circle—and the Revd. George Dyson for murdering her husband, the wealthy English grocer Thomas Edwin Bartlett. On New Year's Eve 1885, Adelaide Bartlett found that her husband had died in the bed they shared in their flat at 85 Claverton Street, Pimlico, London. Edwin Bartlett was found to have chloroform in his stomach. His father suspected that Adelaide, who became intimate with the Wesleyan minister Dyson, had poisoned Edwin, most probably because Edwin had recently amended his will so that Adelaide could remarry in the event of his death. During the trial, which began on 12 April 1886 at the Old Bailey, where Justice Wills was the presiding judge,

Clarke defended Adelaide Bartlett (whose father may have hired Clarke), while Frank Lockwood and Charles Mathews served as Dyson's defense counsel. The attorney general, Sir Charles Russell, who led the prosecution, declared in his opening statement that he would "offer no evidence on the part of the Crown against Mr. Dyson"; Edward Beal, ed., *The Trial of Adelaide Bartlett for Murder* (London: Stevens and Haynes, 1886), 2. The foreman of the jury accordingly stated that Dyson was "Not Guilty." The case has been the subject of several critical studies over the years, including Kate Clarke, *In the Interests of Science: Adelaide Bartlett and the Pimlico Poisoning* (London: Mango Books, 2015).

44. The commentary and examination that follow have been adapted from [anon.], "The Wilde Charges: Trial of Taylor," *Manchester Courier, and Lancashire Advertiser*, 21 May 1895: 8; and [Millard], *Oscar Wilde: Three Times Tried*, 335–48, unless otherwise noted.

45. In British English, the term "public school" refers to an independent, fee-paying secondary school, with particular reference to old institutions such as Eton College (founded 1440), Harrow School (founded 1572), and Winchester College (founded 1382). Marlborough (founded 1843) belonged to a generation of Victorian public schools, including Radley College (founded 1847), that based their teaching on Anglican principles.

46. On Kettner's and the Solferino, see 498–99 above.

47. [Anon.], "Wilde: Case Reopened To-Day at the Old Bailey," *Star*, 20 May 1895: 3.

48. For details about the police raid at Fitzroy Street, see 134–35 and 333 above.

49. The name of Edward Harrington had emerged during the proceedings of both the pretrial hearing and the first criminal trial. It is probable that Harrington was subpoenaed to attend the second criminal trial, since Lockwood called on this individual to make himself known in the courtroom (see 330). Harrington was not called to give evidence.

50. Grain's following cross-examination of Charles Parker has been adapted from [anon.], "Wilde: Case Reopened," 3; and [Millard], *Oscar Wilde: Three Times Tried*, 339–41.

51. The identity of this man remains unknown.

52. Ernest Macklin was an old friend of Taylor's (see 334); it has not been possible to discover information about him.

53. The identity of Clarke remains unknown. Like other allusions to alleged crimes in which Charles Parker was the perpetrator or accessory, this one indicates that Grain had access to sensitive information about the witness's history as a blackmailer.

54. Whitsuntide (also known as Whit Sunday) is the festival in the Christian religious calendar that outside Britain is called Pentecost, which itself falls seven weeks after Easter Sunday. In 1894, Whitsuntide was on 13 May.

55. Northumberland Mansions is situated on Luxborough Street (formerly Northumberland Street), in the Marylebone area of London; in the 1890s, it was regarded as a fashionable address.

56. Millard reports this and the next four exchanges in indirect speech; *Oscar Wilde: Three Times Tried*, 341. I have supplied Grain's questions and answers in direct speech. John Dernbach (also recorded as Durnbach, whom the 1891 Census records as an inmate of the Carter Home for Destitute Boys, Clapham, at age fourteen) counted among the twenty men who were taken into custody during the Fitzroy Street raid in August 1894 (see

134–35 and 333). *Reynolds's Newspaper* reported that Dernbach was a valet; [anon.], "Men in Women's Clothes," 19 August 1894: 8.

57. [Anon.,] "Wilde: Case Reopened To-Day at the Old Bailey," *Star*, 20 May 1895, 3; and [Millard], *Oscar Wilde: Three Times Tried*, 341. Datchet is a village on the River Thames that was traditionally located within the county of Buckinghamshire, though the redrawing of county boundaries in 1974 placed it within Berkshire. The area was historically connected with horseracing. Charles II raced horses at Datchet Mead, next to Windsor Castle. The racecourse at nearby Ascot, Berkshire, superseded the one at Datchet Mead. Queen Anne opened Ascot in 1711. During the libel proceedings, Wilde informed Carson of what he knew about the Parker brothers: "They told me their father lived at Datchet and was a man of some wealth—not wealth exactly, but a man of some fortune there" (Merlin Holland, *Irish Peacock and Scarlet Marquess: The Real Trial of Oscar Wilde* [London: Fourth Estate, 2003], 167).

58. [Millard], *Oscar Wilde: Three Times Tried*, 342.

59. [Anon.], "Wilde: Case Reopened To-Day at the Old Bailey," 3.

60. This detail appears in [anon.], "The Society Scandal: Re-Opening of the Case," 1.

61. The commentary and exchanges that follow have been adapted from [anon.], "Wilde: Case Reopened To-Day at the Old Bailey," 3; and [Millard], *Oscar Wilde: Three Times Tried*, 342–46, unless otherwise noted.

62. [Anon.], "Wilde: Case Reopened To-Day at the Old Bailey," 3.

63. [Anon.], "Wilde: Case Reopened To-Day at the Old Bailey," 3. The letters in question are reproduced in full above (see 77–78).

64. The letter, which had been mentioned previously in court, is discussed on 178, 229, and 508 above.

65. This and the next two sentences have been adapted from [anon.], *The Trial of Oscar Wilde: From the Shorthand Reports* (Paris: privately printed, 1906), 87.

66. [Anon.], "Oscar Wilde: Second Trial at the Old Bailey," *Illustrated Police Budget*, 25 May 1895: 8.

67. It remains unclear what Cotter meant by "utensils." At the time, the term referred to instruments or vessels used for culinary purposes; here, however, it appears to refer to an implement in the bathroom (see notes 242 and 244 below [550]).

68. This and the next eight sentences have been adapted from [anon.], *The Trial of Oscar Wilde*, 88.

69. In some reports, including the *Star*'s, Becker's name is spelled "Becca." The *Illustrated Police Budget* recorded the witness's name as "Emil Paul Vestre"; [anon.], "Oscar Wilde: Second Trial at the Old Bailey," 8. It is likely that the witness was the German-born Adolph Emil Becker, who, according to the 1901 Census, was a hotel proprietor.

70. The commentary that follows has been adapted from [Millard], *Oscar Wilde: Three Times Tried*, 346–48, unless otherwise noted.

71. This and the next two sentences have been adapted from [anon.], "Prosecution of Oscar Wilde: The Second Trial," *Western Mail*, 21 May 1895: 6.

72. The court records note the time of adjournment; National Archives, CRIM 9/16, n.p.. The judge's comment to the jury is noted in [anon.], "Central Criminal Court—May 23," 8; and [anon.], "The Society Scandal: Re-Opening of the Case," 1.

73. The commentary that follows has been adapted from [anon.], "The Society Scandal: Trial of Taylor," *Galignani Messenger*, 22 May 1895: 1; and [Millard], *Oscar Wilde: Three Times Tried*, 349–50.

74. [Anon.], "The Prosecution of Oscar Wilde," *Lloyd's Weekly Newspaper*, 2 June 1895: 4; and [anon.], "Oscar Wilde: Proceedings in Bankruptcy," *St. James's Gazette*, 25 July 1895: 14.

75. [Anon.], "The Society Scandal: Trial of Taylor," 1. The *Star* proceeded to state that Wilde's "counsel . . . were not in attendance," which was inaccurate, since Clarke was in court; the same error appeared in [anon.], "The Wilde Scandal: Taylor Cross-Examined by Sir Frank Lockwood," *Star*, 21 May 1895: 3.

76. Grain's examination of Taylor has been adapted from [anon.], *The Trial of Oscar Wilde*, 89–90, and the commentary has been adapted from [anon.], "The Society Scandal: Trial of Taylor," 1.

77. Taylor presumably meant that he rented one of several subdivided rooms at 13 Little College Street.

78. [Anon.], "The Society Scandal: Trial of Taylor," 1.

79. Lockwood's cross-examination of Taylor has been adapted from [anon.], "The Society Scandal: Trial of Taylor," 1; [Anon.], "The Wilde Scandal: Taylor Cross-Examined by Sir Frank Lockwood," 3; [anon.], *The Trial of Oscar Wilde*, 90–91; [anon.], "The Wilde Charges: Trial of Taylor," 8; and (mostly) [Millard], *Oscar Wilde: Three Times Tried*, 352–53. In a number of places, I have converted indirect into direct speech in order to represent Lockwood's questions and Taylor's replies.

80. The word "burlesque" means a grotesque or derisive imitation; usage became less common in the later decades of the nineteenth century.

81. The exhibition space at Olympia, West Kensington, London, opened in 1886 as the National Agricultural Hall. The Royal Opera House (often known as Covent Garden), Bow Street, in the Covent Garden district of London, opened on its present site in 1732; it was rebuilt several times, and by the 1890s it occupied the third theatre building, which was erected in 1858. Built in the early 1880s, Queen's Gate Hall, located in South Kensington between Cromwell Road and Queen's Gate, was initially used for theatrical performances, society meetings, and social events; in the twentieth century, the building became a Christian Science church.

82. The story of Dick Whittington is a staple of English folklore. It tells a tall tale about Richard Whittington, who became Lord Mayor of London in 1397. The legend, which has various versions and has no bearing on the real Whittington's life, recalls how the orphaned Dick flees his impoverished existence as a scullion in the country. On his way to London, he hears the sound of Bow bells (from the Church of St. Mary-le-Bow in the City of London), which tell him he will become Lord Mayor of London. Pantomimes about Dick Whittington, in which cross-dressing was central to the staging, were popular in the nineteenth century and remain so to this day.

83. Taylor's use of "stood" indicates that the Parker brothers covered the price of a beverage in the bar. The verb "retaliated" means that Taylor reciprocated or returned a service in kind; usage became obsolete after the late nineteenth century.

84. [Anon.], "The Society Scandal: Trial of Taylor," 1; [anon.], "The Wilde Scandal: Taylor Cross-Examined by Sir Frank Lockwood," 3. The identity of Court remains unknown.

85. The Tivoli Theatre of Varieties, which was based in the Strand, London, opened in 1890, and it soon became one of the city's leading music-halls; by 1922, the building was refurbished and reopened as a cinema, which remained in operation until 1957, when it was demolished.

86. Victoria Street is located between Victoria Station and Westminster Abbey in West London; it is not clear at which restaurant Taylor dined with Harrington.

87. There was potential embarrassment in mentioning the name of Maurice Salis Schwabe. As became clear in Wilde's libel case against the Marquess of Queensberry and in both the pretrial hearing and first Crown prosecution above, Schwabe's name was a source of sensitivity (129, 182, and 234–35).

88. The identity of Harold Henry remains unknown.

89. Hunter Street is adjacent to Brunswick Square, in the Bloomsbury district of London.

90. This and the next two exchanges between Lockwood and Parker appear in [anon.], "Taylor Again on Trial: His Story as a Witness," *Echo*, 21 May 1895: 3.

91. On these venues, see 246, 275, 168, and 167 above.

92. This pew was reserved for aldermen and officers affiliated with the City of London Corporation, which is the local authority of the City of London, where the Old Bailey is located. Such officers include the recorder of London (the senior judge) and the common serjeant of London (the second most senior judge).

93. The British phrase "at table" simply refers to the table where the dinner party took place.

94. This sentence appears in [anon.], "Taylor Again on Trial," 3. The identity of the individual with whom Charles Parker allegedly traveled to Paris remained unknown in the proceedings.

95. This question appears in [anon.], "Taylor Again on Trial," 3.

96. Regent Street was located in the World's End district of Chelsea; it later became Stayton Street. The street was one of several that were cleared for two public housing developments, the Cremorne Estate (1956) and the World's End Estate (1977).

97. The police raid took place at 46 Fitzroy Street on Saturday, 11 August 1894 (see 134–35 and 333 above).

98. Arthur Marling, a female impersonator who was dressed in a black-and-gold gown during the Fitzroy Street raid, was also a receiver of stolen goods (see 135 and 517 above).

99. Although a betting man usually means a man who places bets, here the meaning is synonymous with an individual who takes bets, calculates odds, and gives out winnings. The context is more than probably horseracing. Some of the men in Taylor's circle—including Frederick Atkins and James Dennis Burton—were involved in bookmaking.

100. This and the next three exchanges between Lockwood and Taylor appear in [anon.], "Taylor Again on Trial," *Echo*, 3.

101. [Anon.], "The Wilde Scandal: Taylor Cross-Examined by Sir Frank Lockwood," 3.

102. The emphasis appears in [anon.], "The Wilde Scandal: Taylor Cross-Examined by Sir Frank Lockwood," 3; the reporter commented on Lockwood's remark: "It was, of course, true, and Sir Edward had nothing to say at a very irritating juncture."

103. [Millard,] *Oscar Wilde: Three Times Tried*, 364–65. The *Star* records Lockwood's remark differently: "a place taken in this secluded street as a place where debased persons congregated" ("The Wilde Scandal: Taylor Cross-Examined by Sir Frank Lockwood," 21 May 1895: 3).

104. [Anon.], "The Wilde Scandal: Taylor Cross-Examined by Sir Frank Lockwood," 3.

105. The commentary that follows has been adapted from [anon.], "The Wilde Charges: Trial of Taylor," 8; [anon.], "The Society Scandal: Trial of Taylor," 1; and [Millard], *Oscar Wilde: Three Times Tried*, 365–66, unless otherwise noted.

106. [Anon.], "The Wilde Scandal: Taylor Cross-Examined by Sir Frank Lockwood," 3. The "still small voice" refers to the voice of conscience in the Hebrew Scriptures (1 Kings 19:13).

107. [Anon.], "The Society Scandal: Trial of Taylor," 1. The unusual use of "complication" appears in the report.

108. [Anon.], "Wilde Again in the Dock at the Old Bailey," *Star*, 22 May 1895, 3; small changes have been made to punctuation. The members of the sworn jury were recorded as follows (National Archives, CRIM, 9/16):

1. Joseph Richard Smith	5. Thomas Eldridge	9. Henry Thos Blundell
2. Charles Henry Ellis	6. Charles Ernest Breese	10. Alfred Martin
3. Henry Wilson	7. Allan Stewart	11. James Robinson
4. Harry Blanks	8. Joseph Spencer	12. John Wm Scholes

109. The commentary and exchanges that follow have been adapted from [anon.], "Wilde Again in the Dock at the Old Bailey," 2–3, unless otherwise noted.

110. [Anon.], "Wilde Again in the Dock at the Old Bailey," 2.

111. [Anon.], "Wilde Again in the Dock at the Old Bailey," 2. The *Sun* agreed: "Shelley is really their best witness in that he is absolutely free from the taint which attaches to the miserable blackmailers"; [anon.], "Wilde on Trial: He Looks Ill and Haggard," 22 May 1895: 3.

112. This and the next three sentences have been adapted from [anon.], "Wilde Scandal: Second Trial Commenced," *Western Mail*, 23 May 1895: 5.

113. [Anon.], "Wilde Again in the Dock at the Old Bailey," 2.

114. It is not clear if these are Millard's own words or a paraphrase of a report on Lockwood's presentation of the case to the jury; [Millard], *Oscar Wilde: Three Times Tried*, 382. The letters were Wilde's private correspondence with Douglas, which Wood had appropriated from a set of Douglas's clothes in Oxford; for more information on this episode, see 228–29 above.

115. This and the next two sentences have been adapted from [anon.], "Wilde Scandal: Second Trial Commenced," 5.

116. [Anon.], "Wilde Again in the Dock at the Old Bailey," 2.

117. [Anon.], "Wilde Again in the Dock at the Old Bailey," 2.

118. Earlier in the day, Queensberry appeared at Great Marlborough Street Magistrates' Court in connection with the fracas that took place between him and his son Percy Sholto Douglas in Piccadilly on Tuesday, 21 May 1895. The street-fight was widely reported in the press.

119. [Anon.], "Wilde Again in the Dock at the Old Bailey," 2.

120. [Anon.], "Wilde Again in the Dock at the Old Bailey," 2.

121. This and the next two exchanges between Clarke and Shelley appear in [anon.], "Oscar Wilde: His Second Trial at the Old Bailey," *Echo*, 22 May 1895: 3.

122. This and the next three exchanges with Shelley appear in [anon.], "Wilde on Trial," 3.

123. The transcript of the proceedings of the libel trial contains a longer version of this letter, which Clarke noted had been sent from 3 Hildyard Road, Earls Court; Holland, *Irish Peacock*, 230. Wilde's second book of fairytales, *A House of Pomegranates*, appeared—with imposing designs by Charles Ricketts and Charles Haslewood Shannon—from James R. Osgood, McIlvaine, and Co. in November 1891. The *Pall Mall Gazette* asked: "Is A House of Pomegranates intended for a child's book? We confess that we do not exactly know. The ultra-aestheticism of the pictures seems unsuitable for children"; [anon.], "Some Illustrated Gift Books," 30 November 1891: 3. Wilde took unkindly to this review, and he expressed his displeasure in a letter to the editor: "I had about as much intention of pleasing the British child as I had of pleasing the British public"; [early December 1891], in *The Complete Letters*, 503. The parenthetical remark in the *Star*'s report implies that Shelley, not Clarke, read this letter (and, most probably, the others on which Clarke proceeded to cross-examine him) aloud in court; [anon.], "Wilde Again in the Dock at the Old Bailey," 3.

Marguerite, Countess of Blessington was a celebrated beauty, author, editor, and society wit whose salon at her home, Gore House, in Kensington became legendary in the 1830s and 1840s. The novelist and poet George Meredith was renowned for the witty exchanges between his characters in his most famous novels, such as *The Egoist* (1879).

124. The transcript of the libel trial records Clarke reading aloud a slightly longer version of this letter; it notes that Shelley wrote this item of correspondence from Vigo Street (Holland, *Irish Peacock*, 232–33).

125. [Anon.], "The Society Scandal: Trial of Oscar Wilde," *Galignani Messenger*, 23 May 1895: 1.

126. [Anon.], "Wilde Again in the Dock at the Old Bailey," 3. During the libel trial, Clarke read aloud the complete text of the letter in which Shelley makes this comment; Holland, *Irish Peacock*, 233.

127. During the libel trial, Clarke read aloud a letter dated 27 March 1893, which Shelley sent from 3 Hildyard Road, in which he complains about his "harsh existence"; the letter does not mention plans to move to a clerkship in the City of London (Holland, *Irish Peacock*, 233).

128. During the libel trial, Clarke read aloud the full text of the letter from which this comment is taken; Shelley wrote this item of correspondence, which is dated 15 June 1894, from 3 Hildyard Road (Holland, *Irish Peacock*, 235–36). Shelley's desire to "read with a coach" means that he wanted to benefit from private instruction.

129. This and the next sentence have been adapted from [Millard], *Oscar Wilde: Three Times Tried*, 388. Shelley's phrase does not appear in the records of his correspondence that Clarke read aloud at the libel trial and during the first criminal trial.

130. During the libel trial, Clarke read aloud the full text of the letter in which the following sentences appear; he mentioned that the letter was dated 24 April 1894 (Holland, *Irish Peacock*, 234).

131. Clarke's question is reported in [anon.], "Trial of Oscar Wilde: Case for the Prosecution," *Manchester Courier, and Lancashire Advertiser*, 23 May 1895: 6.

132. During the libel trial, Wilde told Clarke that he had given Shelley £5 at the time; it was also noted that in April 1894 Shelley had been earning £50 a year in a commercial office at 1 Dunster Court, Mincing Lane, in the City of London (Holland, *Irish Peacock*, 234).

133. In the libel proceedings, when Clarke read aloud the letter in which Shelley's comment appears, he suppressed Lane's name; the letter is dated 14 June 1894 (Holland, *Irish Peacock*, 235).

134. Also, during the libel trial Clarke had read aloud the complete text of the letter (dated 15 June 1894) in which Shelley made these comments; it was sent from 3 Hildyard Road (Holland, *Irish Peacock*, 235–36). As Wilde pointed out to Clarke during these earlier proceedings, Shelley was referring to a review of Wilde's poem *The Sphinx* (1894), which appeared in the *Daily News*. The disapproving reviewer deplored Wilde's interest in "the hideous sensualities of the old world"; [anon.] "Mr. Oscar Wilde and Edgar Poe," 11 June 1894: 6.

135. The transcript of the libel trial does not record these words in any letter that Shelley sent Wilde.

136. This section of Clarke's cross-examination of Shelley, together with the commentary on Lockwood's subsequent examination of Shelley and with Elkin Mathews's testimony, has been adapted from [anon.], "Wilde Scandal: Second Trial Commenced," 5.

137. This and the next two exchanges between Clarke and Shelley appear in [anon.], "Oscar Wilde: His Second Trial at the Old Bailey," 3.

138. [Anon.], "The Society Scandal: Trial of Oscar Wilde," 1.

139. [Anon.], "The Society Scandal: Trial of Oscar Wilde," 1.

140. [Anon.], "The Society Scandal: Trial of Oscar Wilde," 1.

141. Clarke's question appears in [anon.], "Wilde Again in the Dock at the Old Bailey," 3.

142. The commentary that follows, together with Clarke's cross-examination of Wood, has been adapted from [anon.], "The Society Scandal: Trial of Oscar Wilde," 1, except where otherwise noted. The detective was employed by the Crown to keep watch on Wood.

143. Justice Wills asked Wood to be precise about the kind of commission that Wood's brother made to earn his living; a turf agent took bets at race courses.

144. This and the next eleven exchanges between Clarke and Wood appear in [anon.], "Oscar Wilde: His Second Trial at the Old Bailey," 3.

145. Earlier in the second criminal trial, Taylor stated that Charles Parker had been resident at 72 Regent Street, Chelsea, at the time of the Fitzroy Street raid in August 1894 (see 134–35 above). Charles Parker, however, denied that blackmailing took place at this address (see 353).

146. [Anon.], "Wilde Again in the Dock at the Old Bailey," 3.

147. [Anon.], "The Society Scandal: Trial of Oscar Wilde," 1.

148. Harman Edgar Tidy was a solicitor with offices based at 27 Sackville Street, which is located between Piccadilly and Vigo Street, central London.

149. This and the next five exchanges between Clarke and Wood appear in [anon.], *The Trial of Oscar Wilde*, 96–97, which mistakenly presents Douglas's nickname "Bosie" as "Bogie"; this source also confusingly suggests that parts of Clarke's cross-examinations of Shelley and Wood involve only Shelley.

150. "Varsity" became the colloquial term for university; today, usage—which dates from the mid-nineteenth century—tends to refer to sporting matches between Oxford and Cambridge.

151. Some reports on the libel trial state that there were four letters; see [anon.], "Alleged Libel on Oscar Wilde," *Cardiff Times*, 6 April 1895: 4.

152. Wilde's surviving letters that Wood thieved begin "My Own Boy" and "Dearest of All Boys"; see 77–78 above, and also *The Complete Letters*, 544 and 559.

153. This and the next exchange between Lockwood and Wood appear in [anon.], *The Trial of Oscar Wilde*, 97.

154. [Anon.], *The Trial of Oscar Wilde*, 97. These details are not recorded in any other source. To "toss off" is British sexual slang for masturbation; the *OED* dates usage to the 1730s.

155. The following commentary, together with the two exchanges between Clarke and Charles Parker, has been adapted from [anon.], "Trial of Oscar Wilde: Case for the Prosecution," 6.

156. The commentary that follows has been adapted from [Millard], *Oscar Wilde: Three Times Tried*, 395.

157. This detail has been adapted from [anon.], "Trial of Oscar Wilde," *Evening Standard*, 23 May 1895: 6. Chiswick is located in West London.

158. The time of the adjournment is given in the court records; National Archives, CRIM 9/16, n.p.

159. [anon.], "Wilde: Weak, Ill, and Utterly Dejected in the Dock," *Star*, Special Edition, 23 May 1895: 3.

160. [Anon.], "Wilde: Weak, Ill, and Utterly Dejected," 3.

161. [Anon.], "Wilde: Weak, Ill, and Utterly Dejected," 3.

162. In British English, "shortsighted" equates with the American English use of "nearsighted."

163. [Anon.], "Wilde Convicted: Scenes between Counsel," *Reynolds's Newspaper*, 26 May 1895: 1.

164. [Millard], *Oscar Wilde: Three Times Tried*, 399–400.

165. The cross-examination of Becker that follows has been adapted from [Millard], *Oscar Wilde: Three Times Tried*, 400–1.

166. [Anon.], "Wilde Convicted," 5.

167. [Anon.], "Wilde Convicted," 5.

168. Justice Wills's speech and the commentary that follows on Clarke's response have been adapted from [anon.], "Central Criminal Court—May 20. (Before Mr. Justice Wills.) Prosecution of Oscar Wilde," *Daily Telegraph*, 21 May 1895: 8; and [anon.], "Wilde: Weak, Ill, and Utterly Dejected," 3.

169. [Anon.], "Wilde: Weak, Ill, and Utterly Dejected," 3.

170. "Wilde's Trial: Still Weaving and Unweaving," *Sun*, 23 May 1895: 3.

171. This letter by Wilde is quoted in full at 78 above.

172. [Anon.], "Wilde: Weak, Ill, and Utterly Dejected," 3; small changes have been made to punctuation.

173. Clarke's speech, together with some small sections of the commentary that follows, has been adapted from [anon.], "Central Criminal Court—May 23. (Before Mr. Justice Wills.) Prosecution of Oscar Wilde," *Daily Telegraph*, 24 May 1895: 8.

174. This part of Lockwood's comments has been adapted from [anon.], "Central Criminal Court—May 23," 8.

175. Technically, Justice Wills, if his comments had been reported properly, meant the Court of Crown Cases Reserved (see 514 above).

176. This and the next eight sentences in the commentary have been adapted from [anon.], "Central Criminal Court—May 23," 8.

177. Although Justice Wills did not go so far as to suggest that Shelley suffered from insanity, the decision to discount this witness's evidence related to a larger debate in the English courts about the best principles to observe when such an individual's testimony appeared to be marred by mental disturbance: "If a witness has been allowed by the judge to give evidence, on the assumption that he is competent, but it afterwards turns out, in the course of his evidence, that he really is not so, the evidence which he has already given may be struck out and altogether withdrawn from the jury, who must then try to consider the case as if this evidence had never been given at all"; George Pitt-Lewis, R. Percy Smith, and J. A. Hawke, *The Insane and the Law: A Plain Guide for Medical Men, Solicitors, and Others* (London: J. & A. Churchill, 1895), 243. There were also, as the judge acknowledged, difficulties involved in corroborating Shelley's evidence.

178. The commentary in this sentence and the next two paragraphs has been adapted from [anon.], "Central Criminal Court—May 23," 8.

179. Clarke was reminding the court of a point that Justice Charles, in the first Crown prosecution against Wilde and Taylor, made with reference to Lord Bramwell about the rule that uncorroborated evidence by an accomplice should never provide the grounds for a conviction (see 285 above).

180. [Anon.], "Wilde: Weak, Ill, and Utterly Dejected," 23 May 1895, Clark press clippings, 111 Wildeiana Box 17.

181. The exchange between Clarke and Justice Wills has been adapted from [anon.], "Central Criminal Court—May 23," 8.

182. The time of adjournment is given in the court records; National Archives, CRIM 9/16, n.p.

183. [Anon.], "Wilde: Weak, Ill, and Utterly Dejected," 23 May 1895, Clark press clippings, 111.

184. The commentary that follows has been adapted from [anon.], "Wilde: Cross-Examined for the Third Time," *Star*, 24 May 1895. This long report is taken from Clark press cuttings, 111–17 (this information does not appear in the British Library microfilm, which is presumably an earlier edition of the paper).

185. *Regina v. Meunier* (1894) focused on an alleged French anarchist, Théodule Joseph Constant Meunier, who faced two charges in his home country: murder, and attempted

murder relating to bomb explosions, the one at the Lobau Barracks on 14 March 1892, and the other at the Café Very on 25 April 1893. Chief-Inspector William Meville, who led the hunt for French anarchists in London, arrested Meunier, who had fled to England, at Victoria Station, London, on 4 April 1894. Meunier was committed for trial under the provisions of the Extradition Act 1870. He applied for a writ of habeas corpus in order to authorize his discharge on the grounds that the depositions the French authorities had sent to the English courts referred to some other man named Meunier, not himself. Mme. Bricquot (Meunier's alleged accomplice in the bombings) had made these depositions to the French police. For further discussion, see Constance Bantman, *The French Anarchists in London, 1880–1914: Exile and Transnationalism in the First Globalisation* (Liverpool: Liverpool University Press, 2013), 146.

186. On the Court of Crown Cases Reserved, see 514 above.

187. [Anon.], "Wilde: Cross-Examined for the Third Time," 111.

188. Clarke's speech in this and the next paragraph has been adapted from [anon.], "Wilde: Cross-Examined for the Third Time," 111; parts of this report are in indirect speech.

189. The British judge and politician Sir John Holker, Q.C., who served as Member of Parliament for Preston from 1872 until his death, became the first solicitor general in 1874 (the year in which he was knighted) and attorney general in 1875. In his autobiography, Clarke recalls Sir John as "a powerful advocate, and one of the kindest and most generous of men"; Edward Clarke, *The Story of My Life* (London: John Murray, 1918), 127. In 1877, Clarke served as the defense during the controversial trial for the murder of Harriet Staunton, when Holker was counsel for the prosecution. The trial involved charges for the murder of the heiress Staunton against four individuals whom Justice Hawkins (nicknamed "Hanging Hawkins") sentenced to death by hanging. Clarke produced a highly informed defense of one of the accused, Patrick Staunton (Harriet's younger brother), by presenting medical evidence that claimed the victim had perished because of meningitis and tuberculosis; see J. B. Atlay, *The Trial of the Stauntons* (Edinburgh: William Hodge, 1911), 190–224. A campaign to support the defendants resulted in a pardon in one case, and the commutation of the death sentence to life imprisonment in the three other cases.

190. This and the next two paragraphs of Clarke's speech have been adapted from [anon.], "Central Criminal Court, May 24. (Before Mr. Justice Wills.)," *The Times*, 25 May 1895: 19, unless otherwise noted. The detailed report in *The Times* on Clarke's comments is in indirect speech.

191. This sentence appears in [anon.], "The Trial of Oscar Wilde," *Evening News*, 24 May 1895, Clark press cuttings, 116.

192. The description appears in [anon.], "Wilde: Cross-Examined for the Third Time"; and [anon.], "Wilde Convicted," 5.

193. This commentary, together with the next three exchanges between Clarke and Wilde, has been adapted from [anon.], "Wilde Scandal: Speech for the Defence," *Western Mail*, 25 May 1895: 5.

194. [Anon.], "Wilde: Cross-Examined for the Third Time," 2; and [anon.], "Wilde Convicted," 5.

195. Lockwood's following cross-examination of Wilde has been adapted from [anon.], "Oscar Wilde: Third Day of His Trial," *Echo*, 24 May 1895: 3; and [anon.], "The Trial of

Wilde," *Evening Standard*, 24 May 1895: 2; [anon.], "Wilde Scandal: Speech for the Defence," 5; and [Millard], *Oscar Wilde: Three Times Tried*, 415–30, unless otherwise noted.

196. The detail about the Hôtel des Deux Mondes appears in [anon.], *The Trial of Oscar Wilde*, 100. The hotel, which closed in 1940, was located at 22 Avenue de l'Opéra.

197. This speech appears in [anon.], *The Trial of Oscar Wilde*, 100.

198. Lockwood's question has been adapted from [anon.], "Wilde Scandal: Speech for the Defence," 5.

199. [Millard], *Oscar Wilde: Three Times Tried*, 417–18.

200. At the time, Douglas spent vacations with his mother and grandfather, Alfred Montgomery, at Bad Homburg.

201. This commentary has been adapted from [anon.], "Wilde: Cross-Examined for the Third Time."

202. Lockwood's question appears in this form in [anon.], *The Trial of Oscar Wilde*, 101–2. A snuggery defines a comfortable or cozy space within a home or public house; one of its meanings, which emerged in the late nineteenth century, is a bachelor's den.

203. Wilde's speech takes this form in [anon.], "Wilde Convicted," 5; [anon.], "Wilde: Cross-Examined for the Third Time"; and [anon.], "Wilde: In the Witness Box," *Sun*, 24 May 1895: 3.

204. [Anon.], "Wilde Convicted," 5; and [anon.], "Wilde: Cross-Examined for the Third Time."

205. In 1909, the travel writer Harry de Windt, who attended Wilde's trial, claimed that the dinners that Wilde had hosted for his male companions prompted Lockwood's "unusually merciless and even vindictive cross-examination":

> "I suppose," said Sir Frank, "these suppers you gave were composed of all the luxuries in and out of the season—"
>
> "Pardon me!" politely interrupted the defendant, raising his hand, "but my doctor's orders—"
>
> "Never mind your doctor's orders, sir!" thundered Lockwood, his rosy face now crimson with anger. "Never mind your doctor's orders—"
>
> "Unfortunately for my health, I never do," was the quiet rejoinder, but which, like the prisoner's other witticisms, scarcely impressed either judge or jury in his favour. (Harry De Windt, *My Restless Life* [London: Grant Richards, 1909], 231–32)

There is no account of this exchange in the press. Wilde's quip was similar to one that he made in response to Edward Carson's cross-examination during the libel trial (see Holland, *Irish Peacock*, 170).

206. Westminster, although home to Westminster Abbey and the Houses of Parliament, still had a reputation for the Devil's Acre, one of the worst slums in London. Lockwood may have had in mind this slum, which was associated with prostitution, when inquiring whether Little College Street (located several streets west of the Devil's Acre) was "cheerful."

207. This detail appears in [anon.], "Wilde: Cross-Examined for the Third Time," 113.

208. [Anon.], "Oscar Wilde: Third Day of His Trial," 3; [anon.], "The Society Scandal: Case for the Defence," *Galignani Messenger*, 25 May 1895: 1; [anon.], "Wilde Convicted," 5.

209. [Anon.], "Oscar Wilde: Third Day of His Trial," 3; [anon.], "The Society Scandal: Case for the Defence," 1; [anon.], "Wilde Convicted," 5.

210. This exchange and the subsequent comment from Justice Wills appear in [anon.], "Wilde: In the Witness Box," 3. The *Leeds Times* observed that Wilde commented: "I have never seen those pins. I have bought pearl pins of Henry Lewis and Co., New Bond Street. Harrington was a friend of F. Schwabes [*sic*]" ([anon.], "Oscar Wilde: Severe Cross-Examination by the Solicitor General," 25 May 1895: 8).

211. [Anon.], "Oscar Wilde: Third Day of His Trial," 3; [anon.], "The Society Scandal: Case for the Defence," 1; [anon.], "Wilde Convicted," 5.

212. This and the next exchange between Lockwood and Wilde appear in [anon.], *The Trial of Oscar Wilde*, 102.

213. [Anon.], "Wilde: In the Witness Box," 3.

214. [Anon.], "Wilde Convicted," 5.

215. [Anon.], "The Society Scandal: Case for the Defence," 1.

216. [Anon.], "Oscar Wilde: Cross-Examined for the Third Time,"115.

217. Some newspapers reported Schwabe's name as "Schwartz"; see, for example, [anon.], "Wilde Convicted," 5.

218. [Anon.], "Wilde Convicted," 5.

219. Clarke's presentation of the case for the defense has been adapted from [anon.], "Oscar Wilde: Cross-Examined for the Third Time," 115, 117; and [Millard], *Oscar Wilde: Three Times Tried*, 431–35.

220. This and the next two sentences have been adapted from [anon.], "Wilde: In the Witness Box," 3.

221. [Anon.], "Oscar Wilde: Cross-Examined for the Third Time," 117.

222. [Anon.], "Oscar Wilde: Cross-Examined for the Third Time,"117.

223. [Anon.], "Oscar Wilde: Cross-Examined for the Third Time,"119.

224. [Anon.], "Wilde Scandal: Speech for the Defence," 5. The *Morning* also noted: "There was some applause in court on the conclusion of the learned counsel's speech"; [anon.] "The Trial of Oscar Wilde: Close of the Prosecution," *Morning*, 25 May 1895: 3. It has not been possible to locate a source that provides a fuller account of Clarke's well-received address to the jury.

225. The commentary on Lockwood's presentation of the case for the prosecution has been adapted from [anon.], "Central Criminal Court, May 24," 19; [anon.], "Wilde Convicted," 5; and [anon.], "Wilde Scandal: Speech for the Defence," 5.

226. The prosecution's right to reply (i.e., having the "last word") was established through section 2 of the Criminal Procedure Act 1865 (commonly known as Denham's Act), which stated that whenever there were prisoners or defendants who were defended by counsel, the following procedure was to be followed: "[I]t shall be the duty of the presiding judge, at the close of the case for the prosecution, to ask the counsel for each prisoner or defendant so defended by counsel whether he or they intend to adduce evidence; and in the event of none of them thereupon announcing his intention to adduce evidence, the counsel for the prosecution shall be allowed to address the jury a second time in support of his case, for the purpose of summing up the evidence against such prisoner or prisoners, or defendant or defendants" (28 & 29 Vict. c. 18 s. 2).

The right of reply was amended in section 3 of the Criminal Evidence Act 1898: "In cases where the right of reply depends upon the question whether the evidence has been called for the defence, the fact that the person charged has been called as a witness shall not of itself confer on the prosecution the right of reply" (61 & 62 Vict. c. 36 s. 3).

The provisions of the of the 1865 and 1898 Acts were amended in the Criminal Procedure (Right to Reply) Act 1964:

(1) Upon the trial in any indictment—
(a) the prosecution shall not be entitled to the right of reply on the ground only that the attorney general or the solicitor general appears for the Crown at the trial and
(b) the time at which the prosecution is entitled to exercise that right shall, notwithstanding anything in section 2 of the Criminal Procedure Act 1865, be after the close of evidence and before the closing speech (if any) by or on behalf of the accused. (1964 Eliz. 2 c. 34. s. 1)

Section 10(2) and part III of schedule 3 of the Criminal Law Act 1967 repealed section 2 of Denham's Act.

227. Lockwood most likely used the word "illiterate" loosely here. From the evidence we have, the leading male witnesses could certainly read and write, though their standard of literacy did not compare with that of a highly educated man such as Wilde.

228. Lockwood was referring to English jurist William Blackstone's well-known Latin circumlocution for the "*crime against nature*, committed with either man or beast" (see 6 above).

229. The time of adjournment is given in the court records; National Archives, CRIM 9/16, n.p.

230. [Anon.], "Wilde Trial: Fierce Combat between Counsel," *Star*, 25 May 1895, Clark press clippings, 119: small changes have been made to punctuation. Most of the commentary here and in what follows has been adapted from this source. *Regina v. Read* was a criminal trial that resulted in the hanging of James Canham Read (1855–94). Read was a married pay clerk at the Royal Albert Docks who maintained several mistresses. The court found him guilty of murdering twenty-three-year-old Florence Dennis, who was pregnant with his child, through a shot to the head. The murder took place at Prittlewell, near Southend, Essex, on 24 June 1894. After his arrest, Read was brought before the magistrates at Southend on 9 July 1894. The trial, which lasted four days, followed a few weeks after Lockwood's appointment as solicitor general. In the available press reports, no mention was made of Lockwood's using the solicitor general's privilege of having the right of reply after the defense had made its case to the jury.

Jane White was a sixty-three-year-old midwife who had been charged at the North London Magistrates' Court with causing the death of Elizabeth Fisher (the wife of a medical student) through "an alleged illegal operation" (i.e., abortion); [anon.], "North London," *Evening Standard*, 25 May 1895: 5. As noted below, the Treasury offered no evidence against her. On 9 February 1899, White was tried for the same offense at the Old Bailey. The jury found her guilty, with a very strong recommendation to mercy. The judge pronounced the death sentence. White, however, was reprieved on 13 February 1899; [anon.], "Medico-Legal. Constructive Murder. Conviction of a Nurse: Reprieve," *British Medical Journal*, 18 February 1899: 448.

The black cap was a square cap worn by English judges on certain state or solemn occasions; a judge also wore it when handing down a death sentence.

A coroner's warrant was issued when a coroner had been notified of a suspicious death.

231. [Anon.], "Wilde Convicted," 5.

232. Lockwood's comment and Clarke's subsequent response have been adapted from [anon.], "Conviction of Oscar Wilde: Close of the Sensational Trial," *Western Mail*, 27 May 1895: 5. Lockwood's use of "glamour" relates to the nineteenth-century sense of a "magical or fictitious beauty attaching to any person or object; a delusive or alluring charm" (*OED*).

233. On Apollo and Hyacinthus, see 478 above.

234. This exchange appears in [anon.], "Wilde: Nearing the Crisis," *Sun*, 25 May 1895: 3.

235. [Anon.], "Wilde Trial: Fierce Combat between Counsel," 119.

236. [Anon.], "Wilde Trial: Fierce Combat between Counsel," 119.

237. [Anon.], "Wilde Trial: Fierce Combat between Counsel," 119. In the nineteenth century, a vinaigrette referred to a small bottle (usually made of cut glass) containing a sponge saturated with pungent salts.

238. On section 20 of the Criminal Law Amendment Act 1885 (48 & 49 Vict. c. 69), see 21, 211, and 513 above.

239. [Anon.], "Conviction of Oscar Wilde," 5.

240. [Anon.], "Wilde Trial: Fierce Combat between Counsel," 121.

241. Hearsay remained a vexed area of legal debate in England and Wales during the nineteenth century. See William Wills, *The Theory and Practice of the Law of Evidence* (London: Stevens and Sons, 1894), 5 and 108–9.

242. Vaseline was a comparatively recent product; the American chemist Robert Cheeseborough patented it in the United States in 1872 and in England in 1877. The Cheeseborough Manufacturing Company, based in Perth Amboy, New Jersey, initially sold Vaseline under Standard Oil before distributing its product independently in 1911. The Anglo-Dutch conglomerate Unilever acquired the company in 1987. In the reports on the trials, this is the first occasion when there is a mention of grease and Vaseline, although this part of the proceedings suggests that these substances were alluded to when the staff at the Savoy Hotel first gave their evidence (see 187, 249, and 323–24 above).

243. Like the comments on grease and Vaseline, this is the first time in the reports that commentators allude to diarrhea on the bed linens, which presumably had also been mentioned in the evidence that Wilde gave, as well as in Clarke's previous presentation for the defense (see 378 above).

244. This statement is somewhat opaque. There is a record that Jane Margaret Cotter, who served as a chambermaid at the Savoy Hotel, had found excrement on a bathroom utensil, as well as face powder on the bed linens where the unidentified young man had been sleeping (see 323–24 above).

245. In legal circles, the phrase "to hang a dog" referred (wryly) to the medieval and early modern practices in some European courts of punishing animals for offenses (such as biting and bestiality) that were on occasion deemed to be the responsibility of their owners. See Elisabeth A. Cawthorn, "Dogs and Dogma: Medico-Theory and the Problem of

Rabies in England, 1750–1850," in *Essays in European History: Selected from the Annual Meetings of the Southern Historical Association, 1990–1991*, ed. Carolyn W. White (Lanham, MD: University Press of America, 1996), 3:19.

246. [Anon.], "Wilde Trial: Fierce Combat between Counsel," Clark press clippings, 123.

247. [Millard], *Oscar Wilde: Three Times Tried*, 459. Lockwood's remark is also mentioned in I. Playfair [J. H. Wilson], *Gentle Criticisms on British Justice* (Newcastle upon Tyne: privately printed, 1895), 18. Wilson adds that the jury reached an "unexpected Verdict" (18). Lockwood's comment indicates that he suspected the jury might acquit Wilde and leave him free to flee to France in order to take refuge from the controversy surrounding the trials. Robert Harborough Sherard states that he was sitting behind Lockwood in court and did not hear this remark, but understood the solicitor general to say: "That means an acquittal"; *The Real Oscar Wilde: To Be Used as a Supplement to, and in Illustration of "The Life of Oscar Wilde"* (London: T. Werner Laurie, 1916), 378.

248. [Anon.], "Wilde Convicted," 5.

249. [Anon.], "Oscar Wilde: Gets Two Years' Hard Labour, and So Does Taylor," *Illustrated Police Budget*, 1 June 1895: 8; small change to punctuation. The more common phrase for the jury is "twelve good men and true"; usage dates from the early seventeenth century.

250. [Anon.], "Wilde: The Last Terrible Scene of the Great Trial," *Star*, 27 May 1895: 2.

251. On the Court of Crown Cases Reserved, see 514 above.

252. [Anon.], "Wilde: The Last Terrible Scene of the Great Trial," 2.

253. Several newspapers carried the words "immoral house" or "infamous house" in place of "some kind of brothel"; see, for example, [anon.], "Oscar Wilde: The Last Day of His Trial," *Echo*, 27 May 1895, Clark press cuttings, 137. (This report is probably from a late edition, since it does not appear in the microfilm copy that I consulted.)

254. [Anon.], "End of the Oscar Wilde Case," *Illustrated Police News*, 1 June 1895: 4. Variations in the wording of Wills's speech appear in different newspapers.

255. [Anon.], "Wilde: Last Terrible Scene of the Great Trial," 2. The *Weekly Dispatch* observed: "There was intense excitement when sentence was pronounced; cries of 'Shame! Shame!' were heard from the gallery, accompanied by hisses" ([anon.], "Wilde and Taylor: The Sentences—Closing Scenes," *Weekly Dispatch*, 2 June 1895: 2).

256. Robert Harborough Sherard, "Ultima Verba: With Some Reflections on the Mischief Caused by Pernicious Amnesia—Being an Open Letter to George Bernard Shaw," British Library, Add. MS 81688, fo. 7.

257. Seymour Hicks, *Between Ourselves* (London: Cassell, 1930), 85.

258. Hicks, *Between Ourselves*, 86.

CHAPTER SIX

Epigraphs: [anon.], "The Wilde Case," *Morning*, 27 May 1895: 4; and [anon.], "The Criminal Jailers of Oscar Wilde," *Liberty*, 15 June 1895: 4.

1. See Josephine M. Guy, "'The Soul of Man under Socialism': A (Con)Textual History," in *Wilde Writings: Contextual Conditions*, ed. Joseph Bristow (Toronto: University of Toronto Press, 2003), 58–85.

2. J. Benjamin Townsend states that Davidson's comment comes from a letter dated 25 March 1895, though the sentiment would appear to place it some time later (such as 25 May 1895). The letter is held at Princeton University Library; *John Davidson: Poet of Armageddon* (New Haven, CT: Yale University Press, 1961), 184.

3. Robert Harborough Sherard, *Oscar Wilde: The Story of an Unhappy Friendship* (London: Hermes Press, 1902), 200. The Russian realist artist Vasily Vereshchagin was famous for his war paintings.

4. The image is too roughly drawn to warrant reproduction here; see [anon.], "Oscar Wilde: Gets Two Years' Hard Labour, and So Does Taylor," *Illustrated Police Budget*, 1 June 1895: 8.

5. H. Montgomery Hyde, *Oscar Wilde*, Famous Trials 7 (Harmondsworth: Penguin, 1962), 273. Hyde does not provide a source.

6. [Anon.], "News of the Week," *News of the World*, 5 May 1895: 6.

7. [Anon.], "The Wilde Case: Result of the Trial at the Old Bailey," *News of the World*, 26 May 1895: 1.

8. [Anon.], "Editorial," *Daily Telegraph*, 27 May 1895: 6.

9. [Anon.], "Editorial," *Daily Telegraph*, 6. The adjective "effeminate" is implicitly linked here with homosexuality.

10. [Anon.], "Editorial," *Daily Telegraph*, 6.

11. [Henry Labouchere], "A Righteous Verdict," *Truth*, 30 May 1895: 1331.

12. [Labouchere], "A Righteous Verdict," 1331.

13. [Labouchere], "A Righteous Verdict," 1331. Not surprisingly, Douglas took Labouchere to task; see Alfred Douglas, "To Henry Labouchere," 31 May 1895, Clark Library, Robert Baldwin Ross Collection, Box 85, Folders 15–16.

14. [Anon.], "Notes from London," *Scottish Law Review and Sheriff Court Reports* 111, no. 126 (1895): 180. The "Notes" are dated 30 May 1895. This writer refers to the "hideous tragedy of the Wilde case" (180).

15. [Anon.], "Notes from London," 181.

16. [Anon.], "Notes from London," 180.

17. [Anon.], "Notes from London," 182.

18. [Anon.], "Notes from London," 182.

19. Alfred Douglas, "Oscar Wilde," in *Oscar Wilde: A Plea and a Reminiscence*, ed. Caspar Wintermans (Woubrugge: Avalon Press, 2002), 27.

20. More Adey, "To an Unknown Correspondent," [June 1895], Clark Library, MS Wilde, A233L U58 1895, Box 1 Folder 5. Adey's letter was drafted on notepaper from the Hôtel de la Poste, Rouen. The document, which was prepared for the French press, begins with an apology "for writing . . . in English."

21. Edward Marjoribanks [with Ian Colvin], *The Life of Lord Carson*, 3 vols. (London: Victor Gollancz, 1932–36), 1:230.

22. Marjoribanks, *The Life of Lord Carson*, 1:230.

23. Marjoribanks, *The Life of Lord Carson*, 1:230.

24. [W. T. Stead], "The Progress of the World," *Review of Reviews*, June 1895: 492. In another article, Stead observes that it is "quite extraordinary to discover how virtuous people

become the moment vice is locked up . . . . It is neither a manly nor a noble practice to exult over the bodies of the slain"; "The Innings of the Philistines: After the Fall of Oscar Wilde," *Review of Reviews*, June 1895: 538.

25. [Stead], "The Progress of the World," 493. Stead's comments echo those of George Egerton (see 295–96 above).

26. Edward Carpenter, "To W. T. Stead," 29 June 1895, British Library, Add. MS 81732. Carpenter's pamphlet appeared from the Labour Press Society, Manchester, in 1894. In 1895, the London publisher T. Fisher Unwin planned to reissue *Homogenic Love* with some of Carpenter's other sex-radical pamphlets. In light of Wilde's imprisonment, the company canceled the contract in July 1895. On this matter, in addition to the varied responses in the socialist press to Wilde's conviction, see Sheila Rowbotham, *Edward Carpenter: A Life of Liberty and Love* (London: Verso, 2008), 189–95.

27. Alfred Douglas, "To W. T. Stead," 28 June 1895, British Library, Add. MS 81732.

28. [Anon.], "Wilde: Some of the Mysteries of the Case," *Star*, 28 May 1895: 2.

29. [Anon.], "Wilde: Some of the Mysteries of the Case," 2. The game of noughts and crosses is sometimes known as tic-tac-toe outside Britain.

The answers to the journalist's thirteen questions, many of which have been documented above, are as follows: (1) John Francis Bloxam. (2) John Francis Bloxam. (3) The poet Lionel Johnson, who was Alfred Douglas's schoolmate at Winchester College, introduced Douglas to Wilde (Wilde referred to "a friend of Lady Queensberry and of my own" in the libel trial; Merlin Holland, *Irish Peacock and Scarlet Marquess: The Real Trial of Oscar Wilde* [London: Fourth Estate, 2003], 47). (4) Queensberry was accompanied by Edward James Pape, whose name Wilde mentioned during the libel trial (see Holland, *Irish Peacock*, 57). (5) During the libel proceedings, Wilde did not name Schwabe but handed his name on a piece of paper to Justice Collins; Wilde mentioned that he had met Taylor through this "gentleman," whose rooms, he recalled, were "off Regent Street . . . in Margaret Street on the ground floor" (Holland, *Irish Peacock*, 183). (6) During the pretrial hearing, Justice Bridge prevented Parker from uttering the name of the man who took him to meet Wilde at the Albemarle Hotel (see 169 above). (7) The "gentleman" has never been identified. (8) The composer may have been Cotsford Dick (see 517 above). (9) The "Birmingham gentleman" has never been identified. (10) The identity of the "gentleman" whom Atkins and Burton blackmailed remains unknown. (11) The "two American gentlemen" have never been identified. (12) The "foreign nobleman" may have been Marc-André Raffalovich. (13) The identity of the "elderly City man" remains unknown.

30. [Anon.], "Male Prostitution," *Reynolds's Newspaper*, 26 May 1895: 1.

31. On the Boulton and Park case, the Dublin Castle scandal, and the trial and imprisonment of Edward de Cobain, MP, see 118–19, 467–68, and 300.

32. [Anon.], "Male Prostitution," 1.

33. [Anon.], "Male Prostitution," 1.

34. [Anon.], "Male Prostitution," 1. *Reynolds's* continued to report on the unfairness of Wilde's trials. The paper featured, for example, a letter from "A Woman who Believes in Oscar Wilde"; she commented that Wilde "was condemned before he was convicted"

by a "large section of the press" ([anon.], "About Oscar Wilde," *Reynolds's Newspaper*, 16 June 1895: 5). Christopher Sclater Millard also protested the sentence; "C. S. M." "To the Editor of Reynolds's Newspaper." *Reynolds's Newspaper*, 2 June 1895: 8.

35. Dalhousie Young, *Apologia pro Oscar Wilde* (London: William Reeves, 1895), 6, 39.

36. Young, *Apologia pro Oscar Wilde*, 39–40. Young was not alone in harboring these sentiments. An anonymous letter dated 7 June 1895, signed "Justitia," and sent from the Liverpool Racquet Club to an unknown correspondent, states: "should such [homosexual] acts be punishable by law? If two men choose to indulge in this way with one another, what should law have to do with this matter?" (Clark Library, uncatalogued Wilde MSS).

37. H.M. Prison Pentonville, which opened in 1842, is a men's prison located on the Caledonian Road, Barnsbury, in north London. Designed by Joshua Jebb, it provided a model on which later penitentiaries in London were based.

38. [Herbert Gladstone, ed.], *Minutes of Evidence Taken by the Departmental Committee of Prisons* (London: HMSO, printed by Eyre and Spottiswoode, 1895), 16.

39. [Anon.], "Central Criminal Court—May 25. (Before Mr. Justice Wills.) Prosecution of Oscar Wilde," *Daily Telegraph*, 27 May 1895: 8.

40. [Anon.], "Oscar Wilde: Gets Two Years Hard Labour," 8.

41. [Anon.], "Oscar Wilde: Gets Two Years Hard Labour," 8. In Gladstone, *Minutes of Evidence*, one prison officer reported that "prisoners have to ascend something like 4,500 feet in 6 hours" (332).

42. [Anon.], "Oscar Wilde in Prison: State of His Health," *Morning*, 6 June 1895: 1.

43. [Anon.] "Oscar Wilde's Health in Prison: Official Statement," *Pall Mall Gazette*, 6 June 1895: 7.

44. [Anon.] "Oscar Wilde's Health in Prison," 7.

45. [Anon.] "The Convict Oscar Wilde: Attempt to Procure His Release," *Pall Mall Gazette*, 17 June 1895: 7.

46. Richard Burdon Haldane, *An Autobiography* (London: Hodder and Stoughton, 1929), 167. Flaubert's name was still contentious. In 1857, public prosecutors had taken a case against his novel *Madame Bovary* (1856) for obscenity. Flaubert was acquitted.

47. The list was received by the Home Office on 5 July 1895; National Archives, PCOM 8/432. Walter Pater's *Studies in the History of the Renaissance* (London: Macmillan, 1873), which was retitled in subsequent revised editions as *The Renaissance: Studies in Art and Poetry* (1877, 1888, and 1893), remained one of the strongest influences on Wilde's outlook on art. The works by Newman were *Apologia pro vita sua* (1864), *An Essay in Aid of a Grammar of Assent* (1870), *Two Essays on Scripture Miracles and on Ecclesiastical* (1870), and *The Idea of a University Defined and Illustrated* (1873).

48. Opened in 1851, H.M. Prison Wandsworth for men is located on Heathfield Road, Wandsworth, in southwest London.

49. William Douglas Morrison, "Are Our Prisons a Failure?," *Fortnightly Review* 55 (1894): 468. Morrison had already made similar observations four years earlier: "if the purpose of imprisonment is not only to punish but also to prepare the offender for the duties of society, the system of solitary confinement will not effectually accomplish this task" (William Douglas Morrison, *Crime and Its Causes* [London: Swan and Sonnenschein, 1891], 216).

50. Oscar Wilde, "To Lord Alfred Douglas," [January–March 1897], in *The Complete Letters of Oscar Wilde*, ed. Merlin Holland and Rupert Hart-Davis (London: Fourth Estate, 2000), 735.

51. André Gide, *Oscar Wilde: A Study*, ed. and trans. Stuart Mason [Christopher Sclater Millard] (Oxford: Holywell Press, 1905), 63. Gide's essay first appeared as "Oscar Wilde," *L'Ermitage: Revue mensuelle de littérature* 24 (1902): 401–29. Gide visited Wilde at Berneval-sur-Mer, Normandy, where Wilde settled in late May 1897, in the third week of June that year.

52. J. Robert Maguire, *Ceremonies of Bravery: Oscar Wilde, Carlos Blacker, and the Dreyfus Affair* (Oxford: Oxford University Press, 2013), 54.

53. [Anon.], "A Visit to Oscar Wilde," *Era*, 31 August 1895: 10.

54. [Anon.], "A Visit to Oscar Wilde," 10.

55. Sherard reiterated this comment in *Oscar Wilde: The Story of an Unhappy Friendship*, 206; *The Life of Oscar Wilde* (London: T. Werner Laurie, 1906), 373; and *The Real Oscar Wilde: To Be Used as a Supplement to, and in Illustration of "The Life of Oscar Wilde"* (London. T. Werner Laurie, 1916), 386.

56. Constance Wilde, letter, 13 September 1895, National Archives, PCOM 8/432. The envelope for this letter has not been preserved; the letter was presumably addressed to the secretary of the prison commission.

57. Constance Wilde, "To Richard Harborough Sherard," 21 September 1895, in Sherard, *The Real Oscar Wilde*, 173 (this is a holograph reproduction of the letter). Sherard also transcribed the letter in *Oscar Wilde: The Story of an Unhappy Friendship*, 209–10.

58. Constance Wilde, "To Richard Harborough Sherard," 21 September 1895, 173.

59. W. D. Morrison, "To Richard Burdon Haldane," 11 September 1895, National Archives, PCOM 8/432.

60. W. D. Morrison, "To Richard Burdon Haldane," 11 September 1895. Carbolic soap, which contains phenol, was used as a disinfectant from the 1860s onward.

61. Evelyn Ruggles-Brise, "To Richard Burdon Haldane," 7 October 1895, National Archives, PCOM 8/432.

62. Evelyn Ruggles-Brise, memorandum, 1 October 1895, National Archives, PCOM 8/432. The document contains a note in a different hand stating that Ruggles-Brise requests permission from the home secretary to inform Haldane about the inquiries that have been made into Morrison's claims, adding that there is reason to believe the chaplain's conduct will come to "no good" and that it is time to "transfer Wilde to a country prison." Ruggles-Brise presumably thought that removing Wilde to a prison outside London would diminish the amount of attention that activists such as Morrison had been paying to him.

63. Jeyes Fluid was a widely used disinfectant that the inventor John Jeyes patented in 1877.

64. Ruggles-Brise, memorandum, 1 October 1895.

65. Press clipping from the *Daily Chronicle*, 27 September 1895: 5, National Archives, PCOM 8/432.

66. Press clipping from the *Daily Chronicle*, 28 September 1895: 5, National Archives, PCOM 8/432.

67. H. Montgomery Hyde assumes that this name refers to one of Sherard's brothers; *Oscar Wilde: The Aftermath* (London: Methuen, 1963), 34. Sherard stopped identifying as Kennedy after a family dispute about an inheritance.

68. George Rayner, Principal Warder, H.M. Prison Wandsworth, 16 October 1895, National Archives, PCOM 8/433.

69. A receiving order, which can be made by either a creditor or a debtor, is a petition asking the court to appoint an official receiver to take over the debtor's estate.

70. The official announcement about Wilde's bankruptcy was reported widely in the press. See, for example, [anon.], "Bankruptcy of Oscar Wilde," *Pall Mall Gazette*, 22 August 1895: 7. Maguire gives the breakdown of the total sum as follows: £677 3s. 8d. to cover Queensberry's legal costs; £1,557 16s. 1d. to the trustees of Constance's marriage settlement (this amount includes the compound interest on the unpaid loan of £1,000 that the trust had made to him before his wedding); £500 for an unpaid loan, dating from 1885, from Constance's brother, Otho Holland Lloyd; £414 19s. 11d. to George Alexander for advances given against royalties on *The Importance of Being Earnest*; and £70 16s. 11d. for unpaid bills at the Savoy Hotel (where Wilde had rooms in 1893–94). There was also a sum of £230 owed to sundry vendors. See Maguire, *Ceremonies of Bravery*, 54. Cf. Donald Mead, "Heading for Disaster: Oscar's Finances," *Wildean* 46 (2015): 80–113.

71. This information is in the papers relating to the marriage settlement: see Justice Kekewich, British Library, Add. MS 81754 A–F.

72. Among More Adey's papers held at the Clark Library are several undated accounts of fees paid and monies received in relation to Wilde's affairs; some of these suggest that the individuals who had contributed to the fund included Dalhousie Young (£50); the Cambridge Hegelian philosopher J. M. E. McTaggart (£50); and Digby La Motte, a classics master at St. Paul's School (£50). More Adey, "Various Assorted Papers," Clark Library, MS Wilde, A223Z V312, Box 1, Folder 10. Ross, too, had been attempting to raise the desired sum; he assured Oscar Browning, a fellow at King's College, Cambridge: "No names of subscribers will be made public so none of the charitably disposed need fear lest the appearance of their names might give the impression that they were in any way connected with Oscar Wilde" ("To Oscar Browning," 21 October 1895, in Maureen Borland, *Wilde's Devoted Friend: A Life of Robert Ross, 1869–1918* [Oxford: Lennard, 1990], 510). The sums that had been collected were returned to the donors after Wilde was declared bankrupt in November 1895.

73. Arthur Clifton, "To Carlos Blacker," 24 September 1895, Blacker Papers, Hand's Cove Library, Shoreham, Vermont, quoted in Maguire, *Ceremonies of Bravery*, 59. On 24 August 1895, Clifton had requested an interview with Wilde to discuss the bankruptcy proceedings. The authorities refused. The following month, Clifton stated that he would like to send and receive a letter on this matter. This, too, was declined.

74. Clifton, "To Carlos Blacker," 24 September 1895, 59.

75. Clifton, "To Carlos Blacker," 24 September 1895, 59.

76. R. M. Gover, "To Evelyn Ruggles-Brise," 28 September 1895, National Archives, PCOM 8/432. Hyde notes that Gover was the superintending medical officer of prisons; *Oscar Wilde: The Aftermath*, 27.

77. Frank Harris, *Oscar Wilde: His Life and Confessions*, 2 vols. (New York: privately printed, 1916), 2:334. Wilde told Harris about this experience during a visit on 16 June 1896.

78. Harris, *Oscar Wilde: His Life and Confessions*, 2:336–37.

79. Richard Brayn and David Nicholson, report, 29 October 1895, National Archives, HO/45 24514. The doctors had trained as forensic psychologists.

80. [Anon.], "Oscar Wilde in Court: His Bankruptcy Affairs," *Reynolds's Newspaper*, 17 November 1895: 3.

81. [Anon.], "The Bankruptcy of Oscar Wilde: Appearance in Court," *Daily News*, 13 November 1895: 7. A transcript of the hearing is reproduced in Mead, "Heading for Disaster," 98–101.

82. A. P. H. Helby, memorandum, H.M. Prison Wandsworth, 17 October 1895, National Archives, PCOM 8/433.

83. Helby, memorandum, H.M. Prison Wandsworth, 17 October 1895.

84. Home Office referred letter, 29 October 1895, National Archives, PCOM 8/433.

85. Designed by George Gilbert Scott and William Boyntham Moffatt, H.M. Prison Reading opened in 1844. The institution, which accepted male and female adult prisoners and male child prisoners, was modeled on the separate system pioneered at Pentonville. Public executions took place there until 1868, after which time the death penalty was administered inside. The prison was closed in 2014. The Ministry of Justice put the building up for sale in October 2019.

86. Oscar Wilde, "To Lord Alfred Douglas," [January–March 1897], in *The Complete Letters*, 756–57. Sherard claimed that a man standing on the platform declared: "'By God, that's Oscar Wilde!' and spat in his face"; *Oscar Wilde: The Story of an Unhappy Friendship*, 220.

87. Richard B. Haldane, "To More Adey," 23 January 1896, Clark Library, MS Wilde, H158L A233 1896, Box 29, Folder 30.

88. [Anon.], "Oscar Wilde Secretly Released from Prison at Night Time," *Illustrated Police News*, 29 May 1897: 3.

89. Gide, *Oscar Wilde: A Study*, 66.

90. Gide, *Oscar Wilde: A Study* 67.

91. Gide, *Oscar Wilde: A Study*, 67.

92. Gide, *Oscar Wilde: A Study*, 67.

93. Constance Wilde, "To Lily Wilde," February 1896, Clark Library, MS Wilde, W6771L W613, Box 70, Folder 3. This letter is a copy in Adey's hand. Lily Wilde had visited Oscar on 17 October 1895; during the visit, she informed him of his mother's ailing health.

94. Constance Wilde, "To Lily Wilde," February 1896.

95. The draft of this letter, which is undated, is held at the Clark Library, MS Wilde, A233L W6721 [1896]b, Box 1, Folder 7.

96. Robert Ross, "To More Adey," [30 May 1896], in *Robert Ross, Friend of Friends: Letters to Robert Ross, Art Critic and Writer, Together with Extracts from His Published Articles*, ed. Margery Ross (London: Jonathan Cape, 1952), 39. My quotations, which differ slightly from the text in Margery Ross's edition, follow the original document, which

is held at the Clark Library, MS Wilde, R825L A233, Box 56, Folder 1. Merlin Holland and Rupert Hart-Davis date Sherard and Ross's visit to Friday, 29 May 1896; Wilde, *The Complete Letters*, 654.

97. Ross, "To More Adey," [30 May 1896], 39.

98. Ross, "To More Adey," [30 May 1896], 39-40.

99. Ross, "To More Adey," [30 May 1896], 40.

100. Ross, "To More Adey," [30 May 1896], 40.

101. Ross, "To More Adey," [30 May 1896], 40.

102. Ross, "To More Adey," [30 May 1896], 40 and 41.

103. Ross, "To More Adey," [30 May 1896], 42. By "silly," Ross meant defenseless or powerless.

104. Ross, "To More Adey," [30 May 1896], 42.

105. Ross, "To More Adey," [30 May 1896], 43.

106. Evelyn-Ruggles-Brise, memorandum to Henry Isaacson, drafted by a secretary on 13 June 1896, National Archives, PCOM 8/433. The document was received and signed by Isaacson the following day, and then returned with an enclosed report, which Ruggles-Brise acknowledged on 16 June 1896.

107. Alfred Douglas, "To Ada Leverson," 13 September 1895, Clark Library, MS Wilde, D733L L661, Box 20, Folder 5.

108. Douglas, "To Ada Leverson," 13 September 1895.

109. Douglas, "To Ada Leverson," 13 September 1895. Douglas also remarks in this letter: "I really wish Oscar & I were both dead."

110. Alfred Douglas, "To Her Majesty the Queen," 25 June 1895, National Archives, HO 45/24514. As we see in the same file, on 29 June 1895 an official assured Queen Victoria's private secretary that she had not seen the correspondence, and that it would be left for the home secretary to decide upon taking any action against Douglas.

111. Hughes Rebell, "Défense d'Oscar Wilde," *Mercure de France* 67 (1895): 182.

112. Alfred Douglas, *The Autobiography of Lord Alfred Douglas*, 2nd ed. (London: Martin Secker, 1931), 118.

113. Douglas, *Autobiography*, 118.

114. See Alfred Douglas, "Amoris Vincula," "In Praise of Shame," "In Sarum Close," "Two Loves," and "Sicilian Love-Song," in *Poems/Poèmes* (Paris: Mercure de France, 1896), 19–20, 22–23, 24–25, 104–11, and 120–21, respectively.

115. Oscar Wilde, "To Robert Ross," [30 May 1896], in *The Complete Letters*, 654.

116. Wilde, "To Robert Ross," [30 May 1896], 654, 655.

117. Alfred Douglas, "Une introduction à mes poèmes, avec quelques considérations sur l'affaire Oscar Wilde," *Revue blanche*, 1 June 1896: 486.

118. Alfred Douglas, "To Robert Ross," 4 June 1896, in Richard Ellmann, *Oscar Wilde* (New York: Knopf, 1988), 501.

119. Harris, *Oscar Wilde: His Life and Confessions*, 2:328.

120. Harris, *Oscar Wilde: His Life and Confessions*, 2:330.

121. Harris, *Oscar Wilde: His Life and Confessions*, 2:339.

122. Harris, *Oscar Wilde: His Life and Confessions*, 2:342.

123. Harris, *Oscar Wilde: His Life and Confessions*, 2:343.

124. Harris, *Oscar Wilde: His Life and Confessions*, 2:340.

125. Oscar Wilde, "To the Home Secretary," 2 July 1896, in *The Complete Letters*, 658. Adey had already written to Haldane to see if Wilde might have "use of pen and ink" and an "improvement in diet"; Adey notes that Wilde had been "in the Infirmary several times since his removal to reading" ("To Richard Haldane," 13 April 1896, Clark Library, MS Wilde, A332 H158, Box 1, Folder 2; this document is a draft copy of the letter).

126. Wilde, "To the Home Secretary," 2 July 1896, 656.

127. Wilde, "To the Home Secretary," 2 July 1896, 656. In *The Man of Genius*, which first appeared in Italian in 1888, Lombroso claimed that many male geniuses "showed abnormalities of the reproductive functions"; Cesare Lombroso, *The Man of Genius*, trans. anon., 2nd ed. (London: Walter Scott, 1891), 316. In *Degeneration*, which first appeared in German in 1892, Nordau had already portrayed Wilde as an embodiment of the "egomania of decadentism." Nordau made it clear that artistic geniuses were often perverted; he accused the French poet Paul Verlaine, for example, of "madly inordinate eroticism" (Max Nordau, *Degeneration*, trans. anon., 2nd ed. [London: William Heinemann, 1895], 317, 120). At the time of Wilde's conviction, several commentators claimed that he was an example of a modern degenerate type. To cite one instance, H. W. Massingham in the *Daily Chronicle* stated that the proceeedings had created "a fresh chapter in Dr. Nordau's indictment of 'degeneration,' an appalling picture of the state of mind and heart in which all moral and intellectual perspective becomes blurred and distorted"; [H. W. Massingham], "Editorial," *Daily Chronicle*, 27 May 1895: 4.

128. Wilde, "To the Home Secretary," 2 July 1896, 657.

129. Wilde, "To the Home Secretary," 2 July 1896, 658.

130. Wilde, "To the Home Secretary," 2 July 1896, 659.

131. Oliver Calley Maurice, medical report, H.M. Prison Reading, 3 July 1896, National Archives, HO 45/24514.

132. Copy of "Extract from Visiting Committee Book: Re Oscar Wylde [*sic*]," H.M. Prison Reading, 10 July 1896, National Archives, HO 45/24514. Prison inspectors were not medical specialists. Their duties, which dated from the eighteenth century, involved addressing the conditions of the prisons.

133. Sir Kenelm Digby, memorandum no. A56887, 18 July 1896, National Archives, HO 45/24514. Digby served as permanent undersecretary at the Home Office.

134. W. B. Bury, copy of "Instructions Sent to Governor Reading Prison in the Case of Oscar Wilde," undated, National Archives, HO 45/24514. Bury wrote on behalf of the home secretary.

135. Bury, copy of "Instructions Sent to Governor Reading Prison."

136. On the murder of Laura Ellen Wooldridge, see Angela Buckley, "The 'Thing' He Loved," 5 July 2019, https://victorian-supersleuth.com/the-thing-he-loved/.

137. [Anon.], "Wilde's Prison Life at Reading Gaol": 8, Clark Library, uncatalogued Wilde MSS. This informative memoir, which is written in the pages of a notebook, appears to date from around 1906. There is some possibility that the memoir is by Charles Fleet, who counted among the prison guards and inmates to whom Wilde paid his "debts of honour" (in Fleet's case, £1 10s.) within two weeks of his release.

138. Oscar Wilde, *The Ballad of Reading Gaol*, in *Poems and Poems in Prose*, ed. Bobby Fong and Karl Beckson, *The Complete Works of Oscar Wilde*, 11 vols. to date (Oxford: Oxford University Press, 2000–), 1:197.

139. Oscar Wilde, "To Leonard Smithers, 19 [November 1897], in *The Complete Letters*, 983.

140. Ross made the same error: "Isaacson is a Jew, tall and not unlike the head master of a public school" (*Robert Ross: Friend of Friends*, 43). Isaacson received a Catholic burial.

141. Gide, *Oscar Wilde: A Study*, 70; and Wilfred Hugh Chesson, "A Reminiscence of 1898," *Bookman* 37 (1912): 390.

142. James O. Nelson, quoted in *Manchester Guardian*, 13 October 1914: 5, reprinted in Hyde, *Oscar Wilde: The Aftermath*, 79.

143. James O. Nelson, "To the Commissioners of Prisons," 29 July 1896, National Archives, PCOM 8/433.

144. [Anon.], "Wilde's Prison Life at Reading Gaol," 14.

145. Gide, *Oscar Wilde: A Study*, 71. Wilde had once again requested a prose translation of the *Divine Comedy*; it appears that he received an Italian-language edition.

146. Oscar Wilde, "To More Adey," [25 September 1896], in *The Complete Letters*, 664, 666.

147. Wilde, "To More Adey," [25 September 1896], 666.

148. Oscar Wilde, "To the Home Secretary," 10 November 1896, in *The Complete Letters*, 668.

149. Oscar Wilde, "To Robert Ross," [November 1896], in *The Complete Letters*, 669.

150. Wilde, "To Robert Ross," [November 1896], 669.

151. Wilde, "To Robert Ross," [November 1896], 669.

152. Wilde's list is in Ross's "Prison Letters and Other Documents," Clark Library, W6721L R825 1895–97 bound. Ross may have thought the works of Morrison too contentious to be sent to the prisoner. The list of requests is in Wilde, *The Complete Letters*, 791–93.

153. [Anon.], "Wilde's Prison Life at Reading Gaol," 12.

154. [Thomas Martin], "The Poet in Prison," in Sherard, *The Life of Oscar Wilde*, 390. Sherard did not disclose Martin's identity at the time.

155. [Martin], "The Poet in Prison," 389.

156. Oscar Wilde, "To Thomas Martin," [c. April 1897], in *The Complete Letters*, 798. These fragments are in Ross's collection of "Prison Letters and Other Documents." Martin passed these materials to Ross on 1 March 1898; he asked for a few shillings in return.

157. Martin's comments are in Sherard, *The Real Oscar Wilde*, 260. His letters to Sherard are held at Special Collections, University of Reading Library.

158. [Anon.], "Wilde's Prison Life at Reading Gaol," 7. A third warder at Reading, who published a short memoir of Wilde, also notes: "I always found Wilde extremely good-natured, and he wrote several little things out for me"; [anon.], "In the Depths: Account of Oscar Wilde's Life at Reading, Told by His Gaoler," *Evening News and Evening Mail*, 1 March 1905: 4, and 2 March 1905: 2, in *Oscar Wilde: Interviews and Recollections*, ed. E. H. Mikhail, 2 vols. (London: Macmillan, 1979), 2:331. This warder may have been George Groves.

159. [Anon.], "Wilde's Prison Life at Reading Gaol," 7.

160. [Anon.], "Wilde's Prison Life at Reading Gaol," 15.

161. [Anon.], "Wilde's Prison Life at Reading Gaol," 7.

162. [Anon.], "Wilde's Prison Life at Reading Gaol," 7.

163. [Martin], "The Poet in Prison," 400–1.

164. Alfred Douglas, "To More Adey," 27 September 1896, Clark Library, MS Wilde, D733L A33, Box 15, Folder 1. This is a typescript copy of the original document.

165. Douglas, "To More Adey," 27 September 1896.

166. Douglas, "To More Adey," 27 September 1896.

167. Alfred Douglas, "To More Adey," 30 November 1895, Clark Library, MS Wilde, D733L A33, Box 15, Folder 1. This is a typescript copy of the original document.

168. Douglas, "To More Adey," 30 December 1895.

169. Douglas, "To More Adey," 30 December 1895.

170. Oscar Wilde, "To Robert Ross," [November 1896], in *The Complete Letters*, 669.

171. Wilde, "To Robert Ross," [November 1896], 669.

172. Oscar Wilde, "To Robert Ross," 1 April 1897, in *The Complete Letters*, 782.

173. On 6 April 1897, Ruggles-Brise made this note on the memorandum that Nelson had sent to the Home Office four days earlier; National Archives, PCOM 8/434.

174. Oscar Wilde, "To More Adey," 18 February 1897, in *The Complete Letters*, 678.

175. Oscar Wilde, *De Profundis*, [ed. Robert Ross] (London: Methuen, 1905), 748; cf. Wilde, *The Complete Letters*, 748. Wilde probably had in mind the debate about Jesus Christ's uses of Greek and Aramaic in Alexander Roberts, *Greek: The Language of Christ and His Apostles* (London: Longmans, Green, 1888).

176. Wilde, *De Profundis*, 77; cf. *The Complete Letters*, 748–49.

177. Wilde, *De Profundis*, 12; cf. *The Complete Letters*, 730.

178. Wilde, "To Lord Alfred Douglas," [January–March 1897], 714.

179. Wilde, "To Lord Alfred Douglas," [January–March 1897], 757.

180. Wilde, "To Lord Alfred Douglas," [January–March 1897], 758.

181. Wilde, "To Lord Alfred Douglas," [January–March 1897], 729.

182. The fees for Humphreys's services, as we can tell from Adey's correspondence, were hefty. On both 5 July 1895 and 19 March 1896, Adey parted with 20 guineas to cover the costs of handling Wilde's bankruptcy. Additional sums of £50 were paid on 15 May 1896 and again on 20 June 1896 to cover Wilde's legal affairs.

183. Official Receiver, statement of proofs—admitted amounts of Wilde's bankruptcy, National Archives, B4/429, reproduced in Mead, "Heading for Disaster," 93.

184. Oscar Wilde, "To Robert Ross," 1 April 1897, in *The Complete Letters*, 785.

185. Wilde, "To Robert Ross," 1 April 1897, 785.

186. See Wilde, "To Alfred Douglas," [January–March 1897], 704.

187. Oscar Wilde, "To Robert Ross," 13 May 1897, in *The Complete Letters*, 822.

188. H. Martin Holman, "To More Adey," 10 May 1897, Clark Library, MS Wilde, D733L A233, Box 15, Folder 1. This is a typescript copy of the original document.

189. Holman, "To More Adey," 10 May 1897.

190. Holman, "To More Adey," 10 May 1897.

191. Holman, "To More Adey," 10 May 1897.

192. Wilde, "To Robert Ross," 13 May 1897, 823.

193. Wilde, "To Robert Ross," 13 May 1897, 816. Ricketts's account of the interview is very different; he says that Wilde's "cordial greeting and enquiries might have been spoken in Bond Street" (Jean Paul Raymond and Charles Ricketts, *Oscar Wilde: Recollections* [London: Nonesuch Press, 1932], 46). Ricketts recalls that their lively exchanges touched on various artistic and literary matters.

194. E. Clayton, on behalf of the prison commissioners, "To More Adey," 8 April 1897, Clark Library, MS Wilde, G786L A233, Box 29, Folder 10.

195. More Adey, "To Ernest Flower," 22 March 1897, National Archives, HO 45/24514.

196. Visiting Committee Minutes, pp. 176, 185, 191, Berkshire Record Office, P/RP1/6/1, quoted in Peter Stoneley, "'Looking at the Others': Oscar Wilde and the Reading Gaol Archive," *Journal of Victorian Culture* 19, no. 4 (2014): 469.

197. Oscar Wilde, "To the Editor of the *Daily Chronicle*," 27 May 1897, in *The Complete Letters*, 853. The letter, which appeared the next day, was headlined "The Case of Warder Martin, Some Cruelties of Prison Life." Martin had recently been dismissed from his duties, ostensibly on the grounds that he had given a hungry child prisoner some "sweet biscuits"; *The Complete Letters*, 847.

198. Wilde, "To the Editor of the *Daily Chronicle*," 27 May 1897, 853

199. [Anon.], "Wilde's Prison Life at Reading Gaol," 8. The term "idiot" here refers to a person suffering from permanent mental illness.

200. Oscar Wilde, "To Thomas Martin," [17 May 1897], in *The Complete Letters*, 831. On the plight of the children held on remand, see the coda (439–42).

201. [Anon.], "In the Depths," 2:330.

202. [Anon.], "In the Depths," 2:330.

203. More Adey, "To Evelyn Ruggles-Brise," 16 May 1897, National Archives, PCOM 8/434.

204. More Adey, "To Adela Schuster," 12 March 1898, Clark Library, MS Wilde, A233L S395, Box 1, Folders 2–8.

205. Reggie Turner, "To Oscar Wilde," 18 May 1897, in Wilde, *The Complete Letters*, 837.

206. Oscar Wilde, "To More Adey," 17 May 1897, in *The Complete Letters*, 834.

207. Nicholas Frankel, *Oscar Wilde: The Unrepentant Years* (Cambridge, MA: Harvard University Press, 2017), 4.

208. Adey, "To Adela Schuster," 12 March 1898.

209. Oscar Wilde, "To More Adey," 6 May 1897, in *The Complete Letters*, 809.

210. [Anon.], "Release of Mr. Wilde: Removed Secretly from Reading to Holloway," *Morning*, 19 May 1897, National Archives, PCOM 8/434.

211. [Anon.], "Oscar Wilde Released: Smuggled from Reading to Pentonville," *Pall Mall Gazette*, 19 May 1897: 7.

212. [Anon.], "Oscar Wilde Released," 7.

213. Stewart Headlam, quoted in F. G. Bettany, *Stewart Headlam: A Biography* (London: John Murray, 1926), 132.

214. Headlam, quoted in Bettany, *Stewart Headlam*, 132.

215. Ada Leverson, *Letters to the Sphinx from Oscar Wilde, with Reminiscences of the Author* (London: Duckworth 1930), 45.

216. Bettany recalls Headlam's stating that Wilde asked him to send for a priest at the Jesuit Church of the Immaculate Conception, Farm Street, Mayfair; *Stewart Headlam*, 132.

217. Leverson, *Letters to the Sphinx*, 46.

218. Adey, "To Adela Schuster," 12 March 1898. Adey meant East Croydon, one of the stops along the line from Victoria to Newhaven.

219. Oscar Wilde, "To Robert Ross," 19 May 1897, in *The Complete Letters*, 844.

220. Robert Ross, "Unpublished Preface to after Reading," Clark Library, MS Wilde, R825M3 U58, Box 58, Folder 3, reprinted in Wilde, *The Complete Letters*, 842. The document probably dates from 1911.

CODA

Epigraphs: Oscar Wilde, "To Carlos Blacker," 22 September 1897, in *The Complete Letters of Oscar Wilde*, ed. Merlin Holland and Rupert Hart-Davis (London: Fourth Estate, 2000), 947; More Adey, "To Adela Schuster," 12 March 1898, Clark Library, MS Wilde A233L S395, Box 1, Folders 2–8.

1. Ada Leverson, *Letters to the Sphinx from Oscar Wilde, with Reminiscences of the Author* (London: Duckworth 1930), 45.

2. Oscar Wilde, "To the Editor of the *Daily Chronicle*," 27 May 1897, in *The Complete Letters*, 848. The letter appeared the next day. Martin's letter was published in the *Daily Chronicle*, 24 May 1897: 5.

3. Wilde, "To the Editor of the *Daily Chronicle*," 27 May 1897, 848.

4. Wilde, "To the Editor of the *Daily Chronicle*," 27 May 1897, 849.

5. Wilde, "To the Editor of the *Daily Chronicle*," 27 May 1897, 850.

6. Wilde, "To the Editor of the *Daily Chronicle*," 27 May 1897, 852.

7. [Herbert Gladstone, ed.], *Minutes of Evidence Taken by the Departmental Committee on Prisons* (London: HMSO, printed by Eyre and Spottiswoode, 1895), 28–29.

8. Peter Stoneley, "'Looking at the Others': Oscar Wilde and the Reading Gaol Archive." *Journal of Victorian Culture* 19, no. 4 (2014): 471.

9. Stoneley, "Looking at the Others," 471. Stoneley observes: "The month closest to Wilde's imprisonment for which the prison registers are complete and entirely legible is November 1893" (463).

10. "List of Criminal Cases, Wilde, Oscar Fingal O'Flahertie," National Archives, HO 144/271/A58947.

11. National Archives, HO 144/271/A58947. The documents in the file are stamped 28 May and 31 May 1897. All further quotations from these official documents come from this file.

12. Michael Davitt, "Reading Prison (Discharge of Warder)," *Hansard's Parliamentary Debates*, 4th series, vol. 49, 25 May 1897, cols. 1266–67, and 27 May 1897, col. 1420, https://api.parliament.uk/historic-hansard/commons/1897/may/27/index.html.

13. Oscar Wilde ["Melmoth"], account book, [May–June 1895], Clark Library, uncatalogued Wilde MSS. Martin received at least one additional sum of £6 from Wilde. In a letter to Ross written a few months after Wilde's release, Martin states that he intends to

repay this amount by 25 September 1897 (26 August 1897, in Wilde, *The Complete Letters*, 932). Martin was writing from the Holborn Union Workhouse.

14. George Groves, "To Oscar Wilde," 2 June 1897, in "Prison Letters and Other Documents," Clark Library, MS Wilde, Box W6721L R825 Bound, leaf 25.

15. Oscar Wilde, "To an Unidentified Correspondent," [*c.* 28 May 1897], in *The Complete Letters*, 861. Stoneley suggests that this letter was sent to Bushnell; "Looking at the Others," 476. The text of the letter appeared in the *Newbury Express* on 1 July 1897.

16. Wilde, "To an Unidentified Correspondent," [*c.* 28 May 1897], 862.

17. James O. Nelson, "To Robert Ross," 22 May 1897, in "Prison Letters and Other Documents," leaf 24.

18. Oscar Wilde, "To Major J. O. Nelson," [28 May 1897], in *The Complete Letters*, 862.

19. Wilde, "To Major J. O. Nelson," [28 May 1897], 863.

20. Wilde, "To Major J. O. Nelson," [28 May 1897], 863.

21. Oscar Wilde, "To Reginald Turner," [? 7 June 1895], in *The Complete Letters*, 889.

22. For an account of Cruttenden's career, see Stephen Clifford Wilson, "Oscar Wilde and Arthur Cruttenden: Inside and outside Reading Gaol," *Notes and Queries* 52, no. 1 (2005): 82–84.

23. Wilde, "To Reginald Turner," [? 7 June 1895], 888.

24. Wilde, "To Reginald Turner," [? 7 June 1895], 887.

25. Wilde, "To Robert Ross," [28 May 1897], 858.

26. Wilde, "To Robert Ross," [29–30 May 1897], in *The Complete Letters*, 865. Plans were discussed between Wilde and his wife so that the boys might visit him at Dieppe. There was also the hope that he might see his family in October 1897. But these prospects came to nothing.

27. Ernest Dowson, "To Conal O'Riordan," 16 June 1897, in *The Letters of Ernest Dowson*, ed. Desmond Flower and Henry Maas (London: Cassell, 1967), 387.

28. Dowson, "To Conal O'Riordan," 16 June 1897, 387.

29. Oscar Wilde, "To Ernest Dowson," [? 11 October 1897], in *The Complete Letters*, 957.

30. André Gide, *Oscar Wilde: A Study*, ed. and trans. Stuart Mason [Christopher Sclater Millard] (Oxford: Holywell Press, 1905), 59.

31. André Gide, *Oscar Wilde: A Study*, 72.

32. See Nicholas Frankel, *Oscar Wilde: The Unrepentant Years* (Cambridge, MA: Harvard University Press, 2017); and Matthew Sturgis, *Oscar: A Life* (London: Head of Zeus, 2018), 627–715.

33. Wilde, "To Robert Ross," [28 May 1897], 858.

34. Oscar Wilde, "To Lord Alfred Douglas," 4 June 1897, in *The Complete Letters*, 881.

35. Wilde, "To Lord Alfred Douglas," 4 June 1897, 880.

36. Oscar Wilde, "To Lord Alfred Douglas," 13 June 1897, in *The Complete Letters*, 898.

37. Oscar Wilde, "To Lord Alfred Douglas," 17 June 1897, in *The Complete Letters*, 901.

38. Wilde, "To Lord Alfred Douglas," 17 June 1897, 901.

39. Oscar Wilde, "To Robert Ross," 4 September 1897, in *The Complete Letters*, 934.

40. Oscar Wilde, "To Robert Ross," 21 September 1897, in *The Complete Letters*, 942.

41. Wilde, "To Robert Ross," 21 September 1897, 942.

42. This is the figure that Douglas gives in *The Autobiography of Alfred Douglas*, 2nd ed. (London: Martin Secker, 1931), 152. In December, Lady Sibyl provided funds to defray the debt.

43. Wilde's interview with Rocco first appeared in an Italian edition of *Il delitto di Lord Arturo Savile*, trans. Federigo Verdinois (Naples: Società Editrice Partenopea, 1908), and is translated in Renato Miracco, *Oscar Wilde's Italian Dream, 1875–1900: The Infamous St. Oscar of Oxford, Poet and Martyr Undecided between the Cloister and the Café* (Bologna: Daniami, 2020), 80–81.

44. Miracco, *Oscar Wilde's Italian Dream*, 81.

45. Harry de Windt, *My Note-Book at Home and Abroad* (New York: E. P. Dutton, 1923), 141. Douglas recalls meeting de Windt at this time with Wilde; *Autobiography*, 154–55.

46. Douglas, *Autobiography*, 154.

47. Oscar Wilde, "To More Adey," [27 November 1897], in *The Complete Letters*, 994.

48. Wilde, "To More Adey," [27 November 1897], 995.

49. Oscar Wilde, "To Robert Ross," [? 2 March 1898], in *The Complete Letters*, 1029.

50. Later, in 1929, Douglas claimed that he gave these sums to Wilde; he added that the cheques were drawn by his mother and disbursed by More Adey (see Douglas, *Autobiography*, 323).

51. Logan Pearsall Smith, "To Robert C. Trevelyan," *c.* January 1898, in *A Chime of Words: The Letters of Logan Pearsall Smith*, ed. Edwin Tribble (New York: Ticknor and Fields, 1984), 102. The publisher Leonard Smithers had met with Wilde soon after his release from jail; see 449. Smithers was known for maintaining a list of clandenstine erotica, including the anonymous homoerotic novel *Teleny; or, the Reverse of the Medal* (1893), with which Wilde's name has sometimes been associated.

52. Vincent O'Sullivan, *Aspects of Wilde* (London: Constable, 1936), 69.

53. Oscar Wilde, "To Robert Ross," [? 18 February 1898], in *The Complete Letters*, 1019.

54. Wilde, "To Robert Ross," [? 18 February 1898], 1019.

55. William Douglas Morrison, "Prison Reform: I.—Prisons and Prisoners," *Fortnightly Review* 63 (1898): 781.

56. Morrison, "Prison Reform," 781.

57. Oscar Wilde, *The Ballad of Reading Gaol*, in *Poems and Poems in Prose*, ed. Bobby Fong and Karl Beckson, *The Complete Works of Oscar Wilde*, 11 vols. to date (Oxford: Oxford University Press, 2000–), 1:202.

58. Wilde, *Complete Works*, 1:198.

59. Wilde, *Complete Works*, 1:195.

60. Wilde, *Complete Works*, 1:206.

61. Wilde, *Complete Works*, 1:209.

62. Wilde, *Complete Works*, 1:209.

63. [W. E. Henley], "De Profundis," *Outlook*, 5 March 1898: 146.

64. [Anon.], "New Poem by Oscar Wilde: 'The Ballad of Reading Gaol,'" *Reynolds's Newspaper*, 13 February 1898: 8.

65. Major J. O. Nelson, "To Robert Ross," 12 January 1898, in Robert Ross, *Robert Ross, Friend of Friends: Letters to Robert Ross, Art Critic and Writer, Together with Extracts*

from His Published Articles, ed. Margery Ross (London: Jonathan Cape, 1952), 50. Nelson added that he was "distressed to gather from [Ross's] letter that Mr. Wilde has not succeeded in rescuing himself completely from the slough of the past two years" (50).

66. Edmund Gosse, "To Robert Ross," 21 February 1898, in Ross, *Friend of Friends*, 50.

67. *Hansard's Parliamentary Debates*, 4th series, 4th Session of 26th Parliament, vol. 16, col. 60. https://api.parliament.uk/historic-hansard/commons/1898/apr/04/prisons-bill.

68. Oscar Wilde, "To the Editor of the *Daily Chronicle*," 23 March 1898, in *The Complete Letters*, 1045.

69. Wilde, "To the Editor of the *Daily Chronicle*," 23 March 1898, 1049.

70. Frankel, *Oscar Wilde: The Unrepentant Years*, 194.

71. Robert Ross, "To Leonard Smithers," 9 May 1898, Fales Library, New York University, quoted in Sturgis, *Oscar*, 683.

72. Oscar Wilde, "To Robbie Ross," [July 1898], in *The Complete Letters*, 1090.

73. Constance Wilde, "To Carlos Blacker," 20 March 1898, Blacker Papers, Hand's Cove Library, Shoreham, Vermont, quoted in J. Robert Maguire, *Ceremonies of Bravery: Oscar Wilde, Carlos Blacker, and the Dreyfus Affair* (Oxford: Oxford University Press, 2013), 119.

74. Constance Wilde died on 7 April 1898. On the surgery that the Italian gynecologist Luigi Maria Bossi performed on Constance at Genoa in hopes of relieving nine years of pain that had affected her mobility, see Ashley H. Robins and Merlin Holland, "The Art of Medicine: The Enigmatic Illness and Death of Constance, Wife of Oscar Wilde," *Lancet*, 3 January 2015: 21–22; Robins and Holland suggest that the genitourinary problems she suffered were related to multiple sclerosis and not, as Bossi believed, a uterine fibroid.

75. Chris Healy, *Confessions of a Journalist*, 2nd ed. (London: Chatto and Windus, 1904), 132.

76. Healy, *Confessions of a Journalist*, 133, 134.

77. Healy, *Confessions of a Journalist*, 134.

78. Oscar Wilde, "To Carlos Blacker," [8 March 1898], in *The Complete Letters*, 1035.

79. Wilfred Hugh Chesson, "A Reminiscence of 1898," *Bookman* 34 (1911): 389.

80. Chesson, "A Reminiscence of 1898," 390.

81. Chesson, "A Reminiscence of 1898," 390.

82. Rowland Strong, "In the French Capital," *New York Times*, 19 June 1898: 19. The background to this episode is discussed in Maguire, *Ceremonies of Bravery*, 31–50.

83. Oscar Wilde, "To Robert Ross," 27 June 1898, in *The Complete Letters*, 1085, 1086.

84. Wilde, "To Robert Ross," 27 June 1898, 1086. The reference is to the hypocritical protagonist of *Tartuffe* (1664) by Molière.

85. Wilde, "To Robert Ross," 27 June 1898, 1086.

86. Healy, *Confessions of a Journalist*, 126.

87. Healy, *Confessions of a Journalist*, 126.

88. Nellie Melba, *Melodies and Memories* (New York: George H. Doran, 1926), 79. This episode probably occurred in the middle of 1900, when Wilde was visibly in decline.

89. George Barr Baker, "Criminal Genius in Exile: Picture from His Last Days in Paris," unidentified press cutting, dated 28 November 190[?], in an album of press cuttings, Clark Library, Wildeiana, Box 25, Folder 20.

90. Gustave La Rouge, "Oscar Wilde," *Nouvelles littéraires*, 3 November 1928: 5, and 10 November 1928: 5, in *Oscar Wilde: Interviews and Recollections*, ed. E. H. Mikhail, 2 vols. (London: Macmillan, 1978), 2:462

91. O'Sullivan, *Aspects of Wilde*, 198.

92. Oscar Wilde, "To Reginald Turner," [6 December 1898], in *The Complete Letters*, 1108. Jean Moréas (1856–1910) was a reactionary poet known for the *Symbolist Manifesto* (1886), and Ernest La Jeunesse (1874–1917) was a literary critic and occasional caricaturist, who wrote an important memoir, "Oscar Wilde," *Revue blanche*, 15 December 1900: 589–96.

93. Wilde, "To Reginald Turner," [6 December 1898], 1108.

94. Oscar Wilde, "To Robert Ross," 14 May 1900, in *The Complete Letters*, 1187.

95. Wilde, "To Robert Ross," 14 May 1900, 1187.

96. In his *Autobiography*, Douglas itemizes the amounts of the cheques that he made out to "Melmott, Melmoth or Melmotte from 12th February 1900 to 15th of November that year inclusive" from his account at the National Provincial Bank (322–23). He adds that he gave Wilde £1,000 in 1899 (162). On Wilde's demand that Bosie bestow sums of £1,500 or more, see Frank Harris, *Oscar Wilde: His Life and Confessions*, 2 vols. (New York: privately printed, 1916), 2:516 and 525.

97. Robert Harborough Sherard, *Twenty Years in Paris: Being Some Recollections of a Literary Life* (London: Hutchinson, 1906), 456.

98. Sherard, Twenty Years in Paris, 456.

99. Sherard, Twenty Years in Paris, 456.

100. Sherard, *Twenty Years in Paris*, 457. Wilde was reading an edition of John Howard, *The State of the Prisons in England and Wales* (1777).

101. Frank Harris, *My Life and Loves*, 4 vols. (Nice: privately printed, 1922–27), 4:346.

102. George Bernard Shaw, "To Frank Harris," 4 November 1900, in *Collected Letters, 1898–1910*, ed. Dan H. Laurence (London: Max Reinhardt, 1972), 193.

103. J. P. Wearing records that the play ran for 116 performances; *The London Stage, 1900–1909: A Calendar of Plays and Players* (Metuchen, NJ: Scarecrow Press, 1981), 54. H. Montgomery Hyde suggests that a disagreement between Stella Campbell, who ran the 1900–1901 season at the Royalty Theatre, and Fred Kerr, who took the role of Mr. Daventry, brought the production to an end; "Introduction," in Frank Harris, *Mr. and Mrs. Daventry: A Play in Four Acts* (London: Richards Press, 1956), 3.

104. Vyvyan Holland, "To Fr. Cuthbert Dunne," 14 December 1900, in Papers of Fr. Cuthbert Dunne, Clark Library, uncatalogued boxes. Vyvyan Holland was eventually introduced to Ross, who became a good friend, in 1905.

105. [Anon.], "Death of Oscar Wilde," *Pall Mall Gazette*, 1 December 1900: 6.

106. "Max" [Max Beerbohm], "A Satire on Romantic Drama," *Saturday Review*, 8 December 1900: 720.

107. [Anon.], "Dramatic Gossip," *Athenæum*, 8 December 1900: 768.

108. [George Ives], "In Memoriam Oscar Wilde, Died November 30th, 1900 (for 'Reynolds's')," *Reynolds's Newspaper*, 9 December 1900: 1. Ives signed the poem as "Author of the 'Book of Chains.'" His *Book of Chains* came out in 1897. The English poet A. E. Housman, who came to prominence with *A Shropshire Lad* (1896), was equally appalled

by Wilde's sentence. Housman could not, however, bring himself to publish his trenchant verses on the cruel arbitrariness of the punishment Wilde suffered for his homosexuality, which might as well—as the poetic voice puts it—have been "the colour of his hair." Housman's poem, numbered "XVIII," appeared posthumously in Laurence Housman, *A. E. H.: Some Poems, Some Letters and a Personal Memoir by His Brother* (London: Jonathan Cape, 1937), 226.

109. Robert Ross, "To Louis Wilkinson," 10 December 1900, Clark Library, MS Wilde, R825L W686, Box 58, Folder 2.

110. Charles Ricketts, "To William Anthony Pye," [summer 1912], in *Self-Portrait: Taken from the Letters and Journals of Charles Ricketts*, ed. T. Sturge Moore and Cecil Lewis (London: Peter Davies, 1939), 178.

111. Ricketts, "To William Anthony Pye," [summer 1912], 178.

112. Ricketts, "To William Anthony Pye," [summer 1912]. 178–79.

113. Laurence Housman, *Echo de Paris: A Study from Life* (London: Jonathan Cape, 1923), 56.

114. Richard Ellmann, *Oscar Wilde* (New York: Knopf, 1988), xvii.

115. Albert Crew, *The Old Bailey: History, Constitution, Functions, Notable Trials* (London: Ivor Nicholson and Watson, 1933), 47.

116. "Homosexual Crime," *Hansard's Parliamentary Debates*, House of Lords, 6th series, 19 May 1954, vol. 187, col. 742, https://api.parliament.uk/historic-hansard/lords/1954/may/19/homosexual-crime.

BIBLIOGRAPHY

"A. B. W." [A. B. Walkley]. "The Drama: *Lady Windermere's Fan*." *Speaker*, 27 February 1892: 257–58.

——. "The Drama: *The Importance of Being Earnest*." *Speaker*, 23 February 1895: 212–13.

Account Book for Channon's Stores, Grocery and Provisions, Wines, Spirits and Bottled Beers [1892–95]. British Library, Add. MS 81761.

Adey, More. Correspondence. Clark Library, MS Wilde, Box 1, Folders 2–9.

Advertisement for the Albemarle Hotel. *Truth*, 27 February 1890: 444.

Advertisement for the Hotel Avondale. *Truth* 37 (1895): 930.

Advertisement. *Morning Post*, 27 April 1895: 4.

Allen, W. E. "Blackmailing." *Reynolds's Newspaper*, 18 December 1898: 8.

Althaus, Frederick C. Correspondence. Clark Library, MS Wilde, Box 2, Folder 13.

[Anon.]. "About Oscar Wilde." *Reynolds's Newspaper*, 16 June 1895: 5.

——. "The Abuse of Cross-Examination" *Saturday Review*, 12 December 1891: 657–58.

——. "Alleged Libel on Oscar Wilde." *Cardiff Times*, 6 April 1895: 4.

——. "Alleged Robbery by a Salesman." *Illustrated Police News*, 10 November 1894: 3.

——. "The Alleged West-End Blackmailing: Disclosures by Convicts." *Daily News*, 20 January 1898: 3.

——. *The Arraignment and Conviction of Mervin Lord Audley, Earle of Castlehaven*. London: T. Thomas, 1642.

——. "Arrest of Oscar Wilde." *Daily Chronicle*, 6 April 1895: 6.

——. "Arrest of Oscar Wilde." *Lloyd's Weekly Newspaper*, 14 April 1895: 15.

——. "Arrest of Oscar Wilde." *Manchester Evening News*, 6 April 1895: 3

——. "Arrest of Oscar Wilde." *Western Mail*, 6 April 1895: 5–6.

——. "The Arrest of Taylor." *Illustrated Police News*, 13 April 1895: 3.

——. "The Assizes." *The Times*, 17 July 1891: 10.

——. "At Holloway: How Wilde Fares in Prison." *Sun*, 8 April 1895: 3.

——. "Bankruptcy of Oscar Wilde." *Pall Mall Gazette*, 22 August 1895: 7.

——. "The Bankruptcy of Oscar Wilde: Appearance in Court." *Daily News*, 13 November 1895: 7.

——. "Blackmail." *Justice of the Peace*, 12 February 1895: 99.
——. "Blackmailing." *Sun*, 18 December 1898: 8.
——. "Blackmailing a City Merchant." *Reynolds's Newspaper*, 3 February 1895: 3.
——. "Blackmailing: By W. E. Allen (a Convicted Blackmailer)." *Reynolds's Newspaper*, 18 December 1898: 8.
——. "Blackmailing Gangs: Further Revelations." *Reynolds's Newspaper*, 13 March 1898: 5.
——. "The Censure and 'Salomé': An Interview with Mr. Oscar Wilde." *Pall Mall Gazette*, 29 June 1892: 2.
——. "Central Criminal Court." *Evening Standard*, 27 May 1895. Press cuttings scrapbook, 131. Clark Library, Wildeiana, Box 17.
——. "Central Criminal Court. [Before Charles, J.]. 25, 30 April; 1 May. Reg. v. Wilde and Taylor." *Justice of the Peace* 59, no. 19 (11 May 1895): 296.
——. "Central Criminal Court—May 20. (Before Mr. Justice Wills.) Prosecution of Oscar Wilde." *Daily Telegraph*, 21 May 1895: 8.
——. "Central Criminal Court—May 23. (Before Mr. Justice Wills.) Prosecution of Oscar Wilde." *Daily Telegraph*, 24 May 1895: 8.
——. "Central Criminal Court, May 24. (Before Mr. Justice Wills.)." *The Times*, 25 May 1895: 19.
——. "Central Criminal Court—May 25. (Before Mr. Justice Wills.) Prosecution of Oscar Wilde." *Daily Telegraph*, 27 May 1895: 8.
——. "Central Criminal Court—Monday." *Morning Post*, 7 June 1870: 7.
——. "The Charge against Wilde." *Daily Chronicle*, 25 April 1895: 7.
——. "The Charge against Wilde." *Pall Mall Gazette*, 6 April 1895: 7.
——. "Charge of Libelling Oscar Wilde." *Lloyd's Weekly Newspaper*, 17 March 1895: 5.
——. "The Charges against Oscar Wilde: Another Arrest." *Daily Telegraph*, 8 April 1895: 5.
——. "The Charges against Wilde." *Daily Telegraph*, 8 April 1895: 5.
——. "The Cleveland Street Scandals." *Reynolds's Newspaper*, 25 May 1890: 3.
——. "The Convict Oscar Wilde: Attempt to Procure His Release." *Pall Mall Gazette*, 17 June 1895: 7.
——. "Conviction of Oscar Wilde: Close of the Sensational Trial." *Western Mail*, 27 May 1895: 5.
——. "Court of King's Bench: Thursday, December 7." *Hull Packet*, 19 December 1809: 4.
——. "Criminal Court—May 23." *Daily Telegraph*, May 24, 1895: 8.
——. "Criminal Investigation against a Newspaper." *Reynolds's Weekly*, 22 December 1878: 5.
——. "The Criminal Jailers of Oscar Wilde." *Liberty*, 15 June 1895: 4.
——. "Criminal Libel Action against Queensberry." *Morning*, 4 April 1895: 1.
——. "Death of Oscar Wilde." *Pall Mall Gazette*, 1 December 1900: 6.
——. "The Decadent Guys (A Colour-Study in Green Carnations)." *Punch*, 10 November 1894: 225.
——. "A Doll's House." *Musical World*, 22 June 1889: 398.
——. "The Drama of the Day." *Daily Telegraph*, 12 February 1892: 2.

——. "Dramatic Gossip." *Athenæum*, 8 December 1900: 768.
——. "Editorial." *Daily Telegraph*, 27 May 1895: 6.
——. Editorial. *Sketch*, 17 April 1895: 655.
——. Editorial. *Westminster Gazette*, 17 April 1895.
——. "The Eighty Club." In *The Eighty Club: 1895*, 3–4. London: privately printed, 1895.
——. "End of the Oscar Wilde Case." *Illustrated Police News*, 1 June 1895: 4.
——. "An Essay in Burlesque." *Globe*, 28 September 1894: 3.
——. "Examination of Saturday." *Illustrated Police News*, 13 April 1895: 3.
——. "Extraordinary Action for Libel." *Bristol Mercury*, 20 February 1879: 3.
——. "A Fair within a Fair." *Pall Mall Gazette*, 18 July 1888: 5.
——. "The Government and Mr. Labouchere." *Pall Mall Gazette*, 1 March 1890: 7.
——. "'Guy Domville' at the St. James." *Sketch*, 9 January 1895: 2.
——. "How It Would Work: For Professional Men to Compete by Advertising Methods." *Travelers Record*, July 1892: 8.
——. "Immorality." *South Wales Daily News*, 21 February 1879: 2.
——. "Imperial Parliament." *Evening Standard*, 4 May 1895: 2.
——. "The Importance of Being Oscar." *Sketch*, 20 February 1895: 213.
——. "In Camera." *St. James's Gazette*, 4 April 1895: 3.
——. "In the Depths: Account of Oscar Wilde's Life at Reading, Told by His Gaoler," *Evening News and Evening Mail*, 1 March 1905: 4.
——. "In the Depths: Account of Oscar Wilde's Life at Reading, Told by His Gaoler," *Evening News and Evening Mail*, 2 March 1905: 2.
——. "In the Dock." *Evening News*, 6 April 1895: 3.
——. "In the Dock: Wilde and Taylor Together." *Sun*, 6 April 1895: 3.
——. "In the Matter of the Extradition of Meunier." *The Times*, 12 June 1894: 3.
——. "Indecency and Suicide." *Reynolds's Newspaper*, 18 November 1894: 3.
——. "Journaux et revues." *Mercure de France*, 20 (1896): 389–95.
——. "King's Bench Division: Lord Alfred Douglas's Libel Action—*Douglas v. Ransome and Others*." *The Times*, 23 April 1913: 3.
——. "The Law and the Lawyers." *Law Times*, 1 June 1895: 101–3.
——. "The Law and the Lawyers." *Law Times*, 8 November 1902: 31.
——. "The Legal Point Raised in the Wilde Case." *Law Journal*, 4 May 1895: 285.
——. "London Echoes." *Galignani Messenger*, 6 April 1895: 1.
——. "London Theatres." *Stage*, 10 January 1895: 15.
——. "London, Wednesday, March 1, 1893." *Morning Post*, 1 March 1893: 6
——. "Lord Alfred Douglas Appeals for Fair Play." *Star*, 20 April 1895: 3.
——. "Lord Alfred Douglas Regrets He Did Not 'Correct' His Father." *Sun*, 24 May 1895: 3.
——. "Lord Euston's Case." *Reynolds's Newspaper*, 19 January 1890: 4.
——. "Lord Queensberry and His Son: The Affray in Piccadilly." *Pall Mall Gazette*, 22 May 1895: 7.
——. "Lord Queensberry's Threat." *Pall Mall Gazette*, 6 April 1895: 7.
——. "Male Prostitution." *Reynolds's Newspaper*, 26 May 1895: 1.

——. "Oscar Wilde: Charged with Infamous Conduct." *Reynolds's Newspaper*, 7 April 1895: 1.
——. "Marquis and Oscar Wilde: Criminal Libel Action—Verdict." *Reynolds's Newspaper*, 7 April 1895: 4.
——. "The Marquis of Queensberry and His Son. Police Court Proceedings." *Manchester Courier, and Lancashire Advertiser*, 23 May 1895: 8.
——. "Marriage of Lord Edward Cecil and Miss Violet Maxse." *St. James's Gazette*, 19 June 1894: 6.
——. "Medico-Legal. Constructive Murder. Conviction of a Nurse: Reprieve." *British Medical Journal*, 18 February 1899: 448.
——. "Men in Women's Clothes." *Reynolds's Newspaper*, 19 August 1894: 8.
——. "Miscellaneous Notes." *United Ireland*, 13 April 1895: 1.
——. "Mr. Hichens." *Nottingham Evening Post*, 9 November 1894: 2.
——. "Mr. Justice Wills on the Criminal Law Amendment Act." *Pall Mall Gazette*, 29 May 1886: 14.
——. "Mr. Oscar Wilde and Edgar Poe." *Daily News*, 11 June 1894: 6.
——. "Mr. Oscar Wilde in a Cell at Bow Street." *Paris Herald*, 6 April 1895: 1.
——. "Mr. Oscar Wilde on Woman's Dress." *Pall Mall Gazette*, 14 October 1886: 6.
——. "Mr. Oscar Wilde's 'House of Pomegranates.'" *Pall Mall Gazette*, 30 November 1891: 3.
——. "Mr. Wilde on Mr. Oscar Wilde: An Interview." *St. James's Gazette*, 18 January 1895: 4.
——. "Mrs. Humphry." "Social Echoes." *London Society* 53 (1888): 667.
——. "Mrs. Oscar Wilde at Home." *To-Day*, 24 November 1894: 93–94.
——. "Mrs. Oscar Wilde on Women and War." *Pall Mall Gazette*, 17 April 1888: 8.
——. "New Books." *Illustrated London News*, 8 March 1884: 23.
——. "New Novels." *Graphic*, 15 July 1893: 11.
——. "New Poem by Oscar Wilde: 'The Ballad of Reading Gaol,'" *Reynolds's Newspaper*, 13 February 1898: 8.
——. "The New Renaissance." *Saturday Review*, 4 November 1882: 597.
——. "News of the Week." *News of the World*, 5 May 1895: 6.
——. "North London," *Evening Standard*. 25 May 1895: 5
——. "Notes." *National Observer*, 6 April 1895: 547.
——. "Notes and News." *Oxford Magazine*, 30 November 1892: 120.
——. "Notes from London." *Scottish Law Review and Sheriff Court Reports* 111, no. 126 (1895): 180–82.
——. "Obiter Dicta." *Law Journal*, 13 April 1895: 239.
——. "Occasional Notes." *Pall Mall Gazette*, 23 April 1888: 4.
——. "Oscar and Taylor." *Reynolds's Newspaper*, 14 April 1895, 1.
——. "Oscar Arrested." *Morning Leader*, 6 April 1895: 5.
——. "Oscar at Bow-St." *Morning Leader*, 8 April 1895: 5.
——. "Oscar To-Day: A Startling Cross-Examination by Mr. Carson." *Evening News*, 4 April 1895: 3.

——. "Oscar Wilde." *Echo*, 6 April 1895: 2–3.
——. "Oscar Wilde." *Star*, 26 April 1895: 3.
——. "Oscar Wilde." *Illustrated Police Budget*, 27 April 1895: 8–9.
——. "Oscar Wilde." *Echo*, 27 May 1895. Press cuttings scrapbook, 135. Clark Library, Wildeiana, Box 17.
——. "Oscar Wilde: The Amount of Bail Fixed." *Illustrated Police News*, 11 May 1895: 4.
——. "Oscar Wilde and Taylor at Bow Street." *Illustrated Police News*, 20 April 1895: 1–2.
——. "Oscar Wilde Arrested." *Cardiff Times*, 13 April 1895: 5.
——. "Oscar Wilde Arrested." *Morning*, 6 April 1895: 1.
——. "Oscar Wilde: Arrested at Chelsea." *Echo*, 6 April 1895: 2.
——. "Oscar Wilde at Bow-St." *Morning Leader*, 8 April 1895: 5.
——. "Oscar Wilde at Bow Street." *Globe*, 6 April 1895: 5.
——. "Oscar Wilde at Bow Street." *Paris Herald*, 12 April 1895: 10.
——. "Oscar Wilde at the Old Bailey." *Pall Mall Gazette*, 22 May 1895: 7.
——. "Oscar Wilde at the Old Bailey: Case for the Defence." *Pall Mall Gazette*, 24 May 1895: 7.
——. "Oscar Wilde at the Old Bailey: Scene in Court." *Illustrated Police Budget*, 4 May 1895: 6–9, 11.
——. "Oscar Wilde: Brought Up at Bow-St This Morning." *Star*, 11 April 1895: 3.
——. "The Oscar Wilde Case." *Manchester Courier, and Lancashire General Advertiser*, 24 April 1895: 8.
——. "Oscar Wilde Case." *Morning Leader*, 27 April 1895: 5.
——. "The Oscar Wilde Case." *Portsmouth Evening News*, 27 April 1895: 3.
——. "Oscar Wilde Case." *Weekly Dispatch*, 28 April 1895: 16.
——. "The Oscar Wilde Case." *Western Mail*, 13 April 1895: 5.
——. "The Oscar Wilde Case." *Western Mail*, 25 April 1895: 5.
——. "Oscar Wilde Case: Judge's Summing-Up." *Globe*, 1 May 1895: 5.
——. "The Oscar Wilde Case: Proceedings at the Old Bailey." *Western Mail*, April 1895: 6.
——. "Oscar Wilde: Charged with Infamous Conduct." *Reynolds's Newspaper*, 7 April 1895: 1.
——. "Oscar Wilde: Defends Himself at the Old Bailey." *Star*, 3 April 1895: 3.
——. "Oscar Wilde—£5,000 Bail." *Illustrated Police News*, 18 May 1895: 8.
——. "Oscar Wilde: Fourth Day—Some Surprises." *Star*, 30 April 1895: 3.
——. "Oscar Wilde: Gets Two Years' Hard Labour, and So Does Taylor." *Illustrated Police Budget*, 1 June 1895: 8.
——. "Oscar Wilde: His Second Trial at the Old Bailey." *Echo*, 22 May 1895: 3.
——. "Oscar Wilde in Court: His Bankruptcy Affairs." *Reynolds's Newspaper*, 17 November 1895: 3.
——. "Oscar Wilde in Jail." *Echo*, 8 April 1895: 3.
——. "Oscar Wilde in Prison." *Illustrated Police Budget*, 20 April 1895: 8.
——. "Oscar Wilde in Prison." *Star*, 8 April 1895: 3.
[Anon.], "Oscar Wilde in Prison: State of His Health," *Morning*, 6 June 1895: 1.
——. "Oscar Wilde: Last Scene of the Sensational Trial." *Star*, 26 April 1895: 3.

——. "Oscar Wilde—Latest." *Reynolds's Newspaper*, 19 May 1895: 1.
——. "Oscar Wilde Libel." *News of the World*, 7 April 1895: 7.
——. "Oscar Wilde Libel Case." *Pall Mall Gazette*, 3 April 1895: 7.
——. "Oscar Wilde: More Witnesses Are Called for the Prosecution." *Star*, 29 April 1895: 3.
——. "Oscar Wilde. Mr. Buchanan Replies to an 'Anonymous Coward.'" *Star*, 24 April 1895: 2.
——. "Oscar Wilde: Proceedings in Bankruptcy." *St. James's Gazette*, 25 July 1895: 14.
——. "Oscar Wilde Prosecution: Committal." *Illustrated Police News*, 27 April 1895: 6.
——. "Oscar Wilde Released: Smuggled from Reading to Pentonville." *Pall Mall Gazette*, 19 May 1897: 7.
——. "The Oscar Wilde Scandal." *Manchester Courier and Lancashire General Advertiser*, 8 April 1895: 8.
——. "The Oscar Wilde Scandal." *Supplement to the Manchester Courier*, 20 April 1895: 8.
——. "Oscar Wilde: Second Trial at the Old Bailey." *Illustrated Police Budget*, 25 May 1895: 8.
——. "Oscar Wilde Secretly Released from Prison at Night Time." *Illustrated Police News*, 29 May 1897: 3.
——. "Oscar Wilde: Severe Cross-Examination by the Solicitor General," 25 May 1895: 8.
——. "Oscar Wilde: Third Day of His Trial." *Echo*, 24 May 1895: 3.
——. "The Oscar Wilde Trial: Case for the Prosecution." *Manchester Courier, and Lancashire General Advertiser*, 27 April 1895: 9.
——. "The Oscar Wilde Trial: Case for the Prosecution Closed." *Manchester Courier, and Lancashire General Advertiser*, 30 April 1895: 3.
——. "Oscar Wilde's Arrest." *Illustrated Police Budget Supplement*, 13 April 1895: 7–10.
——. "Oscar Wilde's Case." *Reynolds's Newspaper*, 5 May 1895: 1.
——. "Oscar Wilde's Health in Prison: Official Statement. *Pall Mall Gazette*, 6 June 1895: 7.
——. "Oscar Wilde's Trial." *Morning*, 20 April 1895: 5.
——. "Oscar Wilde's Trial." *Reynolds's Newspaper*, 12 May 1895: 1.
——. "Oscar Wilde's Trial: Further Evidence for the Prosecution." *Morning*, 29 April 1895: 5.
——. "Paddington Fair Countermanded." *Public Ledger and Daily Advertiser*, 3 May 1817: 3.
——. "Pall Mall Gazette Office." *Pall Mall Gazette*, 14 March 1895: 8.
——. "Le plus décadent des décadents." *Pall Mall Gazette*, 4 May 1893: 3.
——. *Poetry of the Crabbet Club*. N.p.: privately printed, 1892.
——. "Police Intelligence." *Standard*, 8 April 1895: 2.
——. "Police Raid on the West-End." *Daily Chronicle*, 14 August 1894: 8.
——. *The Political Libel Actions of Gatty v. Farquharson and Gatty v. the Western Gazette and Pulman's Weekly News Company, Limited: Verbatim Evidence from Official Shorthand Notes*. London: Penny and Hull, 1894.
——. "The Press on 'The Maiden Tribute.'" *Pall Mall Gazette*, 20 July 1885: 11.

——. "The Prosecution of Oscar Wilde." *Huddersfield Chronicle*, 8 April 1895: 4.
——. "The Prosecution of Oscar Wilde." *Lloyd's Weekly Newspaper*, 2 June 1894: 4.
——. "Prosecution of Oscar Wilde: The Second Trial." *Western Mail*, 21 May 1895: 6.
——. "Queensberry." *Star*, 22 May 1895: 3.
——. "Queensberry Case." *Reynolds's Newspaper*, 10 March 1895: 1.
——. "Queensberry Corrects." *Sun*, 6 April 1895: 3.
——. "The Queensberry Divorce Case." *The Times*, 24 January 1887: 4.
——. "Queensberry–Wilde Case." *Daily Telegraph*, 6 April 1895: 3.
——. "The Queensberry–Wilde Case." *Globe*, 28 March 1895: 5.
——. "The Queensberry–Wilde Case." *Illustrated Police News*, 13 April 1895: 3.
——. "Queensberry–Wilde Libel Trial." *St. James's Gazette*, 5 April 1895: 8.
——. "The Raid on a 'Fancy Dress' Ball." *Liverpool Echo*, 30 September 1880: 4.
——. "Release of Oscar Wilde." *Lloyd's Weekly Newspaper*, 12 May 1895: 1.
——. "Release of Oscar Wilde." *Morning Post*, 8 May 1895: 3.
——. "Release of Oscar Wilde: His Bail and Sureties." *Reynolds's Newspaper*, 12 May 1895: 4.
——. "Retribution." *Evening News*, 27 May 1895: 2.
——. "Review of Wilde, *The Picture of Dorian Gray*." *Daily Chronicle*, 30 June 1890: 7.
——. "Sale of Oscar Wilde's Effects." *Daily Chronicle*, 25 April 1895: 7.
——. "Salisbury, the Shuffler." *Reynolds's Newspaper*, 9 March 1890: 4
——. "Satire à la mode." *Pall Mall Gazette*, 27 September 1894: 4.
——. "The Scandals." *Sun*, 20 May 1895: 3.
——. "Scotland-Yard and Street Songs." *Echo*, 29 April 1895: 3.
——. "Second Scene of the Last Phase of the Trial." *Star*, 27 April 1895: 3.
——. "Silk and Stuff." *Pall Mall Gazette*, 4 April 1895: 1.
——. "The Society Scandal." *Galignani Messenger*, 4 April 1895: 1.
——. "The Society Scandal." *Galignani Messenger*, 7 April 1895, 1.
——. "The Society Scandal: Case for the Defence." *Galignani Messenger*, 25 May 1895: 1.
——. "The Society Scandal: Judge's Summing up." *Galignani Messenger*, 1 May 1895: 1.
——. "The Society Scandal: Re-Opening of the Case." *Galignani Messenger*, 21 May 1895: 1.
——. "Society Scandal: Trial of Oscar Wilde." *Western Mail*, 27 April 1895: 5.
——. "The Society Scandal: Trial of Oscar Wilde." *Galignani Messenger*, 23 May 1895: 1.
——. "The Society Scandal: Trial of Taylor." *Galignani Messenger*, 22 May 1895: 1.
——. "Some Illlustrated Gift Books." *Pall Mall Gazette*, 30 November 1891: 3.
——. "St. James's." *St. James's Gazette*, 27 April 1895: 1.
——. "The Stop-Day Action." *Western Mail*, 28 July 1902: 5
——. "Studio and Personal." *Artist and Journal of Home Culture*, June 1894: 192–95.
——. "Summary of News." *Western Mail*, 13 April 1895: 4.
——. "Summary of This Morning's News." *Pall Mall Gazette*, 5 March 1881: 6.
——. "Swinburne and Water." *Punch*, 23 July 1881: 26.
——. "Taylor Again on Trial: His Story as a Witness." *Echo*, 21 May 1895: 3.

——. "The Terrible Scandals in 'High Life.'" *Reynolds's Newspaper*, 1 December 1889: 4.
——. "Theatrical Items." *Globe*, 5 January 1895: 3.
——. "Transcripts (Taken from the Original Shorthand Notes) and Other Material Relating to Oscar Wilde's Prosecution of the Marquess of Queensberry for Criminal Libel in April 1895." April 1895. British Library, Western Manuscripts, Loan MS 122.
——. "To-Day." *To-Day*, 29 December 1894: 241–44.
——. "To-Day." *To-Day*, 5 January 1895: 273.
——. "To-Night's Entertainments." *Pall Mall Gazette*, 27 April 1895: 1.
——. "The Trial of Boulton and Park." *Morning Advertiser*, 10 May 1871: 7.
——. "Trial of Oscar Wilde." *Evening Standard*, 23 May 1895: 6.
——. "Trial of Oscar Wilde." *Lincolnshire Echo*, 27 April 1895: 3.
——. "Trial of Oscar Wilde." *Lloyd's Weekly Newspaper*, 5 May 1895: 4.
——. "Trial of Oscar Wilde." *Morning*, 25 April 1895: 3.
——. "The Trial of Oscar Wilde." *Morning*, 25 May 1895: 3.
——. "Trial of Oscar Wilde: Case for the Prosecution." *Manchester Courier, and Lancashire Advertiser*, 23 May 1895: 6.
——. "The Trial of Oscar Wilde: Close of the Prosecution," *Morning*, 25 May 1895: 3.
——. "Trial of Oscar Wilde: Evidence for the Prosecution." *Morning*, 27 April 1895: 1–2.
——. *The Trial of Oscar Wilde: From the Shorthand Reports*. Paris: privately printed, 1906.
——. "The Trial of Oscar Wilde: To-day's Proceedings." 27 April 1895: 8.
——. "The Trial of Taylor." *Daily Chronicle*, 22 May 1895: 4.
——. "The Trial of Taylor." *Globe*, 21 May 1895: 5.
——. "The Trial of Wilde." *Evening News*, 24 May 1895: 3.
——. "The Trial of Wilde," *Evening Standard*, 24 May 1895: 2
——. [Untitled]. *Morning Post*, 20 March 1895: 5.
——. "Verdict of the Jury—Acquittal of Mr. Ford." *Western Times*, 23 November 1878: 3.
——. "A Visit to Oscar Wilde." *Era*, 31 August 1895: 10.
——. "Wagner's Parsifal." *Illustrated Sporting and Dramatic News*, 22 November 1884: 12.
——. "Wanton Verse." *Saturday Review*, 19 January 1895: 71
——. "The Week." *Athenæum*, 12 January 1895: 57.
——. "West Kent Quarter Sessions." *Maidstone Journal and Kentish Advertiser*, 4 July 1895: 8.
——. "Wilde." *Star*. Special Edition. 1 May 1895: 3.
——. "Wilde." *Star*, 27 May 1895: 2.
——. "Wilde Again in the Dock at the Old Bailey." *Star*, 22 May 1895: 2–3.
——. "Wilde and Friend: Resumed Trial at the Central Criminal Court." *Leeds Times*, 4 May 1895: 2.
——. "Wilde and Taylor." *Echo*, 11 April 1895: 3.
——. "Wilde and Taylor." *Echo*, 19 April 1895: 2.
——. "Wilde and Taylor." *Echo*, 29 April 1895: 3.
——. "Wilde and Taylor." *Reynolds's Newspaper*, 21 April 1895: 5.
——. "Wilde and Taylor." *Sun*, 19 April 1895: 3.
——. "Wilde and Taylor Are Both Committed for Trial." *Sun*, 19 April 1895: 3.

——. "Wilde and Taylor at the Old Bailey." *Sun*, 26 April 1895: 3.
——. "Wilde and Taylor: Conspiracy Charges Withdrawn." *Echo*, 30 April 1895: 3.
——. "Wilde and Taylor: The Sentences—Closing Scenes." *Weekly Dispatch*, 2 June 1895: 2.
——. "Wilde and Taylor: They Appear Again at the Old Bailey." *Echo*, 20 May 1895: 3.
——. "Wilde Appears in the Dock." *Sun*, 20 May 1895: 3.
——. "The Wilde Case." *Morning*, 27 May 1895: 4.
——. "The Wilde Case." *News of the World*, 7 April 1895: 1.
——. "The Wilde Case." *News of the World*, 21 April 1895: 2.
——. "Wilde Case." *Star*, 19 April 1895: 3.
——. "The Wilde Case." *Western Mail*, 8 April 1895: 8.
——. "Wilde Case: Mr. Charles Mathews Applies for Postponement." *Star*, 24 April 1895: 3.
——. "Wilde: Case Reopened To-Day at the Old Bailey." *Star*, 20 May 1895: 3.
——. "The Wilde Case: Result of the Trial at the Old Bailey." *News of the World*, 26 May 1895: 1–2.
——. "The Wilde Charges." *Manchester Courier, and Lancashire Advertiser*, 22 May 1895: 8.
——. "The Wilde Charges: Trial of Taylor." *Manchester Courier, and Lancashire Advertiser*, 21 May 1895: 8.
——. "Wilde Convicted: Scenes between Counsel." *Reynolds's Newspaper*, 26 May 1895: 5.
——. "Wilde, Cross-Examined for the Third Time, Admits that He Was Enormously Fond of Praise." *Star*, 24 May 1895: 2.
——. "Wilde: Cross-Examined for the Third Time," *Star*, 24 May 1895. Clark press cuttings, 111–17, Wildeiana, Box 17.
——. "Wilde Has Been Ill." *Reynolds's Newspaper*, 14 April 1895: 1.
——. "Wilde: Impressive Summing Up by Mr. Justice Charles." *Star*, 1 May 1895: 3.
——. "Wilde in Court." *Sun*, 11 April 1895: 3.
——. "Wilde in the Witness-Box." *Sun*, 24 May 1895: 2-3.
——. "Wilde: The Last Scene in the Trial." *Sun*, 1 May 1895: 3.
——. "Wilde: The Last Terrible Scene of the Great Trial." *Star*, 27 May 1895: 2.
——. "The Wilde Libel Case." *Pall Mall Gazette*, 9 March 1895: 7.
——. "Wilde: Nearing the Crisis." *Sun*, 25 May 1895: 3.
——. "Wilde on Trial: He Looks Ill and Haggard." *Sun*, 22 May 1895: 3.
——. "The Wilde Prosecution." *Daily Chronicle*, 8 April 1895: 7.
——. "Wilde Released: Mr. Vaughan Accepts Bail This Morning." *Star*, 7 May 1895: 3.
——. "The Wilde Scandal." *Star*, 21 May 1895: 3.
——. "Wilde Scandal: Second Trial Commenced." *Western Mail*, 23 May 1895: 5.
——. "Wilde Scandal: Speech for the Defence." *Western Mail*, 25 May 1895: 5.
——. "The Wilde Scandal: Taylor Cross-Examined by Sir Frank Lockwood." *Star*, 23 May 1895: 3.
——. "Wilde: Second Day of the Wilde Trial." *Sun*, 27 April 1895: 3.

——. "Wilde: Some of the Mysteries of the Case." *Star*, 28 May 1895: 2.
——. "Wilde–Taylor." *Reynolds's Newspaper*, 5 May 1895: 1.
——. "Wilde–Taylor." *Reynolds's Newspaper*, 28 April 1895: 1.
——. "Wilde–Taylor at the Old Bailey." *Reynolds's Newspaper*, 28 April 1895: 1.
——. "Wilde–Taylor Case: Evidence of the Prisoner." *Daily Telegraph*, 1 May 1895: 4.
——. "Wilde–Taylor Case: Summing-Up and Result." *Daily Telegraph*, 2 May 1895: 4.
——. "The Wilde–Taylor Case: Trial at the Old Bailey." *Illustrated Police News*, 4 May 1895: 2–3.
——. "Wilde–Taylor: Result of the Trial." *Reynolds's Newspaper*, 5 May 1895: 1.
——. "Wilde the Man." *Morning*, 6 April 1895: 4.
——. "Wilde: To Be Re-Tried at the Next Sessions," *Star*, 2 May 1895: 3.
——. "Wilde Trial: Fierce Combat between Counsel." *Star*, 25 May 1895: 3.
——. "Wilde v. Queensberry." *Daily Chronicle*, 6 April 1895: 6.
——. "Wilde v. Queensberry: The Great Libel Suit." *Daily Chronicle*, 4 April 1895: 6.
——. "Wilde: Weak, Ill, and Utterly Dejected in the Dock." *Star*. Special Edition. 23 May 1895: 3.
——. "Wilde's Career Ended." *Sun* [New York], 6 April 1895: 1.
——. "Wilde's Prison Life at Reading Gaol." 8. Clark Library, uncatalogued Wilde MSS.
——. "Wilde's Trial: The Two in the Dock." *Sun*, 29 April 1895: 3.
——. Wilde's Trial: Still Weaving and Unweaving," *Sun*, 23 May 1895: 3.
——. "Women's Dress: Rational or Fashionable?" *Pall Mall Gazette*, 26 March 1886: 11.
——. "A Yellow Melancholy." *Speaker*, 28 April 1894: 468–69.
Archer, William. *The Theatrical "World" for 1893*. London: Walter Scott, 1893.
——. *The Theatrical "World" of 1895*. London: Walter Scott, 1896.
Atlay, J. B. *The Trial of the Stauntons*. Edinburgh: William Hodge, 1911.
Backhouse, Edmund Trelawny. "The Dead Past." Oxford, Bodleian Library, MSS. Eng. Misc. d. 1223–26.
——. *The Dead Past*. Edited by Peter Jordaan. N.p.: Alchemie Books, 2017.
——. *Décadence Mandchoue: The China Memoirs of Sir Edmund Trelawny Backhouse*. Edited by Derek Sandhaus. Hong Kong: Earnshaw Books, 2011.
Baedeker, Karl. *Paris and Its Environs*. 9th ed. Leipsic: Karl Baedeker, 1896.
——. *London and Its Environs: Handbook for Travellers*. 9th ed. Leipsic: Karl Baedeker, 1894.
——. *London and Its Environs: Handbook for Travellers*. 10th ed. Leipsic: Karl Baedeker, 1896.
Baker, George Barr. "Criminal Genius in Exile: Picture from His Last Days in Paris." Unidentified press cutting, 28 November 190[?]. In an album of press cuttings, Clark Library, Wildeiana, Box 25, Folder 20.
Bantman, Constance. *The French Anarchists in London, 1880–1914: Exile and Transnationalism in the First Globalisation*. Liverpool: Liverpool University Press, 2013.
Beal, Edward, ed. *The Trial of Adelaide Bartlett for Murder*. London: Stevens and Haynes, 1886.
Beale, Joseph Henry. A *Selection of Cases and Other Authorities upon Criminal Law*. Cambridge, MA: Harvard Law Review Publishing Association, 1894.

Beardsley, Aubrey. *The Letters of Aubrey Beardsley*. Edited by Henry Maas, J. L. Duncan, and W. G. Good. London: Cassell, 1970.
Becker, Marie Luise. "Salome—Darstellerinnen auf der modernen Bühne." *Bühne und Welt* 9, no. 1 (1906–7): 439–47.
Beckson, Karl. *Arthur Symons: A Life*. Oxford: Clarendon Press, 1987.
——, ed. *Oscar Wilde: The Critical Heritage*. London: Routledge and Kegan Paul, 1970.
——. "Oscar Wilde and the Green Carnation." *English Literature in Transition, 1880–1920* 43, no. 4 (2000): 387–97.
Beerbohm, Max. *Letters of Max Beerbohm, 1892–1956*. Edited by Rupert Hart-Davis. New York: W. W. Norton, 1988.
——. *Letters to Reggie Turner*. Edited by Rupert Hart-Davis. London: Rupert Hart-Davis, 1964.
——. "Oscar Wilde: By [Max Beerbohm Masquerading as] an American." *Anglo-American Times*, 25 March 1893. In Max Beerbohm, *Letters to Reggie Turner*, 285–92. Edited by Rupert Hart-Davis. London: Rupert Hart-Davis, 1964.
[——]. "A Satire on Romantic Drama." *Saturday Review*, 8 December 1900: 719–20.
Beisly, Martin, Mark Bills, and Rosie Jarvie. *William Powell Frith, R.A. (1819–1909): The Private View at the Royal Academy, 1881*. London: Martin Beisly, 2019.
Bettany, F. G. *Stewart Headlam: A Biography*. London: John Murray, 1926.
Birt, Howard H. "How a London Police Court Is Worked." *Leisure Hour*, January 1899: 191–94.
Blackstone, William. *Commentaries on the Laws of England*. 4th edition. 4 vols. Oxford: Clarendon Press, 1770.
——. *Of Public Wrongs*. Edited by Ruth Paley. In *Commentaries on the Laws of England*. Vol. 4. Oxford: Clarendon Press, 2016.
Blount, Thomas. *A Law-Dictionary and Glossary*, 3rd. ed. London: E. Nutt and R. Gosling, 1717.
[Bloxam, John Francis]. "The Priest and the Acolyte." *Chameleon* 1, no. 1 (1894): 29–47.
Booth, Charles. *Life and Labour of the People of London*. 16 vols. London: Macmillan, 1895–1904.
Borland, Maureen. *Wilde's Devoted Friend: A Life of Robert Ross, 1869–1918*. Oxford: Lennard, 1990.
Bottomley, A. K. "The Granting of Bail: Principles and Practice." *Modern Law Review* 31, no. 1 (1968): 40–54.
Bramwell, George, 1st Baron Bramwell. "Cross-Examination." *Nineteenth Century* 31 (1892): 183–87.
Bristow, Joseph. "'All men kill the thing they love': The Realistic and Romantic Contexts of *The Ballad of Reading Gaol*." In *Approaches to Teaching Oscar Wilde*, 230–47. Edited by Philip E. Smith. New York: Modern Language Association, 2008.
——. "The Blackmailer and the Sodomite: Oscar Wilde on Trial." *Feminist Theory*, 17, no. 1 (2016): 41–62;
——. "Homosexual Blackmail in the 1890s: The Fitzroy Street Raid, the Oscar Wilde Trials, and the Case of Cotsford Dick." *Australasian Journal of Victorian Studies* 22, no. 1 (2017). https://openjournals.library.sydney.edu.au/index.php/AJVS.

——. "Introduction." In *Wilde Discoveries: Traditions, Histories, Archives*, 3–39. Edited by Joseph Bristow. Toronto: University of Toronto Press, 2013).

——. "Introduction: Oscar Wilde and the Cultures of Childhood." In *Oscar Wilde and the Cultures of Childhood*, 1–39. Edited by Joseph Bristow. London: Palgrave Macmillan, 2017.

——. "Oscar Wilde, Ronald Gower, and the Shakespeare Memorial." *Etudes anglaises* 69, no. 1 (2016): 7–22.

——. "Oscar Wilde: The Man, the Life, the Legend." In *The Palgrave Guide to Oscar Wilde*, 6–35. Edited by Frederick S. Roden. Basingstoke: Palgrave, 2004).

——. "Oscar Wilde's Unfinished Society Plays: *Mr. and Mrs. Daventry*, *A Wife's Tragedy*, and *Love Is Law*." In *Oscar Wilde's Society Plays*, 51–74. Edited by Michael Y. Bennett. New York: Palgrave Macmillan, 2015.

——. "Symonds's History, Ellis's Heredity: *Sexual Inversion*." In *Sexology in Culture: Labeling Bodies and Desires*, 79–99. Edited by Lucy Bland and Laura Doan. Chicago: University of Chicago Press, 1998.

Bristow, Joseph, and Rebecca N. Mitchell. *Oscar Wilde's Chatterton: Literary History, Romanticism, and the Art of Forgery*. New Haven, CT: Yale University Press, 2015.

Buchanan, Robert. "Camera Obscura." *Star*, 16 April 1895: 4.

——. "Oscar Wilde: To the Editor of the 'Star,'" *Star*, 20 April 1895: 3

Buckley, Angela. "The 'Thing' He Loved," 5 July 2019, https://victorian-supersleuth.com/the-thing-he-loved/.

Burgess, Gilbert. "'An Ideal Husband' at the Haymarket Theatre: A Talk with Mr. Oscar Wilde." *Sketch*, 9 January 1895: 495.

Butterworth, Arthur Reginald. *The Criminal Evidence Act 1898*. London: Sweet and Maxwell, 1898.

Calloway, Stephen. *Aubrey Beardsley*. London: V&A Publications, 1998.

Carpenter, Edward. *The Intermediate Sex: A Study of Some Transitional Types of Men and Women*. London: George Allen and Unwin, 1908.

——. "To W. T. Stead." 29 June 1895. British Library, Add. MS 81732

Carrington, Charles. Correspondence. Clark Library, MS Wilde, Box 10, Folder 42.

Cawthorn, Elisabeth A. "Dogs and Dogma: Medico-Theory and the Problem of Rabies in England, 1750–1850." In *Essays in European History: Selected from the Annual Meetings of the Southern Historical Association, 1990–1991*. Vol. 3, 16–32. Edited by Carolyn W. White. Lanham, MD: University Press of America, 1996.

Central Criminal Court: After Trial Calendars of Prisoners. 1870. The National Archives, Kew. CRIM 9/16.

Chesson, Wilfred Hugh. "A Reminiscence of 1898." *Bookman* 34 (1911): 389–94.

Clarke, Edward. "Oscar Wilde." Undated. British Library, Add. MS 81758.

——. *The Story of My Life*. London: John Murray, 1918.

Clark, Kate. *In the Interests of Science: Adelaide Bartlett and the Pimlico Poisoning*. London: Mango Books, 2015.

[Coates, Tim, ed.]. *The Trials of Oscar Wilde, 1895: Transcript Excerpts from the Trials at the Old Bailey, London, during April and May 1895*. London: The Stationery Office, 2001.

Cocks, H. G. *Nameless Offences: Homosexual Desire in the Nineteenth Century*. London: I.B. Tauris, 2003.

Cohen, Ed. *Talk on the Wilde Side: Toward a Genealogy of a Discourse on Male Sexualities*. New York: Routledge, 1993.

Cohen, William A. "Wilde's French." In *Wilde Discoveries: Traditions, Histories, Archives*, 233–59. Edited by Joseph Bristow. Toronto: University of Toronto Press, 2013.

Coke, Edward. *The Third Part of the Institutes of the Laws of England: Concerning High Treason; and Other Pleas of the Crown, and Criminal Causes*. London: M. Flesher, W. Lee, and D. Pakeman, 1644.

Coleridge, Samuel Taylor. *Biographia Literaria; or, Biographical Sketches of My Literary Life and Opinions*. Edited by James Engell and W. Jackson Bate. In *Collected Works of Samuel Taylor Coleridge*. 16 vols, vol. 7. Bollingen Series LXXV. Princeton: Princeton University Press, 1985.

Colligan, Colette. "Oscar Wilde's Sex Trials in Paris's Expatriate Press." *Textus* 28, no. 1 (2015): 57–82.

Collins, Richard Henn. "To Edward Carson." 5 April 1895. British Library, Add. MS 81732; copy in RP3046[i].

Cook, Matt. *London and the Culture of Homosexuality, 1885–1914*. Cambridge: Cambridge University Press, 2003.

Crew, Albert. *The Old Bailey: History, Constitution, Functions, Notable Trials*. London: Ivor Nicholson and Watson, 1933.

Croft-Cooke, Rupert. *Bosie: The Story of Lord Alfred Douglas, His Friends and Enemies*. London: W. H. Allen, 1963.

——. *Feasting with Panthers: A New Consideration of Some Late Victorian Writers*. London: W. H. Allen, 1967.

Cuffe, Hamilton. "Letter to Charles Murdoch." In *List of Criminal Cases: Wilde, Oscar Fingal O'Flahertie Wills, Convicted at Central Criminal Court on 20 May 1895 of Gross Indecency and Sentenced to 2 Years' Penal Servitude with Hard Labour. The Public Prosecutor States Reasons why Lord Alfred Douglas Is Not to Be Prosecuted*. April 1895. The National Archives, Kew. HO 45/24516.

[Dallas, Eneas Sweetland]. *Kettner's Book of the Table: A Manual of Cookery, Practical, Theoretical, Historical*. London: Dulau, 1877.

Danson, Lawrence. "Oscar Wilde, W. H., and the Unspoken Name of Love." *ELH* 58, no. 4 (1991): 979–1000.

Darwall-Smith, Robert. "Charles Alan Fyffe: A Victorian Tragedy." *University College Record* 23, no. 1 (2001): 72–84.

Defendant: Queensberry, John Sholto Douglas, Marquis of. Charge: Libel. March 1895. The National Archives, Kew. CRIM 1/41/6.

Derry, Caroline. "Lesbianism and Feminist Legislation in 1921: The Age of Consent and 'Gross Indecency between Women,'" *History Workshop Journal* 86 (2018): 245–67.

De Windt, Harry. *My Note-Book at Home and Abroad*. New York: E. P. Dutton, 1923.

——. *My Restless Life*. London: Grant Ricards, 1909.

Dickens, Charles. *A Tale of Two Cities*. London: Chapman and Hall, 1859.

Dockray, Martin. "The Cleveland Street Scandal 1889–1890," *Journal of Legal History* 17, no. 1 (1996): 1–16.

Donohue, Joseph. *Fantasies of Empire: The Empire Theatre of Varieties and the Licensing Controversy of 1894*. Iowa City: University of Iowa Press, 2005.

Douglas, Alfred. *The Autobiography of Lord Alfred Douglas*. 2nd ed. London: Martin Secker, 1931.

——. *Collected Poems*. London: Martin Secker, 1919.

——. "In Praise of Shame," *Chamelion* 1, no. 1 (1894): 25.

——. "In Sarum Close." In *Collected Poems*, 21. London: Martin Secker, 1919.

——. "Une introduction à mes poèmes, avec quelques considérations sur l'affaire Oscar Wilde." *Revue blanche*, 1 June 1896: 484–90.

——. *Oscar Wilde: A Plea and a Reminiscence*. Edited by Caspar Wintermans. Woubrugge: Avalon Press, 2002.

——. *Oscar Wilde: A Summing-Up*. London: Duckworth, 1940.

——. *Oscar Wilde and Myself*. London: John Long, 1914.

——. *Poems/Poèmes*. Paris: Mercure de France, 1896.

——. "*Salomé*: A Critical Review." *Spirit Lamp*, 4, no. 1 (1893): 20–27.

——. "To Ada Leverson." 13 September 1895. Clark Library. MS Douglas. D733L L661, Box 20, Folder 5.

——. "To Charles Kains-Jackson." 16 May 1894. Clark Library. MS Douglas. D733L K135, Box 20, Folder 3.

——. "To Charles Kains-Jackson." 29 November 1894. Clark Library, MS Douglas. D733L K135, Box 20, Folder 3.

——. "To Frank Harris." 20 March 1925. Harry Ransom Center, University of Texas.

——. "To George Cecil Ives." 11 November 1894. Clark Library, MS Douglas. D733L I95, Box 20, Folder 2.

——. "To More Adey." 3 December 1895, Clark Library, MS Douglas. D733L A33, Box 15, Folder 1.

——. "To More Adey." 8 February 1897. Clark Library, MS Douglas. D733L A33, Box 15, Folder 1.

——. "To More Adey." 27 September 1896. Clark Library, MS Douglas. D733L A33, Box 15, Folder 1.

——. "To More Adey." 30 November 1895. Clark Library, MS Douglas. D733L A33, Box 15, Folder 1.

——. "To W. T. Stead." 28 June 1895. British Library, Add. MS 81732

——. "Two Loves," *Chameleon* 1, no. 1 (1894): 26–28.

——. *Without Apology*. London: Martin Secker, 1938.

Douglas, Francis Archibald Kelhead, and Percy Colson. *Oscar Wilde and the Black Douglas*. London: Hutchinson, 1949.

[——]. The Tenth Marquess of Queensberry. *The Sporting Queensberrys*. London: Hutchinson, 1942.

Dowling, Linda. *Hellenism and Homosexuality in Victorian Oxford*. Ithaca, NY: Cornell University Press, 1994.

Dowson, Ernest. *The Letters of Ernest Dowson*. Edited by Desmond Flower and Henry Maas. London: Cassell, 1967.

Dunne, Fr. Cuthbert. Papers. Clark Library, uncatalogued boxes.

Dynes, Wayne R. "Buggery." In *Encyclopedia of Homosexuality*. Edited by Dynes. 2 vols. New York: Garland, 1990.

Edmonds, Antony. "An Ideal Boy?" *Wildean* 45 (2014): 97–101.

——. "Family Matters Relating to Alphonse Conway." *Wildean* 43 (2013): 87–107.

——. *Oscar Wilde's Scandalous Summer: The 1894 Worthing Holiday and the Aftermath*. Stroud: Amberley, 2014.

Egerton, George [Mary Chavelita Dunne Bright]. "To John Lane." 5 May 1895. Clark Library, MS Wilde. B855IL L265 1895, Box 7, Folder 63.

——. *A Leaf from the "Yellow Book": The Correspondence of George Egerton*. Edited by Terence De Vere White. London: Richards Press, 1958.

Ellis, Havelock, and John Addington Symonds. *Sexual Inversion*. London: Wilson and Macmillan, 1897.

——. *Studies in the Psychology of Sex: Volume II—Sexual Inversion*, 3rd ed. Philadelphia, PA: F. A. Davis, 1915.

Ellmann, Richard. *Oscar Wilde*. London: Hamish Hamilton, 1987.

——. *Oscar Wilde*. New York: Knopf, 1988.

Emsley, Clive, Tim Hitchcock, and Robert Shoemaker. "Historical Background—History of the Old Bailey Courthouse." *Old Bailey Proceedings Online*, version 7.0, November 2019. https:// www.oldbaileyonline.org/static/The-old-bailey.jsp.

Fawcett, Millicent Garrett. "Women's Suffrage." *Woman's World* 1 (1888): 9–12.

Fenwick-Miller, Mrs. [Florence]. "The Ladies' Column." *Illustrated London News*, 29 April 1893: 534.

Financial papers of Oscar Wilde; 1875-1900. Mostly typewritten. Includes: hotel and luncheon bills, including the bill from the Hotel d'Alsace covering expenses of his last days and burial clothing:— publishing contracts. Vol. CXLI A. British Library, Eccles Bequest, Western Manuscripts, 1875–1900, Add. MS 81759.

Fitch, Clyde. "To Oscar Wilde," *c*. 1889. Clark Library, MS Wilde. F544L W6721, Box 26, Folder 41.

Frankel, Nicholas. *Oscar Wilde: The Unrepentant Years*. Cambridge, MA: Harvard University Press, 2017.

Frith, W. P. *My Autobiography and Reminiscences*. 3 vols. London: Richard Bentley, 1887–88.

Fry, Roger. *The Letters of Roger Fry*. Edited by Denys Sutton. 2 vols. London: Chatto and Windus, 1972.

Fryer, Jonathan. *Robbie Ross: Oscar Wilde's Devoted Friend*. London: Constable, 2000.

Garber, Marjorie. *Vested Interests: Cross-Dressing and Cultural Anxiety*. New York: Routledge, 1997.

General Meetings and Trustees Standing Committee—Minutes to Officers 1895 May 01–1897 Dec. 31. British Museum Central Archive, CE 6/4.

Gide, André. "Oscar Wilde." *L'Ermitage: Revue mensuelle de littérature* 24 (1902): 401–29.

——. *Oscar Wilde: In memoriam (souvenirs); le "De Profundis."* Paris: Mercure de France, 1910.
——. *Oscar Wilde: A Study*. Edited and translated by Stuart Mason [Christopher Sclater Millard]. Oxford: Holywell Press, 1905.
——. *Prétextes: Reflexions critiques sur quelques points de littérature et de morale*. Paris: Mercure de France, 1903.
——. *Si le grain ne meurt*. Paris: Gallimard, 1955.
Gill, Charles. Letter to Sir Hamilton Cuffe, 19 April 1895. The National Archives, Kew. DPP 1/96.
[Gladstone, Herbert, ed.]. *Minutes of Evidence Taken by the Departmental Committee of Prisons*. London: HMSO, printed by Eyre and Spottiswoode, 1895.
Gorham, Deborah. "The 'Maiden Tribute of Modern Babylon' Re-Examined: Child Prostitution and the Idea of Childhood in Late-Victorian England." *Victorian Studies* 21, no. 3: 353–79.
Guy, Josephine M. "'The Soul of Man under Socialism': A (Con)Textual History." In *Wilde Writings: Contextual Conditions*, 58–85. Edited by Joseph Bristow. Toronto: University of Toronto Press, 2003.
Guy, Josephine M., and Ian Small. *Oscar Wilde's Profession: Writing and the Culture Industry in the Late Nineteenth Century*. Oxford: Oxford University Press, 2000.
Haldane, Richard Burdon. *An Autobiography*. London: Hodder and Stoughton, 1929.
——. "To More Adey," 23 January 1896, Clark Library, MS Wilde. H158L A233 1896, Box 29, Folder 30.
Hallam, Henry. *Introduction to the Literature of Europe in the Fifteenth, Sixteenth and Seventeenth Centuries*. 4 vols. London: John Murray, 1837.
Hamilton, Edward. *The Destruction of Lord Rosebery: From the Diary of Sir Edward Hamilton, 1894–1895*. Edited by David Brooks. London: The Historians' Press, 1986.
Hansard's Parliamentary Debates. https://api.parliament.uk/historic-hansard/commons/index.htmlhttps://api.parliament.uk/historic-hansard/commons/index.html.
Harcourt, Lewis. *Loulou: Selected Extracts from the Journals of Lewis Harcourt (1880–1895)*. Edited by Patrick Jackson. Madison, NJ: Fairleigh Dickinson University Press, 2006.
Harris, Frank. *Mr. and Mrs. Daventry: A Play in Four Acts*. London: Richards Press, 1956.
——. *My Life and Loves*. 4 vols. (Nice: privately printed, 1922–27).
——. *Oscar Wilde*. New York: Covici, Frede, 1930.
——. *Oscar Wilde: His Life and Confessions*. 2 vols. New York: privately printed, 1916.
Harris, Seymour F. *Principles of the Criminal Law: A Concise Exposition of the Nature of Crime, the Various Offences Punishable by the English Law, the Law of Criminal Procedure, and the Law of Summary Convictions*. 4th ed. London: Stevens and Haynes, 1886.
Havighurst, Alfred F. *Radical Journalist: H. W. Massingham (1860–1924)*. Cambridge: Cambridge University Press, 1974.
Headlam, Stewart. "Personal," *Church Reformer* 14, no. 6 (1895): 124.
Healy, Chris. *Confessions of a Journalist*. 2nd ed. London: Chatto and Windus, 1904.

Healy, T. M. *Letters and Leaders of My Day*. 2 vols. London: T. Butterworth, 1928.
[Henley, W. E.]. "De Profundis." *Outlook*, 5 March 1898: 146.
——. *The Selected Letters of W. E. Henley*. Edited by Damian Atkinson. Aldershot: Ashgate, 2000.
Henry Gaze and Sons (Ltd.). *Gaze's Tourist Gazette* 10, no. 1 (1897).
[Hichens, Robert.] *The Green Carnation*. London: William Heinemann, 1894.
Hicks, Seymour. *Between Ourselves*. London: Cassell, 1930.
Holland, Merlin. *Irish Peacock and Scarlet Marquess: The Real Trial of Oscar Wilde*. London: Fourth Estate, 2003.
——. *The Real Trial of Oscar Wilde: The First Uncensored Transcript of The Trial of Oscar Wilde vs. John Douglas (Marquess of Queensberry), 1895*. New York: HarperCollins, 2003.
——. "Wilde as Salomé?" *Times Literary Supplement*, 24 July 1994: 14.
Holland, Vyvyan. *Son of Oscar Wilde*. 2nd ed. Edited by Merlin Holland. New York: Carroll and Graf, 1999.
Holman, H. Martin. "To More Adey," 10 May 1897. Clark Library, MS Wilde. D733L A233, Box 15, Folder 1.
Hope, Adrian, and Laura Troubridge. *Letters of Engagement, 1884–1888: The Love Letters of Adrian Hope and Laura Troubridge*. Edited by Marie-Jacqueline Lancaster. London: Tite Street Press, 2002.
Houlbrook, Matt. *Queer London: Perils and Pleasures in the Sexual Metropolis, 1918–1957*. Chicago: University of Chicago Press, 2005.
Housman, Laurence. *A. E. H.: Some Poems, Some Letters and a Personal Memoir by His Brother*. London: Jonathan Cape, 1937.
——. *Echo de Paris: A Study from Life*. London: Jonathan Cape, 1923.
Howard, John. *The State of the Prisons in England and Wales*. Warrington: William Eyres, 1777.
Humphreys, Travers. *A Book of Trials*. London: William Heinemann, 1953.
——. "Foreword." In H. Montgomery Hyde, *The Trials of Oscar Wilde*, 7–14. Notable British Trials. London: William Hodge, 1948.
Hunt, Violet. *I Have This to Say: The Story of My Flurried Years*. New York: Boni and Liveright, 1926.
Hyde, H. Montgomery. *Carson: The Life of Edward Carson, Lord Carson of Duncairn*. London: Heinemann, 1953.
——. *The Cleveland Street Scandal*. London: W. H. Allen, 1976.
——. *Lord Alfred Douglas: A Biography*. London: Methuen, 1984.
——. *Oscar Wilde*. Famous Trials 7. Harmondsworth: Penguin, 1962.
——. *Oscar Wilde: The Aftermath*. London: Methuen, 1963.
——. *The Trials of Oscar Wilde*. Notable British Trials. London: William Hodge, 1948.
——. *The Trials of Oscar Wilde*. 2nd ed. New York: Dover, 1973.
Ives, George. *A Book of Chains*. London: Swan Sonnenschein, 1897.
[——]. "In Memoriam Oscar Wilde, Died November 30th, 1900 (for 'Reynolds's')." *Reynolds's Newspaper*, 9 December 1900: 1.

Jackson, Holbrook. *The Eighteen-Nineties: A Review of Art and Ideas at the Close of the Nineteenth Century*. London: Grant Richards, 1913.

[Jerome, Jerome K.]. Editorial. *To-Day*, 29 December 1894: 241.

[Jeyes, Sidney Henry]. "A Study in Puppydom." *St. James's Gazette*, 24 June 1890: 3–4.

Johnson, Paul. "Buggery and Parliament, 1533–2017." *Parliamentary History* 38, no. 3 (2019): 325–41.

"Justitia." "To an Unknown Correspondent." 7 June 1895. Clark Library, uncatalogued Wilde MS.

Juxon, John. *Lewis and Lewis*. London: Collins, 1983.

Kaplan, Morris B. *Sodom on the Thames: Sex, Love, and Scandal in Wilde Times*. Ithaca, NY: Cornell University Press, 2005.

Kekewich, Justice. Note. British Library, Add. MS 81754 A–F.

Kennison, Peter. *Discovering More behind the Blue Lamp: Policing Central and North and South West London*. London: Coppermill Press, 2004.

Kettle, Michael. *Salome's Last Veil: The Libel Case of the Century*. London: Hart-Davis, MacGibbon, 1977.

King, Peter. *Hurstpierpoint College, 1849–1995: The School by the Downs*. Bognor Regis: Phillimore, 1997.

La Jeunesse, Ernest. "Oscar Wilde," *Revue blanche*, 15 December 1900: 589–96.

[Labouchere, Henry]. "Entre nous." *Truth*, 2 January 1890: 8.

[——]. "Entre nous." *Truth*, 23 January 1890: 156.

[——]. "A Righteous Verdict." *Truth*, 30 May 1895: 1331

Lane, John. "A Repudiation." *Western Mail*, 13 April 1895: 5.

Langbein, John H. *The Origins of Adversary Criminal Trial*. Oxford: Oxford University Press, 2005.

Leverson, Ada. *Letters to the Sphinx from Oscar Wilde, with Reminiscences of the Author*. London: Duckworth, 1930.

Levy, [?]. "To Oscar Wilde," 17 April 1884. Clark Library, MS Wilde. L668L W6721, Box 39, Folder 3.

Littlechild, John George. *The Reminiscences of Chief-Inspector Littlechild*. 2nd ed. London: Leadenhall Press, 1894.

——. *The Reminiscences of Chief-Inspector Littlechild*, 2nd ed. London: Leadenhall, 1894.

Lloyd, Constance. "To Oscar Wilde." [*c.* April 1884]. British Library, Eccles Bequest, 81690.

Lombroso, Cesare. *The Man of Genius*. Translated by anon. 2nd ed. London: Walter Scott: 1891.

Longford, Elizabeth. *A Pilgrimage of Passion: The Life of Wilfrid Scawen Blunt*. London: Weidenfeld and Nicolson, 1979.

Louÿs, Pierre. "Sonnet." *Spirit Lamp* 4, no. 1 (4 May 1893): 1.

Mackenzie, Compton. *Literature in My Time*. London: Rich & Cowan, 1933.

Maguire, J. Robert. *Ceremonies of Bravery: Oscar Wilde, Carlos Blacker, and the Dreyfus Affair*. Oxford: Oxford University Press, 2013.

Mahaffy, J. P. *Social Life in Greece from Homer to Menander*. London: Macmillan, 1874.

——. *Social Life in Greece from Homer to Menander*, 2nd ed. London: Macmillan, 1875.
Mallon, Thomas. "A Boy of No Importance." *Biography* 1, no. 3 (1978): 65–81.
Maltby, Edward. *Secrets of a Solicitor*. London: John Long, 1929.
Marjoribanks, Edward [with Ian Colvin]. *The Life of Lord Carson*. 3 vols. London: Victor Gollancz, 1932–36.
Marquis of Queensberry vs. Oscar Wilde Working Papers (Cat. 170), at *Oscar Wilde: L'Impertinent absolu*. Petit Palais: Musée des Beaux-Arts de la Ville Paris. 28 September 2018-15 January 2019.
Mason, A. E. W. *Sir George Alexander and the St. James's Theatre*. London: Macmillan, 1935.
[Massingham, H. W.]. "Editorial." *Daily Chronicle*, 27 May 1895: 4.
Mathews, Elkin. "Mr. Elkin Mathews Writes to Us from Vigo-Street," *The Times*, 8 April 1895: 13.
May, J. Lewis. *John Lane and the Nineties*. London: John Lane at The Bodley Head, 1936.
McCann, Kate. "Turing's Law: Oscar Wilde among 50,000 Convicted Gay Men Granted Posthumous Pardons." *Daily Telegraph*, 31 January 2017.
McCormack, Jerusha Hull. *John Gray: Poet, Dandy, Priest*. Waltham, MA: Brandeis University Press, 1991.
McKenna, Neil. *The Secret Life of Oscar Wilde*. London: Century, 2003.
McKinstry, Leo. *Rosebery: Statesman in Turmoil*. London: John Murray, 2005.
Mead, Donald. "Earnings from Journalism." *Wildean* 45 (July 2014): 76–78.
——. "Heading for Disaster: Oscar's Finances" *Wildean* 46 (2015): 88–103.
——. "Oscar's Finances: The Pillage of the House Beautiful," *Wildean* 47 (2015): 38–55.
Melba, Nellie. *Melodies and Memories*. New York: George H. Doran, 1926.
Menzies, Amy Charlotte Bewicke ["Mrs. Stuart Menzies"]. *Further Indiscretions by a Woman of No Importance*. New York: E. P. Dutton, 1918.
Mikhail, E. H., ed. *Oscar Wilde: Interviews and Recollections*. 2 vols. London: Macmillan, 1979.
Miles, Canon. Correspondence. Clark Library, MS Wilde, Box 43, Folder 17.
[Millard, Christopher Sclater]. *Bibliography of Oscar Wilde*. London: T. Werner Laurie, 1914.
[——]. *Oscar Wilde: Art and Morality—A Record of the Discussion which Followed the Publication of "Dorian Gray."* 2nd ed. London: Frank Palmer, 1912.
[——]. *Oscar Wilde: Three Times Tried*, Famous Old Bailey Trials of the XIX Century. London: Ferrestone Press, 1912.
[——] "C. S. M." "To the Editor of Reynolds's Newspaper." *Reynolds's Newspaper*, 2 June 1895: 8.
Miracco, Renato. *Oscar Wilde's Italian Dream, 1875–1900: The Infamous St. Oscar of Oxford, Poet and Martry Undecided between the Cloister and the Café*. Bologna: Daniami, 2020.
Mix, Katherine Lyon. *A Study in Yellow: "The Yellow Book" and Its Contributors*. Lawrence: University of Kansas Press, 1960.
Morrison, William Douglas. "Are Our Prisons a Failure?" *Fortnightly Review* 55 (1894): 459–69.

——. *Crime and Its Causes*. London: Swan and Sonnenschein, 1891.

——. "Prison Reform: I.—Prisons and Prisoners," *Fortnightly Review* 63 (1898): 781–89.

Mort, Frank. *Capital Offences: London and the Making of the Permissive Society*. New Haven, CT: Yale University Press, 2010.

Mosher, Thomas. "Bibliographical Note." In Rennell Rodd, *Rose Leaf and Apple Leaf*, 97–98. Portland, ME: Thomas B. Mosher, 1906.

Moyle, Franny. *Constance: The Tragic and Scandalous Life of Mrs. Oscar Wilde*. London: John Murray, 2011.

Munday, R. J. C. "Reflections on the Criminal Evidence Act 1898." *Cambridge Law Journal* 44, no. 1 (1985): 62–86.

Murray, Douglas. *Bosie: A Biography of Lord Alfred Douglas*. New York: Talk Miramax Books, 2000.

Nelson, James G. *The Early Nineties: A View from the Bodley Head*. Cambridge, MA: Harvard University Press, 1971.

——. *Elkin Mathews: Publisher to Yeats, Joyce, Pound*. Madison: University of Wisconsin Press, 1989.

"A New Magazine, Entitled the Chameleon." Advertisement. *Athenæum*, 8 December 1894: 805.

Nordau, Max. *Degeneration*. Translated by anon. 2nd ed. London: William Heinemann, 1895.

Norman, C. H. "Letter: Wilde's 'De Profundis.'" *Times Literary Supplement*, 28 September 1928: 745.

——. "Oscar Wilde." *Tribune*, 23 July 1948: 13.

Norton, Rictor, ed. "The Exeter Scandal, 1878." In *Homosexuality in Nineteenth-Century England: A Sourcebook*. Edited by Norton. http://rictornorton.co.uk/eighteen/1878exet.htm.

——. "The Keevil Libel Case, 1879." In *Homosexuality in Nineteenth-Century England: A Sourcebook*. Edited by Norton. http://rictornorton.co.uk/eighteen/1879keev.htm.

"O'Flahertie Wilde, O. H., author: Vol 1." Court of Bankruptcy and Successors: Proceedings under the Bankruptcy Acts, 1895–97. The National Archives, Kew, B 9/428.

O'Sullivan, Vincent. *Aspects of Wilde*. London: Constable, 1936.

[——]. "Walter Pater: By an Undergraduate." *Pall Mall Gazette*, 2 August 1894: 3.

Owen, Roger. *Lord Cromer: Victorian Imperialist, Edwardian Proconsul*. Oxford: Oxford University Press, 2004.

Paley, William, Walter Henry Macnamara, and Ralph Neville. *Paley's Law and Practice of Summary Convictions under the Summary Jurisdiction Acts, 1848–1899*. 8th ed. London: Sweet and Maxwell, 1904.

Pater, Walter. "A Novel by Mr. Oscar Wilde." *Bookman*, November 1891: 59.

——. *The Renaissance: Studies in Art and Poetry*, 2nd ed. London: Macmillan, 1877.

——. *Studies in the History of the Renaissance*. London: Macmillan, 1873.

——. "Winckelmann." *Westminster Review*, n.s. 31 (1867): 80–110.

Pearson, Hesketh. *The Life of Oscar Wilde*. London: Methuen, 1946.

Peck, Charles Fletcher. "A Model Prison." *Pall Mall Gazette* 7, no. 31, 1895: 449–68.

Pennell, Joseph. "A New Illustrator: Aubrey Beardsley." *Studio* 1 (1893): 14–19.
Percy, William. "Gross Indecency." *Encyclopedia of Homosexuality*, Vol 1. Edited by Wayne R. Dynes, Warren Johansson, William A. Percy, and Stephen Donaldson. New York: Garland, 1990: 507.
Pitt-Lewis, George, R. Percy Smith, and J. A. Hawke. *The Insane and the Law: A Plain Guide for Medical Men, Solicitors, and Others*. London: J. & A. Churchill, 1895.
Plato. *Euthyphro, Apology, Crito, Phaedo, Phaedrus*. Translated by Harold North Fowler. 1914; repr., Cambridge, MA: Harvard University Press, 1990.
——. *Lysis, Symposium, Gorgias*. Translated by W. R. M. Lamb. Cambridge, MA: Harvard University Press, 1925.
Playfair, I. [J. H. Wilson]. *Gentle Criticisms on British Justice*. Newcastle upon Tyne: privately printed, 1895.
"Plea of Justification Filed by the Defendant in *Regina (Wilde) v. Queensberry*." Office of Charles Russell. The National Archives, Kew. CRIM 4/1118.
Press cutting from the *Star*, March 1911. Robert Ross scrapbook. British Library, Add. MS 81824: 26.
Prison Commission: Registered Papers. The National Archives, Kew. PCOM 8/434 and HO/24513-24516.
[Pullen, William, ed.]. *Handbook for Travellers on the Riviera: From Marseilles to Pisa*. [Edited by the Revd. Henry William Pullen]. London: John Murray, 1892.
Raffalovich, [Marc] André. "L'Affaire Oscar Wilde," *Archives de l'anthropologie criminelle* 10 (1895): 445–77.
——. *Uranism and Unisexuality: A Study of Different Manifestations of Sexual Instinct*. Translated by Nancy Erber and William A. Peniston, edited by Philip Healy with Frederick S. Roden. Basingstoke: Palgrave Macmillan, 2016.
——. *Uranisme et unisexualité: Etudes sur différentes manifestations de l'instinct sexuel*. Lyon: A. Storck; Paris: Masson, 1896.
——. *A Willing Exile: A Novel*. 2 vols. London: F. V. White, 1890.
Ransome, Arthur. *Oscar Wilde: A Critical Study*. London: Martin Secker, 1912.
Raymond, Jean Paul, and Charles Ricketts. *Oscar Wilde: Recollections*. London: Nonesuch Press, 1932.
Rebell, Hughes. "Défense d'Oscar Wilde." *Mercure de France* 67 (1895): 182–90.
Recommendation for Oscar Wilde's Application. British Library, Add. MS 48341ff., 213, 215.
Reed, J. D. "Wilfred Owen's Adonis." In *Dead Lovers: Erotic Bonds and the Study of Premodern Europe*, 39–56. Edited by Basil Dufallo and Peggy McCracken. Ann Arbor: University of Michigan Press, 2006.
Reed, Jeremy. *The Dilly: A Secret History of Piccadilly Rent Boys*. London: Peter Owen, 2014.
Report of the Committee on Homosexual Offences and Prostitution. London: Her Majesty's Stationery Office, 1957.
Richards, Grant. *Memories of a Misspent Youth*. London: W. Heinemann, 1932.
Ricketts, Charles. *Self-Portrait: Taken from the Letters and Journals of Charles Ricketts*. Edited by T. Sturge Moore and Cecil Lewis. London: Peter Davies, 1939.

Robert Baldwin Ross Collection 1890–1918. Series 4. Miscellaneous 1896–1951. Clark Library, MS Ross, Box 85.

Roberts, Alexander. *Greek: The Language of Christ and His Apostles*. London: Longmans, Green, 1888.

Robins, Ashley H., and Merlin Holland. "The Art of Medicine: The Enigmatic Illness and Death of Constance, Wife of Oscar Wilde." *Lancet*, 3 January 2015: 21–22.

Robins, Ashley H., and Sean L. Sellars. "Oscar Wilde's Terminal Illness: Reappraisal after a Century." *Lancet* 356 (2000): 1841–43.

Rodd, Rennell. *Rose Leaf and Apple Leaf*. Philadelphia, PA: J. M. Stoddart, 1882.

——. *Social and Diplomatic Memories*. 3 vols. London: Edward Arnold, 1922–25.

Rose, David Charles. *Oscar Wilde's Elegant Republic: Transformation, Dislocation and Fantasy in Fin-de-Siècle Paris*. Newcastle upon Tyne: Cambridge Scholars, 2015.

Roseliep, Raymond, ed. "Some Letters of Lionel Johnson." Unpublished doctoral dissertation, University of Notre Dame, 1953.

Ross, Robert. "Introductory Note." In Oscar Wilde, *A Florentine Tragedy: Opening Scene by T. Sturge Moore*, v–x. Boston, MA: John W. Luce, 1908.

——. *Robert Ross, Friend of Friends: Letters to Robert Ross, Art Critic and Writer, Together with Extracts from His Published Articles*. Edited by Margery Ross. London: Jonathan Cape, 1952.

Rowbotham, Sheila. *Edward Carpenter: A Life of Liberty and Love*. London: Verso, 2008.

Russell, Charles. "Letter to the Public Prosecutor." *Daily Chronicle*, 6 April 1895: 6.

Schneider, Wendie Ellen. *Engines of Truth: Producing Veracity in the Victorian Courtroom*. New Haven, CT: Yale University Press, 2015.

Schroeder, Horst. *Additions and Corrections to Richard Ellmann's "Oscar Wilde."* 2nd ed. Braunschweig: privately printed, 2002.

——. "Ερος τον αδυνατον—*L'Amour de l'impossible*: A Graeco-French Collocation in 'The Critic as Artist.'" *Notes and Queries* 40, no. 1 (1993): 52–53.

Schuster, Adela. "To More Adey," 5 December 1895. Clark Library, MS Wilde, S395L A233, Box 61, Folder 1.

Second Report of the Legal Departments Commission: Command Papers. 1874.

Seeney, Michael. *From Bow Street to the Ritz: Oscar Wilde's Theatrical Career from 1895 to 1908*. High Wycombe: Rivendale Press, 2015.

Shakespeare, William. *Shakespeare's Sonnets*. Edited by Katherine Duncan-Jones. The Arden Shakespeare, 3rd series. London: Thomas Nelson, 1997.

Shaw, George Bernard. *Collected Letters, 1898–1910*. Edited by Dan H. Laurence. London: Max Reinhardt, 1972.

——. *Selected Short Plays: Definitive Text*. Edited by Dan H. Laurence. London: Penguin, 1987.

Shelley, Edward. "Letter to John Lane," 7 April 1895. Harry Ransom Humanities Research Center, University of Texas, Austin.

Sherard, Robert Harborough. *André Gide's Wicked Lies about the Late Oscar Wilde in Algiers in January 1895*. Corsica: Vindex, 1933.

——. *Bernard Shaw, Frank Harris, and Oscar Wilde*. London: T. Werner Laurie, 1937.

——. *The Life of Oscar Wilde*. London: T. Werner Laurie, 1906.
——. *Oscar Wilde: The Story of an Unhappy Friendship*. London: Hermes Press, 1902.
——. *Oscar Wilde: The Story of an Unhappy Friendship*. London: Greening, 1905.
——. *Oscar Wilde: Twice Defended from André Gide's Wicked Lies and Frank Harris's Cruel Libels*. Chicago: Argus Book Shop, 1934.
——. *The Real Oscar Wilde: To Be Used as a Supplement to, and in Illustration of "The Life of Oscar Wilde."* London: T. Werner Laurie, 1916.
——. "To A. J. A. Symons," 13 May 1937. Clark Library, MS Wilde, S551L S988 1937, Box 62, Folder 25.
——. *Twenty Years in Paris: Being Some Recollections of a Literary Life*. London: Hutchinson, 1906.
——. "Ultima Verba: With Some Reflections on the Mischief Caused by Pernicious Amnesia—Being an Open Letter to George Bernard Shaw." British Library, Add. MS 81688.
Short, Frederick H. *The Taxation of Costs in the Crown Office*. London: Stevens and Haynes, 1879.
Showalter, Elaine. "It's Still Salome." *Times Literary Supplement*, 2 September 1994: 13–14.
——. *Sexual Anarchy: Gender and Culture at the Fin de Siècle*. New York: Viking, 1990.
Smith, Adam. *An Inquiry into the Nature and Causes of the Wealth of Nations*. 2 vols. London: W. Strahan and T. Cadell, 1776.
Smith, F. E. "Labouchere's Amendment to the Criminal Law Amendment Bill." *Historical Studies* 17 (1976): 165–73
Smith, Logan Pearsall. *A Chime of Words: The Letters of Logan Pearsall Smith*. Edited by Edwin Tribble. New York: Ticknor and Fields, 1984.
Soderlund, Gretchen. *Sex Trafficking, Scandal, and Transformation of Journalism, 1885–1917*. Chicago: University of Chicago Press, 2013.
Speedie, Julie. *Wonderful Sphinx: The Biography of Ada Leverson*. London: Virago, 1993.
[Stead, W. T.]. "The Innings of the Philistines: After the Fall of Oscar Wilde." *Review of Reviews*, June 1895: 538.
[——]. "The Maiden Tribute of Modern Babylon." *Pall Mall Gazette*, 6 July 1885: 1–6; 7 July 1885: 1–6; 8 July 1885: 1–6; 10 July 1885: 1–6.
[——]. "The Progress of the World." *Review of Reviews*, June 1895: 492.
Stephen, James Fitzjames. *A Digest of the Law of Evidence*, 9th ed. London: Macmillan, 1919.
——. *A History of the Criminal Law in England*. 3 vols. London: Macmillan, 1883.
Stephens, John Russell. *The Censorship of English Drama, 1824–1901*. Cambridge: Cambridge University Press, 1980.
Stokes, John. *Oscar Wilde: Myths, Miracles, and Imitations*. Cambridge: Cambridge University Press, 1996.
——. "Wilde Shot." *London Review of Books*, 27 February 1992. https://www.lrb.co.uk/the-paper/v14/n04/letters.
Stoneley, Peter. "'Looking at the Others': Oscar Wilde and the Reading Gaol Archive." *Journal of Victorian Culture* 19, no. 4 (2014): 457–80.

Stratmann, Linda. *The Marquess of Queensberry: Wilde's Nemesis*. New Haven, CT: Yale University Press, 2013.

Strong, Rowland. "In the French Capital." *New York Times*, 19 June 1898: 19.

Sturgis, Matthew. *Oscar: A Life*. London: Head of Zeus, 2018.

Swinburne, A[lgernon] C[harles]. *The Swinburne Letters*. Edited by Cecil Y. Lang. 6 vols. New Haven, CT: Yale University Press, 1960.

Sydenham, Floyer. Advertisement in *The Banquet: A Dialogue Concerning Love—the Second Part*. Edited and translated by Floyer Sydenham. London: W. Sandby, 1767.

Symonds, John Addington. *The Letters of John Addington Symonds*. Edited by Herbert M. Schueller and Robert L. Peters. 3 vols. Detroit, MI: Wayne State University Press, 1969.

Tattersall, Charles. "Genius on Trial: Key Sources Relating to Oscar Wilde at The National Archives." The National Archives, Kew, 3 July 2009. https://media.nationalarchives.gov.uk/index.php/genius-on-trial-key-sources-relating-to-oscar-wilde-at-the-national-archives/.

Townsend, J. Benjamin. *John Davidson: Poet of Armageddon*. New Haven, CT: Yale University Press, 1961.

"Transcripts (Taken from the Original Shorthand Notes) and Other Material Relating to Oscar Wilde's Prosecution of the Marquess of Queensberry for Criminal Libel in April 1895." British Library, Western Manuscripts, Loan MS 122.

Trevor-Roper, Hugh. *A Hidden Life: The Enigma of Sir Edmund Backhouse*. London: Macmillan, 1976.

"Trial of James Jelley (27) January 1894." *Old Bailey Proceedings Online*, version 8.0, 12 August 2019, t18940108-208.

"Trial of John Shepherd, Alias Wood (36) George Moody Alias Mooney (27) George Wilton (48,) June 1895." *Old Bailey Proceedings Online*, version 8.0, 12 August 2019, t18950617-519.

"Trial of John Sholto Douglas, Marquess Of Queensberry, March 1895." *Old Bailey Proceedings Online*, version 8.0, 12 August 2019, t18950325-336.

"Trial of Oscar Fingal O'fflahartie Wills Wilde (40) Alfred Waterhouse Somerset Taylor (33), May 1895." *Old Bailey Proceedings Online*, version 8.0, 12 August 2019, t18950520-425.

"Trial of Robert Cliburn (23), March 1898." *Old Bailey Proceedings Online*, version 8.0, 12 August 2019, t18980307-243.

Upchurch, Charles. *Before Wilde: Sex between Men in Britain's Age of Reform*. Berkeley, CA: University of California Press, 2009.

——. "Full-Text Databases and Historical Research: Cautionary Notes from a Ten-Year Study." *Journal of Social History* 46, no. 1 [2012]: 89–105.

Vivian, Herbert. "The Reminiscences of a Short Life." *Sun*, 17 November 1889: 4.

Walker-Smith, Derek, and Edward Clarke, *The Life of Sir Edward Clarke*. London: Butterworth, 1939.

Walkowitz, Judith R. *City of Dreadful Delight: Narratives of Sexual Danger in Late-Victorian London*. Chicago: University of Chicago Press, 1992.

Wan, Marco. "A Matter of Style: On Reading the Oscar Wilde Trials as Literature." *Oxford Journal of Legal Studies* 31, no. 4 (2011): 724–25.

Warwick Film Productions Ltd. v. Eisinger and Others (1967), 1 Ch. 1969.
Wearing, J. P. *The London Stage, 1900–1909: A Calendar of Plays and Players*. Metuchen, NJ: Scarecrow Press, 1981.
Welldon, J. E. C. "Abnormality and Crime." *Saturday Review*, 17 December 1921: 687.
[Whibley, Charles?]. Review of Oscar Wilde, *The Picture of Dorian Gray*. *Scots Observer*, 5 July 1890: 181.
Whittington-Egan, Molly. *Frank Miles and Oscar Wilde: "Such White Lilies."* High Wycombe: Rivendale Press, 2008.
Wilde, Constance. "Children's Dress in This Century." *Woman's World* 1 (1888): 417.
——. "To Arthur Humphreys," 1 August 1894. British Library, Eccles Bequest 81732.
——. "To Lady Mount-Temple," undated letter. University of Southampton, Broadlands Archive, 57/14/93.
——. "To Lily Wilde," February 1896. Clark Library, MS Wilde, W6771L W613, Box 70, Folder 3.
Wilde, Oscar ["Melmoth"]. account book, [May–June 1895]. Clark Library, uncatalogued Wilde MSS.
——. "The Case of Warder Martin: Some Cruelties of Prison Life." *Daily Chronicle*, 28 May 1897: 9.
——. *Children in Prison and Other Cruelties of Prison Life*. London: Murdoch, 1898.
——. *The Collected Works of Oscar Wilde*. Edited by Robert Ross. 14 vols. London: Methuen, 1908.
——. *The Complete Letters of Oscar Wilde*. Edited by Merlin Holland and Rupert Hart-Davis. London: Fourth Estate, 2000.
——. *The Complete Works of Oscar Wilde*. 11 vols. to date. Oxford: Oxford University Press, 2000–.
——. *De Profundis*. [Edited by Robert Ross]. London: Methuen 1905.
——. *De Profundis, with Additional Matter*. Edited by Robert Ross. London: Methuen, 1909.
——. "The Decay of Lying." *Nineteenth Century* 25 (January 1889): 35–56.
——. *Il delitto di Lord Arturo Savile*. Translated by Federigo Verdinois. Naples: Società Editrice Partenopea, 1908).
——. "The English Renaissance of Art." In *Miscellanies*. Edited by Robert Ross. *The Collected Works of Oscar Wilde*. Vol. 14, 241–78. London: Methuen, 1908.
——. "Epigrams and Aphorisms. 1890." Clark Library, MS Wilde, Box 81, Folder 5, W6721M3 E64 [189–?].
——. "A Few Maxims for the Instruction of the Over-Educated." *Saturday Review*, 17 November 1894: 533.
——. *Intentions*. Translated by Hughes Rebell. Paris: Carrington, 1906.
——. *Lady Windermere's Fan: A Play about a Good Woman*. 2nd ed. Edited by Ian Small. London: Ernest Benn; New York: W. W. Norton, 1999.
——. *The Letters of Oscar Wilde*. Edited by Rupert Hart-Davis. London: Rupert Hart-Davis, 1962.
——. "*L'Envoi*." In Rennell Rodd, *Rose Leaf and Apple Leaf*, 11–28. Philadelphia, PA: J. M. Stoddart, 1882.

——. "Phrases and Philosophies for the Use of the Young." *Chameleon* 1, no. 1 (1894): 1–3.

——. "Phrases and Philosophies for the Use of the Young." In *The Collected Works of Oscar Wilde*. Edited by Robert Ross. 14 vols. Vol. 8, 241–78. London: Methuen, 1908.

——. "A Preface to 'Dorian Gray,'" *Fortnightly Review* 49 (1891): 480–81.

——. *The Picture of Dorian Gray. The Collected Works of Oscar Wilde*. Vol. 1. Paris: Charles Carrington, 1908.

——. *Poèmes en prose*. Translated by Charles Grolleau. Preface by Jacques Desroix. Paris: C. Carrington, 1906.

——. "The Portrait of Mr. W. H." *Blackwood's Edinburgh Magazine* 146 (1889): 1–21.

——. *The Soul of Man*. London: Chiswick Press, 1895.

——. *Two Society Comedies: "A Woman of No Importance" and "An Ideal Husband."* Edited by Ian Small and Russell Jackson. New York: W. W. Norton, 1983.

Wilde (Oscar) News Clipping Albums, Collection of Christopher S. Millard. Volume XI 1910–Volume LXVI 1926–1927. Clark Library, Wildeiana Clippings.

Wills, William. *The Theory and Practice of the Law of Evidence*. London: Stevens and Sons, 1894.

Wilson, James H. *Iscariot's Bitter Love*. London: Headley Brothers, 1912.

——. *"Zalmoxis" and Other Poems*. London: Elliot Stock, 1892.

Wilson, Stephen Clifford. "Oscar Wilde and Arthur Cruttenden: Inside and outside Reading Gaol." *Notes and Queries* 52, no. 1 (2005): 82–84.

Winder, W. H. D. "The Development of Blackmail." *Modern Law Review* 5, no. 1 [1941]: 26.

Wintermans, Caspar. *Alfred Douglas: A Poet's Life and His Finest Work*. London: Peter Owen, 2007.

Wright, R. S. *The Law of Criminal Conspiracies and Agreements*. London: Butterworths, 1873.

Wright, Thomas. "Party Political Animal." *Times Literary Supplement*, 4 June 2014: 14.

Yeats, W. B. "The Tragic Generation." In *Autobiographies*, 219–66. Vol. 3 of *The Collected Works of W. B. Yeats*. Edited by William H. O'Donnell and Douglas N. Archibald. 14 vols. New York: Macmillan and Scribners, 1989–2015.

Young, Dalhousie. *Apologia pro Oscar Wilde*. London: William Reeves, 1895.

Zander, Michael. "Bail: A Re-Appraisal." *Criminal Law Review* (1967): 25–39, 100–110, 128–42.

INDEX